Linguistics
and English Grammar

Linguistics
and English Grammar

H. A. Gleason, Jr.

HARTFORD SEMINARY FOUNDATION

Holt, Rinehart and Winston, Inc.

New York   Chicago   San Francisco   Toronto   London

Preface

Interest in linguistics among English teachers has risen phenomenally in the last few years. The subject is in the air at every professional meeting—sometimes earnestly advocated, sometimes bitterly combatted, often provoking questions, almost always somewhere in the background of any debate on the language section of the curriculum. With increasing frequency linguistics is now intruding even into discussions of the teaching of composition or literature. Staunchly old-fashioned textbook series have had to give it some recognition, and others claim modernity in its espousal. It is no longer responsible behavior merely to ignore it, yet no clear picture emerges from most of the debate. Too frequently linguistics is presented as slightly esoteric.

The resulting curiosity about linguistics and its place in the English classroom is now too great to be satisfied by the short articles appearing in the professional journals, the several introductory pamphlets, or the teachers' guides to the linguistically oriented textbooks. The most pressing questions bear on the relations of linguistics to the more traditional formulations of the subject matter of English—to literature, to composition, and especially to grammar. These questions are too central and too complex to be treated so lightly.

There is, certainly, a need for books that will go beyond what we have in interpreting linguistics to the English teacher and in bringing it to bear on the questions met in the classroom. This book is one linguist's contribution toward meeting this need. It is primarily concerned, as its title is meant to suggest, with the interrelations between linguistics and English grammar. It is not a textbook of either subject, and should not be expected to give a balanced or comprehensive self-contained view of either.

This is in many respects a guide book to English grammars. It is a little like a Baedeker—rather unenlightening reading at home in your own living room, but useful as you travel through the regions described. It should not be read alone, unless you are already so familiar with the territory that you can visualize it as you read. Rather, it should be read with two or three grammars at hand, so that the features pointed out may be identified and examined closely.

English grammars are now both numerous and diverse, differing not only in terminology but also in organization, orientation, and scope. To examine several of them jointly is possible only from a perspective that can penetrate these surface differences and reveal their most basic features. To provide such a perspective is one of the major contributions of linguistics to English studies. A central concern of linguistics is the theory and practice of language investigation and description. In the grammars themselves, general principles are usually tacitly assumed rather than explicitly stated. Indeed, they are often buried under a mass of more obvious features. It is for this reason that a guide book is necessary if grammars are to be correlated or compared on anything other than the most superficial level, and it is for the same reason that such a guide book must be grounded in linguistics.

This book has grown far beyond what was originally envisioned. Even so, much more might be said about every one of the topics included. Several large areas have had to be omitted almost entirely, derivation and inflection among them. Others could receive only passing mention without the critical evaluation that they deserve. Thus, when phonology has had to be brought in, the presentation has been based on the one analysis most widely used in the sources accessible to teachers. To do otherwise would have required three or four more chapters. Syntax is for the schools the heart of English grammar, and so has been made the central concern of the book. A critical discussion of phonology has had to give place to this.

The focus is on those approaches to English syntax which at the present time may be considered live options for the American high school or junior high school. This must call forth various apologies, particularly to British colleagues, who may feel quite justly that the book is provincial in outlook. There was no alternative, however; I am not well enough acquainted with the schools of other English-speaking countries to take a broader approach. There are, however, some parallels. British school grammar is similar in many ways to American, differing most noticeably in the total absence of Reed and Kellogg diagramming. Interesting new developments in English grammar from a "neo-Firthian" point of view have not been discussed. Several important publications from this approach are promised. When they appear they will demand notice, not only in Britain but also in America.

The book divides into three parts, each quite different in nature. Two of these have seemed to some readers marginal or even extraneous. Each demands, therefore, a word of justification or explanation.

English grammars do not simply compete in the present academic market place on the basis of their present virtues, real or imagined. They have histories, and their present positions are the consequences of their pasts. Our preferences are the compounding of our own judgments with the traditions into which we have come through birth and education. The interrelations of the several English grammars can be understood in depth only if their historical background is kept in mind. Hence Part One consists of four historical chapters.

Linguistics and English grammar, so often viewed today as antithetic, have had separate courses only since about 1800. At about the same time, English grammar began to develop the oldest of the schisms still existing within it, that between school grammar and scholarly traditional grammar. In a book concerned with relating currently competing approaches, the starting point for a history must be in the immediate antecedents of these splits. For another purpose, the important and interesting developments of the seventeenth and eighteenth centuries would demand attention.

The tragedy of grammar has been its isolation. We have neither brought external insights to bear on its problems nor allowed it to illumine any other discipline. One luxury we can no longer afford in any curriculum is an isolated, smugly autonomous subject. No discussion of English grammar is fully responsible which does not face interdisciplinary relationships, at least those relationships to other segments of the field of English. Thus Part Three presents six chapters suggesting points of contact and implications.

If it is a complex task to interrelate half a dozen varieties of English grammar, it must be much more so to state in any fullness the relations of these to several other fields, each with its own internal diversities. Obviously I can be only suggestive. I must remind the reader that I write as a linguist, not as a composition teacher nor a literary scholar. For example, I must disclaim any suggestion that I have presented a theory of style. That would be outside my province and my competence. I do advance a few principles, none of them original, which might enter into such a theory. Some might even be basic. There would, however, have to be much more than this in a comprehensive treatment of style, and some overlappings would have to be cleared up. My single objective in this part of the discussion is to demonstrate that English grammar must underlie any significant study of stylistics, and to indicate something of the demands that stylistics must make of grammar. Some other approach to style would, I am sure, set quite comparable requirements.

There is prevalent among English teachers an exaggerated idea of the unsettledness of linguistics and of the disagreements among linguists. We are a pugnacious profession. Our joy in battle easily obscures the consensus that exists. Of what English teachers see of the work of linguists, an unfortunately large part is polemic. This book, however, is not a partisan argument for or against any particular school of linguistics or approach to grammar. I can claim a special neutrality. My own preference and conviction run to stratificational grammar. This has not yet received the development which would make it a possible contender for use in the schools; it is not therefore included in the discussion.

There are many points about which I have been less dogmatic than has been recently fashionable, either among linguists or among English scholars. I have tried, for example, to give a fair presentation of the strengths of school grammar and of diagramming—the latter has fascinated me since seventh grade, and I have continued to use it myself as a convenient and revealing way to visualize a sentence structure. I have been distressed in recent years by the shallowness of most of the attempted defenses of "traditional grammar" which have appeared in professional English journals. It deserves both more discerning criticism and more reasoned defense than it has had. I have also tried to show some of the weaknesses of the "new grammar" as it is commonly presented to English teachers and through them to high school pupils. In particular, I regret that it has so often been justified simply by an appeal to the authority of a new intellectual aristocracy. I belong to that aristocracy and know that in actuality we are all commoners.

At certain places I have taken a very definite stand. Often this conforms to the general consensus of the leaders of the English-teaching profession and of the linguists. But not always. There are places where I find myself set against my colleagues. I hope, therefore, first, that you will weigh everything that is said here critically—I believe that is the best way that my position can establish itself—and second, that you will not quote anything preceded by "Linguists have established that" until you can satisfy yourself that the statement has general support; what you read here is to be taken only as the considered opinion of one linguist.

One of my friends has said that most presentations of linguistics for English teachers are simply collections of warmed-over, secondhand prejudices. In some cases, perhaps, he is right. But I would like to claim that he is wrong of mine. Prejudices there are, of course, but all of them I have made my own, wherever they may have originated. At least most of those which were in the first draft but which I did not hold firmly and with conviction have been eliminated under the proddings of my critics. Those that remain are those I persist in against their advice and urging. Your gratitude must go with mine for this service, as well as for the clarifications of muddy statements, the detection of careless errors, the supplying of examples, and all their suggestions which have strengthened the book.

There is little that is new in this book. Some points I have documented when the source is obvious to me. Other points I have left undocumented because the source will be obvious to every reader. For most points, however, I cannot trace the origin well enough to give credit. Some have been brought to my attention by linguist and teacher colleagues in conversation or debate. Some I have picked up in reading and they have sunk into my general fund of ideas. Not a few have come to me first in class discussion, particularly at the Hartford Seminary Foundation, at Trinity College, and at Bedford and Long Lots Junior High Schools, Westport,

Connecticut. All I can claim to have done is to compile the labor of others. If any credit is due, it must be shared very widely.

It has often been suggested to me that I should write a little book which, to describe it honestly, should be entitled *What an English Teacher Needs To Know To Teach Modern Grammar*. This is not that book. I hope it is part of a small library of books which might collectively be given such a label with one word added at the end: *What an English Teacher Needs To Know To Teach Modern Grammar Well*. To be thoroughly prepared for his work, an English teacher will need to familiarize himself not only with most of the contents of this book but also—the order is of no consequence—with a standard treatment of general linguistics, three or four good English grammars of as diverse approaches as possible, a solid history of the language, an introduction to English phonology (and the general phonetics usually included in such books), and a sampling of the professional literature on the applications of linguistics to English teaching. In addition, he should get some personal experience with exploring the system of the language beyond the limits described adequately in his reading. Some may do all this by home study, a difficult but by no means impossible task. Others will do it by taking three or four respectable academic courses.

The program I have just suggested may easily be misconstrued. It is rather larger than what most have been advocating as either necessary or desirable. Some will feel that I am laying down a course of preparation for specialists within the English-teaching profession. I must insist that this is the minimum I consider necessary for a rank-and-file teacher who wishes to carry out his proper tasks in a workmanlike manner using the best insights of the present day. Specialists we must have also. For them a great deal more is required, perhaps a graduate degree in linguistics.

Suppose someone who had never done anything with English literature in school or college were called on to teach Shakespeare. We would have little patience with anyone who suggested some slim little volume to be read over the weekend as giving all one would need for this task. A good literary history, a solid social history of England, a first-rate critical introduction to Shakespeare, a treatment of the fundamentals of English poetics, an introduction to the drama, and a fair sampling of the professional literature on the teaching of Shakespeare would, it seems to me, be a minimum crash preparation—provided it were combined with a good bit of firsthand experience with Shakespeare's plays. (Some of this we would not ordinarily list in a teacher's qualifications simply because we would expect it of ALL educated Americans.) Such a course of preparation is roughly comparable to what I have suggested above as a minimum for the effective teaching of grammar. So far, nothing but a superficial exposure to school grammar has come to be generally expected of educated Americans. All of the requirements must, then, be included in professional training. The teaching of language, rightly or wrongly, looms at least as large in the American curriculum as does Shakespeare. It would be irresponsible to consider as adequate any preparation for language teaching that is short of what would seem a minimum for the teaching of Shakespeare.

It may be argued that in the practical realities of the English-teaching profession today, what I have outlined is visionary. One hundred thousand high school English teachers cannot immediately be so equipped. This is of course true. But we are approaching the time when a very large part of the corps of teachers will have had the minimum technician's training that workshops and a handful of pamphlets can give. We must start now to work toward the next step. That must involve a higher standard of competence than what we have been resting our recent planning on.

It is for the next step forward that *Linguistics and English Grammar* has been written. I hope that there may soon appear some of the other books that will be needed with it. May it speed the day when English grammar will come into its own as a subject worthily taught, bearing its part in a truly liberal education.

Hartford, Connecticut   H. A. Gleason, Jr.
May 1965

Acknowledgments

Among those to whom the author is grateful for assistance in the preparation of this book are the following, linguists, English teachers, students, friends: Robert L. Allen, Robert C. Austin, Richard W. Bailey, Ford L. Battles, Thomas Creswell, Ella Demers, Madeline Ehrman, W. Nelson Francis, Charles C. Fries, Harjit S. Gill, H. A. Gleason, Frances E. Gleason, Michael A. K. Halliday, V. Louise Higgins, J. Maurice Hohlfeld, Frances Hunter, John C. Hunter, Martin Joos, Ruby M. Kelly, D. Terrence Langendoen, Albert J. Leet, Paul Leser, John C. McLaughlin, Ronald A. Murch, William J. Samarin, George L. Shelley, Flola Sheperd, Roger W. Shuy, Robert P. Stockwell, Hugh M. Stimson, Charles R. Taber, W. Freeman Twaddell, Priscilla Tyler, John Van Scoyoc, Ralph M. Williams, and pre-eminently George P. Faust, whose help has directly affected almost every page. Some of these people have further transmitted to me suggestions from their students, who, though nameless, also deserve our thanks. Miss Tang Shu-Mei wrote out the text of Wang Wei's *Parting*.

Contents

Preface   v

Part One

HISTORICAL BACKGROUND

Chapter I

Grammar in the Schools

Few subjects have had so ambiguous a place in American education as English grammar. This strange position is reflected in the familiar term "grammar school". This has largely passed out of the professional vocabulary of educators, as neither descriptively adequate or really relevant. However, it persists in common usage — especially among older people — as the normal designation for that block of the educational system that precedes high school. If the term had not been coined in the last century, it could never have been in this. In no school today is grammar the conspicuous element. In prestige, it is near or at the bottom among the numerous subjects of the modern curriculum. It would hardly occur to anyone to pick grammar out as the characterizing feature of any level of American education. The term "grammar school" is an anachronism.

Yet it is symbolic of the teaching of grammar, also incredibly anachronistic.

Prevailing concepts of what grammar is, how it should be taught, and how it relates to other subjects are all obsolete, often dangerously so. It is not simply that the same grammar is being taught in the same way and with the same attitudes as fifty years ago. Rather, there has been serious degeneration in content, both qualitatively and quantitatively. Moreover, any improvements in teaching methods have largely failed to alter the basic approach of rule memorization and artificial application to sentences out of context. The significance of grammar in the total educational process has become very obscure. Grammar is one of those rare subjects where improvement might sometimes be made by turning the clock back half a century.

Any such improvement would be small beside what is possible if the school curriculum can be opened to the best insights available today, and to the progress which seems likely in the next decade. For scholarship in grammar is flourishing both in this country and abroad. New and significant results are appearing. Fundamental understanding is being advanced. This scholarship operates under the label "linguistics". It is a broad and diverse discipline, of which English grammar is merely a minor and very specialized branch. It is, indeed, the very breadth of linguistic scholarship which gives promise of rescuing grammar from its narrowness and sterility.

Language is an important feature of human life, the major means of communication, and hence a basic essential in our communicating society. It is an intricate complex of patterns, controlling the forms of words, of sentences, and of whole discourses. All these patterns are held together about a systematic core of patterns, the grammar of the language. Because of its centrality, grammar is a key to our understanding of verbal communication.

If man is to understand himself, he must understand how he communicates. Some fundamental insight into language should be a basic qualification for an educated man. That must be based, in part, on grammar. However, it cannot be founded on "grammar" narrowly confined to a few details judged useful to avoid a handful of selected errors. True grammar is no mere collection of rules, but a system into which the rules fit in a significant and revealing way. The language instruction which is to educate must show clearly this systematic nature of grammar, the interrelatedness of the parts, and something of the complexity of the whole. It is here that linguistics can make its major contribution.

POPULAR ATTITUDES TOWARD GRAMMAR

The American public has a most ambivalent attitude toward grammar. Parents feel their children threatened by any suggestion of change in grammar instruction, and they react promptly and violently. Yet they are attracted by a French course that advertises "no grammar". Such contradictions are possible only because grammar is seldom thought about or discussed calmly and rationally. It is a focus of the anti-intellectual component of the American mentality. A cherished part of the school ritual, it is not really expected to be practically useful in the real world. This deeply ambivalent attitude has very ancient roots in the American school system.

As settlement pushed westward and communities became established, the demand arose for at least rudimentary education for the children. A very characteristic pattern emerged in many areas.[1] Schools were organized

---

[1] The patterns varied in detail from one part of the country to another. The description is composite, but largely based on the Southern Midlands. "Pie suppers" and "patrons" are both Southern Midland terms. The principle of neighborhood responsibility and initiative, however, was widespread.

locally by direct action of the parents. They were financed out of the meager resources of those isolated, largely self-contained communities. The neighbors met together and discussed their needs. After an agreement had been reached, each family contributed what it could. One gave the use of a plot of land. The neighbors worked together to put up a simple building from donated materials. A teacher was hired — often with no more preparation for the job than graduation from a similar school. One family contributed room and board (and chaperonage!) for the teacher. Or, each family "boarded the teacher" in rotation. Salaries were low; the whole community was on a subsistence economy in any case, and cash figured relatively little in their life.

Such a school was in every respect a community enterprise. The school house was a neighborhood center. Here they held "pie suppers" as community get-togethers and as a means of meeting any small expenses not covered by subscriptions for the teacher's salary. The men met together to repair the building when necessary. Everyone watched over the school and its operation, keeping an eye on the teacher, judging her work and behavior. Each year they debated whether to call her back or to seek another.

Today's elementary school may be housed in a building of very modern architecture set on an extensive, well-landscaped tract of expensive suburban land. The equipment is varied and highly specialized. The building was financed by a bond issue floated in Wall Street. All this is a far cry from the unimaginative one-room building on a half acre, its ancestor not many years back.

The organization has changed with the building. Neighbors meeting together to choose a teacher and determine curriculum gave way to the selection of a "school committee". Subscription was supplanted by taxation. In due course the "school committee" metamorphosed into a "board of education". Many of the operational details were delegated to a new professional administration. School districts were consolidated. State supervision of local systems became established and gradually strengthened. The finances became more and more complex. Standards of teacher preparation were raised.

Not everything has changed as much as the outward form. In some areas the parents sending children to a local school are still known as "patrons". Formal authority has been delegated and legally defined. Still, the public has not lost its feeling of direct responsibility for the teachers and the curriculum. The patrons may have a decisive, if informal, part in policy making and even in daily management.

As might be expected, the forces of public opinion have been, for the most part, narrowly conservative. The origins of American mass education were in communities with little specialization. The school teacher came out of the same background as the parents, had much the same education.

and was only in a very limited way more expert. Indeed, some of the parents were often former school teachers themselves, quite willing to share in the guidance of an untrained, inexperienced newcomer.

The picture of the school teacher as not much more knowledgeable than the parents has persisted even into an age where most teachers have extensive specialized preparation. Each parent considers himself as good as an expert,[2] most particularly in those segments of the curriculum which have come down from the one-room schools — reading, writing, arithmetic, and grammar. Opinions run strong on these subjects, not only as to what to teach, but equally as to how to teach it. Whatever questions may be raised are simple and straightforward. There is no suspicion that any element of this basic part of the curriculum might involve complexity beyond the reach of everyday common sense. The typical American can hardly conceive of anyone having any special competence in these rudiments — all there is to know is common knowledge.

The second major root of the modern American educational system was an academic tradition oriented toward college. This was not mass education, but preparation for professional leadership. It also has left its mark on the popular attitude toward grammar.

Hardly had the settlements on the East Coast been planted before colleges were founded, beginning with Harvard in 1636 and William and Mary in 1693. Before American independence there were several in operation. These were supported by a considerable number of academies, set up largely to prepare young men for college entrance. The oldest of these, the Boston Latin School, indicates by its name something of the classical orientation which was characteristic of all of them.

"Colleges" were organized through the West as soon as the settlements became established. The typical frontier college started out with a faculty of two or three. Each of these stood ready to teach any part of the curriculum. The course of studies was the best approximation they could produce to the work at the older eastern institutions.

Students came out of the one-room community schools with little more than the "three R's". Most of the western colleges provided for their needs in an "academic department", with a curriculum based on that of the eastern academies. This included geometry, geography, history, grammar, rhetoric, Latin, and occasionally even Greek.

American secondary education grew from several sources, among them the older eastern academies and the "academic departments" of the frontier colleges. By the end of the nineteenth century, the high schools had been largely separated, administratively, from the colleges and brought

---

[2] Early in this century it was still the practice in many rural areas for school-board members (not professional administrators!) to visit schools unannounced and examine the children in spelling, arithmetic, or any other subject the examiner thought he could handle.

into closer relationship with the elementary schools. But the academic orientation was little changed. Preparation for college remained their controlling objective. Their curriculum was conventional, dictated by the needs of the colleges — though generally with a conspicuous lag.

The position of grammar in this academic tradition was an inheritance from a still earlier system. In the Elizabethan schools of England, instruction was all in Latin and centered on Latin literature. Here grammar had to be taught as a tool. When English was substituted, its grammar replaced that of Latin in the scheme, and inherited much of its position. It was not so much an intellectual subject as an instrument, expected to assist students in writing good English, as formerly grammar had assisted in writing good Latin. However large it may have loomed in the syllabus, its place was always to some degree menial. To an extent not true of any other element in the academic curriculum, grammar was justified by immediate practical ends.

The grammar textbooks used in American schools through the nineteenth century mostly defined grammar more or less in the following manner: "English grammar is the art of speaking and writing English correctly."[3] Late in the century, a definition as "the science of language" came to be given more frequently by textbook writers. In this, they were following the almost universal practice of grammarians other than the authors of school books.

Nevertheless, the old textbook definition continues as the most widely held understanding of the nature and purpose of the subject. Combined with a characteristic interpretation of "correctly", it dominates popular thinking. It is this that motivates the parents' highly emotional desire for grammar teaching for their children.

The close association of grammar with the three R's, the conception of grammar as a tool, and this definition reinforce each other. Together they have been the main forces molding popular attitudes.

The subject is considered closed. That is, the total body of grammatical facts is felt to be fixed, and not particularly large. There are no unsolved problems to be isolated and investigated. Grammar is not conceivably a subject for research or advanced study — any more than is (in the popular notion) arithmetic. The facts are considered to be clear, definitive, and unassailable.

This does not exclude debate about the place of grammar in the curriculum, but it does limit the topics that can be debated. There are conceivable questions as to when and at what rate it is to be taught. For most Americans, however, there is no possible argument as to the content

---

[3] Definitions of this type are largely traceable to Lindley Murray's: "English grammar is the art of speaking and writing the English language with propriety." He is apparently indebted in part at least to Robert Lowth's: "Grammar is the Art of rightly expressing our thoughts by Words."

of the grammar course. Any suggestion that there might be is inevitably misconstrued and taken to be outright rejection of grammar.

This is in sharp contrast to the debate about other subjects. Physics, for example, is known to be rapidly expanding. Physicists are expected to have some special, even esoteric, competence. Almost any American will acknowledge his lack of understanding of physics and feels no embarrassment for it. If he is realistic, he may admit that he does not know everything about grammar — or more likely, that he has forgotten a great deal of grammar. He feels a little guilty about this. His guilt only reinforces his desire that the new generation may learn it more thoroughly. He certainly knows what should be taught. Simply, it is grammar, the whole fixed body of rules. There is no need for expert advice at this point, even if such were conceivably available.

PRESCRIPTIVISM

Coupled with the notion that the body of grammatical knowledge is complete and definitive has been the belief that there exists an absolute standard of correctness. This is thought to be so clear that any educated man should comprehend it immediately. Any failure to conform is evidence of poor education, bad taste, stupidity, or seditious intent to destroy English. In theory this norm is enshrined in the dictionaries and grammars. The author or editor of any such work, of course, is expected to have a fine feel for this standard. His objective must be to provide guidance for the less sensitive. To fail in this is to betray a public trust.

Every new major dictionary has been greeted with violent condemnation in the public press and in literary circles. The recent uproar over *Webster's Third New International Dictionary* was perhaps the most angry and unenlightened.[4] Much of the criticism focused on the inclusion of certain words which anybody (certainly dictionary editors!) should know are bad, among them *ain't* and *finalize*. That these were included could indicate either that the editors were totally incompetent or that they were deliberately undermining the language. Some critics made one charge, some the other, a few inconsistently made both. The irresponsibility of the criticism is shown by the fact that many of the condemned features are found in the Second Edition (generally considered by this year's critics as the last great dictionary[5]) and in many of the current standard desk

[4] A good sample of the comment, pro and con, can be seen in James Sledd and Wilma R. Ebbitt, *Dictionaries and That Dictionary*, Chicago: Scott, Foresman and Company, 1962. This is probably the most significant documenting of American attitudes toward language in this century, and has implications extending far beyond lexicography.

[5] The reception of the Second was only a little less violent than that of the Third. Some journals required a decade or more to reconcile themselves to that edition. Many of these now proclaim that they will stick with the Second as the last symbol of stability in an era of language decadence. The First was similarly condemned when it appeared in 1911.

dictionaries. The more moderate critics were willing to admit that such words exist, but were dismayed that the editors had not seen fit to label them flatfootedly as bad. They could not conceive that the status of such a word could be uncertain. The well-known standard of good English would surely draw a definite line in such cases.

In the entry at *ain't* the following statement is made: "though disapproved by many and more common in less educated speech, used orally in most parts of the United States by many cultivated speakers, esp. in the phrase *ain't I*."[6] This is a statement of fact made with care by a staff of specialists giving full time to observation of current English and supported by a great deal of meticulously gathered data. One might legitimately criticize details of evaluation. Is "disapproved by many" sufficient, or would "disapproved by most" be better? Should it be "many cultivated speakers" or "some cultivated speakers"? But the argument did not go that way. Instead, some simply said that the editors must surely have known (everybody does!) that *ain't* is incorrect and labeled it so without such excessive verbage. Others denied the facts. *Ain't*, they said, is simply never used by cultivated speakers. Indeed, anyone who uses it, by that act excludes himself from the circle. The facts are, however, that people who by every other standard must be judged to be cultivated speakers do use *ain't*. Nothing can be more obnoxious than the facts to someone who has already made up his mind.

The ire of the public has more often been directed to dictionaries than to grammars. No grammar has ever had quite the same prominence as the "Unabridged", the most prestigious book ever produced in America. Public vigilance for grammar finds its target in the curriculum rather than in books. The underlying attitude is the same, as is the cavalier disregard for facts, and often the extreme emotionalism of the reaction. Educational administrators have tended to be cautious.

The market for grammar textbooks has favored those that have been strictly prescriptive. — Some of them have set out to state precisely what is "correct English" and lay down rules by which it can be spoken or written. — Many have devoted even more space to stating in detail what is "incorrect English", and what one should, therefore, avoid in one's own speech and writing, and what one should censor when used by others. The public has wanted books that would shoulder the responsibility of preserving the "purity of the language". In general, grammar textbook writers could be found who would do so.

Not all authors have had this prescriptive orientation. Whenever a writer has tried to make a more moderate statement, his efforts found

---

[6] *Webster's Third New International Dictionary*, Springfield, Mass.: G. and C. Merriam, ad loc, 1961. This statement has commonly been quoted as indicating the editors' approval of *ain't*. Clearly it is intended as nothing but a statement of observed fact.

scant sympathy or understanding. Often, he was misinterpreted and read as an authoritarian, whether he desired it or not. Dictionary compilers have made explicit disclaimers of oracular powers; these have been left unread and forgotten. A grammarian's acknowledgement of any possible openness to doubts about the standards often received the same treatment. To be successful, a grammar textbook had to be either definitely prescriptive or capable of being used as if it were. The public was generally more authoritarian than the grammarians.

Unfortunately the "correct English" visualized by the purists has been something of a will-o'-the-wisp. Johnny in the last row in the ninth-grade English class is expected to develop a sensitivity to correctness, though the models held up for his emulation — from Shakespeare and the King James translators to current writers — seem to have been unable to gain that same insight, and so make egregious errors. The teacher finds it less embarrassing to pass very quickly over certain passages and to keep the children's minds busy with literary questions lest they notice grammar. And in the grammar class, Shakespeare must not be mentioned lest they really do notice his language and ask a question that would be troublesome. Thus is the integration of the English curriculum furthered!

This platonic standard is most capricious. *Ain't I* is vigorously condemned; *am I not* is advocated in its place. The latter is so jarringly snobbish or pedantic to many Americans that they either go to great lengths to recast sentences to avoid anything of the kind, or they substitute *aren't I*.[7] Teachers tend to close their eyes and say nothing unless their attention is directed to *aren't I*. Then they have to say that it really is not good, but at least it is better than *ain't I*. Great attention is given to *who* and *whom*, and rigorous conformity to rules of case is enjoined — in general. But *than whom* is usually tolerated and occasionally taught, even in contexts where *than me* would be instantly condemned in favor of *than I*. English grammar is indeed a bewildering subject!

THE ENGLISH CURRICULUM

The English curriculum is currently thought of as having three main components: literature, composition, and language. This, however, gives only a very partial picture. In the first place, the English curriculum has long been the dumping ground for numerous small, often ill-assorted, matters that someone thought ought to be in the school program somewhere. In some instances these have bulked so large that the central concerns were obscured. In the second place, some of the major components have had less internal unity and coherence than might be desirable.

---

[7] Many speakers have picked up *aren't I* in childhood by imitation of their elders. The substitution was made, then, by their linguistic ancestors. Whoever was ultimately responsible, it remains in origin a deliberate substitution to avoid *ain't I*.

This is particularly true of language. In the upper grades it has tended to consist largely of grammar; in the lower grades of reading and spelling. There may be various amounts of formal instruction in vocabulary. Most other elements are recent accretions and have at best a precarious place.

The most conspicuous feature of the English curriculum after its loose organization is its diversity. The syllabus varies from system to system. The implementation of the syllabus varies even more. English is probably the least uniform and the least coherent major segment in the American public school curriculum.

A generation or two ago the general picture was much the same. The place of grammar in the curriculum varied from school to school, and even from classroom to classroom. It had been practically eliminated from a few schools and drastically cut in some others. It remained strong in most. Indeed, in some it was clearly the dominant element in the English curriculum, receiving more attention than either literature or composition, or even than both together.

Some English teachers were disturbed over this situation. A small segment of the profession, largely acting through the National Council of Teachers of English, were trying to break the stranglehold of grammar on the English curriculum. The National Council itself was weak, and the movement was not particularly effective.

In some schools grammar was started in the grades. In others it was reserved for the last years of high school. Methods of teaching varied, and were constantly debated within the profession. The subject matter, however, was fairly uniform. Though the textbooks varied in many ways, one basic conception of grammar was shared by almost all of them.

Most teachers probably shared the prevailing popular attitude that grammar was primarily a device for producing better writing. Some were content to teach it in a rote mechanical way, apparently satisfied that such teaching would meet the need. Most, however, had at least a slightly more sophisticated notion than prevailed among the general public. Some teachers had a vision much broader than this and were trying to make grammar applicable to composition in new and more imaginative ways.

Some teachers disliked grammar and gave it only perfunctory attention. Others considered it important and put great emphasis on it, teaching it with care and imagination. No single generalization about grammar teaching could cover more than a small part of the profession.

The most serious current difficulty with grammar teaching seems already to have begun to make itself felt two generations ago. Teacher training had been upgraded, formally at least. College preparation was now the norm in the profession. But this had not affected grammar. Grammar was, with a few exceptions, not a serious subject of study in the colleges and universities of America. It was seldom taught, and it was not often the subject of significant research activity.

Lacking university support, the tradition of grammar teaching has had to be maintained within the schools themselves. Grammar was learned in grammar school or in high school, and future teachers got no further instruction in the subject in their college preparation. Any deficiencies in his original learning or retention the teacher had to make up on his own — if he could. That was often difficult. Few sources were available to him beyond the textbooks he was using in class, perhaps supplemented by one or two others on much the same level. These seldom gave the sort of help the teacher needed. Textbooks at advanced levels or solid reference works have been notably few, and mostly poorly known and little circulated in the schools. To have either perspective or confidence, a teacher needs a margin of knowledge beyond the curriculum he is to teach. This can never be acquired without instruction, or adequate books, or both. Few teachers were privileged to have either.

Grammar in the schools was cut off from any intellectual growing edge. This was not true to the same extent of any other segment of the curriculum. Many English teachers, for example, had worked in college or university under first-rate literary scholars. Even the dullest professor in the poorest college had himself studied under a scholar or under someone who had. No English major could be more than a step or two removed from productive scholarship and the attitudes that it engenders. Not all were excited about their field, of course, but many were. The whole effort of literature teaching was continually revitalized by these direct or indirect contacts. By contrast, grammar was intellectually moribund in the American schools and colleges. Research on grammar was almost nonexistent in this country. The research in Europe was hardly known and practically inaccessible. The rare scholar with vital interest in English as language was isolated and often looked upon as eccentric. He could communicate his interest to few, and it could not spread far. For most teachers there was no effective source for revitalization of grammar teaching, even through several removes.

A process of deterioration in grammar teaching has been going on for at least two or three generations. This has continued until we have now reached a situation where very many teachers of English do not understand the grammar they are teaching, and where very few know anything about the subject beyond what is contained in the textbooks their students use.

The curriculum as a whole and all its parts individually have evolved through a long history of experimentation and debate. Numerous cross currents have affected it since the beginnings of American education. Some of these had their origins in the frontier background of the common schools. Some stemmed from the academic tradition of the colleges and secondary schools. Some were merely the temporary fashions of their day. The interactions of all these forces have been complex and far from uniform. Even a broad sketch of the history of the grammar segment of the curriculum would be beyond the dimensions possible in this book.

There are, however, three movements of comparatively recent times which must be mentioned because they form a sequence of developments leading up to the present debate about grammar and linguistics in the curriculum. These are the movements centering about the survey of errors, usage, and the "new grammar".

SURVEYS OF ERRORS

One of the most characteristic movements affecting the schools in this century has been educational research, the statistical study of curriculum, materials, methods, and so on, against certain measurable criteria of usefulness. This has become a standard way of approaching any educational problem. Experiment, evaluation, and statistical interpretation have become familiar devices to every curriculum specialist.

It has usually been assumed that a major purpose of English instruction was to teach "good", "error-free" language. The success of grammar teaching could be measured against this. Grammar might be justified if it could help in preventing "errors" in writing, or if it could contribute in any other way to composing ability. Tests were devised to measure the effectiveness of grammar teaching. The results were for the most part noncommittal, but occasionally definitely negative. It seemed at best that grammar could not be proved to be carrying its load. There was some evidence that it was contributing very little at all to the assumed objectives.

A few teachers and administrators drew the conclusion that grammar should be curtailed or eliminated. A low valuation of grammar sometimes passed into open antagonism. Those who felt grammar to be proven useless scientifically were reinforced by another group whose sole interest lay in literature and who disliked grammar because it was so mechanical and spiritless.[8] Strange bedfellows they were!

Against this antigrammar sentiment, the most effective defense came from the public and from school-board members. They were generally much less impressed by educational research than were the professionals. Grammar had always been in the schools, therefore, they believed, it belonged in the schools. Grammar was generally believed to be indispensible for correct English, and every parent coveted correctness for his children. The public clamor restrained any professional rejection. It also confirmed the antagonism of some teachers and administrators. Grammar was the root of a disproportionate share of their difficulties with the public. In many schools, grammar was cut just as much as curriculum specialists and superintendents thought was politically prudent. The fate of grammar hung

---

[8] A strong expression of this kind of antigrammar position may be found in Sidney Cox, *The Teaching of English, Avowals and Ventures*, 1928, p. 96: "As for books about writing, or about grammar, I do not see how an English teacher can either spare the time for them, or let them affect the student's conception of a *book*."

upon a struggle where neither antagonist understood what was at stake, but where prejudices were strong.

Educational research had cast doubt upon the utility of grammar teaching. But it was only a minority that drew the conclusion that grammar should be dropped. A much larger group interpreted the findings as raising questions about the way in which grammar was being taught. Specific diagnoses varied. So did proposals for reform.

One of the most widely discussed remedies was often labeled "functional grammar".[9] For a couple of decades it loomed large in the professional debates, and in the long run it had a considerable effect on the teaching of grammar, in part by preparing the way for another movement of even greater direct effect.

The common premise was accepted that grammar teaching should help eliminate errors in language use. It was taken as a corollary of this that teaching should focus on those specific points of greatest value for this purpose, that is, on the rules which would be antidotes to the most common and serious errors. Mistakes in children's writing were collected, tabulated, and interpreted statistically in order to guide curriculum planners and classroom teachers in placing proper emphasis. Debate centered about the functionality — that is, the usefulness in preventing solecisms — of particular rules, or about how and when to introduce them to achieve maximum results in improvement of writing. Lists of items to be taught were drawn up by various teachers or committees. The procedure seemed usually to involve evaluating specific rules individually. The focus of attention was on details rather than on system.

The cumulative effect was a shift in the emphasis in grammar instruction and the dropping of certain points completely. A few were eliminated because they were found to be unnecessary — few people make the kind of errors they would correct. A few rules were dropped because they were found to be of little directly discernible benefit in helping children to write or speak better English. More often, the decisions were of a different kind: Certain points were found to require much more attention than they had been receiving. As these were given an increasing share of classroom time, others necessarily had less. Many rules were dropped simply by default. But, however it happened, the trend was toward concentration on a smaller number of points.

As this process went on, the emphasis tended to fall on very specific points and the more general were first neglected and then forgotten. The broader patterns are harder to list, infractions are more difficult to identify, and the tabulations are not so easily interpreted into teaching directives. Many lists of items to be taught as "functional grammar" were almost

[9] "Functional grammar" in this sense must be distinguished from several other uses of the same term, notably that of Jespersen, for whom "functional grammar" was grammar based on the functions of words and word groups. See page 77.

entirely matters of usage of specific forms, of the order of the distinction between *lie* and *lay* and the interdiction against *ain't*. Some of these problems quite properly deserved attention in the curriculum, but the emphasis was often quite wrong.

The consequences of such a movement are inescapable. Language is a system (or a complex of systems). Its grammar must be systematic to be meaningful. Bits and pieces cannot be taught or omitted at will simply because they are individually judged useful or not. As items are dropped the system falls apart. When certain ones are eliminated, it becomes more difficult to teach the remainder. No one would seriously propose omitting from the arithmetic curriculum in the primary grades the teaching of $2 \times 2 = 4$ on the ground that high school students made fewer mistakes with this than with $9 \times 7 = 63$. If the multiplication table is to be taught, it is far better and easier to teach the whole and to teach it systematically. It, like English, is a system.

The grammar taught in the American schools had never put much stress on the system. "Functional grammar" and similar movements of the twenties and thirties emphasized its tendencies to atomism. This led to a remarkable development. While the content of the grammar course contracted markedly, the time devoted to grammar shrank much less, if at all. A great deal more time was needed for the material that was retained. As items were deleted from the eighth-grade syllabus they were replaced by additional review of points presented in the seventh. The curriculum seemed to be approaching the strange condition of being almost entirely review. This yearly reiteration was necessitated by the failure of students to learn. In turn it aggravated the situation by adding boredom to vacuity.

The experience of the schools with "functional grammar" has confirmed that random teaching cannot work. The more grammar is cut, the less successful is the teaching of the remainder. The more disconnected the facts, the more difficult they are to teach. "Functional grammar" with its emphasis on errors, is self-defeating. It is tantamount to the elimination of grammar — simply a longer, slower process to that end. While grammar and usage continued in most schools to occupy a very large block of time, their status deteriorated.

THE USAGE MOVEMENT

The surveys of errors which loomed so large in discussion during the twenties were based on the prevailing notions of right and wrong in language. It was taken for granted that "errors" could be easily identified. The problem was only to ascertain what "errors" were most important.

Not everyone was satisfied, however. The next step was clearly to examine the rules themselves to find out whether they could be justified. The movement for the survey of errors had opened a way. Statistical study might be made of the very validity of the grammatical principles. The wide familiarity with survey methods in the English-teaching profession would assure a hearing that previous antiprescriptive writings had not had.

The result was what came to be known as the "usage movement". The foundations were laid in Sterling A. Leonard's *Current English Usage*,[10] published in 1932, and in Albert H. Marckwardt and Fred Walcott's *Facts about Current English Usage*, published in 1938. These monographs deal with specific points of usage, items like *try and, it's me, no doubt but that, between the four*. In the first study, 230 such expressions were selected. These were submitted to 229 judges, ranging from linguists and English teachers to prominent authors and editors. They were asked to rate them as: formally correct English; fully acceptable English for informal conversation, commercial, foreign, scientific, or other technical uses; or popular or illiterate speech. The evaluations of this panel were tabulated and analyzed statistically. For just under half, a fair consensus was found, and the report accordingly lists some items as standard or substandard. For the remainder, agreement was felt inadequate to make definitive decisions, and the usages were listed as disputable. The disparity between these results and the prescriptions of the textbooks was often extreme.

The study of Marckwardt and Walcott examined the disputable items in the light of evidence gathered in the great dictionaries, *The Oxford English Dictionary* and *Webster's New International Dictionary, Second Edition*, and the fuller scholarly grammars. They found that actual recorded usage provided a criterion in many cases. This study indicated that the opinions of Leonard's panel, far out of accord as they were with what was taught in the textbooks, were nevertheless often quite conservative in the light of prevailing use.

Studies along the same lines have continued in increasing numbers. They have gradually shifted from the methodologies of Leonard and of Marckwardt and Walcott to careful counts of large bodies of text. Often many thousands of pages of printed matter have been meticulously searched for all instances of some sets of competing usages. The professional literature has been full of such studies.[11] Many of them have been of great interest and significance. Recently, much of this work has been gathered and summarized in Margaret Bryant's *Current American Usage*.

This focus of attention on actual observable facts has been most salutary. Many details in the textbooks have been modified or completely restated as a consequence. But much more important has been the change in professional attitudes that has come about. In three decades, the direct

[10] Full bibliographic information on this and other works cited in this section can be found in the Bibliography.

[11] A full bibliography can be found in Margaret M. Bryant, *Current American Usage*, 1962.

observation of language has gained new respect among English teachers. This is evidenced, for example, by the fact that the teachers have been far less frightened by *Webster's Third New International Dictionary* than the editors and contributors to the slick-paper press. It has produced a new openness to innovations in English grammar, particularly when they are clearly based on examination of data.

The usage movement, however, has also had some less desirable side effects. For many teachers, it has strengthened the piecemeal approach that lay behind "functional grammar". In undercutting the old reliance on logic and analogy in favor of facts of usage, it sometimes further attenuated the understanding of grammar as system. Grammar becomes trivial when its systematic organization is destroyed.

With the usage movement, there has grown up a distinction, popular in the profession, between "grammar" and "usage". This has never been sharp, and for some it has been very confused. Often "usage" refers to the more specific details — rules applying to single words or phrases — or to the exceptional and marginal cases. "Grammar" refers to the more general features. Sometimes "usage" verges on style. This distinction might have helped materially to save for grammar the emphasis on system by excluding from grammar the less systematic fragments. That it did not do so is probably evidence that systematic grammar with intellectual content was already moribund through much of the profession when the distinction arose.

The larger part of the usage movement has continued to examine quantities of text for certain preselected details. A branch of the movement turned instead to examining a body of text for whatever might be found in it. That is, in effect, to tabulate actual usage whether it had been called into question or not. Through the thirties this was certainly the weaker of the two prongs of the usage movement. But it held promise. The dominant figure was Charles C. Fries.

Fries was commissioned by the National Council of Teachers of English to conduct a full-scale study to determine what grammatical material should be taught in the schools. After considerable delay the report appeared in 1940 as the *American English Grammar*. His stated objective was reminiscent of many earlier investigations. His method was not. He saw the problem as a much deeper one, and conducted a more comprehensive study than any of his predecessors.

Fries' work was a usage study, but with a difference. He did not examine good writing from reputable authors in an attempt to determine the prevailing standard. Instead, he examined a large body of letters written by quite ordinary Americans of a wide range of backgrounds. He thus did not determine what should be, but what was the actual writing practice of the American public.

In this respect it was more like the old surveys of errors. But the difference here was even more profound. He did not restrict his attention to selected points, but tabulated whatever he found, that is, all aspects of grammar and usage, either "correct" or "incorrect". He thus put "errors" in a new perspective. He was able to show that many notions about them had no real relationship with what actually happens in the practical, unself-conscious writing of normal Americans. Many of the commonly discussed "errors" were far less frequent than had usually been assumed.

He had certain information about the writers and used this to classify his sample. He was thus able to compare letters from people with meager background and poor education with those of professional people, graduated from good colleges, and living in cultural centers. He found far less difference between the two groups than might be expected. Grammatical errors were not the most significant difference between semiliterate and standard written English.

Fries found the two levels to differ most in the meagerness of the language used by the substandard writers. Many useful constructions were apparently not known to them. Their letters showed a very narrow range of expression. If the function of the school is viewed as making writers of standard English out of those who would otherwise fall into the substandard group, this would suggest that the correction of "errors" could be only a minor part of the task at best. Far more important would be training students to use a broader spectrum of the resources of the language. Grammar teaching would have to be constructive rather than merely corrective. This would certainly necessitate a drastic modification of the view of grammar underlying the prevailing teaching.

Indeed, it would require a total restructuring of the content of the grammar curriculum. Fries recognized this:

> It is the point of view of this report that *a study of the real grammar of present-day English has never been used in the schools* and that the conclusions concerning its effectiveness relate only to the type of "grammar" that has been tried. . . .
> This book, therefore, presents a *grammar* of Present-day American English that differs from any that has yet been tried in the efforts to deal with the language practices of students. It contains no rules and definitions of correct English and is not a closed handbook of usage. It does, however, attempt to provide the starting point for a workable program in English language for the schools by its methods and materials.[12]

Moreover, Fries suggested as the third of his major recommendations[13]

---

[12] Charles C. Fries, *American English Grammar*, New York: D. Appleton-Century Company, 1940, pp. 285, 286.

[13] The three are: "A. We must agree upon the kind of English which it is the obligation of the schools to teach. B. We must agree to base our teaching upon an accurate, realistic description of the actual practices of informal Standard English and eliminate from our language programs all those matters of dispute for which there is any considerable usage in informal Standard English. C. We must agree to stimulate

that the English program should be designed to make the student "an intelligent observer of language usage". This, he pointed out, would require reorientation of grammar teaching to put major emphasis on fundamental matters of language structure. It would also demand a very different form of presentation from the traditional statement of a rule, its rote memorization, and then its use in correcting or completing artificially selected sentences. This would have to be replaced by presentation of data, observation, and the formulation of conclusions, as much as possible of the work being done by the students. The two methods of teaching would be very difficult to reconcile within a single program.

The *American English Grammar* had a mixed reception. Many in the rank and file of the profession never saw it. Others ignored it. Some could not understand it. Some rejected it vehemently. It might have had very little effect at all but for the openness slowly and painfully developed by such books as those of Leonard and of Marckwardt and Walcott. Among the leaders of the teaching profession its influence continued to grow.

For some time its significance as a study of usage greatly overshadowed its suggestions concerning the more basic problems of grammar. These could be widely appreciated only after certain other developments had taken place. One of these was increased contact with linguistics.

In the thirties very few English professors, and practically none of the school English teachers, knew very much about the small but growing field of descriptive linguistics. Marckwardt and Fries, however, were both members of the Linguistic Society of America; Fries in particular had been active in the Society from its foundation in 1924. The leaders in the usage movement, thus, had close contact with linguistics. They referred to linguistics in their writings and were instrumental in bringing the discipline to the attention of the profession. However, it required some time before any real understanding of linguistics was at all general, even among the leaders of the English-teaching profession.

THE NEW GRAMMAR

Fries' *American English Grammar* was an important event. It opened up a whole new direction of development. Before 1940 most of the progressives were looking toward the teaching of essentially the same grammar, purged of some meaningless rules, but from a nonprescriptive approach. Fries suggested that a new grammar was needed. Often in the past, changes had been suggested in the terminology, the definitions, or even in the classifications, but most of the suggestions for changes were only in matters of detail. That some radically new type of grammar would

---

among our pupils observation of actual usage and to go as far as possible in giving them a practical equipment for this purpose." Fries, *American English Grammar*, New York: D. Appleton-Century Company, 1940, pp. 289, 290, 291. The quotation in the text is from p. 291, the discussion of proposal C.

be possible was a new idea for most of the profession, and one which would require some time for acceptance. On the whole the grammatical tradition of the schools had been remarkably uniform, and only a small minority of English teachers in America were aware of the grammatical work in Europe.[14] Even fewer were really acquainted with it. There had long been only one type of grammar effectively available to school teachers and curriculum specialists.

Not only had Fries emphasized that such a change was needed; he had also attempted to give at least a partial statement of a new system. His book was not primarily about English teaching, or even about grammar. It actually was a grammatical description of American English. The title was quite fitting. He demonstrated the possibility of a new grammar by presenting a good bit of grammatical information in a new formulation.

The *American English Grammar*, however, does not give a system complete enough to provide the basis for the new curriculum he envisioned. To do so, it would have to have included a description of sentence structure. Fries had originally planned a chapter on syntax. However, he found that an adequate treatment would delay the book greatly (it was already a decade overdue) and increase its size beyond reason. He therefore planned to make up the deficiency by a second book.

It was twelve years before the continuation appeared as *The Structure of English, An Introduction to the Construction of English Sentences.*[15] The delay was probably fortunate. It was a far better book in 1952 than it could have been earlier. Before 1940 American descriptive linguistics had very little to contribute to the analysis or statement of syntax. The decade before *The Structure of English* appeared was one of intense activity in this field. Fries was able to make use of some of the newly developed techniques. He was also able to obtain and use a larger and more satisfactory corpus of data, roughly a quarter million words of recorded and transcribed conversation.

Moreover, the profession was far more receptive. The lessons of the *American English Grammar* were beginning to be assimilated and appreciated, though of course not universally. A few English teachers had begun to read publications on linguistics. There was excitement in foreign language teaching that was spreading through the schools and arousing curiosity. Some of the suggestions of the older book had been tried here and there in the class room. As a result a few English teachers had had some experience with the advantages and problems of a new grammatical approach. Without all this preparation, the new book would have been accepted much more slowly than it was.

[14] Some college courses have made use of some of Jespersen's work. However, it seems that the origin of the ideas taught was seldom made clear to the students.

[15] Full bibliographic information on this and other works cited in this section can be found in the Bibliography.

In the preceding year, George L. Trager and Henry L. Smith, Jr., had published *An Outline of English Structure*. This was independent of Fries' work and approached the problem from a very different point of view. It attempted to cover the sound system, word formation, and syntax, but was much the fullest on the first of these and hardly more than suggestive on the last. The authors were primarily linguists and wrote more for linguists than for teachers.

The two books can, however, be looked on as supplementing each other.[16] It was found that the syntax of Fries could be teamed with the phonology of Trager and Smith to give a usable combination. The "new grammar" now had a sufficient body of material to form a basis for teaching. In the midfifties it looked as though it might emerge and congeal as a new eclectic tradition based on these two sources with certain elements salvaged from older grammars.

The Structure of English, An Outline of English Structure, and the eclectic "new grammar" based on them became topics of discussion at professional meetings. Within a few years, reference to these and to linguistics became almost regular in English curriculum discussions. Experimental teaching began to increase. Rapid expansion awaited only the appearance and general availability of satisfactory textbooks.

The year 1956 saw the first such publications. Two appeared for college "freshman English": Harold Whitehall's *Structural Essentials of English* and Donald Lloyd and Harry Warfel's *American English in its Cultural Setting*. One was written for high schools: Paul Roberts' *Patterns of English*. In the next few years several additional college textbooks appeared. High school materials came out more slowly, mostly in mimeographed and near-print form for local use.

Before the "new grammar" tradition could be consolidated, a new movement within linguistics had appeared and very quickly made itself known among the leadership in the English-teaching profession. This was transformational generative grammar. The first textbook to show any influence from this source was Paul Roberts' *English Sentences* published in 1962. Others are now appearing. These represent a wide variety of approaches. The establishment of a "new grammar" orthodoxy has been effectively forestalled. In the process, further complexity has been injected into an already confused picture.

These new materials are not yet widely known, but their use is spreading.[17] It is not yet possible to claim that results establish their value. Success

---

[16] The use of these two as supplemental is partly artificial. The basic principles on which the two analyses are based are quite divergent. Only the looseness of textbook presentation has made it possible to integrate them into a single statement.

[17] A study published in 1960 found 4 percent of the English teachers in California using some elements of structural grammar in their teaching. This is probably representative. Charles Alva, *Structural Grammar in California High Schools*, 1960, English Journal 49:606.

has been various. Some schools have been well pleased and expect to continue using linguistically oriented materials; others have been dissatisfied and have returned to the old. The causes, of course, are complex. One important factor is certainly the teachers' understanding of the books and their underlying viewpoint. They cannot be taught effectively with only the weak background in school grammar that is normal among English teachers. Nevertheless, many have demonstrated that teachers who are willing to make the effort can attain a working familiarity with the "new grammar" by self-education. Training in linguistics is still not widely available, but is becoming more accessible.

At least as important a factor as knowledge has been attitudes. Lack of commitment has often been contributory to failure, and high enthusiasm to success. All such factors, however, would have similar effects with any new approach, good or bad. It cannot, therefore, be proved that the new materials are superior, but many competent teachers who had better-than-average success with the old have been very favorably impressed with the new and find their satisfaction growing with each reuse. The "new grammar" certainly gives every indication of being a decided improvement.[18]

It is important to remember that the "new grammar" is still operating under real difficulties. So far there are only single books. These are inevitably difficult to articulate into a continuing curriculum. It will be some time before adequate series can be made available. It will require a great deal more work before most of the problems that arise in teaching are understood and can be provided for. Nevertheless, there is every reason to believe that new curricula will gradually evolve to take full advantage of the "new grammar", and that before long all curricula will show more or less of its influence.[19]

"LINGUISTICS" VS. "TRADITIONAL GRAMMAR"

The first introduction to linguistics for most English teachers was in the context of controversy, first over authoritarianism, then usage, and later broadened to include the content of grammar instruction. The opponents of the old doctrine of correctness had brought in the "findings of linguistic science" as the chief witness for the prosecution. It was perhaps inevitable that, for many teachers, linguistics should be rather narrowly identified with antiprescriptivism. In the heat of battle both friends and

[18] It should be remembered that the available textbooks have been somewhat diffident in their approach. In general, they attempt to do little other than what traditional textbooks have done. The full benefit of new insights will not be attained until the scope of the language segment of the curriculum is broadened appreciably. See Chapter 20.

[19] We have already reached a point where few texts, even the most conservative, show no trace of influence from the recent developments in "linguistic approaches" to grammar. In most instances the innovations are small, and sometimes neither well integrated nor well treated. A trend is, however, indicated.

foes emphasized certain features of linguistics disproportionately. As a result, much of the English profession got a constrained and distorted view of the scope and significance of the science. For some it was merely an ally ready to provide arguments with an aura of scientific authority. For the conservatives — including a large segment of the general public — it was merely a pseudoscience created to justify permissiveness in language and to undercut standards.

Much was said about the "principles of linguistics", but most of it was superficial. One of the more popular formulations in the fifties,[20] repeatedly quoted, took the following form:

1. Languages change constantly.
2. Change is normal.
3. Spoken language is the language.
4. Correctness rests upon usage.
5. All usage is relative.

In general, linguists will accept these statements, though many would prefer considerable rewording. No professional linguist would be satisfied with them. To advance them, as has commonly been done, as *"the* principles of linguistics" is certainly a misrepresentation. They are not even adequate as a selection of principles of maximum usefulness to English studies in the schools. They are totally inadequate as a basis for the study of the grammar of any single language, to say nothing of the investigation of language in general. Moreover, they range from fairly obvious, common-sense statements, to ones which are almost Delphic. To dignify such a miscellany with the label "principles" is ridiculous. To describe them as some have, as established by brilliant new research is worse. Linguistics must certainly be based on more than this, and must have produced more than this, or it is no science.[21]

Many of those who appealed to the authority of linguistics had only a second- or third-hand acquaintance at best. Careful, reasoned arguments can easily be degraded as they get farther from their source. Without an understanding of the basic viewpoint of linguistics, special pleaders could easily overstate the case and produce a caricature. In their zeal to make their "linguist" the strongest possible champion against normative teaching in the schools, they made him the sworn enemy of *all* standards. They endowed him, moreover, with the same special wisdom as a baseball star pontificating on nutrition.

[20] This statement seems to be traceable to the National Council of Teachers of English, *The English Language Arts in the Secondary Curriculum*, 1952.

[21] I use the word "science" with diffidence. I do not wish to imply many features of the popular notion of science. Nor do I wish to set linguistics as a science against certain other studies to which the term might not be applied. And, especially, I would not want to suggest that if linguistics is a science that fact gives it any kind of superiority.

The conservatives generally knew no more about linguistics. But they were often quite right in opposing the false authority that was being used against them. Much of it was in fact trite, nonsensical, or illiberal. It often did not require much special knowledge to criticize the caricature presented as "linguistics". From their side, the conservatives were frequently no more careful. They often condemned linguistics as a conspiracy against the English language, against literature, and against all humanistic values. They countered trivial statements of "principles" with slogans and epithets.

Irresponsible journalism has often further confused the issue. Any attack on prescriptivism from an English professor has been considered to have news value of the man-bites-dog variety. Sensational write-ups have often distorted or even fabricated statements. "Professor advocates ain't" has been judged proper reporting of a cautious and carefully phrased statement that children should be taught the kind of language in actual use by good writers. These reports have been the chief sources of information about linguists and linguistics for many of the enraged protectors of language purity, particularly outside the English-teaching profession. Canards have been repeated. The linguistic profession has been defamed. Some literary journals have permitted no rebuttal or clarification. The result has been the growth of a "devil image", ascribing to linguists strange doctrines and perverted motives. Unfortunately, this picture has been propagated by men of stature in the world of letters. Their word has carried weight far beyond its worth. Many English teachers and a large segment of the public have been misled.

The difficulty was compounded as the attention broadened to include the issues raised by the "new grammar". For generations the English profession had not given as much thought to the nature of grammar as to the authority of standards. Teachers were poorly qualified either to judge the new or defend the old. The debate inevitably centered largely on superficialities. Prominent among the latter were terminology and certain gimmicks.

Fries wrote for English teachers and interested laymen. He used no more of the professional terminology of linguistics than he felt absolutely necessary. He also avoided many of the old grammatical terms. He judged the latter often more likely to mislead than to clarify. He therefore abandoned all the familiar designations for parts of speech, replacing them by arbitrarily assigned figures and letters. Thus "noun" seems almost whimsically to be renamed "word of form class 1". Fries wanted to make clear that much more was involved: the boundaries of the class had been redrawn. Most of his classes are different in significant ways from the old parts of speech.

Trager and Smith, too, used a new vocabulary. They were writing primarily for linguists and students of linguistics. They wanted to set their work into a broad framework of a theory of language. Accordingly, they had to use a number of terms unfamiliar in school grammar. However odd they might seem to English teachers, their terms were certainly chosen with care and deliberate purpose.

Many of the presentations of the "new grammar" for English teachers gave undue prominence to these matters of terminology. Before an audience not accustomed to thinking about the presuppositions of grammar, it was certainly easier to argue such concrete points than to struggle with more basic matters. Some of the presentations were made by men who did not themselves understand the subtler points. The result is that "linguistics" is often viewed as largely a matter of neologisms. Somehow, if one can say "word of form class 1" when he means "noun" he is modern. Not a few have merely translated the old content into the new language.[22] Conservatives have been distracted from the real issues in the same way and have often dismissed "linguistics" as mere juggling with labels.

Fries made much of the point that grammatical signals are independent of word meanings. He showed that one can perform grammatical analysis on jabberwocky — indeed, this is precisely what one must do to read Lewis Carroll's poem. He found the use of nonsense words in grammatical sentences to be a very effective device for teaching about structure. Here was another feature that could be presented effectively in a short time, that teachers could carry home from a workshop and use. It became a favorite demonstration of the proponents of "linguistics". Inevitably some teachers have overdone it, using nonsense sentences for the presentation of almost every point. This they have done in the name of "linguistics". "Linguistics" has come to be merely a kind of gimmickry, and any new trick of presentation gets the label.

The "new grammar" has also been advocated for its alleged simplicity. A common and ancient charge against the old school grammar has been its complexity. (Perhaps this is only a reaction to its unreality!) Some teachers are obsessed with the search for a simpler alternative.[23] Some advocates have grandly swept aside the petty details of word-centered grammar, and

[22] Teachers have often asked Nelson Francis for a table of equivalents relating his terms to those of school grammar. His answer that he would not have used new terms if old had been available has frequently been received with incredulity. Yet anyone who assumes that old rules can merely be restated in the new terminology has obviously missed the point entirely, whether he be author or teacher.

[23] This note constantly recurs through the literature on the teaching of English. An extreme example (and one in many ways not representative) is the following: "Teachers of grammar face a real problem in most texts — selection and simplification. These texts vary from 250 to 800 pages and are usually written in *technical terms* by professors who never studied teaching, and perhaps were never effective teachers. They present the subject *as scholars, not as teachers*, and they write as if largely ignorant of the students who use the texts. . . . Most texts are in professorial, technical, or scholarly terms. *Boil them down to everyday talk.* Instead of 'A noun is the name of a person, place, or thing,' let's say, 'Any name is a noun.' " Philip M. Marsh, *How To Teach English*, New York: Bookman Associates, 1956, pp. 72, 73.

have seen everything as summed up in a simple scheme of sentence patterns. This has struck fire with the simplification seekers, and "linguistics" has become a movement for a cleaner, less complex grammar.[24] That anything deriving directly or indirectly from modern linguistics could seem to fill this bill is ironical. One of the great contributions from linguists must certainly be a new appreciation of the marvelous intricacy of human language in general and of the specific devices of individual languages. One of the major criticisms of the grammar of the schools is its superficiality and grossness.

In the advocacy of some enthusiasts, "linguistics" has become the new panacea. Not infrequently English teachers have espoused the new with an assurance that is amazing. It is a new truth, created by some superior beings, the linguists. The task is simply to exorcize some ancient superstitions. The falsity of some claims made for Fries' grammatical system[25] should be patent to anyone who would examine the evidence. It has been said to be the final word and complete in itself. The notion that the body of grammatical fact is small and closed dies hard![26]

Moreover, the new grammar has been set far too sharply in opposition to the old. There are differences, and some are important, but at many points they say the same thing, sometimes in almost identical ways. That each is an effort to describe English should guarantee some resemblance. The differences that matter have often been overlooked, and those that are less significant exaggerated. The whole question has been prejudiced by an unfortunate formulation. The debate has come to be between "linguistics" and "traditional grammar". Both terms are misnomers.

Fries labels his work as a "linguistic approach", explaining that it is "an attempt to apply . . . some of the principles underlying the modern scientific study of language."[27] He was certainly clear on the distinction between the grammar of English that he gives and linguistics, the general study of language. But his label, "linguistic approach", was often misinterpreted. In due course "linguistics" became the popular designation

---

[24] A representative statement is: "Modern linguistics and other approaches to the simplification of our teaching of the language are helping us to sense what is significant in English grammar and usage." Dora V. Smith, *Teaching Language as Communication*, 1960, English Journal 49:171. The same attitude pervades the following: Owen Thomas, *Generative Grammar: Toward Unification and Simplification*, 1962, English Journal 51:94–99, 113.

[25] It must be emphasized that the excessive claims stem from others, not from Fries. He claimed nothing more of his results than that they were "tentative formulations", and only that they covered "the basic matters of English structure". *The Structure of English*, 1952, p. vii.

[26] In spite of Roberts' disclaimer on page 40, it is commonly assumed that the ten sentence patterns described in *English Sentences* provide a complete description. I have heard this explicitly stated by speakers at teachers' meetings, and even more commonly implied. The facts are that a complete grammar of English would be a very large and complex thing. Such a grammar has not yet been closely approximated in any system.

[27] Fries, *The Structure of English*, 1952, p. 2.

not only for the newer systems of grammar but for almost every innovation even remotely similar.

"Traditional grammar" seems both clearer and fairer. It labels the kind of grammar that has been traditional in the schools. But it has also been applied to the work of the English grammarians in European universities. These two should not be confused, for they have little in common. Their terminology is often similar, some statements are much the same, but the underlying attitudes are quite opposed. One is scholarly in its orientation, the other shares much of the anti-intellectualism that has characterized lay American thinking on basic subjects of the curriculum.

Some conservatives have countered the appeal to "linguistics" by enlisting the support of scholarly traditional grammar. This work is impressive. However, it is a *non sequitur* to cite Jespersen, Poutsma, and Kruisinga to justify "traditional grammar" and then conclude that what now prevails in the schools is good. The old curriculum is no more influenced by the results achieved by these men than it is by that of the linguists. Indeed, if the American schools had been open to the work of the scholarly traditionalists, grammar teaching could never have deteriorated to the low state it has recently attained.

The debate between "linguistics" and "traditional grammar" should at least be rephrased. Much more helpful would be a moratorium on such a question, with its almost inevitable oversimplification of issues and its proneness to superficialities. What is needed, rather, is a new effort to understand the basic principles of language and of language description, an examination in some depth of the host of little questions that arise with any system of grammar, and a concerted drive against superficiality and distortion whether it be labeled "linguistics" or "traditional grammar". This requires both an historical perspective and close attention to underlying concepts.

Chapter 2

The Origins of Modern Linguistics

Since very ancient times men have been interested in their languages. As one of the most remarkable, complex, and familiar of human attainments, language has excited their curiosity. It is so much a part of their human existence that to understand themselves they have seen that they must first understand language. At the same time, they have recognized the pragmatic value of the ability to manipulate it well. Accordingly, works dealing in various ways with language are known from most of the ancient civilizations.

In classical Greece and Rome, grammar and rhetoric were subjects of study by all educated men. Practical handbooks were written to guide teacher and student. These started a line of development that has continued down to the present day, dividing and changing in various ways, to give us both grammar and linguistics. In a day when "grammar" and "linguistics" are set against each other as antagonists in debate, it is pertinent to see in some broad sketch how both arose from these ancient roots.

THE STUDY OF LANGUAGE TO 1800

The Western tradition of grammar and linguistics arose among the Greeks. The Greek philosophers concerned themselves quite extensively with discussion of the nature of language. Some held that language was a matter of convention, others that it was inherent in nature. This debate could not be resolved, of course, and is still with us. The discussion impelled some of them to look closely at language. The result was the first efforts to describe Greek. In due course various parts of speech were identified and named and some of the principles of grammar still taught in the schools were set forth.

28

The Romans were not intellectual innovators, but borrowed their learning wholesale from the Greeks. By the time this took place, the main outlines of Greek grammar had already been worked out. The two languages are rather similar in many ways, and it proved possible to transfer this pre-existing system of grammar to Latin with only minor adjustments. The Greek terminology was translated rather literally, ultimately to be adapted from Latin to English and most other languages of Europe.

Through the Middle Ages the scholarship of Western Europe was confined almost entirely to Latin. Grammar, rhetoric, and logic, inherited from the ancients, formed the core of general education. The grammar was, of course, the grammar of Latin as formulated by the late Roman grammarians. Medieval scholarship was not idle, however. The older grammatical tradition was actively restated and reformed to meet the needs of the times. No longer was Latin grammar being taught to students who spoke the language natively. Latin had become a second language for most users, and the textbooks took cognizance of the change. They became more prescriptive, more devoted to laying down rules as to how the language should be spoken and written. In accord with the scholasticism of the times, they were tied more closely to philosophy and logic.

Following the Renaissance, the newer languages of Europe gradually established themselves as vehicles for literature and later for science. Latin, however, remained central in the education of all scholars. The grammarians and rhetoricians only very slowly shifted their attention to the vernaculars. The first treatments of other languages began to appear in the fifteenth century, but it was much later before they became of great importance. The first English grammars appeared in the sixteenth century, and became influential only in the eighteenth.

The first grammars of modern European languages were written on the model of the medieval Latin grammars. This was not only natural, but useful as well. They were written not so much to teach students their own language as to provide a good base for teaching Latin, still the central subject in the curriculum. It was only in the nineteenth century that English and other modern languages displaced Latin, and so became objects of serious study in themselves. Slow as this shift was, the trend through these centuries was clearly to bring a wider range of languages into the purview of grammarians, previously concerned almost exclusively with Latin.

There was another trend that started with the Renaissance which had much the same effect. This was the rediscovery of Greek and Hebrew, and later of other ancient languages. During the Middle Ages all Biblical studies in the West had been based on the Vulgate Latin version. But with the fall of Constantinople a few scholars fled to the West. These refugees reintroduced the study of Greek and of the Greek Scriptures and the Church Fathers. Soon thereafter, Christian scholars began to learn Hebrew from rabbis and to undertake the study of the Old Testament in the original language. With this came contact with another tradition of grammar, ultimately stemming from the ancient Greeks, but transmitted through Syriac and Arabic and molded by languages very different from Latin. Soon other languages of the ancient and recent Near East were being studied. Scholars now had contact with languages quite divergent from Latin or any of the modern Western European tongues. Inevitably their grammatical horizons were widened.

The period of the great explorations brought Europeans into renewed contact with South and East Asia. Acquaintance with the languages, however, was slow in penetrating European scholarship, but by the eighteenth century some were known sufficiently to make some impact. By far the most germinal was Sanskrit. There were very important reasons. One was the high order of linguistic work of the ancient Sanskrit grammarians. Many centuries earlier they had produced a grammatical description which even now has seldom been approached for completeness and precision. The texts themselves are extremely difficult, and not every Sanskrit scholar could get very much out of them. But the grammatical system which is taught in them has so permeated Indian scholarship that no student of Sanskrit could avoid some exposure, however indirect, to the ideas of language deriving from these ancient grammarians. This grammatical work was independent of the older Greek grammar and the tradition stemming from it. It was organized on a very different pattern. Contact with Sanskrit inevitably stimulated European thought about language and grammar.

Sanskrit shows an evident basic similarity to Greek and Latin. Hardly had Sanskrit been introduced to European scholarship than this resemblance was noticed and commented upon. The most frequently quoted observation was made in 1786 by Sir William Jones, who had become acquainted with Sanskrit as Chief Justice in Bengal. He said:

> The Sanskrit language, whatever be its antiquity, is of a wonderful structure; more perfect than the Greek, more copious than the Latin, and more exquisitely refined than either; yet bearing to both of them a stronger affinity, both in the roots of verbs and in the forms of grammar, than could possibly have been produced by accident; so strong, indeed, that no philologer could examine all three without believing them to have sprung from some common source, which, perhaps no longer exists.[1]

The comparison of languages was no new thing.[2] It was already going

---

[1] Quoted here from Otto Jespersen, *Language*, 1922, p. 33.

[2] Mention of a number of early investigations may be found in Holger Pedersen, *The Discovery of Language*, 1931, or in L. H. Gray, *Foundations of Language*, 1939. Special note should be made of S. Gyármathi, *Affinitatis Linguae Hungaricae cum Linguis Fennecae originis grammaticae demonstrata*, 1799. This could with considerable justice be considered the real beginning of modern comparative linguistics. However, it attracted little attention since few scholars in European universities were interested in Hungarian or Finnish.

on actively in various centers in Europe. But observations like that of Sir William called attention to a particularly productive place to carry on the work and fired the imagination of many people. The stage was being set for a rapid new development in language study of far-reaching consequences.

COMPARATIVE GRAMMAR

The first fruits were actually some time in coming. In 1814 R. K. Rask submitted an essay in Danish entitled *Investigations concerning the origin of the Old Norse or Icelandic language.*[3] This established the relationships of Icelandic with a number of other languages of northern Europe by meticulous comparisons both of whole words and of the sounds of which they are composed. Before it was published another work appeared which was destined — largely because it was in German rather than Danish — to have a far greater immediate influence. This was by Franz Bopp: *Concerning the conjugation system of the Sanskrit language in comparison with those of the Greek, Latin, Persian, and German languages.*[4] This consisted of a detailed examination of the verbal endings of these languages, following up one of the similarities which had caught the notice of Sir William Jones and many other scholars of the previous generation.

From this beginning with Rask and Bopp the new discipline of historical linguistics or "comparative grammar", as it was often called, grew rapidly and soon established a very important place for itself in the universities, particularly in Germany. It quickly developed a characteristic and fairly rigorous method by combining the techniques of Rask and Bopp. By 1833 there could already be produced a comprehensive handbook entitled *Comparative grammar of Sanskrit, Zend, Greek, Latin, Lithuanian, Gothic, and German,*[5] setting forth an impressive quantity of solidly established fact. This was the first of a long line of comprehensive handbooks, each building on the others and together erecting an imposing structure of fact and theory.

The methods of this nineteenth-century linguistics are best set forth by means of some examples, though not presented in exactly the form that prevailed a century ago. The verb 'to be' in the present and imperfect tenses has the following forms in the three major classical languages:

---

[3] Rasmus Kristian Rask, *Undersøgelse om det gamle nordiske eller islandske sprogs oprindelse*, 1818.

[4] Franz Bopp, *Ueber das Conjugationssystem der Sanskritsprache in Vergleichung mit jenem der griechischen, lateinischen, persischen, und germanischen Sprache*, 1816.

[5] Franz Bopp, *Vergleichende Grammatik des Sanskrit, Zend, Griechischen, Lateinischen, Litauischen, Gothischen und Deutschen*, 1833–1852.

	Latin	Greek	Sanskrit
I am	sum	eimí	ásmi
thou art	es	essí	ási
he is	est	estí	ásti
we are	sumus	eimén	smás
you are	estis	esté	sthá
they are	sunt	eisí	sánti
I was	eram	êa	ásam
thou wert	eras	êstha	ásīs
he was	erat	êen	ásīt
we were	eramus	êmen	ásma
you were	eratis	ête	ásta
they were	erant	êsan	ásan

There are numerous similarities here, not only in the general grammatical system of the three languages but, even more remarkably, in specific details. It was these details which Bopp studied and which enabled him to write his first monograph on the conjugation system.

The second type of resemblance which attracted attention was that in vocabulary. The following are typical of many more sets:

	Latin	Greek	Sanskrit
father	pater	patēr	pitar
mother	māter	mētēr	mātar
mouse	mūs	mūs	mūṣ
tooth	dent-	odont-	dant
knee	genu	genū	jānu
foot	ped-	pod-	pad-
three	trēs	treis	trayas

Such a list can be greatly extended. In addition, there are many other words in which two of the three languages are similar. Again, the similarities are not merely general, but specific and repeated. For example, in the short list above, two words start with *p* in all three languages, and two with *m* in all three. Many more examples could be found for each of these patterns of similarities. Such resemblances did not seem to have been produced by accident. Moreover, the addition of other languages — Gothic, Lithuanian, Persian, and so on — merely strengthens the case, confirming even minute details.

It was first considered by some that Latin and Greek were descended from Sanskrit. But as evidence accumulated, it became more and more difficult to maintain this position. Linguists debated the relationships, and finally agreed that the three were all daughter languages to one still more ancient speech form no longer directly accessible, and indeed probably never recorded. Linguists turned their attention from merely noting resemblances to attempting to deduce the features of that forgotten language.

There was a parallel available. Italian, French, and Spanish were known to be descended from Latin. They showed the same sort of similarities as did Latin, Greek, and Sanskrit:

	Italian	French	Spanish
father	padre	père	padre
mother	madre	mère	madre
foot	piede	pied	pie

Words starting with *p* in all three languages come from Latin originals which also started with *p*. It was reasonable to guess that the unknown original behind Latin, Greek, and Sanskrit showed the same sort of relationship to these three that Latin was known to show to Italian, French, and Spanish. That is, words that came down with initial *p* in all three languages had initial *p* in the parent. Not all the details are as obvious and straightforward as this. As may be seen by examining the words tabulated above, there are often much more complex relationships. Sometimes very elaborate deductions would be required to establish a reasonable hypothesis. But there were so many evident parallelisms that such deductions had a great deal of evidence on which they could be based and could often be established with considerable security. Working in this way, 'father' has been reconstructed as **pətér-*, 'mother' as **mā́ter-*, and 'foot' as **pəd-*. Words so reconstructed are conventionally marked with asterisks to show that they are not actually attested in ancient records.

It must be emphasized that these reconstructions were not hastily arrived at. Vast quantities of data were accumulated, collated, and very carefully weighed. Not only the three languages of the examples above, but every available language which could be assumed to have the same source was examined. The changes which the sounds of this reconstructed language underwent in the history leading to each known descendant were patiently worked out, and for the most part established by a mass of evidence. Not only the original parent language was reconstructed; various intermediate stages were worked out. The history of each word and each sound was patiently traced through all of these and the changes systematically examined. The main outlines of this reconstruction were completed by the middle of the nineteenth century, but many details are still being worked out and fitted in. This reconstructed parent language is now generally called Proto-Indo-European, conveniently abbreviated PIE. The family of languages descended from it is called Indo-European. English, of course, is among them, and inherits much of its vocabulary and grammar from this source.

There have been tremendous changes in the course of history. Many words have gone out of use, others have been drastically changed, and the grammar has been radically altered by the loss of some features and the development of new patterns. But there was never a sudden metamorphosis transforming one language into another. Only details have changed drastically in short periods of time. The changes of whole languages have been gradual, spread over centuries. English clearly shows many traces of its ancient Indo-European heritage. Looked at from the other side, Indo-European history explains many of the puzzling features of modern English. We can trace whence and how they came, see how they have shifted in nature and function through the centuries, and so tie in even some of the most erratic phenomena with fundamental language processes.

The relationships in the sound system between an earlier and a later language are usually stated in the form of "sound laws". These are statements of the form of: "PIE *p becomes Latin p." or "PIE *p becomes English f." For most linguists during the first fifty years of development of Indo-European linguistics, these sound laws were thought of as stating general tendencies — perhaps very strong tendencies. In most words PIE *p did indeed become Latin *p, but there were known exceptions of various kinds, and the possibility had to be recognized that there might be other exceptions not yet brought to attention.

The sound law "PIE *p becomes English f." has a number of such exceptions.[6] Among them is the following: Latin *septem*, Greek *heptá*, Sanskrit *septá*, English *seven*. Here PIE *p becomes English v. This is not an isolated example; there are a number of others of the same sort. In 1875 Karl Verner published a paper entitled *An exception to the first sound shift*.[7] He showed that a very large number of these exceptions could be explained if notice was taken of the position of the accent in the word — that is, of course, the position of the accent at the time the change occurred. If the accent immediately preceded the *p it became v; if not, it became f.

---

[6] This sound law is usually called "Grimm's law", having first been stated by Jakob Grimm in 1822. It is better described in terms of PIE and Proto-Germanic, that is, without the complications of subsequent changes in English or other Germanic languages. It may be summarized as follows:

PIE		PGmc	
voiceless stops	became		voiceless fricatives
voiced stops			voiceless stops
aspirates			voiced fricatives

There are several regular exceptions:

Voiceless stops remain voiceless stops when immediately following Germanic fricatives.
If PIE voiceless stops are not initial or immediately following a stressed vowel, then PIE voiceless stops become PGmc voiced fricatives.

This second exception is "Verner's law".

[7] Karl Verner, *Eine Ausnahme der ersten Lautverschiebung*, Zeit. für vergl. Sprachforschung, 1875, 23:97–130.

Exactly parallel changes were found with certain other sounds. The older single sound law was replaced by two, and a statement was formulated to specify for any word which of the two applied. Thus a very large and troublesome accumulation of apparent exceptions was eliminated.

It was soon suggested that all irregularities might be amenable to similar treatment. If this were so, there would be no real exceptions. Apparent exceptions would be only cases where the relevant factors had not yet been discerned, but which would in due course prove to be regular after all. In the intellectual climate of the late nineteenth century this was most attractive, particularly to younger scholars. Very soon, controversy broke out around this conclusion.

One party, who came to be called "young grammarians" or "neo-grammarians", maintained that the sound laws were indeed without exception. Repeatedly they found confirmation of the assumption that the exceptions could be explained if they were examined in sufficient detail, and if all relevant factors were taken into account. Sound laws, they concluded, applied invariantly to specific sounds in specific environments, that is, in definable positions within the word: before or after certain other sounds, in accented syllables or in unaccented syllables, and so on.

The conservatives continued to maintain that the sound laws merely represented general tendencies. Within these general tendencies, individual words had their own histories. They might follow all the relevant sound laws precisely, or they might depart from one or more of them in minor — or even occasionally major — ways. What actually happened in each case would be the result of interplay of a number of diverse factors, of which the development of the sound system as summarized in the sound laws would be only one.

Through the eighties the debate was acrimonious, and it has persisted with only gradually diminishing intensity until very recent years. Each party criticized the work of the other minutely. Linguists were, therefore, forced into very careful and detailed scrutiny of the evidence from every side. As sharply opposed as these two positions seem to be, it was nevertheless found in due course that each had something to contribute to the other. Today the lines have largely faded out. Linguists now know that the process of historical development of languages is much more complex than either party envisioned at the height of the controversy.

Through this period of bitter debate, the body of well-attested conclusions about the development of Indo-European languages from their common ancestor has continually grown. The general results must be considered as very strongly established. This is not necessarily the impression a newcomer will get from reading the literature. But it must be remembered that linguistics has come through a series of fundamental debates during which attention has been focused pre-eminently on differences of opinion and on weaknesses in the arguments of others.

DIALECT STUDY

During the nineteenth century the attention of most linguists was focused on standard written languages. Only rarely were spoken languages observed. Linguists were, in general, very little concerned with the variations in form exhibited within vernacular languages. These were, of course, difficult matters to handle within the framework of historical linguistics, particularly as advanced by the neogrammarians.

The opponents of the neogrammarians felt that a variety of factors were at work, of which the development of the sound system was only one. Within this group there arose an increasing interest in dialects, since here seemed to be evidence for a more complex and much less rigid set of processes. Ultimately, this resulted in a conviction among some of them that every word had its individual history which could be disentangled only by tracing out the development of the word in great detail both in time and in space. It would not suffice, therefore, to look simply at a single form of each of the major languages. Rather, as many as possible of the vast number of local dialects should be studied. One of the important tools for the understanding of a word's history would be a detailed mapping of its forms over a wide expanse of territory. This could then be compared with similar mappings of forms of related or interacting words.

Not the first, but certainly the most influential, of the early studies in this field was the work of J. Gilliéron and E. Edmont, *The Linguistic Atlas of France*,[8] which appeared between 1902 and 1910. They recorded the spoken patois in 629 communities scattered fairly evenly over the entire French-speaking area in Europe. The results were presented in a series of over two thousand maps, each showing the geographic distribution of a selected feature. Some of their maps seemed to indicate that words or pronunciations had spread outward from some central point, commonly Paris, rather than occurring by simple linguistic change in each community. Other maps seemed to demonstrate clearly that the development of a word was not always independent of that of similar though unrelated words. The classic case is the word for 'rooster'.[9] In most of the French area this is a derivative of Latin *gallus* 'rooster'. But in a large area in southwestern France this word would be expected to change in such a way as to become identical in form with the word from Latin *gattus* 'cat'. In precisely the area where this might happen, the local dialects substitute other words for 'rooster'. Competition between homonyms seems to have been a controlling force.

With Gilliéron and Edmont, linguistic geography established its usefulness in accounting for intricate developments in language. Much of the strongest opposition to the neogrammarians became increasingly com-

---

[8] J. Gilliéron and E. Edmont, *Atlas linguistique de la France*, 1902–1910.
[9] This example is discussed in L. Bloomfield, *Language*, 1933, pp. 396–398.

mitted to this technique in preference to comparative grammar. There remain to the present lingering traces of the old battles, many of them transferred to differences of opinion between dialect workers and historical linguists or descriptive linguists. One form of this misunderstanding is the frequent rejection by dialectologists of the use of phonemic techniques in their work, and the consequent sharp criticism of the descriptive linguists.[10]

In due course, linguistic atlases of most areas of Europe appeared. These have used a variety of different techniques and studied a variety of problems. Differences of pronunciation, grammar, and vocabulary have been mapped. Some atlases have done a great deal to correlate the language differences with cultural differences. Others have thrown into sharp relief the coincidence of dialect boundaries with older political divisions.

There has gradually accumulated a body of principles for both field work and interpretation, but these lack something of the precision and rigor of the methods of other branches of linguistics. Other linguists sometimes look down on dialect workers as being too preoccupied with data gathering and too little with generalizations and the discovery of basic principles. The dialect geographers, however, must necessarily work with a great deal larger mass of data than most other linguists. Their problems of organizing and digesting all this information are tremendous.

DESCRIPTIVE LINGUISTICS IN EUROPE

Through the nineteenth century the orientation of academic linguists was predominantly historical. Indeed, there was a general conviction that only the history of a language could be studied precisely and scientifically. Comparative studies had to be based on grammars and dictionaries of individual languages, but the linguists gave relatively little attention to the problems of preparing such. They used the existing materials, or they prepared new on the same model. Grammars were continually being rewritten and improved, dictionaries were corrected and expanded, and previously unknown languages were occasionally brought to the attention of the scholarly world. It would be grossly inaccurate to say that no descriptive work was done — rather, there was little thought devoted to the peculiar problems of language description. Moreover, the work on individual languages done by university linguists was almost entirely based on documents and depended heavily on the technical abilities of philologists who often looked more toward literature than toward language. With occasional exceptions, the notion of field work on a spoken language was unknown.

---

[10] A very mild and reasonable rejection of phonemics can be seen in Raven McDavid's chapter in Nelson Francis, *The Structure of American English*, 1958, pp. 492–493. This chapter can be recommended as an excellent introduction to dialect study. It should be noted, however, that there is an increasing use of phonemic techniques in dialectology.

There were, however, other groups of Europeans who faced the problems of unwritten languages. Probably the largest body were the missionaries in Asia, Africa, and the Pacific. Another group were the colonial officials. Asians or Africans who knew European languages were not yet numerous, and every European who lived in these areas had to learn to use some local language. Many of them had to work at a high level in the language. Some seemed to have learned exceedingly well. A number wrote textbooks for their junior colleagues. A few became engrossed in languages and the linguistic problems they met. Many of them had come out of the European universities where they had had some contact with linguistics. Some of them applied what they could of the linguistics they knew to the very different languages of their fields.

One inevitable result was the appearance of a number of works on comparative grammar of non-European languages. An early example was the *Comparative grammar of the Dravidian or South Indian family of languages*, published in 1856 by Bishop Robert Caldwell. This was still in use a hundred years later as a basic textbook in courses in historical linguistics in some Indian universities. That it should be is at once a testimony to the high quality of the book and to the subsequent inactivity in the study of this language family.

Naturally, there was much activity in the description of languages. Large numbers of grammars and dictionaries were compiled. Many were never printed because of low interest, but the list of published works is impressive. Most of the authors followed rather closely the pattern of the grammars familiar to them in European and classical languages. Many of them, however, showed a surprising and very commendable freedom. They often knew the languages they were describing so well that they could not help noticing differences from European languages and refused to distort the material enough to fit it into the conception of a grammar which they had brought with them from Europe.

Unfortunately, the feedback of information from these overseas linguists into the academic circles of European universities was meager. Few professors read widely in these works — after all, the professors were specialists in a very demanding field. But the separation was not complete, and information about the languages of Asia and Africa slowly began to find its way into European linguistics. In due course the work of missionary linguists began to exert some influence in academic discussions. This would ultimately play a small but crucial role in the development of the discipline. In retrospect it is clear that many of the fundamental problems of linguistics would inevitably remain insoluble until the perspective was widened and data from drastically different language systems could be added to the vast store accumulating from the study of Indo-European languages.

There was thus a very considerable amount of descriptive work done during the nineteenth century. It was scattered and not widely known in the profession, but it is a serious mistake to underestimate either its quantity or its significance. It was not, however, based on any well-developed, up-to-date body of special descriptive techniques, nor was it guided by any linguistic theory giving adequate place to the systems of individual languages. Before descriptive linguistics could become a significant branch of the science, it had to develop a conceptual basis in line with the progress in other fields.

The first development in this direction was suggested by the neogrammarian principle. The regularity of sound laws focused the attention of historical linguists on the sound system and specifically on the formulation of sound laws. Since Verner's work of 1875, it had been recognized that sound laws operate differently in different positions within words. Since this is the case, two different sets of correspondences — for example, Latin p equals English f, and Latin p equals English v — might well point back to one original sound in the reconstructed language. For this to be true it was necessary, of course, that the distribution of the two could be precisely defined. In the example just given, one correspondence was found only when immediately preceding the accented vowel, the other in other positions. Two different, usually only partially different, things could have a kind of equivalence in a system.

Phonologic descriptions of modern languages generally consisted of statements about the pronunciation of the letters used in writing the language. They were sets of reading rules rather than true descriptions of sound systems. It had long been known that some letters were, in some languages, pronounced differently under different conditions. Beginning in the late nineteenth century, phoneticians had observed closely the pronunciation of a large number of languages. They found a totally unexpected variation. It seemed that there was no limit to the number of sounds that could be recognized and described, even in the speech of one person. But the native speaker seemed totally unaware of much of this variety. Indeed the speaker commonly insisted that two things were identical when to the phonetician they were obviously, even grossly, different. The discrepancy between the phoneticians' observations and the natives' "feel" required explanation. So did the discrepancy between the almost limitless number of sounds and the much more restricted number of letters in the alphabets.

An answer was slow in coming, and even slower in acceptance. But it finally came out of the insights of the neogrammarians, the phoneticians, and the missionary linguists. Just as numerous different correspondences could point to a much smaller number of basic sounds in the reconstructed language, in the same way, many diverse sounds in speech could point to a small number of significant units in a current spoken language. It would be required, of course, that the environment determine which variant should appear. These units came to be called "phonemes".[11] They were considered to be the basic units in the sound system of a language. The variants were of a much different nature, of very little significance in the system of language.

The phoneme gave a needed rationale for much of what had been done in the past by linguists describing languages. Their judgment had told them that certain sounds should be written alike, even when the phonetician told them they were different. Occasionally they had tried to justify their "inadequate" work by appeal to expediency. Sometimes they had excused themselves with the plea that phonetics was too esoteric a science for use in the field. The new notion of the phoneme could explain why sounds could be alike (that is, the same phoneme) and different (phonetically) at the same time. The practical linguist had not always been correct in detail, but often enough he was correct in general, and there was now good justification for his practice. It was found that the phoneme could also explain some puzzling things about long familiar languages. It was indeed a useful concept.

The phoneme principle gave the first workable basis on which to begin erecting a modern theory of descriptive linguistics. Obviously, a great deal more would need to be done, but here was the essential first step. It was a difficult one, requiring drastic reorientation of thought about language and it was slow in establishing itself. It was well into the twentieth century before the phoneme became widely known. With this, however, descriptive linguistics was established with its own fundamental viewpoint and principle of analysis and desciption.

The first great monument of European descriptive linguistics did not appear until 1939. This was N. Trubetzkoy's *Foundations of Phonology*.[12] This summarized what had been accomplished in Europe toward an understanding of the sound systems of languages on the basis of the phoneme. The stage seemed set for a rapid development.

ANTHROPOLOGICAL LINGUISTICS IN AMERICA

As the university developed in America the study of languages developed also. American professors, many of them trained in Europe, followed the developments there with interest. Through them historical linguistics

---

[11] The phoneme is a fundamentally important concept. A discussion is, however, outside the scope of this book. Readers are referred to the literature on linguistics, particularly to H. A. Gleason, Jr., *An Introduction to Descriptive Linguistics*, 1961, Chs. 16–21; Robert A. Hall, Jr., *Introductory Linguistics*, 1964, Chs. 14–20; Charles F. Hockett, *A Course in Modern Linguistics*, 1958, Chs. 2–13; R. H. Robins, *General Linguistics; An Introductory Survey*, 1964, Ch. 4.

[12] Nikolai Sergieevich Trubetskoi, *Grundzüge der Phonologie*, 1939, or the French translation by J. Cantineau, *Principes de phonologie*.

came to have a place in the American universities, but only in a few institutions did it grow into any great strength or status. The one notable American linguist of the nineteenth century was W. D. Whitney, professor of Sanskrit at Yale University from 1854 until his death in 1894. Not only did he establish Sanskrit studies in this country, but he made notable contributions to linguistic theory. The most characteristic development of linguistics in America, however, was to come over a generation later from a very different source: anthropology rather than classical or oriental studies.

In this country there has always been a great interest in the American Indian. A great deal of amateur work, starting in very early years, was devoted to describing Indian customs and languages. This varied greatly in quality, but occasional publications were good and important. The first Bible published in what was to become the United States was a translation into Massachusetts by John Eliot (1664). About the same time, Roger Williams, better known as the founder of Rhode Island, wrote and published a grammar of Narragansett. Many others followed in the two centuries before professional work became significant.

Early in the twentieth century, anthropology came to be recognized in the American universities. The great pioneer was Franz Boas, who became the first professor of anthropology at Columbia University in 1899. For many years he dominated the discipline in America. He was a very active, meticulous, and productive field worker. He insisted on the same careful, detailed, and comprehensive work from his students. He trained them to gather facts in abundance, and to exercise considerable restraint in generalization. For Boas, language and culture were both within the scope of anthropology. All of his students received training in both linguistics and cultural anthropology. Many of them continued to work in languages. His students were the nucleus around which descriptive linguistics developed in America. Boas thus set a pattern for American linguistics which has held very nearly universally up to very recent times. It was closely allied with anthropology, indeed often being considered simply as a specialized branch. Field work with informants — recording and analyzing an unwritten tongue — has been both the basic training and the most characteristic activity of American linguists.

In 1911 there was published the first volume of the *Handbook of American Indian Languages*. This contained descriptions of a number of speech forms, mostly written by Boas' students, and a long introduction by Boas himself, in which he set forth the principles he followed in his field work and taught to his students. This is the first monument of American anthropological linguistics, and one in every way characteristic of the discipline in the first years of its development.

The next great American linguist, Edward Sapir, was a student of Boas. He was likewise an excellent field worker with a deep insight into the languages he analyzed. Unlike many of his fellow anthropologists, he was widely read in European linguistics and had a broad outlook on language. Sapir was much more ready to generalize and to propose wide-ranging theories than was Boas, but he was no less insistent on the importance of extensive and careful field work. Different as the two men were at many points, they were agreed that the basic data must be gathered from informants. In 1921 Sapir published a little book entitled *Language*. This was designed as a popularization and has recently been republished as a paperback. While written well and simply, it revealed profound insights and became immensely influential in the training of young linguists.

The anthropological linguists concentrated their attention on the languages of the American Indians. Many of these languages had had very little if any previous description. When earlier publications were available, they were often inadequate and sometimes seriously incorrect, though some could be useful if interpreted with care. Documentary sources — written literature or already collected folklore — were seldom available, and often enough poorly done. American Indian linguists tended to ignore all such sources. They preferred to devote their efforts to field work while native speakers were still available. Indeed, they developed a general distrust of written materials. This attitude was often deepened by their experiences with traditional grammars of European languages. It came to be a dogma with them that only speech is language; writing is only a reflection — often very imperfect — of speech.

In describing an Indian language, the field worker's first task was to devise some method of recording it. Under Boas, anthropological linguists used a phonetic notation that came to be fairly well standardized, but appeared esoteric to others. Relatively minute differences of pronunciation were meticulously recorded. This led very often to perplexing variation in grammatical forms. This did not greatly worry Boas, who insisted on close attention to detail, however complex the data might become. But some, particularly Sapir and his students, were eager to discern underlying patterns and were impatient with the phonetic confusion.

In the early twenties the concept of the phoneme, which had been slowly developing in Europe, came to the attention of some Americans. It was found to bring a new order into this phonetic chaos and was soon adopted by Sapir and his followers. It gave them a new basis for recording languages and a new theoretical undergirding for their work. Boas and those of his students not influenced by Sapir did not accept the new theory and continued meticulous phonetic recording and description of languages in the old format.

Boas had set up a standard outline for description. The first topic was always the sound system. With the acceptance of the phonemic principle, this pattern was continued. The first major section of a grammar was a description of the phonemic system. This was a continuation of the Boasian tradition, but it was reinforced by a new theoretical foundation. Sapir's theory of descriptive linguistics was based on the phoneme. The sound system was not, therefore, simply a convenient place to begin; it was the necessary starting point.

Through the next three decades the understanding of the phoneme gradually evolved, but its primacy was seldom questioned. American linguistics was almost universally grounded on the phoneme. Dissent did not become significant until the appearance of generative grammar in the late fifties.

Linguists in the heritage of Sapir soon began to reach out for comparable concepts that would regularize their treatment of grammar and establish it on a comparably firm base. Soon they developed the idea of the morpheme, the smallest unit of word formation. Its origin was in an analogy with the phoneme. The morpheme might vary in form from one position to another, provided some suitable conditioning could be stated. For example, an English plural noun like *dogs* was considered to consist of two morphemes, a stem *dog* and a suffix *-s*, or rather of two bits of speech spelled in these ways. No further division is possible without destroying the identity of the units. The plural suffix varies in form. Three common ones can be heard in *dogs*, *cats*, and *fishes*. These are all one morpheme because the conditions under which each will appear can be clearly defined.

With this new unit as a base, anthropological linguists were able to make great advances in the description of word formation. They found this to be immensely complex in some languages, rather simple in others. The second division in the new model of descriptive statement, after a section dealing with the phonemes, would be one describing the morphemes and their combination to form words. This became known as morphology. The universally accepted outline of a grammar included phonology, morphology, and syntax, in that order, though techniques for handling syntax were still rudimentary and that section was often very sketchy.

American Indian languages differ widely among themselves. Field linguists were strongly impressed by the diversity in structure that they observed, even among neighboring languages. They developed an expectation of finding new and different features, and enjoyed exhibiting them to each other and to their students. Naturally, they preferred to write up their descriptions in such a way as to show the individuality of the language in the clearest light. They insisted that each language must be described in terms of its own structure. This insistence became a cardinal doctrine.

Earlier work on American Indian languages, mostly by amateurs, had often tended to force the facts into a grammatical mold familiar in European languages. This was clearly a distortion, and professional linguists developed a very suspicious attitude toward any similarity to the traditional grammar, particularly that of Latin. Sometimes they leaned over backwards to avoid the old categories or the old manner of description. This customary suspicion was to be of great importance when, later, linguists of this background turned their attention to English.

Working as they did with languages using very different conceptual categories than does English, American linguists became acutely conscious of the great difficulty of translation. Using informants whose knowledge of English was sometimes limited, they found that their recorded meanings for utterances were often inadequate and sometimes downright misleading. The traditionally oriented grammars commonly parrotted the classical grammatical definitions — usually meaning-based — and then tried to identify the same familiar parts of speech in the Indian language on the basis of these definitions. All these experiences conspired to create a suspicion of meaning. The movement of thought among American anthropological linguists was toward total rejection of meaning as a basis for analysis. Some of the leaders in this development found it necessary to apologize for the use of meaning as a "convenient shortcut", while others struggled valiantly to eliminate it from their procedures. In due course another characteristic American tenet was established: Meaning is not relevant for linguistic analysis.[13]

As American anthropological linguistics came of age it was strongly marked by insistence on field work, by the dogma that only speech is properly language, by strict allegiance to the phoneme and the morpheme as the basic units of analysis, by an insistence that each language must be described in its own terms (sometimes, even, a blind faith that such a procedure could never lead to certain Latin-grammar-like types of description), and by a very marked distrust or total rejection of meaning as a tool of analysis or statement. Some of these convictions are characteristically American; others are more strongly emphasized in this country than in Europe. The combination gave American descriptive linguistics a stance quite different from that of its European counterpart.

GENERAL LINGUISTICS

By the nineteen thirties several well-marked subdisciplines had developed within linguistics. We have traced the development of three of them: The oldest and still dominant branch was historical linguistics or comparative grammar, largely devoted to the Indo-European language family. In most universities this was the only branch that had attained any academic status, and for many people "linguistics" meant simply Indo-European comparison. Second was the much younger branch known as dialect geography or geographical linguistics. This had established itself in a few universities, but in most was either unknown or overshadowed by its older

---

[13] This has been a fruitful source of misunderstanding. The objection is to basing analysis on meaning, not, for most linguists, to the study of meaning. See page 58.

sister. It was still largely in the data-gathering stage, though important principles were beginning to emerge. The third was descriptive linguistics. This had originated more or less independently in Europe and America. The antecedents were rather different in the two centers, and the developments showed clear evidence of this. Little interchange of ideas had taken place, and when, as with the phoneme, the Americans had accepted an idea of European origin, they had quite thoroughly reinterpreted it in line with their own quite different background. On both continents descriptive linguistics was yet to receive academic recognition except in a very few centers. The general scholarly public was hardly aware of its existence.

These three subdisciplines might easily have drifted apart. There were several reasons why they did not. Many of the workers and most of the leaders in the two younger branches had had extensive training in the older historical linguistics. Some of the workers in historical linguistics, and the number has tended to increase, had had some training in either dialect geography or descriptive linguistics or both. This came about, in part, because of the lack of academic recognition for the newer branches; research workers in these fields had to attach themselves to the older established subjects. There has been a common heritage in the three branches, and the training of linguists has been such as to maintain this as a unifying factor.

The scientific societies and the learned journals have not differentiated themselves to match these subdisciplines of linguistics. For example, in the United States the oldest society (dating from 1924) is the Linguistic Society of America, and the leading journal its publication *Language*. The society was founded by a group including historical linguists and anthropological linguists, and has continued to include persons studying language from every scholarly point of view. From the start *Language* has published papers representing every branch of the discipline active in this country.

Still more important as unifying factors have been the outstanding efforts to state the principles of the science. The influential systematizations have generally taken cognizance of all available information about language. Naturally, those produced in the nineteenth century were largely restricted in their material to historical linguistics, since very little else was sufficiently developed to contribute. But even these generally took the widest feasible view of their subject. As results began to appear from other approaches to language, they found their place in summary statements. Two major formulations deserve mention as having definitely molded and unified modern linguistics, one in Europe pre-eminently, and the other in America.

Ferdinand de Saussure was a leading figure in linguistics in the French-speaking countries in the early years of this century. Though he published little, he was a very provocative and inspiring teacher. In 1911 he delivered a course of lectures on general linguistics which particularly fired the imagination of his hearers. Shortly thereafter, he died. A group of his students reconstructed his lectures from their class notes and published them in 1916 as the *Course in General Linguistics*.[14] In this, de Saussure showed a remarkably broad understanding of language. He made a clear distinction between the historical and the contemporary. He saw historical and descriptive work as partners in advancing the understanding of language. He drew a distinction between language (a system) and speech (a concrete act).[15] These two distinctions were crucial in providing a basis for the developing European theories of descriptive linguistics.

De Saussure's lectures are certainly the most important single European publication in linguistics in this century. (The qualification "European" may be only a bit of American provincialism!) Every subsequent worker on the Continent has been influenced by them, some very heavily. Indeed, much of modern linguistic studies in Europe is best understood as continuation of his work. The *Course in General Linguistics* continued to be read, closely studied, and debated. (The book is obscure at some very important places, but this is probably the result of the rather strange process that brought it to print rather than deficiencies in de Saussure's original presentation.) European linguistics cannot be understood without some grounding in de Saussure.

The great synthesizer in America was Leonard Bloomfield. His training, both in this country and in Germany, was in Indo-European linguistics and his early career was as a professor of German. The appearance of a speaker of Tagalog at the University of Illinois impelled him to attempt a study of that language. In 1917 he published a volume entitled *Tagalog Texts*, which included as a preface a very detailed description of the grammar of the language. This remains one of the important contributions to the theory of syntax. Later he came in contact with the Menomini Indians in northern Wisconsin, learned their language, and wrote a number of important papers on Menomini and on the comparative study of the Algonquian languages of which it is one. He thus combined training and experience in both historical and descriptive linguistics. His comparative work included both the filling out of details in the long-established field of Indo-European and pioneer work on an American Indian language family. He was intimately acquainted with the descriptive work of the anthropological linguists, and combined that with his familiarity with the work of the ancient Sanskrit grammarian, Panini.

Out of this broad background Bloomfield produced in 1933 his book, *Language*. This summarized the whole field as it had developed up to that time — descriptive, historical, and geographical. Not only did he work these divergent approaches together into a remarkably consistent presenta-

---

[14] Ferdinand de Saussure, *Cours de linguistique générale*, 1916. Now available in an English translation by Wade Basking, *Course in General Linguistics*.

[15] In French, *langue* and *parole*. These have become established as technical terms and are used with French spellings in many English publications.

tion but he made in the book a number of brilliant and productive innovations.

Almost immediately, *Language* became the standard handbook for American linguists. For the next two decades it was the basic textbook in the training of young linguists, and the constant reference of older workers. Its influence was so pervasive that American linguistics is sometimes referred to, mostly by Europeans, as "The Bloomfield School". Some parts of *Language* are now obsolete, but for the most part they have been superseded by newer developments that arose out of Bloomfield's work and followed lines that he first suggested. On some other topics it remains useful and important. The importance of Bloomfield's *Language* as a molder of the discipline is so profound that it must still be closely studied by any serious student of linguistics.

Chapter 3

The Last Two Decades in Linguistics

The Second World War was a turning point for linguistics. It broke just as important new developments in the field were getting under way. At first, of course, it halted progress in many centers, cut the lines of communication between workers in different countries, dispersed linguists, and generally disrupted academic life and the calm pursuit of research and theoretical discussion. Much of this damage will never be repaired, and the loss of life or productivity of many linguists was tragic. But it also started new lines of development and cleared the way for reorganization and rebuilding when the war was over.

APPLIED LINGUISTICS

Prewar American linguistics was very largely taken up with the problem of recording and analyzing the disappearing American Indian languages. The profession was a small one; the members were scattered thinly through the universities, most of them officially employed in some other capacity. They were, however, excited by their young and rapidly progressing discipline and intimately acquainted with each other. It was a dynamic group, but one receiving little recognition.

Language teaching was, of course, an established feature of the school system. In high schools the concentration was on Latin, French, Spanish, and German. Very few other languages were even considered. In the colleges and universities, Greek was often taught and in a few institutions one or two other European languages were added. The orientation in almost all schools was toward literature. The method of teaching elementary languages was the traditional one of grammar rule, vocabulary, and translation exercise. Professional language teachers knew little of any other method, and in any case saw their task as that of preparing the students to read literary material as quickly as possible. The schools generally considered thorough training in literature both essential and sufficient for the work of teaching.

The war suddenly brought a demand for instruction in a large number of languages previously untaught. A few language teachers courageously tried to work through the available textbooks and teach some exotic tongue as they had long taught French or Spanish. Some of them had fair success, but it was a harrowing experience both for teachers and students. Others, of course, were completely lost when taken away from their familiar territory.

The linguists were also called on. They were accustomed to starting from scratch on a new language with only a native informant. They were able very quickly to prepare preliminary analyses, setting up phonemic transcriptions which could be used in preparing class materials. They were committed to the primacy of speech over writing, and so were not at all distressed by the requirement that they teach spoken language rather than written. Their experience as language teachers was in some cases very limited, but they had strong convictions as to how it should be done. They were not at all hesitant about jumping in. Often they could effectively cover up their real deficiencies by their great self-confidence and ebullient enthusiasm. Soon a large part of the small cadre of descriptive linguists were hard at work teaching Japanese, Arabic, and a number of other languages, for the most part learning a step ahead of the class and producing lesson materials under terrific pressures.

That the program was successful was a miracle, in view of the severe handicaps. In the emergency the linguists had proved themselves, and now had the basis for recognition. This very success, however, presented its own problems. The public press was soon carrying sensational stories of the "Army Method" of language teaching. It was widely hailed as a panacea. All sorts of extravagant claims were made. Not all of them could possibly stand in the light of later peacetime teaching. On the whole, linguists basked in the unaccustomed praise, and all too easily accepted the adulation. The reaction was inevitable.[1] In some circles, linguists were considered patent medicine hawkers, given to irresponsible pronouncements, and thoroughly naïve in their approach to teaching. The air is not yet clear of the extreme claims made nor of the negative reactions they provoked.

It was an important beginning, however. Since the war, linguists have been increasingly involved in applied linguistics. Soon after the Armed Forces Language Programs were terminated, the universities began broad-

---

[1] This reaction was, in part, stimulated by the "devil image" that had arisen around linguistics in connection with the battles over prescriptivism in English. See page 24.

ening the range of languages taught. In some institutions there was a basic shift in objectives and methods. Many of the courses in spoken languages, particularly in those not taught before, are now managed by persons trained in descriptive linguistics. The National Defense Education Act of 1958 accelerated this process and provided extensive support for research on "neglected languages" and for the preparation of teaching materials.

Not only have professional linguists taken a larger part in language teaching, but language teachers have increasingly had instruction in linguistics included in their training. Courses in introductory linguistics have been established in a large number of universities. Language majors are more and more being encouraged to take them. Linguistically oriented courses in the structure of the languages to be taught have become common. Modern linguistics is beginning to be felt very strongly in the foreign-language teaching profession.

A parallel situation has been developing in English. Since the war linguists have given increasing attention to English grammar and to the many other linguistic problems in English studies. At the same time, there has been a sharp increase in the reading of linguistics among English students. Many English departments have made courses in introductory linguistics available to their students. Some have made them requirements for degrees.

Before the war there was very little attention given in America[2] to the problems of teaching English as a second language. The rapid increase of foreign students in American universities forced these institutions to make some provision for this. The development of foreign aid programs soon brought heavy demands for English teaching abroad. In a very short time, the teaching of English as a second language developed as a new profession. Linguistics has had a place in this from the beginning.

Much of the initiative for expansion of applied linguistics has come from the leadership of the Modern Language Association. Under their sponsorship there has been established in Washington a Center for Applied Linguistics.[3] This serves as a clearing house, disseminating information about programs in various institutions in America and abroad, advises various agencies on language problems, and carries on a program of research and development of materials.

Language teaching has naturally been the field in which the greatest opportunities for application of linguistics have been found. Beyond this,

---

[2] The British have a much longer history of active work in teaching English as a foreign language. Moreover, their efforts have increased markedly since 1945. Some of this work is excellent and deserves to be better known, not only among Americans teaching abroad but also among English teachers in American schools. A few such books are included in the Bibliography.

[3] The Center for Applied Linguistics is at 1755 Massachusetts Avenue, N.W., Washington 6, D.C. The Center publishes the *Linguistic Reporter*, a useful and inexpensive bulletin on current activities in the field.

linguists have been called on to advise mathematicians in communicating basic ideas to students, to assist in indexing chemical names, to aid in designing telephone communication systems, and to help in a number of other unusual projects. These are rather special instances, of course, but indicate something of the wide range of problems on which linguistics impinges. Certainly the range will continue to expand. More normal and frequent applications include the design and revision of writing systems, the teaching of reading, translation, and speech therapy.

PUSHING BACK THE FRONTIERS

The American linguist of the forties and early fifties was an incurable optimist. Progress in his discipline had been rapid and seemed to be accelerating. His analytic procedures were being codified into ever more incisive instruments for field work. There was an appearance of elegance and certainty in his theories that he missed in neighboring disciplines. Some linguists claimed, rather extravagantly, that theirs was the most precise of the social sciences. The evidence could indeed be read to support this contention.

The phoneme theory had been established in America under the leadership of Edward Sapir in the twenties. It was reformulated, clearly stated, and made a central point in his synthesis by Leonard Bloomfield. Since that time it had been further sharpened in a number of important papers, the terminology had been developed, and techniques of analysis had been refined. Descriptions of languages, appearing in increasing numbers, showed the utility of the phoneme for clear and succinct treatment of phonology.

Bloomfield's phonemes were roughly what we familiarly know as consonants and vowels. He was aware of the significance of stress and intonation, and refers repeatedly to them, designating them collectively as "modulation". His statements, however, are often vague because he lacked a means for precise description. In the forties, the phoneme principle was brought to bear on stress and intonation. In several languages, among them English, these systems were described in terms of a small number of stress and pitch phonemes. It was confidently expected that many other languages would soon be given "complete" phonologic descriptions. For most American linguists, it became a standard operational assumption that every pronunciational feature that had any linguistic relevance could and should be analyzed in terms of phonemes. The meaning of the term "phoneme" was extended to include basic functional units of several new types.

Encouraged by this success with intonation, a few linguists turned their attention to the various features — drawl, whisper, overloudness, and so on — which are popularly known as "tone of voice". These they considered to be just outside the limits of language proper. They expected thus to push the frontier of scientific phonological analysis outward a further step.

Morphology made similar progress. Bloomfield's treatment had been far less satisfactory than his phonology. For one thing the morpheme concept was newer and less thoroughly worked out when he took it up in 1933. Through the forties there was intense activity, the definitions were tightened, the procedures sharpened, and applications patiently explored. Morphology seemed to be following the same line of development as phonology. If anything it was moving more rapidly, catching up with phonology that had preceded it. The problems of describing word formation seemed on their way toward an ultimate solution.

The great frontier was in syntax. Most of the older work was far from satisfying. Bloomfield's *Language*, the conventional bench mark, was quite inadequate. The chapters on syntax contained a number of acute observations, suggested a number of new techniques, but seemed to lack integration. Surely, in the optimism of the age, all that was needed was to find the great principle that would unlock syntax and provide the base for an advance similar to that of phonology and morphology.

A number of approaches were tried, but the most promising seemed to be one of those suggested in *Language*. Bloomfield had observed that an English-speaking person faced with a sentence like *Poor John ran away.* would divide it into two parts: *poor John* and *ran away*. Each of these he would again divide into two. The resulting four elements would be constituents of the sentence, though not directly. A proper analysis would not be in terms merely of these four. Rather, it would take account of the two successive levels of structure as shown by the successive divisions of the sentence. Each time a sentence or a portion of a sentence is divided there are found two constituents. In turn each of these, if it can be divided at all, has two constituents. Bloomfield suggested that any complex form (ranging from a long sentence to a multielement word) could be described in terms of its constituents and the grammatical features by which these are joined. The important notion here is that of levels of structure. A sentence is made of parts which are made of parts and so on until ultimate indivisible pieces are reached. Only one level should be described at a time. The constituents at the level currently under consideration are called "immediate constituents" in contrast with the "ultimate constituents" into which they may be divided.

During the forties this notion of immediate constituent structure was followed up and systematized. Many linguists contributed by discussion and by exemplification. The first effort to give a comprehensive treatment of the syntax of a language on the basis of immediate constituents was Eugene Nida's *Synopsis of English Syntax*. This was written more as an experiment with the technique than as an effort to contribute to English grammar, though, of course, it was both. Others tried the method, and variations of it, on a variety of other languages.

With a sentence like the one Bloomfield had used, the structure seemed clear, and there was little dispute that the way suggested was indeed the correct division. Many English sentences, however, presented problems. Linguists disagreed on their analysis, but there was no clear criterion to settle the matter. The application of the technique to other languages often left the linguist hesitant in making a choice or dissatisfied after it had been made. There was need for procedures which would unambiguously establish the correct division on the basis of observable patterns in the language. There was equal need for full formulation of the theory of immediate constituents. This finally came in the late forties, and it seemed to many that the conquest of syntax now lay open before the profession.

At the beginning of the fifties confidence was running high. Many linguists felt that a new synthesis of the discipline was needed and that a suitable time was rapidly approaching. This would continue the Bloomfield tradition taking into account the results achieved in two decades. Indeed, some spoke of the need for a "revision of Bloomfield", not a replacement but an updating. No one, however, felt able to undertake the task.

This tremendous progress had been achieved by extending and sharpening techniques stemming from Bloomfield or through his *Language* from earlier workers. The trend was toward more and more consistent use of one uniform technique of description and toward extending its scope to wider and wider areas. There were two important aspects of this, the element and construction technique, and the "allo- and -eme" principle.

From a simple-minded point of view an English past tense form such as *walked* is most easily described in terms of adding *-ed* to the basic form *walk*. Equally obviously, the easy way to describe *ran* is in terms of a vowel change from *run*. These are two basically different techniques. Earlier American linguists had not felt embarrassed by the difference and wrote of grammatical processes and affixes in the same description. Much of the sharpening of morphological techniques during the forties consisted of eliminating statements of change or process. The preference was clearly toward a form of statement where all grammar is described in terms of elements — morphemes or constructions of morphemes — which are added together. But any complete description of a language like English must treat verbs of the types of *walk* and *run* together. Various expedients were experimented with to bring *ran* into the same pattern: *run* plus some element.

The immediate constituent approach fits nicely into this pattern. Constructions are described as formed by joining two elements, the immediate constituents of the construction. This new construction is now an element which can enter, as an immediate constituent, into some still larger construction. The technique can be repeated over and over to build up sentences of any required degree of complexity.

Bloomfield had described "modulation" (stress and intonation) as marking the relationship between constituents in a construction. Full consistency required that these features should also be treated as elements added to the rest. To do this, it would be necessary to analyze stress and intonation in terms of phonemes and morphemes, that is, in a way strictly parallel to the treatment of the more familiar elements of speech. Such analyses have been published for a number of languages, and they provide the basis for a consistent element-and-construction treatment. Not all linguists have, however, been convinced either of the soundness of the premises or of many details of the descriptions.

The phonemic principle was based on the observation that some audible phonetic differences had functional significance in a language, while others did not. A phoneme came to be regarded as a class or group of sounds. In the forties the term "allophone" became popular for these nondistinctive variants which exist within a phoneme. Soon after, "allomorph" was proposed to designate the nonsignificant alternates of a morpheme. In due course, "alloword", or, more elegantly, "allolog", appeared to label such variants as *have* and *'ve*. Finally, at first largely as professional slang, linguists began to talk in general of "allos" and "emes" and of the "allo and eme principle".

This proliferating terminology is symptomatic of a viewpoint that was becoming more and more pervasive in the thinking of linguists. It centered in the proposition that the objective of analysis was to separate significant entities ("emes") from nonsignificant variants ("allos"), or equivalently, to distinguish significant variation from nonsignificant.

Earlier linguists had been content to say that *-ed* became voiceless when added to *walk*. The combination of the element and construction principle with the "allo and eme principle" led to the fashion of saying that the past tense suffix had three forms (allomorphs), /-d -t -id/. A verb stem like *walk* requires the second of these. No change is described, just a choice of the appropriate allomorph. Processes of all kinds were being thoroughly exorcized from linguistic descriptions.

THE UNIFICATION OF DESCRIPTIVE LINGUISTICS

The war scattered European scholars. A little band of them came to this country and set up a small French university in exile in New York City. Among them were a few linguists whose orientation was within European traditions. Together with Americans in the metropolitan area they organized the Linguistic Circle of New York. This organization has had a constantly widening influence. Though it continues to hold its meetings in New York, it is now national or even international in scope.

Its journal, *Word*, is one of the leading periodicals in linguistics. The Linguistic Circle of New York from the first was a meeting place for European and American viewpoints and techniques. Graduate students trained in the universities in New York City were exposed to teaching in both traditions. As they have moved out to other schools they have been instrumental in interpreting European positions in this country. *Word*, similarly, has tended to bring together the two approaches.

With the close of the war, scholarly interchange became possible again. American linguists began reading European publications more intensively and Europeans were able to obtain American publications more freely. The two developments in descriptive linguistics, very largely isolated from each other before, now began to interact to their mutual benefit. Some ideas which originated in Europe have been taken up by American linguists, and some American positions have become influential in Europe. The two have not yet merged, but it is clear that the movement is in that direction, and the differences — and even more important, the misunderstandings — are diminishing steadily.

The two traditions differed in significant ways in their approaches to many problems. One result of the interchange has been, in America at least, a much greater flexibility. For example, American anthropological linguists were very rigid in demanding that a description present phonology, morphology, and syntax in that order. Other outlines were rarely tried, and the few experiments were not well received. At the present time, American linguists are employing many different organizations in their descriptions. Some of these are proving very interesting and fruitful.

Another result has been a tremendous theoretical ferment. Prewar American linguists were much more interested in field methods than in theory. They tended in general to take the attitude that, if they could find good workable techniques, the basic issues would take care of themselves. Indeed, much American linguistic "theory" was just overelaborate description of field procedures. On the whole, the Europeans were less well equipped for field analysis (many of them had no interest in field work at all), but they had a better understanding of the theoretical problems. Under the impetus of new ideas from abroad, Americans were forced to examine their basic assumptions far more critically. Some positions that before the war were considered established beyond reasonable debate were re-examined and found to require reformulation or extensive amendment.

The interaction of widely different viewpoints inevitably produced a hybrid swarm of new ideas. There are among American linguists far more competing positions than ever before. There is, of course, agreement on many points, but there is sharp debate on many issues, and sometimes significant difference of emphasis even within areas of general consensus. The discussion promises to further our understanding of the nature of language, but the rethinking of fundamental issues is sometimes painful and often arduous.

For the student, or the interested outsider, the present ferment makes special difficulty. There is a confusion of voices. Limited reading in linguistics shows near chaos. It is very hard to trace the areas of general agreement through the conflicting positions on details. Only close familiarity with the literature, and with the writers, can put it all in perspective and reveal the fundamental unities. It is no wonder that many English teachers have had difficulty in understanding what linguistics is.

Not only is there theoretical ferment; there is also terminological confusion. As descriptive linguistics arose in two centers isolated from each other, two separate systems of terminology developed. All too often these used the same terms but in slightly different meanings. When the two traditions began to mix, not only were the two terminologies brought together but the resulting reinterpretation of basic theory produced a new proliferation of terms and of meanings for old terms. Some of these were, of course, unnecessary, but they have been used in important publications and must be reckoned with. The weeding out of unneeded terminology is a process that goes on unceasingly in every discipline (as indeed it does in nontechnical subjects also). But in recent years in linguistics it has not been able to keep up with the growth. Unfortunately, there is no suitable up-to-date dictionary to guide a beginner. A student must find his own way through the jungle unassisted.

THE TRANSFORMATIONAL-GENERATIVE APPROACH

As we have seen, the postwar advances in syntax were largely based on the immediate constituent technique. There are, however, some facts about sentences which are at least obscured, if not totally overlooked, in this approach. One of these is the relationship, clearly felt by a fluent speaker of the language, between certain pairs of sentences of rather different apparent structures. Thus, if a speaker of English were asked to match up the following sets of sentences he would do it with no hesitation, and he would do it in exactly the same way any other speaker would:

Where are you going?	*That is a book.*
What is that?	*I like that one.*
Which one do you like?	*I am going tomorrow.*
Are you going tomorrow?	*I am going home.*

If large numbers of sentences of these two types are examined and matched up, it will be found that a precise description can be made of the relationship between the sentences of such pairs. The description is grammatical in form. That is to say, it does not depend on any understanding of meaning, but it does require recognition of parts of speech and of sentence structures. Regular rules can be formulated which will tell in exactly what kind of words the two sentences will differ, and exactly what differences of word order will appear. As they might first be formulated, not all the rules are simple, but with continued work it proves possible to simplify them in rather interesting ways.

Such pairs of sentences are agnate.[4] The rules that relate them are called transformations. Quite a number of transformations can be found and described for English, and the whole set would serve to link together many rather extensive sets of sentences.

Though known and used — in a lax, unsystematic way — by traditional and school grammarians, transformations received no attention from linguists until the fifties, when Zellig Harris[5] began making use of them and started the process of formalizing the procedures and providing a theoretical basis.

In 1957 Noam Chomsky published a little book, *Syntactic Structures*,[6] which proposed to use transformations as an instrument for the description of syntax. Some sentences were to be described in the established ways, or nearly so, as being built up of immediate constituents. The remainder would be formed from these by transformational rules. Such rules would be formulated as processes operating on one structure to produce another. This proposal ran directly counter to much of the development in American linguistics since Bloomfield, where the trend had been to eliminate process statements.

Chomsky's proposal was certainly the most radical innovation in linguistics for some decades. Naturally, it became the center of much discussion and even of heated controversy. Nevertheless, it has exerted a profound influence on the thinking of all American linguists, whether they have accepted Chomsky's reasoning or not. A few have become enthusiastic supporters of the new technique. A great deal of work is going on along the lines suggested. It is pertinent to note that a large part of this is directed to the English language, with the result that there is certainly much more research on English grammar underway today than at any previous time.

The work of this group does not simply add a new set of tools to the grammarian's kit. Chomsky calls into question some of the basic tenets

---

[4] This term is not used by the transformational-generative linguists. See Chapter 9.

[5] Zellig S. Harris, *Co-occurrence and Transformation in Linguistic Structure*, 1957, Language 33:283–340. Though Harris' work is the starting place for Chomsky's, there are fundamental differences between the two approaches.

[6] Though already obsolete at many points, this remains the basic work in transformational-generative grammar. Much of the later work will remain unintelligible until *Syntactic Structures* has been mastered.

of the older group of descriptive linguists.[7] In *Syntactic Structures* he examines what he considered to be the basic principles of other linguistic approaches and finds them wanting. He claims to have proven that no grammar which stops short of using transformations in forming sentences can possibly fulfill what he considers to be reasonable objectives for a grammar. Not everyone is convinced by his proof. Not a few linguists would reject some of the premises from which he proceeds.

Chomsky does not claim that his approach to grammar will do what descriptive linguists have long striven to do. Rather he sets forth new and different objectives. He considers certain of the old objectives impossible of attainment by any method. For him a grammar is a set of rules that will generate sentences. That is, by following the rules of a proper grammar all grammatical sentences in the language can be found, but no ungrammatical ones will appear. To do this, the grammar must start from an agreed standard starting point, and by the application of one rule after another, in an order rigidly fixed by the grammar, lead explicitly to a correctly formed sentence. By allowing choices (which must be explicitly presented) at most places, it is possible for a reasonable set of rules to lead to the very large number of sentences known to exist in a language.

The key word here is "generate". Because of this, one common designation for the approach is "generative grammar". It is also referred to as "transformational grammar". Neither is entirely satisfactory. It is easily possible to prepare grammars which use transformations, but which are not at all generative. Moreover, grammars can be generative without the use of transformations. The best term, therefore, for a grammar of the kind advocated by Chomsky is "transformational-generative grammar".

NEW FRONTIERS

American linguists have often insisted that analysis and description — or at least the latter — should be carried out with the minimum appeal to meaning. Some, as we have seen, have attempted in various ways to eliminate the use of meaning completely.

Nonlinguists, particularly those with an interest in literature, have often been perplexed or distressed by this insistence. Probably no stand of the linguist is harder for the outsider to understand than this. Many of the critics are people with no interest in language apart from meaning. They have little sympathy for anyone who would brush meaning aside. They can hardly expect any useful results from work based on such a premise. Against

---

[7] It is not altogether clear that the tenets Chomsky has so incisively criticized were actually held by many linguists in the form he imputes to them. Moreover, many of the arguments advanced in *Syntactic Structures* no longer hold in view of widespread modification of the techniques and theory of transformational-generative grammar in recent years.

the linguists they would advance certain facts: The conveying of meaning is a major function of any language. Access to meanings is certainly the most usual reason for anyone studying a language, either his own or another.

Actually, few linguists would deny either statement. They certainly recognize the importance of meaning in language. They are not rejecting meaning. Rather they are insisting that meaning must be studied as a separate system, not confused with the grammar. Conversely, grammar must be studied separately. Linguists have maintained that if grammar and meaning are confused from the beginning, neither can be adequately analyzed. Some have asserted that the study of meaning must be based on, and hence follow after, a sound formal analysis of the grammar. Only in this way, they say, can a really penetrating understanding of meaning be attained.

For such linguists, the study of meaning stands on their agenda as a task to be taken up as soon as their studies of grammar are advanced enough to support it. This must mean after real progress has been made in syntax. Meaning certainly is tied up with contexts wider than single words. A grammar restricted to units smaller than sentences has very little to offer. An even broader grammatical base would, of course, be desirable.

In recent years some descriptive linguists have begun the first probing into the structure of meaning on the basis of grammatical analysis. To date the results have not been spectacular. Some small steps, however, have been taken. A variety of different techniques have been used. Some have studied the combination of words that can occur together, attempting to set up semantic classes that can be defined in relation to one another. Others have studied folk taxonomies, the ways in which more general terms cover definable sets of more specific ones. Others have looked into the sets of contrasting terms to ascertain the relationships that exist in such cases. Still others have tried to analyze the components of meaning that differentiate the members in vocabulary sets. No one of these has attained very comprehensive results, though each has contributed some useful bits of information. There is nevertheless considerable promise here. The number of fragmentary approaches that have been found and tried is reassuring. As these are combined with one another and compared, additional experiments will be suggested. It seems likely that the next few years may see the beginning of a productive new area of development in linguistics.

A second challenging frontier is the study of grammatical features of stretches longer than individual sentences. Linguists have long been aware that there are features, very much like what have always been considered grammar, which operate over sequences of sentences. The use of pronouns, for example, is in part controlled by the context in which the sentence as a whole is found. The use of English articles is quite different in an opening sentence than elsewhere. And, of course, sentence introducers like *however, on the other hand,* and so on, are obvious cases. There are grammatical features, then, which are determined by the place of the sentence in a whole discourse.

Linguists, nevertheless, were forced to restrict their attention to smaller units. Only these were they able to handle effectively. Often enough, this has had to be the word. As techniques for syntactic analysis have been gradually developed, the limit has usually been set, rather conventionally, at the sentence. Some few have felt that this is the natural limit of grammar which cannot safely be transgressed. Most have considered it a temporary expedient, imposed only by the shortcomings of present techniques of analysis.

During the fifties a few linguists started probing into the grammar of sequences longer than sentences. This necessitated development of radically new methods, always a slow process. Results have, accordingly, been slow in coming. Yet what has been achieved holds great promise, and interesting and significant developments seem very likely in the near future. The potential value of this work to English studies cannot be overestimated. It may well provide a solid foundation for significantly improved approaches to both literature and composition.

INTERDISCIPLINARY CONTACTS

One of the most conspicuous trends in scholarship in the postwar period has been the increased interaction between disciplines. There is more use within one science of the results attained in another; there is more attention to problems along the borderlines; there are more instances of joint attack on problems that two disciplines formerly worked on separately; in some cases, even, there is a tendency to merge and reorganize disciplines. In all of this, of course, linguistics has been involved.

In America, linguistics has always had close contact with anthropology. Before linguistics found recognition in the university organization many linguists were trained in anthropology departments. Conversely, the training of anthropologists was ideally conceived as including some linguistics, and at least a course in "Language and Culture" was very nearly standard everywhere. The larger departments often had strong offerings in linguistics. Anthropological field work often necessitated learning a hitherto unworked language, and the recording of "texts" — folklore and native accounts of the culture — was a frequent activity of the field worker. The interpretation of the materials so gathered required some facility in language analysis. Not infrequently a brief sketch of the language was included in an ethnographic description.

The large number of tribes and cultures with which they worked necessitated some organization. Anthropologists found a linguistic classification convenient. Many of them had worked on language comparison in the hope of establishing relationships; others used the results of work by linguistic specialists.

Linguists, for their part, found anthropological techniques and anthropological results essential in their own field work. They had to record the meaning of the materials they collected, and that could only be done in terms of the culture of the speakers.

Under these circumstances it is not surprising that anthropologists and linguists became greatly interested in the relationships between languages and cultures. Different peoples react to the same situation in quite different ways, so much so that the most elemental behavior can easily be misinterpreted by the outsider. Languages describe the same situations in entirely different manners, selecting different factors to specify and organizing the statements in incommensurable patterns. Could there be a connection? Do languages affect or control nonlanguage reactions? Unfortunately, no clear cases simple enough for accurate analysis have been found. The question remains an open one, and because of its inherent interest, a tantalizing one. There has been a great deal of informed careful speculation.

Certainly the most suggestive writer on this topic was Benjamin Lee Whorf.[8] Not only are his ideas provocative and his examples perceptively interpreted, but he writes appealingly. His work was done before the period under discussion here (he died in 1943), but it was in the fifties that it came into wide discussion among anthropologists and linguists and exerted a great influence on the thought in both fields.

The question is one of much broader interest. In a period when the base of literature courses is being widened to include material from many cultures, it has direct bearing on the study of literary works. Whorf's writings are distinctly stimulating, and should be more widely known and read by people in the field of English. They must be understood as speculation, but as germinal speculation.

Contact has been growing rapidly between linguists and psychologists, and has led to the development of a well-organized borderline discipline, psycholinguistics. Psychologists see their subject matter as human behavior. Since language is one of the most important aspects of behavior, the areas open to cooperative examination are many and deep-reaching: among others, bilingualism, language learning, speech pathology, cognition, speech perception. Many of these in turn have direct bearing on other problems, including many questions of language curriculum. As the work in the new field of psycholinguistics progresses, the bearing will become ever more evident.

Perhaps the most significant activity at present is the research on

[8] The most interesting papers may all be found in John Bissell Carrol (ed.), *Language, Thought, and Reality, Selected Writings of Benjamin Lee Whorf*, 1956.

language learning in children. Linguists and educators have long had diametrically opposed notions, neither of them particularly well grounded in perceptive research. Linguists have frequently maintained that a child of six coming to school for the first time knows his language, by which they mean, of course, the basic structures. Children, they said, are able to put together sentences accurately and effectively. Their vocabulary, the linguists were sure, is not as large as that of adults, but very much larger than others imagined. In any case, for linguists, vocabulary is a more or less incidental aspect of language, coming and going with the needs of the speaker.

The educators tended to think much more in terms of vocabulary. The estimates in the literature were quite various: One extreme story credited the six-year-old with only 300 to 600 words. The task of the school was visualized, more or less, in terms of teaching language, pre-eminently vocabulary, but also the power of expressive sentence formation. The linguists saw the task of the school rather as that of teaching the child to connect spoken and written language — that is, to write what he already knew, and to read, identifying from the printed page what he could already understand.

The recent research of child-language specialists has shown that both views were seriously oversimplified. The process of learning a language is far more complex than either had imagined. The educators had erred, basically, in assuming a far too simple notion of language; the linguists underestimated the complexity of the learning process; the laymen, of course, failed at both points.

There are now a number of centers where research is being conducted by groups aware of both the linguistic and psychologic dimensions of the problem. Carefully controlled observation and some ingenious experimentation are slowly building a much more adequate appraisal of the child's actual command of language and the processes by which it is built up. School English curricula will soon have a far more realistic baseline on which to build.

Even more recent and less developed has been cooperative work between linguists and sociologists. Language is a crucial instrument in interpersonal interaction. Both linguists and sociologists have long been aware of this and have concerned themselves with this dimension. The work on both sides has tended to superficiality. The language signals that operate here are far more complex than the sociologist has realized. The social processes involved are more intricate than the linguist has assumed. Obviously joint attack, making use of the insights of both disciplines, is badly needed.

These three do not exhaust the fields coming into growing contact with linguistics. Geography and history have an old tie, now deepening. Philosophy, the parent of Greek linguistics, is increasingly concerned with language and now beginning to take account of the work of linguists. Indeed, almost every discipline has some possible connection with linguistics, however tenuous.

LINGUISTICS IN THE MACHINE AGE

Like everything else, linguistics is becoming mechanized. The tape recorder has given a whole set of new techniques to the research worker. In its train has come a large variety of other machines which analyze various aspects of speech, or even simulate speech for experimental use. Electronic gear has become as much a part of modern linguistics as elaborate glassware was of classical chemistry.

For the most part, the tape recorder and other electronic machines are merely new tools to do the old jobs. Perhaps they do them slightly better. Sometimes they only lull the linguist into overconfidence. But there can be no question of their over-all usefulness, and the great increase in productivity that they have brought.

Other machines, however, have brought really new problems. Most noteworthy is the electronic computer and the proposal to use it in machine translation. We are faced with an ever-mounting output of publication in every subject and a wider and wider range of languages in which it appears. Scholarship in every field is choked with the volume of it. New ways must be found of making this material accessible. One of the gravest problems is that of language. Translation seems the only real answer, but it is slow and incredibly expensive when done by hand. Can it be done cheaply and rapidly by machine?

Some think it can, and a great deal of effort is being expended to build a machine that will do it. The problems that seem most difficult are not with the machine itself. Immensely sophisticated computer techniques are already available, and more are developed every year. What instrumentation problems have not been solved seem soluble in the not too distant future. The most puzzling problems are with the languages.

A human translator works in a way that we do not understand at all. He looks at a sentence in, say, Russian, senses what it means, and then writes a sentence in English that means the same thing. But how does he do this? How does he know what the Russian sentence means? How does he go about putting together the English sentence? Such questions multiply almost without end.

A Russian grammar and a dictionary certainly give part of the answers. They tell us some very important things about the Russian language, things that the translator either knows when he starts, senses somehow as he goes along, or looks up in the grammar or dictionary when he gets stuck. A translation machine will have to have built into it most, if not all, of this various equipment of the human translator.

But while the existing grammars and dictionaries are useful to the human translator, they are not at all to the machine. Machines are really very unintelligent, or at least they have no imagination. Everything must be told them precisely and explicitly. A good translator uses human judgment that the machine cannot. Every little detail of the process will have to be worked out and stated in the form of detailed rules which the machine can follow blindly, passing at the direction of the rules from step to step. The machine will not only have to be given the rules; it will also have to have the correct rule picked out for it every time. A new kind of grammar and a new kind of dictionary are indispensable.

The kind of language tools needed in machine translation would be of no conceivable use in the classroom. Even when translated into plain English from the mathematical-looking symbols that the machine reads best, they would be incredibly uninspiring reading. The dullest conventional grammar would be concise and sparkling by comparison. We cannot expect any direct contribution from machine-translation research to English studies.

But the indirect contribution might be considerable. Mechanical translation is focusing attention on some details of language structure that have long been taken for granted. There are coming to light some inadequacies in existing grammars which handicap the human user also, but which had long escaped attention. The characteristics of grammars are becoming better understood as they are pushed to their limits. The English student may profit from this, much as the conservative driver profits from the tests that run automobiles like his for endless hours at high speeds over tracks designed to torture the machine as no public road ever does.

THE LINGUISTICS PROFESSION

The linguistics profession has grown rapidly. One convenient measure is membership in the Linguistic Society of America: In 1930, six years after organization, there were 398 members; in 1940, 552; in 1950, 829, and in 1960, 1768. These figures, of course, include many for whom linguistics is a quite secondary interest. The group within the membership that would consider themselves as primarily linguists, and who have some active involvement in the discipline, is considerably smaller, but their numbers have grown at about the same rate. The number of persons in other fields who have at least a general acquaintance with the work of linguists, but not enough involvement in linguistic activities to be attracted to the society, has grown even more rapidly.

In the thirties there were only a handful of universities which offered graduate work in linguistics. In some of them this was primarily in Indo-European historical linguistics and attracted very few students. In others it was included in the anthropology department and was hardly known outside that department. Even single introductory courses in general linguistics were available in very few institutions and seldom had much enrollment.

At the present time several new graduate programs in linguistics are opening each year, though the universities having them are still distinctly a minority. Most of the existing programs have both descriptive and historical work. Introductory courses are available at most universities, and enrollment is increasing rapidly. Where there is no linguistics department as such, these courses are offered in the English department, the anthropology department, or a language department. Even where linguistics departments exist, other departments commonly cooperate closely and give additional work in the field. Linguistics courses are beginning to be available to undergraduates. In a few schools it is becoming possible to major or minor in the discipline.

In 1928 the Linguistic Society of America inaugurated a Linguistic Institute which meets each summer on some university campus. Its original purpose was to make available courses in linguistics to students whose universities offered no work in the field. It attracted many prominent linguists as teachers and visitors and became a forum for exchange of ideas among leaders in the profession and a fertile source of new advances. It was the most important element in the recruiting and training of many of today's leaders in linguistics. The need the institute was organized to meet is no longer urgent. Nevertheless, it has grown in enrollment and course offerings through the years. It serves today largely to make highly specialized courses available to students from universities with more modest offerings. A few universities have continued summer programs of the same type when the institute has moved on from them. The opportunities for training in linguistics have thus grown tremendously, both in regular university programs and in summer schools.

The demand for linguists has grown too. With increased teaching of linguistics, the requirements here have multiplied severalfold. With increased teaching of non-European languages there has arisen a very heavy demand for linguists who can direct these programs, prepare teaching materials, supervise class work, and conduct basic research. It is quite a reversal from the days when linguists supported themselves by teaching French, German, or Latin under academic administrations which did not understand their interest in obscure languages and tolerated it only because they expected professors to be queer. Numbers are employed in government and in a wide variety of private research institutions. At least two thousand, many, however, only semitrained, are serving throughout the world under missionary societies, analyzing obscure languages, translating, preparing literature, and advancing literacy.

The linguists themselves are a very diverse group of people, and so cannot readily be characterized. A well-trained and experienced American descriptive linguist generally has a command of several languages other than English, usually at least one of them non-European. He has had lesser contact with a number of others ranging from careful study of someone else's grammatical sketch to a few weeks of intensive field work. He often has a rather thorough knowledge of the grammar of a language which he speaks only slightly or not at all, a phenomenon which is often most perplexing to the nonlinguist. He has a disconcerting way of larding his argument with examples from a vast range of the most out-of-the-way speech forms, tacitly assuming that his listener knows something about Kwakiutl or Menomini, for example — and if his listener is a linguist, he probably does! He knows how to approach an unknown language and work rapidly toward a comprehensive outline of its structure. He tends to approach a problem in English grammar in much the same way.

The typical linguist knows something of the historical development of at least one language family, usually Indo-European. He is acquainted with the major results of dialect geography, and probably has a good ear for dialect differences in his own and perhaps some other language as well. Above all, he is fascinated by the intricacies of linguistic phenomena and their variations and enjoys probing into them. He will often digress to pick up and comment upon some little feature in something he himself or anyone else present happens to say.

American linguists meet together in the Linguistic Society of America, the Linguistic Circle of New York, and a multitude of local clubs and seminars. They see each other at professional meetings in disciplines neighboring their own: the American Anthropological Association, the Modern Language Association, and many others. They serve together on committees concerned with language teaching, research coordination, publication, and so on. They visit each other. Everywhere they "talk shop". Ideas diffuse through the whole profession. Nothing of basic importance can be found in child-language research that does not ultimately reach the field worker struggling with some remote African tongue. Somehow the interesting discoveries in a machine translation project reach the comparativist working on Indo-European reconstruction. Often new results are widely known before they can be published. The most important tool of the profession is, as in any other, the grapevine.

It is this constant interchange of facts and theories that makes linguists what they are and gives unity to the field. It is also this that leaves the outsider so puzzled when he must work with them. To really understand linguists and linguistics one must get into the circle and participate in the interchange.

Chapter 4

English Grammars

The origins of linguistics and modern English grammar are the same. Both grew out of the speculations of the Greeks. Both were transmitted through the Latin grammars of the medieval period and transformed during the Renaissance by the broadening interest in language. The divergence between linguistics and grammar came only in the eighteenth and nineteenth centuries. Even so, the separation has never been complete — some grammarians and some linguists have maintained contact and interchange of ideas. But often enough, any influence from one profession to the other was restricted to a few workers and much attenuated before it reached most others. Today the two are drawing closer again. We may expect that they will benefit mutually by the increased flow of ideas from one to the other.

Grammatical scholarship, itself, has not been able to preserve its own unity. The lines of development have branched, and some branches have lost contact with others for considerable periods. There is, thus, a wide range of diversity in English grammar, and unfortunately a great deal of misunderstanding between grammarians.

THE EIGHTEENTH CENTURY

The eighteenth century was a period of great interest in the English language. It had only recently attained full respectability as a medium for arts and letters, and was just beginning to be used in science. British intellectuals cherished for it the same regularity and stability that they saw in the classical languages. They debated the means by which this might be brought about. For some time there was considerable sentiment for an academy which could regulate the language. But in the latter half of the century the preference was running toward providing for English all the apparatus of scholarly study — particularly dictionaries, grammars, rhetorics — that they judged would make its rationale evident and provide a standard enforced by reason. To provide these attracted the attention of some of the best minds in England.

Samuel Johnson is perhaps the best known of those who labored at this task. In 1755 he published his *Dictionary of the English Language*. Often considered the beginning of English lexicography, it was actually only one of a number of dictionaries produced in that century, and was clearly dependent on some of its predecessors. Nevertheless, it did make some notable innovations, and must be considered as the most important work of its kind in the period. Johnson also wrote a brief grammar, but it was not much used and was of no continuing significance.

Joseph Priestley as a young man showed great ability as a scholar in oriental languages. He became a voluminous writer on a variety of subjects ranging from theology to chemistry. It is for his contribution to the development of the latter science — actually theories of no permanent importance — that he is best known today. In 1761 he produced *The Rudiments of English Grammar*,[1] a small but remarkably original book, destined to be condemned by more dogmatic grammarians for nearly a century.

Robert Lowth also started as an orientalist and gained some fame for his studies in Old Testament literature. He was appointed professor of poetry at Oxford, and later Bishop of London. In 1762 he published *A Short Introduction to English Grammar*.[2] This book has a position in the history of English grammar much like that of Johnson's dictionary in lexicography. It was not the first, but beyond all others it was influential in setting the pattern.

Both Priestley and Lowth are far better known for their other accomplishments than for their work on grammar. Indeed, many encyclopedia entries on the two men fail to mention it at all. Yet their grammatical contributions have been more enduring than most of their other works. The English-speaking world has long held grammar in low esteem and grammarians in even lower!

There was a remarkable diversity in point of view among the eighteenth-century grammarians. Lowth and Priestley represent extremes.

Lowth was an authoritarian, politically, ecclesiastically, and in matters of grammar. He says:

---

[1] This went through several editions; I have seen only the second, of 1771.

[2] This went through several editions; I have used "a new edition, corrected", of 1775.

> The Principal design of a Grammar of any Language is to teach us to express ourselves with propriety in that Language; and to enable us to judge of every phrase and form of construction, whether it is right or not. The plain way of doing this is to lay down rules, and to illustrate them by examples. But, besides showing what is right, the matter may be further explained by pointing out what is wrong.[3]

And this he proceeds to do. To each rule is added a fair number of quotations which illustrate it. These are drawn from a wide range of authors, all carefully identified. Shakespeare, Milton, Pope, Addison, and Dryden appear most commonly, but there are many others less frequently cited. To many of the rules are also added examples which, in Lowth's opinion, are erroneous or questionable. (He is quite careful to condemn some flatly and merely suggest that others seem to him probably incorrect.) These are drawn from much the same list of authors. It is noticeable that the many quotations from the King James Bible are almost all "errors", and that, churchman that he was, he had some rather harsh criticism for the Book of Common Prayer.

The criteria which he uses in selecting correct constructions are nowhere specified clearly. There seem to be several. In part it is universal grammar — the speculations about the logic of language which arose in the previous century and remained very popular in his time. He does not, as has been charged, simply take over Latin grammar *in toto*; at many places he specifically points out sharp differences between the two languages. For example, he notes that English differs from Latin and Greek in having only two cases, and he prefers "possessive" to "genitive" because of the divergence in use between English and Latin. The influence of Latin (in places it is strong!) comes not directly but through universal grammar, since Latin, as the best known grammatical system, had a heavy influence in the development of the latter set of ideas. But he does not slavishly follow universal grammar either: He specifically rejects the difference between "absolutely neuter verbs" like *sleep* and "actively intransitive verbs" like *walk*, saying, "But however these latter may differ in nature, the construction of them both is the same: and Grammar is not so much concerned with their real, as with their Grammatical, properties."[4]

Another criterion is apparently usage. When the evidence from "good authors" is overwhelmingly for a given pattern, he accepts it. And, of course, he then condemns the minority. He seems to have shared the common view of his time that the English language was deteriorating, and so preferred the usage of older authors against that of more recent. He subordinated usage to logic or universal grammar, but it is unfair to say that his system rejected usage completely.

Lowth also deferred to the opinions of other grammarians, particu-

[3] Robert Lowth, *A Short Introduction*, 1762, p. x.
[4] Lowth, *A Short Introduction*, p. 62.

larly James Harris and his *Hermes, or a philosophical inquiry concerning Universal Grammar* of 1751. In general, Lowth applies all the resources of his scholarship to finding an appropriate rule, and having found it, endows it with all the authority he can muster.

Priestley's approach to English grammar is quite different. He was certainly strongly under the influences of universal grammar — it was, after all, an important part of the intellectual climate of his time, from which no one might escape entirely. But he was thoroughly committed to the primacy of usage over authority, and tried to give considerations of logic always the second place. He says:

> It must be allowed, that the custom of speaking is the original and only just standard of any language. We see, in all grammars, that this is sufficient to establish a rule, even contrary to the strongest analogies of the language with itself. Must not this custom, therefore, be allowed to have some weight, in favor of those forms of speech, to which our best writers and speakers seem evidently prone?[5]

In his grammar he tried consistently to record what he had observed, refraining from judgments of absolute right or wrong. It is interesting to note that he was politically and ecclesiastically liberal as well, a free church preacher and a leader of the protest against rigid Calvinism. His house and the chapel where he preached were burned by a mob angered at his sympathy with the French Revolution.

Contrary to the fashion of the day, Priestley was no admirer of Greek and Latin, though he knew them both well. Indeed, he had some rather hard things to say about the needless complexity of Greek, and lesser criticisms of Hebrew, Latin, and several modern languages. His approach to language was remarkably broad and critically perceptive. He saw problems that few later grammarians were aware of. Basically, his was the scientific attitude of observation, critical evaluation, and generalization.

THE SCHOOL TRADITION

Lindley Murray was an American lawyer of somewhat doubtful patriotism during the Revolution. At the close of the war, he emigrated to Britain, settled in Yorkshire, and devoted himself to writing. At the request of the teachers in a girls' school in York, he compiled and published in 1795 his *English grammar adapted to the different classes of learners.*[6]

The rising interest in English among the intellectuals had filtered down into the schools. English was supplanting Latin as the chief subject of study. English grammar had to take over the educational functions of Latin gram-

---

[5] Joseph Priestley, *The Rudiments of English Grammar*, 1771. The quotation is from the Preface to the second edition.

[6] Editions, both British and American, are numerous. I have seen several, but not the first.

mar. Soon after Lowth's grammar was published it found its way into the schools where it was popular for many years. Several other grammars of the same general type were also used. They did not, however, really meet the need. They had been directed at the learned public, not at school children. They gave no exercises or even directions for practical classroom use. Teachers were puzzled by their lack of decisiveness — Lowth, as dogmatic as any, not infrequently leaves questions open. And, most serious, the several grammars in use did not all agree. The teachers in York wanted something suited to the school, decisive and dependable. Murray's grammar met their needs, and apparently the needs of many others. It immediately became popular and dominated the schools for decades.

In 1797 Murray published two companion works: *English exercises adapted to Murray's English grammar* and *Key to the exercises adapted to Murray's English grammar*.[7] The first is advertised as "consisting of Exercises in Parsing; — Instances of False Orthography; — Violations of the Rules of Syntax; — Defects in Punctuation; — and Violations of the Rules respecting perspicuous and accurate Writing. Designed for the Benefit of Private Learners as well as for the Use of Schools." This subtitle gives an impression of the nature of classroom instruction as Murray conceived it.

Murray's books were immediately successful and remained for fifty years the leading textbooks in the field. The *English grammar* went through at least fifty editions, and in an abridgment appeared in at least one hundred and twenty more. Piracies and thinly disguised imitations appeared in numbers. Millions of copies were printed in America, and it was the standard textbook throughout the country.

Murray organized grammar under four heads: (1) Orthography, which included general observations on the alphabet and the sounds of the letters, syllabification, and spelling rules. (2) Etymology, which treated the parts of speech individually. Murray lists nine: article, substantive, adjective, pronoun, verb, adverb, preposition, conjunction, and interjection. There is also a brief treatment of derivation. (3) Syntax, which again takes up each part of speech, adding a treatment of the participle. He here gives explicit rules for parsing and a number of fully parsed examples. (4) Prosody, which covered rules for correct and expressive reading and the general principles of versification. Appended are a treatment of punctuation and "Rules and observations for promoting perspicuity and accuracy in Writing". Much of this material lay outside the bounds of grammar as conceived by Lowth or Priestley, but was of obvious utility in the schools.

Murray frankly appeals to expediency in determining his rules. He recognizes that there are only two case forms in the noun, but considers it easier to teach three, since there are three in the pronoun. His grammar

---

[7] I have seen only later editions.

deals almost entirely with words — their classification and forms comprising etymology, and their uses constituting syntax. His syntax includes only twenty-two rules, each copiously illustrated. Almost nothing is said about the order of words.

In the United States the spirit of the times was isolationist in educational matters. The American language was being given its own character independent of British English. 1828 saw the appearance of Noah Webster's *American Dictionary of the English Language.* This was only one of a number of nineteenth-century dictionaries, most of which were committed to stressing American usage, and which collectively helped to establish American spelling as different at many points from British. The production of school books, requiring less labor and originality, was still more active. Spelling books, readers, arithmetics, and grammars poured out of the publishing houses. For grammars, Murray's provided the preferred model. His system was followed in general, though rules and definitions were commonly rephrased or rearranged and occasional additional rules appeared. Excepting Murray's, textbooks from England were largely excluded from the market, and the influence of British grammatical work after 1800 was slight. There gradually developed an American tradition in grammar.[8]

This was most emphatically a school tradition. Almost without exception the publications were intended for classroom use. Most writers were teachers themselves, or former teachers turned professional textbook compilers, producing books in several subjects. These were not always in English or what we would call "language arts" — at least a dozen authors of grammars are known to have written arithmetics as well. The critical public was composed of school teachers and school board members. Their acceptance insured success for a few books, sending them through edition after edition. Their rejection made most of them failures. There was a strong selection in the direction of teachability by teachers who knew only one type of grammar and toward conformity to the prevailing ideas on language.

Conservative as the school systems were, they did not maintain absolute uniformity. By the middle of the century there had taken shape, alongside the system based on Murray, a second approach emphasizing "analysis". By this was meant the examination of sentences as wholes, their classification, and particularly the identification of the major sentence elements. All this was a definite departure from the older system, which emphasized the parsing of individual words, generally giving all words in

---

[8] The British school grammar tradition is rather similar, though apparently of largely separate development. It can best be seen in the following, still in occasional use, though only once slightly revised: J. C. Nesfield, *English Grammar, Past and Present,* 1898. Numerous other books continue the same tradition, and are mostly heavily indebted to Nesfield, either directly or indirectly.

a sentence equal attention, and said very little if anything about sentences as wholes.

In sentence analysis, subjects, verbs, and objects were identified, typically, as single words. They constituted the central framework of the sentence. Other words were considered as modifying these and hence secondary; they received much less emphasis. In any case the order of attention was from major elements to modifiers, rather than in the order of appearance as in Murray's directions for parsing.

Graphic devices were developed to indicate sentence structure. By 1850 a system of diagramming had appeared.[9] This recognized some twenty-six patterns, of which those in the diagram are examples.

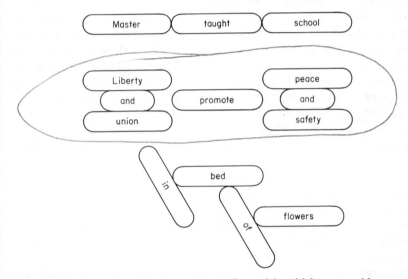

(Note that in presenting the last pattern, the article which we would assume to precede *bed* was omitted. Presumably the attention is, for the presentation, directed away from such a modifier.)

By the end of the century this system had been modified to give rise to the pattern of diagramming still familiar. Alonzo Reed and Brainerd Kellogg[10] seem to be responsible for the final steps. Little more was required than substituting lines for balloons, elaborating a few details, and adding characteristic separators between different elements: ——+—— between subject and predicate, ——⊥—— between verb and direct object, ——\—— between verb and predicate nominative. The major sentence elements were put

[9] Stephen W. Clark, *Analysis of the English Language*, 1851, p. 54–55. I have not seen this; the diagrams I have are courtesy of Professor Priscilla Tyler.

[10] Alonzo Reed and Brainerd Kellogg, *Work on English Grammar and Composition*, 1877. Later editions were under the title *Higher Lessons in English*. I have seen only the edition of 1909.

on a single straight line, the modifying elements were hung on this, thus indicating clearly their subordinate status. To further emphasize the importance of the subject, verb, and object this line was drawn heavier. Such a diagram serves as an excellent representation of sentence structure as conceived by the advocates of "sentence analysis".

Through the latter half of the nineteenth century and into this, school grammars tried various combinations of the analysis and parsing approaches. This gives a deceptive appearance of diversity. Actually, the underlying conception of grammar was much the same in all, and the material fairly standardized. Only the emphasis differed appreciably. As this could be further shifted by the teacher, the grammars were all very nearly interchangeable in the classroom.

For school grammar in its modern form, the two most important units are the word and the sentence. These are the direct heirs of the two competing approaches through the nineteenth century, the parsing of words and the analysis of sentences. Intermediate units include the clause and the phrase — the latter term being restricted very largely to the prepositional phrase. Apart from these two, there is very little attention to any unit larger than the word or smaller than the sentence. Sentence elements, except for prepositional phrases, are generally single words.[11] The "complete subject", that is, the simple subject plus its modifiers, has only an uneasy place at best.

School grammar makes much of the classification of words into parts of speech. The system is really very uniform, though the number varies from seven to ten. There are three long standing debates: Some grammarians recognize the article as a separate part of speech; most consider it simply a variety of the adjective. The participle is sometimes treated independently; others divide its consideration among the discussions of the noun, adjective, and verb. The interjection is sometimes omitted, since it is not intimately involved in sentence structure and therefore is not considered properly a part of speech.

The discussion of each part of speech is characteristically opened by a definition. Some of these seem to be in terms of meaning, others of use. But the parts of speech are described largely in terms of their places[12] relative to other words. That is, even when the definitions are meaning-based, the terms are actually used as labels for function. Some of the school grammarians are very explicit on this point. For them, every word that appears as subject of a sentence is a noun, appearance notwithstanding. Nouns simply cannot occur as modifiers; that function is reserved for adjectives

[11] Certain closely knit word groups, for example, an auxiliary and a verb, are treated as sentence elements.

[12] "Places" must be understood as 'places within grammatical structures', not as 'places within sequences of words'. The former is a more sophisticated idea than the latter. School grammar deals with sentence structure rather than with word order.

and adverbs, and these two are sharply distinguished by the part of speech that they modify.

Sentences are classified in two ways: as declarative, interrogative, exclamatory, and imperative; or as simple, compound, complex, and (sometimes) compound-complex. Much of the interest in the first of these classifications arises from the need for teaching conventions of punctuation. The second is a feature of the sentence analysis approach and provides a framework for identifying and naming clauses.

Sentence patterns are kept as few as possible by liberal use of the notion of understood elements. This makes it possible to treat many special types within the framework already provided for other kinds. Thus, imperative sentences are conformed to the declarative patterns by considering the subject as being *"you* understood''. Indirect objects are commonly treated as prepositional phrases with *"to* or *for* understood". Sentences which cannot be brought into the basic subject-predicate patterns by this device are excluded from attention or ruled against as improper.

School grammars show little interest in word order. The older books hardly mention the matter except to point out that it can be varied, particularly in poetry. Recent texts do little more.

Traditional school grammar has been closely associated with prescriptivism. Rules have been taught in the schools, not as descriptions of what actually occurs, but as legislation establishing what should be said and written. Some of the rules have been handed down for many years, though they have no apparent connection with actual usage either past or present. Some are flatly in opposition to usage in even "the best authors", a constant source of embarrassment in the teaching of literature. This prescriptive viewpoint was widely held in America through the nineteenth century. The school boards could be expected to favor the books that took an unequivocal stand for "good English". Today, many at least want to "play it safe".

But it would be a mistake to assume, as is commonly done, that prescriptivism was a necessary feature of school grammar or the universal position of textbook writers. The grammarians were probably — as are their present-day successors — on the average more open-minded on the matter of grammar and usage than the general public, and in particular, than the poorly trained teachers and school boards that chose the books. Among the grammarians were both rigid authoritarians and flexible observers of usage. In one of the early competitors of Murray's *Grammar* we find:

> The established practice of the best speakers and writers of any language is the standard of grammatical accuracy in the use of that language.
> Language is conventional, and not only invented, but, in its progressive advancement, *varied* for purposes of practical convenience. Hence it assumes any and every form which those who make use of it choose to give it. We are,

therefore, as *rational* and *practical* grammarians, compelled to submit to the necessity of the case; to take the language as it *is*, and not as it *should be*, and bow to custom.[13]

We can, however, easily imagine the average teacher seizing rather on the following statement: "A rule describes the peculiar construction or circumstantial relation of words, which custom has established for our observance." This might easily be interpreted contrary to the finer print just above it. All the grammars could be TAUGHT as authoritarian pronouncements, whatever the position of the writer. Prescriptivism is characteristic of the schools more than of the system of school grammar.

THE EUROPEAN SCHOLARLY TRADITION

Stemming also from Lowth, Priestley, and their contemporaries is another grammatical tradition. This developed almost entirely in Europe, more in fact on the Continent than in Britain. The molders were not teachers in a provincial school system, but university scholars, mostly professors of English in Germany and the Netherlands. It was shaped not for native-speaking school children, but for specialists in English language and literature, many of them having some other mother tongue. It developed through a host of technical articles in learned journals, solid handbooks, and multivolumed reference grammars. In each case all the apparatus of careful scholarship was used: bibliographic references, critical evaluation of the work of predecessors, and thorough documentation by citations from English literature. For all these reasons, it is best labeled as "scholarly traditional grammar".

While the American school tradition shows a remarkable consensus on basic questions, the European scholarly tradition has been prolific in its diversity. There has been the interplay of many very divergent points of view. There are many differences in interpretation of details, and there is a variety of terminology. It is not, therefore, easy to characterize scholarly traditional grammar in any useful way. Only some very general tendencies can be noted, and exceptions can be adduced readily enough for any of them.

Since the major formulations of this tradition are much fuller than those produced in the school tradition, it is not surprising that it penetrated much deeper and often reached into areas of uncertainty or controversy. School grammar sets forth a system of very definite answers; the scholarly tradition raised many unanswered questions. In part this reveals the different predilections of school teachers and continental scholars working in disparate intellectual climates toward basically unlike goals. In part it reflects different materials. The school grammarians had a narrow corpus

---

[13] Samuel Kirkham, *English Grammar in Familiar Lectures*, 1832, pp. 17, 18. This was one of the very popular textbooks in the first half of the nineteenth century.

of accepted sentences, the European grammarians a large and growing body of literary excerpts, since each worker gathered additional citations from English literature. The grammarians felt a responsibility to all this cumulation. Much of this collecting, unfortunately, was of oddities, and this biased the sample toward the unusual, and greatly increased the difficulties of interpretation.

Much of the work of the scholarly traditional grammarians has suffered from the lack of an adequate framework within which they might assess the relevance of the examples studied. Only an adequate basic outline continually examined in the light of a general theory of language could provide this. But few gave any attention to such questions. The general structure was accepted from past authors without as much critical consideration as it deserved. The focus of attention for the European grammarians has always been strongly on the details, particularly the uncertain or controversial points that marked the boundaries of current knowledge.

The general framework of scholarly grammar is conservative. It is organized around parts of speech and sentence elements. The old apparatus of tense, mode, and voice is used in discussing the verb, though sometimes aspect is treated separately. There is some freedom, however, in the list of tenses, and more readiness than in the school grammar to recognize forms like *goes* and *is going* as more than mere varieties of the present. The noun is treated in terms of cases. Some grammarians, because of their historical bias, find in modern English the same list as in Old English — not, however, the Latin list. There is often some discussion of word order, but commonly this is confused because too much prominence is given to unusual arrangements found in poetry.

The European scholarly tradition culminates in three great grammars produced in the first part of this century: Henrik Poutsma, *A Grammar of Late Modern English*;[14] Etsko Kruisinga, *A Handbook of Present-day English*; and Otto Jespersen, *A Modern English Grammar on Historical Principles*. The first two have each been through a number of editions, growing in size with each. They are accordingly cited under a great variety of dates. Poutsma began in 1904, Kruisinga in 1909. Jespersen is in seven volumes published from 1909 to 1949.

Poutsma and Kruisinga represent what may perhaps be thought of as the central position in traditional grammar, generally conservative, very detailed, and thoroughly documented. A convenient one-volume handbook in the same line is that of R. W. Zandvoort, *A Handbook of English Grammar*.

Jespersen is the one great traditional grammarian who gave attention to the general framework of grammar and made considerable innovations.

---

[14] Full bibliographic information on this and other works cited in this section can be found in the Bibliography.

He based his treatment of syntax almost completely on meaning, with rather odd results at many places. He classified the words of sentences into ranks: primary for the main sentence elements, secondary for their modifiers, and tertiary for modifiers of secondaries. His terminology is also divergent in many details. Jespersen's system can be most conveniently seen in his one-volume *Essentials of English Grammar*.

The authors of the great European reference grammars, like most of their co-workers who produced smaller critical studies, were acquainted with linguistics. Some had a very deep understanding of the subject. Indeed, Otto Jespersen wrote extensively in the field. His *Language; its nature, development, and origin* has been widely used as an introductory textbook.

The linguistics which they knew, of course, was largely historical and focused on Indo-European. Many of them were thoroughly trained in Old English and other Germanic languages. They were thoroughly acquainted with the historical development of English and its dialects. The result is a historical orientation which is very prominent in most of their work. Since the body of evidence that had been gathered ranged over a long period of English literature, this historical orientation was very useful. It gave them a framework within which to arrange their citations and a basis for assessing some of the differences.

Descriptive linguistics developed late in Europe. It did not, therefore, have much impact on European traditional grammar until after the appearance of the great reference grammars. It is, however, now beginning to be felt, and we can be sure that the character of the tradition will alter as a result.

While the scholarly tradition has centered in Europe, it has not been unknown in America. On the whole the school textbook writers have been little influenced by it, even when they have been acquainted with some of these grammars. But in the universities it has had a greater following, particularly in recent years. Some college textbooks have made appreciable use of the work of the continental grammarians, and a few have been based largely on it.[15] Jespersen has probably had more influence in this way than the others.

A few Americans have contributed to the discussion and one major reference grammar in this tradition has appeared in the United States. This is George O. Curme's *A Grammar of the English Language*, planned as three volumes. Only two, *Syntax* and *Parts of Speech and Accidence* have been published, however. This has the usual historical orientation. It appeared too early (1935, 1931) to be greatly influenced by descriptive linguistics. It is, however, careful to note stress differences when pertinent. It cites a great number of recent examples, including many from newspapers

---

[15] For example, Margaret M. Bryant, *A Functional English Grammar*, 1959.

and magazines, a source commonly overlooked by continental grammarians. Unfortunately, Curme is sometimes led into difficulties by his heavy reliance on meaning.

STRUCTURAL GRAMMAR

As descriptive linguistics arose in America, a few English professors were aware of the movement and followed its development. One of these was Charles Carpenter Fries of the University of Michigan. From the twenties onward he urged upon his colleagues the necessity of rethinking the content of the grammar course in the schools. There was, however, very little available that would serve to replace the existing scheme.

In 1952 Fries published *The Structure of English*, designed to meet this need. As its subtitle, *An introduction to the construction of English sentences*, suggests, it is almost entirely devoted to syntax. It attempts to build a new treatment of the subject on the basis of a large body of recorded spoken English. This, however, is presented in conventional spelling and analyzed much as written material might be.

Fries rejects the traditional parts of speech. Instead he defines four major form classes and fifteen groups of function words. No one of these corresponds particularly well with any traditional category. For example, Class 1 contains nouns plus some (not all) pronouns; Class 2 contains most verbs, but the auxiliaries and some superficially similar forms are excluded. He was not afraid to set up very small groups of function words: *not*, for example, forms a group by itself.

Formal characterizations are attempted for these categories. Class 1 includes all words that can be used in a sentence like:

The _____ is/are good.

This is supplemented by seven other criteria, including the occurrence of a plural form, the use with -'s, use following determiners (articles, and so on) and prepositions. The four form classes are described as having large and unlimited membership. The fifteen groups of function words are defined by listing. While the lists are not complete, it is implied that exhaustive lists could easily be worked out and would not be greatly larger.

Because his categories do not correspond with the traditional parts of speech, Fries does not use the familiar terminology. Instead he gives arbitrary labels: "Class 3", "Group A", and so on. For some people this has been the most obvious feature of the Fries scheme, and they have tended to dismiss it as mere juggling of labels. Others have acted as if mere dropping of "noun" for "Class 1" has constituted progress.

A number of basic sentence patterns are described by formulae using his arbitrary symbols. For example, D 1 2-d 4 symbolizes sentences of the pattern of *The pupils ran out*. These formulae are of value in focusing attention on the pattern rather than on the specific words. Certain words are described as "modifying" others. (Fries always uses quotes around this and related words, apparently to avoid implications of a meaning-based definition of "modify".)

This seems to be a direct inheritance from either school grammar or European scholarly traditional grammar or both. But he does not put the same emphasis on single-word main sentence elements as do the older systems.

After a number of sentence patterns have been discussed, there is a brief treatment of immediate constituents. It is claimed that the immediate constituent structure can be found from the structure signals and the class membership of the major words, no recourse to meaning being necessary. This chapter gives a crucial point in Fries' understanding of grammar. Without immediate constituents, most of the description of function words becomes rather irrelevant. The function words are not the structure of the sentence; they are only signals of that structure. The successive layers of immediate constituents do define the structure of the sentence directly.

The emphasis in *The Structure of English* is clearly on sentence structure. For this reason the whole system is best known as "structural grammar". Looked at from the point of view of school grammar, it was a new and radical innovation. Hence it became known among English teachers and school administrators as the "new grammar". Because of Fries' insistence on the principles of linguistics — he meant, of course, as a device for establishing a grammatical analysis — the scheme also came to be identified as "linguistics", and is commonly so called by English teachers today.

Linguists generally look on Fries' work as a small step in the right direction but a rather timid one. In particular they consider as extremely conservative his failure to use phonemic notation for his examples or to give more than passing attention to intonation.

A sober appraisal of Fries' structural grammar must, I think, consider it more nearly as scholarly traditional grammar than as in the mainstream of linguistics. It is, of course, much influenced by descriptive linguistics, particularly by the Bloomfieldian point of view of the thirties and forties. Like the work of the linguists, it is based directly on a sample of actual usage collected for the purpose. But neither of these characteristics would set it off from traditional grammar. The European grammarians are more cognizant of historical than descriptive linguistics, but that is historical accident. The traditional grammarians also gathered a sample and based their work on observation of it.[16] Fries' material is merely less in total quantity though much more homogeneous than that of the traditionalists.

---

[16] Even the better school grammars did the same: "We have considered hundreds of suggestive letters written us by intelligent teachers using the book. We have examined the best works on grammar that have been published recently here and in England. And we have done more. We have gone to the original source of all valid authority in our

Fries is like the grammarians of Europe in knowing and referring to a great deal of older work. To be sure, his references are mostly highly critical. They are restricted to the earlier part of the book where he examines and discards many definitions of the sentence and of the parts of speech. When he comes to building his system, he proceeds independently.

Fries differs from the older grammarians of the scholarly tradition in showing much more concern for the basic structure of the grammar. His innovations are almost entirely here, rather than in details. Indeed, the easiest criticism to level against his work is grossness. A great deal of refinement in detail will be needed before it can be considered adequate. Much of that refinement, however, can be accomplished by working along the same lines as Fries. Structural grammar must be judged not as a complete system, but as a skeleton. Perhaps no more could legitimately be expected in one publication. Unfortunately, there has not been much work expended on filling out and perfecting the scheme. Structural grammar stands today very nearly where Fries put it in 1952.

THE LINGUISTS ON ENGLISH

American linguists have frequently turned to English for examples to use in exposition of linguistic principles. In this way, they can find materials readily understandable to their students. Moreover, they reveled in applying successfully to English, French, or Latin the same techniques of analysis and statement that they had used in the field with Kwakiutl, Navaho, and Menomini. To do so was an effective protest against the popular insistence on a fundamental difference between "primitive" and "civilized" or "advanced" languages. It is an item of dogma among the anthropological linguists that all languages are basically the same, and hence amenable to the same methods.

Bloomfield's *Language* makes use of many English examples. They appear in every part of the book. The approach to English, however, is fragmentary. Examples are adduced where it fits the author's purpose, but there is no attempt to work the whole into a balanced, comprehensive description of English as a language. That is, of course, quite justifiable:

---

language — the best writers and speakers of it. That we might ascertain what present linguistic usage is, we chose fifty authors, now alive or living till recently, and have carefully read three hundred pages of each. We have minutely noted and recorded what these men by habitual use declare to be good English. Among the fifty are Ruskin, Froude, Hamerton, Matthew Arnold, Macauley, De Quincey, Thackeray, Bagehot, John Morley, James Martineau, Cardinal Newman, J. R. Green, and Lecky in England; and Hawthorne, Curtis, Prof. W. D. Whitney [a linguist!], George P. Marsh, Prescott, Emerson, Motley, Prof. Austin Phelps, Holmes, Edward Everett, Irving, and Lowell in America. When in the pages following we anywhere quote usage, it is to the authority of such men that we appeal." Alonzo Reed and Brainerd Kellogg, *Higher Lessons in English*, 1909, p. 11. This is from the "Author's note to edition of 1896".

Bloomfield made no pretense of writing other than a presentation of general linguistic principles. English was for him only a side issue.

During the war many American linguists found themselves teaching languages. They had insisted that two languages had to be taken into account in planning lessons, the one being taught and the mother tongue. Ability to speak a language involves automatic conformity to a set of precise patterns. To establish this with a person who already has a strongly established set of language habits is difficult. There is constant danger of conforming the new patterns to the old. To avoid this, linguists have asserted, students must be made aware of some features of their mother tongue. Lesson planners must take the total structure of the students' first language into account. Classroom teaching of language in the light of such convictions increased the interest of linguists in English. Some of them found themselves giving close attention to English phonology and grammar.

In the development of the Bloomfieldian tradition during the forties, several of the significant papers dealt with major sections of English structure. Some of them were written primarily with theoretical points in mind, but they all had the effect of advancing understanding of the language. English had an advantage for this purpose in that other linguists had equal access to the data, and could therefore more effectively weigh the theoretical points at stake. Debate and discussion tended to center on these papers rather than others based on less widely known languages. This gave these contributions a key place in advancing analytic techniques. One series of papers dealt with the English phonemic system, gradually evolving an analysis of the vowel system. Others dealt with English verb inflection. Many points were widely discussed among linguists but not formally published. All this work prepared the way for a synthesis generally in the Bloomfield tradition.

The first important attempt to give a comprehensive description of English within the framework of American descriptive linguistics was that of George L. Trager and Henry Lee Smith, Jr. This was published in 1951 as *An Outline of English Structure*. It represented in many ways the culmination of the linguistic developments since Bloomfield.

As might be expected, the *Outline* gives a very thorough treatment of the sound system including stresses, pitches, and junctures. This analysis rather quickly came to be more or less the standard among linguists in America. Not every one accepts it in every detail, of course, but many do, and most understand enough of it that it is an effective basis for discussion. It claims to cover all varieties of American English, and most of those of other countries, within one system, and thus to serve as part of the description of the English language rather than of some single dialect.

The treatment of English morphology is just over a third as long as that of the phonology. But in that space they give rather adequate coverage of the inflection and make some suggestions toward a technique of description of derivation. They point out that the latter would require a very lengthy statement for full treatment.

The discussion of syntax is even shorter, hardly more than a few hints. The deficiency here is not the reflection of any lack of interest on the part of the authors (they have since been working on a major treatment of English syntax) but of the state of the art. Trager and Smith in 1951 were just beginning to work out their techniques for syntactic analysis, and still had some rather fundamental problems to settle.

Beyond syntax in what they labeled "metalinguistics", they could merely make a general programmatic statement of additional topics they felt should ultimately be investigated. Among them are the social implications of phonological and grammatical differences, certain peculiar phonological features which they later labeled "voice qualifiers", and the general problem of relationship between language and the rest of culture.

The authors were not unaware that there was a great deal of previous work on English grammar, particularly on English syntax, where their own treatment was weak. They might have used some of this to fill out the gaps. But they chose to approach the problem independently, in much the same way as they would approach a previously undescribed American Indian language. In part this was because of a desire to demonstrate what their technique could do, and in part it was because of the difficulty of integrating into their over-all scheme results obtained from a totally different approach. The traditional grammars had been largely based on written English, and whatever was said about spoken English had been fitted into the matrix set by the literary language. For Trager and Smith only speech is really the language; writing is merely a reflection of speech, and often quite imperfect at that. Therefore, from their point of view the traditional grammars had approached the problem backwards; the results were suspect and everywhere seriously incomplete. Trager and Smith judged it worthwhile to put the old work aside and approach the problems afresh. Only in this way could they put together a new framework not seriously distorted by the shortcomings of the old grammars.

It is in the treatment of grammar that the *Outline* breaks new ground. This is based solidly on the English sound system. In particular, Trager and Smith called attention to the grammatical significance of stresses, pitches, and junctures (collectively called "suprasegmentals"). These had never before been given much more than passing notice. They suggested that the grammatical analysis could only be made by following clues presented by these suprasegmental phonemes. For example, they showed that in a sentence like

Long Island is a long island.

there is a difference in stress between the proper name and the sequence of adjective and common noun. This signals a difference in the grammatical construction of the two, a difference which is systematically associated with the two stress patterns. Any other stress pattern would mark another construction. The stress, here as throughout English, they maintained, is the major marker of certain specifiable types of syntactic relationships.

In much the same way, intonation patterns mark other syntactic constructions, generally larger ones. They tie together the smaller, stress-marked constructions into units of the general size and type of sentences and clauses. Older descriptions of English necessarily missed much of the structure, they claimed, by overlooking these suprasegmental features entirely, or by using only a partial and often approximate analysis of stress.

This type of analysis, based directly on the phonology, has come to be known as "phonologic syntax".[17] The impact of this work on those attempting to bring new grammatical concepts into English teaching has been very great. For many this approach is considered almost synonymous with "linguistics". It does not, however, reflect the position of all American linguists, probably not of a majority. Few of the others will deny the importance of the suprasegmentals, but many feel that the "phonologic syntax" position tends to magnify their significance beyond what is warranted.

In 1958 Archibald A. Hill published his *Introduction to Linguistic Structures; from sound to sentence in English*. This was intended to do two things: serve as an introduction to linguistics, and present a more thorough framework for English grammar. It carries the technique of "phonologic syntax" far beyond what is done by Trager and Smith in the *Outline* — so far, some linguists believe, as to show certain fatal defects.

The work is useful, however, since the syntax is given a fairly comprehensive and detailed treatment. The major patterns are all examined, and at some points many fine details are covered. Some matters are treated that are not easily found even in the most comprehensive handbooks. Of course, patterns of stress and intonation are carefully recorded throughout and made the basis of much of the presentation.

Criticism of Hill's analysis by linguists has been heavy. Much of it accepts his avowal that he does pronounce certain sentences as described, but suggests that the pronunciation is not general in the United States. A thoroughly adequate grammar on this basis will certainly have to meet this type of criticism by investigating many dialects and establishing in detail the range of stress and intonation patterns that are associated with each construction from area to area.

The great advance in syntactic method in the forties was the further development of immediate constituent analysis. Prior to its codification

---

[17] The term "phonologic syntax" is not used by those linguists to whose work it is applied.

there were a number of experiments with describing languages in these terms. One of the important ones was Eugene A. Nida's *A Synopsis of English Syntax*. This was completed as a doctoral dissertation in 1943, but not formally published until 1960. In the meantime it circulated in a limited way in several dittoed or mimeographed editions. One of these was put out for the use of teachers of English in Afghanistan, and another with notes in Japanese for teachers in Japan. A few linguists in America had copies, but it was hardly known among the English profession in the United States. This is unfortunate because it is a useful supplement to Fries and to Trager and Smith. Now that it is available certain shortcomings are quite obvious, and they may give a wrong impression of its value.

Nida attempted to describe English syntax by a thorough application of the immediate constituent technique. Each construction was described as consisting of two parts (very rarely three or more) of specific types and in a definable relation. Long sentences are described in terms of many layers of such simple constructions, one within another.

Nida's presentation is in outline form, with little explanation or comment. For this reason it is rather difficult to follow. It does contain a very large amount of material, probably covering a wider range of English sentence types than any other grammar yet produced by a linguist in America. It does not, however, take account of the suprasegmentals. Nida was aware of their importance, but wrote before there was an adequate analysis that he could use.

In addition to the major studies of the grammar of English, there have been a number of important contributions by linguists dealing with smaller segments. Some of these certainly are of first importance as contributions to English grammar, though they await integration into a general grammatical system. Only examples can be mentioned here. W. Freeman Twaddell published in 1960 a small pamphlet, *The English Verb Auxiliaries*. This examines the features generally treated as tense, voice, mode, and aspect. It shows that the system operates in a much different way than had been supposed by others, either traditional grammarians or linguists. This has been, perhaps, the place where the charge of latinization of English grammar has been most deserved. Strangely, those who have made the charge have been little less guilty than those they accused.

There have been a number of studies of the order and classification of the modifiers with nouns. These have shown a far greater richness of interesting features than traditional grammars would lead one to expect. There are a number of different classes or subclasses of such modifiers and they show rather complex relationships.

Finally there is the work of the transformational-generative grammarians. This group has not yet produced a major description of English as a whole, or even a very full outline, but they are working actively on various parts of the system. Almost all the basic theoretical discussion of the approach is illustrated with English examples. There are a number of journal articles dealing with specific details, and more are appearing continually. The most comprehensive single publication to date is that of Robert B. Lees, *The Grammar of English Nominalizations*. The problem discussed in this is the structure of items like *washing machine, dog biscuit, powder puff*, and so on. These are described in terms of derivation by series of transformations from certain whole sentences. As background for this presentation, Lees gives a somewhat fuller outline of English sentence structure than is available elsewhere on a transformational-generative basis. It is, of course, somewhat sketchy and unbalanced, since it is intended to give adequate coverage only to the sentence types needed for the main purpose of the book.

Transformational-generative grammar, then, has not yet given us a systematic presentation of English syntax even at the level of moderate detail. But it does hold out a promise of such a grammar, or perhaps of several such grammars. And that promise is reasonably firm. We may soon see a major contribution.

CAN WE FIND A SYNTHESIS?

A number of analyses of English grammar are currently competing, somewhat unequally of course, for acceptance. Among them are school grammar, several varieties of scholarly traditional grammar, structural grammar, phonologic syntax, immediate constituent analysis, and transformational-generative grammar. Such a list does not exhaust the possibilities, as there are other approaches current among linguists, but not yet tried on English in any comprehensive way. There are perhaps others not yet investigated at all. Transformational-generative grammar, the most recent and perhaps the brashest challenger, shows signs of developing a number of variants. No serious student of English grammar can dismiss any of these summarily. Certainly he should not condemn any of them without understanding the issues at stake.

The several types of grammars differ at various levels. Some of the most obvious differences are only superficial and relatively unimportant. Among these are certain matters of terminology or form of expression. Unfortunately, these can easily be magnified out of all proportion, and in some instances have become most misleading. Certainly, any such difference can be overcome by patience and charity.

At a deeper level are differences in technique of description. These are not necessarily incompatible, though most linguists and grammarians have a strong preference for neat uniformity of analysis and statement. Perhaps an ideal grammar should use several different techniques. But if so, their relationships must be clearly understood. Otherwise there will be at least appearances of conflict, and perhaps looseness at the seams.

At a still deeper level there are more fundamental issues: the nature of language and the wider processes of communication, the nature and function of grammars, the epistomological bases of analysis, definition, and statement. These are easily glossed over and forgotten. The history of English grammar will show many instances when this has happened. But these differences cannot be permanently suppressed. Sooner or later they rise up to plague a grammarian who does not face them squarely.

There are many parallels in our situation today to that faced by the teachers in York in 1795. There is a confusion of voices in English grammar at a time when there is increasing interest in language and when the schools are undergoing rapid change. Teachers do not see all the relationships between the competing systems, nor their significance to the student and his educational future.

We would like to find some way to present English grammar so that it is both teachable and intellectually respectable. The easy way, of course, would be to find another Lindley Murray who would cut through the confusion and formulate a definitive system. This would then become the beginning of a new and probably equally stultifying grammar tradition.

Instead, we should somehow open the schools to the best insights of all approaches, from grammarians and linguists alike, so that students can sense something of the marvelous complexity of language system and the problems and challenge of linguistic investigation.

Part Two

TOPICS IN ENGLISH SYNTAX

Chapter 5

Structure and System

Certain basic premises are shared by all types of grammar and by modern descriptive linguistics. One of these is that sentences have structure. Lowth, for example, knew this and based his treatment of syntax on it. He starts his discussion with:

> A Sentence is an assemblage of words, expressed in proper form, ranged in proper order, and concurring to make a complete sense.
> The Construction of Sentences depends principally upon the Concord or Agreement, and the Regimen or Government, of Words.[1]

At least three principles of sentence structure are mentioned: order, concord, and government. A page later he sets forth another: "A Phrase is two or more words rightly put together, in order to make a part of a Sentence; and sometime making a whole sentence." That is to say, sentences have structures within structures. Lowth made more of this point than did most of his successors, but none followed out the implications to their limit.

Sentence structures show great diversity. A second premise shared by linguists and grammarians is that underlying all this variety there is system.[2] It is, therefore, possible to make statements which apply to all sentences or to a large and definable set of sentences. This Lowth does not

---

[1] Robert Lowth, *A short introduction*, 1762, p. 118.
[2] I am distinguishing structure and system. The first is characteristic of connected discourse, the second of language. Both are usually called "structure" by American linguists, and this dual use of the term seems to be a source of confusion. British linguists have generally kept the two separate. My distinction is similar, but not precisely identical, to that made in Britain.

state explicitly, but that he even attempted to write a grammar indicates that he would have accepted the premise had it been put to him.

These two are old premises. They do not need to be replaced, and very little modification is called for. But it is desirable to follow their implications more comprehensively and consistently. Here modern linguistics can make its greatest contribution to English grammar. Wide experience with many languages and basic concern with fundamentals have led the linguist to more thorough exploration of structure and system than has been usual in the past. Earlier grammarians have focused their attention more on the details of one language.

SENTENCE STRUCTURE

At first sight a written sentence is a collection of words arranged in a row on the paper. A spoken sentence seems to be a group of words occurring one after another in time. They are connected somehow: if they are jumbled, the sentence is destroyed or changed. A sentence might be likened to a railroad train: a series of cars, each one coupled to the one before and the one following. This is the first impression, but it is quite wrong. The structure is always more complex. Every part is somehow tied in with the others, but it is not necessarily adjacent words that are directly linked.

As a simple example we may take a familiar bit of written English of a quite unliterary sort. To the right is a common highway sign. Its meaning is clear enough — the sign has been carefully designed so that it can be read at a glance. However, it cannot be read in the conventional way from top to bottom: *Children slow crossing* somehow completely obscures the meaning. But Americans accustomed to the conventions of highway signs would never read it that way. As they immediately recognize, it is not three words in a row. *Children* goes with *crossing*, and the two together stand as an explanation of the command *slow*. This is signaled on the sign by the two sizes of lettering, which obviously connect *children* and *crossing* and set them off against *slow*. Some of the usual signals of written English, notably certain features of word order and all punctuation, are discarded. But they are replaced by the special conventions[3] of highway signs which serve the same purpose in different ways.

CHILDREN
SLOW
CROSSING

---

[3] A designer is not necessarily aware of the structural significance of these conventions, any more than most speakers are aware of the structure signals in their speech. Moreover, they grew up by trial and error, rather than any deliberate planning, and are not at every point efficient indicators of structure.

Shown below are two signs which set aside or misuse the conventions. One is without the size difference. It does not seem to carry the meaning clearly or forcibly. We may guess that the difficulty arises from the absence of signals of structure. The second has a different word written large. It does not, therefore, mean the same thing as the standard sign. The meaning is puzzling, rather than unclear. Structure is signaled, but the result seems inappropriate or ridiculous. The failings of the two signs are different, and they point up in two ways the significances of the difference in lettering as a device to signal which words go together.

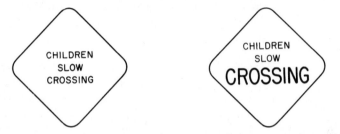

In a more usual context — almost anywhere except on a highway sign — the message of the original sign could be conveyed by the same three words. But they would have to appear in a more rigidly fixed order, either *slow children crossing* or *children crossing slow*, certainly not *children slow crossing*, as on the sign. Word order usually plays a more important part in signaling than it does on highway signs. But order alone is not enough. Consider a sign like the following, written in nearly conventional form for ordinary English:

SLOW CHILDREN CROSSING

This can be read in two different ways, giving opportunity for a rather threadbare joke: "Where do the fast children cross?" The problem is simply one of linking the words correctly. The signals are inadequate, and two alternative readings seem fairly reasonable. They can be indicated in the mathematician's notation: *Slow (children crossing).* or *(Slow children) crossing.* In the first, *children* and *crossing* go together and then the two go with *slow*. In the second *slow* and *children* go together and then the two go with *crossing*.

In standard written English the two would be distinguished by punctuation, but this is not as straightforward as the mathematician's bracketing. The first would be: *Slow, children crossing.* The comma separates *slow* from the rest, thus effectively joining *children* and *crossing*. In this sentence the comma is obligatory. *Slow children crossing*, without the comma, would indicate *(slow children) crossing*. The indication of structure is indirect; it rests on the absence of the comma that is obligatory in the other possibility.

Consider what happens if this set of three words is read aloud. Apart from reading it simply as a list, there are two[4] distinctly different ways of pronouncing it, each quite unambiguous. When we speak, there are signals in the intonation which mark the structure we intend. The simplest to observe is a pauselike feature, technically a terminal, occurring at the point where the comma is written in: *Slow, children crossing*. This terminal might be thought of as separating the two major parts, but this is not all. Spreading over *children crossing* is a single intonation contour and this serves to tie them together in one unit. In the other reading, a terminal may come between *children* and *crossing*, separating them, while an intonation contour joins *slow* and *children*.

Lettering differences on signs, punctuation in normal written English, and intonation in speech do much the same thing: they mark some features of structure, in most cases enough to suggest the whole. They do not usually mark all the structure simply and directly — part is marked, if at all, only indirectly. The intonation patterns and the punctuation patterns do not necessarily indicate the same selection of features. It is not, therefore, always possible to equate them.

Sentences cannot be punctuated simply by following the intonation. Rather, the signals given in speech must be used to understand the structure, and then punctuation can be supplied which marks this structure. Even when marks do come where terminals are heard, the whole structure must be understood to guide the choice. On the other hand, passages cannot be well read by mechanically placing terminals at punctuation marks. The choice of terminals and of intonation contours can be guided only by an understanding of the full structure.

With only three elements, there are very few possible structures, so that the example just discussed is about as simple as any can be. If there are more pieces, there are very many more ways of organizing them. With only a few words the possibilities mount up into the thousands. Some fairly effective system of signals is imperative.

In every intelligible bit of English, spoken or written, there must be signals which indicate at least the major features of the structure. Somehow the reader or hearer uses these to pick out a structure that fits, very often exactly what the writer or speaker intended. Once in a while a sentence permits two or more structures to be seen in it. Such a sentence is amgibuous. A simple example is the following:

On the shelf were the old-fashioned ladies' hats.   (1)

Any American who hears or reads this sentence immediately gets an idea of what it means. But what he understands could be either of two mean-

---

[4] There are more than two ways of reading such a sentence, some of them ambiguous. Additional ones would only complicate the statement, not require basic changes, and so can be overlooked in this presentation.

ings. Some people will notice this. Anyone who does will ask himself such a question as: "With what does *old-fashioned* go, with *ladies* or with *hats?*" Perhaps in the context there is a clue which will answer the question. If not, the sentence is unresolvably ambiguous. This sentence is so because the structure signals which it provides are not quite sufficient to answer all our questions about what pieces go together. Nevertheless, there are structure signals in the sentence — many of them. Any English speaker knows without much doubt that the first *the* goes with *shelf*, and that *on* goes with *the shelf*, and so on. It is impossible to put together a sentence in English that does not contain features marking the largest part of its structure — unless we produce a mere collection of words that cannot properly be called a sentence. Structure and structure signals are indispensable and unavoidable in English, as in any language.

STRUCTURE SIGNALS AND VOCABULARY

It is important to note that the structure and the structure signals of a sentence like the example above are characteristically English. We cannot talk about the structure of sentences in general. To know English means, basically, to be able to discern the structure of an English sentence. Other languages use different structures and signal them in different ways. For example, the following are two normal Panjabi sentences:

mere dost ne tòbi nu nale kol jande wekhɪa cacaji nal. (2)

kheḍda pɪa si məndɪr nalde mədan wɪc mere pài da ləṛka khɪddo. (3)

Both these sentences will be completely meaningless to most readers of this book. Some parts of each are structure signals; these will not be easy to translate individually. Nor would a translation be helpful. What would be needed to make these intelligible would be an explanation of how the signals indicate structure, and what the structures are. But to give this would require the exposition of a very large part of the total system of Panjabi grammar. Other parts of the two sentences are easier to translate. For example, *dost* means 'friend', *tòbi* means 'washerman'. (Of course, to cover all the details, a great deal more than this would be required, but this much is at least helpful.) Restricting our translating to this second type of feature, we may half-translate sentence (2): (Hyphens merely mark the boundary between English and Panjabi when they fall into the same word.)

mere *friend* ne *washerman* nu *stream* kol *walk*-de *see*-a *uncle* nal. (4)

Now we know, to express it very loosely, what the sentence is about: a friend, a washerman, a stream, an uncle, and the acts of walking and seeing. But the sentence does not make sense. Who walks? The friend, the washerman, or the uncle? Who sees? We do not know the answers to these or to many other similar questions. It is not enough to understand the main words. We must also grasp their relationship, that is, the structure. There are plenty of structure signals (the parts left untranslated); they would answer our questions if we knew Panjabi grammar. Since our translating has not changed the structure, (4) is still a Panjabi sentence. It is not intelligible to one who knows only English.

We can try it the other way around with sentence (3):

$$My \text{ pài-}'s \text{ lərka } was \text{ kheḍ-}ing \text{ khıddo } on \text{ } the \text{ mədan } near \text{ } the \text{ məndır.} \quad (5)$$

The process of half-translating to get sentence (5) is very different from that to get sentence (4). Structure signals cannot be translated individually, as a general rule. Instead we translated[5] the whole set of Panjabi signals into an equivalent set of English signals. In sentence (4) we translated the main words one by one.

In sentence (5) it is very clear how the words go together, but we have no idea what the sentence is about. Yet an American, without knowing the untranslated words, would be able to make up some additional sentences like:

> *The* lərka *was* kheḍ-*ing* khıddo.   (6)
>
> *My* pài *has a* lərka.   (7)
>
> *The* mədan *is near the* məndır.   (8)
>
> *It was on the* mədan *that my* pài-*'s* lərka *was* kheḍ-*ing* khıddo.   (9)

Of course, we do not know what these sentences mean either. But we can be reasonably sure that they are just as good sentences as (5). Most of the words that can fit into the pattern that we judge sentence (5) to represent are the kind of words that can fit just as well into the patterns of these additional sentences. That this is so is a fact about English that the native speaker senses. The patterns are valid whether we know the words in them or not.

But this is not the whole story. Either the following is acceptable:

> *My* pài-*'s* lerka *was* khıddo kheḍ-*ing on the* mədan *near the* məndır.   (10)

or the following is:

> khıddo *was being* kheḍ-*ed by my* pài-*'s* lerka *on the* mədan *near the* məndır.   (11)

But if (10) is acceptable, (11) cannot be, and vice versa. There is an am-

---

[5] Separating the translating process into two parts is, of course, an oversimplification, but not otherwise a distortion. Different aspects of a passage do require different treatments. Especially is it true that structure signals must be translated in interconnected sets, never singly. The major vocabulary can be treated more individually, though seldom as much so as has been done here. A legendary schoolboy rendering of the opening of *De Bello Gallico* shows what can happen when context is completely ignored: "All Gaul is quartered into three halves."

biguity in sentence (5); the structure signals that have been translated are not quite enough. The question is, what is *khɪddo*? If it is what is traditionally called an "adverb", then sentence (10) is appropriate, but if it is a noun, sentence (11) is.[6] It is not necessary to know what it means, only what part of speech (and in many instances what subdivision of a part of speech) it is. Whatever structure signals there are in words like *friend, walk, good* are all matters of their part of speech, not of their dictionary meaning. We must have a part of speech classification to fully understand the structure.

The original Panjabi sentences can be fully translated as:

> *My friend saw the washerman walking with Uncle near the*
> *stream.*   (2)
> *My brother's boy was playing ball on the field near the temple.*   (3)

We now see that *khɪddo* means 'ball'. In sentence (5) it was a noun, hence sentence (11) was right, not sentence (10). But it is not the meaning of *khɪddo* that tells us this, but the fact that it is a noun. If the translation of sentence (5) had turned out to be something like the following, sentence (10) would have been acceptable:

> *My brother's boy was playing quietly on the field near the temple.*   (12)

Please note that the question was: What part of speech is *khɪddo* in sentence (5)? This is an English sentence, and it is reasonable to ask of any word in it what English part of speech it may be. *Khɪddo* must be treated in this sentence as an unfamiliar English word.[7] We do not ask: What part of speech is *khɪddo* in sentence (3)? That is a Panjabi sentence, and the question would have to be answered in terms of Panjabi parts of speech, which may be vastly different from those of English.

We understand sentences because we know two things: 1) the structure signals and the ways they operate, and 2) the meanings of the remaining words. Both are necessary, but in very different ways.[8] Of course,

---

[6] There are other less likely possibilities for this word, but the same type of argument would hold for each. For example, Robert Allen suggests the pattern: *My father's friend was waxing eloquent on the subject near the end.* Here an adjective occupies this place. Such a pattern would merely provide some additional alternatives alongside sentences (10) and (11).

[7] Anyone who has lived abroad will understand the possibility of an English sentence containing numerous non-English words: *We had puri, dal-bhat, and kofta for dinner.* And conversely. I once overheard the following in a Hindi telephone conversation: *ek first-class special reservation hæ.* That this is Hindi is shown by the fact that the structure signals, including the two function words, are Hindi, even though all the major vocabulary is English.

[8] As will be shown in Chapter 8, the function words and major vocabulary are not quite so sharply distinct as is suggested here. Every word has some structure-signaling function, but some much more than others. Most have lexical meaning. Nevertheless, there is a group which preponderantly signals structure, and another group in which this is only a minor function.

in our native language, we do not ordinarily separate the meanings of words from the structure signals in this way. When we read a sentence or listen to one, we do not focus our attention first on one and then on the other. Rather we notice the words and their meanings and the structure signals all together. When either is not quite clear or simple, we use clues from one to help us with the other. Because this is so, we tend to overlook the fact that we are doing two different things when we listen to a sentence, or read one from a book. But to understand the process we must look at the two parts separately.

The structure signals are mostly extremely familiar. We have been using most of them constantly since early childhood. Many of them are very common, occurring over and over in everything we read or hear. A structure signal which is not thoroughly familiar is a very infrequent occurrence. Because of their great familiarity and pervasiveness, we give them very little attention. The structure signals are like the air we breathe, so constantly around us that we are almost entirely unaware of them.

The vocabulary, however, presents a different situation. Every day we meet new words. Often we are puzzled by them. Just as frequently we see or hear old acquaintances now nearly forgotten, and we are a little unsure of our memory. At other times we run into old friends in such strange contexts that we hesitate to believe they could mean what we have always assumed they did. Actually, we come upon new words or new meanings for old words much more frequently than we realize. In most cases we guess their meanings well enough for our purposes at the moment and never notice them. The context usually tells us all we need. It is, then, only the exceptional instance when strange words come into our awareness, but these alone are enough to make us feel that there are all manner of difficulties with words.

If we pick up a book in a subject not familiar to us, we may find it totally incomprehensible. If we overhear a professional conversation outside our own field, it may be largely unintelligible. Correctly, we diagnose our trouble as one of vocabulary. This is the source of most of our conscious language difficulties as experienced adult speakers of the language. Yet it was not always so for us — as young children we had to struggle with structure.

Americans tend to think of learning a new language as a matter of learning hosts of new words. Actually, the major problem is learning new structures and new structure signals. Not only is this the important task; it is also the more difficult. We all know foreigners who have learned a marvelous store of English words, but who can seldom put them together into a good, intelligible sentence. Their language learning efforts have been concentrated in the wrong place.

Four paragraphs above it was said that the structure signals are mostly extremely familiar. One significant qualification must be made to that statement: They are familiar as long as we are listening to the kind of English we customarily hear, or are reading the kind of literature we customarily read. With these we have had sufficient experience that all the signals have become thoroughly familiar.

However, if we read or listen to a radically different type of English, we may find an appreciable number of structure signals with which we are not at all familiar. High school students very often have this experience in their first reading of Shakespeare. Structural problems are as significant as lexical, but far less often noted by editors of school editions.

In all reading, the vocabulary problems may be very obvious to the reader, the structural problems unnoticed. As he labors through a difficult sentence, he may go repeatedly to the dictionary for words that he really knows, not recognizing that his trouble is elsewhere. In some instances, if he would give the same careful attention to the structure signals and the structure, his difficulties would be resolved. Unfortunately, far fewer people have a reference grammar at hand than have a good dictionary. Not many would know how to use one effectively if they had it.

If an author gives as careful attention to his sentence structure as to his choice of words — and many do — a meticulous reader should do likewise. Excessive concern with vocabulary, so characteristic of Americans (the greatest dictionary buyers on earth!), should not divert attention from grammatical problems. When a passage warrants close reading, a thorough knowledge of sentence structure may help materially in understanding precisely what a sentence means, pointing out subtleties which might easily be overlooked.

Grammar is for most of us a neglected aspect of language, one that we use constantly but seldom think about. This is permissible enough for some people, but not for those whose business is thinking about language. The process of communication can never be thoroughly understood until we see how sentence structure contributes to it. For an intelligent approach to literature or composition, there must be the ability to bring the niceties of English grammar into awareness at will. There is no need to parse or analyze every sentence. But it is essential to be able to recognize a structural difficulty when it is encountered and to understand some of the devices available to resolve it.

LANGUAGE SYSTEM

Every acceptable English sentence has a structure. A grammarian would like to be able to describe that structure for any sentence that comes before him. He cannot, however, face each separate sentence as an independent problem. To do so would be meaningless. Rather, in analyzing any given sentence he must make use of the knowledge gathered from his examination of many other sentences. The structure of a sentence is not simply a property of that sentence alone, but is also a reflection of some underlying system which characterizes all the sentences of the language. Sentences have structure only because the language has system.

The language system lies behind the structures of the sentences of the language. The native speaker senses it and conforms new sentences to it. He cannot state it, however. It cannot be seen directly until a grammarian somehow succeeds in abstracting it and describing it. A grammar is a description of a language system — or, in most cases, an incomplete approximation of such a description. A grammar is adequate to the extent that it makes possible the discovery and statement of a useful description of structure for any given sentence in the language.

The following sentence was used as an example above:

On the shelf were the old-fashioned ladies' hats.   (1)

We would like to describe its structure. A number of things must be done. One part of the task would be to state what words go together. The description, therefore, might include, along with much other information, the following: "The first *the* goes with *shelf*. *On* goes with *the shelf*. . . ." Such a set of statements would apply only to this specific sentence. Add to the material under consideration:

On the table were the old-fashioned ladies' hats.   (13)
On the chair were the old-fashioned ladies' hats.   (14)

The fragmentary description given of sentence (1) can be amended so that all three sentences are covered in one statement: "The first *the* goes with *shelf, table,* or *chair*. *On* goes with *the shelf, the table,* or *the chair*. . . ."

Obviously, such an approach can be carried a great deal farther. Somewhere in the two descriptions already suggested there must appear the word *"hats"*, probably at several places. Instead we might say *"hats, bonnets, coats, purses,* and so on." If this is done, the description would cover a considerable number of sentences including:

On the chair were the old-fashioned ladies' coats.   (15)

And, we might replace *"on"* by a list, *"on, under, near, beside,* and so on." This would add still more possibilities, including:

Under the sofa were the old-fashioned ladies' bonnets.   (16)

This is a rather strange sentence, but, perhaps, only because we do not expect to find bonnets under sofas. But it could happen, and if the unexpected did occur, this might be just what we would say to describe it. So we accept this as a good English sentence. The strangeness is not in the sentence, but in the situation it suggests.

There is no reason to put in just the three lists of alternatives mentioned above; at every place there are a number of other possibilities. The more general description would not mention single words anywhere, but always speak of lists. But there is a grave difficulty. The description is getting longer and longer, and accordingly harder and harder to follow. There is only one way to save the situation. We need some convenient, reasonably short designation that would identify the groups of words we are referring to and enable us to avoid repeating long lists. For our present purpose the traditional terminology will do; "singular common noun" and "preposition" will serve adequately. On this basis the following will be part of the description: "The first article goes with the following common noun. The preposition goes with the following combination of article and singular common noun. . . ." This is certainly an improvement.

We can think of this as a description of a set of sentences, all of which follow a common pattern. This can be stated in terms of a formula which replaces words by labels for parts of speech, but preserves the order:

> Preposition — Article — Singular Common Noun — Linking
> Verb — Article — Adjective — Plural   Common   Noun,
> Possessive — Plural Common Noun.   (17)

Formulas of this sort, commonly using abbreviations, are given in many textbooks. They are often known as "sentence patterns". Such a sentence pattern as (17) covers sentences (1), (13)–(16), and many others, including:

> *In the forest were the eccentric hermits' residences.*   (18)
> *Along the way are some wealthy merchants' shops.*   (19)
> *Inside the thimble were the purple elephants' helicopters.*   (20)

All of these are a little strange, and sentence (20) might cause us to hesitate. As an English sentence it is certainly a ridiculous example, hardly worth describing. But there is only a difference of degree between this sentence and (16), or, for that matter, sentence (1). We might want to talk about bonnets under the sofa, but it is rather unlikely. Helicopters inside the thimble seem even less likely. But people do write fantasy, and fantasy in English is different from fantasy in Zulu, because it must follow English grammatical patterns. Sentences no more probable than (20) do occur. When they appear, our grammar must be able to handle them. So we can overrule objections to any of these sentences. The formula (17) represents a group of English sentences graded from fairly useful to utterly ridiculous, but all grammatically acceptable.

Some textbook writers have assumed that a formula like (17) is adequate to set forth a sentence pattern, but it is not. It fits sentence (1) well enough, but that sentence is ambiguous — it has two possible structures. A sequence of words which fits the formula may have either of these structures, or both. The difference is most easily seen by comparing two sentences which fit the formula but show different structures:

> *On the shelf were the elderly ladies' hats.*   (21)
> *On the shelf were the moth-eaten ladies' hats.*   (22)

In (21), *elderly* clearly goes with *ladies*. In (22), *moth-eaten* just as clearly goes with *hats* or some element containing *hats*. In (1) *old-fashioned* can be construed either like *elderly* or like *moth-eaten*. A simple formula is not, therefore, sufficient; there must be, in addition, some description of what elements go together.

However, this is not sufficient either. Consider the following sentence:[9]

> *Flying planes can be dangerous.*   (23)

It is quite clear that *flying* and *planes* go together. But there remain two possible interpretations based on the two possible structures. These two parallel the following two sentences:

> *Raving maniacs can be dangerous.*   (24)
> *Blasting rocks can be dangerous.*   (25)

Again using traditional terms, *blasting* is a participle and *rocks* is most probably its complement. But *raving* must be a modifier of *maniacs*, because it comes from an intransitive verb which cannot have a complement. *Flying* may be a modifier of *planes*, or *planes* may be a complement of *flying*. To state the structure adequately the relationships must be identified. Among the components of the language system must be a number of contrasting constructions which can unite pairs of elements.

From the point of view of the language system, constructions join elements of particular kinds, not specific elements. For example, the complement construction joins a verb and a following noun. Obviously, any statement of this sort can be no better than the classification of parts of speech on which it rests. The organization of words into parts of speech is part of the system of a language, and an important one.

The discussion of the last few paragraphs might imply that listing sentence patterns and describing them would be adequate to present a language system. It would not. In the first place it is not feasible. The total number of sentence patterns of the kind given at (17) is incredibly large. It is not thousands or even millions, but far beyond that. We can easily pick out a reasonable list of very common patterns. These would account for a respectable number of the sentences we meet, particularly if we restrict our reading to very simple literature. But an English grammar must have a higher objective than that. It should account for very nearly every English sentence that we come upon, provided only that it is a

---

[9] This example is from Noam Chomsky. It has been widely used as an instance where structural methods are inadequate. For this purpose, the choice is unfortunate. In one interpretation *flying* is head, in the other, *planes*. No full structural description could fail to distinguish.

properly formed sentence. And the grammar must be of manageable size. Enumerating sentence patterns will not meet these conditions.

Moreover, it is nearly meaningless to describe individual sentence patterns independently. They are patterns because they are made up of parts that occur over and over in the language. A sentence pattern is built up out of constructions. There are a considerable number of these, but far less than the immense number of sentence patterns. Once the constructions are known and understood, additional sentence patterns can be made up at will by simply seeking new combinations which follow the rules of the system.

It is this system that our grammars describe. It is necessarily quite abstract. Its features are classifications of words and other elements, constructions, and rules for combining constructions. These are all things that we can discern recurring in sentence patterns and underlying sets of sentences. They cannot be found directly.

One might object that, if grammar is as abstract as this, it is not a reasonable subject to teach young children. The best answer to this argument is that in one sense children already know it long before we would start teaching grammar. Children coming to first grade already talk. That is, they make sentences — most of them quite new, created on the spot to meet the need of the moment. They are able to understand English — that is, to listen to a sentence and figure out its structure and, hence, its meaning. Of course, they cannot do this with any English sentence whatever; their knowledge of the language does have limits. But even the most poorly endowed of them has an incredibly wide variety of patterns that he can and does use, and most children frequently put together new patterns just as do adults. The six-year-old child certainly knows a great deal of the system of his language.

A young child cannot explain how he does all this. He cannot even tell us how a certain sentence means what it does. But he does know what it means, and he can make sentences to mean what he wants to say, at least some of the time. His major deficiency is not in a knowledge of the system, but only in the ability to talk about it. A grammar rule is actually much more concrete than the behavior which it describes. When we teach grammar, we are only teaching how to talk about familiar things.

THE THREE SYSTEMS

It would be complex enough if a sample of speech had just one structure reflecting just one system in the language. But it does not. All speech has at least two structures running along concurrently and reflecting at least two language systems.

Probably the most obvious system is the one we sometimes call grammar. We can think of it as controlling the ways we put words together into sentences. Actually, this is a rather primitive view of grammar, and it must be amended immediately. First, grammar does not have to do simply with words, but also with certain groups of words. We are accustomed to think of compound or complex sentences not as made up directly of words, but of clauses which in turn are composed of words. Phrases consisting of two or more words can act as units in sentences. All this is basically correct, and there are many more instances of the kind than those which grammars ordinarily describe. Sentences are typically composed of structures within structures, sometimes through many levels. Even in the simple three-word sign with which this chapter started, it was found that two of the three words had to be grouped together as a structure within the larger structure. Only by doing this could we grasp the meaning of the sign. The sign maker had deliberately designed his work to assist us in seeing the correct grouping.

As a second amendment we must note that some words are obviously divisible into parts with which grammar must be concerned. Plural nouns have suffixes, past tense verbs have their suffixes, nouns can be made by adding -ness to adjectives, or verbs can be made by adding -ize to certain adjectives or nouns. All these are facts of grammar. The real units of grammar, therefore, are often smaller than words, though some words have only one such unit. The linguist calls these pieces "morphemes".

Grammar, then, is the system built upon the morphemes and their relationships. It comprehends the patterns by which morphemes are built into words, and the kinds of words that result, the patterns by which words are built into phrases and the kinds of phrases, and so upward through many groups for which traditional grammar does not supply a convenient term.

It has long been customary among linguists and grammarians to divide grammar into morphology, dealing with the structure of words, and syntax, dealing with larger structures. This division is not wholly satisfactory — some syntactic constructions in English reach down to involve parts of words — but if interpreted freely, it is still convenient and useful.

Another system in language has to do with the sounds that we use when we speak. It is known among linguists as "phonology". We commonly think of the sounds of the language as of two kinds, consonants and vowels. But there are also features of stress and intonation. All these together constitute the phonology. The units are known to many linguists as "phonemes".

The phonemes go together to form syllables. The syllables are put together to form what we might call "words", since they are commonly identical with the words composed of morphemes and described in the grammar. But the identity is not complete, and some linguists are careful to discriminate between phonologic words and morphologic words. The words of the sound system go together to form breath groups and various other larger units.

None of this "going together" is haphazard. The patterns are fairly definite, regular, and characteristically English. Ask an American child to recite some utter nonsense and listen carefully. You will recognize that it is English nonsense — that is, that the sounds are English, and that they are put together in much the same way as they would be in normal English sentences. They must be, because the child knows no other patterns and because these are so deeply engraved in his neural system that he cannot easily escape their control. The nonsense of a Chinese child will sound different; it will conform just as closely to Chinese sound patterns.

Linguists very generally agree that a language has both a phonological system and a grammatical system. They differ, however, in the way they view the relationship between the two. For some, morphemes are composed of phonemes, and the larger units in a passage are both phonological and morphological.[10] For others, the phonological and grammatical systems are separate from the smallest units to the largest, though closely parallel and occurring together in any sample of language. In this view, morphemes are not composed of phonemes but are represented by phonemes. Numerous intermediate positions are also held, and there are many minor variations in each. These differences are important, but they are marginal to the main interest of this book. Rather than attempt a full discussion, which would require many pages, the remainder of this section will be based on the second of the two views mentioned. Fuller statements representing a variety of positions can be found in the linguistic literature.

Linguists are also not agreed as to whether two systems are enough. Some (probably a minority in America) consider that there must be a third. This is coming to be called "semology".[11] A sentence not only has a pronunciation and a grammatical structure, but also has a "meaning". Part of what is commonly called "meaning" can be defined by observing situations in which the sentence is used. This lies outside language. Another part of "meaning", however, seems to be organized within language. There are patterns of distinctions which English forces its speakers to make. For example, whenever a noun is spoken it must be assigned to either singular or plural. There is no such demand in a number of languages, and, in some languages which lay down similar requirements, the details are very different. Words form systems of contrast that sometimes follow and sometimes cut across differences of grammar. These are all fragments of the semological system. Like the phonological and grammatical systems, the semological system we know and use is characteristically English.

---

[10] The "phonologic syntax" approach is based on this assumption. See page 84.

[11] Semology is called "content" in H. A. Gleason, Jr., *An Introduction to Descriptive Linguistics*, 1955.

The three systems, phonology, grammar, and semology, must interact with each other in complicated ways. Since every sentence must conform to the patterns of all three, it has three structures simultaneously. These somehow find their audible expression in one sequence of sounds. These sounds are not part of the structure, nor are they part of the system. They are only a medium through which structure and system can be presented to the hearer.

Behind the sounds and somehow manifested through them is a phonologic structure of successive speech sound symbols and accompanying stresses, transitions, pitches, and terminals. All these are built into syllables and various larger sequences. These units, large and small, and their interrelations, constitute the phonologic system. It obviously is affected in various ways by the physiology of speech production and the acoustic characteristics of the actual physical sounds. It is, however, none of the latter, but a system of a wholly different sort manifested through the phonetic facts.

In turn, behind the phonology is another structure, of morphemes, words, phrases, sentences, and the multifarious relations between such units. The grammar is distinct from the sound system, but the latter in some way manifests the grammatical structures.

Again, behind the grammar is a third system, of meaning contrasts and patterns of sense organization, the semology. It is still very poorly understood. Yet we suspect that the relationship of semology to grammar is much the same as that of grammar to phonology.

The relation between these structures in a sentence is primarily one of manifestation. One system gives realization to another. Each system finds its own realization outside itself, in another system of the language or just outside language in physical sound. As the attention is transferred from one system to another there is always this complex and elusive relationship, never real identity or equivalence.

Historically, the three systems of language have interacted with one another and with the systems just outside language — for example, the physical realities of speech. This interaction has gone on as the language has changed, so that each system is fairly well adjusted to the others in which it finds manifestation or which it manifests. Change anywhere in a language may require change elsewhere to maintain the balance.

Looked at without historical perspective, the changes and mutual adjustments which produced and maintain the equilibrium are not seen as facts of the system. Each part operates under its own regulations and imposes certain restrictions on other parts. Another system must respect these restrictions, but may have in its own organization some device to circumvent their effect.

For example, English phonology does not allow certain sequences of consonants, $^\times$/pz bs sz/. It is impossible, therefore, for English grammar to use either /s/ or /z/ as a suffix applying uniformly to all words whatever consonant they may end with. The English plural suffix, therefore, must have alternative forms in order to comply with this phonologic restriction. The spelling does not show this (the restrictions in spelling are very generally parallel, but not necessarily identical in detail). English plurals *tips* /tips/, *nibs* /nibz/, and *hisses* /hisiz/ show three forms of the plural suffix to accommodate to the restrictions of the phonology.

Each of the three systems must be individually complex in order to provide for its own needs while under pressure from two sides. The three collectively, that is, the language, must be even more complex. And it is. All languages are complex, English not much more nor much less than any other.

This is the picture of language that emerges from the studies of linguists. It would seem to a newcomer in the field unduly complex. For him, talking is an ordinary everyday activity, engaged in freely and extensively by almost every member of society. It is carried on with the minimum of concentration, usually with none at all on its mechanism. Certainly this popular impression is inadequate. It may be carried on without conscious attention, but this is not evidence for its simplicity. Linguists, psychologists, physiologists, and others are finding new complexities every year. Language is, in fact, one of the most intricate of all systems of human behavior.

Perhaps, indeed, the fact that we do so much of our speaking unconsciously is one reason for its complexity. An automatic gear shift is a more complex bit of machinery than the old-fashioned stick shift. Additional automation means additional equipment. Language is a very highly automated system, and it performs a very elaborate set of functions.

Language must convey all the complex organization of observations, ideas, and plain prejudices on which society and culture rest. It must reveal our individual moods, social status, origin, and appraisal of the situation in which we find ourselves. It must enable us to interact both with close friends and total strangers promptly and effectively. All this is complicated enough.

But language must do more than this. It must continually adjust itself to new needs. No language can be a fixed system of words and patterns. It must be open to receive new words and new structures, and to change the old. Change is inevitable, since language functions in a society in ceaseless flux. The continual change in language produces inevitable maladjustments in the system. The language must repeatedly repair itself, restoring and maintaining equilibrium by additional changes to counterbalance those forced upon it by changed environment. A language that could not adjust would deteriorate.

A language is, to this extent, like a biological organism, a bundle of interacting systems maintaining a dynamic equilibrium known as homeostasis.[12] No simple system can do this. There must be a network of inter-actions tying all parts together, and tying every pair of parts together in a number of ways. It is perhaps a reasonable speculation to insist that language, as we know it, with all its complexities, is very close to the simplest possible system which can maintain homeostasis in the face of the intricate set of external forces that impinge on it.

SPEECH AND WRITING

Every functioning language has three systems. But in a language like English this is not all. There is in addition a writing system.

Consider the position of a scholar somewhere outside the English-speaking world. He has learned to read English easily, and perhaps does so regularly. He corresponds with colleagues abroad using written English, and occasionally he writes a paper for one of the international scholarly periodicals. His own language is not widely known, so he writes in English. But he never learned to speak English, and is very ill at ease when anyone tries to speak it to him. For him, English, in effect, has no phonology. And yet it functions effectively; he is able to keep up with the literature of his discipline and to contribute to it, all by use of English. The English he uses has three systems: a writing system, a grammar, and a semology. Without some such structure it would fail him.

Written English functioning in isolation from spoken English is an aberrant phenomenon. Most people literate in English speak it also. But that it can occur, however rarely, is interesting and significant. Its occurrence demonstrates that written English has three systems, much as does spoken English. The writing system that fills out the tripos is worthy of close investigation.

The elements of the writing system include letters, numbers, punctuation marks, spaces, and the rules by which they are combined into larger and larger structures. For example, there is the simple and familiar rule that after *q* there must always be a *u*, and the less familiar ones that words do not end in *v*, or that double *k* is adjusted to *ck*.[13] These are comparable, but in detail quite unrelated, to such rules of the phonology as that no word begins with /ŋ/.

---

[12] The term "homeostasis" seems to have been first used in linguistics by Martin Joos. The concept is a very important one, and the term is useful, but the analogy with biological systems must not be carried too far.

[13] Except that when two *k*'s come together in a compound, both remain. Many of these rules can be found in any comprehensive treatment of spelling, but seldom is any distinction made between rules dealing with arrangements of letters (technically, tactic rules), those dealing with the representation of sounds by letters (spelling rules), and those dealing with the representation of letters by sounds (reading rules). A thoroughly satisfactory description of the writing system would require that these three be carefully distinguished.

Written English has its own grammar. It is not exactly like that of spoken English, though in broad outlines and many details the resemblance is very close. Yet there are differences. The most frequently noticed are instances in which written English is ambiguous, but spoken is not. *Parking is restricted to customers only after 9 a.m.* In speech intonational signals would indicate clearly whether this is . . . *(customers only) after 9 a.m.* or . . . *customers (only after 9 a.m.)* There is no way of showing this in written English other than by a drastic reorganization of the sentence: *After 9 a.m. parking is restricted to customers only.* or *Only after 9 a.m. is parking restricted to customers.*

A more important type of grammatical difference is most easily noticed in the frequency of certain constructions. The nonrestrictive relative clause, which many writers use extensively, is very rare in most spoken English, and totally unused by many speakers. This difference reflects the fact that it is not at all a normal construction in colloquial English, the rare uses being only intrusions of literary patterns into speech.

Some details of written grammar are adjusted to the restrictions of the writing system, just as some of those in spoken grammar are adjusted to the requirements of the phonology. A house without a well is *welless*, or *well-less*, but not ×*wellless*. Since the conventions of the phonology and the writing system are frequently quite different, the adjustments do not match at all closely. All of the examples cited of differences between written and spoken grammar are minor, but there are enough of them that the total effect is appreciable divergence.

Written English also has its semology. We know very little about either this or its spoken counterpart, and so cannot say how similar they may be. As a guess, I would expect them to be hardly different, if at all.

What then is one to do in making a complete description of English? Very likely one description will serve jointly for the semology of the two. Just as one grammar can be extended to cover several styles of speaking, so the grammatical statement can be extended to cover both written and spoken English. There will need to be separate notes on some matters, for example, the rules for making noun plurals. Spoken English uses three variants of the plural suffix /-s -z -iz/ where written English uses only two: *-s* and *-es*, and the rules do not easily match up. Structure signals will also require some separate discussion.

But nothing of this kind will do for the remainder. We must have a thorough description of the phonology of English in its own terms. That means we must describe how English is spoken on the basis of the phonemes and their patterns, not of letters. And we must have a description of the writing system of English in its own terms, that is, of the basic units of the writing system, not of the phonemes.

Separate descriptions of the two, however, are not enough. To these must be added a statement of the interrelations between the two. This might take the form of a set of spelling rules stating how phonologic features are represented in writing, or of a set of reading rules stating how written structures are to be pronounced. The need for such a description results from the very important connections that exist between the two. First, the phonology and the writing system are parts of a single language. Each interacts with the grammatical system, and hence is subject to some of the same forces from this direction. No apparatus as highly integrated as a language can be fully comprehended until the relations are understood between each main component and all the rest.

Second, the users of the language constantly relate the two in various ways. They write down "what they hear". This is often a kind of two-part translation much like that used above.[14] The vocabulary items are translated individually. /téybil/ becomes *table;* /ríyd/ becomes *read* or *reed*. (Translation always involves some of these cases where context has to be brought in to select between two or more possible equivalents.) /místər/ becomes *Mr*. But we cannot do the same with the structure signals. We listen to the intonation, stress, and all the associated signals over a long stretch. We decide that /^{2}hwàt + də + ^{4}yúw + sêy$^{1\searrow}$/ is a question. That calls for an initial capital and a question mark: *What do you say?* The intonation put emphasis on the subject; should we mark this in writing? If we decide we should, we italicize one word: "What do *you* say?" In either case the whole system of signals in the one is translated into a whole system of signals in the other.

When we read we reverse the process. Only proofreaders and Victor Borge read — that is, read individually — the punctuation marks.[15] The normal process is a difficult task. Some people do it well, and some do not. Strangely, many Americans who cannot "read expressively" still read silently with great success. They know what the book is about, they understand sentences. They just do not translate well. Many of us are more like the foreign scientist than we think. We often read written English without translating, and sometimes we do not even know how to translate into our mother tongue.

---

[14] Reading written material and transcribing speech are usually thought of more nearly in terms of simply changing the physical form. This simplistic notion is the root of many confusions, both in using English and in teaching it. If the close parallelism between spoken and written English in certain features is remembered, the notion of translation gives a much better understanding of these processes. For one thing, it will focus more attention on the structure signals of the two systems. Between any two language forms, these are always the hardest to translate. They are also the area of greatest difference between the two forms of English. It is, therefore, not surprising that they are the hardest to teach and learn in the written language.

[15] Occasionally, names of punctuation marks are borrowed into speech and used for emphasis. In turn, this colloquial use may be reborrowed into written dialogue: *I told you you can't go and you can't go, period!* This is a little like *the hoi polloi*, or the *Rio Negro River*, or my favorite supermarket product, *chile con carne with meat*. One signal is carried over from another language and then duplicated by an essentially equivalent signal within the second.

Nevertheless, translation is part of the normal process of reading, and not infrequently of writing. We sit at the typewriter pecking mutely, but continually asking ourselves, "How will that sound?" When two language systems are constantly linked by translation, they are inevitably affected — mutually. English phonology is constantly under pressure from the writing system; so-called "spelling pronunciations" are an evidence. And the writing system is constantly under pressure from the phonology; spelling reform and spelling errors are evidences.

We may take a partial analogy from a man walking a dog. Each has his own desires, and his own habits of travel. They are commonly at cross purposes and constantly compromising with each other. But they can never get any farther apart than the length of the leash. English has a fairly long leash.

So a full description of English must include a description of the phonology and of the writing system, each in terms proper to itself, and in addition, a description of the interrelations, even the interactions, between the two.

WHAT DOES GRAMMAR TREAT?

Grammar says some very important things about sentences, but it does not concern itself with everything that can be said. For example, it is no grammatical question whether a sentence is true or not. *The sun is hot. The sun is cold.* These are both grammatical sentences, even if contradictory. Indeed they are structurally equivalent, since they are built on precisely the same grammatical pattern. A good grammar must be able to describe both true and false sentences; both are used, and both are part of normal English speech behavior.

Another sentence may give the impression of trying to say something true and yet be ungrammatical: *The sun are hot.* A grammar should not only indicate that this is ungrammatical, but also point out precisely at what point it deviates from the patterns and suggest a correction.[16] In this case there are at least two alternative ways to make it grammatical: *The suns are hot. The sun is hot.* If the second of these represents what the framer wanted to say, the sentence is presumably true. The first is also grammatical, but it is a little difficult to determine whether it is true or not. The uncertainty arises because we are not quite sure what is being talked about. It is impossible to judge a sentence as true or false except in some relevant context. We do not know what circumstances might bring forth this sentence, and so cannot judge it. Yet a sentence is grammatical or

---

[16] A grammar may suggest a correction, but only one which will make the sentence grammatical. Good writing or good speech involves much more than grammaticality. A grammar, therefore, is not competent to insure language appropriate to some situation of use. See the discussion of standards on page 472.

not without any reference to the situation of speaking. All that is needed to judge it is within it, in its structure, and in the language under whose rules it is framed.

Other sentences pose the same problem in a much more serious way. *The suns are delicious.* It is a little harder to imagine any situation where this is relevant, but there may well be one or more in which it is entirely appropriate.[17] But the grammarian need not worry. If the situation should arise where this sentence were called for, it could be said. And it would be — indeed, it is — grammatical.

We can go on, step by step, producing less and less probable sentences. These require more and more imagination to produce a context making them useful. But if they follow the structural patterns of English, they are grammatical, and a grammar must describe them.

An English grammar is under no obligation to consider any of these other dimensions of usefulness. On the contrary, it must not. If our grammars described only sentences which were known to be useful or true, our grammars would have to be revised every year. New situations arise continually and call for kinds of statements that before were totally inconceivable. Sentences that once occurred only in science fiction are now real, serious, or even prosaic.

Nor is grammar concerned with good language manners. The following statement must be accepted as good grammar: *Teacher is an old crab.* But it is certainly not good manners in most situations.

Grammar is concerned with only one feature of sentences — their conformity to the system of the language. As a grammarian, one can only ask whether or not they are properly constructed in terms of that system. Whether sentences are truthful, appropriate, polite, meaningful, or anything else is no concern to the grammarian as grammarian.

Some of these things, however, are the concern of English teachers. The scope of English is far wider than grammar. But they must recognize that when they give attention to these other dimensions they are not working with grammar. The traditional school distinction between gram-

---

[17] For example, a plate of cookies of three kinds, cut as stars, crescents, and circles. Such a situation is unlikely, perhaps, but it should be remembered that incredibly unlikely events are really commonplace, and language must be able to cope with them.

The paradox that unlikely events are commonplace arises from a misunderstanding of terms. For example, there are well over six million license plates consisting of two letters followed by up to four digits, the common pattern in my state. Of all these possibilities, it might be considered most improbable that I should get BD 470. But every number is equally improbable (that is, unforeseeable), so that it is inevitable that every car will bear a highly unlikely number. Many other happenings are the same: a highly improbable event is almost a certainty. Language must be able to deal with these as they occur. This means simply that language must be able to accommodate the unforeseeable. That is, there must be the minimum advance commitment as to what it can or cannot describe. As a matter of fact, we are able to describe anything which happens, even if previously totally unimaginable.

mar and usage is an attempt at discrimination. It is inadequate because there are more factors than can be comfortably accommodated under just two heads. The distinction, also, is often fuzzy because the definitions of the two have been inexact and inappropriate. English grammar has commonly been diluted in the schools by being made to cover too wide and too incongruous a collection of sentence pathologies. The student loses because inadequate diagnosis cannot be a basis for adequate treatment. Many language difficulties are misidentified, and therefore wrongly prescribed for.

But grammar suffers even more. Grammar is a system, or it is nothing but meaningless fragments. The system will never be seen clearly until foreign intrusions are removed. Grammar can only make sense when we are rigorous about the field of discourse. Grammar must deal with structure and system, and it must present them structurally and systematically.

Chapter 6

Parts of Speech

School and traditional grammars recognize much the same system of parts of speech for English. These are typically eight: noun, pronoun, adjective, verb, adverb, preposition, conjunction, and interjection. A few grammarians have divided one of these or merged two. Jespersen has grouped the last four together as subclasses of particles. But even the most radical has not departed far from the usual system.

Latin is usually described in terms of the same eight parts of speech. Indeed, both the classification and the terminology currently used in English are developments through universal grammar from Latin grammar and, hence, ultimately from the work of the Greek grammarians. This is one of the places where ancient grammatical tradition has been most firmly entrenched in the treatment of modern English.

In their field work with American Indian languages, anthropological linguists have met very different language systems. These have often necessitated descriptive frameworks radically different from those of European languages. Frequently the parts of speech have been found to be fewer in number and aligned in quite unfamiliar ways. Anthropological linguists became predisposed to favor, wherever possible, fewer categories of much broader definition and to relegate differences not covered in this way to subclass status.

Many American Indian languages had earlier been described by untrained amateurs. They often used precisely the traditional eight parts of speech, however difficult it may have been to identify some of them. Descriptions in such terms were often patently unsuitable. These grammars had the effect of prejudicing anthropological linguists even more strongly against the eight-part system. The latter came to be, for them, a prime symbol of uncritical cramming of a language into an alien mold. They were naturally suspicious when they saw this system used for English.

When linguists examined the definitions given for the eight parts of speech, their suspicions were strengthened. They had become highly distrustful of meaning-based language description. The school grammars seemed to define a noun as "a name of a person, place, or thing". Such a definition was regarded as unworkable and misleading and became one of the chief targets of criticism.

Linguists and all grammarians, however, agree on a very fundamental point: There must be some classification of words, or of some other basic units, into parts of speech or some functionally equivalent system of classes. (Some linguists have so disliked the term "part of speech" because of its associations with traditional systems, that they have rejected it in favor of "form class" or "morpheme class" or the like.) Every linguist who has worked with English has, therefore, had to face the problem of delimiting the parts of speech and, in most cases, of defining or characterizing them.

It is with the different classifications and different designations for the classes that the most immediately obvious departures from traditional and school grammars can be seen in the work of the linguists and the structural grammarians. Minor differences can easily be magnified and major points overlooked.

THE BASIS OF CLASSIFICATION

There are several bases on which definitions can be made. The traditional definition of the adverb is in terms of syntactic use: "An adverb is a word that modifies a verb, adjective, or another adverb." That of the noun is in terms of meaning: "A noun is a name of a person, place, or thing." Some recently proposed definitions have been in terms of inflection: "A noun is a word which forms a plural by adding -s or the equivalent." Many of the classes could be defined in any of these three ways.

Some grammars have seemed to use different techniques for defining different parts of speech.[1] Inconsistency might result in overlapping cate-

---

[1] Generally the noun and verb have been "defined" in terms of "meaning", the remaining parts of speech in terms of syntactic use. Whether this inconsistency is real or only apparent depends on an author's understanding of these statements.

Some authors did not intend the descriptions of the noun and verb as definitions. These two were assumed in the definitions of the remaining parts of speech, but were not themselves defined. Instead, there is given a rough description, only enough to give a reader an approximate identification. There is a certain validity in this treatment. To give syntactic definitions of all the parts of speech is inevitably circular in a way that vitiates all the definitions.

Most school grammar textbook writers, however, did not understand this distinction, and so considered the descriptions of noun and verb as definitions on a par with the others, thus rendering all the definitions as inadequate as the two on which the remainder are based.

gories or in uncovered gaps. Indeed, some grammars quite clearly suffer from either or both of these difficulties.

Yet no one type of definition seems fully satisfactory by itself. As a result, many grammarians have tried to combine several techniques into elaborate definitions, carefully drafted to avoid at least the most serious gaps and overlappings. This is not, however, an easy matter. The several criteria are often in conflict. The difficulties in working them together harmoniously can best be seen from some simple examples:

Table presumably names a thing, it is inflected for plural by adding -*s*, and it occurs in typically noun positions in sentences. By any definition, *table* is a noun. *Handshake* meets the inflectional and syntactic definitions, but seems to state an action more than name a thing. (Unless, of course, a thing is defined simply as anything named by a noun — an interesting circularity!) *Perseverance* may name a thing — the application of the definition is quite unsure; it does occur in typical noun positions in sentences; but it does not seem to have a plural. *Cattle* has the opposite trouble; it does not seem to have a singular and it shows no evidence that it is inflected for plural — it somehow just IS plural, witness: *The cattle are lowing.* *Handshake, perseverance,* and *cattle* are examples of words that are nouns by some definitions, but not by all. There are many more. Because of these, the choice of basis of definition may be crucial.

Certainly the least promising type of definition is that based on meaning. In the first place, it is hard to draw the lines clearly and decisively. We do not at present have sufficiently precise techniques for delimiting and classifying the meanings of words. No definition based on meaning will be clear enough in its application to satisfy any but the least critical user. As a matter of fact, the traditional meaning-based definitions of school grammar do not seem to be actually applied, even by the authors of the books, because they would not serve the needs. Parts of speech are identified in some other way, perhaps not consciously recognized by the identifier, and then the definition is used merely to legitimize the decision.

But that is not the most crucial objection to meaning-based definitions. There are some cases where it is possible to consider sets of words as having similar meanings. Therefore, some fairly well-marked meaning-based word classes can be set up. However, these often would not be the sort that we need for a grammar. For example, the meanings of *no* and *not* are nearly identical. In any meaning-based scheme, these two words would, most likely, have to go together. But they are not interchangeable in sentences. They have nothing in common grammatically. If we set up a part of speech containing these two, we cannot use that part of speech in the grammar. There would be very little grammatical that we could say about it.

A meaning-based class such as that containing *no* and *not* might, however, have some real and important utility in some other problem.

It may turn out to be a very significant semantic class. Probably any structural approach to English semology will have to start by setting up a system of classes of words appropriate to the task at hand. Almost certainly any such set of classes will be different from those needed in grammar. We are here considering parts of speech as classes to be used in a grammatical statement. Meaning-based classes no matter how well established, will not serve this need.

To be useful in grammar, the parts of speech must be based on structural (that is, grammatical) features of the words classified. There are, however, two quite different possibilities: 1) The criteria might be found within the word — in types of inflection, derivational suffixes, or other features. For example, a noun might be defined as a word that takes a plural in -s or the equivalent, or is formed by the suffixes -ance, -ness, or -ity. By such a definition, handshake is a noun because there is a plural handshakes, and perseverance is a noun because it is formed by the suffix -ance. No such definition will help with cattle, which we somehow would like to see included. 2) The criteria might be found outside the word — in its use in sentences. Thus a noun might be defined as any word that can occur in a frame such as: The ____ is/are good. Handshake and cattle fit this with no question. But does perseverance? — The perseverance is good. This sentence seems a little odd. This might be for any number of reasons: because we cannot think of an occasion to use such a sentence and so are badly handicapped in judging whether it would be acceptable; or because we have selected a bad frame to use as a test. It will require a very sophisticated use of carefully selected frames to avoid many difficulties of this sort.

Probably some much more elaborate definition will make it clear that perseverance is indeed a noun, just like table, handshake, and cattle. Certainly a good definition, be it morphologic or syntactic, will be a very difficult thing to design, and perhaps also quite complex to operate.

Notice that the difficulties with the definitions come at different places. Cattle poses a problem for one; perseverance does not. Perseverance was a crux for the other; but this had no difficulty with cattle. Perhaps a joint definition could exploit the potentialities of both. Any word which meets either criterion or both would be a noun. This has its difficulties also. In general, however, this has been the procedure of good scholarly traditional grammar, insofar as it has examined the question at all. (Traditional grammarians have tended to concentrate their attention elsewhere and accept the parts of speech rather uncritically.) Even an involved joint definition will probably leave a small list of difficult cases that must be assigned more or less arbitrarily.

A different technique has been employed by Trager and Smith[2] and

[2] George L. Trager and Henry Lee Smith, Jr., An Outline of English Structure, 1951. In this publication the dual classification is very carefully followed.

linguists in their tradition. They set up two systems of classes. One is based on inflectional criteria. In it are distinguished nouns, personal pronouns, adjectives, and verbs. These are defined as words showing the following types of inflection:

> *man   man's   men   men's*
> *I   me   my   mine*
> *nice   nicer   nicest*
> *go   goes   went   gone   going*

The remaining words, which show no inflection at all, are classed together as particles.

Trager and Smith's second system is classified by syntactic criteria. In it are found nominals, pronominals, adjectivals, verbals, adverbials, prepositionals, and so on. The two sets of terms are carefully distinguished by using the suffix *-al* on all syntactic terms. In general, nouns are also nominals, verbs are also verbals, and so forth. The two systems do not match exactly, however; if they did there would be no need to treat them as separate systems.

Such a distinction between two systems of classification has certain merits. When adhered to carefully, it makes clear exactly what is being talked about. It helps to avoid the dangers of jumping to syntactic conclusions on inflectional evidence, and vice versa. It gives a simple system for statements about syntax.

Unfortunately, some of the suggested labels present terminological difficulties. For example, "verbal" has long been established in another meaning. "Prepositional" seems to many unnecessary, since "preposition" is available and not needed in the morphology-based system. "Adjective" is a very much smaller class than that usually known by this name. Partly for such reasons, most grammarians have rejected Trager and Smith's scheme, often with the protest that it is too elaborate and awkward. Others see no need for the complexity of two partly parallel classifications. Such criticism is not wholly justified — after all the facts of English are complex, and no simple system of parts of speech can be expected to be adequate.

There is another criticism, possibly much more cogent. This divorcing of the two may be, in part, an abdication of responsibility. Syntax and inflection are different, of course, but they are part of the same grammar. They should be worked into the most completely integrated statement possible. Trager and Smith's system, perhaps, makes too much of the difference between morphology and syntax, and not enough of differences between various levels of syntax.

Fries in *The Structure of English*[3] does not really define his form

---

[3] Charles C. Fries, *The Structure of English*, 1952. See his Chapters 5, 6, and particularly 7.

classes. For each he does give a list of "characteristics" — eight of them for Class 1 (roughly equivalent to nouns plus some pronouns), and several of these are themselves complex. These are found partly in word form and partly in syntactic uses. Most of those based on word form are stated in terms of contrasts with other items. For example, Class 1 is characterized by a number of "contrasts of form" with Class 2, among them: *arrival* and *arrive*, *departure* and *depart*, *delivery* and *deliver*, *acceptance* and *accept*. The characterizations as a whole are involved, overlapping, and incomplete. They cannot be considered as definitions, but they are no less useful for that fact.

It may, indeed, be presumptuous to assume that definitions can be written at all. Many linguists today are very dubious about the feasibility of defining such elementary notions as parts of speech. But word classes certainly can be characterized. That is, features can be listed by which, taken singly or in combination, most words can be assigned to an appropriate part of speech. Occasional refractory cases may defy any such easy classification, but the difficult cases are generally recognizable as such by the fact that they fit the characterizations in ambiguous or conflicting ways.

Some people might protest that such characterizations are merely definitions that do not define, differing from proper definitions only in that they are unsuccessful. There is some justice in the charge, but no great cogency. Characterizations are both useful and feasible. Definitions are probably not possible, at least for unlimited classes like Fries' four major form classes.

With small classes, a special kind of definition is possible. This consists of merely listing the members. The personal pronouns, for example, can be exhaustively listed. There are eight that all Americans use: *I, you, he, she, it, we, they, who*, plus two others that are somewhat less general: *thou*, and one occurring only in speech and represented in dialect writing as *y'all*, or something like that. (The latter is normally spelled *you* by its users.) For some classes, for example prepositions, it is a little harder to claim that any list is actually exhaustive. But there is no doubt that a list can easily be compiled that includes most prepositions, even one approaching very closely to being exhaustive.

Such a list is a kind of definition when complete; when incomplete it is a kind of characterization. It says in effect: Any additional items must be basically similar to the elements already in the list. The features by which that similarity is to be judged are not specifically identified, but they are clearly implicit. New items can be added if they seem to "fit in" or to "belong". The characterization is informal, but effective. Native speakers of English can easily judge, in most cases, since they sense correctly what is common to any reasonably homogeneous list, whether they can specify what they feel or not.

Whatever may be the formal technique of definition or characterization in use in the classroom, the actual working principle has always been identification by matching lists. A child presented with a word and asked whether it is a noun does not often answer the question by applying the definition he has learned. Rather he compares it with words that he knows to be nouns and judges whether there is any detectable similarity. Previous classroom presentations have in effect provided him with a standard list of nouns for comparison.

The technique of characterizing parts of speech by listing typical examples should receive more formal recognition. The classification of words by matching lists on a basis of general resemblance should be explicitly taught. Few books do this. But many teachers do present the parts of speech this way, unfortunately often with a bit of remorse or apology. They feel that it is really not the correct procedure, but a shortcut or compromise. Actually, it may be the only feasible technique — the one used, often unconsciously, by all who identify parts of speech successfully.

Obviously, this procedure works best with parts of speech of maximum homogeneity. The "adverb" of school grammar covers a remarkably diverse group of words. If students have special difficulty in learning to recognize "adverbs", it may not be due to any specific deficiency in the definition — after all, none of the other definitions is much better — but to the fact that the group is so heterogeneous that they cannot get any feel for it. It would be reasonable to expect a far better result with more homogeneous parts of speech, even if it means a considerable number of additional classes to learn.

INTERSECTION OF CLASSES

It is commonly assumed[4] that each word in the English vocabulary belongs inherently to some specifiable part of speech. Only a little inquiry will show that the situation is far from that simple. Three examples will bring out the problem:

Run may be found showing typical verb characteristics, as in: *The boy ran away.* Here it occurs in a verbal inflected form, the so-called past tense, and as the head word in the predicate, the most typical verb function. *Run* can also be found showing evident noun behavior, as in: *The boy made three runs.* Here it occurs in a plural form, as a direct object of a verb, and with a modifier commonly used with nouns. An excellent case can be made out for considering *run* as either verb or noun.

---

[4] This assumption is in strange contradiction to the principles of school grammar, where words are generally assigned to parts of speech strictly on the basis of their position in the sentence. Thus, all words modifying nouns are by definition adjectives, however they may be assignable in other instances. This conflict is seldom faced squarely — and never resolved — in school grammar textbooks. It is, however, sensed by the students and is the root of much of their difficulties with parts of speech.

Bear shows both verb and noun behavior in much the same way: *The Greeks bore gifts. He saw three bears.*

The is common as a noun modifier: *The dog bit the man.* It is called adjective, article, or determiner in various systems of English grammar. *The* also occurs immediately before comparative adjectives, often not followed by nouns, and often paired with a second similar occurrence: *The more, the merrier.* In this position it is commonly labeled as "adverb" Most grammarians recognize that these two uses of *the* are sharply distinct.

These three examples are parallel in many ways. In each case the part of speech can only be recognized when the word occurs in a context. But there are also sharp differences that any speaker of the language senses. Some will insist that the three are not at all comparable. In any case, it will not do to ask, "What part of speech is *run? Bear? The?*" Or at least, we have no right to expect a simple answer, nor even the same kind of answer in all three instances.

The common solution of the lexicographer is to consider that each of these three spellings (or pronunciations) represents two or more different words, and each of these words falls into a clearly identifiable class. We find in *Webster's Third New International: run*$_1$, a verb; *run*$_2$, a noun; *run*$_3$, an adjective; *bear*$_1$, a noun; *bear*$_4$, a verb; *the*$_1$, the definite article, and *the*$_2$, an adverb. Grammatical information, pronunciation, etymology, definitions, and examples of usage are given separately for each. This is certainly convenient for the dictionary user. There are enough differences in meaning and usage that separate definitions would be required in most instances anyway. Indeed, the dictionary also lists *bear*$_2$, another verb, and *bear*$_3$, another noun. The dictionary user can easily identify from the context which part of speech he is concerned with, so separation by part of speech is a convenient way to organize the numerous definitions for him. The entries with similar spellings are immediately adjacent, so that it is easy to refer from one to the other if desirable.

If there are two or more words with the same spelling, there remain two distinct possibilities. Either the two are related, or they are simply alike by accident. The latter is probably the case with *bear*, meaning respectively 'an animal' and 'to carry'. It is not simply that there is no apparent connection in meaning. Someone might make out a case for some relationship: perhaps that bears are animals that carry things, or something of this kind. This is farfetched, and, more significant, it is isolated. We do not know of many other pairs of noun and verb that are related in anything like this same way. With *run* it is quite otherwise. Indeed, it would not be far wrong to say that *run*$_1$ and *run*$_2$ have the same meaning; only the grammar is different. *He ran. He made a run.* These sentences are very nearly synonymous, but differently structured. The meaning of *run* can be put into the sentence in two places, one requiring a verb and the other a noun. We would like to consider the two words as related to assist us in describing such sentences and the relationship between them.

A grammar does not describe isolated phenomena. That run_1 and run_2 seem similar is not grammatically pertinent unless such similarity is a recurrent pattern in the language. Examination of a few pages of a large dictionary will reveal a multitude of identically spelled verbs and nouns. Comparable cases can be found following *run*, at *rupture, rush, rusk, russet, rust, rustle*. Some, but not all, of these parallel *run* in use:

> He rushed for it.
> He ran for it.

> He made a rush for it.
> He made a run for it.

Other pairs parallel *run* less closely:

> He ruptured it.

> He made a rupture in it.

Both of these patterns, and many others, are recurrent, in that many pairs of verbs and nouns are related in exactly parallel ways. Any such pattern can be formulated as a rule of grammar, and a very large number of verbs are related by some such rule to an identically spelled noun. But in addition, there are many other pairs of verbs and nouns which are not related by a recurrent pattern. $Bear_1$ and $bear_4$ seem to be an instance of the latter kind. Whatever relationship may exist between these two is not grammatical.

The relationship between run_1 and run_2 must be looked at in two ways. First, it must be compared with other pairs of verbs and nouns: *arrive* and *arrival, deliver* and *delivery, decide* and *decision, idolize* and *idol, beautify* and *beauty, enrage* and *rage, shelve* and *shelf, house* and *house, permit* and *permit, man* and *man, try* and *try, toy* and *toy*. These are organized here into four groups: 1) The noun seems to have a suffix. It can be thought of as formed from the verb by the addition of the suffix. 2) The verb seems to have a suffix or prefix. It can be described as formed from the noun by the addition of the suffix or prefix. 3) The two differ in final consonant or in stress. Which is best considered as derived from the other is less clear. 4) The two are alike in form.

This mass of data (there are thousands of cases of various kinds) must be described in a complete grammar of English. It is part of the morphology, more specifically of the derivation patterns.

Second, the related uses of verb and noun to produce more or less synonymous sentences must be described: *He delivered. He made a delivery. He decided. He made a decision.* Such pairs of sentences are grammatically related in a formally statable way. They may be said to be agnate. This relationship deserves description because it is a grammatical fact of the language and because it is of great practical significance in offering an alternative wording for the same ideas. It thus offers an important resource for stylistic manipulation. Chapter 9 will examine this relationship and Chapter 18 will discuss something of its practical significance.

The situation with *the* is different from either *run* or *bear*. In the first place, there seems to be little profit in asking whether *the*₁ and *the*₂ mean the same thing. Both are function words, items which have little meaning in the ordinary sense of the term. The closest thing to meaning in such words is grammatical function. In this, of course, they differ profoundly.

Nor will it be profitable to look for parallels of the sort we found with *run*. *The*₁, the definite article, is the only member of the class. Even if we take a larger comprehending class, that of articles in general, there are few fellow-members. *The*₂ is labeled by the dictionary as an "adverb", but it shares few typical "adverb" uses. If the classification is drawn sufficiently tightly to be useful, *the*₂ is also unique or very nearly so. It is a hopeless quest to seek another pair related to each other as are *the*₁ and *the*₂. It is meaningless to consider them as related in anything but form.[5]

It is quite common for function words to raise this question. Many of them show very diverse uses. It is customary to refer to this phenomenon as "class cleavage". That is to say, *the* exhibits class cleavage by occurring in two classes, article and some special group of "adverb". The relationship of these words cannot be considered as a grammatical fact, but the possibility of confusion must be taken account of in a grammar. These are the words that most particularly signal structure. Class cleavage may produce a special kind of ambiguity in the signaling. A full grammar must, accordingly, list the instances of function words with class cleavage. It should call attention to the other signals that may or may not resolve the ambiguity. For example, *the* can be ambiguous only if immediately followed by a comparative. A full statement of the patterns will remove most possibilities of confusion.

One possible answer to the problems presented by *run, bear, the,* and many other words, then, is to make three kinds of statements: *Bear,* noun and verb, are a pair of accidental homonyms, of no grammatical significance, and adequately handled in the grammar by a general note that homonyms do exist. *Run,* the noun, is derived from *run,* the verb by a morphological process that must be described. The alternation between the two plays a part in certain sentence relationships and must be described. *The*₁ and *the*₂ are two separate words, each of which must be described separately and in some detail, as function word members of small or one-member classes. The coincidence in form between the two must be noted, and the means of discriminating them stated.

There is a second totally different way of accounting for overlapping

---

[5] They are also, of course, related in history. However, in this chapter we are avoiding historical considerations as far as possible. The history of the two forms is interesting, pertinent for some purposes, but irrelevant for classification of *the*₁ and *the*₂ into parts of speech.

patterns of word use. This involves setting up more classes of words. *Criticize* fits all the verb characterizations and no others. It may be called a verb. *Acquaintance* has only noun uses, and can be called a noun. *Run* would be neither verb nor noun, but a member of a separate class of words combining verb, noun, and adjective uses. *Out* would go into a class that combines adjective, preposition, noun, and adverb uses: *The batter was out. He went out the door. The outs were jealous. He struck out.* This solution has been proposed by some linguists, but never actually applied in a full treatment of English. It would soon be found unworkable. There would be too many such combination classes. Moreover, every grammatical statement would be excessively complicated by the new classes. Plural formation would have to be described for nouns, words of the class of *run*, words of the class of *out*, and many others. Though occasionally proposed in the literature, this solution can be eliminated as a possibility.

A third possible answer would be to follow to the full the common feeling that words do inherently belong to parts of speech. Thus *run* might be a verb, always and unchangeably, but occasionally used in noun positions. This does not seem to be feasible for a thorough and systematic description of English. But traces of it do appear in school grammar.

This idea is at the root of some difficulties with English usage. Purists commonly become very much upset over the traffic sign that reads "GO SLOW". *Slow*, they say, is an adjective; it is common but slovenly usage to employ adjectives as adverbs; certainly this should never be done when a real adverb is available. Highway engineers are not maintaining the purity of the language. (I hope they are maintaining the safety of the streets. That seems to be more properly their job!)

As a matter of fact the purists are wrong, historically. (The historical argument becomes pertinent only as an answer to the charge of relaxing old and time honored standards.) The Old English adjective and adverb could be distinguished clearly. The course of language history changed both into modern *slow*. Historically, *slow* in *go slow* is an adverb, and need not be supplanted by a much younger, upstart, fellow-adverb *slowly*. Descriptively, *slow* is in well-established use as an adverb, and this use is supported by excellent parallels: *He worked hard all day.* Compare: *He worked hardly all day.*

The proposal that pairs of words like *run*, the noun, and *run*, the verb, are related also seems to raise a historical question, but this is a misinterpretation. To say that *run₂* is derived from *run₁* is not intended as a historical statement. Actually, the two go back to Old English in separate histories, as do some but not all of the parallel pairs. It is not historically correct, therefore, to consider either to be derived from the other within the last millennium. But a descriptive grammar does not claim to be a presentation of history. It is a device to summarize current facts conveniently. It is useful to consider *run₁* and *run₂* as intimately related in present-day English. In fact, they are connected in the mind of every speaker who uses them both. He cannot avoid being influenced by one when he uses the other. They are connected by similarities of meaning and patterns of use. The grammarian must record these connections, and the easiest way in many cases is in terms of derivation, but he is not talking about history, only about the system of current English.

THE EIGHT "PARTS OF SPEECH"

Any assortment of English grammars will show perplexing diversity. This will most often be immediately apparent in the list of parts of speech. Jespersen[6] gives only six; Fries[7] has nineteen. Some of the differences are only superficial, often mere matters of terminology. Some are much deeper, reflecting divergent approaches or totally different bases of classification. School grammar typically defines eight parts of speech, each with a reasonably standard and familiar label. These can form a convenient framework within which to show some of the major points of disagreement.

Four classes are recognized by very nearly every grammarian, and generally under much the same names: noun or substantive, verb, adjective, and adverb. These are approximately Fries' "major form classes" 1, 2, 3, and 4. There are, however, some significant differences in the ways these are delimited.

Fries and his followers have included some of the pronouns within the noun class.[8] Of course, there is little or no morphological justification for this. Pronouns do not have plural forms comparable to those of nouns. *We* is plural of *I* only in a very special sense. *They* can be called a plural, but, if so, it is shared by three contrasting singulars, *he*, *she*, and *it*, a very un-nounlike behavior. *You* is unmatched; the one form is commonly labeled plural, but there is little more than a historical basis for this. Excepting *it* and *you*, the personal pronouns have separate subjective and objective (or nominative and accusative) case forms; no nouns have.

The syntactic justification is hardly any stronger. Both nouns and pronouns occur as subjects of verbs: *John came. He came.* But so do many other types of elements: *To err is human. Over the fence is out.* Nouns com-

---

[6] Otto Jespersen, *Essentials of English Grammar*, 1933, p. 66ff. He lists: substantives, adjectives, verbs, pronouns, particles, and numerals. It is not entirely clear, however, whether he intends numerals as a separate class or as a subclass of pronouns.

[7] Fries, *The Structure of English*. Fries' classes are designated by arbitrary symbols, so need not be listed here. They are discussed below.

[8] Fries, *The Structure of English*, p. 76–79. On page 119, Fries discusses the inclusion of pronouns with nouns in his Class 1, but does not really establish any strong basis for it. One reason for this is the mixed nature of the list of "substitutes" which he gives. It includes some words, for example *others*, which do clearly shown noun characteristics, as well as true pronouns. "Substitution" is not an adequate basis for classing words together within a part-of-speech scheme. See Chapter 8, "Types of Meaning and Meaninglessness".

monly have modifiers, and these are of many types. Pronouns very rarely do, and the possibilities are very restricted. *The good food* is not paralleled by *the good it*, though *only food* is paralleled by *only it*. Pronouns very seldom enter derivational constructions; nouns often do.

Pronouns are commonly said to substitute for nouns. This is not strictly correct.[9] *My new house is white.* Not: *×My new it is white.* But: *It is white.* *It* substitutes, not for the noun *house*, but for the noun phrase *my new house*. Only when a noun phrase consists of one single noun do we have the appearance of a pronoun substituting for a noun: *James is a lawyer. He is a lawyer.*

On the whole, it does not seem really profitable to merge the noun and personal pronoun classes in this way. There are many points of difference between them and very few similarities. A grammar that recognizes structural levels — that is, one which carefully distinguishes between words and phrases — would find no real usefulness in a class joining these two. The grouping of nouns and pronouns together must be considered one of the weak points of Fries' system, but one that is easily corrected.

The major question with the verbs is the status of the various auxiliaries. Traditional grammars generally consider these as a special group of verbs. Structural grammar and the treatments of most linguists separate them. No grammar of consequence fails to give some recognition to the special characteristics of the group. If they are included among the verbs, they are always recognized in the subclassification.

In the matter of details, however, there is very considerable variation. Hardly any two grammars agree on the total list of auxiliaries, or upon their detailed classification. The reasons are clear enough. These elements can only be classified in connection with a precise and detailed treatment of the structure of the verb phrase. This has been one of the difficult points in English grammar, but recent work seems to be clearing it up. This question will not be further discussed here, but deferred to Chapter 13.

The adjective is more of a problem. In general, school grammars have tended to treat as adjectives all words that modify nouns. There are, however, many types of noun modifiers in English. Two treatments are possible. These numerous types can be considered as separate parts of speech, or they can be recognized as subclasses within the adjective class.

Some school grammars separate the article, sometimes defined as only *the* and *a/an* and sometimes including a few others. Other school grammars

---

[9] The statement that pronouns substitute for nouns is more nearly correct within a school-grammar frame of reference than elsewhere. In school grammar, headed phrases are closely identified with their heads. Thus in the example given, *it* might be said to substitute for *house*, and in so doing to exclude modifiers. The statement becomes wholly wrong when it is carried over into another kind of grammar without the necessary change. This has commonly been done in efforts to introduce the "new grammar" into the schools.

recognize the article as a special type of adjective. Further subclassification on a grammatical basis is rarely given and never important in the treatment of articles. School grammar, it should be remembered, is little concerned with discrimination between types of modifiers. As a result little can be said about internal structure of noun phrases.

Fries[10] in effect excluded some words from the adjective class of school grammar and divided the remainder into two groups: class 3, which some of his followers have labeled "adjective", and group A, which he called "determiners". There are sharp and significant differences. Determiners do not occur with words of the class of *extremely: the extremely good ice cream*, but not ×*the extremely five houses*, or ×*extremely the men*. Moreover, almost all the determiners are alike in showing some restrictions as to the type of nouns with which they can occur: *a man*, not ×*a men; all men*, not ×*all man; few men*, not ×*few water; much water*, not ×*much men*.[11] Most determiners cannot occur in other adjective positions: *Water is wet*. But not ×*Water is the*.

However, Fries' list of determiners is very far from homogeneous. The group must either be divided or subclassified, if any detailed study of the patterns of their use is to be made. Traditional grammars, structural grammars, and most linguistic grammars are all alike in stopping short of an adequate classification. What is given in most is not even adequate for the rather gross abbreviated treatment that can be given in a brief grammar curriculum.

The division or subclassification of Fries' determiner class must provide a means to describe various combinations of these words that are in use. For example, in the following phrases all but the nouns are determiners according to Fries: *all the men, the several men, all the several men, all his friends, his several friends, all his many friends*. In none of them can the order of words be altered, and a full grammar must be able to describe the facts. To do so, some further division or subclassification is required. As a first approximation, the following groups can be distinguished, mostly on the basis of occurrence in sequences of determiners: 1) determiners that can occur in sequences, but only as the first member — *all, both;* 2) determiners that can occur as the first or second of two or as the second of three — *the, his, that;* 3) determiners that can occur only as the last in sequences of two or three — *several, many;* 4) determiners that do not ordinarily occur with other determiners except occasionally with numerals — *every, each, any;* 5) the numerals — *two, twenty;* and 6) the "indefi-

---

[10] Fries, *The Structure of English*, pp. 82–83, 88–89, 126–132.

[11] There have been shifts in these patterns within the last three centuries, so that some of the collocations occurring in older literature are no longer used. *Much men*, for example, will be accepted by some, but only as archaic. *Much people* in the King James Version generally becomes *many men* in modern translations, for example in Num. 20:20.

nite article" which most often occurs as the only determiner in a phrase, but may occur in certain very special combinations: *many a*. A fuller treatment can be given only in connection with a detailed description of noun-phrase structures.

One other type of modifier requires some attention. Most school grammars consider the word *car* in *the car salesman* as an adjective, perhaps noting that it is related to the noun *car*. A few consider it as a noun used as an adjective; in such a statement "adjective" means precisely the same as "modifier of a noun" and is not a label for a part of speech at all, but for a syntactic position. In any case *car* is very different from *young* in the *young salesman*. School grammars seldom note the difference and have no effective way to account for it when they do. Most scholarly traditional grammars and most treatments by linguists consider *car* as a noun, even when modifying another noun.

There are ample reasons to do this. Any noun whatever can be used in this way. All of them have very different behavior from true adjectives. Nouns do not allow the use of *extremely: the extremely young salesman*, but not ×*the extremely car salesman*. They are quite fixed as to position, coming only directly before the head noun: *Motor bus* is entirely different from *bus motor*. But *the young and old inhabitants* is only stylistically different from *the inhabitants, young and old*.[12] Noun phrases with adjectives are agnate to sentences using the same adjectives as subjective complements. It is possible to transform one into the other: *the young salesman* ⇒ *The salesman is young*. But *the car salesman* does not correspond with any sentence: ×*The salesman is car*.

All of this suggests that modifiers like *car* have very little in common with those like *young*. The only possible basis for classifying them together is a very rigid insistence that all modifiers of nouns are by definition adjectives.

The "adverb" is certainly the least satisfactory of the larger traditional parts of speech in English. Many attempts have been made to redefine it, almost always through separating various smaller groups. There is little agreement, however, probably because the use of many of the words involved is not yet adequately understood. The problem warrants a fuller discussion in the next section.

Finally there are a variable number of smaller parts of speech. Some of these are fairly well delimited in traditional grammars, and give little trouble. Prepositions, for example, present no particular difficulty except for occasional confusion with similar "adverb" forms. Others, like the pronouns, are often divided, distributed over other classes, or reorganized in various ways.

---

[12] There are a few instances in which noun modifiers of nouns do invert in much the same way as adjectives: *all radio and television programs* or *all programs, radio and television*. These seem best treated as being in transition from nouns to adjectives.

There are two general extremes. Jespersen groups together as particles all except nouns, verbs, adjectives, adverbs, and pronouns. In general these are all alike in having no inflection, and being usually single morphemes. He then gives some subdivision of the particle group.

Other grammarians have set up very large numbers of small groups. Fries, for example, lists fifteen in all. Even so, some of these clearly need further division, and many need subclassification.

These smaller groups of words can all be labeled as "function words". On the whole, the classification of the function words will depend very heavily on the type of syntactic description that is used. We cannot, therefore, expect very close correlation between the classifications in different grammars until some of the basic questions in English syntax have been agreed upon.

THE "ADVERB"

The "adverb" is an excellent example of a traditional category that does not fit well in English. Ironically, it is one that is always defined functionally in the school grammars: "An adverb is a word that modifies a verb, an adjective, or another adverb." This is the type of definition that many linguists have insisted is proper, and which they would like to give to every part of speech.

The difficulty from the linguist's point of view, then, is not in the form of the definition, but in the fact that there is no homogeneous group of words which fits the definition. The traditional "adverbs" are a miscellaneous lot, having very little if anything in common. Some fit part of the definition, but not other parts. Some fit the whole definition but far exceed its limits. The linguist almost invariably divides this assemblage into several groups which are not related to one another.

It is instructive to compare Fries' classification[13] at this point. His Class 4 consists of words that in the older grammars would be called "adverbs". They can be characterized as usually modifying verbs, predicates, or sentences, but not true adjectives. Seven of his fifteen groups of function words contain items labeled "adverb" in at least some traditional or school grammars. (Some receive no discussion at all in many grammars.) Names are supplied from other sources:

Group C. containing only *not*, the Negator
Group D. containing words like *very*, Intensifiers
Group H. containing only *there*, an Expletive
Group I. containing words like *when, where, why*, Interrogators
Group J. containing words like *nevertheless, therefore*, Connectors

[13] Fries, *The Structure of English*, pp. 83–86, 92–94, 97–103, 132–141.

Group K. containing *well, oh, now*, Attention Signals

Group L. containing *yes* and *no*, Responses

The old "adverb" class is thus divided among eight new classes. Each is more homogeneous, and it is therefore possible to say a great deal more about each class without endless qualifications. Still, some of the groups that Fries uses are not yet sufficiently homogeneous for best results. Group I is a particularly troublesome one. He puts together all question words. These behave like several other classes, but all of them also mark the sentence as a question. Undoubtedly it is necessary here to have some kind of cross-cutting classification.[14] *When* would then be classed in two ways, as an adverb (Fries' Class 4) and as an interrogator. *Who* similarly would be classified as a pronoun and as an interrogator. Traditional grammars often suggest this by using labels like "interrogative adverb" and "interrogative pronoun", but, unfortunately, they do not regularize it, and do not exploit the possibilities fully.

Fries' work was in the right direction, but some details must be corrected, and the direction pursued much further. The aim must be a system of word classes characterized by maximum homogeneity within the classes.

Three moderate-sized groups of "adverbs" must certainly be separated out from the class if it is to be made workable. They are better treated as independent parts of speech rather than as subdivisions of a comprehending "adverb" class.

The first of these may be called "intensifiers". This class includes such words as *very, extremely, rather*. It constitutes the larger part of Fries' Group D. Intensifiers modify adjectives or adverbs. They do not modify verbs. This latter restriction is so strong that it gives a useful criterion for distinguishing adjectives from participles. For example, the following two sentences are superficially similar: *He is interesting. He is coming.* If an attempt is made to insert *very*, the difference is immediately apparent. *He is very interesting.* but not ×*He is very coming. Coming* is clearly a verb form (a participle), while *interesting* is an adjective. In another context *interesting* can be a participle, in which case *very* cannot be added: *He is interesting a client in some insurance.* But not ×*He is very interesting a client in some insurance.*

The second group that must be excluded from the adverbs may be called "limiters".[15] This class includes words like *only, just, even*. Fries includes these with intensifiers in his Group D. Limiters modify phrases of all kinds, noun phrases as well as others: *Only his first model ever worked properly.* (*Only* modifies *his first model.*) *Only John was at home.* (*Only*

---

[14] Cross-cutting classification is necessary in several places, and so should be considered as quite normal. See Chapter 8, "Types of Meaning and Meaninglessness".

[15] The analysis here and the term "limiter" are from Seymour Chatman, *Pre-Adjectivals in the English Nominal Phrase*, 1960, American Speech 35:83–100.

modifies *John* — a one-word noun phrase.) *I think it must have been the man downstairs — only he would do that.* (*Only* modifies *he*, a pronoun substituting for the noun phrase *the man downstairs.*) *Only in Los Angeles do they drive like that.* (*Only* modifies the prepositional phrase *in Los Angeles.*) *The bus runs only occasionally.* (*Only* modifies the adverb *occasionally.* This can, however, be considered as a one-word phrase, since it parallels multiword phrases: *The bus runs only on holidays.*)

A third group that must be excised from the old adverb class may be called "sentence introducers" or "sentence connectors". This class includes words like *nevertheless, however, furthermore.* They fall into Fries' Group J. They come at various places in sentences. In many places they must be set off from the remainder of the sentence by terminals or commas.

There are a number of words which must be excluded from the "adverb" class, but which do not fall into any clearly definable group. Among them are *not, there* (as in: *There once was a man.*), *the* (as in: *The more, the merrier.* See page 121.)

After these excisions what remains of the old adverb class is very much more homogeneous, but not yet entirely satisfactory. Lacking anything better, the term "adverb" can be retained for this class. These words largely modify verbs or verb phrases, whole predicates or whole sentences.

It is instructive to note how this excision would alter the old school definition: "An adverb is a word that modifies a verb, adjective, or other adverb". Most of the "adverbs" which modified adjectives or "other adverbs" have been reassigned as intensifiers. The remainder are mostly limiters. (*Your paper even now is only fair. I want it just perfect.*) This would suggest that the definition might become: "An adverb is a word that modifies a verb." Certainly, this would be a better definition, since it suggests a more homogeneous group. It must be remembered that this definition presupposes the base-and-modifier analysis which underlies school grammar, in which modifiers of phrases are considered as modifying the head word in the phrase. Adverbs modify verbs, predicates, or whole sentences, but verbs can be considered as heads of predicates and sentences. Only in an amended school grammar could we use such a definition as: "An adverb is a word that modifies a verb."

Even then another amendment would have to be made to such a definition. Many "adverbs" can modify nouns. These typically follow the noun immediately: *The man downstairs, a junior year abroad, a desire within.* School grammars, of course, have considered these not as "adverbs" but as adjectives. However, they differ from true adjectives in that they do not take intensifiers, nor do they occur in the typical adjective position — between the determiner and the noun, as in *a famous man.*

This narrowed adverb class still is far from homogeneous. A good deal of subclassification is called for. The groups, however, have not as yet been clearly demarcated. Perhaps further study will produce a better scheme. The sharpest distinction seems to be between two groups that have different places in clause structure.

The first subclass may be called "emphatic adverbs" or "preverb adverbs". The class includes such words as *always, usually, certainly*. Their typical use is to give some sort of general emphasis to the sentence or to express some sort of reservation. Examples are: *I certainly will go. I always like ice cream. Well, he usually does.*

The typical position for the emphatic adverb is in the verb phrase, usually immediately before the first auxiliary. They may also follow the auxiliary, but only if either the auxiliary or the adverb is stressed in speech. The typical position for the remaining groups of adverbs is final after the verb phrase and after the complement. These, however, are only the typical positions, and adverbs of either group can be found in various places in the sentence, often with intonational differences. These may be illustrated by examples including *certainly*, an emphatic adverb, and *rapidly*, an adverb of the other type.

The typical positions are illustrated in the following:

> *He certainly will run.*
> *He will run rapidly.*
> *He will certainly run.*

All these sentences would normally be said with a single intonation contour. Emphatic adverbs can also occur in final position, but here they are usually separated by a terminal, and the whole sentence is then said with two contours:

> *He will run, certainly.*

On the other hand, both types of adverbs can be moved to initial position. Here *rapidly* must be set off by a terminal, whereas *certainly* may be but usually is not:

> *Rapidly, he will run.*
> *Certainly he will run.*   or   *Certainly, he will run.*

Emphatic adverbs are one subclass; the remainder, though sharing certain features of distribution, seem best divided into at least three subclasses. The criterion here is the interrogative to which they answer. Manner adverbs, like *rapidly, unobtrusively, precariously, nicely*, answer questions containing *how*. Temporal adverbs, like *now, soon, afterwards, immediately*, answer questions containing *when*. Locative adverbs, like *here, abroad, outside, nearby*, answer questions containing *where*. There are other differences, but these are hard to define precisely. For example, some verbs never take manner adverbs, but do take locatives.

SUBCLASSIFICATION

School grammars traditionally list eight parts of speech. Fries in *The Structure of English* lists nineteen. Several of Fries' groups could easily be divided. The process might be carried to considerable lengths, each new subdivision being in some significant way justifiable. A new difficulty would appear. Similarities between some of the groups are important, but would become less and less clear. Both large and small groups have advantages to the grammarian. Fortunately, the two can be combined by setting up a few large groups, some of which are subdivided, yielding many minor groups.

School grammars give some recognition to this. Nouns are subclassified as common and proper, adjectives as descriptive or definitive, verbs as transitive or intransitive. This is necessary, since, while many things can be said about nouns in general, there are additional things that must be said about each of the divisions alone. Subclassification of this sort is, however, used very sparingly by the school grammarians. Newer treatments tend not only to realign the classes, but also to introduce further subclassification.

A part of the new insights of the linguists can be incorporated into the framework of traditional grammar through subclassification. But this must be done with care. As shown above, the old "adverb" class contains a number of quite disparate elements. One possible device would be to delimit these several groups as subclasses of "adverbs" — perhaps treating Fries' eight groups this way.

There are, however, two serious difficulties. First, some of Fries' function word groups are drawn from two or more of the old traditional parts of speech. They would either be split and the fragments made subclasses of the appropriate major groups, or some realignment of the major groups would be forced.

Second, some of the fragments of the old "adverb" class have nothing significant in common. If all the groups are maintained within the whole, the major class remains as lacking in usefulness as ever. At least some of these groups must be taken out of the "adverb" class if the latter is not to be grammatical deadwood.

On the other hand, we cannot simply dismiss "adverb" or its traditional delimitation. For one thing all the dictionaries label items "adv.", following the older formulations. Students must understand this in order to use the dictionaries. And, of course, they must understand the limitations of the term. The old labels, when they must be abandoned, must still be taught, not as facts of grammar, but as facts of the history of grammar. The inclusive "adverb" must disappear from our curriculum as a working part of speech, but the old scheme must be understood in much the same way that Ptolomaic astronomy must be understood.

The trend among linguists studying English is clearly toward more —
and more complicated — subdivision of the major parts of speech. This
is at least as important as the realignment of the parts of speech themselves. Improvement in grammatical formulations comes in part from
refinement of the classification.

The transformational-generative grammarians are currently leading
the way in this. Every paper of theirs, it seems, involves the further sub-
subclassification of some subclass. In the welter, it is a little difficult to
see the broader outlines or to understand the significance of the work.
Nevertheless, this extension of classification will certainly prove to be one
of the important contributions of the movement. Many of their divisions
and redivisions can be shown to have just as great usefulness and validity
within some other grammatical framework as within transformational-
generative grammar.

Perhaps the transformational-generative grammarians tend to overdo
subclassification. Some of their minutest divisions may be really outside
the proper province of grammar. Certainly they could not avoid making
some mistakes in their rapid advance. But their work will surely produce
something worthwhile. Some of that will come from their careful attention
to word classification.

It is perhaps ironic that the transformational-generative grammarians
are contributing most heavily to other approaches precisely at the point of
subclassification. They are addicted to labeling nongenerative grammars as
"taxonomic". But no previous group ever approached the elaboration of
their taxonomies!

THE SUBCLASSIFICATION OF NOUNS

Grammarians have always subclassified nouns under two heads:
proper and common. One reason for insisting on this has been the importance of the distinction for the conventions of capitalization. But it is
grammatically important as well, though the value of the distinction is
blurred unless some further subclassification is made.

Proper nouns fall into two very clearly marked subdivisions. One very
rarely occurs with a determiner; the other usually has *the*. Once this distinction is made, many of the grammatical distinctions between either
group and the common nouns can be stated fairly clearly and straight-
forwardly. Without the distinction, the rules for use of determiners are
seemingly chaotic. Since the use of determiners is a very important grammatical matter, the subclassification is crucial.

The two groups contrast directly: *Connecticut* is a state; *the Connecticut*
is a river. *Erie* is a city; *the Erie* is a railroad. *Hartford* is a city; *the Hartford*
is an insurance company. In areas where these pairs of names are known,
the distinction is immediately apparent to everyone. The differing use of

determiners distinguishes them infallibly in most environments. But in a place where no noun can have a determiner, for example, as a noun modifier of another noun, they can be confused. In *New Haven passengers* we do not know whether the reference is to passengers on the New Haven railroad, or passengers going to or from the city of New Haven.

There is a much more important distinction among the common nouns. Some, often called "count nouns" because they can occur with numerals, are used as either singular or plural. Others, usually called "mass nouns",[16] do not have this distinction. When used as subjects, mass nouns take singular verbs. The determiners used with mass nouns, however, are more nearly like those used with plural count nouns than like those used with singulars.

In general count nouns refer to discrete, individual objects; mass nouns to substances, qualities, and the like. The distinction, like all grammatical distinctions, however, is partially arbitrary. *Pebbles* are no more countable than *gravel*, yet we say: *The pebbles are . . ., Gravel is . . .; two pebbles*, but not *×two gravels*. It is simply a convention of English that *pebble* is a count noun, usually plural, whereas *gravel* is a mass noun.

The grammatical importance of the distinction comes out immediately when an effort is made to discuss the use of determiners. The patterns are markedly different for the two types of nouns. They may be hinted at by a tabulation of grammatically comparable constructions.

the man is	*the men are*	*the water is*
a man	*men*	*water*
this man	*these men*	*this water*
—	*few men*	*little water*
every man	*all men*	*all water*
one man	*two men*	—
some man	*some men*	*some water* (*some* stressed)
—	*some men*	*some water* (*some* unstressed)

All these are quite common and usual constructions.[17] All deserve close attention in any reasonably complete grammar. Most of these constructions cannot be described meaningfully unless the three types of nouns, singular count, plural count, and mass, are separated. None of them is well described in the school grammars.

[16] There are a few nouns that do not clearly fall into either subclass, and must accordingly be thought of as belonging to an additional small subclass. A familiar example is *oats*. This behaves in many ways like a normal plural count noun, but does not occur with numerals: *×two oats* (though this would be possible meaning 'two kinds of oats'). While plurals usually occur with *many*, the usual form is *much oats*. *Goods*, *riches* are other examples. Another, somewhat similar, small subclass includes such words as *intelligentsia*.

[17] The tabulation does not exhibit all the possibilities, witness: *Man is mortal.* However, such uses are clearly specialized, and so require expansion of the description rather than basic revision.

This is not purely an academic matter. Students do make occasional errors, sometimes interesting and puzzling ones, in the use of these constructions. An excellent example is: *Liberal education is one which . . .*[18] This was marked wrong on a student paper. The writer demanded an explanation of the difficulty, and was of course entitled to it. But without recognition of the mass noun-count noun distinction, none could be given. *Liberal education* is here a mass noun. *One* can only substitute for a count noun. In this construction, subject and subjective complement must agree.

There can be no question that the contrast between mass and count nouns is a crucial one in English. It cannot be avoided or glossed over in any account of English grammar that goes beyond the broadest outline. But a very interesting question can be raised as to how it is to be treated.

There is a very puzzling aspect of the distinction. Many words are commonly used both as mass nouns and as count nouns. Sometimes there is a profound difference of meaning: *Iron is a metal. An iron is an instrument for pressing clothes.* Or the difference may be subtle and almost undefinable: *education* vs. *an education.* In the largest number of cases, however, the difference is quite systematic. *Beer* as a mass noun refers to a certain substance. In a restaurant, *a beer* often means one glass of beer. Most nouns commonly referring to substances can be used as count nouns referring to a portion of that substance. Another use is to mean one particular kind of the substance. Thus a customer, unable to choose between two brands, might say: *I don't care; one ice cream is as good as another.* When a noun is most commonly used as a count noun, it can be made into a mass noun with the meaning 'the substance of which the object is made'. If you eat *an egg*, you may get *egg* on your tie. The shifting of nouns from mass to count and from count to mass seems to be a fairly regular and productive pattern in English. It must, therefore, be considered a grammatical fact, and it demands a grammatical description.

Are there limitations to this shifting? At first sight there seem to be. Certain nouns seem only to occur in one type, others only in the other. But it is soon found that many of the ones with both uses are very much more frequent in one than in the other. The less frequent use occurs only in rather unusual circumstances. *Water* as a mass noun is common and widespread; as a count noun is nearly restricted to waiters. Even if the restaurant usage had not been observed, the pattern would remain and this use might arise at any time. Perhaps some of the other words would also show both uses if sufficiently unusual situations were conceived. This seems to be the case. For example, *book* and *shelf* are both fairly typical count nouns. With the present vogue of speaking-animal stories, we can imagine one featuring a mother termite concerned over her child: *Johnny is very choosey about his food. He will eat book, but he won't touch shelf.* This

---

[18] I owe this very interesting example to John Hunter, in whose class it occurred.

is farfetched, of course. But it does suggest that every noun, given the right context, can occur in either type of usage, count or mass.

If it is true that every common noun can occur in both patterns of use, the count-mass distinction is not one that divides the nouns of English into two separate subclasses. Rather it is one, like the plural-singular distinction, that affects all, or nearly all, nouns. Indeed, it is like number in other respects. For one thing it is these two distinctions together which control the use of determiners in noun phrases.

The semantic contrasts within both distinctions are generally regular. But in both there are erratic instances. For example, if early in the evening a man says the following, he is using the plural *boys* in a very special sense: *I'm going out with the boys.* But *boys* is also, probably more frequently, used in its normal predictable meaning. Most nouns lack any such specialized use of the plural. So likewise with *iron*. If the count noun has a meaning not predictable from the mass noun, this is clearly specialized even if common. As a count noun it can also be used in the normal sense of a portion or a kind. A raw-materials salesman might say to a manufacturer: *I think I have an iron that will exactly meet your specifications.*

There are nouns that are very rarely used as count nouns. Paralleling these are nouns that are very rarely used as singulars. *Trousers* is an example. We might say, then, that an English noun potentially occurs in three numbers, singular, plural, and mass. Some occur in all three, some in only one — any one, some in two — most often singular and plural. The limitations are perhaps partly grammatical, but largely arise from the lack of appropriate contexts.

This is a somewhat radical suggestion viewed from the vantage point of any of the systems of grammar presented in textbooks. It needs rather thorough testing before anyone would urge its adoption in a curriculum. But it deserves that testing, and will indeed get it. One of the chief functions of linguistics in English grammar is to call into question each of the "facts" which grammars have recorded, to test them minutely and extensively, and to accept or reject them on the basis of their ability to clarify the system of the language. From some, valuable new insights will come. This may be a case of this kind; no one can yet tell. In scholarship, nothing can be considered finally fixed.

This distinction in noun uses must be taken account of somewhere in the system of grammar. It might be in the subclassification of nouns, or it might be in the system of number, or it might be in some other place. We must be prepared for basic restructuring, but we must insist that every significant feature find a place.

Chapter 7

Syntactic Relations

The description of the syntax of a language must include two major components: a classification of the words and other elements, and a statement of their relations. There are a variety of techniques to meet the latter need, and grammarians have shown different preferences among them. The various techniques emphasize different features of syntactic structure and sometimes reflect differences of fundamental viewpoint of the authors.

In this chapter, for convenience of presentation, attention will be restricted to simple sentences or single clauses. All the fundamental questions can be seen clearly without the additional complexities of compound and complex sentences. Some of the latter will be discussed in Chapter 14.

THREE TECHNIQUES

Three related techniques for describing structure are in common use among traditional grammarians and many linguists. The basic differences and similarities are best indicated by contrasting their treatments of a sample sentence:

The three old ladies upstairs own a boxer dog with a mean temper.   (1)

This is a sentence of the familiar subject-verb-direct object type. One approach would start by identifying these three major sentence elements, where possible as single words: *ladies* is subject, *own* is verb, and *dog* is direct object. These three together constitute the sentence base, *ladies own dog*. The remaining sentence elements are all modifiers[1] of one or the other of these three: *the, three, old*, and *upstairs* modify *ladies*, and *a, boxer*, and *with a mean temper* modify *dog*. *With a mean temper* is a prepositional phrase and functions as one unit in modifying *dog*. Within it are a preposition *with*, its noun object *temper*, and two modifiers of *temper: a* and *mean*.

The term "sentence base" or, perhaps better, "clause base" is not widely used, though the concept is fundamental. It will provide the best label for the approach, which we will call the base-and-modifier technique. This is characteristic of the school grammars, and in presenting this type of analysis we will follow the conventions of the school tradition.

A second approach also recognizes (1) as a subject-verb-object sentence and starts by recognizing these elements. They are not, however, identified as single words: *the three old ladies upstairs* is the subject, *own* is the verb, and *a boxer dog with a mean temper* is the direct object. Two of the three require further analysis. They are both noun phrases. A noun phrase is considered as having a number of slots or positions, for each of which there can be specified appropriate fillers. One of these — the one which is most generally filled[2] — is designated the head; the others are modifiers. Other constructions, however, may not have a single position that can be designated head. When a head is present, the slots can most easily be designated by counting outward from it. In the convention followed here, N − 5 should be read as "N minus 5" and means the fifth slot before the noun. This slot is filled by certain types of determiners. Only as much of the scheme is given here as is needed to explain the example.[3]

---

[1] Throughout this book, I use "modify" to mean 'grammatically dependent upon' or 'grammatically subordinate to'. This seems to be the actual use of most school grammarians, though their definitions are quite otherwise: "To modify means to describe or to make more definite the meaning of words." John E. Warriner, *Handbook of English, Book Two*, 1951, p. 6. "The term 'modify' in grammar means 'to qualify, limit, or restrict.'" R. W. Pence and D. W. Emery, *A Grammar of Present-day English*, 1963, p. 6.
   Many linguists and some English teachers have rejected the terms "modify", "modifier", and "modification", replacing them by "is attributive to", "attributive", and "attribution". I find the old terms just as usable, and the new open to every objection that can be brought against the old. That the usual definitions are unworkable is no obstacle — so are the definitions of, say, the noun. If linguists can continue to use the word "noun" for essentially the same class of words as the school grammarians, I see no reason not to continue "modify" for essentially the same relationship.
   I do not attempt a new definition, because modification seems to be one of the fundamental grammatical concepts that cannot be defined, only exemplified.

[2] This should not be taken as a definition of "head", but simply as an observation about noun phrases. *The poor* can be considered as a noun phrase without the head noun.

[3] In this scheme, N − 3 is filled by specifiers (*other, same, chief*), ordinal numbers, and superlative adjectives: *the two other new books, the three best literary contributions*. N − 6 is filled by predeterminers (*all, both*, and *half*): *all those men, half the time*. The positions after the head are less clearly distinguishable, and many details are still uncertain.

Slots	N − 5	N − 4	N − 2	N − 1	N	N + 1	N + 2
Fillers	Deter-miners	Numerals	Adjec-tives	Nouns	Nouns	Adverbs	Prepositional Phrases
	the	*three*	*old*	—	*ladies*	*upstairs*	—
	a	—	—	*boxer*	*dog*	—	*with a mean temper*
	a	—	*mean*	—	*temper*	—	—

To make effective use of a description which distinguishes a number of types of modifiers, it is necessary to use a classification of parts of speech that makes relatively precise discriminations. "Adjective" therefore is used here in a very narrow sense; many of the other modifiers would be called "adjective" in most grammars. The fillers permitted in N + 1 position include only a part of the class of adverbs, locative adverbs.

Numerals like *three* and adjectives like *old* differ in several respects. For example, only *old* can be modified by words like *extremely*: *the three extremely old ladies*, but not ×*the extremely three old ladies*. They occupy two different columns in the tabulation because they can freely occur together, but only in the indicated order: ×*the old three ladies* is not normal English. Numerals always precede adjectives. The first phrase does not contain a noun modifier; if it did it would have to appear between *old* and *ladies*, since adjectives always precede nouns. Moreover, as the tabulation indicates, numerals precede noun modifiers: *the three boxer dogs*. Nothing can come between a noun modifier and the head noun; this is the implication of the slot designation N − 1. A label like N + 2 implies that these modifiers can occur immediately after those found in N + 1 position or after the head noun, but nowhere else.

Fillers for many of the slots can be either single words or phrases. In *the twenty-seven very fierce Saint Bernard dogs*, the N − 4, N − 2, and N − 1 positions are all filled with phrases. A full grammar would include a description of numeral phrases and adjective phrases as well as noun phrases.

The sentence as a whole is described in terms of a construction having at least three slots, the subject, verb, and direct object. Each of these three may be filled by either a single word, in which case no further analysis is required, or by a phrase, in which case the construction of each phrase is described in terms of a series of slots and the appropriate fillers. This technique is repeated until ultimate constituents are reached. In the sentence under discussion, one construction is a prepositional phrase, in which there are only two slots — one always filled by a preposition and the second usually by a noun phrase. This noun phrase, in turn, is analyzed in terms of the same construction pattern as the other, and is shown in the tabulation above. This approach is best labeled as the slot-and-filler technique.[4]

---

[4] Tagmemic analysis is a slot-and-filler technique combined with certain charac-

Apart from the fact that the slot-and-filler description is commonly carried out to greater detail (as with the modifiers of nouns), it differs from the base-and-modifier technique in one significant way. In one the modifier is added to the major sentence elements; in the other the modifiers are within and part of the major sentence elements. School grammars sometimes pay respect to this in passing by differentiating between the "simple subject" (that is, *ladies*) and the "complete subject" (that is, *the three old ladies upstairs*). But the complete subject is given little importance in most school textbooks.[5]

The third approach is less concerned with such major sentence elements. It operates on the assumption that most constructions will have only two parts. The sentence is accordingly divided into *the three old ladies upstairs* and *own a boxer dog with a mean temper*. These two are called the immediate constituents (often abbreviated ICs) of the sentence.[6] In turn, each of these is divided into its immediate constituents. The second is cut into *own* and *a boxer dog with a mean temper*. The three major sentence elements have appeared, but not as coordinate parts of the sentence. One is an IC of the sentence, the other two are not, but are ICs of the predicate. At each stage of the analysis only the ICs, that is the IMMEDIATE components of the construction are relevant. Notice also that there is no requirement that the parts be equal in size; seven words have been cut into one and six. Each fraction of the sentence is examined in turn and cut into two until ultimate indivisible units are reached.

Alternatively the description might start with the separate words of the sentence. The first step would be to unite as constructions those pairs of words judged to be most closely connected: *old ladies, boxer dog,* and *mean temper*. Then treating these as units on a par with the remaining single words, the process is repeated. The next constructions to appear are: *three old ladies, a boxer dog,* and *a mean temper*. And so on. The outcome of the two approaches, from words to larger and larger constructions and from the sentence to its parts and the parts of the parts, will in most cases be exactly alike.

The IC and slot-and-filler techniques are alike in building up larger constructions from smaller, rather than hanging extra elements on a basic skeleton. They differ in several ways. The IC approach builds out of pairs

---

teristic views of the general nature of language systems. The latter are outside the scope of this chapter, so that the description of the slot-and-filler technique will serve to describe tagmemic methods, except for a different set of notational and terminologic conventions.

[5] It is perhaps indicative that there is nowhere, to my knowledge, any mention of a "complete object". If the complete subject were given a central place, consistency would demand recognition of a number of other comparable elements, but only the complete predicate is ever mentioned, and when it is, it is always rather casually.

[6] ICs are called "pattern parts" in Paul Roberts, *Patterns of English*, 1956.

of units wherever possible. The slot-and-filler technique has no restriction as to the number of constituents in a construction. The IC approach, therefore, often goes through more steps from word to sentence, but they may be much simpler steps. The slot-and-filler technique must describe many unfilled slots, for example, the N − 4 (numeral) and N − 2 (adjective) slots in *a boxer dog*. The IC approach, however, does not do this— each construction is described as complete in itself. The IC technique emphasizes the relation between the partners in a construction; the slot-and-filler technique emphasizes the place of each component in a larger whole.

REED AND KELLOGG DIAGRAMS

The sentence discussed above can be diagrammed, following the usual practice in the schools as follows:

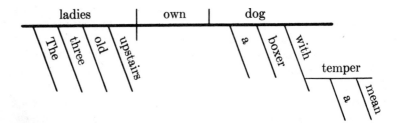

This system seems to have been brought to its familiar form by Alonzo Reed and Brainerd Kellogg,[7] and is perhaps best designated by their name. In the schools it is generally known simply as "diagramming", there being no other system from which it must be distinguished.

The Reed and Kellogg scheme was designed to reflect the base-and-modifier description which prevailed in American school grammar. With varying amounts of modification,[8] much of it simply abridgment, it continues in use in many school textbooks. It has received very little attention from linguists or university scholars, and is peculiarly the property of the public schools and of English departments strongly oriented toward the

---

[7] Alonzo Reed and Brainerd Kellogg, *Higher Lessons in English*, 1909, new edition. There were earlier editions in 1877, 1885, and 1896, but I have not seen these. Exactly the same system of diagramming is used in Homer C. House and Susan Emolyn Harman, *Descriptive English Grammar*, 1950, second edition.

[8] It is instructive to compare any of the current textbooks for high school use with Reed and Kellogg or House and Harman. In most cases there has been a great deal of abridgment and simplification. This not only increases the number of sentences that cannot be diagrammed but also results in a loss of usefulness in the resulting diagrams. Pence and Emery, *A Grammar of Present-day English*, is a college-level textbook presenting a comprehensive and responsible modification of Reed and Kellogg diagramming.

public schools. Indeed, linguists have tended to dismiss it out of hand.[9] But it is actually a very effective device for exhibiting the school grammar analysis of English sentences, and so will be used here as a convenient tool in contrasting the base-and-modifier technique with others. In any case, any fundamental deficiences of diagramming are deficiencies of the underlying analysis or of misuse in the schools, not of the graphic device.

The clause base is represented by a horizontal line. This is drawn heavier than all other parts of the diagram to indicate its primary importance. It is divided into sections, each representing one of the major sentence elements. There are four patterns:

Fish | swim	subject—verb (no complements)
Farmers| grow | food	subject—verb—direct object
Grass | is \ green	subject—verb—subjective complement
They |elected / president | Washington	subject—verb—objective complement—direct object

It is interesting to note that, as Reed and Kellogg diagram the last type, the objective complement is placed before the direct object, rather than in the order in which it normally occurs in sentences: *They elected Washington president.* Their reason for doing this is significant. The objective complement is related to both the verb and the direct object, and so stands between them. Indeed, as they point out, the verb alone does not express the action, but the verb plus the objective complement does. In a sense the latter is a part of the verb of which *Washington* is the direct object.

Reed and Kellogg diagramming is not concerned with word order at all, only with word relationships. That in three of the patterns above the words are arranged in normal sentence order is incidental. The verb, since it is related both to the subject and the complements, must go between. The normal sentence order meets this condition in most cases, and is therefore arbitrarily conventionalized. In English there are many pairs of

---

[9] A few years ago, I inquired among a number of linguists and linguistically oriented English professors. I found none that claimed to know anything about diagramming, and few that could cite a source for definitive information.

Most English teachers in the schools can draw diagrams, but few know anything of its origin and history, and, more seriously, few understand the basic rationale. As a result it has generally been taught as a meaningless mechanical operation, thoroughly disliked by most teachers and almost all students.

Diagramming has, therefore, become a focus of criticism of old-fashioned grammar teaching. Much of both the attack and the defense has been based on ignorance, and is quite beside the point. The major difficulty with Reed and Kellogg diagramming has been prevailingly bad teaching.

sentences containing the same words in different orders. When these are alternative arrangements with the same structural relations, the two are diagrammed alike. When there is a difference of structural relations the diagrams are different:

They took the book away. ⎫
                          ⎬
They took away the book. ⎭

They rolled it up.

They rolled up it.

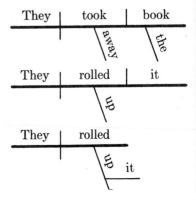

Moreover, when a sentence is ambiguous, that is, when one sequence of words has two or more possible analyses, there are two or more diagrams to indicate the possible structures:

(They wanted to dance, so . . .)

They rolled up the rug.

(He spilled the marbles, and . . .)

They rolled up the rug.

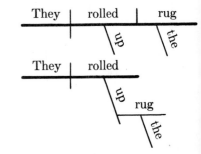

The "neglect of order" has been severely criticized as a deficiency in the system, but it is not necessarily a shortcoming. Sentences diagrammed alike are only stylistically different. Ordinarily one can be substituted for the other with no change of meaning. The diagrams point out this grammatical equivalence, just as they provide a means of exhibiting ambiguity. They may be valuable precisely because they go behind order to exhibit structure which is only partly signaled by order. Teachers using Reed and Kellogg diagrams seem seldom to have utilized, or even seen, their possibilities in discussing style.

The following devices are used in Reed and Kellogg diagrams. (Arrows indicate the features under discussion.)

1. Major sentence elements are written on a horizontal base line. This is drawn heavier than the other lines in the diagram.

Boys love candy.
⇨ Boys | love | candy

2. The subject and predicate, the two essential sentence elements, are separated by a short vertical line crossing the base line. It is, of course, the "simple subject" and "simple predicate" that are so written.

Dogs bark.

3. A **direct object** is marked by a short vertical line rising from the base line and separating it from the verb.

John enjoys tennis.
John | enjoys | tennis

4. A subjective complement is marked by a short line rising from the base line and slanting to the left (pointing back at the subject). Predicate nouns and predicate adjectives are not distinguished. Nor are adverbs which school grammar would consider as adjectives in this position.

Mother seems well.
Mother | seems \ well

5. An objective complement is marked by a short line rising from the base line and slanting to the right (pointing ahead toward the object). Nouns and adjectives are not distinguished. A variant, perhaps commoner than the original, is to diagram the objective complement after the direct object, in which case the marker slants to the left.

Jane considers him foolish.
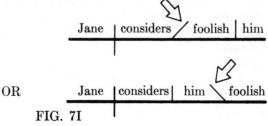
Jane | considers / foolish | him

OR   Jane | considers | him \ foolish

FIG. 7I

6. Modifiers are generally written on slant lines hung below the base line. There is usually no distinction between various types of modifiers. Those hung from verb lines are "adverbs". Those attached to the subject and noun complement lines are all considered as "adjectives", following the usual definitions of school grammar.

The big black bear ran away quickly.

7. Prepositional phrases have two basic components, and are accordingly written on a pattern of two lines.[10] They are modifiers, and therefore one line is slanted. On this is written the preposition, since this is the mark of its being a modifier. They contain nouns or verbs (infinitives with *to* are treated as prepositional phrases), and so the second line is horizontal, like the noun and verb lines of the base.

My friend in London went to Paris.

8. Participles are single words having both "adjective" characteristics and verb characteristics. They are, therefore, written on a single line which bends from the adjective slant to the horizontal position used for verbs.

Growing children bring increasing troubles.

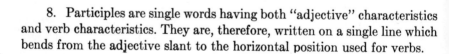

9. Gerunds[11] are considered words partaking of both noun and verb characteristics. Both of these are usually diagrammed with horizontal lines, so the gerund gets two horizontal segments with a slight break between.

---

[10] A number of recent textbooks do not distinguish between the two-line pattern for a prepositional phrase and the bent line for a participle.

[11] "Gerund" is a term widely used in school grammars, but not considered as distinct from "participle" by many modern grammars.

He learned by doing.

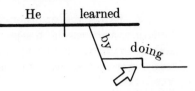

10. The horizontal lines of the participles, gerunds, and prepositional phrases containing verbs can be prolonged and bear a complement. This is separated by the same dividers as are used on the base line. The line, however, differs from the base line in being light.

The child was rewarded
   for being good.

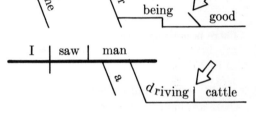

I saw a man driving cattle.

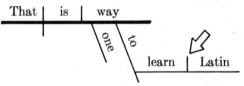

That is one way
   to learn Latin.

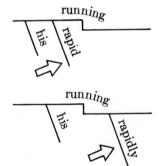

11. Below any horizontal line may be hung slant lines for modifiers. In the case of the gerund, these are carefully segregated. "Adjectives" hang before the break (the noun portion of the line) and "adverbs" after. This is one of the very few instances where types of modifiers are distinguished.[12]

his rapid running

his running rapidly

[12] Very few current school textbooks observe this distinction. It is, however, indicative of the care taken by some school grammarians, and also revealing of fundamental points of view.

12. Expletives, or other elements of loose connection to the sentence structure, are written on separate lines, usually above the main diagram, and always light. If they seem to relate to some particular part of the sentence, they may be joined by a dashed line.

Indeed, he returned as a hero.

There is nothing here.

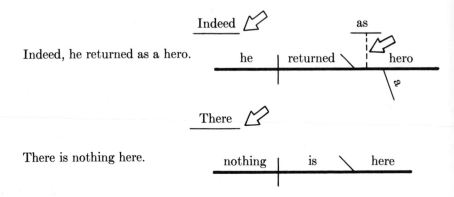

13. Compound elements are written on forked lines. Modifiers of the whole are hung on the single stem, modifiers of individual parts are hung on the separate forks. The forking may be at either or both ends.

I saw John and Mary.

They saw and heard the thief.

The old men and young boys came.

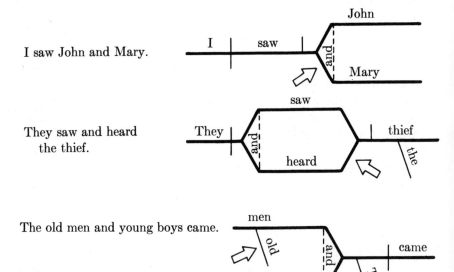

14. Conjunctions are written on dashed lines joining the parts connected.

The old and gray man had a brown and white cow.

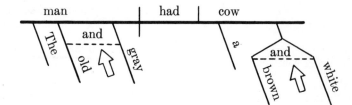

15. Appositives are inserted in parens after the elements with which they are in apposition.

My brother, John, plays tennis.

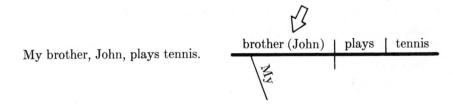

16. Understood elements are diagrammed as if present, and an X is written in their place.

Bring paper, pen, and ink.

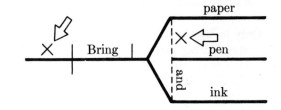

17. Indirect objects and nouns in adverbial use are diagrammed as phrases, but without a preposition and without X. The explanation usually points out the parallelism between *Give me it* and *Give it to me* as justification for the phrase line. Nevertheless, they are diagrammed as without a preposition,[13] rather than as having an understood preposition.

---

[13] "If we change the order of the words, a preposition must be supplied; as 'He gave a book *to me*.' . . . When the indirect object precedes the direct, no preposition is expressed or understood. . . . The idiom of the language does not often admit a preposition before nouns denoting measure, direction, and so on. In your analysis you need not supply one." Reed and Kellogg, *Higher Lessons in English*, 1909, p. 80. Many recent textbooks do insist on supplying a preposition (for example, "*to* understood") in the indirect object at least.

He gave me it.

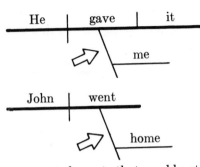

John went home.

Three minor devices are provided to connect elements that would not otherwise fit together conveniently. They are required more by the geometry of the diagram than the structure of the sentences:

18. A short horizontal line connects one slant line to another. It is most often used to connect an "adverb" (intensifier) to an adjective.

Very good food disappears
    extremely rapidly.

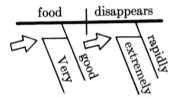

19. A pair of short lines joins a modifier to both lines of a prepositional phrase to indicate that the phrase as a whole is modified, not merely the preposition.[14]

Only in Los Angeles is
    the weather perfect.

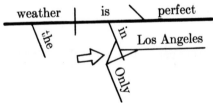

20. A stilt is used to put phrases, gerunds, participles, or clauses on horizontal lines. It is not needed when a gerund is object of a preposition. (See the example at 9)

[14] Some textbooks attempt to make a distinction between examples like that in the text and those of the following type:

just inside Los Angeles

That is, they distinguish between those where the "adverb" modifies the whole phrase (preposition and noun) and those where it modifies the preposition alone. However, criteria to make this distinction are difficult to find, and none of the books is clear on the matter.

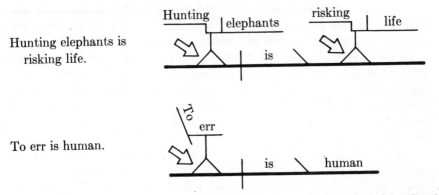

Hunting elephants is
risking life.

To err is human.

This short list comprehends all the devices which are used by Reed and Kellogg in diagramming clauses.[15] At least three of the twenty are simply mechanical provisions for connecting pieces, rather than indication of structures. The remainder indicate the range of constructions recognized in school grammar.

IMMEDIATE CONSTITUENT DIAGRAMS

There are a number of methods of diagramming structure by immediate constituents. Probably the simplest and most generally useful is that known as the tree diagram. The following is an example:

The three old ladies upstairs own a boxer dog with a mean temper.

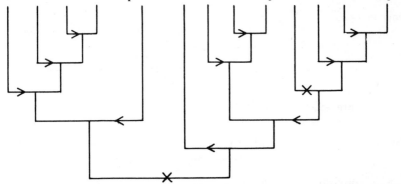

[15] Reed and Kellogg diagramming is far less successful in showing the structure of compound and complex sentences than in handling simple clauses. The devices used consist of little more than variants of those shown: Some clauses are placed within others by means of stilts. Others are connected by dashed lines. The difficulties arise when one word serves two functions, both of which should be recognized in the diagram. For example, a word may be an important structural element within one clause and also serve as a mark of connection of that clause to another. In these instances, there seems to be little agreement in conventions, and some books are hardly able to maintain their own internal consistency.

In such a diagram each horizontal line represents a construction and each vertical line a constituent. The vertical lines at the top represent the ultimate constituents, in this case words. The lowest horizontal line represents the largest construction, the sentence. As the sentence is not a constituent of anything, there is no vertical line leading down from it. The vertical lines at each end of a horizontal line represent the two immediate constituents of that construction. Each constituent consists of all those words that can be reached by going up the tree from the line that represents it.

It is not sufficient merely to show what elements are connected. In addition it is necessary to indicate the kinds of constructions. Nida,[16] whose system of marking ICs we will follow unless otherwise indicated, does so by the use of four marks representing four very broad construction types.

The first type is the modifier-head construction.[17] This is marked by an arrow pointing toward the head. English has a very considerable number of kinds of modifier-head constructions. A few examples are:

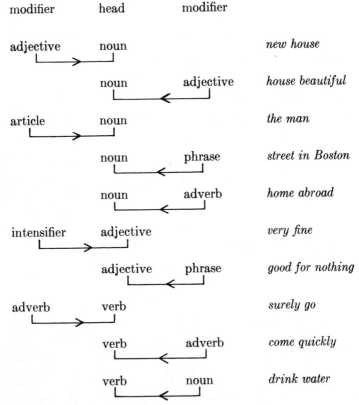

modifier	head	modifier	
adjective	noun		*new house*
	noun	adjective	*house beautiful*
article	noun		*the man*
	noun	phrase	*street in Boston*
	noun	adverb	*home abroad*
intensifier	adjective		*very fine*
	adjective	phrase	*good for nothing*
adverb	verb		*surely go*
	verb	adverb	*come quickly*
	verb	noun	*drink water*

[16] Eugene Albert Nida, *A Synopsis of English Syntax*, 1960.
[17] Also called "endocentric".

Head-modifier constructions are always grammatically equivalent, or nearly equivalent, to the head.[18] For example, an adjective-noun construction will enter many of the same constructions as a noun alone. *The (new house)* is closely parallel to *the house*; both are article-noun constructions, with *new house*, itself an adjective-noun construction, acting as the noun in the first.

The second major type is that in which neither constituent is head. These nonheaded[19] constructions are also of a number of kinds. They are indicated by an X. Examples are:

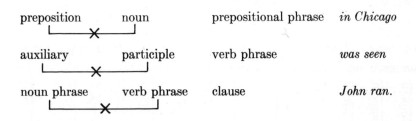

first constituent	second	construction	
preposition	noun	prepositional phrase	*in Chicago*
auxiliary	participle	verb phrase	*was seen*
noun phrase	verb phrase	clause	*John ran.*

It would probably be better in analyzing sentences to distinguish several kinds of nonheaded constructions, rather than mark them all alike. These constructions are not grammatically equivalent to either of their immediate constituents.

The third major type of construction is that in which both constituents are grammatically similar to the whole.[20] Neither is then a modifier, and it is only a matter of taste whether they should be considered as having two heads or none. These are marked with an equal sign:

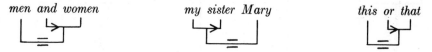

men and women   *my sister Mary*   *this or that*

The fourth type is composed of loosely connected constructions,[21] often very difficult to define. These are marked as follows:

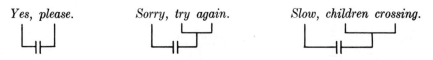

Yes, please.   *Sorry, try again.*   *Slow, children crossing.*

---

[18] This statement is commonly used as a definition of the head and of the head-modifier construction type. Since, however, the notion of grammatical equivalence on which it rests is at least as difficult as the notion of a head of a construction, it does not seem particularly useful to attempt such a definition.

[19] Also called "exocentric".

[20] Also called "coordinate".

[21] Also called "paratactic".

Nida's system of marking must be considered minimum. For many purposes it would be desirable to mark on the basis of a more detailed classification. Indeed, it is often convenient to add to the diagrams labels for some or all of the constructions and some or all of the constituents. The following is only partly labeled, in that several slightly different constructions are all indicated as "nominals". Each piece of the sentence bears two labels, one as construction and one as constituent. The difference is important. Note that three constructions are labeled "noun phrase"; they are all alike internally and hence represent the same construction. They enter into different constructions, and hence are different types of constituents. They are, therefore, labeled as "subject", "direct object", and "object [of preposition]" respectively.

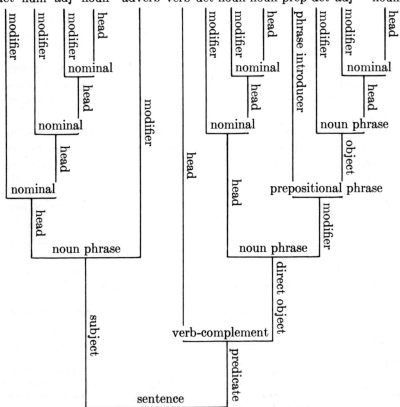

This may be collapsed into a slot-and-filler diagram:

The three old ladies upstairs own a boxer dog with a mean temper.

det num adj noun   adverb verb det noun noun prep det adj   noun

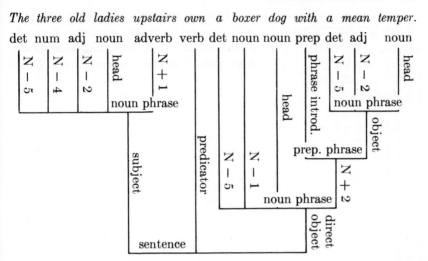

Of the two, the slot-and-filler diagram is more explicitly labeled. Four different types of modifiers are distinguished: N − 1, N − 2, N − 4, and N − 5. The equivalent distinction should be made in the IC diagram by distinguishing four different kinds of nominals: perhaps nominal$_1$ for *boxer dog*, nominal$_2$ for *old ladies*, nominal$_4$ for *three old ladies*, and nominal$_5$ for *a boxer dog.*[22] However, this seems awkward, in large part because the constructions labeled "nominal" seem to be much less significant than most of the others. The charge might be made that the IC diagram shows too much structure. This question will be further examined below, where the problems of cutting are discussed.

Reed and Kellogg diagrams are fairly well established as standard representations of the base-and-modifier analysis. There is no equivalent standardization of any graphic representation of IC structure. A number of quite different-appearing systems of IC diagramming are in use. Some of the differences are only in the physical form of the diagram.[23] Others reflect some modification of the underlying analysis.

[22] The designations for types of nominals have been chosen to indicate the correlation with the slots. Thus nominal$_1$ is a construction consisting of a head and a modifier which in another description would be labeled as occupying slot N − 1. The description would have to say, for example, that nominal$_4$ is composed of a numeral and a nominal$_3$, a nominal$_2$, a nominal$_1$, or a noun. It is necessary in a full grammar to distinguish these types of nominals and to make these complex statements in order to exclude such constructions as ✗*two three men*. The latter would seem to consist of a numeral and a nominal$_4$.

[23] For example, one in which spaces indicate elements is used in Charles F. Hockett, *A Course in Modern Linguistics*, 1958, p. 152, and H. A. Gleason, Jr., *An Introduction to Descriptive Linguistics*, 1961, p. 130. This type of diagram is useful for certain special purposes (for example, step-by-step translation as shown by Hockett, p. 151, or showing constructional parallels as in Gleason, p. 130). They are, however, in every way equivalent to tree diagrams, which are easier to draw.

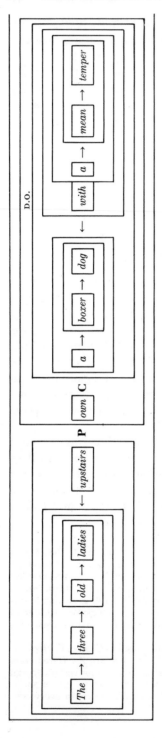

Perhaps the most interesting difference in IC analysis is in the treatment of coordinating conjunctions. Nida diagrams phrases with these like *men and women*. But this is

not entirely satisfactory; *and women* is not coordinate with *men*, but *women* is. Therefore, the coordinate construction should be marked as joining the two words, *men, women*. If this is done, *and* must be recognized as something other than a full partner in the construction. Indeed, many speakers of English would feel that it is really more of a marker of a construction than an element in one. This can be indicated by diagramming it *men and women*.

The line from *and* is dashed to indicate that it participates in a different way than do the words tied in by solid lines. The dashed line runs to the equal sign to indicate that *and* marks the coordination. It is in effect the embodiment of the coordination in the spoken or written form.

There is a question, of course, as to how far this technique should be carried. A few words are very nearly pure structure signals: *to* in *want to go*, or *of* in *City of New York* (compare *New York City*). If *and* is to be diagrammed as a structure signal, these certainly should be also. Other words are somewhat marginal cases. The decision as to where to draw the limit must be partly arbitrary. But there is, of course, something arbitrary in any system of diagramming which tries to present structure in a simple and decisive way.[24]

An example of a technique of diagram-

[24] Arbitrariness is not, therefore, a criterion for rejecting a system of diagramming. Reed and

ming IC structure that is basically a different graphic form is that used by
Francis.[25] He refers to his diagrams as "Chinese boxes". The sentence we
have been using would appear as shown at the left of page 156.

The symbols between the boxes mark constructions. The following
are distinguished: Modifier-head construction (the arrow points toward
the head)

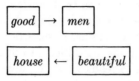

Subject-predicate construction (the P always faces the predicate)

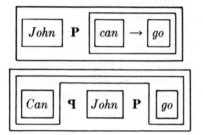

Verbal element-complement construction (The C always faces the complement)

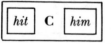

Coordination

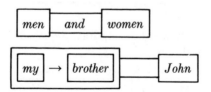

Preposition-object construction

[25] Nelson W. Francis, *The Structure of American English*, 1958, p. 294ff.

The complement is further marked by the following abbreviations above the box: DO direct object, IO indirect object, SC subjective complement, OC objective complement.

It is evident that this scheme treats conjunctions as structure signals rather than constituents since they are written within the construction symbol. Prepositions are given special status not quite the same as other constituents. No example is given by Francis of a loose construction type, such as Nida marks⊣ ⊢. Francis discriminates more constructions, even though fewer types of sentences are discussed.

"Chinese box" diagrams are difficult to draw neatly, and, when complex, are relatively hard to read. They do, however, have one great value. They clearly indicate the notion of constructions being nested within constructions. Because of this, they might be useful as an introductory teaching device. Their function would be to assist in the presentation of the immediate constituent concept.

A "Chinese box" diagram is easily converted into a tree diagram. To do so proceed as follows: From the center of the bottom line of any box draw a line downward until it meets the bottom line of another box. Draw a line along the lower line of the box to join the new vertical lines that terminate on it. Construction symbols written between boxes should be dropped down to the line immediately below them.

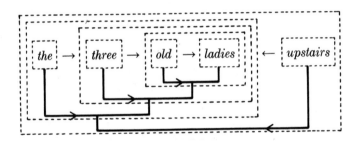

If a conjunction is indicated, draw a dashed line downward from it to the next horizontal line.

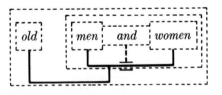

If the bottom line of a box is not straight, but goes up and over another box, the horizontal line will be carried straight across but will be broken to cross a vertical line without connecting. Only one of the two construction symbols needs to be retained.

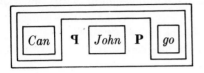 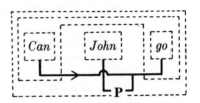

The result of these operations is a tree diagram that differs from those of Nida only in using different marks for a few constructions. That this can be done by simple mechanical rules demonstrates the essential identity of the two types of diagrams.

CUTTING

A satisfactory IC diagram of a sentence is dependent on some reasonable and consistent procedures for dividing constructions into their ICs, that is, for what the linguist calls "cutting". The procedures must be consistent; otherwise structural similarities of sentences may be disguised or wholly hidden. The cuts should also reflect the real and significant patterns of the language system. To meet the first condition is relatively simple. A set of cutting rules can be formulated so that a particular pattern of cutting is specified for every situation — at least for every common situation. Such rules do not automatically meet the second condition, however.

Fries gives the general outline for a set of cutting rules in his *The Structure of English*. These have been taught in some recent textbooks,[26] and form the basis of most presentations which introduce the notion of ICs. They may be summarized as follows:

After the parts of speech have been identified and the various structure markers have been found, there are six rules for the actual cutting.

1. Cut off any sequence signals.
   However, | that is probably the best he can do.
   In any case, | I won't do it.

2. Cut off any adverbial clause that stands at the beginning of the sentence.
   If you go, | I'll be left alone.
   When he dies, | his son will be a millionaire.

3. Cut between the subject and the predicate.
   Albert | was certainly the outstanding student in the class.
   That funny old man with the long white beard | tripped.

4. Cut off any modifiers of the head noun of the subject, one by one.

[26] Paul Roberts, *Patterns of English*, 1956, pp. 106–153. See also pp. 25–27 in the *Teacher's Guide* (bound into the teacher's edition). Note that Roberts avoids examples with auxiliaries.

      a. First those following the noun, beginning with the most remote.

that funny old man | with the long white beard

someone |₂ there |₁ who can take care of it

that is:

someone there | who can take care of it

then:

someone | there

      b. Then those preceding the noun, beginning with the most remote.

that |₁ funny |₂ old |₃ man

his brother's |₁ very efficient |₂ secretary

  5. Cut off any modifiers or complements of the verb head of the predicate, one by one.

      a. First those that precede the verb, beginning with the most remote.

certainly | saw him yesterday

probably |₁ never |₂ would |₃ have |₄ done that

      b. Then those that follow the verb, beginning with the most remote.

done | that

saw |₂ him |₁ yesterday

  6. Following similar procedures cut all word groups that were treated as single units in previous cuttings.

very | efficient

my | brother's

These rules, of course, presuppose others which identify how much of a sequence of words is to be treated as a single modifier. Fries does not state these explicitly, but many of them are clearly enough implied in his discussion. Occasionally there will be some difficulty:

the man in the car | I saw yesterday

OR *the man | in the car I saw yesterday*

The problem in this case is in the ambiguity of the construction, and either analysis might be correct. Labeling it as structurally ambiguous and saying that there are two different ways to analyze it into ICs are essentially equivalent statements of the problem.

Fries' rules for cutting are open to a number of criticisms. These are of at least three different kinds: First, they are inadequate at many points. Second, they may be incorrect at certain points. Third, they may not always be relevant. Each type of criticism deserves some discussion.

The last rule merely says "following a similar procedure". This is vague. An example will show its inadequacy. *Much better than average* is best considered as an adjective phrase containing two modifiers, one preceding and one following. We are given a rule for noun phrases (the following is cut first) and a rule for verb phrases (the preceding is cut first). The rules as formulated do not indicate which model is to be followed with an adjective phrase. That is, they do not decide between:

much |₁ *better* |₂ *than average*
much |₂ *better* |₁ *than average*

In a noun phrase like *a better house than average*, it would be possible to consider *than average* as modifying the remainder. In this case the cutting can proceed according to Fries' rule:

a |₂ *better* |₃ *house* |₁ *than average*

But it would seem preferable to consider *than average* as modifying *better*, and *better . . . than average* as being a single modifier in the noun phrase. In this case the rules are not adequate. Fries makes no provision for a modifier surrounding the head. Should this adjective phrase be cut off before *a* (as a modifier following the noun would be), or after *a* (as would a preceding modifier less remote from the head)? The two possibilities are:

A. *a* |₁ *better house than average*
    a |₁ *better . . . than average* |₂ *house*
B. *a . . . house* |₁ *better . . . than average*
    a |₂ *house* |₁ *better . . . than average*

Many other cases of the same type of deficiency can be cited. But all such difficulties can easily be remedied by adding the necessary provisions to the rules.

The second kind of difficulty may also be shown by examples. In a few cases the rules given by Fries may produce what seem to many people to be incorrect cuts. For example, his rules would produce the following:

I |₁ *can* |₂ *see* |₃ *it.*

But a good case[27] can be made for the following, in which *can see* is a verb phrase having *it* as direct object:

I |₁ *can* |₃ *see* |₂ *it.*

Nida has several examples where he follows the second pattern of cutting. Fries does not actually give any example with an auxiliary in his chapter on immediate constituents, so that it is not certain exactly what he intended. But if the second pattern is preferred, the rules can easily be amended to cover:

---

[27] This is the traditional analysis. Most linguists have preferred Fries' cutting in a case like this. However, the situation is far more complex than it seems at first sight, and a much more complex cutting is possible and very probably necessary. For this see Chapter 13.

　　5. Cut off any modifiers or complements of the verb head of the predicate, one by one.

　　　　a. First those other than auxiliaries that precede the verb, beginning with the most remote.

　　　　b. Then those that follow the verb, beginning with the most remote.

　　　　c. Then the auxiliaries.

Fries' rules seem to imply that cuts must come between words, and so the example *my brother's* above was cut *my | brother's*. This seems clearly wrong as will be shown in the next section. The correct cut must be *my brother | -'s*. Again the rules can be amended to cover this case.

Both types of criticism already raised — that the rules are inadequate and that they are wrong in specifiable places — can easily be corrected. They are criticisms of the specific set of rules, not of the general principles of analysis. It is probably unfair to consider Fries as intending his rules to be much more than a preliminary formulation, open to corrections and expansion. However, the important question is whether the rules are relevant, even after all necessary additions and corrections have been made. That is to say, does the order of cutting actually matter in all the places where the rules specify an order? This is at least doubtful.

In a sentence like the following, practically every linguist or grammarian will agree that the first cut should be as shown:

　　　The 8:15 train to New York | will not run.

But there will be no such agreement as to the order of further cuts in either the subject or the predicate. A great deal can be said for either of the following:

　　　the | 8:15 train to New York
　　　the 8:15 train | to New York

or even:

　　　the . . . train to New York | 8:15

Furthermore, there seems to be no clear argument for any of the three possibilities:

　　　will | not run　　　(apparently Fries' solution)
　　　will not | run
　　　will . . . run | not

In almost any sentence the same thing will be observed. Some cuts are very clear and widely accepted; others seem much less certain and not generally agreed upon. Moreover, the unclear ones seem to be much less significant structurally.

Perhaps the greatest difficulty is with cutting off complements.[28] Fries' rules demand:

(They) elected Washington | president.

But many grammarians (often not using the terminology of ICs) have insisted that *president* goes more closely with *elected* than does *Washington*. This would be equivalent to a cut:

elected . . . president | Washington

Similarly, Fries' rules would require:

(They) gave |₂ Frank |₁ money.

The interesting fact is that many of the arguments other than order which can be adduced to support Fries' rule in one sentence support the opposite in the other. For example, in one case the more remote complement can be dropped, in the other the nearer:

They elected Washington.	*They gave money.*
×They elected president.	*×They gave Frank.*

The most important fact here is not that there are two possible solutions each supportable by arguments, but that there seems to be no particular purpose that is served by making a choice between them. There are certainly three constituents in each predicate, and these three are significant. But there seems to be no great value in recognizing a constituent consisting of the verb and one of the two complements. It might be much better to cut immediately into three constituents:

elected | Washington | president
gave | Frank | money

In general the IC approach has insisted that MOST constructions have exactly TWO constituents. Occasional exceptions are made, the most familiar one being for constructions like *foot-pound-second*. In all such, the three constituents are coordinate. This is not the case in the predicates just discussed. To cut them into three or more constituents directly seems to be a departure from normal IC practice. It is, of course, a switch toward slot-and-filler technique. If the shorter forms like *They gave money* are described in the same framework as *They gave Frank money* (in this case, by saying that the indirect object is lacking, or the like) the method is fully that of the slot-and-filler approach. The latter technique avoids the necessity of deciding order of cuts (or of making cuts) in precisely those places

---

[28] See the discussion of clause patterns in Chapter 13. Predicates such as those shown seem far better cut into three parts at one stage.

where it seems most debatable and least useful. Earlier in this section[29] we saw that the difficulties of full labeling could be avoided by the same change of method. Here are two clear advantages of slot and filler over rigidly dichotomous IC description.

THE WORD AS A SYNTACTIC UNIT

It is commonly assumed that the unit of sentence structure is the word. Indeed, the usual delimitation between morphology and syntax is based on this idea. The grammar within words is morphology; the building together of words into larger structures is syntax. However, there are some places where the words, as usually recognized, are not syntactic units.

The simplest of these is the so-called "possessive" form of the noun. This is traditionally treated as a case form — one of only two — a last remnant of the characteristic Indo-European noun inflection. This it is historically, but it has been very basically reoriented in modern English. Compare the following:

> *Fred's three brothers*
> *his three brothers*
> *the three brothers*

Fred's seems clearly to occupy the same place in the noun phrase as does *his* or *the*, the N − 5 position. This is the place characteristic of determiners, and it seems entirely appropriate to consider *Fred's*, like *his* and *the*, a determiner. Only one determiner can occur in this position in any one phrase. The following are, therefore, all impossible:

> ×*his the three brothers*
> ×*the his three brothers*
> ×*Fred's the three brothers*
> ×*the Fred's three brothers*

---

[29] See pp. 154–155. At that place it was suggested that IC analysis introduced more structure than a slot-and-filler analysis, but that some of it seems to be of very minor significance. This is equivalent to saying that there is too much cutting. There are, however, certain constructions where repeated binary cutting is contrastive, and hence necessary to account for significant structures. This is true of any sequence of noun modifiers of nouns. Contrast:

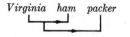

But some other constructions with nouns in the possessive seem to require the presence of two determiners:

> *his neighbor's three brothers*
> *the neighbor's three brothers*
> ×*neighbor's three brothers*

These are, however, no exception. The two determiners are not syntactically on a par, since it is quite clear in the first example that *his* is not a determiner for *brother*, but for *neighbor*. By analogy, the same thing is probably true in the second also: *the* is to be construed with *neighbor*, not with *brother*. In each case, then, *brother* has only one determiner. The difficulty with the third example is that *neighbor* is a kind of noun (singular count) that usually has a determiner.

Now consider the following sentence:

> *The King of England's wife is the queen.*

Certainly *wife* must be the head of the subject, and if so *the king of England's* (the whole phrase!) is the determiner in N − 5 position before it. The sentence is clearly about the king's wife, not about England's wife. With what does -'*s* go? Not with *England*, nor with *king*, but with the whole phrase *the king of England*. This ending can be attached to a single word (as in *Fred's*) or to a phrase consisting of several words. We may conclude that it goes with the phrase *his neighbor* in *his neighbor's brothers*. That is to say, the cut must be between -'*s* and the whole phrase, that is, within a word even when there are two or more words.

An excellent confirmation of this is heard in colloquial English. In speech -'*s* is attached to any sort of noun phrase, those ending with the head noun, those ending with another noun, and those ending with a word not a noun.

1) *the very old man's beard*
2) *the man in the store's pencil*
3) *that man there's car*
4) *a friend of mine's house*

Traditional grammar has generally treated -'*s* as a case suffix on a noun. For this reason, examples like those labeled 3) and 4) have been considered totally ungrammatical, and those like 2) highly suspect. As a result neither type occurs very often in literary English, nor in carefully planned spoken English. But both are fairly frequent in speech, including the speech of highly educated people. I have heard them used in discussion on the floor in professional meetings of English teachers. We have here an example (there are many others) of a traditional grammatical formulation, not wholly in accord with the patterns of the language, making itself felt to a limited extent in changing the actual usage. As always, the change has been partial, largely restricted to written, even to carefully edited, English.

If the cut is always to be between *-'s* and the noun phrase, such words as *man's*, *store's*, *there's*, and *mine's* have no status as syntactic units. It is only the accidental fact that some noun phrases have only a single word (for example, *Fred*) that makes it possible for a word with *-'s* ever to be a syntactic unit.

In a description following the base-and-modifier technique, the issue is usually of little significance. The head noun of the included phrase is, of course, considered as the modifier of the main noun. Any subordinate modifiers are considered as secondary. The *-'s* as the mark of subordination is attached to the noun. The common type of possessive phrase can be diagrammed as follows:

Phrases of type 2) and 3) would, however, cause difficulty. I have never seen one of these diagrammed, and so do not know how the Reed and Kellogg system would handle them.

The *-'s* functions in many ways exactly like a preposition. (It is, of course, partially synonymous with *of*.) It differs only in following the object rather than preceding, and being joined in conventional spelling, rather than written as a separate word. Reed and Kellogg diagramming is not, in general, concerned with order, but only with structural relationships. It might, therefore, be a real improvement to diagram *-'s* in the same way as a preposition. This would make the relationships clearer and provide a solution for all types of possessive phrases:

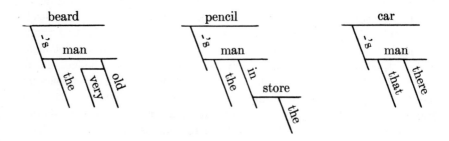

These are now diagrammed exactly like their synonymous equivalents:

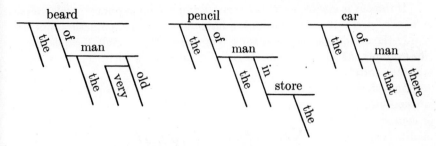

With other types of diagramming there is no great difficulty:

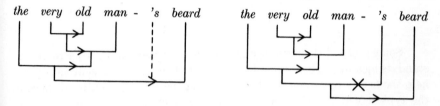

Chapter 8

Structure Signals

Some grasp of the structure of a sentence is essential in order to understand its meaning. There must be some sort of signals in the sentence which help the hearer or listener to discern that structure. As a matter of fact, in the typical sentence there are a number of such signals, often more than are necessary to mark it clearly. Structure signals are of many kinds: the parts of speech, word order, function words, affixes, stress and intonation or word division and punctuation. Only in very special cases does one of these alone suffice to mark structure unambiguously. More typically, all types of signals cooperate, supplementing and reinforcing one another.

REDUNDANCY IN SIGNALS

Because there is so much reinforcement and duplication, it is often possible to omit various structure signals more or less completely, relying on those which remain. The familiar example is the special written style used in headlines and telegrams. Here most function words are omitted, capitalization loses its distinctive value, and punctuation is omitted or curtailed. The result may, of course, be ambiguity. The now classic example[1] is:

SHIP SAILS TOMORROW

If this is recast into normal written form, at least one function word must be added. This addition immediately removes the ambiguity. There must be at least two ways to fill it out, corresponding to the competing meanings of the original:

The ship sails tomorrow.
Ship the sails tomorrow.

[1] C. C. Fries, *The Structure of English*, 1952, p. 62. Similar examples can be found in almost any newspaper.

This example, while far from unique, is certainly unusual. Most head-lines and telegrams are quite clear, or only exceptionally misinterpreted. The signals provided by the function words are dispensable because they are in effect duplicated by others which remain in headline style. Indeed, the example just cited would be less ambiguous in use than it is when cited out of context. One of the two interpretations is highly unlikely except in a telegram addressed to a sail-maker or ships' chandler. If context is given, most ambiguous examples become appreciably less ambiguous.

We tend to think of statements as either ambiguous or unambiguous. Is it, then, meaningful to speak of something as becoming less ambiguous? If we consider that a sentence either has a meaning or has two meanings, or none, or several, then "more ambiguous" and "less ambiguous" are unacceptable. But the facts are that sentences do not HAVE meanings in some fixed and determinable way. In practice they suggest meanings to the hearer or reader. An unambiguous sentence is one which suggests one meaning with such overwhelming probability that the chance is very small that any other will be perceived. An ambiguous sentence is one which sug-gests two or more, each with sufficient probability that there is a significant chance of a hearer or reader deciding upon it. In almost any sentence there is some chance, perhaps exceedingly small, of an unusual meaning being accepted. In this sense, then, sentences can be more or less ambiguous.

As a general rule, structure signals do not specifically label sentence structures. They merely indicate that a certain type of structure is possible. For example, the function word *the*, one of our commonest signals, usually precedes a noun. (There are constructions, all relatively infrequent, where this is not the case.[2]) The occurrence of a *the* in a sentence, then, indicates a relatively high probability that one of the following words will be a noun. Normally the noun will follow very soon, perhaps as the next word, though there are often adjectives or other modifiers between *the* and the noun. The determiner never signals which of the following words is the noun, and occasionally the noun may follow at some considerable distance. Moreover, even if the noun were identified conclusively, the structure would not necessarily be specified completely. Nouns occur in sentences in various functions. The presence of a single structure signal, therefore, does not identify a structure, but only suggests a number of possibilities. Often it enables a hearer or reader to assess roughly the probability of each of several structures.

The same thing is true of the parts of speech of the major vocabulary items. Not many English words can be assigned unambiguously to a single part of speech. For most of them, however, one part of speech is very much more probable than any other. Few words are at all common in more than

---

[2] The clearest examples are those similar to: *The more, the merrier. The* may also occur in nominal phrases which lack nouns: *The poor we have always with us.* Here *poor* seems best treated as an adjective, though some grammarians would consider it a noun.

two or three. Some sort of a guess is, therefore, possible as to the part of speech of every English word, even out of context. Various signals outside the word, including the possible parts of speech of nearby words, weight the probabilities and generally allow a reliable guess as to the classification of a word in context.

How this works can be seen clearly by looking more closely at the telegram cited above: SHIP SAILS TOMORROW. The problem arises because SHIP can be either a noun or a verb, SAILS either a noun or a verb, and TOMORROW either an adverb or a noun. Eight structures would be possible taking all combinations, but most of these are evidently impossible or quite unlikely. For example, any sequence containing two verbs, particularly these two, is improbable and would invariably have some other pattern of affixes than —— ——s, perhaps —— ——ing as in *keep going*. Noun — Verb — Noun is a common enough pattern (DOG BITES MAN), but SHIP is the wrong kind of noun for this pattern, and TOMORROW is much more likely to be an adverb than a noun in any case. Only two patterns seem to fit: Noun — Verb — Adverb, and Verb — Noun — Adverb. Both work well. But substitution of almost any synonym for either SHIP or SAILS would eliminate the ambiguity:

SHIP DEPARTS TOMORROW   SEND SAILS TOMORROW
STEAMER SAILS TOMORROW   SHIP CANVAS TOMORROW

The ambiguity, then, arises from the fact that both SHIP and SAILS can be either noun or verb, in fact the correct kind of verb, and further that both the grammatically possible sentence patterns make acceptable sense with these particular words.

Now consider the insertion of a *the*. The probability of the following word being a noun is increased appreciably. At the same time the probability of the same word being a verb is greatly diminished. Verbs, other than forms with the *-ed* or *-ing* endings, seldom stand between determiners and nouns. In whatever position the *the* is inserted, it serves to greatly increase the probability of one interpretation and to decrease that of the other even more. Once *the* is added, either form is a typical unambiguous sentence — one in which one structure is very much more reasonable than any other. But even so, no one can guarantee that no other interpretation is possible. Once in a while sentences which seem quite clear turn out to be open to some unexpected analysis, and, occasionally, this strange structure seems actually demanded by the context.

When a telegram like SHIP SAILS TOMORROW is reformed into normal written English, a determiner is inserted. But there is another equally important change. The first letter is capitalized in contrast to the remainder, and punctuation is added. These are important structure signals in written English. Even without them, the sentence structure would be quite adequately marked. In most instances, punctuation and capitalization merely reinforce the other signals. But there are occasions, of course, when these signals help materially in marking structure of otherwise inconclusively marked sentences.

If instead of normal written form, the transfer is made to normal spoken form, other signals are added. These consist of patterns of stress and intonation. Nothing can be said by a speaker of English without these accompaniments. However, their very ordinariness should not cause anyone to discount their importance. Stress and intonation carry a much greater share of the signaling load in speech than do capitalization and punctuation in written language. They may be viewed as corroborating a decision made from other signals, but it would in many cases be better to think of them as the primary signals, most of the others serving to reinforce a decision based on the stress and intonation.

If all the available structure signals are taken together, many sentences are effectively unambiguous. Indeed, many of them are so redundantly marked that a good part of the signals might easily be dispensed with. It is this fact that makes possible ordinary spoken and written communication. Hearing conditions are seldom perfect. The spoken message comes to the hearer at a very rapid rate, several words a second, with all the accompanying stress and intonation patterns. The hearer must interpret it as it comes. Only rarely can he store part of it to meditate over at leisure.

Seldom can all the signals be perceived infallibly and evaluated correctly. Instead, the accomplished hearer depends on picking up just enough to meet his needs. Whatever is missed is no loss; the remaining signals will carry the message. A less-accomplished hearer (for example, a recent learner), less thoroughly conversant with the signals, cannot do this. He is more vulnerable to difficulty from bad hearing conditions. The speaker, for his part, must take care as he speaks that enough signals are given that the hearer can understand, allowing for the inevitable loss. Spoken language, to be intelligible under normal conditions, must be redundant. The structure signals must overlap and reinforce one another.

Written language is somewhat different. The reader can adjust his speed so that he perceives an adequate part of the signals provided. He can go back and look again when anything is unclear, or when a later passage seems to contradict his interpretation of an earlier. Therefore, less redundancy is needed. The writer can be more parsimonious. He can expect the reader to pick up almost all the signals that are given. He will, indeed, often deliberately avoid giving the same oversupply that he would unhesitatingly provide in speaking.

By the same token, the writer has an obligation to greater accuracy and precision. Errors are not so easily covered up and compensated for. The reader demands more care and exactness in written material than he has any right to expect in speech. Most written English is edited, often very meticulously; most spoken English is extempore and unplanned. This is as it should be: the system of written English has grown up around a norm of editing and permanence; that of spoken English around a norm of temporary improvisation.

This difference between spoken and written English is fundamental. They meet different requirements in different ways. One provides the maximum amount of structure signals to overcome difficulties in transmission and still guarantee an adequate minimum at the hearer's end. The other uses a minimum of signals with much higher precision and efficiency. It is, therefore, an immature kind of writing which follows closely the patterns of spoken English. Mature writing is different. It is better adjusted to the peculiar conditions of written communication, and is characterized by far greater economy and precision than is either possible or required in speech.

The teaching of composition must involve making students aware of the differences in the basic functioning of the two systems, and it must impart specific skills in using the devices employed in good written English. This is not alone a requirement for "creative writing"; good straightforward exposition requires a far different kind of attention to details than comes with normal fluent speaking. Moreover, reading beyond the most elementary level involves learning to see and evaluate structure signals more precisely than is needed in speech, relying less on the redundancy so necessary for understandable spoken communication.

INTONATION

Almost every written sentence, particularly if isolated from its context, can be read in more than one way, often in a number. These differ in most cases only in intonation. They may carry, however, subtle but significant differences of connotation, though in some instances a native speaker is left in doubt as to whether two alternative pronunciations are alike in their implications or not. Moreover, there are obvious differences in intonation from one dialect to another. Occasionally, these cause difficulties in communication, but more often they are taken in stride, and the loss of meaning, if any, is hardly noticed.

These complexities obscure the importance of intonation as a structure signal. Few speakers of English have any accurate idea of the extent to which they actually depend on it for the understanding of speech, and even fewer are able to make any significant observations about it. The variations in patterns also render the written discussion of intonation peculiarly difficult or even risky, since every example adduced can be misidentified.

Not only are there difficulties in identifying the phenomena that are under discussion, but there are also a number of unresolved problems in the analysis of intonation, some of them of basic theoretical or practical importance. Probably no segment of language has been so resistant to systematic formulation or so variously interpreted by investigators. The disagreements have ranged from details of statement to fundamental questions of the place of intonation in the total system of a language. But there has been general agreement on the importance of intonation as a system of structure signals in speech.

The most widely recognized unit in this system is the intonation contour, a pattern of pronunciation which spreads over a portion of speech of from one to perhaps a dozen syllables in length. Each contour has a clearly marked end, after which, if speech continues, another contour follows. For the present, we may indicate an intonation contour simply by a line drawn above the words to which it applies and marked at its termination with an arrowhead.

While this symbolization overlooks many features, it will serve to make clear the first of the two important functions of intonation contours: to delimit certain stretches of speech. For example, the following sentences, though containing the same words in the same order, are quite different:

$$\overrightarrow{\hspace{4cm}}$$
John Henry is coming tomorrow.

$$\overrightarrow{\hspace{1cm}}\ \overrightarrow{\hspace{3cm}}$$
John, Henry is coming tomorrow.

The most obvious difference is the presence of one intonation contour spreading over all five words in the first, but two contours dividing the second into two unequal parts. A native speaker of English recognizes this as signaling a division between *John* and the rest of the sentence in the second pronunciation. A second pair of examples shows much the same contrast:

$$\overrightarrow{\hspace{4cm}}$$
When is the coffee ready?

$$\overrightarrow{\hspace{1.5cm}}\ \overrightarrow{\hspace{2.5cm}}$$
When? Is the coffee ready?

As a matter of fact, examples of this kind are not easy to find. Most sequences of words can be divided into major syntactic units in only one way. When contours are deployed in different ways over the same words, it is most often only a matter of alternative pronunciations of sentences that are structurally the same. These facts must not be interpreted as suggesting that the delimiting function of intonation is unimportant. Intonation might well bear a very heavy share of the burden of marking structure without often doing so alone. Hearing conditions are seldom perfect, and the hearer is always faced with an elaborate task in detecting and interpreting all the signals that are presented to him. He does not pay equal attention to all. There is some reason to believe that he puts his heaviest reliance on the intonation, often conforming his understanding of other signals to the basic outline he derives from it. Many of the features which, it would seem, might allow him to guess the intonation are, instead, guessed at from the intonation.

In reading, of course, the process is reversed. Intonation is not given on the printed page, but a host of other signals are. A skilled oral reader is one who can accurately and facilely supply a series of intonation contours to fit the other markers of structure given in a passage. Such a person, reasoning from his feel for the nature of the oral-reading process, is likely to underestimate the significance of intonation as the dominant structure signal in speech.

A really crucial experiment to demonstrate the importance of intonation is difficult to design. On the one hand, intonation is an inevitable feature of spoken English; there is no way to speak a sample without it. The best one can do is to use a set of intonation contours totally out of step with the syntax of the passage. Few people, if they understand the passage, can do this easily, and most will introduce additional distortions of other kinds when they try. The best way is to read the words as a list, putting a separate contour on each, the so-called list intonation. To read a passage in this way effectively disguises the structure, so that a hearer, if he listens to it as he ordinarily would to speech, may not understand it at all.

On the other hand, the experimental situation may cause a literate person to shift to a quite unnatural way of listening. Instead of relying on intonation as he normally would, he changes to a kind of auditory reading. He listens for the individual words, visualizes them, and then, as it were, reads from his image. He makes use of structure signals in much the same way that he would if they were presented to him in print. That a literate person can understand passages read aloud in list intonation is not evidence that intonation is of minor importance. Instead, the fact that the operation is extremely tiring, and hence can only be continued for a short while, is evidence that this way of understanding speech is very unnatural. It is more comparable to the way we understand messages spelled out orally, than it is to the way we normally listen.

Deliberate use of list intonation is not a very important phenomenon, but a similar unintentional distortion is. One type of poor reading is characterized by recognition or sounding out of individual words, one by one. The child then reads them aloud to himself, some or even many of them with individual listlike contours. When he does group words under a contour, the grouping may be out of accord with the writer's intended structure. Word recognition may be accurate and fluent, but comprehension poor.[3] The intonation patterns supplied by such a reader do not reinforce other structure signals, but contradict them. Intonation is such

---

[3] As a matter of fact, word recognition is usually poor. A reader of this kind cannot make use of the contextual clues which are so important in word recognition, even for the best readers.

a powerful signal in spoken English that the new reader cannot disregard it. His interpretation of the passage is inevitably strongly influenced by the intonation which he supplies as he reads. If that does not connect words in a meaningful way, the child is unlikely to perceive any meaning. If habits of listlike reading become entrenched, his understanding is permanently impaired by distortions of his own making.

From the very beginning, reading instruction must help the child to respond to graphic signals of structure much as he already responds unconsciously to speech signals, and hence to supply a meaningful intonation contour. As he later learns to read silently, the perception of structure must continue to play a part, though the oral interpretation of structure in terms of intonation recedes. The child must learn to use all the structure signals in written English by first translating them into the correct structural patterns of fluent normal speech.[4] Any failure here has serious, perhaps lifelong, consequences.

Delimitation of structurally significant stretches of speech does not exhaust the functions of intonation. In many instances a number of different intonation contours are possible as accompaniments to the same sequence of words. In such cases, the choice may signal something of the nature of the construction, or may alter the meaning in some way. Intonation, therefore, has also a distinguishing function.

To demonstrate this, it will be necessary to use a somewhat less crude transcription of the intonation, one that will show the contrasts between contours. Instead of a straight line, we will use a line that rises and falls with the pitch of the voice, writing it over a dotted line which may be taken as indicating a normal pitch of the particular speaker. These transcriptions are still schematic, omitting a great deal of detail.

Among the possible renditions of the examples discussed above are the following:

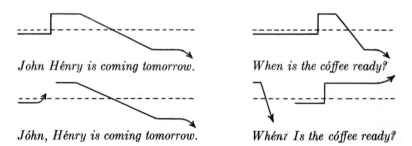

John Hénry is coming tomorrow.   *When is the cóffee ready?*

Jóhn, Hénry is coming tomorrow.   *Whén? Is the cóffee ready?*

---

[4] The model of translation suggested on pages 95–97 was shown on pages 110–111 to apply to the relationship between speech and writing. One significant contribution which linguistics may make to reading instruction may center on some such formulation as this. Reading teachers are, of course, aware of the problem, but can probably profit from a more sophisticated and penetrating formulation of it.

The single contour which spreads over *John Henry is coming tomorrow* and marks it as a single structure is very similar to that which does the same thing with *when is the coffee ready*. It starts at the average pitch, rises at the syllable bearing the main stress of the sentence, and then falls until the end is low and trails off. When these sequences of words are cut into two pieces, however, the results are different. *Henry is coming tomorrow* receives much the same intonation as before — the preliminary stretch at average pitch is merely missing, there being nothing before the main stress. *When is the coffee ready?* and *Is the coffee ready?* are both questions, but quite different in meaning. This is partly signaled by the use of entirely different contours.

Many of the contrasts between intonation contours are matters of sequence signaling. That is, the contour not only delimits certain stretches within the stream of speech but also gives some indication of the connection of many of the pieces to those that precede or follow. For example, a contour delimits each clause in the following passages. In addition, the contour on the first clause marks it as included in the same sentence with the following, or as forming a separate sentence:

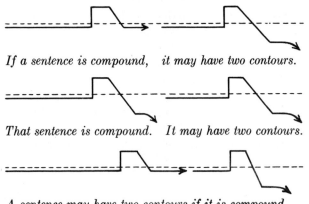

If a sentence is compound,   it may have two contours.

That sentence is compound.   It may have two contours.

A sentence may have two contours if it is compound.

In the first example, the contour on *if a sentence is compound* does not directly mark it as a subordinate clause, but only as an element that is somehow incomplete without some following element. As the third example shows, this initial incomplete clause may be the main clause. The same contour is often used on the subject of a sentence, and then usually signals that a predicate is to follow:

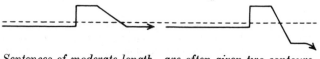

Sentences of moderate length   are often given two contours.

As the Bloomfield tradition developed during the forties and fifties, it was insisted that everything linguistically relevant in speech must be separated into its phonologic and its morphologic (or grammatical) aspects. Moreover, everything which is phonologically significant must be statable in terms of phonemes and their arrangements, and everything grammatically significant in terms of morphemes and their arrangements. English intonation can be readily shown to be significant on both levels. There must be, the Bloomfieldians reasoned, morphemes of intonation and these must be analyzable into phonemes.

The two contours on *John Henry is coming tomorrow* and *when is the coffee ready* differ in what seem to be trivial respects. The high point is nearer the end in one, nearer the beginning in the other. This seems to be determined by the position of the word that gets the main stress in the sentence. The two are best considered as only variants of the same fundamental contour, that is, as two allomorphs of one morpheme. Much the same can be said for that on *Henry is coming tomorrow*. Here the stressed syllable is initial in its contour, and the prestress portion seems to be automatically dropped. This contour can be considered another allomorph of the same morpheme. The situation is parallel to that with the plural morpheme, /-iz/ in *noses* /nowziz/ and /-z/ in *eyes* /ayz/, where the form of the suffix is predictable if the environment is known.

After allowance has been made for such environmental variation, the contours can be seen to be essentially morphemes. It is they that seem to signal structure or to carry meaning — that is, the contours perform the grammatical functions of the intonation system.

According to standard Bloomfieldian views, the phonemes of intonation should be found by comparing minimal pairs of contours, that is, by examining contours that are morphemically different but alike in all but some single feature of pronunciation. The following dialog includes two such minimal pairs:

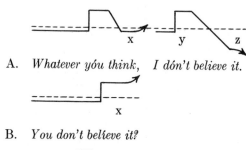

A. *Whatever yóu think,   I dón't believe it.*

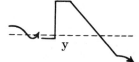

B. *You don't belíeve it?*

A. *Nó,   I dón't believe it!*

Two contours differ only in the pitch level at the points marked x; two others only at the points marked y. These two minimal pairs, provided they can be corroborated by others like them, establish three contrasting pitch levels. That at z is a fourth, seeming to contrast with the two marked x. We can be less sure of this from the data at hand because there is another difference which must be taken account of. However, similar comparison of many contours under properly controlled conditions will lead to the identification of four contrastive pitch levels. Each of these is subject to some variation (omitted in our diagrams, but a real hurdle for the analyst just getting into the problem). Much of this is predictable, and can be taken as allophonic. The four pitch levels are, therefore, phonemes. In the most familiar transcription these are written /1 2 3 4/.[5]

A second kind of contrast can be found between contours, at the end, in the portion indicated by arrowheads in the examples above. Three kinds can be recognized. These are sometimes transcribed as / | ‖ # / and named from their symbols "single-bar juncture", "double-bar juncture", and "double-cross juncture". An alternative transcription uses /→ ↗ ↘/ with the names "sustained terminal", "rising terminal", and "fading terminal". The differences are only in symbols and terminology.

The phonetic manifestations of these terminals are complex and little understood. Most obvious are features of timing. The preceding vowels, or in some cases consonants, are lengthened in various degrees. /↗/ is heard by many as accompanied by a sudden short rise in pitch, and /↘/ by a longer fading out of pitch and voice. Terminals are commonly interpreted as pauses, but they are not necessarily even accompanied by any cessation of speech. When a pause does occur, however, one of the terminals always precedes.

In most instances there are only two or three places in a contour where pitch contrasts are significant. A contour can, therefore, be indicated by symbols for two or three pitch levels and one terminal. The way in which these are conventionally written can be illustrated in the dialog used above:[6]

A.   ²Whatever ³you think²↗ ²I ³don't believe it¹↘
B.   ²You don't ³believe it³↗
A.   ³No²↗ ²I ⁴don't believe it¹↘

These contours may be abstracted as /2 3 2 ↗/, /2 3 1 ↘/, /2 3 3 ↗/, /3 2 ↗/, and /2 4 1 ↘/.

---

[5] The analysis of intonation and stress followed here was first fully formulated in George L. Trager and Henry L. Smith, Jr., *An Outline of English Structure*, 1951. It has subsequently been followed in a large number of publications, sometimes with minor modifications. Perhaps the best introduction to this analysis is to be found in James Sledd, *A Short Introduction to English Grammar*, 1959.

[6] Several other readings of this dialogue are possible. One with ³I don't believe it¹↘ is perhaps commoner but less useful for our purposes.

Intonation may delimit constructions, it may distinguish one from another when they are superficially alike, and it may mark the connection of one unit to another within the largest structures of speech. These are grammatical functions, and intonation is pre-eminently a structure-marking system. Yet intonation also has nongrammatical functions. It may reveal something of the emotional state of the speaker, it may single out some element in a passage for special prominence, or it may indicate some semantic twist, as when *yes* is said in a way that clearly means 'no' or 'maybe'.

Nonlinguists certainly exaggerate these latter uses of intonation, often being largely unaware of its grammatical significance. Most often this is done by assigning the rubric "emphasis" to an ill-assorted collection of phenomena. Often what is so labeled is really structure signaling. For example, one way to make a sentence emphatic is to use /2 4 1 ↘/ where /2 3 1 ↘/ might otherwise be appropriate. It is the choice of the one when both are grammatically possible that marks emphasis. But, on the basis of this, we tend to label as emphatic every sentence with the high pitch transcribed /4/, among them the last line of the dialog above. We might attempt to show this "emphasis" in writing "I *don't* believe it!", with italics and the exclamation point. If this sentence is emphatic at all, it is only in a very special sense, for the choice of /2 3 1 ↘/ or /2 4 1 ↘/ is not presented here. After a confirmation question like *You don't believe it?*, /2 4 1 ↘/, or some similar contour, must be used. In this context, therefore, the contour at least verges on being merely a sequence signal, showing that the sentence is indeed advanced as an answer to the preceding question, that is, that the dialog continues normally.

Such examples could be multiplied. They show first that the common understanding of the function of intonation is at best partial, inadequate as a basis for investigating the structure of speech, and second that it is exceedingly difficult to draw a line between the grammatical and non-grammatical uses of intonation. Yet no adequate analysis will be possible until this discrimination can be made satisfactorily.

One reason for our difficulty lies in the grammarian's preoccupation with sentences. Intonation is no respecter of sentence boundaries. The connections signaled extend from sentence to sentence, even from speaker to speaker within a dialog. But if this makes the elucidation of intonation difficult, it also makes it challenging. The structure of discourse is a frontier for linguistic research today. Intonation may well be one of the keys.

STRESS

There is a second system of structure signals peculiar to speech. This consists of stress phenomena. As with the intonation, this system combines two grammatical functions. It may assist in delimiting certain units in a sentence, and it may serve to identify the constructions that are so delimited.

The latter function is the easier one to demonstrate. There are many sequences of two morphemes of the type of *round* plus *house*, *black* plus *bird* (an adjective followed by a noun) or, less often, *goose* plus *egg* (two nouns). With nearly equal stress — the dictionary would mark them as 'round 'house, 'black 'bird, 'goose 'egg — these are noun phrases. They mean precisely what one would predict from the meaning of the elements: 'a house which is round', 'a bird which is black', 'an egg laid by a goose' (because the meaning is thus predictable the dictionary does not list these!). But if the stresses are less nearly equal — the dictionary lists them as 'round,house, 'black,bird, and 'goose ,egg — these are compound nouns, and the meaning is not predictable: 'a structure for sheltering railroad engines', 'a specific kind of bird', 'zero'. There is a discernible difference in the stress in the two meanings, and it is this difference which enables a speaker of English to distinguish the two, at least when hearing conditions are good. Note, however, that the stress difference does not signal the meaning directly. Rather it indicates the construction. Noun phrases usually have predictable meanings; compound nouns more often do not. The stress merely marks the contrast between noun phrases and compounds.[7]

Looked at from another point of view, these contrasts enable us to establish phonemes of stress. The difference between the dictionary marking with ' and with , is clearly phonemic. A third phonemic stress is that which the dictionary leaves unmarked. Minimal pairs are hard to find, but compare the nickname *Blacky* — 'blacky — with 'black,bird. Both have two syllables. They differ in the stress on the second.

This system of stress markings allows the dictionary to make all the distinctions which are necessary for its purposes. But when attention shifts from single words to phrases it becomes necessary to make one further distinction. For most speakers, the two stresses in noun phrases like *black bird* are not equal. The weaker of the two is always stronger than that in the compound *blackbird*. It is, therefore, an intermediate stress for which the dictionary system provides no symbol, since it does not need to distinguish it from primary.

American linguists have been accustomed to marking stress with a different set of marks: /´/ and /ˆ/ for the stronger and weaker varieties that the dictionary marks ', /ˋ/ for what the dictionary marks ,, and /ˇ/ for the stress left unmarked in the dictionary. They are called primary, secondary, tertiary, and weak.

Using these marks, noun phrases are either *bláck bîrd, róund hôuse, góose êgg,* or *blâck bírd, rôund hóuse, gôose égg.* Which of the two patterns

---

[7] The relation of stress to construction is more complex than stated here, but the general principle is valid.

occurs is determined by the context. Both are normal patterns for phrases, only rarely occurring in compounds. The compounds are *bláckbìrd, róundhòuse, góose ègg*. We can abstract the stress contours: /ˈˆ/, /ˆˈ/, and /ˈˋ/.

Another example of the function of stress in distinguishing different constructions of the same elements can be seen with sequences of morphemes like *set* plus *up*. With /ˋ ˈ/, this is a verb phrase consisting of a verb stem and a closely associated "adverb". Though it is possible for a word or phrase to come between, the two elements are so closely connected that the combination can be called a two-word verb. With /ˈ ˋ/, it is a compound noun, usually written as one word *setup*. Stress here has a distinguishing function, though one rather different from that in the examples first discussed. There is no contrast in the internal relationships of the two elements, but only in the external relationships of the resulting compound, that is, in its part of speech. A similar contrast is used with a number of other pairs, one a verb and one a noun. Many of these are always written solid and are either unanalyzable in English or consist of a prefix and a stem that does not occur by itself. The verbs generally have /ˇ ˈ/ and the nouns /ˈ ˇ/: *permit, conduct, survey,* and so on.

Monosyllabic nouns pronounced in isolation always have primary stress, as indeed have all words. Two monosyllabic nouns in a noun modifier and head noun construction may have either /ˆ ˈ/ or /ˈ ˆ/— the choice is usually determined by the context. Thus when *góose* and *égg* are joined into a noun phrase, one of the primary stresses must be reduced to secondary, giving *góose êgg* or *gôose égg*. Two longer nouns may be joined in the same way. In such an instance, there must be a similar reduction of stress. Normally this affects only the primary stress. *Bláckbìrd* plus *tráp* gives either *blâckbìrd tráp* or *bláckbìrd trâp*. Adjectives joined to nouns behave in much the same way, thus *bláck* plus *bírdtràp* gives either *blâck bírdtràp* or *bláck bîrdtràp*.

The same thing is true if the elements being combined are themselves phrases rather than single words. For example, in isolation the phrase *mòre béautĭfŭl* would normally be pronounced with /ˋ ˈ/, the weak stresses on *béautĭfŭl* being unaffected. If this is combined with *gírls*, only one of the primaries is changed. One possibility is *mòre bêautĭfŭl gírls*. A similar sequence of words with a different stress pattern can be obtained by combining *móre* plus *béautĭfŭl* plus *gírls*. One possible result is *môre bêautĭfŭl gírls*. The contrast in stress patterns on the two pronunciations of *more beautiful girls* indicates a difference in internal construction. /ˆ ˆ ˈ/ marks a noun phrase with two modifiers; /ˋ ˆ ˈ/ marks a noun phrase with one modifier itself containing a modifier.

Stress, thus, has a combination of delimiting and distinctive functions somewhat similar to that of intonation, but operating in much smaller constructions.[8] Some of the possibilities can be more clearly seen in the following noun phrases. *More* and *odd* are alike in that each can be either a modifier within the noun phrase directly, or a modifier within a phrase which is itself a modifier. They differ in the position which they take, both in the noun phrase as a whole and in the included modifying phrase. The structure signaled is diagrammed in both slot-and-filler and IC techniques:

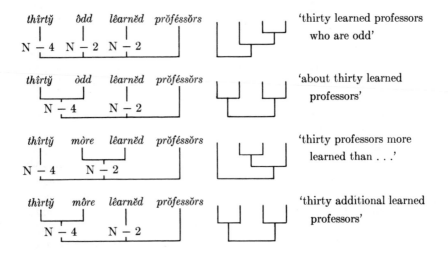

'thirty learned professors who are odd'

'about thirty learned professors'

'thirty professors more learned than . . .'

'thirty additional learned professors'

The overlapping and intersection which has just been illustrated poses problems in dividing stress patterns into morphemes. Many individual stresses have a part in two or more structures, in each contributing to the signaling of relationships. There is, accordingly, little agreement as to the best way of formulating the facts, though most linguists agree in recognizing the importance of stress patterns as structure signals. The disagreements go beyond simple matters of technique of description, since stress is a crucial case in the discussion of the relation of phonology and grammar. Most of this discussion is outside the scope of this book, and could not in any case be fully treated in the space available.

THE CONVENTIONS

Replacing the stress and intonation of speech, there are found in writing a number of structure signals which are collectively referred to as

---

[8] Closely associated with stress, particularly in its delimiting function, is a phenomenon known as open transition or plus juncture. This is in some respects like a terminal, hence some linguists speak of four junctures in English. Open transition is one way of accounting for the contrast between *grade A* /greyd⁺ey/ and *gray day* /grey⁺dey/ or *missed rain* /mist⁺reyn/ and *Miss Trayne* /mis⁺treyn/.

"the conventions". These include punctuation, capitalization, and word division. The two whole systems, stress and intonation on one hand and conventions on the other, are counterparts in the sense that they perform the same functions in the two forms of the language. But it must be emphasized that the parallel is only general; the individual elements do not match.

Punctuation has a delimiting function, much as does intonation. Each mark serves to divide one portion of the text from another. Two very basic differences are very easily overlooked, however. First, a punctuation mark stands at the point of division; intonation contours spread over stretches, and it is the termination of one and the start of another that marks the boundary. Literate people are tempted to give too great prominence to the terminals, taking them, on the analogy of punctuation marks, to be direct indications of division points. Terminals are integral parts of whole contours, and it is the whole contour that signals structure. Second, it is possible to have two or three punctuation marks at the same boundary, marking two or three levels of structure. Intonation contours cannot be superimposed in this way, and the marking of a hierarchy of structures must be much more complex and indirect. It is, however, provided for by a large selection of contours which not only delimit but also mark certain relationships between successive spans of speech.

There are also many differences in detail. The two systems do not always cut in the same places. Simple sentences of moderate length provide an excellent case in point. Such sentences frequently carry two intonation contours, one over the subject and the second over the predicate, thus clearly marking the break between the two major sentence constituents:

^{2}*The three old ladies* ^{3}*upstairs*^{2} $\rightarrow$ ^{2}*own a boxer dog with a* ^{3}*mean temper.*^{1}↘

There may be more than two, in which case some additional cut within either the subject or the predicate is marked. The following seems to me a somewhat more natural reading:

^{2}*The three old ladies* ^{3}*upstairs*^{2} $\rightarrow$ ^{2}*own a boxer* ^{3}*dog*^{2} $\rightarrow$ ^{2}*with a* ^{3}*mean temper.*^{1}↘

The rules of punctuation, however, allow nothing at all comparable. Such a sentence has terminal punctuation, of course, but no single punctuation mark can come between subject and predicate in any normal sentence. The reason for the proviso "single" is that under some circumstances a sentence modifier may be inserted between subject and predicate. In this case it is usually punctuated by commas on both sides, though dashes, parens, or the like are equally possible. All these, however, must occur in pairs; they are AROUND[9] some element rather than BETWEEN subject and predicate.

> ^{2}*The three old ladies* ^{3}*upstairs,*^{2} → ^{1}*they* ^{1}*say,*^{1} → ^{2}*own a boxer dog with a* ^{3}*mean temper.*^{1}↘

Punctuation also has a distinguishing function. The simplest example is the contrast between the period and the question mark. These are essentially alike in their major delimiting function, both coming at the end of sentences. They mark two kinds of sentences. Intonation may do much the same thing, but there are differences both in the classification of sentences and in the way they are marked.

For example, statements and questions consisting of the same words may be distinguished in writing solely by punctuation and in speech solely by intonation:

> ^{2}*It's* ^{3}*raining.*^{1}↘ ^{2}*It's* ^{3}*raining?*^{23}↗

It is tempting to assume that /2 3 3 ↗/ is the speech equivalent of the question mark. There are, however, large numbers of questions, including most of those which start with "*wh*-words", that most commonly have /2 3 1 ↘/ intonations; these are also written with the question mark. The same words may also be said with the /2 3 3 ↗/ contour, but always with a different meaning. Punctuation does not distinguish the two types of questions:

> ^{2}*What* ^{3}*is it?*^{1}↘ ^{2}*What* ^{3}*is it?*^{23}↗

The use of contrasting intonation contours, then, does not coincide at all closely with the use of contrasting punctuations. Each system must be described in its own terms. The translation equivalence between them can be stated effectively only after each system is understood.

In written English, if a sentence requires two punctuation marks, the second one is usually a period, this being the typical final mark. The first one may be a comma, a semicolon, or a dash. In spoken English, there is no comparable rule. We may take /2 3 1 ↘/ as a typical final contour. It is often preceded by /2 3 2 →/, a pattern which signals connectedness or incompletion. For example:

> ^{2}*Whatever you* ^{3}*do*^{2} → ^{2}*is all right with* ^{3}*me.*^{1}↘

But it is also possible to have two closely linked contours of which the first is /2 3 1 ↘/ and the second /1 1 1 ↘/ or /1 1 2 ↗/. The latter is a contour which signals connectedness, but often to a preceding stretch, which may have a final contour.

> "*It is raining*," *said Fred.* ^{2}*It is* ^{3}*raining*^{1}↘ ^{1}*said* ^{1}*Fred*^{1}↘

---

[9] One member of a pair of surrounding punctuation marks may be displaced by a higher-ranking mark and so disappear, but this in no wise vitiates the principle.

Intonation allows us to put "emphasis" on some particular element in the sentence. The normal literary punctuation does not.[10] The exclamation mark can go only at the place where some other final punctuation might go, and so serves to put emphasis on the sentence as a whole. This is basically different! The function of localized emphasis is discharged by italicizing, or the like. This is used much more sparingly than the various emphatic intonation contours. Moreover, italics have other functions totally unrelated to emphatic intonation, for example, to mark unassimilated foreign words.

Word division and hyphenation are comparable in many respects to the stress patterns of speech, but no equation of details is possible. Almost any of the numerous stress patterns that join pairs of elements can be found paralleled by words written with a space, or hyphenated, or written solid. Looked at from the point of view of spoken English, these conventions are haphazard or unreasonable. From the point of view of marking structure in written English, they are a little better, but still not entirely consistent. For example, compound adjectives are commonly written with a hyphen when the corresponding compound noun is solid: *red-headed woodpecker, a redhead.* There is often very little justification for the presence or absence of a hyphen as in the old question about the reason for the hyphen in *bird-cage.*[11] Other things being equal, hyphenation implies closer joining than space, and solid writing even closer, but many special situations arise.

Capitalization not infrequently serves indirectly to distinguish different structural patterns that are distinguished in speech by differences of stress, but this is fortuitous. Its major function is to mark a class of words — proper nouns. Many of these, particularly familiar ones,[12] take a stress contour appropriate to compounds. The same elements when not capitalized are a sequence of adjective plus noun, or noun plus noun, and receive the appropriate stress pattern. The difference can be heard in pairs like *White House, white house, New Jersey, new jersey, Long Island, long island.*

The use of capitalization to distinguish proper nouns is a useful signal, though often redundant since proper nouns have different patterns of

[10] There is an interesting punctuation convention in scientific writing largely unknown elsewhere. An exclamation mark in parens is inserted after a word or phrase to give a kind of emphasis at that particular point: *The normal* (!) *literary punctuation is different.* This indicates that the statement very specifically applies to normal usage, implying that another pattern also occurs but must definitely be considered exceptional. Similarly: *The normal* (?) *literary punctuation is different.* This would indicate that the writer has some doubt as to whether this is actually normal or not. He is questioning this one fact, but asserting the remainder of the sentence.

[11] It is for the bird to sit on!

[12] For example, *White House, Long Island, Red Bank, Main Street.* Almost all of these vary from speaker to speaker. However, the most familiar usually take stress patterns typical of compounds; the less familiar take phrase patterns. A shift in an individual's pronunciation can often be observed as a name becomes familiar.

determiners. If the class of every word could be marked, instead of being merely suggested, much of the structural ambiguity that occasionally plagues written English would disappear. This would be tantamount to appending to every written sentence a partial parsing. Perhaps if only one class can be marked, the proper noun is the most useful, since it is the class of words most often unknown (as specific vocabulary items) to the reader. When presented with a sentence like the following:

> The party camped in Zandfontein.

the reader immediately recognizes the class of *Zandfontein*, whether he has ever seen it before or not. The sentence is, therefore, not structurally comparable to:

> The party camped in desperation.
> The party camped in tents.

A strange proper name preceded by *in* is probably a place name.[13] If he needs further information, the reader turns without hesitation to a gazetteer or an atlas, rather than to a dictionary.

The German system is rather different, but also very useful to the reader. All nouns are capitalized and only a short list of very familiar words other than nouns are so treated in the interior of sentences. Thus a whole major class of words is clearly marked in most occurrences. There is, of course, no such direct marking of nouns in spoken German.

Capitalization of proper names in English, or of all nouns in German, and the marking in both languages of all questions with a question mark are examples of structure signals in written language that have no exact counterparts in speech. They do not suggest equivalents in spoken language which in turn suggest structure. Instead they signal (or suggest) grammatical structures directly. Written language is, at least at these points, autonomous, not simply a reflection of speech.

PARTS OF SPEECH AND FUNCTION WORDS

In Chapter 5 a very sharp distinction was drawn between major vocabulary and function words. They were presented much as the bricks and mortar making up sentences — materially different from one another, and quite distinct in function. A similar distinction is made in many recent books on English, particularly those heavily influenced by Fries. The classification certainly has a valid basis, but it can easily be overdrawn.

As a matter of fact, the grammatical properties of the two kinds of words are not different in kind, only in degree. The two are joined as

---

[13] Proper names preceded by *the* are often applied to a different kind of feature. *The party camped on the Pravara.* The most likely interpretation here would be that the Pravara is a river. Compare pages 134–135.

opposing ends of a continuum by intermediate types where the characteristics of function words and major vocabulary can be seen together. Every
word carries some grammatical significance. Most words also carry some
semantic function, that is, some lexical meaning. In function words the
semantic quality is overshadowed by the grammatical. In the major vocabulary the balance is the other way. There are not two types of words so much
as two functions, semantic and grammatical, which are present together in
most words, but in different proportions.

Vocabulary items are not individually of grammatical significance. To
state the grammatical structure of a sentence it is necessary, among other
things, to replace the words by designations of the grammatical class to
which each belongs. This has the effect of leaving the grammatical dimensions unaltered, but separates and discards the lexical. At the same time the
relationships between the various elements must be examined and stated.

Not having before us a fully worked out classification of the parts of
speech and their subclasses, it will be more convenient to ask, not about
the grammatical structure of a sentence, but whether two sentences are
grammatically similar. The following two seem to be identical; the differences which there are between them are entirely lexical:

He saw the bird.   *She heard the cat.*

Whether or not that judgment or any similar decision will prove correct
depends, of course, on the part-of-speech classification which is used. We
might merely identify each word in terms of the broadest possible classes.
This would certainly bring the two sentences above together, and it would
put with them the following:

They hated my dog.

Or, instead, we might mark each word with the most minute subclassification. In this case, these three would no longer be grammatically equivalent,
since *the* and *my* would certainly go in different subclasses, but the first
two sentences might still be grammatically similar.

The easiest way to interpret these facts is in terms of different degrees
of grammatical similarity. Sentence pairs which are alike under the most
minute labeling are highly similar; those which are alike only under the
coarsest are only slightly similar. Of course to be highly similar, two sentences must also have these elements arranged in the same manner, as
might be shown by having identical structural diagrams. We can count
those sentence pairs as partly similar where the structural diagrams are
largely the same, but with perhaps an additional minor branch in one, or
some other small difference in detail.

Function words are often thought of in a quite different way. Here
the individual words are assumed to have grammatical significance. But

if examined further, many of the function words prove much like the major vocabulary. Compare the sentences:

The man is at the corner.   *The man is near the corner.*

These seem grammatically equivalent. The only difference is in the specific identity of the two contrasting function words, *at* and *near*. The sentences are grammatically identical because *at* and *near* in these sentences belong to the same class of function words. The two sentences mean different things. The contrast between them does not seem basically different from that of each of them with the corresponding one of:

The boy is at the corner.   *The boy is near the corner.*

Such pairs of sentences are grammatically identical because *man* and *boy* are both nouns and members of the same subclass. The grammatical function of a word like *at* or *near* is a matter of the class to which it belongs, just as is the case with *man* or *boy*. The difference, if there is any, is simply in the size of the classes. This must be accounted a rather minor difference.

The following two sentences seem to be structurally similar:

A friend came to see me.   *My friend came to see me.*

They are structurally similar rather than identical, because *a* and *my*, while both determiners, belong to different subclasses. Again, the grammatical properties of determiners depend, as in all other words, on the class and subclasses, or even sub-subclasses, to which they belong. It will bring a welcome measure of consistency and neatness into our work if we consider all words as having a place in the classification, and state all grammatical relationships in the same format, as holding between members of classes, rather than between individual words, or between a specific word and a class.

Many of the function words belong to very small classes. Five of Fries' fifteen groups contain only a single member, and another only two. A revision of this classification would not only add many words not listed, but would differentiate many more groups, so small classes would certainly remain. Even when there are only a handful of members, it is often necessary to subclassify them. As a result a very large number of function words belong to classes or subclasses containing only a single member. This is, for example, the case with *the*. Traditional and school grammars assign this to the very small group of articles (sometimes as an autonomous part of speech, sometimes as a subclass of adjectives). They further designate it as "the definite article". Labeling *the* in this way is tantamount to setting it up as the only member of a subclass or sub-subclass.

Not infrequently in grammars the major words are referred to by class names — noun, verb, and so on — but the function words are quoted. Thus we read descriptions of constructions of *the* with nouns, or of *will* with a verb. With *the*, there is no serious damage. Such statements can be thought of as merely careless or abbreviated ways of referring to the sub-class of the definite article. But to speak of *will* rather than a designation of its class or subclass may cause some trouble. It may obscure whether the features discussed are properties of all modal auxiliaries, or more specifically of that subclass of modals containing *will*. The confusion is of no great importance until we attempt a very detailed and rigorous description. Then it may matter very much.

Most of the special peculiarities of function words are all consequences of the fact that they are largely members of very small classes or subclasses. But there is a great deal of variation in the size of classes among them. Not all, by any means, have unique members. It is this fact that accounts for the intergradation between function words and other vocabulary.

Small classes are mostly closed. It is possible to list all members of the definite article class; there is just one: *the*. This has been the fact for some time in English, and will very likely continue for some time. The class is stable. It is possible to list all the members of the subclass of determiners including *my;* they are the following eight or nine: *my, our, your, his, her, its, their, whose,* and, for some kinds of English only, *thy*. The list is nearly as stable, but we have recently had a change when *thy* fell out of general use to be preserved only in special forms of the language. However, from generation to generation, this subclass is still remarkably stable.

It is not possible to list all the nouns. No two speakers have exactly the same list; that of any one speaker is changing constantly as he learns new ones and forgets old. The total vocabulary is continually receiving accessions, most of them nouns. Such a list is an open one; it can always be added to. Not only is the class of nouns an open class, but so are most of its subclasses. The difference between open classes and closed is not sharp. The class of prepositions is an example of intergradation. It has many of the characteristics of a closed list. All those in common use are known to all Americans; new ones appear very infrequently, so that it is reasonable to expect that the list next year will be the same as it is now; the total is not very large, though over a hundred. There are, nevertheless, marginal cases. The word *anent* is a familiar friend of crossword puzzle fans, and well known to those who read copiously in older literature, but it is used by very few people today, and is totally unknown to many. There are many other such examples. New prepositions do appear at long intervals. It is, therefore, more difficult to draw the limits around this class than around that containing *my*, but much easier than around the class of nouns. The prepositions are a partially closed class, and stand as an intergrade between function words and typical major vocabulary items.

TYPES OF MEANING AND MEANINGLESSNESS

Lexical meaning is associated in some way with the number of items in the class. Only those words belonging to fairly large classes may have very strong lexical meaning. The word *the*, therefore, has little, since it is the only member of its subclass, and because the class as a whole is a relatively small one. Most function words belong to small classes or sub-classes, and therefore tend to have very little lexical meaning. But the examples which can be claimed to have none at all are few and require special comment. One type is exemplified by *to* in contexts like *want to swim*. Since no other element can occur in this position — that is, since this particular *to* is a unique member of a grammatical class — it has no lexical meaning. There is nothing nongrammatical which is lost if only *want* and *swim* are given. The second type of meaningless function words will be mentioned below.

While words in large classes MAY have heavy lexical meaning, they do not necessarily have it. Moreover, if one of the larger classes, say count nouns, is examined it will be found that the members differ widely, not only in the extent to which they have precisely definable meanings, but in the nature of their meanings. There are four partially intergrading types that can be mentioned here:

The one usually thought of as typical includes such items as *tree, finger, sun, pencil*. These can be given the usual kind of dictionary definition in terms of reference to the "real world". It does not matter for our present purposes that many of these will require two or more definitions to reflect a certain amount of variability in meaning. A native speaker can assert that he "knows" what *tree* means, even if the lexicographer finds this claim a bit naïve.

A second kind includes such words as *thingumabob, gizmo, dofunny*.[14] These have no fixed meaning that can be defined in a dictionary in the same way. But they have a fixed use, and the native speaker understands this. They are used to refer very specifically to some definite object, but not necessarily always the same one. They are used when the speaker has forgotten the proper term or never knew it. They are given a fairly precise contextual definition at the moment of use to hold for the duration of that discussion only.

> *You know that thingamajig on the front of the vacuum cleaner — the little plastic one. Well, it just broke off.*
> *Just turn the little dofunny on the gizmo behind where the tape goes in. If that doesn't fix it, nothing will.*

[14] This type of word might be called "indefinite specifics". They are in general indefinite in meaning, but in any given context they are always precisely specific. They are always defined by context, never by anaphora. In this they are basically different from substitutes, which are typically defined by anaphora.

The third kind of noun is typified by *one*. This is a substitute. It may be used to replace any count noun, singular or plural, but typically only when the noun it replaces is in the context and would otherwise be repeated. Much more rarely it will be used when the correct noun has not been said, but is clear from the situation. In the sentence just above, *the little plastic one* means, of course, *the little plastic thingamajig*.

Such a list is an open one. [that is, *an open list*]
If you would like some grapes, I'll pick you out some good ones.

This substitute noun fits the traditional definition of a pronoun. (Actually, true pronouns do not fit since they substitute not for nouns but for noun phrases. We cannot ordinarily say ˣ*the little plastic it*.) *One* is a noun because it follows the syntactic patterns of nouns, and because it has a nounlike plural *ones*.

The last type is exemplified by *thing*.[15] This is the generalized inanimate count noun. It does not carry any specific meaning, and it has no meaning other than that which inheres in its class, that is, it is inanimate and count. In its typical use it makes a very broad and vague assertion. But often it merely fills out the pattern when a noun is required grammatically, contributing minimally to the meaning of the whole.

It was a funny thing to do.
Let's put first things first.

In the first example, the word that matters is *funny*. But this is an adjective, and the sentence pattern requires a noun; *thing* is supplied to fill the breach. In the second, the meaning that is to be conveyed is suggested by *first*. But the sentence requires a noun as direct object of *put; thing* is supplied, and *first* is subordinated to it.

Several of these types are found in other word classes. *So-and-so* and *John Doe* are specified unknown personal proper nouns. *So* and *such* are substitute adjectives.

He is very talented, and so is his sister.
If Alaska is cold, Siberia is very much more so.
He is always talking about orange-spotted purple sea lions, but I don't think there is any such animal.

---

[15] The old "definition" is interesting: "A noun is the name of a person, place, or thing." Since *thing* is a completely generalized inanimate count noun, this would be a definition of sorts if completely generalized members of all other subclasses were also listed. *Person* might be construed as a somewhat unsuccessful effort to cover one large set of animate count nouns, but there is no representation of mass nouns. However, as a definition, even this would run the other way. *Thing* is semantically nearly empty. It cannot define the grammatical class, but can itself be defined only in terms of that grammatical class: A thing is that which is named by any inanimate count noun.

Do, do so, do it, and a few others are substitute predicates. They replace a verb and its complements.

> *He plays pool every Saturday, but I never do.*
> *If you go swimming, be careful to do so in a safe place.*
> *He said he couldn't possibly finish planting the petunias, but now it looks like he can do it.*

The generalized verb is much like the generalized noun, but often presents a clearer case for semantic emptiness.

> *She did the dishes.*   *He did the honors.*

Do in these sentences means just that action which is obvious enough from the direct object. *Washed the dishes* would have meant very little different, but would have been much more redundant. A more interesting case is seen in the following.

> *She did the wash.*   *She did a big wash.*
> *She did three washes.*

In the first we might have had the meaning-carrying verb *washed.* But strangely, *wash* as a noun is more specific than *wash* as a verb. The noun refers almost exclusively to laundry. There is an advantage, therefore, in using *wash* as the direct object. However, if this is done, a verb must be supplied to fill the pattern. This verb need make no semantic contribution; all the necessary meaning is already suggested by *wash,* so *do* is supplied simply to fulfill the grammatical requirement. If it is desired to specify quantity or size, a numeral or an adjective must be used. This requires a noun head; so *wash* must be the object. We cannot easily replace *did three washes* by *washed three times.* The latter has a number of likely meanings, and the desired one does not seem the most natural interpretation. *Washed largely* is impossible; *did a big wash* is clear and explicit. *Do* in all these sentences has minimal meaning, but does perform an essential grammatical function. There are other verbs that do the same thing in certain circumstances.

> *Philip took a nap.*   *Philip napped.*
> *Philip took a long nap.*   *?Philip napped long.*

The generalized use of *thing* is most obvious when teamed up with a generalized use of *do:*

> *He has done great things.*
> *I don't know what is the best thing to do; but do something.*

In one kind of English, *on* is the generalized preposition. As such it connects a phrase in a way that is evident from the context, not inherent in the meaning of *on*. The following give just a small sample of the range of possibilities. In all of them, *on* contributes little or nothing to the meaning. In careful speech and in literary writing, many of these uses are avoided.

> *Call me up sometime on that deal. I think we can talk business.*
> *Fried eggs over on two.*
> *He's always doing things on the sly.*
> *Don't try anything on me.*
> *You don't have anything on me.*

There are at least two extreme cases of generalized function words — so generalized that they carry no meaning whatever. These are the auxiliary *do* and the article *a*. (The auxiliary *do* must be distinguished from the verb *do;* they are both generalized, but they operate in quite different patterns.)

Do is used wherever the grammar requires an auxiliary, but none is at hand. It serves simply to fill out the patterns. There are several situations of this kind: In modern English, *not* follows the first auxiliary. Several types of questions place the first auxiliary before the subject. General sentence emphasis can be made by putting the main stress on the auxiliary.

He will go.	*He will not go.*	*Will he go?*	*He wíll go.*
He has gone.	*He has not gone.*	*Has he gone?*	*He hás gone.*
He went.	*He did not go.*	*Did he go?*	*He díd go.*
He goes.	*He does not go.*	*Does he go?*	*He dóes go.*

Do as an auxiliary never has any meaning. It never changes the meaning of the sentence in which it occurs. All it ever does is to fill out the grammatical patterns of the language by providing an auxiliary when one is needed for the operation of some rule, such as that on the placement of *not*.

A is the generalized determiner. Certain constructions require a determiner. Among these are most noun phrases with singular count nouns, certain phrases with *certain, few, little,* any phrase starting with *hundred, thousand, dozen. The, my, some,* or any of the several other determiners are used when the structure or meaning calls for them. But if none of these is used, *a* is supplied to fill the gap. *A* does not mark a following noun as singular. It is simply the obligatory presence of a determiner that does this. *A*, however, can only occur in constructions where a determiner is obligatory, and, therefore, it SEEMS to mark singular nouns. As a matter of fact *a* can occur in phrases with plural and mass nouns as heads.

A few are coming.	×*A few is coming.*
A number of men are here.	
A little milk is enough.	
A dozen eggs are about right.	

(It is traditional to say that *a* is construed with *dozen*, and that the locution is short for *a dozen of eggs*. Apart from the fact that the long form sounds very queer to most Americans, this analysis gets into serious difficulties with the verb agreement. Either *eggs* is subject, in which case *of* is impossible, or *dozen* is subject, in which case it must be plural!) *A* has no function whatever other than those which are common to all determiners and characterize the class. It is the perfectly generalized word.

Chapter 9

Relation and Process

Sentences have structure; languages have system. These are related facts, each making possible the other. Language system involves regularly recurring patterns in sentence structures. Grammar is feasible only because describing a manageably small set of recurrent relationships between elements provides tools to describe the structures of a very large number of sentences.

Such recurrent patterns within sentences, however, do not exhaust the system of a language. There is an additional set of relationships that grammar must describe, and this is at least as large and diverse. These exist between pairs of sentences — not sentences joined together in larger structures, but alternative sentences which, in some sense, may occur in place of each other. The native speaker is aware of these relationships, and much of his language behavior is based on them.

Partly for this reason, they are the key to language analysis. The structure of an individual sentence, or the system of the language, can be found only by comparing sentences, thus learning which pairs show these relations. Just as structure and system are mutually interdependent, so are structure and relation. Or, the same thing can be said another way: The system of a language reflects both the structure of individual sentences and the relations between pairs of sentences.

In recent years it has become popular among some linguists to state one kind of relation between sentences in terms of transformations, processes by which one sentence can be altered into another in a regular and grammatically significant way. It is important, however, to maintain a distinction between the relations that exist as part of the language system and the manipulations which the language user employs as he, perhaps only figuratively, moves about through that language system. A trip is not part of a highway system, though only the highway system makes it possible.

This chapter will deal primarily with two kinds of relations existing between sentences or other constructions and basic to the grammatical system of the language. These will be called enation and agnation. The chapter as a whole may be taken as a definition of the two relations and of the processes which are associated with them.

SENTENCE SIMILARITIES

Consider the following four sentences:

The dog bit the man.	(1)
The dog seemed rather unpleasant.	(2)
The cat ate the canary.	(3)
The man was bitten by the dog.	(4)

There seems to be some sort of relationship between sentence (1) and each of the other three, though the relationship is quite different in each case. Not every relationship that can exist between sentences is grammatically pertinent. The grammarian's first problem, therefore, is to decide which of these pairs are grammatically related.

Sentences (1) and (2) show a kind of compatibility in meaning that would make it not at all surprising for the two — or sentences very much like them — to appear in the same discourse, even fairly close together. It is, after all, just what we would expect if, when a dog bites a man, some witness might consider that dog unpleasant. But this connection is either an observation about dogs or about human reactions to dogs and not, certainly, about sentences as phenomena of language. As such it can hardly be judged to be grammatical. If sentences (1) and (2) did occur in the same discourse, there might well be some language pattern that would relate them as successive elements in the same larger structure. In this case the relationship between the two would become a grammatical matter, and a complete grammar of English would have to describe the mechanisms involved. But outside any comprehending discourse structure, there seems to be no grammatical relationship between these two, any more than there is a grammatical relationship between such a pair of words as *babies* and *cry* until they are put together into a sentence like: *Babies cry.* The only grammatical relationship between sentences (1) and (2) is potential, and then of the kind we have called structure.

Sentences (1) and (3) are structurally similar. Indeed, if each is parsed or diagrammed, the result is exactly the same:

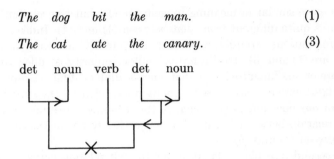

The   dog   bit   the   man.   (1)

The   cat   ate   the   canary.   (3)

det   noun   verb   det   noun

Any grammatical description of either in terms of parts of speech, syntactic relationships, and structure signals would apply without change to the other. The only difference between them is in the vocabulary: *cat* vs. *dog*, *eat* vs. *bite, canary* vs. *man. Cat* and *dog*, for example, are both nouns and, furthermore, members of the same subclass of nouns. That is, they are grammatically identical. While the structure of individual sentences may be described in terms of specific elements within them, grammars must generalize and treat sentences in terms of classes of words (parts of speech) and classes of constructions.

The relation between sentences (1) and (3) is a precisely definable one, whereas the term "structurally similar" seems open to rather imprecise use and interpretation and is not, therefore, an adequate label for the relation. We will call it enation, and say that sentence (1) is enate to sentence (3). We will symbolize the facts by the use of the identity sign ≡:

The dog bit the man.   ≡   *The cat ate the canary.*   (1, 3)

This relation works both ways. It is, therefore, equally true that sentence (3) is enate to sentence (1).

If two sentences are enate, this implies that there is a manipulation which a grammarian or a speaker can apply to alter one into the other. This is substitution. Between (1) and (3), three substitutions are involved: *cat* substitutes for *dog*, *eat* for *bite*, and *canary* for *man*.

The relation between sentences (1) and (4) is of quite a different sort, but equally obvious to any native speaker of English. The sentence patterns are very different; no amount of forcing will bring them together. Parsing or diagramming does not, therefore, immediately reveal the relation as it did between (1) and (3). Yet the relation is evident to any fluent speaker of English in spite of the difference in structure.

A first impression might suggest that the resemblance is in meaning, rather than in structure. Indeed, a case can be made that sentences (1) and (4) mean the same or very nearly the same. Yet this is certainly inadequate to describe the situation, as may be seen if we compare sentence (5):

The collie attacked the visitor.   (5)

198 TOPICS IN ENGLISH SYNTAX

This is quite similar in meaning to sentence (1), but the relation between the two is quite different from that between (1) and (4). Indeed, when we compare relations carefully, we find that (1) and (5) are enate in the same way as are (1) and (3). To this latter kind of similarity is added another by the more or less fortuitous fact that the vocabulary items in similar places in the two sentences are loosely synonymous. That is, the substitution of *collie* for *dog* does not greatly change the meaning. Meaning may be part of the relation between (1) and (4), but certainly not in the same way as it is between (1) and (5).

A second possible explanation for the felt relation between sentences (1) and (4) is in the vocabulary. Leaving the function words and affixes aside, this is identical in the two. Yet this alone is not adequate. Compare the following, which also has precisely the same vocabulary:

> *The man bit the dog.* (6)

Certainly (6) is not related to (1) in the way that (4) is. For one thing, the meaning is not the same. Nor is the communicative function — as everyone knows, one of these sentences is news; the other is not. Actually, sentence (6) is related to (1) in exactly the same way as is sentence (3), that is, they are enate. *Dog* in (1) and *man* in (6) are of the same class and have identical structural relationships with other elements in their sentences. The same is true of *man* in (1) and *dog* in (6).

Neither similarity in meaning nor similarity in vocabulary alone will account for the resemblance which a native speaker senses between sentences (1) and (4). Perhaps the combination might. Yet the relation seems more direct than this — complex to state, perhaps, but ultimately resting in just one feature of the two sentences. It is a grammatical relation, that is, a relation between two grammatical structures. Derivative from it is a grammatical process, a manipulation which works on the grammatical structure and converts one member of the pair into the other. This manipulation is quite different from substitution, and, indeed, sentences (1) and (4) are characterized by the fact that no substitution is involved in changing one to the other. This process is called a transformation. It can be symbolized by a single-headed double arrow:

> *The dog bit the man.* ⇒ *The man was bitten by the dog.* (1, 4)

So defined, every transformation[1] has its converse:

> *The man was bitten by the dog.* ⇒ *The dog bit the man.* (4, 1)

Transformations are the consequence of relations that exist between sentence patterns in the language. The relation is the basic thing, and it will be useful to have a means of describing it, or of referring to it without

[1] Some linguists use the term "transformation" in a much broader sense. Some of the processes included may not be reversible.

speaking in terms of processes or manipulations. We will say that two sentences are agnate;[2] between agnate sentences there exists the relation of agnation. This can be indicated by the double-headed double arrow:

> The dog bit the man. ⇔ The man was bitten by the dog.   (1, 4)

If one sentence is agnate to another, then the reverse relationship is also true. It is this symmetry which makes the double heads appropriate.

ENATION AND FRAMES

Two sentences may be said to be enate if they have identical structures, that is, if the elements (say, words) at equivalent places in the sentences are of the same classes, and if the constructions in which they occur are the same. This is hardly a definition, since it is completely circular, but it does give some indication of what we have in mind when we use the word "enate". It also explains why the relation is not widely discussed in grammars — it is so directly a consequence of the classification of words into parts of speech and the identification of constructions (both essential in a grammar) that little is added by a discussion of enation.

On the other hand, the notion, usually stated in a different way, is basic to language analysis. Traditional grammarians have seldom stated how they determine the part of speech to which a word belongs. Fries, however, and with him many linguists, attempts to be quite explicit. The chief technique is one of frames. A frame is really nothing more than a summary of a set of enate sentences. This may be seen by the fact that the operation by which a frame is used is substitution, the process converting one enate sentence into another.

For example, adjectives might be defined in terms of a frame such as:

> That man is...   (7)

This is equivalent to a set of enate sentences:

---

[2] "Enate" and "agnate" are here proposed as new technical terms in linguistics. They are derived from Latin enatus 'related on the mother's side' and agnatus 'related on the father's side'. They seem appropriate designations for two contrasting types of relations, neither of which can exist without the other.

In my opinion, precision is served by making a clear distinction between relations which are static and inherent, facts of the language system, and processes which are dynamic and describe behavior rather than the language system. For practical purposes, it may often be more convenient to talk of transformations rather than of agnation of constructions, but, in theory, the linguist must describe the system of the language rather than the behavior of the user, and, especially, than the normalized behavior of a highly conventionalized user who operates more nearly like an analytic linguist than an ordinary human being.

I find "agnate" by far the more useful of the two. "Enate" is necessary largely as a counterpoise, an essential lemma in a discussion of the sort attempted in this chapter. In other contexts I would not be surprised if "enate" were very little used.

That man is old.
That man is young.
That man is skillful.
That man is pleasant. etc. (8)

If these are in fact enate, it is true that *old, young, skillful, pleasant,* and so on are all of the same class, in this instance, that of adjectives.

The use of frames as tests of word classification presents difficulties from several directions. First is the fact that most frames are by no means diagnostic. The one just suggested is rather poor, and the shortcomings are very quickly evident as it is used. For example:

That man is going.
That man is inside.
That man is captain. (9)

Here what seems to be the same frame is filled by a verbal form, an adverb, and a noun. It would be quite reasonable to say that in the three sentences in (9) the constructions are not the same as in (8), that is, that the sentences are not really enate. The question is, however, how can the analyst know whether he is or is not keeping the frame constant as he inserts words into it?

Such a frame as (7) also fails from the other side. There are many adjectives that do not fit:

×*That man is golden.* (10)

and many others where at least some doubt arises:

That man is ethereal. (11)

One who knows the language can see immediately that the problem is some sort of incompatibility between *man* and these adjectives. But, of course, one who knows the language this well could probably dispense with the frame in most cases anyway.

There is a fairly obvious way to avoid the second difficulty. This is to use not one frame such as (7) but a series of frames:

That idea is...
That flower is... (12)

To qualify as a set of equivalent frames, it is required that they all be enate. In this instance this means that *man, idea, flower,* and so on must all be of the same class. That is to say, we can use frames to establish the class of adjectives only if we have already established at least one other class, say, nouns.

To avoid the first difficulty, we should rely not on any single frame, but on the agreement of several frames. Thus in addition to (7) we might test in (13):

He is a/an...man. (13)

Old, young, skillful, pleasant, and many other adjectives fit this frame readily enough. Most of the other elements that fit (7) do not. Thus ×*He is a captain man.* seems at least somewhat strange and can be rejected. There are, of course, elements that will fit (13) but not (7), for example, *university,* and these must be excluded also. The combination of (7) and (13) is far more successful in defining the class of adjectives than either alone, but it is not entirely satisfactory. *Inside* will fit both, but is probably not to be considered an adjective.

Of course, other frames are better than either (7) or (13). For example, both of these can be greatly improved in usefulness by simply adding *very:*

That man is very...   *He is a very...man.* (14)

But no single frame can be made infallible. The ones that most successfully select only adjectives miss most of the class, and any one that identifies most of them includes a large number of nonadjectives.

A native speaker of English will sense immediately that *inside* is different from other elements which will fit both (7) and (13). He bases this feeling on a comparison of the following PAIRS of sentences:

That man is inside.   *He is an inside man.* (15)
That man is young.   *He is a young man.* (16)

There is a relation between the sentences in each pair, but the relations are quite different. *Old, skillful, pleasant,* and many others can, however, be inserted to form sentence pairs which will be found to be related in exactly the same way as the pair with *young* in (16). This is a far more discriminating test than simple substitution in frames, no matter how many frames are brought in for corroboration.

The relation that connects the sentence pair in (16), or the frames (7) and (13) from which it is formed, is that of agnation. A pair or set of agnate frames is grammatically more pertinent than any collection of assorted frames. We have seen that another difficulty can be met by using enate frames. To meet both difficulties, then, we must use a two-dimensional set of frames, that is, a set related in one direction by enation and in the other by agnation. Every individual frame in the set must be tied in to the whole set through both relations. If instead of (7) and (13) we use the improvements suggested at (14), we may indicate a fragment of such a satisfactory set of frames as follows:

$$\textit{That man is very}\dots \quad \Leftrightarrow \quad \textit{That is a very}\dots\textit{man.} \quad \Leftrightarrow \text{etc.}$$
$$\textrm{|||} \qquad\qquad\qquad \textrm{|||}$$
$$\textit{That flower is very}\dots \quad \Leftrightarrow \quad \textit{That is a very}\dots\textit{flower.} \quad \Leftrightarrow$$
$$\textrm{|||} \qquad\qquad\qquad \textrm{|||}$$
$$\textit{That idea is very}\dots \quad \Leftrightarrow \quad \textit{That is a very}\dots\textit{idea.} \quad \Leftrightarrow \qquad\qquad (17)$$
$$\textrm{|||} \qquad\qquad\qquad \textrm{|||}$$

etc.

Such a system of frames is useful largely because it reflects the two dimensions along which the grammatical system of a language is organized, dimensions on which the relations are enation and agnation.

AGNATION

Pairs of sentences with the same major vocabulary items, but with different structures (generally shown by differences in arrangement, in accompanying function words, or other structure markers) are agnate if the relation in structure is regular and systematic, that is, if it can be stated in terms of general rules. As with the introductory statement in the last section, this is not a definition that will resolve in advance the question as to whether any given pair of sentences are related and how. Until a grammar is worked out, that must be determined largely by the "feel" for the language that a native speaker has, or that a foreign analyst attempts to acquire. There are, however, some general principles which help, and which may guide that "feel" into more effective and efficient analysis. These are basically interconnections between patterns of enation and agnation.

Agnation is not a unique relation between isolated pairs of sentences. It is based on the pervading patterns of the language. It is, therefore, always a recurrent thing, involving large numbers of sentences. Groups of sentences can be found which are agnate to each other. Within each group the sentences are enate. The two kinds of sentence similarities are thus paired, so that neither can be stated clearly without the other. This is a second reason for identifying and labeling enation, even though it might seem to add nothing to the notions of class membership and constructional identity which must be in a grammar in any case.

This interdependency, then, provides a rough test, simultaneously, for for both enation and agnation. A very small sample is provided by the following set of constructions:

$$\textit{He saw it.} \quad \Leftrightarrow \quad \textit{It was seen by him.}$$
$$\textrm{|||} \qquad\qquad \textrm{|||}$$
$$\textit{He heard it.} \quad \Leftrightarrow \quad \textit{It was heard by him.}$$
$$\textrm{|||} \qquad\qquad \textrm{|||}$$
$$\textit{He felt it.} \quad \Leftrightarrow \quad \textit{It was felt by him.} \qquad\qquad (18)$$

Such an illustration is, of course, very fragmentary. There are a large number of other words that can be substituted for *see, hear*, or *feel* in the two sentence patterns shown. In every instance, provided the structure is not inadvertently altered, the result is another pair of agnate sentences. There are, moreover, other transformations that might be applied, giving rise to further columns in the array. The diagram can, thus, be widely extended in both dimensions.

If, however, we start from a pair or set of sentences which do not have identical structures, however similar they may look, no such extensive display can be set out.

A stranger was seen by the man.	×*A stranger was seemed by the man.* (19)
⇕	
The man saw a stranger. ×≡	*The man seemed a stranger.* (20)
	⇕
×*The man saw to be a stranger.*	*The man seemed to be a stranger.* (21)

The two sentences in (20) seem to be similar in structure, and one not well acquainted with English might take them to be enate. The two have, however, entirely different agnate relations. (19) and (21) show sentence patterns agnate to one of the sentences of (20), but not to the other. We must conclude that the relation between the pair of sentences (20) is entirely superficial and of no grammatical significance. Any adequate grammar would have to distinguish two constructions (traditionally direct object and subjective complement) and assign the two verbs to different subclasses (traditionally transitive and copulative or linking). It is hard to see any usefulness in a grammar which stops short in either respect.

Constant checking of one type of sentence relation against the other is a basic technique of language analysis. We can guess that a child learning his language uses much the same procedure, probably in a very haphazard and unsystematic way, of course. But if a child perseveres — and a child does work hard at language learning for several years — this random comparison leads to subconscious control over the patterns. The adult analyst must proceed methodically, seeking out the transformations that may confirm or deny an apparent enate relation, and conversely. Ultimately, the grammarian takes account in his statement of those relations which seem to fit into an interconnecting system ramifying far and wide through the language. He seeks other explanations for any superficial similarities which seem isolated or unpatterned. In the same way, the child takes into his speech habits those patterns which he finds to interrelate and confirm one another.

There has been much debate among linguists as to the proper use of meaning in linguistic analysis. Everyone has recognized that there are dangers, and so undisciplined use of meaning is generally avoided. Some linguists have gone to great lengths to minimize or even eliminate any employment of meaning. Most have recognized the necessity of some use of meaning, if nothing more than merely to ascertain that two utterances are the same or different.

Of the various kinds of meaning that might be used, one of the most widely accepted has been one which is actually only disguised agnation. For example, *new* and *school* in *the new house* and *the school house* are considered by most grammarians to be grammatically nonequivalent. There are several types of evidence: One is the fixed order of the two when they occur together: *the new school house*, not *×the school new house*. A second is the different possibilities of adding modifiers: *the very new house*, not *×the very school house*, at least not in the "meaning" of a house that is somehow more intensively "school" than another. A third is the "meaning" difference in the two constructions. One "means" *the house which is new*, the other something more like *the house which is for school*, but certainly not *×the house which is school*. The "meanings" are actually agnate constructions, sometimes rather loosely stated.

Perhaps the most common use of this device under the guise of "meanings" has been with series of noun modifiers. In an example with several nouns in sequence, there is always a problem in finding the right cuts among them, that is, the right organization into immediate constituents. "Meaning" is one of the usual tests. *An amusement park ticket seller* is considered to "mean" (that is, be agnate to) *a ticket seller at an amusement park*, not *×a park ticket seller* somehow involved with *amusement*. Indeed, this latter possibility is so remote that the proper form does not easily suggest itself. That is, no construction *a park ticket seller Y amusement*, with *Y* as a suitable structure marker, is known. Another possibility would be *a seller of amusement park tickets*. The original phrase is, therefore, in a rather inconsequential way, ambiguous. In speech the two possible "meanings" could often be distinguished by a difference in stress patterns, and, if the speaker cared to make the structure explicit (he would probably think of it as "meaning"), he could always do so by stress and intonation.

A Farmington Avenue grocery store "means" *a grocery store on Farmington Avenue*, not *×an avenue grocery store in Farmington*, nor *×a store carrying Farmington Avenue groceries*. These relations indicate the IC cuts, since transformations typically involve the rearrangement of constituents, rather than the moving of odd fragments of constructions. Thus, we know that the structure must be:

Farmington   Avenue   grocery   store

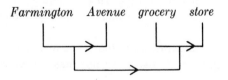

PARTIAL ENATION

Up to this point we have assumed that sentences either are enate, or they are not. There are two ways in which this absolute dichotomy might be modified.

First, we have said that, to be enate, two sentences must have elements of the same class in corresponding places. Classification of words or constructions is not, however, simple and clear-cut. Within some parts of speech it is useful to recognize subclasses, within some of the latter sub-subclasses, and in a few cases several more steps are possible. We have discussed only examples in which there is no question — the words belong to the same group, however finely they are classified. If the words in two sentences belong to the same class, but to different subclasses, would they be enate? Or, to the same sub-subclass, but to different sub-subsubclasses?

Probably the most useful way to answer this is to agree to use the term "enate" only if the two elements are of the same type down to the finest subdivision recognized in the grammar at hand. This would not be the same in every instance. The problem is then changed in nature. Instead of recognizing degrees of enation within one grammar, we must recognize some quality of a grammar that varies from one statement to another. We will call this delicacy.

For any given language, grammars can be written at various levels of delicacy, that is, with various amounts of detail. This does not imply that a grammarian is free to choose whether he will include each separate detail or leave it out. The systematic nature of language precludes that. For example, in English a more detailed treatment of the determiners presupposes a more detailed classification of nouns, and vice versa. These two parts of the grammar must be kept in balance. Much the same is true at many other places. It seems certain that every part of an ideal grammar would be in balance with every other part, though one might choose to compile a more delicate or a less delicate grammar.

Moreover, a more detailed grammar must be only an enlargement and refinement of a less detailed. One cannot flatly contradict the other, but only say something that the other leaves unsaid or be more specific where the other makes a general statement. A grammarian has a great deal of freedom. He has a choice of technique of description, of degree of delicacy, and occasionally of treatment of individual points. Yet the facts of the language impose certain restraints. A responsible grammarian, moreover, will try to write his brief sketch to give it maximum compatibility with an encyclopedic description. In any case, a short grammar need not find its only justification in expediency. The system of the language points out certain features as basic and others as secondary, and a grammar which describes only these central features will have justification in the organization of the language.

More important for our present discussion is a second way in which two constructions can be partially enate. It is perhaps best introduced by some examples:

That man lives in the white house. (22)
That man lives in the grayish house. (23)
That man lives in the brick red house. (24)

As words, *white* and *grayish* are entirely equivalent — both are adjectives and of the same minor subclass. On this basis, (22) and (23) are enate. But if we analyze further, they are not equivalent: *White* is simple and indivisible; *grayish* consists of a stem *gray* and a suffix *-ish*. If we consider the structure within the word, (22) and (23) are not enate. Which should we do? Actually, we can do both. These sentences are enate to the word level of structure, but not beyond.

In certain respects, *brick red* is grammatically equivalent to either *white* or *grayish*, if, of course, it can be taken as a unit. To do so, we need only recognize *brick red* as a phrase (specifically, an adjective phrase). Then (24) is enate to (22) and (23) to the phrase level.

Partial enation in this second sense is an indispensable tool in syntactic analysis. It is a second means of recognizing intermediate constituents of sentences. It is particularly useful in delineating the nesting of constructions within constructions. We will use the symbol ≅ to indicate partial enation of this kind, that is, identity in a significant part of the structure of the two samples, but not complete identity.

There is one kind of partial enation that requires special notice. This is the case where, in IC terms, one sentence has a complex element in place of a simpler one in the other, and the simpler one is included in the complex one as head. In such a case, the larger construction is said to be an expansion of the shorter, and the term expansion is also used of the process by which the longer is produced. For example:

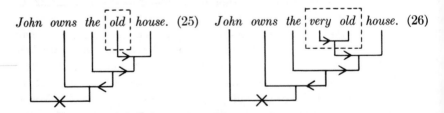

Note that the structures of the two sentences are exactly alike outside the dashed line of the diagram. This line includes a phrase, composed of a single word in (25) and of two words in (26). The sentences are, therefore, partially enate. Moreover, it will be found that the agnate relationships of the two sentences are parallel. The difference is merely that between *old* and *very old*, with the shorter expression included in the longer as its head. On this basis, either the phrase *very old* can be labeled as an expansion of *old*, or the whole of sentence (26) can be called an expansion of (25).

There are various other ways in which sentence (25) can be expanded, among them the following two:

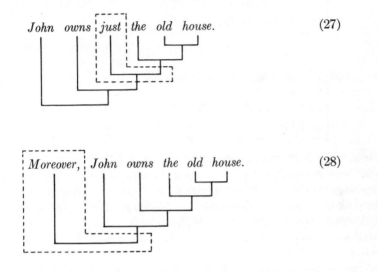

(27)

Moreover, John owns the old house.

(28)

The added structure has been marked off with a dashed line. In each case the remaining structure has not been changed.

If sentence structure is looked at from the point of view of slot-and-filler description, expansions fall into two groups. In one there is added an extra layer of structure. In the other, the existing structure is merely filled out.

John owns the old house.

(25)

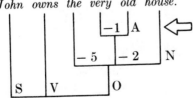

John owns the very old house.

(26)

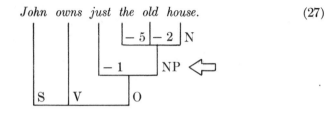

(27)

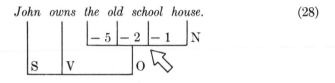

(28)

Sentence (28) has the same structure in slot-and-filler terms as does (25), though one more place has been filled. (There remain several additional places that might be filled without adding another layer of structure.) Sentences (26) and (27), however, have additional layers of structure to accommodate the extra words. (*Just*, for reasons not apparent here, is best treated as a modifier of the noun phrase as a whole, not as part of the phrase.)

That two sentences are alike but for an additional word is not sufficient to show that one is an expansion of the other. There are a variety of possible relationships in such cases. Something of the complexity of the problem can be seen by examining a phrase, *the same old house*. This is ambiguous in written English, though the two possible structures are usually distinguished in speech by stress. One is related both to *the old house* and to *the same house*, having one more slot filled in each case. The other is a true expansion of *the same house*, but not directly related to *the old house*, though it seems to differ only in a single word. The following diagram will show the relations. Stresses are marked. Notice how tertiary stress on *ŏld* marks it as a modifier of a preceding element, not of the following noun.

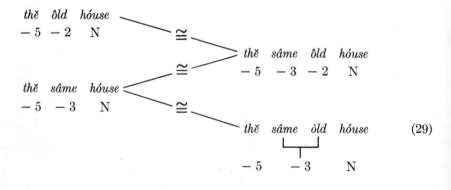

(29)

TYPES OF AGNATION

Agnation was described earlier as a relation between sentences having identical major vocabulary and different structures relatable by general rules. This deserves further exemplification, closer attention to some details, and some modification.

A typical pair of agnate sentences is:

> *To err is human.* ⇔ *It is human to err.*   (30)

There are only two major vocabulary items here, *err* and *human*. The remainder are function words associated with structure patterns which connect *err* and *human* and integrate them into a sentence. This can be done in at least the two ways shown in (30). The two sentences can be considered agnate because in general any sentence of the form of either can be matched by one of the form of the other:

> *To forgive is divine.* ⇔ *It is divine to forgive.*   (31)
> *To murder is unlawful.* ⇔ *It is unlawful to murder.*   (32)

Agnate sentences like those at (30) differ in at least two obvious ways: The major elements (*err* and *human*) occur in reversed orders. The function words are different. Both word order and function words are structure signals, and we might expect them to differ, since any two agnate sentences must differ in structure.

Since function words show such differences in agnate sentence pairs, they must often be specified in any description of the relation. This fact will help to delimit the class of function words. They can be identified as just that group of words that must be specified in stating transformations or in describing agnation patterns. For example, if it is agreed that the two sentences in (30) are agnate, we must consider *it*, at least as used there, as a function word. This principle will not settle all of the marginal cases, but it will help with many. It is merely a reflection of the fact that the system of grammar includes a dimension characterized by agnation, with the result that grammatical statements not taking this into account are incomplete and often needlessly difficult.

There are other pairs of agnate sentences which seem to differ only in the order of elements:

> *I must see this.* ⇔ *This I must see.*   (33)
> *It is raining!* ⇔ *Is it raining?*   (34)

The appearance, however, is deceiving. There is often a difference in intonation. This is the case in both (33) and (34). Intonation contours are another type of structure signal, and thus quite comparable to function words. As in (34) there may be a difference in punctuation.

There are rarer cases in which there is no discernible difference in function words or intonation. This may be the case with the following:

John is here. ⇔ *Here is John.*   (35)

There is, however, still a clearly indicated difference of structure, since the order of elements — particularly when of well-marked classes — is itself a structure signal.

An interesting relation is that seen in such pairs as:

She washed. ⇔ *She did the wash.*   (36)

We have already commented on this pattern as an example of the use of *do* as a generalized verb, that is, as a member of a major form class that nevertheless qualifies as a function word. If we take (36) as agnate, and if we understand that words which must be specified in describing a transformation are function words, then this assignment is confirmed.

As has been pointed out many times, the part of speech (and subclass, of course) is the only thing about the typical vocabulary item which is grammatically pertinent. A transformation such as that which changes one sentence of (36) to the other maintains the vocabulary element *wash* unaltered in a fundamental sense, but does alter its structural relations. It draws a line between the mutable and the immutable, as it were, within the word *wash*, between its lexical identity and its grammatical class. The first remains invariant, the second is a structure signal and can be altered in a transformation.

Most transformations involve more than one kind of change. Structure signals may be added, subtracted, or simply altered. Any kind of signal can be involved: function words, generalized members of major form classes (a special kind of function word), grammatical affixes, derivational affixes, intonation and stress, (or punctuation and word division), word order, class membership. The basic vocabulary items, however, remain in some significant sense unaltered.

The following three sentences are related:

It is a better than average house.
It is a better house than average.
It is a house better than average.   (37)

These may be considered either as partially enate or as agnate. The over-all structure is the same: pronoun-verb-noun phrase, with the same constructional patterns. They are, therefore, enate down to the phrase level. The only difference is in the internal structure of the noun phrase, and the apparent agnation of the three sentences can be seen to rest in the noun phrases. If just the latter are separated out, they show all the characteristics of agnation:

a better than average house
a better house than average
a house better than average   (38)

This example calls for the first modification of our original description of
agnation. It will be better to consider that any construction can be agnate
to another of the same kind, provided only that it is large enough to have
some internal structure. We have seen examples of sentences and of noun
phrases.

There is another very significant fact about (38). These are not only
agnate, but also grammatically equivalent. In any context in which the
phrase *a better than average house* can appear, the other two are also possible.
When this is so, the patterns of agnation have a stylistic significance; a writer
or a speaker is presented with a choice, and the way he chooses contributes
to the style of the passage. Though all are possible in any context where
any one is, there may be a preference of one sort or another for a certain
alternant in some specific context. This will, however, be a preference, not
a requirement absolutely excluding all others. This preference is a matter
of stylistics also.

Exactly the same thing is true of larger constructions. The pair of sentences (30) is an example. The members of such a pair are interchangeable
in larger constructions, say, in paragraphs. The structure of a paragraph
is not greatly changed by making such an alteration in any sentence within
it. But the style may be significantly affected. Indeed, just such possibilities
for variation in sentence structure constitute one of the most valuable
resources of the language. They are the primary foundation for style.

Other types of agnate sentence pairs, however, have much less stylistic
significance. Statements and questions, for example, are clearly related,
yet they have quite different "meanings" — in this case, quite different
functions in communication. One gives information; the other asks for it,
but in so doing may suggest an answer. Once in a while, a question may be
used where a statement would perhaps be more usual. In such instances,
we may speak of rhetorical questions, and consider them as a rather specialized stylistic device.

Agnate sentence pairs, or the transformations which describe their
relations, can therefore be classified (with considerable intergradation) into
two groups. At one extreme, the selection is made on the basis of style,
the choice being free of semantic or grammatical restrictions. At the other,
"meaning" in one of its many forms determines the choice, and there is
little possibility of stylistic significance.

There is another quite different type of transformation. This relates
two constructions which are not on the same grammatical level. A common
variety joins a sentence and a phrase:

The house is new.	⟺ *the new house*	(39)
The man is outside.	⟺ *the man outside*	(40)

In many such instances, the phrase is an expansion of a phrase within the sentence. Thus, *the new house* is an expansion of *the house*. In other cases, the phrase is totally different in type from any part of the sentence:

The boy runs.	⟺ *the boy's running*	(41)

Agnation is not limited to sentences or constructions of smaller size. Another possibility is the joining of a single sentence and a sequence of sentences, that is, a structure composed of two or more sentences:

The passer-by who found the purse got a reward. ⟺	(42)
The passer-by found the purse. He got a reward.	(43)

The major vocabulary items are all the same. Their order and the accompanying function words indicate a difference in structure. Many other parallel pairs might be found, so the relation is recurrent; presumably it can be stated by a general rule. Though we are not accustomed to thinking of a sequence of sentences as a construction, there is good reason to do so in the case of (43). The pair, then, fits our description of agnation.

It is informative to cut apart the two clauses in (42) and match them with the two sentences in (43):

the passer-by got a reward	≅ *He got a reward.*	(44)
who found the purse	≅ *The passer-by found the purse.*	(45)

If either pair of fragments is looked at by itself, the relation is seen to be partial enation. *He* or *who* is substituted for *the passer-by*. A major vocabulary item, thus, is present in one and missing in the other. When in context, however, the situation is different; everything in (42) is preserved through the transformation and appears in (43), and vice versa. One vocabulary item, *passer-by*, merely shifts its position from one fragment to another. A shift in position within a construction is characteristic of agnation. Compare the shift of *man* from direct object position in (1) to subject position in the passive sentence (4).

Words like *who* and *he* are a special type of function word having as one major function the marking of double involvement of that for which some vocabulary item stands. Thus, in these sentences, *he* and *who* are alternative ways of indicating that the passer-by was both the finder of the purse and the recipient of the reward. They have a second function as part of larger patterns which signal grammatical relationships between two major parts of the structure (the two pieces separated out in (44) and

(45)). These can be joined in at least two different ways, and *he* and *who* participate in distinguishing these.

An alternative way to indicate the double involvement would be to use the noun *passer-by* twice. This would have the incidental effect of dropping one of the signals of connection between the two clauses, and, thus, it would be a move in the direction of disassociating them. Other indications of connection occur in the determiners. Changing *the* to *a* will further separate the two. The following, then, is not a construction, but only a listing of two unrelated sentences:

> *A passer-by got a reward. A passer-by found a purse.* (46)

The only grammatical relation these have, other than the fortuitous circumstance that they are enate, is the potential one mentioned in the discussion of sentences (1) and (2) at the beginning of this chapter. With the application of suitable signals of sequencing,[3] they might enter into some comprehending structure. Without that, they can only occur together in a list.

It is perhaps more usual, even so, to consider transformations as working between clauses. What is involved here can be seen from another example:

> *My friend whom I told you about is coming tomorrow.* (47)

From this sentence we can excise a clause: *whom I told you about.* Looking only at this clause, we know that there must be a related sentence of the form: *I told you about....* The blank must be filled by a noun phrase, but there is no evidence within the clause as to what that might be. However, the fact that the clause appears as a modifier of *my friend* in (47) tells us that the sentence must be: *I told you about my friend.* To put it rather oddly, the *whom* signals that the sentence related to this clause has a noun phrase which can be found by looking just outside the clause at the noun phrase preceding *whom.*

Earlier in this chapter, it was suggested that the "meaning" of a construction might sometimes be a more explicit agnate construction. Thus *automatic lathe operator* "means" 'an operator of automatic lathes', whereas *automatic dish washer* "means" 'a dish washer that is automatic'. In the same way, the "meaning" of *whom I told you about* can be thought of as 'I told you about my friend.' The "meaning" of *He got a reward.* is 'The passer-by got a reward.' Whenever words like *he* or *who* occur in a passage,

---

[3] Note that the signals are seldom simply added function words, but much more often involve substitution, generally of elements which characteristically have dual functions, such as pronouns, generalized nouns or verbs, determiners, and so on. This means that there is inevitably a kind of distortion involved in discussing the grammar of sentences taken out of longer contexts unless these substitutions are allowed for.

the "meaning" can be found only by looking elsewhere in that passage to supply a suitable noun phrase.

Of course these related constructions are not the meaning, but only bits of language from which the meaning is more directly deducible. That is, they are more easily interpretable structures. The actual interpretation must involve operations outside of grammar. But these cannot be applied directly to the actual form of sentences or longer passages in many instances. The grammar must assist somehow in finding some underlying structure which can be more easily related to meaning.[4] The notions of sentence relationship presented in this chapter go part of the way toward doing this.

To examine the question simply in terms of sentences or clauses, however, is to impose disastrous limitations. The structures that signal meaning grammatically almost invariably run beyond clauses and beyond sentences, and must be handled within a framework which can accommodate much longer passages.

CHAINS OF TRANSFORMATIONS

Any two of the following six sentence pairs can be said to be agnate. Arrows have been drawn in to indicate the relations.

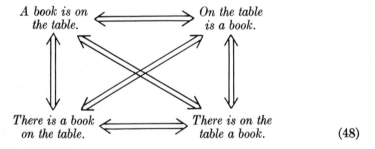

(48)

Each of the sentences on the right is related to the opposite one on the left in the same way. The most prominent feature is the difference in order of the two phrases, *a book* and *on the table*. This can be expressed in a skeleton formula as:

$$X\,Y \Leftrightarrow Y\,X \tag{49}$$

---

[4] This approach to semantics has been developed largely within the transformational-generative framework. See particularly Jerrold J. Katz and Paul M. Postal, *An Integrated Theory of Linguistic Descriptions*, 1964. They discuss a type of rule — "projection rules" — which purport to relate an interpretation to an underlying grammatical structure. A similar thing can be done within the stratificational framework, the semologic structure being that which is most directly relatable to something outside language which can for this purpose be considered an interpretation. Those frameworks which distinguish only phonology and morphology must, of course, base any semantic work directly on the structure of actual morphemes as they stand in the passage, and, therefore, have considerable difficulty with such questions.

The two sentences at the right are related to each other in the same way as are the two at the left. This may be formulated, roughly, as follows:

$$...is... \Leftrightarrow There\ is...\ ... \tag{50}$$

Moreover, the two diagonal pairs are related in the same way, and both can be represented by the same formula:

$$X\ is\ Y \Leftrightarrow There\ is\ Y\ X \tag{51}$$

These three formulae specify, in a rough way adequate for our present purposes, the patterns that join these four sentences. They work equally well, of course, for many other similar sets with different vocabulary.

Formulae such as these can be made more precise and given a place in a grammar. However, before this is done a step toward simplification should be taken. The third formula is really only a summation of the first two. This may be expressed algebraically:

$$(X\ is\ Y \Leftrightarrow There\ is\ Y\ X) = (X\ Y \Leftrightarrow Y\ X)$$
$$+ (...is... \Leftrightarrow There\ is\ ...\ ...) \tag{52}$$

Rather than describe sentence pairs such as those on the diagonals in (48) as joined by a single relation, we can state the facts in terms of two successive relations. In this way the total number of patterns to be described can be reduced. The reduction may materially simplify the final grammatical description.

In earlier chapters the point was made that sentence patterns cannot feasibly be listed. There are far too many of them to be manageable — so many, indeed, that they cannot be fully itemized, no matter how large the grammar. A grammar, therefore, must describe the simpler constructions which in various combinations comprise the sentence patterns. The relations between sentences are also extremely numerous. In many instances, however, they can be considered as complex chains of relations. The only feasible way to write the section of the grammar dealing with agnation is to analyze the observed relations into the elemental relations that occur. To alter one sentence into another may, then, require the application of a chain of transformations. The grammar must list the separate transformations (or the underlying relations) and also state the ways in which they can be combined into chains.

Of the six relations indicated in (48), two have been shown to be complex. As such, they need not be listed, but the sentences concerned must be described as connected by a chain of two. The remaining four relations are of only two types. These facts can conveniently be indicated by a diagram like (48), but with the diagonal arrows removed:

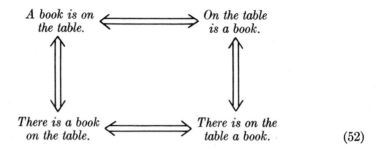

(52)

It must be understood that parallel arrows represent the same relation. The diagonal pairs are clearly seen to relate by a chain of agnations, in each case a chain of two. There are two routes between each diagonal pair. These two routes merely represent the application of the same two transformations in two orders. For this type of relation, the order in the chain is of no significance.

Longer chains are easy enough to find. For example, there are three yes-or-no questions agnate to the set of four sentences shown in (48). These can all be fitted together into one system of agnation by means of three relations, the two shown in (52) and one more: X is Y $\Leftrightarrow$ Is X Y? Representing this new relation by a diagonal arrow, the interrelations of the seven sentences may be diagrammed as follows:

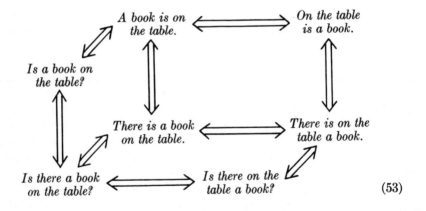

(53)

Any pair of sentences in this set are agnate. Any two not connected by a single arrow are joined by a chain of relations. Nine pairs are connected by a chain of two. Between three pairs of sentences, the chain consists of three successive relations. In each of these cases, the chain can be traced out along four different routes, each representing a different order of application of the transformations. For example, two of the sentences of (53) might be connected as follows:

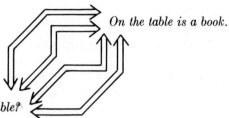

On the table is a book.

Is there a book on the table? (54)

We must not overlook the restrictions. Mathematically, we would expect that there would be six routes between such pairs of sentences, that is, six orders in which three transformations might be applied. Two are missing. The source of this limitation is evident. Three of the four sentences enter directly into only two of the three relations; the other four enter directly into all. Restrictions are significant; they are the stuff of which grammars consist.

We ordinarily think of grammar as rules stating what CAN go together. For example, certain sequences of words are described as possible. But such statements are meaningful only if some other combinations CANNOT occur.[5] So likewise, some chains of sentence relations are possible, others not. In the example under discussion, while all three relations can occur together, there are certain orders in chains which seem to be excluded.

The grammatical system of a language consists of just such facts. The agnation relations between English sentences form an organized system of a kind much like that of other facets of grammar. As we shall see, the facts can be considerably more complex than those in this first sample. For a complete and systematic statement, the rules will need to be framed in a more sophisticated manner.

For another example of a chain of relations, consider the following sentence pairs. In each the position of the sentence stress has been marked.

He will see a ghóst. ⇔ *Will he see a ghóst?* (55)
He will see a ghóst. ⇔ *He wíll see a ghost.* (56)

If we indicate only the sentence elements that have to be specified, these can be formulated roughly as follows:

$Subj + Aux + \ldots$ ⇔ $Aux + Subj + \ldots$ (57)
$\ldots + Aux + \ldots$ ⇔ $\ldots + Aúx + \ldots$ (58)

That is to say, in (55) the auxiliary (*will*) is transposed to a position before

---

[5] We are so accustomed to hearing "can" and "cannot" in prescriptive contexts that such statements are open to misinterpretation. This paragraph is intended to be purely descriptive in orientation. "Can" and "cannot" are used merely to state generalizations or hypotheses based on observation of normal language behavior and vulnerable to overturn or limitation by further observation of normal language behavior in the same language type.

the subject (*he*). In (56), the sentence stress is moved onto the auxiliary; otherwise it would be on the last word in the sentence.

The following two sentence pairs seem closely parallel to (55) and (56):

> *He saw a ghóst.* ⟺ *Did he see a ghóst?*   (59)
> *He saw a ghóst.* ⟺ *He díd see a ghost.*   (60)

The parallelism between (55) and (59) or between (56) and (60) would suggest that the same relations are involved. But the formulations in (57) and (58) cannot, by themselves, describe the relations in (59) and (60). One possibility is to interpose a third, but nonoccurrent, sentence. So expanded, these sets of sentences can be compared directly with those that seem parallel:

> *He saw a ghóst.* ⟺ ˣ*He did see a ghóst.* ⟺ *Did he see a ghóst?*   (59)
> *He will see a ghóst.* ⟺ *Will he see a ghóst?*   (55)

> *He saw a ghóst.* ⟺ ˣ*He did see a ghóst.* ⟺ *He díd see a ghost.*   (60)
> *He will see a ghóst.* ⟺ *He wíll see a ghost.*   (56)

It is now evident that (59) does share with (55) the relations formulated by rule (57), and the other two share the relation formulated by rule (58). In addition, (59) and (60) share another relation which can be formulated as follows:

$$Verb + \text{-}ed \Leftrightarrow do + \text{-}ed + Verb \qquad (61)$$

We must understand, of course, that *saw* equals *see* + *-ed* and *did* equals *do* + *-ed*. The intermediate sentence — ˣ*He did see a ghóst.* — with stress on *ghóst*, is not acceptable present-day English.[6]

The relation (61) never alone links any two sentences, both of which occur in normal modern English. It occurs only as one member in a chain of relations. The others in these chains may, however, occur by themselves linking quite normal sentences. Such sentence pairs must contain auxiliaries, as do, for example, the sentences in (55) and (56).

All this is equivalent to describing *do* as a meaningless auxiliary. It is meaningless because there cannot occur two contrasting sentences exactly alike except that one has auxiliary *do* and one does not. Only elements that contrast can be said to have meaning. *Do* is used only when the grammar requires an auxiliary and no other is at hand. That is, *do* occurs only in sentences which are linked by agnate relations of the kind just described to sentences which do not contain an auxiliary.

---

[6] See Chapter 16 for a discussion of the changes in the use of auxiliary *do* between Elizabethan times and the present.

MIXED CHAINS

A pair of sentences can be related by a chain of relations of two kinds. Many examples present themselves; the following is typical:

A *book is on the table.* $\Leftrightarrow$ *There is a book on the table.*

$\;|||$ $\qquad\qquad\qquad\qquad\qquad$ $|||$

A pencil is in the box. $\Leftrightarrow$ *There is a pencil in the box.* $\qquad$ (62)

The diagonal pairs in (62) are related by a chain of one agnation and one enation. This is of very little interest, except as the system from which it is taken is useful as a means of checking relations for grammatical pertinence. No one is likely to give it a second thought.

The situation is quite different, however, with certain other chains of substitutions and transformations. The relations linking some kinds of questions to equivalent statements are examples:

$\qquad$ *She can bake a pie.* $\qquad\qquad$ *What can she bake?* $\qquad$ (63)

Any description of the relation here will have to note both a difference in the major elements (*pie* is only at the left) and a difference in structure signaled by a contrast in order. The description will be most satisfactory if these can be separated, that is, if the relation can be analyzed into a chain, each member of which is either of one type or the other. The description of the relation in (63) must involve at least two steps, perhaps more.

There is another, somewhat rarer, type of question that is also related in some way:

$\qquad$ *She can bake what?* $\qquad$ OR $\qquad$ *She can bake a what?* $\qquad$ (64)

This is used to express astonishment, disbelief, or occasionally merely to ask for confirmation. It almost always echoes an immediately preceding statement by another speaker:

A. *She can bake a pie.*
B. *She can bake a whát?*
A. *You heard me — a pie.* $\qquad$ (65)

This type of question is most likely to be heard following an unusual or unexpected statement:

A. *Podunk High School just beat Army by six touchdowns.*
B. *Podunk High beat whó?* $\qquad$ (66)

Such questions focus incredulity upon one particular part of the whole sentence. They leave the rest minimally changed except sometimes, as in (66), to delete grammatically unessential parts. The commoner type of question, often used dispassionately in asking for information, recasts the whole sentence.

The relations between the statement and various kinds of questions seems best diagrammed more or less as follows:

$$She\ can\ bake\ a\ pie. \equiv She\ can\ bake\ a\ what?$$
$$\Updownarrow$$
$$^{\times}can\ she\ bake\ what \equiv Can\ she\ bake\ a\ pie?$$
$$\Updownarrow$$
$$What\ can\ she\ bake? \tag{67}$$

$$He\ taught\ Latin. \equiv He\ taught\ what?$$
$$\Updownarrow$$
$$^{\times}he\ did\ teach\ Latin$$
$$\Updownarrow$$
$$^{\times}did\ he\ teach\ what \equiv Did\ he\ teach\ Latin?$$
$$\Updownarrow$$
$$What\ did\ he\ teach? \tag{68}$$

In (67) the longest chain of relations is four; in (68) it is five. This seems excessive at first sight, since some of the intermediate forms are unused. But it turns out to be simpler in the long run to describe the system in this way rather than skip the intermediate steps. For one thing, it makes possible treating the following set of sentences in an exactly parallel way. In turn this seems to fit satisfactorily with the native speaker's "feel".

$$Mary\ will\ write\ it. \equiv Who\ will\ write\ it?$$
$$\Updownarrow$$
$$^{\times}will\ who\ write\ it \equiv Will\ Mary\ write\ it?$$
$$\Updownarrow$$
$$Who\ will\ write\ it? \tag{69}$$

The two questions with *who* in (69) look very much alike. Their profound difference is shown by their different places in such a scheme of sentence relations. In spoken English, the two types would have contrasting stress and intonation patterns. The surprise question is rarely written except in dialogue where the context will usually serve to identify it. It is, therefore, of little consequence that it is in some instances, as (69), identical in spelling with the more usual yes-or-no question.

Sentence relations range from simple to complex, with the latter often analyzable as combinations of simpler ones. These elemental relations are grammatical features, part of the system of the language, and hence within the domain of grammars. Even a severely abridged presentation of the patterns of English must, if it is to be representative of the whole, present some selection of material from this part of the system. Sentence relations, moreover, have a significance in other fields of English studies that also demands that they be given attention.

It has become almost axiomatic among linguists that there is a grammatically correct way in any language to say anything which the speakers of that language will have need of saying. Occasional limitations are found to be largely in the vocabulary, and, hence, easily remediable. If we consider the transmission of information as the function of language, then it is clear that every language is adequate.

At this level, however, languages are not merely adequate — they seem recklessly extravagant. Most simple messages can be conveyed not in one acceptable way, but in several, perhaps scores or hundreds. All of these are equally effective at the rudimentary level of communicating information. Much of this variety of expression arises from patterns of sentence relation. These provide alternative ways of framing sentences, and specify to the speaker of the language the basic semantic identity of sets of forms. Another part comes from the existence of synonyms or near synonyms. All of it gives a language a capacity much greater than that needed for simple transmission of messages.

This flexibility makes it possible for a speaker or writer to rise above the level of mere message framing and to use the choices in language to add other qualities to his discourse. With skill he can suit it to the subject, the situation, and the audience, adjusting it simultaneously in several separate and sometimes conflicting respects. He can make it lucid, confused, precise, vague, or ambiguous — perhaps as he desires and thinks appropriate, perhaps only as his personal limitations restrict his full use of the apparatus. Some people can do all these things simultaneously and add a final touch of artistry.

All these ways in which a speaker or writer can vary his language, still keeping his basic message unchanged, we usually call style. It is simply the exploitation of the flexibility of the language. As such it is rooted in the sets of synonymous words and constructions which the language provides.

Any increase in skill with language has two major components. One is an increased repertoire of choices, the addition of patterns and the clearer sensing of the relations between patterns. The second is growing sensitivity to the implications of these choices, greater ability to select in an effective way. Grammar can give some guidance for the first of these, but since sentence relations are basic to language flexibility, it must be a kind of grammar that directs attention to sentence relations.

Chapter 10

Generative Grammar—*1*

Scholarly traditional grammars, school grammars, structural grammars, and most modern linguistically oriented grammars all deal with much the same problems. The statements, despite very obvious differences in detail, are all organized in much the same way. They share more of their basic assumptions than is ordinarily realized. It is, therefore, profitable to compare them, point by point. Indeed, this is just what has been done in Chapters 5 to 8. The comparison will be resumed in Chapter 13.

A grammar can, however, be organized in a quite different way. One possibility produces what is known as a generative grammar. Even when dealing with the same problems, the approach is so different from that of those already discussed as to make point-by-point comparison difficult or even meaningless. Moreover, generative grammars characteristically deal with a slightly different range of problems, or at least place the emphasis differently among the problems. For these reasons, generative grammars were not brought into the comparisons in Chapters 5 to 8. However, they are beginning to have a heavy impact on thinking about English structure, and must not be neglected. It is necessary to compare the whole structure of a generative grammar with that more or less common to the other types discussed in this book.[1]

To do so, we will first present a sample. This will be a restricted grammar of English. By this is meant one which does not purport to account

---

[1] These nongenerative grammars can conveniently be called "descriptive". Of course, no such designation is particularly satisfactory, but this term has been used in this sense, and no better is at hand. Descriptive grammars deal, however successfully, with the problem of providing an analysis for a given sample of language (say, a sentence), as opposed to generative grammars which generate or produce sentences (the two operations are not the same; see the discussion at the end of this chapter), but do not provide any explicit equipment for finding an analysis for a given sentence.

for all the sentences of English, but only for a small and selected sample. The claim will be made, however, that for those sentences within its purview the sample grammar gives correct results. This claim can be examined, and something of the problems of validation of a generative grammar seen.

The sample grammar presented here is generative, but not transformational. It is not, therefore, of the type most widely discussed today. But it does share many of the interesting features of the transformational-generative type of grammar. It will serve to illustrate some of those features, and to relate generative grammars more easily to the types discussed earlier. In the next chapter the place of transformations in a generative grammar will be exemplified and discussed.

A SAMPLE GENERATIVE GRAMMAR

The sample grammar will be presented in the algebra-like notation commonly used in generative grammars. Two conventions must be explained before the grammar can be read:

The arrow, →, may be interpreted in either of two ways. Perhaps most basic would be something like "may consist of". That is, an expression like $S \rightarrow NP + VP$ may be considered to mean "an S may consist of an NP plus a VP". The meanings of the symbols, S, NP, and VP will be discussed at a later point. For the present, the question is best avoided; they are just expressions that occur in the grammar. Since such statements as $NP \rightarrow Det + N_2$ and $VP \rightarrow \text{-}ed + V_3$ also occur in the grammar, it follows that S may consist of $Det + N_2 + \text{-}ed + V_3$. As other statements of the grammar are considered, still more complex equivalents of S may be found.

For convenient practical use, the grammar can be considered as a set of rules directing an operation by which sentences are produced. In this way of looking at it, it is most appropriate to read the arrow, →, as "rewrite ... as ... ". That is, $S \rightarrow NP + VP$ may be read "rewrite S as NP plus VP". In a similarly convenient way, S, NP, and VP are simply symbols that are manipulated on paper, written, and then replaced by something else. That is, wherever S occurs in the calculation, it may be replaced by $NP + VP$, and it must be replaced by something, so that it disappears as the sentence is produced.

To produce a sentence, that is, to calculate with the grammar, the first step is to write down S, the agreed starting point. Then on the next line, representing the second step, some equivalent expression is put down. This is gotten by finding in the grammar a rule that tells something by which S can be replaced. That is, we look for a rule starting $S \rightarrow$. If there is more than one such rule, we may choose any one we please. From the point of view of the grammar they are all equally good. One such rule is $S \rightarrow NP + VP$. If this rule is selected, the second line of the calculation will read $NP + VP$. The next rule to be used must be either one that starts $NP \rightarrow$ or one that starts $VP \rightarrow$. For each, there are several possibilities, each leading to a different result in the third line. One is selected, say $NP \rightarrow Det + N_2$. The expression to the right of the arrow is written in the place in the sequence occupied by NP. VP must be carried down unchanged through this step. The result on the third line is $Det + N_2 + VP$.

There may be two or more ways of rewriting one symbol (that is, one structure may consist of two or more different sequences of lower-ranked structures). For example, the sample grammar includes the following three rules:

$$NP \rightarrow Det + N_2$$
$$NP \rightarrow N\text{-}prop$$
$$NP \rightarrow Pr$$

Sets of alternatives like this make it possible for one grammar to lead to a considerable variety of sentences. To make the alternatives clear, it is convenient to group them all together, and indeed to gather the three rules into one statement:

$$NP \rightarrow \begin{bmatrix} Det + N_2 \\ N\text{-}prop \\ Pr \end{bmatrix}$$

Braces used in this way will indicate alternatives. In some rules (the lexical rules) alternatives have been written in one line separated by commas. The difference in mode of writing is just a matter of convenience.

In producing a sentence it is preferable to apply one rule at a time through much of the process. This helps to keep things straight and to avoid certain very easy confusions.

Each group of rules is numbered for easy reference. A few numbers have been skipped. They are held for a later point where more extensive grammars covering additional types of sentences will be presented. In this way, equivalent rules will have the same numbers in the three sample grammars to be examined.

P1 $\quad S \rightarrow \begin{bmatrix} NP + VP \\ Interj \end{bmatrix}$

P2 $\quad VP \rightarrow \begin{bmatrix} \text{-}ed + V_3 \\ \text{-}s + V_3 \\ Mod + V_3 \end{bmatrix}$

P4 $\quad V_3 \rightarrow \begin{bmatrix} have + \text{-}en + V_2 \\ V_2 \end{bmatrix}$

P5 $\quad V_2 \rightarrow \begin{bmatrix} be + \text{-}ing + V_1 \\ V_1 \end{bmatrix}$

P6 $V_1 \rightarrow \begin{cases} V\text{-}i \\ V\text{-}t + NP \\ V\text{-}b + NP \\ V\text{-}l + AP \\ be + NP + \text{-}'s \\ have + NP \\ be + \text{-}en + V\text{-}t \end{cases}$

P9 $NP \rightarrow \begin{cases} Det + N_2 \\ N\text{-}prop \\ Pr \end{cases}$

P13 $N_2 \rightarrow \begin{cases} AP + N_2 \\ N_1 \end{cases}$

P14 $N_1 \rightarrow \begin{cases} N_2 + N_1 \\ N\text{-}c \end{cases}$

P16 $Det \rightarrow \begin{cases} D \\ NP + \text{-}'s \end{cases}$

P17 $AP \rightarrow \begin{cases} Int + Adj \\ Adj \end{cases}$

The first part of the grammar above consists of ten sets of rules, a total of twenty-seven rules. Each provides a rewriting of one of ten symbols, S, NP, VP, V_3, V_2, V_1, N_2, N_1, Det, AP. The rules must be applied until none of these symbols remain, that is, until the rules cannot be applied any further. The result will be a formula consisting of symbols representing certain function words, *have* or *be*, certain affixes, *-ed*, *-s*, *-en*, *-ing*, and *-'s*, and symbols representing certain parts of speech or subclasses, *Interj*, *Mod*, *V-i*, *V-t*, *V-b*, *V-l*, *N-c*, *N-prop*, *Pr*, *D*, *Int*, *Adj*. Each rule in the first part of the grammar replaces one single symbol, sometimes simply by another symbol, sometimes by a sequence of two or three. These rules may be called phrase-structure rules. For convenience they have been numbered with a prefix P to identify them as phrase-structure rules. They may be referred to more briefly as P-rules.

The second set of rules are lexical rules, and will be designated L. We will not number them, but they might be labeled L1, L2, and so on. Each rule consists of a list of words in a particular part of speech or subclass. They are the items which can replace the symbols remaining after the P-rules have been applied completely. The lexical rules must be applied until no class symbols remain. This limited grammar has eight parts of speech, one with two subclasses and one with four. A more elaborate grammar would recognize many more, and might subdivide several of those shown here. The total number of lexical rules might be several times this. Each list can be expanded — some very greatly, some by the addition of only a very few words. We list only enough examples for our immediate purpose.

L   *V-i*   → {*walk, swim, run, breathe, sleep*}
       V-t   → {*catch, strike, visit, buy, congratulate*}
       V-b   → {*be, become, remain, seem*}
       V-l   → {*be, seem, look, appear, feel*}
       N-c   → {*man, boy, wife, husband, brother, sister, dealer, car,*
                             bread, sports, city, lady, dog, temper, boxer}
      N-prop → {*James, Peter, Mary, Pauline, Fido, Spot*}
       Pr   → {*he, she, it, someone*}
       D   → {*the, a, this, that, each, every*}
       Int   → {*very, extremely, quite, too, less*}
       Adj → {*good, bad, new, old, lazy, ambitious, beautiful, young*}
       Mod → {*will, would, can, could, might*}
       Interj → {*yes, no, ouch, wow*}

After the lexical rules have been applied, the result is a string of suffixes, function words, and vocabulary items all connected by plus marks. The suffixes need next to be attached to the proper words and to be brought into proper form. For this purpose an additional type of rule is required. We will call them M-rules, which can be thought of as meaning "morphologic rules".[2] These rules combine stems and affixes producing words of normal spoken or written form. The M-rules should properly be worked out in some considerable detail, but throughout this chapter and the next our attention is focused on other parts of the grammar. Just enough of the M-rules will be given to suggest their effect. Anyone acquainted with English can fill out the rules in a crude form by analogy.

M   *-s + have* → *has*   *-ed + have* → *had*
     -s + be   → *is*   *-ed + be*   → *was*
     -s + walk → *walks*   *-ed + walk* → *walked*
     -s + swim → *swims*   *-ed + swim* → *swam*
             etc.   etc.
    -en + have → *had*   *-ing + have* → *having*
    -en + be   → *been*   *-ing + be*   → *being*
    -en + walk → *walked*   *-ing + walk* → *walking*
    -en + swim → *swum*   *-ing + swim* → *swimming*
             etc.   etc.
        he   + *-'s* → *his*
        she   + *-'s* → *her*
        someone + *-'s* → *someone's*
        man   + *-'s* → *man's*
                   etc.

---

[2] These rules are usually referred to as "morphophonemic" rules. "Morphophonemic", however, is one of the most vexed technical terms in linguistics. In no two systemizations of linguistic theory is it used in the same way. Transformational-generative linguists have used it to apply to all the process covered by a comprehensive final set

M-rules differ from the other two types in frequently having two or three symbols before the arrow. That is, a sequence of symbols is rewritten, sometimes by a single word, sometimes by a sequence.

This grammar, then, consists of three kinds of rules, P, L, and M. It falls into three sections, each containing only one kind of rule. While it would be possible to apply certain lexical rules before all the phrase-structure rules are exhausted, nothing would be gained. Something would be lost. With careful separation of the rules into three sets, it is much easier to keep things straight, to avoid confusion, and to understand the process.

PRODUCING SENTENCES

The production of a few sentences by operation of the grammar will show how it works. The numbers at the left indicate the rule that has been used to obtain the result in the same line. In the first example, the elements introduced at each rewriting have been marked by underlining. These underlinings are not a normal part of the calculation, being strictly unnecessary. Otherwise the list of successive stages of sentence production is very much like what one would ordinarily write as the process goes forward.

	S
P1	$NP + VP$
P2	$NP + \underline{\text{-}ed} + V_2$
P4	$NP + \text{-}ed + \underline{have + \text{-}en} + V_2$
P5	$NP + \text{-}ed + have + \text{-}en + \underline{be + \text{-}ing} + V_1$
P6	$NP + \text{-}ed + have + \text{-}en + be + \text{-}ing + \underline{V\text{-}i}$
P9	$\underline{Det + N_2} + \text{-}ed + have + \text{-}en + be + \text{-}ing + V\text{-}i$
P13	$Det + \underline{AP + N_2} + \text{-}ed + have + \text{-}en + be + \text{-}ing + V\text{-}i$
P13	$Det + AP + \underline{N_1} + \text{-}ed + have + \text{-}en + be + \text{-}ing + V\text{-}i$
P14	$Det + AP + \underline{N\text{-}c} + \text{-}ed + have + \text{-}en + be + \text{-}ing + V\text{-}i$
P16	$\underline{D} + AP + N\text{-}c + \text{-}ed + have + \text{-}en + be + \text{-}ing + V\text{-}i$
P17	$D + \underline{Int + Adj} + N\text{-}c + \text{-}ed + have + \text{-}en + be + \text{-}ing + V\text{-}i$

There remains in the last string of symbols nothing which can be rewritten by the P-rules. Therefore, this part of the calculation is finished, and we must turn to the L-rules. After five rules have been applied, one at a time, the string is as follows, with no remaining word-class symbols:

L $the + very + lazy + man + \text{-}ed + have + \text{-}en + be + \text{-}ing + sleep$

---

of rules. In this are included most of the rules equivalent to the morphology and the phonology of other linguists. "Morphophonemic" in their use, then, may be taken to mean the combination of these two systems of structure rather than any borderline portion of either or any bridge between the two. We can very appropriately call the M-rules of these two chapters morphologic because the phonologic (or graphemic) details are not to be discussed.

Finally, M-rules must be applied to attach all affixes to the appropriate stems and give the resulting words the correct form. Each of these rules has the effect of reversing the order of two elements. It just happens that English suffixes are often best introduced into the string before the stem.

$$the + very + lazy + man + \underbrace{-ed + have} + \underbrace{-en + be} + \underbrace{-ing + sleep}$$

M   *The   very   lazy   man   had   been   sleeping.*

The M-rules must also include some provision to introduce capitalization and punctuation. These will merely be assumed here, but could be formulated in a complete grammar.

The same sequence of steps can be shown in the diagram below. Each symbol is shown only where it appears for the first time. Each element is joined by a line to all those elements which represent it below.

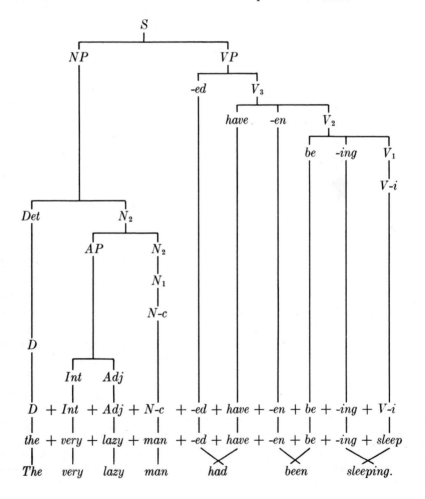

The diagram so produced is a representation of the structure of the sentence in terms of immediate constituents. Every element is labeled. The operation of producing a sentence produces a structural analysis for that sentence simultaneously. The structural analysis is implicit in the operation. For this reason the structure is sometimes referred to as a "derivation".

Another example will show how the grammar can produce short sentences. The rewritings are given and the derivation is diagrammed alongside.

S

P1 $NP + VP$

P2 $NP + \text{-}s + V_3$

P4 $NP + \text{-}s + V_2$

P5 $NP + \text{-}s + V_1$

P6 $NP + \text{-}s + V\text{-}i$

P9 $Pr + \text{-}s + V\text{-}i$

L $he + \text{-}s + sleep$

M $He \quad sleeps.$

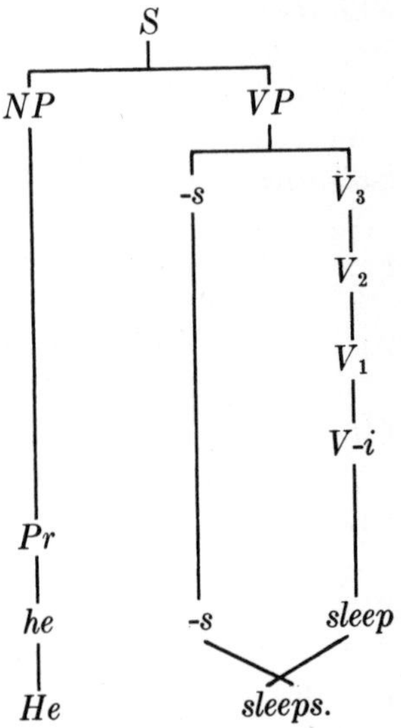

Comparison of this example with that on page 228 will quickly reveal the source of the difference in structure. To produce *He sleeps.*, the shortest alternative has been selected at every place where the rules allow a choice. To produce the longer sentence, longer alternatives have been elected at some of the places where a choice is presented. A still longer sentence may be produced by always choosing the longest option. The reader is invited to try this for himself.

If it is desired to produce a complete sentence, the operation is begun with S. If only part of a sentence is desired, this can be produced by starting with one of the other symbols. To illustrate certain features of the grammar we can work with such small pieces. This may save space and confusion and keep the point under discussion in focus. For example, a noun phrase can be produced starting with NP as follows:

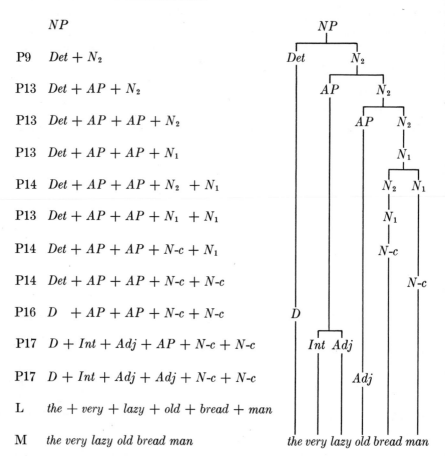

	NP
P9	$Det + N_2$
P13	$Det + AP + N_2$
P13	$Det + AP + AP + N_2$
P13	$Det + AP + AP + N_1$
P14	$Det + AP + AP + N_2 + N_1$
P13	$Det + AP + AP + N_1 + N_1$
P14	$Det + AP + AP + N\text{-}c + N_1$
P14	$Det + AP + AP + N\text{-}c + N\text{-}c$
P16	$D + AP + AP + N\text{-}c + N\text{-}c$
P17	$D + Int + Adj + AP + N\text{-}c + N\text{-}c$
P17	$D + Int + Adj + Adj + N\text{-}c + N\text{-}c$
L	$the + very + lazy + old + bread + man$
M	*the very lazy old bread man*

Rule P13 has an interesting peculiarity. The same symbol, N_2, appears on both sides of the arrow. As a result the rule can be applied over and over. In the example above, P13 has been applied twice to bring in two adjective phrases. It might have been used in this way three or more times. In this manner, phrases like *the very beautiful lazy young lady* can be produced.

Rules that can be applied successively more than once are called recursive. They are an important feature, because they make it possible for a grammar of limited size to produce sentences of unlimited length. Of course, a sentence with seven adjectives in a row would be most unusual English. No recursive rule is ordinarily reapplied without reasonable limit. However, even used very judiciously, a few recursive rules can greatly increase the length and variety of sentences generated by a given grammar.

Our sample grammar has three recursive rules or sequences of rules. The two rules P9 and P16 are another instance. They are as follows:

P9 $NP \rightarrow Det + N_2$
P16 $Det \rightarrow NP + \text{-}'s$

Combined they read:

$$NP \rightarrow NP + \text{-}'s + N_2$$

NP occurs on both sides of the arrow, so the combination is recursive. The following is an example which will illustrate a possible effect of such recursiveness:

										NP
P9								Det		$+ N_2$
P16								$NP + \text{-}'s + N_2$		
P9							Det	$+ N_2$	$+ \text{-}'s + N_2$		
P16						$NP + \text{-}'s + N_2$	$+ \text{-}'s + N_2$			
P9					Det	$+ N_2$	$+ \text{-}'s + N_2$	$+ \text{-}'s + N_2$		
P16				$NP + \text{-}'s + N_2$	$+ \text{-}'s + N_2$	$+ \text{-}'s + N_2$			
P9		Det	$+ N_2$	$+ \text{-}'s + N_2$	$+ \text{-}'s + N_2$	$+ \text{-}'s + N_2$			
P16	$NP + \text{-}'s + N_2$	$+ \text{-}'s + N_2$	$+ \text{-}'s + N_2$	$+ \text{-}'s + N_2$			
P9	Pr	$+ \text{-}'s + N_2$	$+ \text{-}'s + N_2$	$+ \text{-}'s + N_2$	$+ \text{-}'s + N_2$			

Then must follow sufficient applications of rules P13 and P14 to replace every N_2 by $N\text{-}c$. L-rules may then replace Pr and each $N\text{-}c$ by an appropriate word. Then M-rules combine $\text{-}'s$ with the adjacent stem as follows:

$$he + \text{-}'s + sister + \text{-}'s + husband + \text{-}'s + brother + \text{-}'s + wife$$

     his   *sister's*   *husband's*   *brother's*   *wife*

In the application of rules P13 and P14, modifiers might have been introduced. The result could be very complex phrases like:

his younger sister's new husband's oldest brother's second wife

Still longer ones are possible, but it is difficult to find combinations that make sense.

Rule P14 is also recursive, but in a still more interesting way. N_1 appears on both sides of the arrow as it stands. In addition, N_2 appears on the right and this may be developed into N_1. That is, the rule is doubly recursive. As a result a sequence of nouns can be produced in more than one way. There is accordingly more than one structure. The following two derivations illustrate:

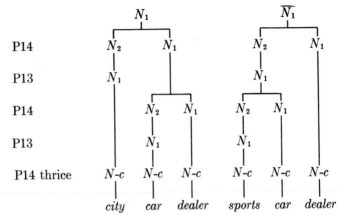

City car dealer and *sports car dealer* are the same over-all construction (both N_1), but differ significantly in internal construction. Considerably more variety of structure is possible with longer sequences of nouns. And these occur: *automobile seat cover manufacturer, express highway interchange caution sign, Parent-Teacher Association school traffic safety committee chairman.*

Moreover, this recursive feature will allow the generation of graphically identical sequences which not only have different internal structures, but also may represent different over-all constructions,[3] for example, an N_2 and an N_1:

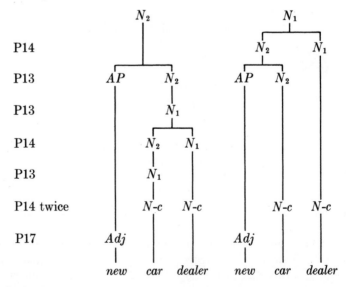

---

[3] Because P14 is recursive, the difference between an N_2 and an N_1 is not particularly significant. The principle is, however, important. Things that look alike need not be alike, either in internal structure or in distributional possibilities.

One of these means a 'new dealer in cars', the other, a 'dealer in new cars'. Why this should be so is quite evident from the derivations.

The example illustrates in a very simple manner the way in which a generative grammar handles structural ambiguity. Whenever two different sequences of rules or different ways of applying the same rules lead to the same words (superficially the same sentence) by different derivations, there are considered to be two sentences. The outward form is ambiguous. To take advantage of this, a generative grammar should be designed so that there is only one derivation for any one sentence unless it is, in fact, ambiguous.[4]

CORRECTING AND EXPANDING THE GRAMMAR

Such a grammar can be tested only by operating it to produce a sample of sentences, examining them, and determining whether they seem acceptable to competent native speakers. Consider the following example:

	S
P1	$NP + VP$
P2	$NP + \text{-}ed + V_3$
P4	$NP + \text{-}ed + V_2$
P5	$NP + \text{-}ed + V_1$
P6	$NP + \text{-}ed + V\text{-}t + NP$
P9	$Pr + \text{-}ed + V\text{-}t + NP$
P9	$Pr + \text{-}ed + V\text{-}t + Pr$
L	$she + \text{-}ed + visit + he$
M	*She visited he.*

This sentence, though produced strictly according to the rules of our restricted grammar, is not a proper English sentence. Here, then, is a test of the grammar in which it fails. It must either be rejected or amended. Since it has otherwise guided the production of quite acceptable sentences, amendment is the preferable course.

What is required is some rule or set of rules that will select what many grammars call the "objective form" of the pronoun whenever it appears as the direct object of a verb. What came out as *he* can be seen to be the direct object by tracing it back to the NP which was introduced by rule P6. At that point, then, something must be done that will mark this NP as one which must lead to *him* rather than to *he*. Two possibilities present themselves. For the present grammar one would be to reformulate the rule

[4] This innocent-seeming requirement is sometimes difficult to fulfill. A large-scale generative grammar may be a very formidable undertaking. However, the requirement is not peculiar to generative grammars. Descriptive grammars should not give two descriptions of the same fact without making clear that there is overlap.

in P6 to read $V_1 \rightarrow V\text{-}t + NP + \text{-}m$. Then a new set of M-rules can be added as follows:

M he $+ \text{-}m \rightarrow him$ $she + \text{-}m \rightarrow her$
        $someone + \text{-}m \rightarrow someone$ $man + \text{-}m \rightarrow man$
                                                              etc.

Now the last part of the derivation will appear:

P6 $NP + \text{-}ed + V\text{-}t + NP + \text{-}m$
P9 $Pr + \text{-}ed + V\text{-}t + NP + \text{-}m$
P9 $Pr + \text{-}ed + V\text{-}t + Pr + \text{-}m$
L $she + \text{-}ed + visit + he + \text{-}m$
M $She \quad visited \quad him.$

Another method would work just as well, except that it would require adding a new P-rule very much like P6. This would be to reformulate the relevant part of P6 as follows: $V \rightarrow V\text{-}t + NP_m$, that is, setting up a new kind of construction rather than merely adding an extra element. Then the rule that would be needed could be either of the following:

$$NP_m \rightarrow \begin{bmatrix} Det + N_2 \\ N\text{-}prop \\ Pr + \text{-}m \end{bmatrix} \qquad\qquad NP_m \rightarrow \begin{bmatrix} Det + N_2 \\ N\text{-}prop \\ Pr_m \end{bmatrix}$$

With the first, there would be needed the same new M-rules, though the grammar is now so formulated that it will not be necessary to include $man + \text{-}m \rightarrow man$, and so on. With the second, there will be needed instead a new L-rule: $Pr_m \rightarrow \{him, her, \ldots\}$. Which of these, or of some other possibilities, is selected by the grammarian may be affected by important considerations as the grammar is expanded. But as it now stands, all these work equally well.

The grammar presented above does not generate negative sentences. It will be instructive to see how it might be amended to do so. We shall restrict our attention to the kind of negative sentence exemplified by:

The very lazy man had not been sleeping.

That is to say, we shall not ask for any new type of sentence, except that a *not* negating the predicate should be introduced into the proper place if desired.

Not can follow an auxiliary. This may be *have* introduced by rule P4, *be* introduced by rule P5, or *be* introduced by one alternative in P6. *Not* can also follow a *Mod* (modal) introduced by P2. *Not* can follow *be* as a main verb introduced by three alternatives in P6. Examples of these follow:

It | *has not come.*	(*have* from P4)
It | *is not coming.*	(*be* from P5)
It | *is not caught.*	(*be* from P6, $V_1 \rightarrow be + -en + V\text{-}t$)
It | *will not come.*	(*Mod* from P2)
It | *is not good.*	(*be* from P6, $V_1 \rightarrow V\text{-}l + AP$)
It | *is not a man.*	(*be* from P6, $V_1 \rightarrow V\text{-}b + NP$)
It | *is not his.*	(*be* from P6, $V_1 \rightarrow be + NP + \text{-}'s$)

Not thus appears in at least four places in the sentence structure, but only in one place in any single sentence. These positions can be shown as follows:

It will be very difficult to insert *not* into the phrase-structure rules so that it will come in exactly these places, but in only the correct one of them in any given instance. However, *not* always comes after the first word in the verb phrase. It will, therefore, be possible to introduce *not* by a rule that puts it at the beginning of the *VP*, and then supply an M-rule[5] that will move it to its proper place. One way to do this would be to expand rule P2:

$$P2 \qquad VP \rightarrow \begin{cases} \text{-}ed & + V_3 \\ \text{-}s & + V_3 \\ Mod & + V_3 \\ \text{-}ed + not + V_3 \\ \text{-}s \; + not + V_3 \\ Mod + not + V_3 \end{cases}$$

Then we must add the following set of rules:

$$M \qquad \begin{array}{lll} \text{-}s & + not + have & \rightarrow \{has \; not, \;\; hasn't\}^6 \\ \text{-}ed & + not + have & \rightarrow \{had \; not, \;\; hadn't\} \\ \text{-}s & + not + be & \rightarrow \{is \; not, \;\;\; isn't\} \\ will & + not & \rightarrow \{will \; not, \;\; won't\} \;\; \text{etc.} \end{array}$$

---

[5] This is a somewhat unusual form for an M-rule. Actually it is a covert T-rule. Compare the treatment of *not* in Chapter 12.

[6] With *have* as a main verb there are two negative forms; *he doesn't have* and *he hasn't*. Only the latter is provided for in these restricted grammars. A slight addition to the rules could provide for the other.

The rules can now be tested. It will suffice to develop *VP:*

	VP	VP
P2	$-ed + not + V_3$	$-ed + not + V_3$
P4	$-ed + not + have + -en + V_2$	$-ed + not + V_2$
P5	$-ed + not + have + -en + V_1$	$-ed + not + V_1$
P6	$-ed + not + have + -en + V\text{-}i$	$-ed + not + V\text{-}i$
L	$-ed + not + have + -en + sleep$	$-ed + not + sleep$
M	$\underbrace{had \ not}$ $\underbrace{slept}$	*?*

The first example works out quite satisfactorily with the rules already provided, as do many others. However, we have as yet no M-rule which will apply in a situation like that in the second example. An addition to these rules is called for, but this cannot be of the same simple form as the M-rules we have already seen. The proper final form for the second example is either *did not sleep* or *didn't sleep.* Such forms occur whenever neither *have* not *be* is present. The M-rule, therefore, must specify that both are absent. We have done this by use of a minus sign in the formula. This is inconvenient, but if this solution is not accepted, some other, involving even greater departures from established patterns, will be required.

M	$-s + not - have - be \ \rightarrow \ \{does \ not, \ \ doesn't\}$
	$-ed + not - have - be \ \rightarrow \ \{did \ not, \ \ didn't\}$

Another expansion of the grammar seems most desirable. As first presented, it included no plurals. Some considerable readjustment of the grammar will be required to provide for subject-predicate agreement.[7]

One way to do this would be to have a rule which introduces a plural morpheme in the vicinity of certain nouns. Let us use *pl* to symbolize this. Then we might have a set of M-rules of the form:

M	$boy \ + pl \rightarrow boys$
	$man + pl \rightarrow men$

The question is where and how to introduce this. Clearly something must be done at the very beginning in P1. At this point, the subject and predicate of the sentence separate, and thereafter each is developed independently. However, there must be agreement between subject and predicate, and this must be provided for at the time of separation. One way to handle the problem would be to introduce the same mark of plurality into both halves of the sentence. We might, then, change P1 to include the following as alternatives:

$$P1 \qquad S \rightarrow \begin{bmatrix} NP & + & VP \\ NP + pl + pl + VP \end{bmatrix}$$

[7] In the sample grammars, provision will be made only for sentences with strict subject-verb agreement. (This is within our prerogatives in writing a restricted grammar!) In actual fact, agreement is much more complex in English, witness: *Two and two is four. A dozen eggs is enough. A dozen eggs are enough.*

Then later there would be pairs of rules like the following:

M $- pl + -s + have \rightarrow has$
$+ pl + -s + have \rightarrow have$

That is, the presence or absence of pl would help to determine the form of the first word in the verb phrase.[8]

However, this solution is not satisfactory, even within our restricted grammar, for at least two reasons. First, it does not provide everything that is needed in the development of noun phrases. For example, the following string might be produced: $D + N\text{-}c + pl$. To this we must apply the L-rules. Among possible outcomes would be:

$a + boy + pl$
M $a\ boys$

Somehow we must provide some guidance in selecting a D so that a, *each*, or *every* does not appear before a plural noun. All our L-rules, so far, have been quite straightforward. For any given symbol, any of the listed words can be substituted wherever it occurs. It would be a totally new kind of L-rule if it required us to look ahead, find the $N\text{-}c$ (it might be some distance off), be sure it is the right $N\text{-}c$ (not a noun modifying another noun), and then look to see if there is a pl following it. So we must have two lists of determiner words, one for each kind of noun. Let us call them D_s and D_p.[9] The two lists will overlap. D_s will include all that can precede singular nouns, and D_p all that can precede plural nouns. D comes from *Det*. We must also have two kinds of *Det*, *Det*$_s$ and *Det*$_p$. The distinction can be established in P9, where *Det* comes from NP. If the contrast between singular and plural can be carried down from here both in the line that leads to D and in the line that leads to $N\text{-}c$, agreement will be automatic. Within our conventions, we cannot do this if NP is marked as plural by a following pl. The rule would have to be something like:

$NP + pl \rightarrow Det_p + N_2 + pl$

But we want each P-rule to involve only one symbol to the left of the arrow. The only way to accomplish this is, in effect, to combine NP and pl into one symbol, that is, to have two kinds of NP, NP_s and NP_p, one singular and one plural. Then P1 would read in part:

P1 $S \rightarrow \begin{cases} NP_s + VP_s \\ NP_p + VP_p \end{cases}$

---

[8] These rules need not be stated in exactly this form. It would be preferable to avoid the specification of the absence of an element. This can be done in several ways. Probably the easiest is by adding an element sg to mark singular.

[9] It will suffice for our present purpose to distinguish only singular and plural. In a less restricted grammar further subdivision would be required, and provision would have to be made for mass nouns. See page 135.

A similar argument with reference to VP points in the same direction. We need to have an indication of plurality not only at the beginning of the VP to insure the correct agreement of the verb phrase with the subject, but in addition must have it in at least one other place. In P6, predicate nouns are introduced. These must be made to agree in number with the subject. The first solution, writing pl in both the subject and the predicate, will not work. Distinguishing two kinds of VP, VP_s and VP_p, however, will meet the need.

Unfortunately, as can be seen from the expanded grammar in the next section, this is practically equivalent to writing two parallel grammars, one for singular sentences and one for plural. To make this parallelism as clear as possible, we have used the same numbers for pairs of similar sets of rules. In the second sample grammar there are fourteen numbered sets of P-rules. Ten of these are actually double sets of rules, one for singular subjects and one for plural. One more is a triplet, a set for singular, a set for plural, and a third set to make possible correct forms of pronouns in complements and prepositional phrases. One is the rule which divides the grammar into two streams. Only two sets of rules are not directly involved in the singular-plural dichotomy. A further problem would have arisen if the pronoun I had not been carefully avoided.[10] It is instructive to see what must be done to bring this in, and the reader is urged to experiment with it.

The grammar has been further expanded to bring in three additional types of noun modifiers, postnoun modifiers, numerals and related words, and specifiers. P10, P11, P12, and P15 are added to accomplish this. One further step would be to make P9 recursive to allow two postnoun modifiers as in *the man upstairs in bed*, but the obvious way to do this — $NP \rightarrow NP + PNM$ — leads to some minor difficulties with pronouns. These can, of course, be worked out, but only by adding additional rules. The grammar as it stands is adequate for our present purposes, however.

One new convention has been added merely to shorten the statement. In the first sample grammar, P4 was given as:

$$P4 \qquad V_3 \rightarrow \begin{Bmatrix} have + \text{-}en + V_2 \\ V_2 \end{Bmatrix}$$

That is, V_3 is always replaced by V_2 with or without $have + \text{-}en$. We can more compactly show this by enclosing optional elements in parens, allowing the two alternatives to be collapsed into one statement:

$$P4 \qquad V_3 \rightarrow (have + \text{-}en +) \; V_2$$

The two forms of statement are absolutely equivalent.

---

[10] It should be reiterated that this expanded grammar is also restricted — severely so. Not only are whole sections of the English grammatical system omitted, but every section that is mentioned has had many significant features overlooked.

THE SECOND SAMPLE GRAMMAR

P1
$$S \rightarrow \begin{bmatrix} NP_s + VP_s \\ NP_p + VP_p \\ Interj \end{bmatrix}$$

P2 $VP_s \rightarrow \begin{bmatrix} \text{-}ed_s + (not +) V_{3s} \\ \text{-}s + (not +) V_{3s} \\ Mod + (not +) V_{3s} \end{bmatrix}$ $VP_p \rightarrow \begin{bmatrix} \text{-}ed_p + (not +) V_{3p} \\ \text{-}0 + (not +) V_{3p} \\ Mod + (not +) V_{3p} \end{bmatrix}$

P4 $V_{3s} \rightarrow (have + \text{-}en +) V_{2s}$ $V_{3p} \rightarrow (have + \text{-}en +) V_{2p}$

P5 $V_{2s} \rightarrow (be + \text{-}ing +) V_{1s}$ $V_{2p} \rightarrow (be + \text{-}ing +) V_{1p}$

P6 $V_{1s} \rightarrow \begin{bmatrix} V\text{-}i \\ V\text{-}t + NP_m \\ V\text{-}b + NP_s \\ V\text{-}l + AP \\ be + Adv\text{-}l \\ be + \begin{Bmatrix} NP_s \\ NP_p \end{Bmatrix} + \text{-}'s \\ have + NP_m \\ be + \text{-}en + V\text{-}t \end{bmatrix}$ $V_{1p} \rightarrow \begin{bmatrix} V\text{-}i \\ V\text{-}t + NP_m \\ V\text{-}b + NP_p \\ V\text{-}l + AP \\ be + Adv\text{-}l \\ be + \begin{Bmatrix} NP_s \\ NP_p \end{Bmatrix} + \text{-}'s \\ have + NP_m \\ be + \text{-}en + V\text{-}t \end{bmatrix}$

P9 $NP_s \rightarrow \begin{bmatrix} N_{5s} (+ PNM) \\ Pr\text{-}s \\ N\text{-}prop \end{bmatrix}$ $NP_p \rightarrow \begin{bmatrix} N_{5p} (+ PNM) \\ Pr\text{-}p \end{bmatrix}$

$NP_m \rightarrow \begin{bmatrix} N_{5s} (+ PNM) \\ N_{5p} (+ PNM) \\ Pr\text{-}m \\ N\text{-}prop \end{bmatrix}$

P10 $N_{5s} \rightarrow (Det_s +) N_{4s}$ $N_{5p} \rightarrow (Det_p +) N_{4p}$

P11 $N_{4s} \rightarrow (one +) N_{3s}$ $N_{4p} \rightarrow (Num +) N_{3p}$

P12 $N_{3s} \rightarrow (Spec +) N_{2s}$ $N_{3p} \rightarrow (Spec +) N_{2p}$

P13 $N_{2s} \rightarrow \begin{bmatrix} AP + N_{2s} \\ \text{-}en + V\text{-}t + N_{2s} \\ \text{-}ing + V\text{-}i + N_{2s} \\ N_{1s} \end{bmatrix}$ $N_{2p} \rightarrow \begin{bmatrix} AP + N_{2p} \\ \text{-}en + V\text{-}t + N_{2p} \\ \text{-}ing + V\text{-}i + N_{2p} \\ N_{1p} \end{bmatrix}$

P14 $N_{1s} \rightarrow \begin{bmatrix} N_{2s} + N_{1s} \\ N\text{-}s \end{bmatrix}$ $N_{1p} \rightarrow \begin{bmatrix} N_{2s} + N_{1p} \\ N\text{-}p \end{bmatrix}$

P15 $PNM \rightarrow \begin{bmatrix} Adv\text{-}l \\ Prep + NP_m \end{bmatrix}$

P16 $Det_s \rightarrow \begin{bmatrix} D\text{-}s \\ \begin{Bmatrix} NP_s \\ NP_p \end{Bmatrix} + \text{-}'s \end{bmatrix}$ $Det_p \rightarrow \begin{bmatrix} D\text{-}p \\ \begin{Bmatrix} NP_s \\ NP_p \end{Bmatrix} + \text{-}'s \end{bmatrix}$

P17 $AP \rightarrow (Int +) Adj$

L $V\text{-}i$ →   {*walk, swim, run, breathe, sleep*}

       $V\text{-}t$ →   {*catch, strike, visit, buy, congratulate, own*}

       $V\text{-}b$ →   {*be, become, remain, seem*}

       $V\text{-}l$ →   {*be, seem, look, appear, feel*}

       Mod →   {*will, would, can, could, may, might, should*}

       $N\text{-}s$ →   {*man, boy, wife, husband, brother, sister, dealer, car,*
                           bread, sports, city, lady, dog, temper, boxer}

       $N\text{-}p$ →   {*men, boys, wives, husbands, brothers, sisters, dealers,*
                           cars, cities, ladies, dogs, tempers, boxers}

       $N\text{-}prop$ →   {*James, Peter, Mary, Pauline, Fido, Spot*}

       $Pr\text{-}s$ →   {*he, she, it, someone*}

       $Pr\text{-}p$ →   {*they, we, you*}

       $Pr\text{-}m$ →   {*him, her, it, someone, them, you, me*}

       $D\text{-}s$ →   {*the, a, this, that, each, every*}

       $D\text{-}p$ →   {*the, some, these, those*}

       Num →   {*two, three, four, many, few, umpteen*}

       $Spec$ →   {*same, different, other, certain, first, next, last*}

       Adj →   {*good, bad, new, old, lazy, ambitious, beautiful,*
                           young, mean}

       Int →   {*very, extremely, quite, too, less, exceptionally*}

       $Adv\text{-}l$ →   {*upstairs, there, here, yonder, outside, ashore*}

       $Prep$ →   {*in, on, with, at, by, near, away from*}

       $Interj$ →   {*yes, no, oh, well*}

M $\text{-}ed_s$ + *have*   → *had*

       $\text{-}ed_s$ + *be*   → *was*

       $\text{-}ed_s$ + *not* + *have*   →   {*had not, hadn't*}

       $\text{-}ed_s$ + *not* + *be*   →   {*was not, wasn't*}

       $\text{-}ed_s$ + *not* − *have* − *be* →   {*did not, didn't*}

       $\text{-}ed_s$ + *walk*   → *walked*

       $\text{-}ed_s$ + *swim*   → *swam*   etc.

       $\text{-}ed_p$ + *have*   → *had*

       $\text{-}ed_p$ + *be*   → *were*

       $\text{-}ed_p$ + *not* + *have*   →   {*had not,   hadn't*}

       $\text{-}ed_p$ + *not* + *be*   →   {*were not,   weren't*}

       $\text{-}ed_p$ + *not* − *have* − *be* →   {*did not,   didn't*}

       $\text{-}ed_p$ + *walk*   → *walked*

       $\text{-}ed_p$ + *swim*   → *swam*   etc.

       $\text{-}s$ + *have*   → *has*

       $\text{-}s$ + *be*   → *is*

       $\text{-}s$ + *not* + *have*   →   {*has not,   hasn't*}

       $\text{-}s$ + *not* + *be*   →   {*is not,   isn't*}

       $\text{-}s$ + *not* − *have* − *be* →   {*does not,   doesn't*}

       $\text{-}s$ + *walk*   → *walks*

       $\text{-}s$ + *swim*   → *swims*   etc.

-0	+ have	→ have	
-0	+ be	→ are	
-0	+ not + have	→ {have not, haven't}	
-0	+ not + be	→ {are not, aren't}	
-0	+ not − have − be →	{do not, don't}	
-0	+ walk	→ walk	
-0	+ swim	→ swim	etc.

-en	+ have	→ had	
-en	+ be	→ been	
-en	+ walk	→ walked	
-en	+ swim	→ swum	etc.

-ing	+ have	→ having	
-ing	+ be	→ being	
-ing	+ walk	→ walking	
-ing	+ swim	→ swimming	etc.

he	+ -'s	→ his	
she	+ -'s	→ her	
it	+ -'s	→ its	
someone	+ -'s	→ someone's	
they	+ -'s	→ their	
we	+ -'s	→ our	
you	+ -'s	→ your	
man	+ -'s	→ man's	
men	+ -'s	→ men's	
boys	+ -'s	→ boys'	
Peter	+ -'s	→ Peter's	etc.

A TEST OF THE EXPANDED GRAMMAR

The expanded grammar can be tested by using it to produce a number of sentences, which can then be checked against the feel of a native speaker. We will try only one example. There is no need to list off all the steps in full. The derivational diagram appears on page 242.

This is, of course, the same sentence as was discussed in Chapter 7. It is instructive to compare the tree diagram with that on page 154. It will be seen that they are alike except for two features — the labels and one line, set apart here by the use of dashes.

In Chapter 7 no notice was taken of suffixes or other parts of words. Indeed, a sentence without visible verbal suffix was selected so that the issue might be avoided. This generative grammar might have been designed to further avoid the question. Instead of writing $VP_p \rightarrow \text{-0} + V_{3p}$ in P2, we might have written simply $VP_p \rightarrow V_{3p}$, leaving the zero out. This would have caused difficulties at a later point to make *are* come out instead of *be*, and to get a simple rule to produce *do not*. Probably some ingenuity

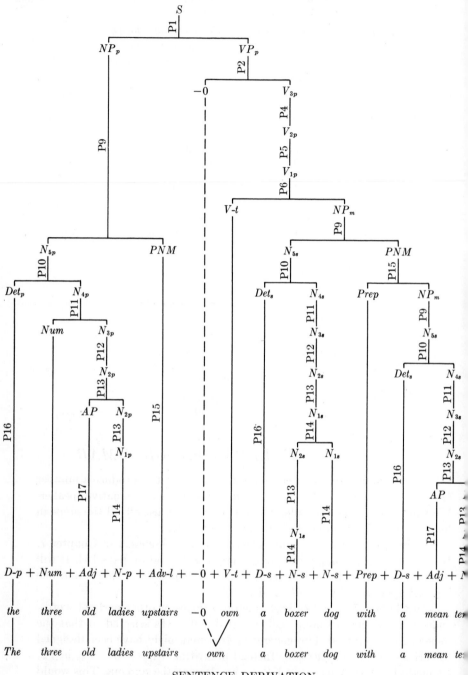

SENTENCE DERIVATION
WITH SECOND SAMPLE GRAMMAR

would find a strategem. Generative grammarians sometimes seem particularly prone to clever devices, some of which hardly reflect any significant reality, but which do produce the desired end. Their grammars are sometimes a bit like robots — they move like men, propelled by solenoids and stepping motors, not muscles. Perhaps the zero is itself simply one of these tricks. We cannot judge until we examine the full system, and evaluate all the consequences of every analysis.

Apart from the questions that are raised by zero, the problem is certainly real in other sentences. Had this been "past" tense, there would have been an -*ed* behaving in much the same way. This could not be overlooked. We shall see in Chapter 13 that a solution comparable to that in our generative grammar has much to commend it, not only in a generative grammar but also in one on the IC or slot-and-filler plan.

All this means, then, that the generative grammar just presented is essentially equivalent to the description of sentences in IC terms discussed in Chapter 7. That is, the two statements would be entirely equivalent if the one were elaborated to cover verb phrases, and the other to cover various details discussed before and overlooked here. A generative grammar is often no more than a different format in which to present a grammar. It is not necessarily different in any more essential way. Any adequate descriptive grammar can be restated in generative terms, and conversely.[11]

But this difference of statement has some interesting features and deserves some closer attention.

EXPLICITNESS

A native speaker of English manipulates very elaborate structures with ease and precision. He does this subconsciously in ways of which he is largely unaware, unless they are brought to his attention by formal instruction in grammar, or by deliberate, disciplined introspection and experimentation.

A grammar may be viewed as an effort to give explicit account of what it is that the native speaker does, or rather of certain facets of this behavior which we consider to be language structure. The speaker, of course, has an excellent command of the patterns. With occasional lapses, he operates them well. But he cannot describe them, and is generally unaware of their complexity, or even of their existence. The grammarian's

---

[11] This is certainly true of the type of generative grammar discussed in this chapter. It is not so obviously true of a transformational-generative grammar. The latter cannot be restated in a simple "Bloomfieldian" descriptive format — none but the simplest transformational rules can be accommodated. There is required an additional "level", "stratum", or "system" of some kind. There is, however, more than one way of providing this. None of these have been sufficiently elaborated to present in a book such as this. It is my personal conviction that the model coming to be known as stratificational grammar offers the best possibilities.

task is to formulate these patterns explicitly. The significant word here is "explicitly".

A completely explicit grammar would describe the processes in such detail that one might follow the statements precisely and mechanically, using nothing outside the grammar, and by so doing duplicate the activity of the native speaker or some part of it. Such a grammar would be explicit in that everything needed would be formulated within it.

Or a grammar might require supplementation at various points by "common sense" or the user's "language feel". Many points might be formulated in greater detail or exactitude than the naïve native speaker could describe them. Perhaps some would be treated in meticulous fullness. But there would be some parts of the whole that would be either omitted or sketchily treated. In use, the grammar would require some kind of supplementation at all the latter points.

As a matter of fact, all the grammars that we have, traditional or modern, are to some measure of the second type. They are usable by people who know the language, at least a little, but not by others. That is, they can be used only by someone who can provide direction for some part of the process where the grammar itself is deficient. This is not to say that they are not useful. Given the proper circumstances, they may have very great utility. Moreover, for certain purposes a fully explicit grammar might be an awkward tool. It would give help both where needed and where completely unnecessary.

But this is not to suggest that a fully explicit grammar is not a goal that grammarians should pursue. There are, indeed, many reasons why they should seek ways of attaining maximum explicitness. Though such grammars may not have direct practical value, they would certainly have theoretical value, and probably considerable indirect practical value.

Generative grammars are one effort toward increased explicitness in grammatical statement. The sample grammar presented above, limited as it is, gives some hints as to what such explicitness is like. Except for a few *etceteras* in the M-rules (purely a space-saving device since it is obvious how the full statement could be given) this grammar is very highly explicit. Given the grammar and an understanding of the basic operations ("rewrite as" and the notion of alternatives) it enables one to produce a considerable corpus of sentences.

It is quite another matter, however, if a sentence is given and its grammatical analysis sought. The generative grammar does not give any specific help for such a task. A person acquainted with English who has used the grammar a number of times builds up some familiarity with its rules and their organization. He observes the consequences of various choices. He is then able to guess at appropriate alternatives to produce a desired result. He can produce a sentence, compare his result with the given sentence, modify his procedures a little, and ultimately find a sequence of rules that will produce a sentence identical with the given one. Then the tree diagram produced by the rules can be taken as presumably the analysis which he has been seeking. Notice, however, that the process here is almost entirely based on the speaker's "feel" — feel for the language and familiarity with the grammar. A purely generative grammar gives no explicit help for this task at all. It is explicit only for the task for which it is designed.

Moreover, the apparatus which is built into this type of grammar to provide the necessary explicitness for its own purpose (for example, the double set of rules for singular and plural in this sample) adds appreciably to the difficulty of finding the correct procedures to produce a replica of a given sentence. The difficulty is not great in a very restricted grammar (like even our expanded version), but increases rapidly in severity as the grammar is made more complete. A generative grammar of the type we have been examining would become very difficult to manage if it approached the degree of completeness which we might consider minimal for any practical use.

Generative grammars achieve their high level of explicitness by concentrating on one task of grammar only: "generating sentences". By this concentration they become less and less useful for many other tasks — that is, among other things, they become less explicit. This lessened usefulness is the result of a special kind of complexity.

The complication in the grammar — for example, the multiple sets of rules — are the consequences of two things: 1) the demands of explicitness, and 2) the limitation to three types of rules, P, L, and M. As we shall see in the next chapter, some more elaborate types of rules can assist materially, particularly as the scope of the grammar is increased, but the problem remains a serious one. While new types of rules certainly help to avoid some of the complexity which would plague any large-scale expansion of the sample grammar given here, they introduce new types of complexity of their own. Often enough they simplify the generation of sentences but at the expense of making it still harder to see what alternatives to choose in order to reach a predetermined goal.

GENERATION

A number of symbols occur in the simple generative grammar we have been discussing. All of them are presented without the usual type of definition, and most of them without any hint of a gloss. Some, of course, do suggest an obvious interpretation — NP looks like an abbreviation of Noun Phrase, and all symbols with N, and some kind of subscript or appendage, look as though they label kinds of nouns or nominal constructions. At best these suggestions are mere mnemonics. The grammar would have been just as effective if the symbols had been selected completely at random. In this case, their form would not have given this comfortable feeling of familiarity which we have with NP, but would leave us still more curious about definition.

As we saw in Chapter 6, one method of "defining" parts of speech is by listing, complete listing in some classes, exemplificatory listing in others. On this basis, the L-rules can be considered as "defining" parts of speech or subclasses. We have followed a convention of writing all subclasses by a part-of-speech abbreviation and a subclass indicator joined by a hyphen.[12] As a part of speech, then, V ("Verb") is characterized as the sum of V-i, V-t, V-b, and V-l. In a fuller grammar, of course, many more subclasses would occur, but the principle would be the same. The problem of overlap, a thorny one with descriptive grammars, is neatly sidestepped: *seem* is simply listed both as V-b and as V-l. This causes no trouble for a generative grammar, but it is one of the things that contributes to the difficulty when we try to use a generative grammar to find an analysis for a given sentence.

In much the same way, AP (suggestive of "Adjective Phrase") is "defined" by rule P17 and the proper L-rules. That is, an AP is either an Adj or an Adj preceded by an Int: an Adj is something like *good, bad, new*, and so on; and an Int is something like *very, extremely*, and so on. These three sets of rules come as close to a definition of AP as we have any right to expect. In similar ways, other rules or other combinations of rules define each of the symbols in the grammar.

This means that the whole set of rules characterizes S. If S is taken to mean something like "sentence" (more properly "sentence covered by this grammar") then the grammar "defines" sentence. This is precisely what a generative grammar is designed to do: to define the notion of a sentence in English.

Borrowing a term from mathematics, the grammar can be said to "generate" sentences (S). The term "generate" is simply a synonym of "define" as it has been used in the last few paragraphs. It is a preferable term, because such a use of "define" is a bit loose; it would be better to restrict the term "define" to another more specific meaning.

A generative grammar is, of course, one that generates. That is, it says that each and every sequence of words that conforms to the statements in the grammar is a sentence. A complete generative grammar would make an additional claim: that only such sequences were sentences. That is, a complete generative grammar would claim that its S is identical to the totality of sentences in the language.[13] The kind of restricted generative

---

[12] Some of these symbols are from Paul Roberts, *English Sentences*, 1962. The pattern he follows has been generalized.

[13] It is customary to claim that a generative grammar ideally generates all "well-formed" sentences in the language. It is difficult to give any precise meaning to "well-formed". Obviously, an ideal generative grammar would define it. Short of that, "well-formed" may be taken to mean 'in the judgment of a grammarian, properly within the domain of a grammar'. I have avoided the term in the text, but by so doing have missed some of the flavor of typical discussions of generative grammar.

grammar discussed above merely claims that its S is identical to a subset of sentences in the English language.

"Generation" does not, therefore, mean the physical production of sentences. The latter is accomplished by some other instrumentality — a man or a machine — operating with a generative grammar. GENERATION IS THE IDENTIFICATION OF A SEQUENCE OF WORDS AS A SENTENCE IN THE LANGUAGE. A generative grammar does not generate one sentence now, and another at another time. Rather, it generates all the sentences it is capable of at all times. The mere fact that the grammar exists is sufficient for it to generate. A grammar is a special kind of definition, albeit a very complex one, rather than a machine.

To read $\rightarrow$ as "rewrite as" is simply to adapt a generative grammar to a practical operation, the one practical operation that demands no great reorganization or restatement of the rules. It requires only reinterpretation of the operator symbols, $\rightarrow$, { }, and so on. The rules of the grammar are stated in a form which allows it to be read either as a set of propositions generating sentences or as directions for producing sentences. It should be noted, however, that these two ways of reading the rules are logically quite different.

STRUCTURE LABELS

The two diagrams on pages 154 and 242 are each labeled as fully as possible. In the first, two kinds of labels are carefully distinguished. Each constituent is labeled in terms of its part in some higher construction, and each construction is labeled. The labels, therefore, look two ways, toward the next larger construction and toward the next smaller. Thus, *the three old ladies upstairs* is labeled as subject, that is, as one partner in a comprehending construction labeled sentence, and as noun phrase, that is, as a construction consisting of a certain kind of head with certain kinds of attributives. On page 242 there are also two kinds of labels typified by NP and P1. NP is very close to noun phrase, and is defined by the grammar in terms of the elements which may compose it, though they bear no such labels as head and attributive. P1, labeling the step that leads to NP from S, indirectly (but only indirectly) identifies this constituent as subject. P1 is a rule of the form $S \rightarrow NP + VP$, and this is implicitly equivalent to a statement that a sentence may consist of a subject and a predicate. However, it is interesting to note that the labeling provided by a derivation such as that on page 242 is explicit with regard to only one kind of label. The labeling looks in only one direction, from a construction to its constituents. Indeed, the more usual practice is to omit labels such as P1 from the diagram. They contribute very little, since P1 must always designate the operation that leads from S.

There is a second difference: On page 242 four different labels, N_{4s},

N_{3s}, N_{2s}, and N_{1s} are applied to *boxer dog* as a unit. But on page 154 this is labeled merely as head in a construction and as some kind of a nominal. That is, though the generative grammar applies only one type of label, it applies very many more examples of them.

If one runs through the rules of the generative grammar, the origin of the extra labels in this phrase will immediately be apparent. Each of the first three represents an unexploited opportunity to add a modifier to the phrase. For example, where the diagram is labeled N_{3s}, there might have been added *other*, giving *another boxer dog*. Where N_{2s} stands there might have been added something like *new*, giving *a new boxer dog*. N_{1s} represents the opportunity to add a noun modifier; this was taken. If it had not been, the result would have been simply *a dog*. These several symbols, then, are comparable to the prenoun slots in a slot-and-filler description of a noun phrase. The numbering used was selected so that they would match in detail.

An IC analysis is sometimes thought to avoid the description of unfilled slots. The latter are considered serious disadvantages in a slot-and-filler description. If we take the tree diagram on page 242, as we must, as a more explicit IC diagram, we see that there is no real difference. The failure to note unfilled slots is simply a lack of explicitness in the usual IC description.

This suggests that we might construct a generative grammar of a slot-and-filler type. For example, P2, P4, and P5 are easily condensed into a single rule:

$$V_s \rightarrow \begin{bmatrix} \textit{-ed}_s \\ \textit{-s} \\ Mod \end{bmatrix} + (\textit{have} + \textit{-en} +) \ (\textit{be} + \textit{-ing} +) \ V_{1s}$$

Since one of the set of alternatives in the first slot is obligatory, as is the V_{1s}, these are not in parens. Another set of rules might be condensed as follows:

$$NP_s \rightarrow (\textit{Det}_s +) (\textit{one} +) (\textit{Spec} +) \left(\begin{Bmatrix} AP \\ \textit{-en} + \textit{V-t} \\ \textit{-ing} + \textit{V-i} \end{Bmatrix}^n + \right) N_{2s}(+ \textit{PNM})$$

Here we have used a new convention: the superior ^{n} indicates recursiveness. Any number of the structures within the parens may be used in one phrase. The formula combines rules P9, P10, P11, P12, and P13 into one (though still maintaining parallel rules for singular and plural). We did not attempt to include P14 also, because this shows a peculiar type of recursiveness that would be difficult to handle by the convention used in the $N - 2$ slot.

If the rules were thoroughly worked over and brought into this form with the use of parens, a new generative grammar could be compiled.

It would have fewer rules than the one presented on page 239, but the rules would be more complex. If used to produce sentences, the derivations would compare in detail with diagrams like that on page 155. That is to say, such a generative grammar would stand in the same relationship to a slot-and-filler grammar as the generative grammar above stands to an IC grammar. It would be merely a generative restatement of the descriptive grammar.

Chapter 11

Generative Grammar—11

The sample generative grammars in the last chapter used only three kinds of rules: phrase-structure (P), lexical (L), and morphologic (M). The most widely discussed types use at least one more: transformational rules (T).

The second sample grammar was rather complex, even though limited in its coverage to a very small part of the language. It shows promise of much greater complexity if it is made more complete. It is not unreasonable to ascribe at least part of the complexity to the restricted apparatus which was employed, combined with the exacting demands of explicitness. If so, expansion of the grammar without undue increase in complexity can be accomplished only by using more types of rules or by relaxing the requirement of explicitness.

There are, in fact, a number of other types of rules. Each of these has its own peculiarities and its own usefulness. Various combinations of these might be used. Generative grammars, therefore, can be produced with very diverse properties. There is no one kind of grammar that can be so labeled, not even one kind that can be called transformational. As used in discussions of generative grammar, "transformation" covers a variety of kinds of rules. Some are comparable to the rules which alter a sentence into an agnate sentence. That is, they are transformations in the sense of Chapter 9. Others are quite different in certain details. All, however, do have some features in common. Within a generative grammar they all function in more or less the same way, so that it is reasonable to treat them together as T-rules.

The presentation will be based on a sample transformational-generative grammar. This will be, as far as possible, similar to the nontransformational grammars of Chapter 10. In this way, comparison will be facilitated. Comparable rules will be numbered the same, and the symbols used will be largely the same. However, it will cover a few kinds of sentences that were not provided for in the grammars of the last chapter. In discussing them, some of the problems they would present in a nontransformational grammar will be indicated.

There is only one new symbol in the P-rules, §. This is required for certain T-rules, and will be explained with them.

THE THIRD SAMPLE GRAMMAR

P1 $S \rightarrow \begin{cases} NP + VP \\ Interj \end{cases}$

P2 $VP \rightarrow PreV + V_3$

P3 $PreV \rightarrow \begin{cases} §No + \text{-}s + §Aux \\ §No + \text{-}ed + §Aux \\ \qquad Mod \end{cases} (+ not)$

P4 $V_3 \rightarrow (have + \text{-}en +) \ V_2$

P5 $V_2 \rightarrow (be + \text{-}ing +) \ V_1$

P6 $V_1 \rightarrow \begin{cases} V\text{-}i \\ V\text{-}t + NP + \text{-}m \\ V\text{-}b + NP§ \\ V\text{-}l + AP \\ be + Loc \\ be + Poss \\ have + NP + \text{-}m \end{cases}$

P7 $NP \rightarrow N_6 + No$
       $NP§ \rightarrow N_6 + §No$

P8 $No \rightarrow \begin{cases} sg \\ pl \end{cases}$

P9 $N_6 \rightarrow \begin{cases} N_5 \ (+ §PNM) \\ N\text{-}prop \\ Pr \end{cases}$

P10 $N_5 \rightarrow (Det +) \ N_4$

P11 $N_4 \rightarrow (Num +) \ N_3$

P12 $N_3 \rightarrow (Spec +) \ N_2$

P13 $N_2 \rightarrow \begin{cases} §AP + N_2 \\ N_1 \end{cases}$

P14 $N_1 \rightarrow \begin{cases} N_2 + N_1 \\ N\text{-}c \end{cases}$

P15 $Loc \rightarrow \begin{cases} Adv\text{-}l \\ Prep + NP + \text{-}m \end{cases}$

P16 $Det \rightarrow \begin{cases} D \\ §Poss \end{cases}$

P17 $AP \rightarrow (Int +) \ Adj$

P18 $Poss \rightarrow NP + \text{-}'s$

Only the following symbols are new or redefined. For others use the L-rules already given.

$$N\text{-}c \rightarrow \{man,\ boy,\ wife,\ husband,\ brother,\ sister,\ dealer,\ car,\ city,$$
$$lady,\ dog,\ boxer,\ temper\}$$
$$Pr \rightarrow \{he,\ she,\ it,\ they,\ we,\ you,\ someone\}$$
$$Num \rightarrow \{one,\ two,\ three,\ four,\ many,\ few,\ umpteen\}$$

The T-rules are discussed individually below. They may be listed here for easy reference.

T1   OPT
$$NP + X + V\text{-}t + NP + \text{-}m \Rightarrow NP + X + be$$
$$\quad 1 \quad\ \ 2 \quad\ 3 \qquad 4 \qquad 5 \qquad 4 \quad\ 2 \quad\ \text{f}$$
$$+\ \text{-}en + V\text{-}t + by + NP + \text{-}m$$
$$\quad\ \text{f} \qquad 3 \qquad \text{f} \qquad 1 \qquad 5$$

T2   OBL
$$No + (X +)\ \S No \Rightarrow No + (X +)\ No$$
$$\quad 1 \qquad 2 \qquad 3 \qquad 1 \qquad 2 \quad 1\ \text{in}\ 3$$

T3   OPT
$$by + NP + \text{-}m \Rightarrow \text{nil} \quad \text{Condition: } by \text{ from T1}$$

T4   OBL
$$\S Aux + (not +)\ have \Rightarrow have\ (+\ not)$$
$$\quad 1 \qquad 2 \qquad 3 \qquad 3\ \text{in}\ 1 \qquad 2$$
$$\S Aux + (not +)\ be \quad \Rightarrow be \quad (+\ not)$$
$$\quad 1 \qquad 2 \qquad 3 \qquad 3\ \text{in}\ 1 \qquad 2$$

T5   OPT
$$NP + PreV + V_3 \Rightarrow PreV + NP + V_3$$
$$\quad 1 \qquad 2 \qquad 3 \qquad 2 \qquad 1 \qquad 3$$

T6   OPT
$$NP \Rightarrow who$$

T7   OBL
$$X + who\ (+\ \text{-}m)\ (+\ Y) \Rightarrow who\ (+\ \text{-}m)$$
$$1 \qquad 2 \qquad\ 3 \qquad 4 \qquad 2 \qquad\ 3$$
$$+\ X\ (+\ Y)$$
$$\quad 1 \qquad 4$$

T8   OBL
$$\S Aux + V_1 \Rightarrow \text{nil} + V_1$$

T9   OBL
$$\S Aux \Rightarrow do$$

T10   GEN
$$\S AP + N_2\ \&\ (D +)\ N_2 + Y + be + AP$$
$$\quad 1 \quad\ 2 \qquad\qquad 2 \qquad\quad 3$$
$$\Rightarrow AP + N_2$$
$$\quad 3\ \text{in}\ 1 \quad 2$$

T11   GEN
$$\S AP + N_2\ \&\ (D +)\ N_2 + Y + V\text{-}i$$
$$\quad 1 \quad\ 2 \qquad\qquad 2 \qquad\quad 3$$
$$\Rightarrow \text{-}ing + V\text{-}i + N_2$$
$$\quad [\text{f} \qquad 3]\ \text{in}\ 1\ \ 2$$

T12   GEN
$$\S AP + N_2\ \&\ (D +)\ N_2 + Y + V\text{-}t + (Z +)\ N\text{-}c$$
$$\quad 1 \quad\ 2 \qquad\qquad 2 \qquad\quad 3 \qquad\qquad 4$$
$$+\ No + \text{-}m \Rightarrow N\text{-}c + \text{-}ing + V\text{-}t\ +\ N_2$$
$$\qquad [4 \qquad \text{f} \qquad 3]\ \text{in}\ 1 \quad 2$$

T13 OPT $N\text{-}c + \text{-}ing + V\text{-}t + N_2 \Rightarrow \text{-}ing + V\text{-}t$
　　　　　　 1　　　2　　　3　　　4　　　2　　　3
　　　　　　 $+ N_2$
　　　　　　 4 [1 $\Rightarrow$ nil]

T14 GEN $\S AP + N_2 \ \& \ (D+) \ N\text{-}c + Y + V\text{-}t + (Z+) \ N_2$
　　　　　　 1　　　2　　　　　　　3　　　　　　4　　　　　　 2
　　　　　　 $+ No + \text{-}m \Rightarrow N\text{-}c + \text{-}en + V\text{-}t \ + \ N_2$
　　　　　　　　　　　　　　　 [3　f　　 4] in 1　2

T15 OPT $N\text{-}c + \text{-}en + V\text{-}t + N_2 \Rightarrow \text{-}en + V\text{-}t$
　　　　　　 1　　　2　　　3　　　4　　　2　　　3
　　　　　　 $+ N_2$
　　　　　　 4 [1 $\Rightarrow$ nil]

T16 GEN $\S Poss + N_4 \ \& \ (D+) \ N_4 + Y + be + Poss$
　　　　　　 1　　　2　　　　　　　　2　　　　　　　　3
　　　　　　 $\Rightarrow Poss + N_4$
　　　　　　 3 in 1　2

T17 GEN $N_5 + \S PNM + No \ \& \ N_5 + Y + be + Loc$
　　　　　　 1　　　2　　　3　　　1　　　　　　　 4
　　　　　　 $\Rightarrow N_5 + No + Loc$
　　　　　　 1　　3　　4 in 2

T18 GEN $N_5 + \S PNM + No \ \& \ N_5 + Y + have + NP + \text{-}m$
　　　　　　 1　　　2　　　3　　　1　　　　　　　 4　　　5
　　　　　　 $\Rightarrow N_5 + No + with + NP + \text{-}m$
　　　　　　 1　　3　　　[f　　4　　　5] in 2

No M-rules will be given because a full and systematic set is beyond the scope of the present discussion. A partial listing has already been given on pages 240 and 241. Together with a few passing mentions in the text, these will suggest enough for our purposes.

AGREEMENT IN NUMBER

One of the most conspicuous features of the second grammar of Chapter 10 was the parallel sets of rules for sentences with singular and plural subjects. This is missing in the sample transformational-generative grammar. The function of securing subject-verb agreement is discharged by a totally different mechanism.

The first element in this is a pair of rules, P7 and P8. One of these inserts a number marker *No* at the end of every *NP*, including of course, the subject. The second allows two values for this, *sg* (singular) and *pl* (plural).[1] A more complete grammar might have to recognize further

---

[1] Again it must be pointed out that we are assuming complete regularity of agreement and a simple two-way number system. Neither assumption is justified by anything beyond the restrictedness of this grammar.

possibilities. These two rules, when combined with the proper M-rules, will take care of number inflection in nouns.

The second element in the number agreement apparatus is introduced by rule P3. In some instances this leads to §*No* as the first symbol in the predicate portion of the string. This is a new type of symbol, not found in the grammars of Chapter 10. It stands for an empty slot that must be filled by a number marker. A T-rule will be needed to fill this slot. It can be set up so that the slot will be filled by an *No* exactly matching that of the subject. Then proper M-rules will produce the correct morphologic form of the verb or auxiliary. These M-rules will make use of this number marker, now in the predicate structure.

A tentative formulation of this slot-filling T-rule is as follows:

$$...No + §No... \Rightarrow ...No + No...$$
$$\quad 1 \qquad 2 \qquad\qquad 1 \quad 1 \text{ in } 2$$

The suspension marks indicate that the elements we are concerned with may be preceded or followed by other symbols, but that we are not concerned with them. Ordinarily this need not be noted. The digits written below the symbols identify them. There are two symbols at the left, arbitrarily marked "1" and "2". At the right there are also two symbols. The first is marked "1", indicating that it is the same as that so marked at the left. The second is marked "1 in 2". This indicates that the element marked "1" is here in the position in the structure of the slot marked "2". That both symbols at the right are now marked "1" indicates that they are identical. Note that the formula at the right no longer contains an empty-slot symbol. This has now been filled, and the string contains only symbols for proper elements.

The purpose of the whole process is to assure a correct match. The rule given will obtain this result, provided that the proper *No* is used. It would be easily possible to have a string of symbols containing two different number indicators. The following is a conceivable intermediate stage in the production of a very common sentence type:

$$N_6 + No + §No + \text{-}s + §Aux + V\text{-}t + N_6 + No$$

We want the verb to agree with the subject, not with the direct object, as might happen in this example if the wrong *No* is selected. One thing that will distinguish the two is position in the string. At this stage many of the complications of sentence structure which may occur in final sentences have not yet been introduced. The P-rules always develop the subject in its usual position preceding the verb, the direct object following the verb. Moreover, only the subject can come before the verb. The P-rules will not permit more than one *No* in the subject. (The subject develops from an *NP* by some combination of rules P7 to P14. It will be seen that *No* appears only in rule P7, and that this rule is not recursive, that is, nowhere does a second *NP* appear derived from an *NP*.)

This makes it an easy matter to select the correct *No*. It must be the only one before the predicate, that is, the only one preceding the §*No* to be filled. The rule can identify the correct *No* simply by relative order.

T-rules are not applied until after all P-rules and L-rules. P8 replaces *No* by either *sg* or *pl*. Therefore, when this slot-filling T-rule is applied, the string will not contain the symbol *No*. This is taken care of by another convention of transformational-generative grammars. A symbol in a T-rule formulation stands either for itself (as does §*No*) or for any symbol or chain of symbols that has replaced it. Only *sg* or *pl* can replace *No*. The conditions for the application of this T-rule will be met if either *sg* or *pl* is found in the proper place. A convenient way to express this is to say that *No* stands for any part of the string "dominated by" *No*, that is, anything which has replaced *No* in the rewriting, or, anything that can be traced back to *No* in the derivation. This means that such T-rules can be applied only if the derivation is known. This is a fundamental difference between T-rules and P-rules or L-rules. A symbol can be rewritten by the latter no matter what its origin.

How this operates is most easily understood by looking at a specific example. The derivation is slightly abbreviated.

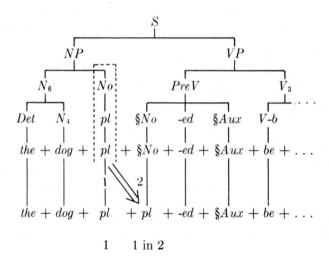

1   1 in 2

A dashed line has been added to the diagram to indicate the part of the structure dominated by *No*. Digits have been added to identify the parts which are involved in the transformation. Among the pertinent M-rules will be: *dog + pl → dogs, pl + -ed + be → were*. (The symbol §*Aux* can be disregarded in this instance. A rule will be given below that will justify doing so.) The result will be: *The dogs were...* Had the other choice been made at P8, *sg* would have appeared in the string for *No* and this would have been moved into §*No*. The end result would be: *The dog was...*

Part of the derivation was left incomplete. This was to be filled out by a predicate nominal. Here again agreement is required. The remainder of the derivation will show how this can be accomplished:

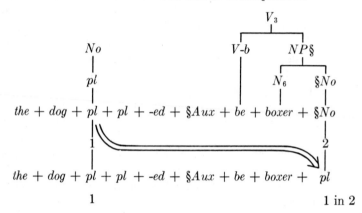

The M-rules will now operate to produce the sentence: *The dogs were boxers.*

In just one respect is the transformation different in the second application. A string of symbols not involved in the rule is interposed between the *No* and the §*No*. As stated above, the rule properly applies only when the two are adjacent. A slight change is called for. The symbols X, Y, and Z will be used in formulations of T-rules to designate any element or sequence of elements that does not need to be specifically identified. The second agreement can be obtained by the use of a rule of the form:

$$No + X + §No \Rightarrow No + X + No$$
$$1 \quad 2 \quad 3 \qquad 1 \quad 2 \quad 1 \text{ in } 3$$

These two formulations can be combined into one by the use of parens. The conventions are a little different from those in the P-rules, however. When an element occurs in parens on both sides of the double arrow, it means that the rule applies whether the element is present or not, but if it is present it must be kept and must be put into the place indicated. Both operations to obtain agreement in number, therefore, can be guided by one rule:

$$\text{T2} \qquad No + (X +) \, §No \Rightarrow No + (X +) \, No$$
$$1 \quad 2 \quad 3 \qquad 1 \quad 2 \quad 1 \text{ in } 3$$

One very minor feature must be noticed. We have used the symbol *NP*§ to mean an *NP* which is to be developed in such a way that a slot will appear instead of the usual element. We have treated the rule involved as only a minor variant of the more usual rule P7.

PASSIVE SENTENCES

Another difference between the grammars on pages 239–241 and on pages 251–253 is much less conspicuous, but just as interesting. In P6 one alternative has been deleted. There is now no P-rule corresponding to:

$$V_s \rightarrow be + \text{-}en + V\text{-}t \qquad\qquad V_p \rightarrow be + \text{-}en + V\text{-}t$$

In the second grammar these would lead to passive sentences, such as: *The men were congratulated.*

Passive sentences are generally agnate to active sentences. In a transformational grammar this provides a way to generate them. The T-rule may be formulated as follows:

$$
\begin{array}{cccccccc}
\text{T1} & NP & + \ X & + \ V\text{-}t & + \ NP & + \ \text{-}m & \Rightarrow & NP & + \ X & + \ be \\
& 1 & 2 & 3 & 4 & 5 & & 4 & 2 & f
\end{array}
$$

$$
\begin{array}{cccccc}
& + \ \text{-}en & + \ V\text{-}t & + \ by & + \ NP & + \ \text{-}m \\
& f & 3 & f & 1 & 5
\end{array}
$$

The following abbreviated derivation will illustrate how this rule operates:

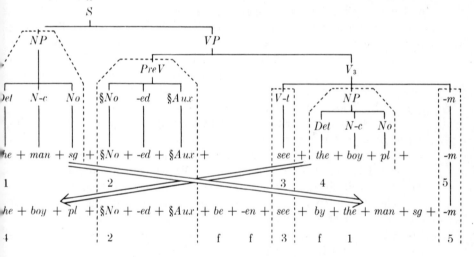

Then T2 must be applied to bring about the subject-predicate agreement:

$$
\begin{array}{c}
\boxed{No} \\
+ \ boy \ + \ pl \ + \ \S No \ + \ \text{-}ed \ + \ \S Aux \ldots \Rightarrow the \ + \ boy \ + \boxed{pl}+ \ pl \ + \ \text{-}ed \ + \ \S Aux \\
1 \qquad\qquad 3 \qquad\qquad\qquad\qquad\qquad\qquad\qquad 1 \qquad 1 \ in \ 3
\end{array}
$$

With proper application of M-rules and a further T-rule which removes the §*Aux*, this becomes: *The boys were seen by the man.* If T1 were not applied,

T2 and the proper M-rules would give the sentence the form: *The man saw the boys*. These two sentences are agnate; the rule T1 is a formal generative statement of the relation between them.

It is evident that the two T-rules so far given must be applied in the proper order. They have been numbered to indicate this. The passive transformation, T1, must be applied before the agreement rule, T2. Otherwise, the verb will agree with the original subject rather than the new subject. The result might be a sentence like: ×*The boys was seen by the man*. This necessity of ordering is characteristic of T-rules, but not of P-rules.[2] The latter can be applied at any time, provided only that the proper symbol is available to be rewritten. T-rules must be applied in the correct order. A grammar must specify this order. The easiest way to do so is to number the rules. The numbering of P-rules was simply for ease in referring to them and for convenience in using them. The numbering of T-rules is often of great significance in the grammar. They should be applied in strict numerical order. Failure to do so may result in improperly formed sentences. Moreover, many T-rules can be applied only once. If they can be applied several times, the grammar must specify this fact. P-rules are always applicable just as many times as the proper symbol appears.

T-rules are of two kinds, optional and obligatory. This difference is very important. T1 is an optional rule. It can be applied or not as the operator elects. If it is applied, a passive sentence results. If not, a nonpassive sentence is produced. These two sentence types are agnate. Agnate sentences are generally related by optional T-rules. Most of the transformations in the sense of Chapter 9, therefore, are statable as optional T-rules.

T2 is an obligatory rule. It must be applied in every sentence containing a §*No*, that is, every sentence not containing a *Mod* (before which §*No* does not appear) nor consisting of *Interj*. In some sentences it may be needed twice. If T2 is not applied, §*No* will remain in the sentence. No M-rule will fill it, remove it, or bring it into normal language form.

The obligatory or optional nature of a rule is essential information for the grammar user. It is, therefore, customary to indicate this for every rule. On pages 252 and 253 and in the text hereafter, this has been done by the abbreviations CBL and OPT after the rule number.

The passive sentence is appreciably longer than the agnate nonpassive. The derivation makes clear the source of the increased length. Every element is carried over, and three elements, two function words and one affix, are added by the transformation. The latter are structure signals. They have been marked in the derivations and in the rules by a small f. See page 209.

In Chapter 10, passive sentences were introduced in the phrase structure by a rule of the form $V_1 \rightarrow be + \textit{-en} + V\textit{-t}$. This will generate a differ-

---

[2] The P-rules considered thus far are context-free and do not require ordering, but context-sensitive rules do. See page 271.

ent kind of passive than will T1. There might just as well have been given a rule of the form $V_1 \rightarrow be + -en + V-t + by + NP_m$. The latter would produce sentences comparable to those using T1. Of course, both rules might have been given, allowing the user a choice.

In a transformational-generative grammar the matter is quite different. A T-rule might be given that would lead directly to either type of passive sentence. Both might be given, just as in the nontransformational grammar. However, the two rules are very much the same. The duplication would be wasteful. A better option is to provide a basic passive rule which leads to the longer form and then to give a second rule which allows a part of the sentence to be cut out and discarded.

Such a rule can be formulated within our restricted grammar as follows:

T3 OPT $by + NP + -m \Rightarrow$ nil   Condition: *by* is from T1

Applied to the sentence derived on page 257, this rule will produce *The boys were seen.* Without T3 the result would be *The boys were seen by the man.* The condition must be appended to the rule to prevent application to such a string as that underlying *It was put by the fireplace.* or *He put it by the fireplace.*

Some transformational-generative grammars make considerable use of rules of this kind. They are called deletion transformations.[3] Sentence fragments (*Nice day.*), commands (*Come here.*), and various other short utterances are described in terms of dropping elements from longer strings.[4] This bears close resemblance to the school-grammar technique of postulating "understood" words in many sentences. If anything, transformationalists use it more than school grammarians.

QUESTIONS

The sample generative grammars in Chapter 10 did not attempt to cover questions. There was good reason; questions cause excessive complications in a grammar restricted to the kinds of rules used there. In most instances, part of the *VP* precedes the subject. That is, the *VP* is discon-

[3] Deletion transformations are not transformations by the definition of Chapter 9. The first three T-rules represent three very different kinds. Such a lack of homogeneity is commonly found in the transformational component of generative grammars. Often enough, this portion of the grammar is the dumping ground for everything which does not conveniently fit elsewhere. (In Chapter 10, we used the M-rules in the same way, with equally poor theoretical justification.)

[4] Some linguists now consider that only certain specific elements should be deleted. These are generally indefinites, as *someone, somewhere, sometime,* and so on. Thus, they might derive *The boys were seen.* from *The boys were seen by someone.*, from *Someone saw the boys.* This makes it possible to reverse deletion transformations. But there are grave difficulties when sentences are examined in context. Neighboring sentences commonly make it perfectly clear what would have to be considered as deleted. It is almost never *someone.* See page 213.

tinuous. It would be necessary to make the first rule in the grammar include some such option as the following:

$$S \rightarrow VP, \, part \; 1 + NP + VP, \, part \; 2$$

Then each part of the VP would be developed independently. To do this explicitly would present extraordinary difficulties. Part 1 might include various elements, but these could not be duplicated in part 2. There would be a problem rather similar to that presented by number agreement, but in some ways much more complex. To insure compatibility of the two parts of the VP, a number of parallel sets of rules would have to be provided. P1 would, then, require a rule like that just suggested for each of them. This is not impossible, only exceedingly awkward and bulky.

Questions are much more easily handled in a transformational-generative grammar. P-rules can produce the sentence parts in any convenient order. Then T-rules can be used to rearrange them. This can be done in several ways. Two possibilities will be described here, the one used in our sample grammar and an alternative.

The basic rule in the sample grammar is:

$$\text{T5 OPT} \qquad \underset{1}{NP} + \underset{2}{PreV} + \underset{3}{V_3} \Rightarrow \underset{2}{PreV} + \underset{1}{NP} + \underset{3}{V_3}$$

The effect of this rule is simply to move the $PreV$ to a new position before the subject. Along with this there must be another change which will ultimately become evident as a change of intonation or punctuation. In a full grammar this must be stated somehow, but we will leave it implicit. No provision for either intonation or punctuation has been included in any of our sample grammars,[5] so the lack here does not affect the comparison between them.

The application of T5 may be illustrated as follows:

$$
\begin{array}{ccccc}
\boxed{\begin{array}{c} NP \\[4pt] the + man + sg \\[4pt] 1 \end{array}} & + & \boxed{\begin{array}{c} PreV \\[4pt] will + not \\[4pt] 2 \end{array}} & + & \boxed{\begin{array}{c} V_3 \\[4pt] come \\[4pt] 3 \end{array}} \quad \Longrightarrow
\end{array}
$$

$$
\begin{array}{ccc}
PreV & NP & V_3 \\[6pt]
will + not + the + man + sg & & come \\[6pt]
\quad\; 2 \qquad\qquad 1 & & 3
\end{array}
$$

---

[5] Most transformational-generative grammarians differ profoundly from other linguists in the way they treat phonology. Nowhere is this more evident than in respect to stress and intonation. Even a very superficial discussion here would demand a full chapter.

This ultimately yields: *Won't the man come?* T5 is an optional transformation. If it is not applied the ultimate outcome may be: *The man won't come.*

This transformation makes clear the reason for a feature of the grammar that might seem puzzling. In Chapter 10, P2 was given in the following form:

$$VP \rightarrow \begin{bmatrix} \text{-}ed & + (not +) \ V_3 \\ \text{-}s & + (not +) \ V_3 \\ Mod & + (not +) \ V_3 \end{bmatrix}$$

In the third sample grammar this is split into two rules, P2 and P3:

$$VP \rightarrow PreV + V_3$$
$$PreV \rightarrow \begin{bmatrix} \S No & + \text{-}ed + \S Aux \ (+ \ not) \\ \S No & + \text{-}s \ + \S Aux \ (+ \ not) \\ & Mod & (+ \ not) \end{bmatrix}$$

As far as the phrase structure is concerned, nothing seems accomplished by this split. The new apparatus, $\S No$ and $\S Aux$, might just as well have been inserted into the old P2 rule. The same result would always be obtained in one less operation.

If, however, P2 and P3 are combined into one rule, T5 becomes very difficult to state clearly. $\S No$, *-ed*, *-s*, $\S Aux$, *Mod*, and *not* all have to be specified. Since no one of these is always present, though at least one occurs in every sentence, and since various combinations occur, this is very difficult to do succinctly. If P2 and P3 are separated, *PreV* becomes available, and T5 is simply stated in terms of this one symbol in place of the complex combinations of six.

The reason for giving P2 and P3 as separate rules, therefore, is simply to provide a convenient label for what seems to be a more or less natural unit. The phrase-structure portion of the grammar should identify and label all the significant units. Another example can be seen in rules P7, P8, and T2.

Other kinds of questions can be produced by additional rules that follow T5:

T6	OPT	$NP \Rightarrow who$							
T7	OBL	$X + who \ (+ \text{-}m) \ (+ \ Y) \Rightarrow who \ (+ \text{-}m) + X \ (+ \ Y)$							
		1	2	3	4	2	3	1	4

For example:

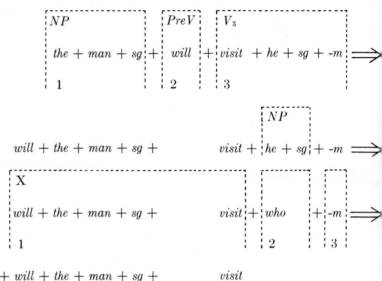

who + -m + will + the + man + sg +   visit

(Each string of symbols is marked only to show how the next T-rule applies.) When the proper M-rules are applied, this will give: *Whom will the man visit?* This is a generative statement of the same analysis as was described briefly on page 220.

The alternative set of rules to produce questions involves the addition of one more option in the phrase structure:

Alt P1 $S \to \begin{bmatrix} NP + VP \\ Q + NP + VP \\ Interj \end{bmatrix}$

The three transformational rules are as follows:

Alt T5 OBL $Q + NP + PreV + V_3 \Rightarrow Q + PreV$
                      1   2   3   4   1   3
                   $+ NP + V_3$
                      2   4

Alt T6 OPT $Q + X + NP \; (+ \text{-}m) \; (+ Y) \Rightarrow Q$
                      1   2   3   4   5   1
                   $+ NP \; (+ \text{-}m) + X \; (+ Y)$
                      3   4   2   5

Alt T7 OBL $Q + NP \Rightarrow who$

Rule Alternate T7 is obligatory after Alternate T6, but must not be applied unless the latter has been. That is, Alternate T7 properly applies only to an *NP* which has been brought to a position immediately after *Q* by Alternate T6.

The same question can be produced by this set of rules as follows:

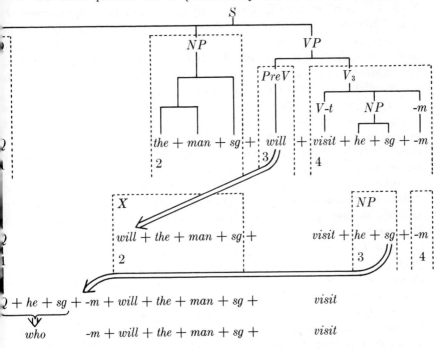

After the first transformation, this might be developed to: *Will the man visit him?* After the second, the third is obligatory. After the last, the string might become: *Whom will the man visit?*

The two sets of rules for questions lead to exactly the same results. They cannot be built into the same grammars, of course. Rather, they must be looked on as fragments of two separate transformational-generative grammars. The two are not greatly different, of course, but at many other points similar variations in organization, statement, or principle are possible. The cumulative effect of many variations could be rather extensive difference. There is no one transformational-generative grammar of English, any more than there is one single descriptive grammar or one scholarly traditional grammar.

Both grammars must somewhere present a choice between two courses, one leading to a declarative sentence and the other to a question. The grammarian may elect where he wishes this choice to appear. In the third sample grammar this comes in the form of an optional transformational rule; in the alternative it comes at the very beginning of the phrase-structure rules in the form of an additional option in P1. The introduction of Q into a string of symbols commits the sentence in advance to undergo the transformation T5, which must be formulated in the alternative grammar to specify Q. Otherwise the rule is exactly the same in the two grammars. However, since the choice should be presented only once, Alternate T5 is obligatory, whereas its counterpart in the main grammar is optional. The difference in treatment of yes-or-no questions forces a difference in the treatment of further questions. T6 is equivalent to Alternate T7, and T7 is equivalent to Alternate T6. In each case the order must be fixed, but in the two grammars it must be different. There are, of course, also minor differences in the form of the rules.

These technical differences of the order and statement of the rules imply an underlying difference in the way questions are viewed. The third sample grammar treats questions and the equivalent statements as very closely related, sharing the same structure in every detail up to the point where T5 can be applied. The difference between declarative and interrogative is purely transformational. The alternative grammar treats the difference as a fundamental one in the structure of the sentence. Whatever similarities there may be are subordinated to a difference introduced at the very highest level.

The best known summary of transformational-generative theory is Noam Chomsky's *Syntactic Structures*, published in 1957. There are many differences in notation and other details between the sketch of English grammar there presented and that in this chapter. However, the treatment of yes-or-no questions in *Syntactic Structures* is basically that of T5 here. One of the arguments Chomsky advanced for transformational-generative grammar was that it recognizes and accounts for the relations between pairs of sentences that are here called agnate. Descriptive grammars were said not to do so, and indeed to be incapable of doing so. This argument does not apply to a transformational-generative grammar using Q to produce questions.

Transformational-generative grammar is young. Its theory and practice are developing rapidly. There have been many changes since *Syntactic Structures*. Some are only refinements in detail; a few are fundamental. Among the latter has been a shift toward the type of treatment represented here by the alternative grammar for questions. Not everyone has followed this trend, but a number have. The change is significant because it represents an alteration in the view of an important sentence relationship.

One reason for the shift is in the difference that is felt between such sentence pairs as:

A book is on the table. ⇔ There is a book on the table.
A book is on the table. ⇔ Is a book on the table?

The first pair differ largely stylistically. The second pair differ in meaning. Some linguists feel that a transformational-generative grammar should recognize this by treating the two differently. One way to do this is to make the difference of meaning determined by a choice in the P-rules, leaving only differences of style to be determined by optional T-rules. This, of course, means an increase in the number of obligatory T-rules. Helpful as it is to keep meaning-bearing differences distinct from stylistic ones, this change does obscure or conceal certain agnate relations which are of significance in the language.

There is one serious shortcoming of rule T6 (or its equivalent, Alternate T7) as stated previously. It calls for a change of *NP* to *who*. In the example used this works well, but with others it would not. As is well known, *who* can be used only in place of certain kinds of *NP*; others require *what*. A fully worked out grammar would have to provide for the proper choice. There is only one way to do so within the framework adopted here. Two or more kinds of *NP* must be recognized. Then T6 would become a set of parallel rules:

$$\text{T6} \quad \text{OPT} \qquad NP_{personal} \Rightarrow who$$
$$NP_{impersonal} \Rightarrow what$$

This distinction cannot be introduced for the first time in this rule. To do so would destroy the complete explicitness that is sought in a generative grammar. The distinction must be made before the L-rules, so that it can also guide the choice of nouns. This means that it must appear somewhere in the P-rules. But to put it there introduces new complications.

Generative grammars characteristically require very detailed subclassification of the word and construction classes.[6] They must have a far more highly developed taxonomy than other grammars. For a fully worked out grammar, a simple classification of nouns into personal and impersonal will not suffice. It is hard to predict just how much finer a division is required, but there would certainly have to be some. Moreover, all of this would have to be built into the grammatical rules at many places. It will require some ingenuity to avoid new involvement in parallel sets of rules comparable in some ways to that in the second sample grammar.

AUXILIARIES

The basic question transformation involves moving the first part of the *VP*, *PreV*, to the position before the subject. In the examples, sentences

---

[6] In part this is the result of using only a single set of labels (see pages 247–248), thus requiring the information of two partially independent taxonomies to be compressed into one. In part it is probably the result of the failure to distinguish between grammar and semology. If each were to require a classification of some sort, these would necessarily be at least partly independent. If, then, these were superimposed, the intersections would be a set of classes more complex than either alone. This cannot, as yet, be conclusively demonstrated, since we lack a semologic classification complete enough to be useful in examining the question.

were selected with the modal *will*. This effectively avoided another problem: The word to be moved may be a modal, *have*, *be*, or in the absence of all of these, *do*. Only modals are introduced directly into *PreV*. For the others our sample grammar provides a slot §*Aux* within *PreV*, and a set of rules by which the correct element can be moved into this slot. The first of these is:

$$
\begin{array}{llll}
\text{T4} \quad \text{OBL} & \S Aux + (not +) \; have & \Rightarrow & have \; (+ \; not) \\
& \;\; 1 \qquad\quad 2 \qquad\; 3 & & \text{3 in 1} \quad\;\; 2 \\[4pt]
& \S Aux + (not +) \; be & \Rightarrow & be \;\; (+ \; not) \\
& \;\; 1 \qquad\quad 2 \qquad\; 3 & & \text{3 in 1} \quad\;\; 2
\end{array}
$$

The following abbreviated derivation will show how this works. T2, T4, and T5 have been applied, the latter in order to show the effectiveness of T4.

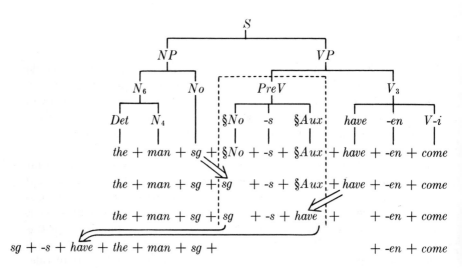

With the application of the appropriate M-rules, this will become: *Has the man come?* If the M-rules were applied before the last transformation (T5), the result would be the agnate statement: *The man has come.* The effect of the first two transformations is to bring together under *PreV* exactly the assortment of elements which must be moved to form a question, namely, the suffix -*s*, the element of number agreement *sg*, and the auxiliary *have*. While the question transformation (T5) might have been stated in terms of these three elements individually, there is an obvious advantage in joining them together as one unit.

If there is no modal or *have* or *be* in the sentence, §*Aux* will remain in the string, since T4 is inapplicable. Additional rules must be provided

either to insert *do* or remove the symbol entirely. The following chart
indicates the desired outcome:

declarative   interrogative

ative

$NP + X + \S Aux + V \Longrightarrow$ $X + \S Aux + NP + V \Longrightarrow$

$NP + X + \qquad\quad V$ $X + \quad do \quad + NP + V$

tive

$NP + X + \S Aux + not + V \Longrightarrow$ $X + \S Aux + not + NP + V \Rightarrow$

$NP + X + \quad do \quad + not + V$ $X + \quad do \quad + not + NP + V$

In the three constructions enclosed in the box, *do* must be inserted in $\S Aux$.
In the one outside, $\S Aux$ must simply be dropped from the string. The
rules must discriminate between constructions in the way shown. Since
with positive sentences, there is a difference between statements and questions, the rules must come after T5, which establishes the structural difference between the two sentence types. The rules must take account of the
presence or absence of *not*. It turns out to be best to have two rules. One
will fill $\S Aux$ with *do;* the other will drop $\S Aux$ out of the string when not
needed. There is one simple feature of the constructions that correlates
with the change that is needed. In positive statements $\S Aux$ immediately
precedes V_1 (V_1 here means *V-i*, *V-t*, or any verb). In the other types,
either *not* or *NP* or both come between. We can use this feature to distinguish the cases. The first rule, therefore, is as follows:

T8   OBL $\S Aux + V_1 \Rightarrow nil + V_1$

This rule merely discards the $\S Aux$ slot unfilled if it immediately precedes
the verb. This is then followed by:

T9   OBL $\S Aux \Rightarrow do$

This inserts *do* into the $\S Aux$ slot if it is still present in the string, that is,
if it has not been filled by rule T5 or discarded by T8.

How these rules work is best shown by an example. We use a sentence
like that used in the discussion on page 266 except that *have + -en* is
omitted.

$man + sg + sg \quad -s + \S Aux + come \Longrightarrow sg + -s + \S Aux + the + man + sg + come$

$man + sg + sg + -s + \qquad come \qquad sg + -s + \quad do \quad + the + man + sg + come$

These lead through proper M-rules to:

The man comes.   *Does the man come?*

There is one more place where *do* may be required in English. General sentence emphasis is shown in speech by shifting the primary stress to the auxiliary. A full grammar of English would, of course, provide detailed rules for this. We will not do so here, but will point out some of the requirements that must be met. The basic rule to introduce sentence emphasis must precede T8, that is, it must apply before §*Aux* is discarded. Moreover, it must somehow block the operation of T8. The obvious way to do this would be by placing something between §*Aux* and V_1. This could be a special marker of emphasis, say *Emph.* Then at some later point there would be a rule or rules which would shift the stress to the word immediately before *Emph.* The latter might best be provided for in the M-rules. With these hints, the reader can work out the rules for himself and find a suitable place for each in the sequence of rules.

It is instructive to compare the treatment of auxiliaries in the second sample grammar. This made no provision for questions, so that some of the thornier problems with auxiliaries did not arise. It did, however, include negative sentences. Therefore the problem of auxiliary *do* had to be met. This could not be done within the conventions of the P-rules. It was consequently shifted off into the M-rules. Even here it gave some trouble, as it required a form of rule that was special and suspiciously ad hoc. It would have been more troublesome if the M-rules had been fully formulated. If not overtly handled by a transformational rule, *do* must be covertly treated in this way.

It is common in transformational-generative grammars of English to view the structure of the verb phrase in a quite different way. Roberts' *English Syntax* can represent this treatment.[7] He gives the following rules, from which certain alternatives not relevant for the present discussion have been eliminated. His symbols have been used, but the equivalent symbols in the sample grammars of this book are shown at the right.

$$VP \rightarrow Aux + verbal \qquad\qquad verbal = V_1$$
$$Aux \rightarrow tense + (M) + (aspect) \qquad M = Mod$$
$$tense \rightarrow \begin{cases} present \\ past \end{cases} \qquad\qquad \begin{matrix} present = \text{-}s \\ past = \text{-}ed \end{matrix}$$
$$aspect \rightarrow (have + part) + (be + ing) \qquad part = \text{-}en$$

The way in which these rules differ from those of this chapter is best seen by comparing the derivation of a single example:

[7] Paul Roberts, *English Syntax*, 1964.

Third Sample Grammar   Roberts' *English Syntax*

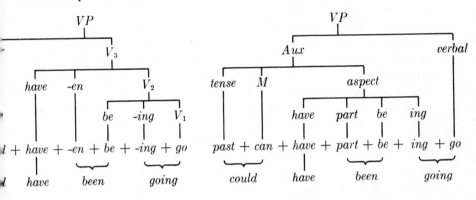

The major difference is in the position of the structures *have* + *-en* and *be* + *-ing*. Roberts and many others include them within *Aux*. This allows the question transformation to be phrased in terms of moving *Aux*, but it raises the necessity of removing *have* or *be* or both in some cases. In the sample grammars in this book, *Mod* is included in *PreV* (roughly equivalent to Roberts' *Aux*) and a provision is made for moving *have* or *be* into *PreV* if needed.

It is instructive to compare Roberts' transformational rules labeled T-af, T-do, T-yes/no, T-A with T4, T5, T8, T9 in this chapter. It will be seen that there are certain advantages in each of the two treatments, so that it is difficult to make a definite decision between them. Ultimately, the difference rests in very free use of symbols for slots in this chapter and very limited use of such in Roberts' book.[8]

DETERMINERS

As pointed out in Chapter 10, the objective in a generative grammar is absolute explicitness within the set task, that is, the generation of sentences. It is reasonable to ask, therefore, how far this sample grammar has attained this goal. There is no doubt that at many points it has been highly successful. There are many others about which there must be reservations or even a firmly negative report.

Perhaps the most serious shortcoming is with regard to the determiners. In Chapter 10, two overlapping lists of determiners were given. The rules provided that with a singular noun selection would be made from one, with plural nouns from the other. In this way constructions like ×*every men* or ×*these man* were excluded. The device by which this was

---

[8] The only one in Roberts' grammar is *Comp* in the rule beginning *VT* — (not *Comp* in the rule beginning *VI* —; unfortunately, this symbol is used twice with two meanings). Constructions with Roberts' *Comp* are not included in our sample grammar, but see page 312 ff.

accomplished, parallel grammars, was far from satisfactory. At a simple level, however, it was effective.

The transformational-generative grammar in this chapter avoids the use of parallel rules. This is certainly an improvement. At the same time, it leaves the determiners in a single group, with no device available to assure proper selection. There is no way to avoid *this men* or *those man* except the good judgment of the user. The grammar is not wrong in that it does not force an incorrect choice. Neither is it right since it does not automatically insure a correct choice. It is simply inexplicit. In a generative grammar that is a highly undesirable condition.

There are devices available to a transformational-generative grammar by which at least some improvement in explicitness at this point is possible. None of them, however, is simple. None can conveniently be included in a grammar of the desired dimensions. Merely to give a number of rules without explanation or exemplification would be of little use. Proper presentation would bulk too large. It is better merely to point out the difficulty and hint at possible solutions.

Short of parallel grammars, from P7, where number first appears, to P11, where it last affects selection within noun phrases, the only possibility is some sort of transformational rules. One possibility would be to change rule P16 to read: *Det* → §*D*. Instead of a determiner being introduced in the phrase-structure rules, a slot would come in. This would commit the generation to certain transformational rules by which a proper determiner could be selected. It would bypass the lexical rules, and enable the choice to be based on a wider range of conditioning factors.

The transformational rules for determiner selection might take account of the class of the noun, the number, the presence or absence of any element that seemed pertinent, or any other factor. Quite a number of rules might be required. They would probably be of diverse types. Some of the rules would be like those for *do*. If after all other rules had been gone past there still remained a §*D*, *a* would be inserted. *A* and *do* have much in common as very generalized members of their classes, elements which are used when something is needed but no other item is available.

It would be quite appropriate to introduce determiners into sentences in some such way. They are largely function words, rather than lexical units. Thus, treatment in a way parallel with nouns or verbs seems to be a little extreme. To introduce them solely by grammatical rules rather than by lexical might well be the best solution.

A little reflection will show why transformational rules can provide for the correct selection of determiners more easily than any elaboration of the phrase-structure rules in the third sample grammar. The problem is, stated simply, to make the determiners appropriate to their context. T-rules can be formulated to take context into account. The kind of P-rules we have used cannot; they must apply without discrimination wherever and whenever a given symbol appears. This, however, is not the only difference between the two types of rules, so that we can conceive of another kind having only this one feature of transformational rules, but otherwise meeting all the restrictions that we laid on phrase-structure rules. That is, they must do nothing more than rewrite one symbol by another or by a string of others (T-rules may affect any number of symbols and in various ways); and they must operate in terms of the symbols actually in the string when they are applied (T-rules, as it were, look up into the derivation to take account of symbols already rewritten). A first crude attempt might reformulate one of the rules from the third sample grammar as follows:

$$\text{P10} \quad N_5 \rightarrow Det_s + N_4 \quad \text{if } N_5 \text{ is followed by } (\S PNM) + sg$$
$$Det_p + N_4 \quad \text{if } N_5 \text{ is followed by } (\S PNM) + pl$$

Rules of this kind are called context-sensitive; those used in the sample grammars are context-free.

Context-sensitive rules have an important difference from context-free rules that arises as a consequence of the statement of context: They must be ordered. Thus, our restatement of P10 must apply after P8 has brought either sg or pl into the string, and before any other rule has changed or moved sg or pl. This requirement causes little difficulty in this case, but, in others, the proper ordering of the rules may be very important, and sometimes difficult to determine.

The restatement of P10 just given should not be considered as a starting point for revising the third sample grammar into a fourth based on context-sensitive rules. Some better place could be found to introduce the needed distinctions; this one is merely convenient to illustrate the technique in a simple way. Indeed, it would be necessary not simply to add contextual qualifications to the existing rules, but to restructure the whole set rather basically. Context-sensitive rules are very highly interdependent, and a considerable part of the total structure of the grammar must be considered in framing each of them. Unless this is done, no effective use can be made of their special properties.

Most recent work in transformational-generative grammar has been based on context-sensitive rules. Partly as a result of this choice, the resulting grammars have been quite different at certain points from most IC descriptions, which generally prefer the type of analysis most easily formulated in context-free rules. Nowhere is this more evident than in the treatment of the noun-phrase.

Some hint of the difference can be seen in Roberts' *English Syntax*. This gives a rule $NP \rightarrow Det + N$, superficially very much like P10 in this chapter. However, *Det* is made to dominate elements which the analysis of page 140 would assign to slots $N - 3$, $N - 4$, and $N - 5$; whereas in the sample grammars N_4 dominates $N - 3$ and $N - 4$. That is, Roberts' treatment associates numerals and specifiers more closely with the determiners. This will facilitate treatment of determiner selection by means of context-sensitive rules.

The rules in *English Syntax* are not stated as context-sensitive. This seems to be primarily because Roberts does not attempt the requisite degree of explicitness. In a textbook it is perfectly legitimate to omit certain details or to treat some parts of the subject matter less thoroughly than others. The comments in the text, however, are frequently of a kind that would most easily be stated strictly by adding context restrictions to the rules given. In short, the grammar seems to be a transformational-generative one, using context-sensitive phrase-structure rules but without formal statement of the contextual conditions. If the book is used primarily to give some idea of how a transformational-generative grammar operates, it would be useful to complete the statement of a sample rule or two, since an important feature of the approach is otherwise hidden.

Chapter 12

Generative Grammar—III

The transformational rules discussed in Chapter 11 all involved various changes within simple sentences. They restructured sentences, filled slots, or deleted unessential parts. Just the handful of such rules in our sample grammar could be seen to have considerable power and versatility in producing sentences.

There are many sentences which combine the basic structures of two or more clauses. The most transparent examples are some of the familiar types of compound and complex sentences, such as:

If he buys a car, we can come.

The obvious way to generate such a sentence would be by some rule combining the strings that underlie the following:

He buys a car. We can come.

Rules of the kind that can do this are known as generalizing transformations.

The usefulness of generalizing transformations is not restricted to such obvious cases. Other sentences have small remnants of one sentence structure embedded in another. These can also be generated in the same manner, part of the structure being discarded in the process. Indeed, this sort of transformation can be used to insert single words into a sentence, either as additions to a sentence structure or to fill slots provided to receive them. The latter kind are well illustrated by the seven generalizing transformations included in our third sample grammar. All of these introduce noun modifiers that in the earlier sample grammars were brought in directly by the P-rules.

NOUN MODIFIERS

The phrase-structure rules in our sample grammar provide three noun-modifier slots to be filled by T-rules. These differ from the other slots (§No and §Aux) in that there is no source within the string itself from which these can be filled. Something must, accordingly, be brought in from outside the sentence. It is pointless to select this from a list; this would be no different from the usual lexical rule. We will always extract such fillers from whole-sentence strings. The string from which it is taken must help in some way in insuring that the selection is appropriate. That means that certain requirements must be laid down for the strings. These must be defined in terms of elements beyond those which are needed. The most usual requirement is that certain sentence elements match in the two sentence strings involved. This can be shown by writing digits below symbols in the formulations.

The rules for this type of transformation must always specify two structures, sentences or sequences of constituents that might be found in sentences. These will be joined by the sign &, which can be read as "combined with" or the like. The string preceding & is to be preserved; either something is to be added to it or some slot in it is to be filled. The string after & will provide certain pieces; in the process some (or even a large part) of its structure may be lost.

These conventions can be illustrated in one of the rules from the sample grammar:

$$T10 \quad GEN \qquad \underset{1}{\S AP} + \underset{2}{N_2} \ \& \ (D+) \underset{2}{N_2} + Y + be + \underset{3}{AP}$$

$$\Rightarrow \underset{3 \text{ in } 1}{AP} + \underset{2}{N_2}$$

This is one option in filling an §AP. This is done by taking an AP out of a sentence with a predicate adjective. This source sentence[1] must be selected so that the N_2 in the subject matches the N_2 immediately following the §AP. (That is, the nominal which the AP will modify when inserted into §AP.) This requirement is indicated by marking both N_2 in the rule with the digit 2 below them. In the source sentence there may be a determiner before the N_2; this possibility is indicated by $(D+)$. There will also be a PreV and perhaps an auxiliary of some sort after N_2. We need not concern ourselves with these elements, and so they are marked Y (identity unspecified and immaterial). Something must be there, so it reads Y, not (Y). There must also be a main verb be just before the AP.

---

[1] Roberts in *English Sentences* labels the structures involved in generalizing transformations as "consumer sentence", "source sentence", and "result sentence". In *English Syntax* he uses "matrix string" and "insert string", and seems to dispense with the third term.

While a great deal of detail is specified about the source string, most of it will be discarded. Only the AP is contributed to the resultant sentence. The N_2, of course, will be there, but continuing the N_2 of the receptor phrase. In effect the rule says "use as a modifier only such an AP as can be used as a predicate adjective after *be* with the noun it will come to modify as subject". Some prefer to use source sentences with the verb *seem*. If this is your preference, merely substitute *seem*, or even V-b, for *be* in the rule.

The receptor structure is a phrase, or part of a phrase. It can occur in a number of places in sentences. For this reason nothing more was specified than that it consist of an §AP and an N_2. Almost paradoxically, the rule retains the structure of that which has least structure, and discards the structure and most of the material of the complete sentence. Of course, in use the rule will be employed to insert an AP into a sentence of which §$AP + N_2$ is only a small part.

T10 may be used with strings such as underlie the following:

I saw a...canary. & The canary is yellow. $\Rightarrow$ *I saw a yellow canary.*
The...interstate highway is open. & The interstate highway is new. $\Rightarrow$ *The new interstate highway is open.*

It does not apply to combinations such as the following:

The...interstate highway is open. & The highway is new.

The N_2 of the two sentences are not identical as the rule requires. Full demonstration of the operation of this rule need not be given here, as there are examples worked out in detail in Figures 6, 7, and 8, later in this chapter.

The sample grammar gives four rules for filling §AP. The other three can profitably be given with an example apiece.

$$\text{T11   GEN} \quad \underset{1}{\S AP} + \underset{2}{N_2} \;\&\; \underset{}{(D+)} \underset{2}{N_2} + \underset{}{Y} + \underset{3}{V\text{-}i}$$
$$\Rightarrow \underset{[f \quad 3] \text{ in } 1}{-ing + V\text{-}i} + \underset{2}{N_2}$$

The brackets are used to tie together $-ing + V$-i, which together fill slot 1. The element marked f is a structure signal introduced by the rule and not coming from either of the two interacting strings.

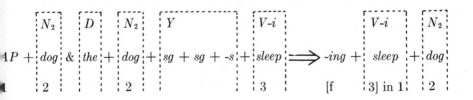

This might be used to introduce a modifier into a sentence like:

$$he + sg + sg + \text{-}ed + see + the + \text{§}AP \qquad + dog + sg + \text{-}m$$
$$he + sg + sg + \text{-}ed + see + the + \text{-}ing + sleep + dog + sg + \text{-}m$$

These can be expressed in a rough way as equivalent to:

He saw the...dog. & The dog sleeps. ⇒ *He saw the sleeping dog.*

The same rule would be used with the chains of symbols underlying:

the...stone & The stone rolls. ⇒ *the rolling stone*
the...tone & The tone falls. ⇒ *the falling tone*
the...dog & The dog barks. ⇒ *the barking dog*

$$
\begin{array}{llll}
\text{T12 \quad GEN} & \text{§}AP + N_2 & \& \quad (D+) \ N_2 + Y + V\text{-}t \\
& \quad 1 \qquad 2 & \qquad\qquad\quad 2 \qquad\quad 3 \\
& + (Z+) \ N\text{-}c + No + \text{-}m \\
& \qquad\qquad\quad 4 \\
& \Rightarrow N\text{-}c + \text{-}ing + V\text{-}t \quad + N_2 \\
& \quad\ [4 \qquad f \qquad 3]\ \text{in}\ 1 \quad 2
\end{array}
$$

Note that the *No* after 4 is dropped. These nouns will always be singular in the resultant phrase. An example follows:

$$
\text{§}AP + \boxed{N_2 \atop dog} \ \& \ \boxed{D \atop the} + \boxed{N_2 \atop dog} + \boxed{Y \atop sg} + sg + \text{-}s + \boxed{V\text{-}t \atop bite} + \boxed{N\text{-}c \atop man} + \boxed{No \atop pl} + \text{-}m
$$

$$
\quad 1 \qquad\quad 2 \qquad\qquad\qquad\quad 2 \qquad\qquad\qquad\qquad\qquad\qquad 3 \qquad 4
$$

$$
\Longrightarrow \boxed{N\text{-}c \atop man} + \text{-}ing + \boxed{V\text{-}t \atop bite} + \boxed{N_2 \atop dog}
$$

$$
\qquad\quad [4 \qquad\quad f \qquad 3]\ \text{in}\ 1 \quad 2
$$

This might be used to fill the slot in the same sentence as used above. This would be equivalent to:

He saw the...dog. & The dog bites men. ⇒ *He saw the man-biting dog.*

The same rule would be used with the chains of symbols underlying:

the...girl & The girl loves fun. ⇒ *the fun-loving girl*
the...cat & The cat hunts mice. ⇒ *the mouse-hunting cat*
the...man & The man writes poetry. ⇒ *the poetry-writing man*

In addition to examples of this sort, participles from transitive verbs can be found modifying nouns without an accompanying noun of the type marked 4 in the formula. These can best be generated by a deletion:

T13 OPT $N\text{-}c + \text{-}ing + V\text{-}t + N_2 \Rightarrow \text{-}ing$
          1   2   3   4   2
                $+ V\text{-}t + N_2$
                  3   4 $[1 \Rightarrow \text{nil}]$

This may be applied to the resultant from the transformation shown above:

$$\boxed{N\text{-}c} \atop \boxed{man} + \text{-}ing + \boxed{V\text{-}t} \atop \boxed{bite} + \boxed{N_2} \atop \boxed{dog} \Longrightarrow \text{-}ing + \boxed{V\text{-}t} \atop \boxed{bite} + \boxed{N_2} \atop \boxed{dog}$$

The resultant phrase is *biting dog*. This can be seen to be structurally different from *barking dog*, since the two have different transformations involved in their generation.

T14 GEN $\S AP + N_2 \ \& \ (D+) \ N\text{-}c + Y + V\text{-}t + (D+) \ N_2$
           1   2   3   4   2
                $+ No + \text{-}m \Rightarrow N\text{-}c + \text{-}en + V\text{-}t \ \ \ + N_2$
                                 [3   f   4] in 1   2

An example follows:

$$\S AP + \boxed{N_2} \atop \boxed{dog} \ \& \ \boxed{N\text{-}c} \atop \boxed{flea} + \boxed{Y} \atop pl + pl + \text{-}s + \boxed{V\text{-}t} \atop \boxed{bite} + \boxed{D} \atop \boxed{the} + \boxed{N_2} \atop \boxed{dog} + sg + \text{-}m$$

$$\Longrightarrow \boxed{N\text{-}c} \atop \boxed{flea} + \text{-}en + \boxed{V\text{-}t} \atop \boxed{bite} + \boxed{N_2} \atop \boxed{dog}$$
$$[3 \ \ \ f \ \ \ 4] \text{ in } 1 \ \ 2$$

This might be used to fill the slot in the same sentence, equivalent to:

He saw the...dog. & Fleas bite the dog. ⇒ *He saw the flea-bitten dog.*

The same rule would account for the following relationships:

> *the...rug* & *Moths eat the rug.*   ⇒ *the moth-eaten rug*
> *the...cart* & *A horse draws the cart.* ⇒ *the horse-drawn cart*
> *the...boy* & *Love smote the boy.*   ⇒ *the love-smitten boy*

Just as with the last rule, shortened forms are commonly found. These are easily generated by the use of a deletion transformation. This is of the same form as T13. It will be used in accounting for examples like these:

> *the...man* & *Illness struck the man.*   ⇒ *the stricken man*
> *the...house* & *The owners abandoned the house.* ⇒ *the abandoned house*

In the second sample grammar on page 239 a nontransformational rule was given in many ways equivalent to T11: $N_2 \rightarrow -ing + V\text{-}i + N_2$. This will produce very much the same results. There was also given an equivalent to T14 followed by T15: $N_2 \rightarrow -en + V\text{-}t + N_2$. There might also have been supplied rules comparable to T12 followed by T13, and to T12 and T14 alone. One difference would be noticeable in any case. Whatever of these possibilities might have been given, each would require a separate and self-contained rule. In the transformational-generative grammar, however, the tendency is to use chains of rules, for example, a generalizing transformation followed by a deletion, rather than single rules, for many of the types. In a more complete grammar, some of the operations which have been described by single rules might be decomposed into chains of operations.[2]

Possessive modifiers of nouns are provided for by §*Poss* and the following rule:[3]

T16   GEN   §$Poss + N_4$ & $(D +) N_4 + Y + be + Poss$
    1 2   2   3
     ⇒ $Poss + N_4$
     3 in 1 2

This may be applied as follows:

---

[2] See the discussion of chains of relations in Chapter 9. For example, T14 might be restated to follow T2. If this were done, T15 might become unnecessary, its function being discharged by T3.

[3] Alternatively, possessives can be obtained from transformations of the following general nature: *John has a dog.* ⇒ *John's dog.* This makes possible grammatical discrimination between several "meanings" of the possessive construction: *John's strike-out won the game for him.* vs. *John's strike-out lost the game for him.* The details, however, are complex, and too involved for inclusion here.

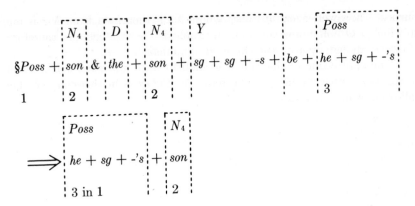

This is the means by which a possessive might be inserted in the following:

...*son came. & The son is his.* ⇒ *His son came.*

As it stands, this rule is adequate in most cases. However, with six pronouns it gives incorrect results. The M-rules might be set up in either of two ways. One would produce:

...*son came. & The son is mine.* ⇒ ×*Mine son came.*

The other would produce:

...*son came. &* ×*The son is my.* ⇒ *My son came.*

One way to avoid this difficulty would be to add another element following *Poss* in one position and to arrange the T-rules so that it does not also appear in the other. There would then be different M-rules applying in the two situations, conditioned by the presence or absence of this element. The reader is invited to determine which is the best place to put it, how to introduce it, and how to reformulate T16 to take advantage of it.

A very large variety of words and constructions can occur in English as postnoun modifiers. Our sample grammar has provided only one slot, §*PNM*, and only two rules for filling it. A full grammar would have more than one slot and a much larger number of rules.

$$\text{T17 GEN} \quad \underset{1}{N_5} + \underset{2}{\S PNM} + \underset{3}{No} \ \& \ \underset{1}{N_5} + Y + be + \underset{4}{Loc}$$

$$\Rightarrow \underset{1}{N_5} + \underset{3}{No} + \underset{4 \text{ in } 2}{Loc}$$

For various reasons it was necessary to place rule P7 introducing *No* before P9 introducing §*PNM*. As a result §*PNM*, when it occurs, comes between N_5 (and hence *N-c*) and *No*. It will be more convenient in the M-rules to to have these two adjacent. T17 and T18 are accordingly formulated so that they interchange §*PNM* and *No*. This is incidental to their main purpose. However, every instance where No is separated from $N\text{-}c$ is one to which a $\S PNM$-filling rule must be applied. The stratagem is, therefore, effective, though open to the charge of gimmickry.

The application of this rule is straightforwaid and need not be given in full here. An example may be found in Figure 8 in this chapter. The following would illustrate:

> *the man... & The man is outside.*   ⇒ *the man outside*
> *the man... & The man is in the house.* ⇒ *the man in the house*

The second rule for filling $\S PNM$ is as follows:

$$\text{T18}\quad \text{GEN}\qquad \underset{1}{N_5} + \underset{2}{\S PNM} + \underset{3}{No}\ \&\ \underset{1}{N_5} + Y + have + \underset{4}{NP} + \underset{5}{\text{-}m}$$

$$\Rightarrow \underset{1}{N_5} + \underset{3}{No} + \underset{[f}{with} + \underset{4}{NP} + \underset{5]\ \text{in}\ 2}{\text{-}m}$$

The following is an example:

N_5		No	N_5		Y	
the + man	+ §PNM +	sg	& the + man	+	sg + sg + -ed	+ have +
1	2	3	1			

NP		N_5	No	NP	
a + dog + sg	+ -m ⟹	the + man +	sg + with +	a + dog + sg	+ -
4	5	1	3 [f	4	] in 2

This might be used to insert a modifier in the following situation:

> *The man...came. & The man had a dog. ⇒ The man with a dog came.*

Another example, given in full, may be found in Figure 8.

The sample grammar gives two rules for postnoun modifiers. This in effect means that it recognizes two types of such modifiers. Certain examples from the two use the same prepositions and appear superficially much the same:

> *the dog with the man*
> *the dog with the mean temper*

The first might be generated by rule T17. The source of the modifier would be a sentence like: *The dog is with the man.* This is a locative phrase, since it seems to be a quite reasonable answer to such a question as: *Where is the dog?* The second is quite different. It does not seem to come from any sentence of the type: ×*The dog is with a mean temper.* It is not a locative. Rather the generation must involve T18 and a source sentence like: *The dog has a mean temper. With* in this phrase does not trace back through an L-rule to *Prep.*

The nontransformational grammar could not easily make this distinction. It merely gave one rule for postnoun modifiers as $PNM \rightarrow Prep + NP_m$. This would lead to both types indiscriminately. To avoid the possibility of producing sentences like ×*The dog was with a mean temper.*, the rules did not permit any prepositional phrases after *be.*

This sample transformational-generative grammar meets only part of the problem, however. It accounts for certain prepositional phrases occurring in both positions, while others occur only as noun modifiers. It does not fully specify which combinations of preposition and noun phrase belong in each category. Thus *Loc* could be developed into *with a mean temper* through the rules as they now stand. The list of prepositions given in the L-rules was restricted to ones known to occur in locative phrases. But this is not enough. Only certain *NP* can occur in locative phrases. A fully explicit grammar would have to be so organized that these could be distinguished in some way. In short, the sample grammar, with all the advantages of close restriction to preselected constructions, is not fully explicit and cannot be made so without a great deal of elaboration. Nevertheless, at some points at least, the prospects are better with the transformational grammar than with the nontransformational.

A SAMPLE DERIVATION

Each rule in the sample transformational-generative grammar on pages 251–253 has now been discussed. The operation of the grammar as a whole is best shown by giving the full derivation of a moderately involved sentence. For this purpose, we will use the one which was diagrammed in several different ways in Chapter 7 and produced by the second sample grammar on page 242.

It will be seen that the process involves putting together parts from five different sentences. One provides the over-all framework. The general structure of the finished sentence is largely that developed in this sentence by means of the phrase-structure rules and two obligatory transformations. Three of the sentences contribute only a word apiece. One provides one phrase and its internal structure.

As the derivation must be given in a series of diagrams (Figs. 1–8), it is a little difficult to see exactly how every separate operation fits into the whole. The following flow chart will give the general picture. Sentences are given in it in ordinary orthographic form, with unfilled slots shown by ellipses. The numbers indicate in which of the series of eight figures the sentence in question is produced.

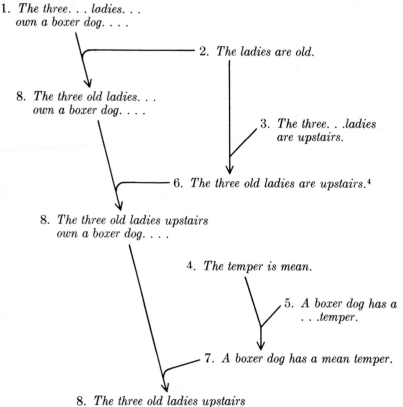

1. *The three. . . ladies. . .*
   own a boxer dog. . . .

2. *The ladies are old.*

8. *The three old ladies. . .*
   own a boxer dog. . . .

3. *The three. . .ladies*
   are upstairs.

6. *The three old ladies are upstairs.*[4]

8. *The three old ladies upstairs*
   own a boxer dog. . . .

4. *The temper is mean.*

5. *A boxer dog has a*
   . . .temper.

7. *A boxer dog has a mean temper.*

8. *The three old ladies upstairs*
   own a boxer dog with a mean temper.

Three generalizing transformations are used: T10, T17, and T18. In a fuller grammar at least one more would be used to introduce the noun modifier of a noun, *boxer*. *Three* might also be introduced by a transformation of some sort. The derivation given may, therefore, be somewhat oversimplified. On the other hand, details will differ somewhat from one type of transformational-generative grammar to another. The derivation shown may, therefore, not be the simplest possible.

---

[4] It would seem more in accord with the native speaker's "feel" to use as a source sentence *The old ladies live upstairs.* We cannot do so within the limits of this restricted grammar, however. No rules have been given for introducing *Loc* after *V-i*. Such rules are very difficult. (The whole matter of adverbial elements of this kind is poorly understood. Perhaps the rules would be simple enough to frame if we had the facts. Certainly, they must be difficult to frame if we do not!) Nor has a suitable transformation been given. One virtue of a generative grammar is that it makes quite evident certain of our makeshifts.

ration of: *The three . . . ladies . . . own a boxer dog . . . ..*

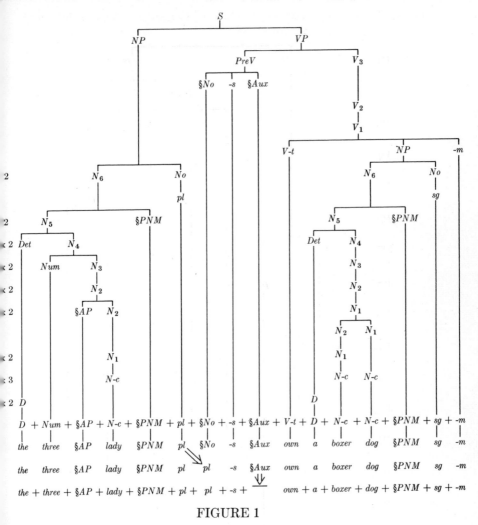

FIGURE 1

ALTERNATIVES

Our sample grammar falls into two main components, the phrase-structure (P-rules) and the transformational (T-rules). Between the two, but of minimal grammatical significance, is the lexical (L-rules). A final component consisting of the M-rules is outside the scope of our discussion. The division of a transformational-generative grammar into these components is of fundamental theoretical significance. Certain grammatical matters are provided for in one section, others in another. However, there are many places where the grammarian can choose between alternative ways of handling the facts.

Generation of: *The ladies are old.*

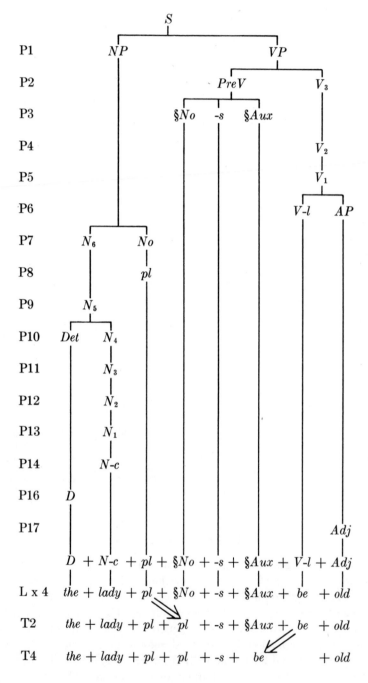

FIGURE 2

Generation of: *The three . . . ladies are upstairs.*

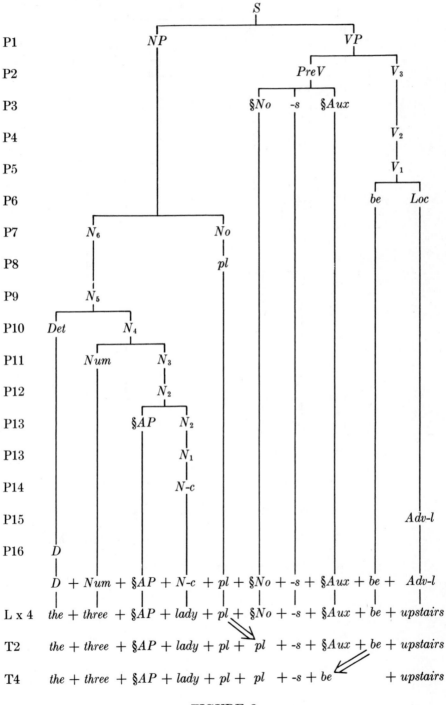

FIGURE 3

Generation of: *The temper is mean.*

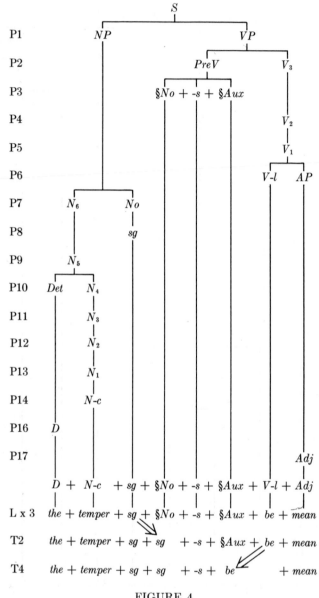

FIGURE 4

Generation of: *A boxer dog has a . . . temper.*

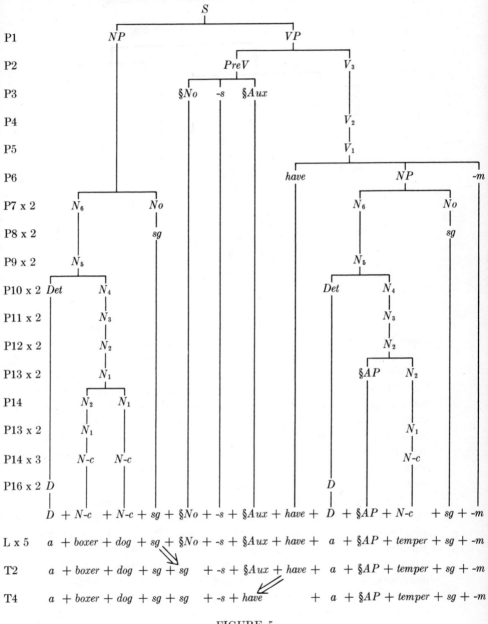

FIGURE 5

Generation of: *The three old ladies are upstairs.*

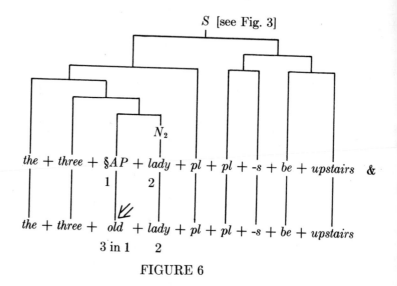

FIGURE 6

We have already seen that alternatives are possible (page 262). At that place two different sets of question transformations were compared. They were evidently similar in some respects, but different in many details and in their over-all place in the grammar. One made no distinction whatever between interrogative and declarative sentences in the phrase structure, but brought this contrast in through an optional transformation. The other grammar committed the sentence to become either a question or a statement at a very early stage. The typical question structure, however, was actually developed much later by transformations. A third possibility, very difficult in the case of questions, would be to introduce the question structure in the P-rules, obviating the need for any transformation.

With noun modifiers, all three possibilities are available. We have seen two of them. In the second sample grammar, these were all taken care of strictly within the P-rules and the L-rules. (There were, of course, no T-rules!) In our third sample grammar, the P-rules brought slots into the string, thus committing the sentence to transformational introduction of modifiers. The third possibility would be to leave noun modifiers entirely to the transformational section of the grammar.

Such a grammar presents some interesting features. We will give a sample rule, conformed as nearly as possible to the conventions of writing rules that have been used in these chapters:

$$D + N_2 \ \& \ D + N_2 + Y + be + AP \Rightarrow D + AP + N_2$$
$$1 \quad 2 \quad \ \ 1 \quad 2 \qquad \qquad \quad 3 \qquad \quad 1 \quad 3 \quad \ 2$$

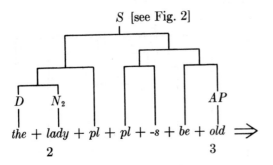

S [see Fig. 2]

D N_2 AP

$the + lady + pl + pl + \text{-}s + be + old \implies$
2   3

FIGURE 6 (*continued*)

This rule differs fundamentally from our T10 in that it actually adds to the structure of the sentence. T10 merely fills out a pre-existing structure. In a tree diagram, the sample grammar leaves a stump to be completed; this alternative rule grafts a new branch in where there was no hint of one before. Roberts' *English Syntax* uses rules of this general type (not, however, a rule precisely like that given above).

Such rules will permit some simplification of the P-rules. P13, which has no other function than to provide slots for adjective phrases (§*AP*) when desired, can be dropped completely. Sentence structure also becomes simpler in a way. Modifiers are merely hung onto the structure, rather than constituting an integral part of it. Other features of the grammar, however, may be more complex.

This is reminiscent of the base-and-modifier technique of school grammar and of some traditional grammars. This was described in Chapter 7 as one of the three basic techniques of description in use in English grammars. The other two, less distinct from each other than they are from base-and-modifier, are the immediate-constituent and the slot-and-filler techniques. We have already seen that generative grammars can be constructed on either of the latter two. We now see that all three can be so used. Indeed, all three have been used.

Roberts' *English Syntax* introduces a number of elements into sentences in this way, among them relative clauses. His rule, restated in the form we have been using in this chapter, is as follows:

Generation of: *A boxer dog has a mean temper.*

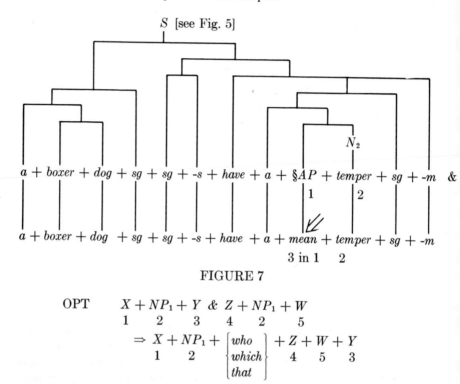

FIGURE 7

OPT $X + NP_1 + Y$ & $Z + NP_1 + W$
          1   2   3   4   2   5
     $\Rightarrow X + NP_1 + \begin{bmatrix} who \\ which \\ that \end{bmatrix} + Z + W + Y$
          1   2   4   5   3

We did not include a rule for relative clauses in our sample grammar,[5] but it can easily be seen how such a rule should be framed. It will be like T17 and T18 in involving §*PNM*, and in restructuring a previously generated clause into a relative clause by substituting a relative pronoun (*who*, *which*, *that*) for a noun phrase and reordering the elements. The relative clause then is inserted into §*PNM*.

Roberts' rule for relative clauses adds a whole new branch to the tree diagram for a sentence, whereas a rule using §*PNM* merely fills out a branch, the stump of which is already in the tree.

Much has been said of the fundamental differences between "generative grammar" and other approaches. These statements can be misleading. Transformational-generative grammars do have basic differences from nontransformational descriptive grammars. The difference lies in the use

---

[5] These sample grammars were framed to exclude what are traditionally called compound and complex sentences. Discussion of these structures is deferred to Chapter 14. However, transformational-generative grammars draw the line in a different way. Simple sentences including modifiers are considered more similar to complex sentences than either are to simple sentences without modifiers. The delimitation of scope in the sample grammar is, therefore, very artificial appearing in the transformational-generative framework.

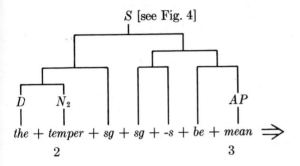

S [see Fig. 4]

D N_2 AP

$the + temper + sg + sg + \text{-}s + be + mean \Rightarrow$

2   3

FIGURE 7 (*continued*)

or nonuse of transformations or some equivalent device to describe agnation. It does not lie in the use or nonuse of the generative form of statement. The two are separate questions. Chapter 10 showed the possibility of a grammar that is generative but not transformational. Chapter 9 made some suggestions about one form of a grammar that would be transformational, but not generative.[6]

In our sample transformational-generative grammar we have introduced noun modifiers directly from source sentences into their final position in the noun phrase in one step, using a single transformation. In a more detailed grammar this would not be the most efficient way in which to do this. It is not possible here to give a full and rigorous statement, even of one chain of transformations. However, the general nature of the problem can be suggested by giving sentences in orthographic form. For example, adjectives can be introduced through such a sequence of steps as the following. Compare this with the derivation in Figures 6, 7, and 8. To avoid a confusing side issue, we will not use slots.

[6] No one has yet produced a grammar that is transformational but not generative. This, however, is no argument. So far all we have of transformational-generative grammars are restricted sketches, often not much more comprehensive than that presented in these two chapters, or treatments of isolated topics, some very thoroughly done but not necessarily relatable to other similar fragments. Thus we really do not have a grammar of English on either model.

Neither should this statement be construed as claiming that the form suggested in Chapter 9 is necessarily suitable for such a nongenerative transformational grammar. That remains to be seen. Chapter 9 is not intended to suggest a form for a grammar, but only to insist that agnation must be taken account of somehow. There certainly is more than one way to do this.

Insertion of modifiers into: *The three . . . ladies . . . own a boxer dog. . . .*

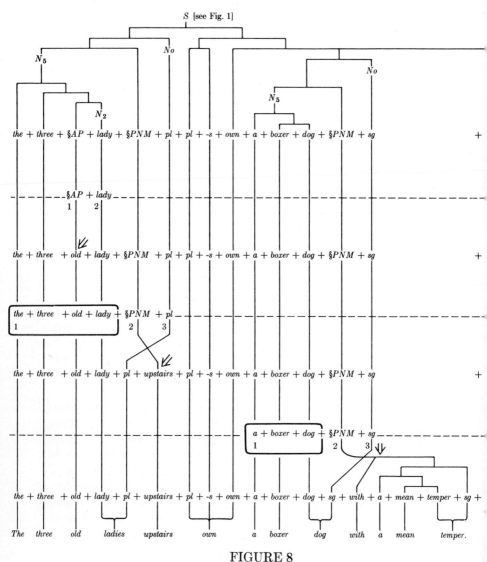

FIGURE 8

the three ladies & The ladies are old.

The first step is to combine these in the form that preserves the largest part of the structure. This is the relative clause:

the three ladies who are old

The next transformation deletes the relative, *PreV*, and *be*:

the three ladies old

On the facing page is given the main sentence as generated in Figure 1. The derivation is labeled only where needed to identify elements specified in transformational rules. Below are shown the three steps by which modifiers are added:

old by T10 from *The ladies are old.*

upstairs by T17 from *The three old ladies are upstairs.*

with a mean temper by T18 from *A boxer dog has a mean temper.*

At each step the relevant parts of the main sentence are singled out, complex elements being enclosed in boxes. The resultant string is shown on the following line.

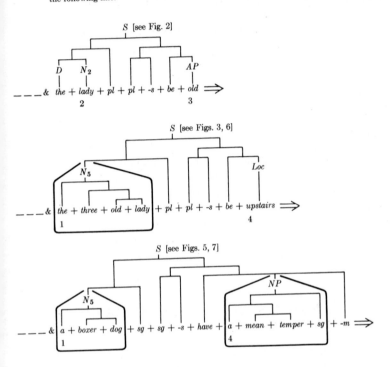

The final string and the final sentence form are shown at the bottom. The structure of the sentence can be seen by tracing up through the figure to the abbreviated tree at the top.

FIGURE 8 (*continued*)

Noun phrases of this general type are possible. When adjective phrases are long they are preferred over the type with the adjective phrase in N − 2 position. When, however, the adjective phrase is short, the preference runs very strongly for the N − 2 position. The last step, therefore, is to move the adjective to a prenoun position:

the three old ladies

Such a procedure is complex, if looked at simply from the point of view of producing a single sentence. It does have certain advantages. Both intermediate steps are needed. A full grammar would have to provide rules generating all three patterns of modification. A rule like T10 might be found to duplicate other rules in a wasteful manner. Replacing T10 with a chain of rules would avoid a great deal of this duplication. Each separate rule might be appreciably simpler than the one given. Indeed, the total complexity of the several rules in the chain might be little if any more than that of the single rule it replaces.

Moreover, the same rule might be found to figure in more than one such chain. For example, our T11 might be replaced by a chain operating more or less as follows:

> *the dog & The dog is barking.*   (*bark* is *V-i*)
> *the dog which is barking*
> *the dog barking*
> *the barking dog*

The last two steps are essentially identical to the last two steps introducing an adjective. Very probably the rules could be formulated in such a way as to apply to both cases. There might be considerable economy in such an alternative.

Finding the optimum set of rules for a grammar is not a simple, straightforward matter. Any grammar can be reorganized in various ways. There is always a possibility that some reorganization will simplify.

REASONS FOR USING TRANSFORMATIONS

It has just been shown that there are three basic approaches open to the grammar compiler in treating certain structures. One uses optional transformations, one uses obligatory transformations after the course is set in the phrase structure, and the last does not use transformations at all. All three seem live options in some parts of the grammar. The question may, therefore, legitimately be raised: Why use the more complicated mechanism to introduce noun modifiers, for example. Four reasons can be mentioned.

Two rules in the sample grammar, T12 and T14, suggest one reason. These transformations introduce rather complex modifiers into the noun phrase. To be sure, the rules of Chapter 10 could be expanded to cover constructions like *the flea-bitten dog*. However, still more complex constructions are possible. The ultimate amount of expansion might be considerable. For every construction of this type there is an agnate sentence which would also have to be generated. Use of transformations such as T12 and T14 will make it possible to handle much of the structure of the complex noun modifiers and the agnate sentences in the same description. The problem becomes particularly acute when full explicitness is demanded. That is to say, the advantages of transformational treatment are greater and much more obvious in a generative format than in the looser descriptive statement.

A second reason, very much like that just given, has been commonly cited. It can most easily be set forth in a specific context. There are numerous limitations on the combinations of adjectives and nouns that are permitted. These run strictly parallel in the two constructions joined by T10. For example, *red vacuum* and the corresponding sentence, *The vacuum is red.*, seem both to be beyond the limits of normal usage. If the grammar can be set up in such a way as to exclude the sentence, a transformational-generative grammar will also automatically exclude the agnate phrase. One statement will thus do at least twice as much work as it might otherwise. Examples of this sort can be multiplied, so that the total increase in efficiency might be very great.

It can be argued that the difficulty with *red vacuum* and similar collocations is semologic or semantic rather than grammatical. The question is thus raised as to the limits of grammar. There is no general agreement on this issue either within the group of linguists preferring the transformational-generative approach or outside it. However, in general those linguists using transformational-generative methods have tended to push the limits of grammar much farther out than have others. Perhaps their methods encourage them to do so. Some of them seem to have the ambition to encompass all morphology and syntax and all semology within one single statement which they would label "grammar". They have criticized descriptive linguistics because the usual types of grammars do not exclude as ungrammatical such phrases as *red vacuum*.

Other linguists feel that such collocational restrictions are not properly within the domain of grammar. This is not to say that they are irrelevant or uninteresting, but only that they are properly treated by some other device. There has been no agreement as to what this might be. I would, myself, consider that they should be treated as a part of language system, but in a separate section, the semology. It seems to me that any effort to handle in the same framework such restrictions and some that are clearly and elementarily grammatical must necessarily bring confusion.

A third reason stems from constructional homonymity and similar phenomena. There are many instances where identical-appearing phrases seem to have some sharp underlying difference that the native speaker senses. *Sleeping car* superficially resembles *sleeping dog*, but otherwise the two are quite dissimilar. As we have seen, the latter can be produced by the use of a transformation such as T10 on a string such as stands behind *The dog sleeps*. There is no comparable source sentence related to *sleeping car.* Instead, this must be produced by some totally different rule, not included in our sample grammar, probably from a sentence such as *The car is for sleeping.* The difference that the native speaker feels is in their quite different sets of agnate relations. These are reflected in the transformational rules by which they might be generated.

This is certainly a valid argument for a transformational-generative as against a nontransformational grammar such as was presented in Chapter 10. It is not, however, an argument for a generative grammar as against a descriptive grammar. That is a totally different issue, though the two have been quite generally confused in recent debates.

There is a fourth reason that is very nearly compelling in this particular sample grammar. Either noun modifiers must be introduced by T-rules or the grammar must be very extensively reorganized. For example, rule T2, the rule to provide for agreement of the predicate with the subject, depends on there being only one *NP* before the verb. This is workable only because §*PNM* and §*Poss* which often contain *NP* are filled after T2 has been passed. If noun modifiers were introduced through the phrase structure rules as they were in Chapter 10, some other device would be needed to obtain agreement. This might be the parallel grammars used there. It might be a transformational rule. In the latter case some care would be required to phrase the rule in such a way that it would select the correct *No* on which to base agreement. This would certainly be complicated. The familiar errors of incorrect verbal agreement often arise because of the difficulty of identifying the correct noun on which to base concord. If it were required to formulate the criteria in the explicit form used in a generative grammar, the difficulty would be compounded.

This fourth reason is tantamount to saying that in a generative grammar one is not necessarily free to choose the most advantageous solution at each specific point, basing the decision on some narrow examination of that point and its immediate consequences. A generative grammar is a very tightly integrated apparatus. Each rule must be formulated or evaluated with regard to the whole. It does not follow that the more complex statement of a rule will always be required; generally the proper form of statement will have advantages in the narrow as well as the broad view. It does mean that the complexity and efficiency of the grammar as a whole is a more important issue than the evaluation of any individual rule.

COMPLEXITY

Undoubtedly the reader has already been struck by the difference between our sample grammars in over-all complexity. A few specific differences have been commented on. It remains to compare them as wholes. The second and third sample grammars are not identical in scope — it would have been very difficult to make them so. Nevertheless, even after due allowance has been made for slightly wider coverage in the transformational version, the nontransformational grammar seems far less cumbersome. The production of the same sentence on page 242 and in Figures 1–8 further strengthens this impression.

It must be remembered that both are severely restricted grammars. They do not purport to cover more than a very narrowly circumscribed segment of the language. They are intended as merely illustrative. Each can be expanded to cover more constructions. Each will become more complex as it is enlarged. The telling consideration is not the comparative complexity within the present artificial limits. Much more significant is that at some larger size where the grammars become practically useful.

It is difficult to estimate the complexity of a grammar as yet unwritten. Nor is it necessary. All that is ultimately pertinent is the comparative complexity of the two. This can be foreseen more easily. Each grammar can be expanded a certain small amount and the increase in complexity observed. The rate of increase in complexity with enlarging scope may be estimated. That of the nontransformational grammar will be greater than that of the transformational. This means that, as both grammars are expanded, the margin between them will diminish. Sooner or later the complexity of the nontransformational generative grammar will overtake and pass that of the transformational one. Thereafter, the comparison will be reversed. We do not know exactly how soon that will happen. It might be well before a really comprehensive scope was reached.

As between the two types of generative grammars, therefore, the preference must rest with that discussed in Chapters 11 and 12. That is not to say that there might not be a better type of generative grammar. Nor does it demonstrate that a generative grammar is better than a nongenerative. The choice between generative and nongenerative is, in some instances at least, simply a choice of form of statement (see p. 243). In any case it rests largely on the purpose for which the grammar is to be used, and cannot be settled in the abstract.

In a sense, the transformational-generative grammar has not been fairly presented. Our sample is entirely too small to indicate the true nature, the basic problems, or the real advantages. This misrepresentation, however, was necessary. The treatment had to be confined to two chapters rather than allowed a whole book. Nevertheless, there is an important lesson in this: The transformational-generative model is not efficient on a restricted scale. It is like a diesel engine — fine for heavy duty, but hopeless to run a motor scooter.

In the final analysis, the one great advantage of a generative statement is explicitness. No other form has yet approached it in this quality. When full explicitness is useful (and there are many such situations), a generative grammar demands consideration and may often be clearly the type to be preferred. The values of explicitness sometimes warrant the cost in complexity.

Very seldom is any fully generative type of grammatical statement worthwhile when its advantages over other forms — primarily its explicitness — are not to be exploited. The complexity introduced to attain these advantages cannot then be justified.

It must also be said that some of the complexity which many people see in a transformational-generative grammar is really only strangeness. A quasi-algebraic notation is not a usual form of expression for many in the English-teaching profession. It may repel, confuse, or frighten some. It can, however, be learned by anyone who will give a little time to the task. Learning a new form of expression can be rewarding, as anyone knows who has really studied a foreign language. English teachers might profitably think of the generative notation as a foreign language worth acquiring. It will open up to them a new world of thought and put into a new perspective their old ways of speaking about the language.

Another part of the complexity is undoubtedly due to our general inexperience. Generative approaches are a recent development. New and better ways of handling various details of structure are appearing. Very likely we have not yet found the best form for stating many of the facts. More succinct and more revealing formulations will certainly continue to be discovered. Some of the complexity, therefore, is only transient.

A large part of the complexity is due to the effort to be fully explicit. For many people, driving a car is a routine unconscious operation. But try to describe the process, or even some small segment of it. How, for example, do you stop the car so that it comes to rest just before the white line marking a cross walk? To describe the operation at all is fairly difficult. To do so with high explicitness is a very real challenge. Yet stopping is only one part of driving, and driving is a far less complex operation than speaking. A grammar is designed to describe language. To do so explicitly should involve us in complexities.

After due allowance for all these sources of complexity, or of apparent complexity, it remains that the greatest source is in the language itself. English, like every other natural language, is complicated. A description of any sort, if it is to be true to the facts, must be intricate. A generative grammar underscores this, because it cannot so easily pass difficulties by in silence.

Chapter 13

Clause Patterns

Most English sentences consist of one or more clauses. A clause contains a subject, a verbal phrase (perhaps of a single word), and sometimes one or more complements. The latter are traditionally described as elements needed to complete the meaning of the verb. Perhaps it would be better to think of them as elements required (or permitted) by the formal nature of the verb. There are several kinds of complements, and they may occur in various combinations. One convenient way to describe the facts is in terms of clause patterns.[1] For example, the commonest pattern in ordinary English is probably one consisting of a subject, a verb phrase, and a direct object.

> *Ghana | exports | cocoa.*
> *The Eskimos | build | dome-shaped snow houses.*
> *He | may be mowing | the lawn.*

There are a number of such clause patterns. Each has important grammatical peculiarities of its own. An adequate understanding of English sentence structure must be based on a suitable description of these patterns. Unfortunately, no treatment adequate for the need has yet been produced. The identification and proper characterization of the clause patterns is, therefore, one of the major frontiers of knowledge in English grammar. This is a topic on which information is badly needed, where work is actively

---

[1] These are more usually called "sentence patterns", but since they apply only to simple sentences (and then only because the clause and sentence are not distinguished) or to the components of compound and complex sentences, the term "clause pattern" is certainly preferable. It will be shown in this chapter that "predicate pattern" is in some ways still better.

going on, and where progress may well be slow, since the patterns are numerous and intricate.

ROBERTS AND SCHOOL GRAMMAR

In his two books *Patterns of English* and *English Sentences* Roberts[2] gives considerable attention to "sentence patterns" — much more than in most books used in high school English. Clause patterns are, therefore, probably best known to teachers today in the form in which he presents them.

In *Patterns of English*, six are described and numbered:

I.   *Birds sing.*
II. *Birds are beautiful.*
III. *Canaries are birds.*
IV. *Canaries eat worms.*
V.   *She gave him money.*
VI. *I believed him honest.*

In addition he mentions patterns used in questions and commands, and some with "the subject after the verb". These are treated as secondary, and receive only incidental mention. Each of his six basic patterns is copiously exemplified. Exercises are provided to insure that the students obtain a thorough mastery of each. The title of the book perhaps indicates something of the importance attached to them.

In *English Sentences*, Roberts expands the list to ten. The same numbering is maintained for the first five. Pattern VI is divided into two, one in which the objective complement can be either an adjective or a noun, and one in which it can be only a noun. The latter is designated VII. Patterns II and III are restricted to verbs other than *be* (which is not considered a verb), and three new patterns are established to cover important uses of *be*.

School grammar puts less emphasis on patterns as such. Instead, the discussion generally centers on several types of complements. At least the following are named in most fairly complete expositions: subjective complement (with two varieties, predicate noun and predicate adjective), direct object, indirect object, and objective complement. Often each of these is the subject of a chapter, almost always of some extended treatment.

Reed and Kellogg diagramming is the device in school grammars which focuses attention most effectively on over-all clause structure. This system does in effect highlight clause patterns by providing four basic lines on which the main sentence elements are to be arranged, and to which other elements are to be appended. These basic lines may be taken as representing

---

[2] Paul Roberts, *Patterns of English*, 1956. Paul Roberts, *English Sentences*, 1961.

clause patterns. Reed and Kellogg diagramming, therefore, provides a convenient apparatus for comparing Roberts' patterns with the treatment of school grammars.

The following tabulation gives the numbers of the patterns as used in both of Roberts' books, a statement of the elements in the pattern (generally using traditional terms), an example, and the appropriate Reed and Kellogg diagram. It will exhibit clearly the similarities and differences among the three treatments.[3]

Patterns of English	English Sentences		
I.	I.	Subject + intransitive verb	
		Fish swim.	*Fish | swim*
II.	II.	Subject + linking verb + subjective complement (predicate adjective)	
		Bulldogs look fierce.	*Bulldogs | look\ fierce*
	IX.	Subject + *be* + subjective complement (predicate adjective)	
		Grass is green.	*Grass | is\ green*
III.	III.	Subject + linking verb (*V-b*) + subject complement (predicate noun)	
		Boys become men.	*Boys | become\ men*
	X.	Subject + *be* + subjective complement (predicate noun)	
		Dogs are animals.	*Dogs | are\ animals*
	VIII.	Subject + *be* + subjective complement (predicate adverbial)[4]	
		James is outside.	*James | is \ outside*
IV.	IV.	Subject + transitive verb (*V-t*) + direct object.	
		Farmers grow food.	*Farmers | grow | food*

[3] Neil Postman, Harold Morine, and Greta Morine, *Discovering Your Language*, 1963, give only four. Unfortunately, their numbering is different from that of Roberts. Their 1 equals Roberts' IV; 2 equals III; 3 equals II; and 4 equals I.

[4] A label such as "predicate adverbial" is not to be expected in school grammar. Words like *outside* are considered adjectives when modifying nouns or in the subjective predicate position. Pattern VIII cannot, therefore, be separated from III.

V.   V.   Subject + transitive verb (V-g) + indirect object + direct object

She gave him money.

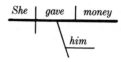

VI.   Subject + transitive verb (V-c) + direct object + objective complement

VI.

They called him Paul.

Bob considered Jim foolish.

VII. Subject + transitive verb (V-e) + direct object + objective complement

They elected him president.

While there is a well-established name for the characteristic complement in pattern V, "the indirect object", Reed and Kellogg do not give it a place on the main line. This is perhaps the most notable difference between their treatment and that of Roberts' *Patterns of English*. The failure to give a more basic place to the indirect object is surely a deficiency in the system of sentence diagramming, and one which does not necessarily reflect a parallel shortcoming in the school grammar on which it is based. For this reason, the deficiency has often been noticed, and several schemes have been proposed to remedy it. One solution would be simply to add a new kind of marker to indicate that an indirect object follows. The following has been used:[5]

She gave him money.

The other difference is that Roberts assigns clauses with predicate adjectives and those with predicate nouns to different patterns (II and III), whereas Reed and Kellogg diagram them alike. This difference is trivial, since school grammars do recognize the difference, and no great advantage can be seen for different diagrams. Moreover, it is interesting to note that even in his expanded system, Roberts does not make the same distinction between adjectives and nouns in the objective complement slot. Clauses with either are VI.

The differences between school grammar and Roberts' *Patterns of English* are not, therefore, great, except in the matter of emphasis. They

---

[5] I do not know the source of this, but have a vague memory of seeing it somewhere. In any case, it or something like it would be an improvement!

present much the same analysis. But the fact that Roberts shifts attention from individual complements to whole patterns is important, and one of the valuable contributions of the book.

One notable fact about these clause patterns is that each occurs with a characteristic type of verb. Both traditional grammar and school grammar have recognized this and provide terms for several kinds of verbs. Three of these are in general use: Transitive verbs are all those which take a direct object. Intransitive verbs are all those which do not take a direct object. Among the latter a special subdivision, linking or copulative verbs, take a subjective complement. School grammars do not have special terms for the subclasses of transitive verbs that take indirect objects or objective complements. Both lacks are unfortunate, since they have contributed to obscuring an important fact: Only a relatively small number of verbs occur in each of these patterns.

Patterns V and VII are alike in having two complements, often of very much the same appearance. The verbs themselves sometimes provide the most important clue to distinguish the two, and thus to discern the correct meaning. Compare:

The Board assigned him a secretary.   (Pattern V)
The Board elected him a secretary.   (Pattern VII)

Sometimes interesting problems arise because the same verb can occur in both:

She made him a good husband because she made him a good wife.
He called her a taxi.   *He called her a fool.*

In *English Sentences*, Roberts provides designations for the verbs occurring in the several patterns. The three well-established and commonly used terms, transitive, intransitive, and linking, are employed. In addition, symbols are provided for four others, each based on a typical member of the group: *V-b* from *become* (a special subdivision of linking verbs), *V-g* from *give*, *V-c* from *consider*, and *V-e* from *elect*. Transitive verbs are abbreviated *V-t*, but strangely the obvious forms *V-i* and *V-l* for intransitive and linking verbs are not used. *Be* is not considered a verb on the grounds that its peculiarities are so great that it would have to be a special subclass in any case.[6]

---

[6] *Be* is morphologically very aberrant. That, however, should not be considered pertinent at this point. Syntactically it is unique also, but not in a way that should separate it from the class of verbs, but the converse. *Be* is a generalized verb, or rather the generalized member of a set of subclasses including *V-b* and *V-l*. In much the same way, *do* is the generalized member for another set of subclasses including *V-i* and *V-t*.

PATTERNS AND TRANSFORMATIONS

Roberts' *Patterns of English* says a little — but only implicitly — about transformations. Certain patterns are treated as secondary to his six basic patterns. But in *English Sentences* these subsidiary patterns are described explicitly in terms of transformations based on his ten basic patterns. Much of the reason for using the longer list of basic patterns lies here. Transformations can be stated only in terms of the structure of the sentences involved.[7] It is desirable to have the sentences which can be involved in different transformations clearly distinguished from one another.

Roberts lists three separate patterns for clauses with *be*. These might all be treated alike, or they could be considered as minor varieties of one basic pattern. However, the three figure quite differently in a set of transformations which Roberts makes basic to his treatment of noun phrases.

IX.   *Grass is green.*   ⇔ *green grass*
VIII. *The man is outside.*   ⇔ *the man outside*
X.   *The girl is a servant.* ⇔ *servant girl*

Subjective complements transform into modifiers of nouns. The three types above come from three different sentence patterns by similar transformations. These three types of modifiers can be distinguished by their transformational sources. One type, noun modifier of nouns, comes from a variety of sources. Of these, pattern X is certainly one of the least frequent. Another important source is pattern VIII, but by means of a quite different transformation:

VIII. *The food is for dogs.* ⇔ *dog food*

This diversity of sources for noun modifiers reflects the common difficulty of interpreting them. Indeed, there is frequent ambiguity. Note the phrase "noun modifiers" in the last sentence. This might be either of the following:

noun modifier ⇔ X.   *The modifier is a noun.*
noun modifier ⇔ IV. *The modifier modifies a noun.*

The latter would be parallel to many other examples:

soap salesman ⇔ IV. *The salesman sells soap.*

Note also that earlier in the paragraph the ambiguity was resolved by writing "noun modifiers of nouns", greatly increasing the presumption that the source is pattern X.

Another reason for listing VIII as separate from the others is seen in the *"there* transformation".

---

[7] See Chapter 9. Transformations are one way of formulating sentence relations, or even relations between sentence patterns.

VIII.   *A man is here.* ⇔ *There is a man here.*

This does not work with other patterns having *be* in the verb place:

IX.   *Grass is green.*   ⇔ ×*There is grass green.*
X.   *Dogs are animals.* ⇔ ×*There are dogs animals.*

Simplicity of description, then, is served within Roberts' technique by carefully distinguishing among these several clause patterns.

A somewhat more general distinction must be made between patterns IV, V, VI, and VII as a group and all the rest: I, II, III, VIII, IX, and X. The first group are all involved in the passive transformation, the latter are not:

IV.   *Farmers grow food.* ⇔ *Food is grown by farmers.*
II.   *Bulldogs look fierce.* ⇔ ×*Fierce is looked by bulldogs.*

That four of these patterns are alike in being involved in passive transformations is sufficient justification for the traditional grouping of the verbs concerned as transitive (of which some grammarians recognize a number of further subdivisions). It is also part of the justification for labeling one element in each pattern as the direct object. Transitive verbs are those which have direct objects. Direct objects may become subjects when transitive verbs become passive. The definitions of the two terms are mutually interdependent.

While patterns IV, V, VI, and VII are alike in having agnate passive constructions, there are some significant differences among them. For example, pattern V is alone in having two passives:

V.   *She gave him money.*   ⇔ *Money was given him by her.*
   ⇔ *He was given money by her.*

This is not true of patterns VI and VII, which also have two complements:

VI.   *They called him Paul.*   ⇔ *He was called Paul by them.*
   ⇔ ×*Paul was called him by them.*
VII.   *They elected him president.* ⇔ *He was elected president by them.*
   ⇔ ×*President was elected him by them.*

This difference alone would justify treating pattern V as distinct from the others, but there are also further differences in the transformations applying to the three patterns that confirm the distinctions.

Both direct and indirect objects may become subjects through a passive transformation. They differ, however, in other behavior. The most familiar is the relation of the indirect object to a prepositional phrase. Actually this divides the *V-g* class into three subclasses:

She gave him money.   ⟺ *She gave money to him.*
She bought him a ticket.   ⟺ *She bought a ticket for him.*
She asked him a question.   ⟺ *She asked a question of him.*

There is no prepositional phrase agnate to a direct object.

A second difference between direct and indirect objects is in the possibilities of omission. Of the four combinations that might be expected, only three are possible:

V.   *She gave him money.*
       She gave   money.
      ×*She gave him*
       She gave.

Instead of the rejected possibility, a form with the preposition can be used:

She gives regularly to the Community Chest.

The matter is perhaps better put the other way: If a verb like *give*, which normally is used in pattern V, has only one complement, this is interpreted as a direct object. Thus, if a native speaker heard a sentence like *She gave him.*, additional information might be sought by asking: *Who did she give him to?* not *What did she give to him?*

The phrase with *by* can usually be omitted in a passive sentence. When this is done, passives of pattern VII are very closely parallel to pattern III, and indeed show many similarities in transformational relationships:

VII.   *They elected him president.*   ⟺   *He was elected president.*
III.   *He became president.*

When a sentence in pattern V is made passive by making the indirect object the subject, the old direct object remains as a complement. The sentence is now in many ways parallel to pattern IV:

V.   *They gave him money.*   ⟺   *He was given money.*
IV.   *He received money.*

School grammars have labeled the complement after such passives as the "retained object". There seems to be no particular reason to use this term, however, since it is merely the direct object in a special situation.

ADDITIONAL PATTERNS

Roberts recognizes that there are further patterns that he does not treat, and he mentions a few briefly so that students will not get the idea that the ten listed exhaust the possibilities.[8] That he discussed no more is, of course, the result of his judgment as to the proper amount of material to lay before students in a single treatment of English grammar. Opinions will differ as to where this line should be drawn — perhaps some would prefer to include more. In any case, there are others of some importance in the language, and a teacher should certainly be aware of at least a few more. Questions may well come up in class about some of them, since several are fairly common. We will here mention only a few. Just for convenience of discussion, Roberts' numbers will be continued.

Sentences of pattern IV have direct objects. They can undergo a passive transformation by which the direct objects become subjects. There are a few verbs which occur in clauses looking very much like pattern IV, but which cannot be made passive.

> Smith lacks money. ⟷ ×Money is lacked by Smith.
> Bad luck befell him. ⟷ ×He was befallen by bad luck.

This restriction is certainly not semantic. Compare the following sentences of very similar meanings which do have passives:

> Smith needs money. ⟷ Money is needed by Smith.
> Bad luck struck him. ⟷ He was struck by bad luck.

We must recognize the clauses without passives as representing a separate pattern. Most grammars do not distinguish this, but treat it in the same way as pattern IV. It seems at least as distinctive as some of the patterns which have been given separate treatment:

XI. *She resembles Jane.*

$$\text{She} \mid \text{resembles} \mid \text{Jane}$$

There are rather few verbs that occur in this pattern: *lack, befall, resemble, have.* However, one of these is very common. Most sentences with *have* as main verb do not have passives:

> Smith has money. ⟷ ×Money is had by Smith.
> John had a headache. ⟷ ×A headache was had by John.

There are, however, passive sentences with *have.* These commonly lack an agnate nonpassive. Apparent nonpassive counterparts seem to have a somewhat irregular relationship. For example:

> Good souvenirs can be had if you are an astute shopper.
> You can have good souvenirs if you are an astute shopper.

---

[8] Paul Roberts, *English Sentences*, 1962, p. 40. This paragraph has unfortunately gone unnoticed all too often. I have heard experienced English teachers with local reputations as leaders in the movement for "linguistics" base their presentation in professional meetings on the notion that Roberts' ten sentence patterns are exhaustive.

These two sentences do not mean the same thing in the way such pairs of passive and nonpassive sentences usually do. Indeed, the idiomatic way to change this passive into an active would involve changing the verb also:

> *You can get good souvenirs if you are an astute shopper.*

In passive sentences, *have* means 'get, obtain, take possession of'. This meaning is unusual in nonpassive sentences, but does occasionally occur. In nonpassive sentences, *have* generally means 'be in possession of, hold, own'. Because the two ranges of meanings are correlated with two different patterns of grammatical use, we must recognize two different homonymous verbs. *Have* meaning 'own' is used in pattern XI. *Have* meaning 'get' is used in pattern IV, more often in the passive, but not exclusively so.

A very much larger number of verbs fall into the following pattern:

XII. *Jim walked miles.*

Traditional grammars (the more thorough ones at least) treat the last element in such sentences as an "adverbial objective". There are many kinds of these; this type is perhaps best designated "complement of measure". Such a complement cannot be confused with a direct object because of the lack of a passive. The pattern differs from XI in that very different assortments of forms can occur in the two complement positions.

Cost, last, and *take* have a complement of measure and may have an additional complement, for which no label is established. The latter is reminiscent of the indirect object in many respects,[9] but neither of the complements is involved in a passive transformation.

XIII. *It cost me plenty.*

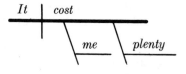

> *That will last me years.*

> *It will take me an hour.*

Restricted as this pattern is, occurring with only a few verbs, it is nevertheless rather frequent and decidedly useful.

---

[9] It is commonly so treated in school grammars.

A few verbs take two objects, either of which can occur alone, and both of which act very much like direct objects. Some school grammars describe these under the rubric of "double objects". Common verbs include *ask*, *tell*, *teach*, and *strike*.

> XIV. *She taught me Latin.*
> *They asked me a question.*
> *He struck the rock a blow.*
> *He told me a lie.*

Reed and Kellogg diagramming in its original form makes no provision for double objects as such. Most school grammars treat the first of the complements as an indirect object. However, sentences with indirect objects but without direct objects are not normal. The following types of sentences are, however, quite usual:

She taught Latin.	*She taught me.*
They asked a question.	*They asked him.*
He struck a blow.	*He struck the rock.*
He told a lie.	*He told me.*

One possibly useful addition to the diagramming conventions is the following to indicate double objects:[10]

The following two sentences seem superficially very much alike and are traditionally diagrammed in exactly the same way:

> *They looked at noon.*
> *They looked at houses.*

However, the second of these has a passive, while the first does not:

> *They looked at noon.*   ⇔ *×Noon was looked at by them.*
> *They looked at houses.*   ⇔ *Houses were looked at by them.*

To be sure, this passive is widely condemned by editors and some teachers, among other reasons, because it is a major source for prepositions at the ends of sentences. However, the construction does occur rather commonly in all kinds of English. It is recognized as legitimate by most traditional grammarians, who often label a combination such as *look at* as a "prepositional verb" and an element in the place of *houses* as a "prepositional-object". By contrast, *noon* in the example above is the "object of a preposition". School grammars seldom discuss prepositional verbs adequately, but a few do recognize this passive construction as legitimate.

[10] R. W. Pence, *A Grammar of Present-Day English*, 1947, p. 321.

Clauses with prepositional verbs may be considered as representing a separate pattern:

XV.   *They looked at houses.*

This pattern is very similar to IV, and the "prepositional object" is only little different from the direct object. However, there are some situations in which the two do not behave alike. Moreover, the structural contrast between the two patterns with prepositions after verbs, as in the above examples, needs to be made clear and the possibilities of ambiguity pointed out. For these two reasons, pattern XV is usefully distinguished from IV.

To meet even ordinary needs adequately, a dictionary must list *look at* and many others of the same kind. It does not suffice to give the meanings separately for *look* and *at*. The combination has its own meaning and usage, different from what might be expected from its constituents. The unit, lexically, is the two words together. They also function as a closely knit unit in the grammar. This might well be recognized in a small departure from standard practice in diagramming:

$$\text{They} \mid \text{looked } \text{at} \mid \text{houses}$$

instead of the usual:

$$\text{They} \mid \text{looked}$$

Some of the peculiarities of prepositional verbs are shared by another group sometimes called "separable verbs". Indeed the two are not always clearly distinguished in dictionaries. In separable verbs, a verb and a following adverb form a unit which must be treated lexicographically. This adverbial element can come either before or after the object. The two orders are basically equivalent and so are diagrammed alike:

XVI.   *They looked up Jim.*

   They looked Jim up.

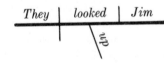

Only one order is possible with pronouns:

   They looked him up.   ×*They looked up him.*

XV and XVI contrast in that *at* and *houses* in XV cannot be inverted:

   They looked at houses.   ×*They looked houses at.*

A further variety of verb seems to combine features of both these last groups. They have an adverbial element of the sort found in separable verbs and a prepositional element. *Put up with* is an example. It is not clear how these verbs should be treated, nor what patterns they are found in.

In addition to various kinds of complements, there are some other elements which can be found in sentences and which merit brief mention here. Among them are elements which are traditionally called "adverbial". In school grammars these are always treated simply as modifiers of the verb. Some of them can be freely added to any clause type, or just as freely omitted. For example, *generally* can be added to many sentences, and other grammatically similar elements can be added in the same place to all:

I.   *Fish generally swim.*
II.   *Bulldogs generally look fierce.*
III. *Grass generally is green.*
IV.   *Farmers generally grow food.*   etc.

On the other hand, other types of adverbial elements are controlled in various ways by the verb. This can work in two ways.

The verb *put* (not as part of a prepositional or separable verb) seems to require some sort of a locative expression:

He put it here.   *He put it on the table.*
He put it somewhere.   *He put it where you wanted it.*
×He put it.

In a sense, then, these locative elements are complements of *put*, and perhaps deserve as much attention in describing sentence patterns as the elements mentioned in the last several pages.

Conversely, some verbs do not allow certain types of adverbial elements. Most linking verbs, for example, do not admit adverbs of manner.

×Bulldogs look fierce rapidly.

It is possible that all the clause patterns listed above should be further described as permitting or excluding adverbs of manner, and in some instances subdivided on this basis.

We do not as yet have adequate information on the use of these various types of adverbial elements. It is, therefore, not possible to set up a list of clause patterns which takes them into account, nor is it possible to say whether such a procedure is either worthwhile or feasible. Two things are requisite: a thoroughgoing investigation of the possibilities with a large sample of verbs, and an adequate classification of the adverbial elements themselves. These two are, of course, mutually dependent. Here is a problem that calls for much research.

PATTERNS WITH TWO VERBS

Some simple sentences have two verbs:

He stopped talking.

Any verb whatever can occur as the last in such a series. Only a short list can occur in the initial position. The latter verbs are called catenatives[11] from the fact that they form chains of verbs. Such chains most often contain only two verbs, but much longer sequences are possible. All but the last must be catenatives.

> *He wanted to finish talking.*
> *He decided to begin trying to stop smoking.*

Long chains of verbs merely repeat catenative constructions. The last example combines the patterns that might be found in such sentences as:

He decided to begin.	*He decided to buy the car.*
He began trying.	*He began to walk away.*
He tried to stop.	*He tried to forget his past.*
He stopped smoking.	*He stopped working years ago.*

The first and fourth of these are quite different from the second and third. These two constructions are representative of a very considerable number that can be found with catenatives.

The second verb in the chain (either a catenative or not) may take various forms paralleling *speak, to speak, speaking, spoken*. This second verb can have whatever complements it would normally have if it were the only verb in the clause:

> *They wanted to elect John president.*
> *They stopped giving Jimmy any allowance.*

This second verb, together with its accompanying complements and modifiers, must be considered as a complement of the catenative which precedes it. In some patterns there may be an additional element in the sentence between the catenative and its verbal complement. This is normally a pronoun or a noun phrase. In some respects it seems to be a complement of the catenative verb. In others it seems to have a close relationhip with the verbal element which follows. In some instances the catenative verb may be made passive, in which case this nominal complement becomes the subject. In other cases this is not possible. Combining all these possibilities, the following patterns are found:

[11] W. F. Twaddell, *The English Verb Auxiliaries*, 1960.

	Verbal complement only	Verbal and nominal complement Passives possible	Verbal and nominal complement Passives impossible
base		*He let me speak.* (*I was let speak.*)	*He had me speak.*
to	*He wanted to speak.*	*He helped me to speak.* (*I was helped to speak.*)	*He wanted me to speak.*
-ing	*He stopped speaking.*	*He stopped me speaking.* (*I was stopped speaking.*)	*He had me speaking.*
-en	*It got spoken.*	*He heard his name spoken.* (*His name was heard spoken.*)	*He had his name spoken.*

In addition, there are clauses which have the second verb in the bare base form, but which must have *to* in the passive:

> *He made me speak.*
> (*I was made to speak.*)

Any such tabulation of patterns, however, is only a first approximation to a useful classification. It does show the combinations of forms that can occur, but something more is needed. That this is so is shown by the following examples:

> *He started to speak.*   *He started speaking.*
> *He stopped to speak.*   *He stopped speaking.*

The two sentences with *started* are very similar in meaning; the two with *stopped* are quite different. We might expect that this difference in meaning would reflect some difference of grammatical behavior between the two catenatives *start* and *stop*. This is in fact the case. With *stop*, *to* may be replaced by *in order to* with little, if any, change of meaning. With *start*, *in order to* is quite unusual and gives a very different meaning from *to*:

> *He stopped to speak.*   *He stopped in order to speak.*
> *He started to speak.*   *He started in order to speak.*

The catenatives followed by *to* can be divided into two groups on the basis of whether *in order to* is substitutable or not.

A full study of the relations of these catenative patterns will probably show a number of other distinctions of this type which are not recognized in the chart above. Perhaps also some of the patterns will turn out to be more closely related than the chart indicates. Indeed, the whole system may need to be organized in some drastically different way.

As we have seen, many catenatives take two complements, one a noun or pronoun and the other a verbal form. These combinations of complements are agnate to clauses containing the noun or pronoun as subject and having the verb in the predicate.

> *(He let) me speak.*   ⇔ *I spoke.*
> *(He helped) me start the car.* ⇔ *I started the car.*

Another similar-appearing type of sentence, often very much more formal, should be compared:

> *(He stopped) my speaking.*   ⇔ *I spoke.*

Separating out the complements, the following patterns of agnation are found:

> *I spoke.*   ⇔ *me speak*
>   ⇔ *me to speak*
>   ⇔ *me speaking*
>   ⇔ *my speaking*
> *His name was spoken.*   ⇔ *his name spoken*

It would be tempting to consider the phrases at the right in this tabulation to be used as complements of catenative verbs. In one case this works well:

> *He | stopped | my speaking.* ⇔ *My speaking was stopped by him.*

This is parallel to:

> *He | stopped | the noise.*   ⇔ *The noise was stopped by him.*

These are clearly normal three-part sentences of pattern IV.

This does not work with the others:

> *He | stopped | me speaking.*   ×*Me speaking was stopped by him.*

The failure of the passive transformation indicates that this is not pattern IV. *Me speaking*, whatever else it may be, is not a direct object. Indeed, *me speaking* cannot be any other kind of complement. It does not behave in sentences as one unit, but as two. *Me* is a complement of the direct object type, as shown by the fact that it becomes a subject when the sentence is made passive. *Speaking* is a separate complement which remains a complement in the passive. *Me speaking, me speak, me to speak,* and *his name spoken* are none of them constituents of any kind. They are sequences of units, occupying two slots in the clause patterns in which they occur. That they are agnate to sentences does not insure that they have any grammatical unity. The perceived unity is only in the sentences to which they are related.

These relations can be used in a generative grammar as a device to account for sentences with catenatives. A sentence like

> *He stopped me speaking.*

is derived from two others:

He stopped + §NP + -ing + §V₁ & I speak.

To rule P6 on page 251 should be added at least three more alternatives:

$$V_1 \rightarrow \begin{bmatrix} V\text{-}cat_1 + \S NP + 0 & + \S V_1 \\ V\text{-}cat_2 + \S NP + to & + \S V_1 \\ V\text{-}cat_3 + \S NP + \text{-}ing & + \S V_1 \end{bmatrix}$$

These recognize three subclasses of catenatives, here arbitrarily numbered. Then there can be added a T-rule of the following general form:

$$V\text{-}cat + \S NP + X + \S V_1 \ \& \ NP + Y + V_1$$
$$1 \quad\quad 2 \quad\quad 3 \quad\quad 4 \quad\quad\quad 5 \quad\quad\quad 6$$
$$\Rightarrow V\text{-}cat + NP + X + V_1$$
$$1 \quad 5 \text{ in } 2 \quad 3 \quad 6 \text{ in } 4$$

SUBJECTS

It has been traditional to define the subject of a sentence as being a noun, to which some grammarians have added "or a noun equivalent". Actually a great many kinds of subjects are used. A listing of some of the possibilities — probably not exhaustive — has some interest. In all examples, the subject is first and is marked off from the remainder of the sentence by a vertical line.

The most common type of subject is a noun phrase. There is, of course, considerable variety in the internal structure of noun phrases, and this variety can be seen in subjects. Probably the most frequent pattern is a noun preceded by a determiner, but the determiner may be lacking, or from one to several other modifiers may be added:

Determiner plus noun	*The library* | *closes at ten.*
Noun alone	*Man* | *is mortal.*
Noun with modifiers	*The chief export of Brazil* | *is coffee.*
	Pure, unalloyed gold | *is too soft for jewelry.*

Complex types of noun phrases can be formed by coordinating two or more noun phrases or by joining them in apposition. Though quite different in their internal structure, these constructions are best considered on the level at which they enter sentence patterns as noun phrases:

Two nouns	*Mary and Martha* | *are sweet little girls.*
Two nouns with their modifiers	*A deteriorating old car and some spare parts* | *ornamented the side yard.*

Two nouns jointly modified   *Ill-matched cups and saucers* | *were*
                                    on the table.
Noun phrases in apposition   *My old friend, Bill Jones,* | *is a*
                                    plumber.

Pronouns are elements which replace noun phrases, and are accordingly frequent as subjects. Most often they stand alone, but a few types of modifiers may occur with them:

Pronoun   *He* | *wrote that just yesterday.*
Pronoun with relative clause   *He who hesitates* | *is lost.*
Pronoun with predeterminer   *We all* | *will be there.*

There are various noun-phrase-like structures which lack head nouns. Most types of prenoun modifiers can occur, either with additional modifiers or without. In some cases, it is clear that the head word is not a noun because, though there is no evidence of a plural ending, the subject is clearly plural both in its verb agreement and its meaning:

Headed by adjectives   *The poor* | *are always with us.*
                                    All the rich | *avoid Coney Island.*
Headed by specifiers   *The same* | *were in the files.*
Headed by numerals   *Those three* | *look good to me.*
Headed by possessive phrases   *Mr. Smith's* | *is better than mine.*
                                    Mine | *is a fifty-six Ford.*
Headed by determiners   *Some* | *like it hot.*
Headed by predeterminers   *Both* | *have the same trouble.*

Determiners and predeterminers in such patterns can, of course, be treated as pronouns, and most frequently are. However, they fit rather interestingly into a sequence of types of phrases which look like noun phrases progressively decapitated. In each of the types, the additional modifiers are restricted to those which might precede the head word if it were a modifier in a normal noun phrase.

Some of the determiners cannot stand alone as subjects, but must be attached to certain nouns which are so generalized as to be empty of meaning:

Determiners with empty nouns   *Anything* | *will do.*
                                Everybody | *is going to the picnic.*

A few verbs never, or only very exceptionally, take noun phrases as subjects. But, as English sentences typically have subjects, a meaningless formal element, *it*, is used. This is usually considered a pronoun, but if so, is a most unusual one. Pronouns are generally thought of as replacing noun phrases. This *it* does not — no noun phrase seems to be possible for it to have replaced:

Empty subject   *It | is raining.*

Similar to this formal *it* are the *it* and *there* which stand before the verb in certain types of inverted sentences. Some grammarians treat these as subjects; others consider the phrase or clause that follows as subject and these as expletives.

Expletives   *It | is kind of you to ask.*
                                      (⇔ *To ask | is kind of you.*)
                                      There | are other fish in the sea.
                                      (⇔ *Other fish | are in the sea.*)

Two types of sentences have no subject at all. The first is imperatives, usually treated in school grammars as having "*you* understood" as subject. The second is the "sentence fragment", usually considered as of marginal correctness at best. Fragments are of very frequent occurrence in some kinds of speech, but generally avoided in formal writing. Certain examples, however, are more often said without the subject than with it, even in fairly formal discourse:

No subject   *Come with me.*
                                      Serves him right!

Clauses are very frequent as subjects, either introduced by a *wh*-word or by *that*. It is notable that *that* is never omitted from a clause in the subject position as it commonly is elsewhere:

Wh-word clause   *Whatever I do | is always wrong.*
That clause   *That it could be so | seemed incredible.*

Direct quotations may be subjects. These may be sentences, longer passages, or fragments. In short, there is no grammatical restriction whatever on what can be quoted. For this reason, it is imperative that these be described as quotations, not as words, sentences, and so on.

Quotation of a sentence   *"I think so," | is just what he said.*
Quotation of a word   *"Is" | is what I mean, not "has".*

Very similar is the use of any bit of language whatever in talking about language.

Identification of a word   *The | is a determiner.*
Identification of an affix   *-Ed | is pronounced in many ways.*

If such occurrences are not carefully distinguished from normal speech or writing, utter confusion results. Any part of speech whatever would have to be listed as a possible subject in an English sentence.

Under normal circumstances, however, a number of other parts of speech besides nouns and pronouns do occur as subjects. Beside those already listed the simplest case is adverbs and adverbial prepositional phrases:

Adverb	*There*	*is much too close.*
	Once	*is enough!*
Adverbial phrase	*Right now*	*is when I want it.*
Prepositional phrase	*Over the fence*	*is out of bounds.*

Verbs or verbs with complements are frequently used as subjects, but always with some special marker. There are two of these, *to* and *-ing*. The verb together with one of these is traditionally treated as a unit. When marked with *to* it is an infinitive; when marked with *-ing* it is a gerund.

Infinitive	*To err*	*is human.*
Infinitive with complement	*To ride the roller-coaster*	*was exciting.*
	To have been elected class president	*was a great honor.*
Gerund	*Seeing*	*is believing.*
Gerund with complements	*Giving beggars money*	*is foolish.*
	Trying to stop smoking	*was a tribulation.*

Infinitives and gerunds may be accompanied by noun phrases or pronouns that in other contexts might be subjects — that is, the combination is agnate to a clause containing subject and predicate. With an infinitive, these are marked by *for*; with gerunds by the possessive marker *-'s*. Infinitives, but not gerunds, can also be preceded by a *wh*-word.

For + nominal + infinitive	*For him to laugh*	*was the last straw.*
	For Samuel to teach Latin	*would be a joke.*
Possessive + gerund	*His laughing*	*was the last straw.*
	Dick's incessant talking	*distresses me.*
Wh-word + infinitive	*What to say*	*was a problem.*
	How to mix the stuff	*wasn't clear to me.*

Throughout this list there are possibilities of coordination, mentioned only in connection with noun phrases. Any two forms that are grammatically equivalent can be coordinated. Thus, two noun phrases can be joined, but not a noun phrase and an adverb. This is one device to show the grammatical equivalence of a pronoun to a noun phrase, or of a prepositional phrase to an adverb:

Two noun phrases	*The policemen and the firemen*	*are meeting on the diamond Saturday.*
Noun phrase and pronoun	*My Latin teacher and I*	*had a long talk.*

| Two prepositional phrases | *Over the bridge and down the road | makes a delightful walk.* |
| Prepositional phrase and adverb | *To the school and back | is a full mile.* |

With this in mind, it is interesting to note that two infinitives or two gerunds may be coordinated, but not an infinitive and a gerund:

Two infinitives	*To bask in the sun and to swim a little	seemed to be all he wanted to do.*
Two gerunds	*Playing ball and talking about cars	are his chief interests.*
An infinitive and a gerund	*×To bask in the sun and swimming a little ×Playing ball and to talk about cars*

This suggests that there is a rather fundamental grammatical difference between infinitives and gerunds even though both constructions can be conceived as primarily devices to use verbs in nonpredicate positions.

Of these numerous types of subjects, not every one can be found in all of the clause patterns listed earlier in this chapter. Still, most of them can be found in several patterns, and most of the patterns can have several of them. It would, therefore, materially complicate matters if the clause patterns were to specify the types of subjects involved. Each of them would have to be subdivided; for example, pattern I would have at least the following varieties:

Nominal + intransitive verb	*The pale moon	rose.*
Verbal + intransitive verb	*To lose this game	will hurt.*
Clause + intransitive verb	*Whoever did that	will suffer.*
Adverbial + intransitive verb	*Outside the circle	doesn't count.*

The list of clause patterns is already long — this further elaboration would appreciably diminish its utility. But it is not at all necessary. The clause patterns can perhaps better be restricted to one important function: that of formulating the combinations of verb classes and complements that occur. The types of subjects are a different problem. The clause patterns are, then, really predicate patterns, or still better, patterns of the unit consisting of verb and complements which may function as a predicate, or as a complement with a catenative verb, or with *to* or *-ing*, as a subject.

This is the unit which was labeled V_1 in the sample generative grammars discussed in Chapters 10 and 11. The patterns we are discussing as clause patterns in this chapter would all be listed in rule P6. The form of that rule given on page 251 may be equated with the clause patterns as follows:

$$V_1 \rightarrow \begin{bmatrix} V\text{-}i \\ V\text{-}t + NP + \text{-}m \\ V\text{-}b + NP\S \\ V\text{-}l + AP \\ be + Loc \\ be + Poss \\ have + NP + \text{-}m \end{bmatrix}$$

Roberts' pattern I

IV

III

II

VIII

(XI)

PREDICATE INTRODUCERS

In the following sentences, a bar has been placed after the subject, and another one before the main verb, dividing them into three pieces:

He | will | undertake the job.
The men | can | give you that information.
He | must | try to do it.

The subject was discussed in the last section; our attention here is on the other two components. The third part of each sentence above can also occur as a complement after catenative verbs:

I won't let him | undertake the job.
They made him | give you that information.
I'll have him | try to do it.

When these verbs plus complement complexes are themselves complements, they are not preceded by elements like *will, can, must*. The latter occur only as the lead-in word in predicates. They never occur in subjects or in complements or anywhere else, except when a whole clause occurs in these places. We shall label them as predicate introducers. They have the function of signaling that the verb-complement complex which follows is a predicate. Without one of these or some equivalent, the verb and its dependent elements would be something else.

Not all clauses fall as easily into these three parts: subject, predicate introducer, and verb-complement complex. The following represent a common type. Only the boundary between the subject and the predicate is marked.

The boys | walked home.
They | gave him money.
They | tried to stop.

While no predicate introducer precedes the main verb, these predicates are not of a form that can occur as complement of a catenative. But there are verb-complement complexes very much like them that can:

I made him | walk home.
I made her | give him money.
I made him | try to stop.

The predicates above differ from these verb-complement complexes only in that something has been added to the lead-in word — the "past tense" suffix *-ed* (or an equivalent vowel change). We may bring these predicates into the same pattern by considering *-ed* as another predicate introducer. This does not precede the complex, but is added to its first word. A bit of rearranging will make it possible to cut in a way quite parallel to our first examples:

The   boys | -ed | walk   home.

Exactly the same thing will be the case with sentences of the following kind:

The boy walks home everyday.
The boy | -s | walk home everyday.

A comparable sentence with a plural subject presents more of a problem. Here there is no suffix visible. However, if we take the liberty of claiming that a suffix is there but not visible, these can be brought into the pattern too.

The boys walk home everyday.
The boys | -0 | walk home everyday.

We have written a zero for the suffix. This looks like a rather desperate artifice, but it does turn out to have some merit. The two suffixes *-s* and *-0* are alike in a great part of their meaning; one occurs with singular third-person subjects, the other with other subjects. It is now possible to say that all ordinary predicates have a predicate introducer either as the lead-in word or as a suffix on the lead-in word.

There is one justification for claiming that there is a predicate introducer where we have written *-0*, and that this is not entirely fictitious. This is the behavior of verb-complement clusters that begin with *be*. These show a clear contrast in form between the instances in which there is no introducer and those in which the introducer is *-0*.

I am first.	*I	-0	be first.*
They let me be first.	*They let me		be first.*
I was first.	*I	-ed	be first.*
You are first.	*You	-0	be first.*

Of course, this occurs only with *be*. This would be a very slender base for an analysis except that *be* is a very common first element in verb-complement complexes. It is not only the main element in the verb phrase in many sentences but it is also the commonest of the verbal auxiliaries.

The full list of predicate introducers in ordinary English is as follows:

can	*could*
shall	*should*
will	*would*
may	*might*
must	

-ed

-s/-0

And for some speakers, *need*, *dare*, and *ought*.

The predicate introducers have been listed in two columns. All those in the second column may carry the general meaning of unreality — *I would have gone, but...* indicates that the speaker really did not go. Those in the first column lack this meaning.[12] Each of the introducers, except *-s/-0*, has also a specific meaning or set of meanings. These have to do with time, obligation, possibility, and so on. All of them are quite elusive and hard to define, but this is not unusual for small structurally important closed sets. The nine that are words are very typically function words.

The suffix *-s/-0* has no meaning other than that shared by the whole set. It is a perfectly generalized member. It signals, by virtue of being a predicate introducer, the beginning of a predicate. But it says nothing about time or any related notion. It is commonly called the "present tense" suffix or something of the sort. But this is an error. It is used in situations where time is immaterial, or already adequately indicated, or quite general. Perhaps the commonest use is to indicate general habit:

> *He goes to the beach every summer.*
> *He gets up at six o'clock, regularly as clockwork.*

It is also used to indicate general truths:

> *What goes up comes down.*
> *The sun rises in the east.*

It is also used to describe specific events when the time is evident from the context and hence it is not considered necessary to be specified:

> *So the Greeks sail against Troy and lay seige to the city.*
> *If anybody asks where I am, I'm in New York till Tuesday.*

---

[12] On the basis of this, it is possible to segment the four in the second column: *could* = *-ed* + *can; should* = *-ed* + *shall; would* = *-ed* + *will; might* = *-ed* + *may*. As a matter of fact, most linguists do so. The statement of the patterns must then be reformulated. Some problems are cleared up; others are rendered more difficult. While it is unquestionable that the relations between *could* and *can* and so on, must be accounted for, it seems to me that they are better treated in another way. For a thorough discussion of the whole system from the other approach, see Martin Joos, *The English Verb*, 1964.

Comparable in many ways to the predicate introducers are two other elements occurring in the same position and indicating exactly the opposite. Verb-complement complexes occurring as subjects must have one of the introducers, *to* or *-ing*. These may also introduce complements, though some complements consist of complexes with no introducer. The contrast between the two is hard to define. In some circumstances, *-ing* is more general, *to* more specific.

I like swimming.	*I like to swim.*
Seeing her was a pleasure.	*To see her was a pleasure.*

The second sentence in each pair is more likely to refer to a specific occurrence. However elusive the difference may be, the function shared by the two is evident. They indicate that a following verb-complement complex is a subject, a complement, or some similar constituent.

A predicate must have a predicate introducer in other than an imperative sentence. This seems to be one of the hard and fast rules of English sentence structure. Most predicates have undoubted verbs, and the predicate introducers are related to them. But there are some sentences in which there is no significant verbal element in their meaning. These are sentences of patterns VIII, IX, and X.

Over the fence is out of bounds.

Such sentences seem to have only two significant elements, the subject and the subject complement. Interestingly enough, it is precisely this type of sentence which has the widest range of subject types. That is to say, almost any two things can be put together in this way to make a clause. The requirement that there must be a predicate introducer still holds. It is most often the generalized one, *-s/0*. But this cannot stand alone. The stem *be*, the most generalized verb or verb like stem is supplied. *Is, are,* and *am* are the forms assumed by the combinations of *be* and *-s/-0*.

VERBAL AUXILIARIES

In addition to predicate introducers, there may be verbal auxiliaries standing before the verb. The following example shows the maximum number possible:

has been being eaten

This rather easily divides into eight pieces, technically morphemes:

have   -s   be   -en   be   -ing   eat   -en

With so many, we might reasonably expect that they would not enter directly and simultaneously into the structure of the verb phrase. Rather, there should be some subassemblies, combinations of parts which serve as one constituent at some higher level. Of the eight elements, -s is clearly the predicate introducer. It marks the predicate as a whole, and we must therefore consider that the phrase as we have it consists of two parts, the predicate introducer and all the rest as a single unit. To show this clearly, it will be necessary to rearrange the order, as we have seen above:

-*s* | *have be -en be -ing eat -en*

The auxiliary *have* can precede the auxiliary *be*, always in the form of *been*, or the main verb. The latter is always in the form known as the "past participle", that is, the form that is conveniently indicated by the symbol -*en*. Since *have* and -*en* are so inseparably linked, we may consider that together they form a constituent. It is necessary, again, to rearrange order, with the following result:

-*s* | *have -en* | *be be -ing eat -en*

The auxiliary *be* is followed either by a form with -*ing* or a form with -*en*. There is a very considerable difference in meaning between the two usages. *Be* followed by -*ing* indicates a very puzzling range of meanings which we will label "limited duration". *Be* followed by -*en* indicates passive. Moreover, if both occur in the same phrase the order is fixed: *be be-ing eat-en*, not *be be-en eat-ing*. It would seem appropriate to consider the constituents to be *be* and the associated inflectional element on the next word. This forces further reordering:

-*s* | *have -en* | *be -ing* | *be -en* | *eat*

The verb phrase consists, then, of five constituents, of which one (the predicate introducer) is clearly not coordinate with the rest. There does not seem to be any particular virtue in attempting to determine immediate constituent structure otherwise. Verbal auxiliaries are involved in three preverb positions.

Another convenient way of portraying the situation is as follows:

-*s*						predicate introducer
have	*-en*					present relevance
	be		*-ing*			limited duration
		be			*-en*	passive
				eat		main verb
have	*-s*	*be*	*-en*	*be*	*-ing*	*eat* *-en*

Such an arrangement has the advantage of preserving the order and showing the constituents. The line between the predicate introducer and the rest indicates the higher rank of that cut.

No longer sequence of auxiliaries is possible. It is, however, common to have what looks like a longer sequence of elements in that it has one more word:

will have been being eaten   *will* | *have -en* | *be -ing* | *be -en* | *eat*

This is longer only in appearance. Two of the predicate introducers are suffixes on the first word, *-s/-0* and *-ed;* the remainder form words of their own.

There is one other verbal auxiliary, *do.* This is followed by the base form of the main verb: *does go, did try.* Very rarely does it occur before *be,* and then it indicates clearly that it is indeed the base form, not a form with *-0:*

> *Do be good!*

Do occurs only with the predicate introducers *-s/-0* and *-ed,* never with modals. Its function is simply to provide a base to which these can be attached when they must be separated from the main verb. Obviously it is not needed if *have* or *be* are present because they can serve this need, nor if modals are present since these do not require a base, being independent words in their own right.

The three auxiliary-suffix combinations have important functions in signaling certain sets of meanings. These are subtle and require some care in formulating. The description which follows is restricted to some of the more frequent meanings, and must not be taken as exhaustive.

The simplest one to define is the passive. This signals that the subject has the same relationship to the action of the verb as would the direct object if there were no indication of passive and if there were a direct object.[13] That is not really a definition of its meaning, however, so much as a definition of a very important agnate relationship. Nonpassive verbs with direct objects are agnate to passive verbs with subjects. The meaning of the transitive verb-direct object relationship is not easy to describe, and perhaps it is not really profitable to try to do so. The familiar statement is that the direct object is the recipient of the action. But that seems meaningless in such instances as

> *I see stars.*   *I enjoy beauty.*

The important part of the statement is that the relation of subject to passive verb is the same as that of nonpassive verb to direct object if there is one. Vague as this relation may be, that between subject and nonpassive verb is much more so. The latter seems to be definable only as the other possible relation when a direct object is present. Thus two kinds of relation to the action named by *drive* are commonly specified in sentences containing that verb:

---

[13] English has three types of passives: 1) the subject is agnate to a direct object, 2) the subject is agnate to an indirect object, 3) the subject is agnate to an object of a preposition. For a full statement, these paragraphs would have to be expanded and qualified to cover all three. There would, however, be no change in basic principles.

> *I drive.*   *The car drives easily.*

Either can be the subject. Only one can be the direct object:

> *I drive the car.*

The opposite arrangement is clearly saying something very different, if it is possible at all:

> ?*The car drives me.*

Because the verb without the passive indicator, *be -en*, does not indicate anything specific about the relation of subject to action, we do not use the term "active". Verbs without *be -en* are better labeled simply "nonpassive", a noncommittal term matching the indefiniteness of the meaning.

Have -en may be said to mark present relevance. In general it implies that the action started or took place in the past, but that it either continues to the present, or its effects continue. Compare for example:

> *I lived in Nebraska for ten years.*
> *I have lived in Nebraska for ten years.*

The second implies that the speaker still is a resident of Nebraska, the first does not, and perhaps even gives a fairly strong implication that he no longer is. That is somewhat unusual. Generally the form without *have -en* is noncommittal about present relevance. Compare, for example, the following:

> *He went down town. I don't know where he is.*
> *He has gone down town. I don't know when he'll be back.*

The most difficult to interpret is *be -ing*. There are two major elements in its meaning, duration and limitation. Which meaning is more prominent depends, as much as anything, on the specific verb. With one like *explode*, for example, which normally refers to a single momentary act, *be -ing* indicates duration, or perhaps duration produced by a sequence of separate events. Compare:

> *The gun shop caught fire. All the ammunition exploded.*
> *The gun shop caught fire. The ammunition was exploding when the fire engines got there.*
> *She dropped a glass and broke it.*
> *She has been dropping glasses and breaking them all day.*

Other verbs have duration inherent in their meaning. With these, the notion of limitation is prominent in the *be -ing* forms:

He teaches Latin.
He is teaching Latin this year, but I don't know what he will do next.
Last year he taught French, but this year he's teaching Latin.
He lives in San Diego.
He is living in San Diego now, but I think he will come back here.
He lives well.
He's living on borrowed time.

Some verbs have so strong an implication of continuous duration that the use of *be -ing* is hardly appropriate.

He knows a lot of important people.
×*He is knowing a lot of important people.*
Two and two equals four.
×*Two and two is equaling four.*
Perhaps: *He seems to be equaling his best past performance, but I don't think he can keep it up for ten full laps.*

Still other verbs are commonly used in situations where duration of the act is totally irrelevant. Often these are instances where the mere saying is effective.

I proclaim this National Dog Biscuit Week.
I declare you man and wife.
The psychiatrist pronounced him sane at the time of the crime.

But in another context duration or repetition is possible:

That psychiatrist has been pronouncing too many people sane recently.

Following out of the notions of duration and limitation is a third, simultaneity. This pattern is the commonest way of indicating a present tense, that is, action simultaneous with the speaking or effectively so.

What are you doing? Just playing.
He's teaching just now. Can I have him call you back?
The leaves are turning red. Winter will soon be here.

This idea of simultaneity is, of course, compatible with the past *-ed*. The combination often indicates action simultaneous with some other in the past.

When I came in he was trying to light the lamps.
When I was coming in, he tried to light the lamps.

The difference in these two sentences indicates a difference of focus. One act is something of an attendant circumstance simultaneous with the other.

The complex interplay of the ideas of duration, limitation, and simultaneity with the inherent meanings of the verbs and the circumstances of speaking makes the *be -ing* form a difficult one for foreign learners. Indeed, it is one of the most common sources of errors for accomplished foreign speakers. Native speakers learn most of the patterns in childhood, fortunately. The problems of semantic definition are always difficult. The English verbal system is an interesting type example of one kind of complexity.

Chapter 14

Joining Clauses

English words are joined together into phrases, the phrases into clauses, and the clauses into sentences and larger structures. Of the larger units, the sentence has received by far the most attention, probably a great deal more than it deserves. Structures both larger and smaller have been relatively neglected. Much of the structure of clauses has been described as applying to sentences by focusing on one-clause sentences and neglecting the distinction between the two levels of structure. On the other hand, the sentence has been the traditional upper limit of grammar. Larger units are discussed only on a basis of logic, semantics, rhetoric, or aesthetics, generally without any awareness that there might be grammatical features worthy of description. But there most certainly are. A really adequate grammar must describe all detectable levels of structure without confusing them.

A full outline of the ascending levels of structure above the clause is not yet possible, and would be out of place here in any case. However, it is worthwhile to point out in a rather general way some of the devices by which clauses are connected and some of the attendant modifications within clauses.

THE SENTENCE

School grammar developed out of the interaction of two approaches that competed through much of the nineteenth century. The older parsing approach emphasized the word as the fundamental unit of language. The analysis movement put its focus on the sentence. As a result of this history, words and sentences have been the basic units of school grammar.

Both are difficult to define, the sentence particularly so. The textbooks always attempt definitions, but these are never satisfactory.[1] Some linguists have tried definitions of the general form of that given by Bloomfield: "each sentence is an independent linguistic form, not included by virtue of any grammatical construction in any larger linguistic form."[2]

Since, however, what are traditionally recognized as sentences DO enter larger constructions, such a definition, if rigorously applied, identifies units much larger than what is desired. The sentence is probably undefinable, short of a very extensive set of statements — a whole grammar, in fact. Yet this should not dismay anyone. Few basic grammatical concepts can be defined easily. It would seem best to abandon the attempt, and to apply the effort to more promising endeavors.

The interest of school grammarians in the sentence derives in part at least from the fact that it is the unit which determines the placement of certain punctuation marks. There are several kinds of end punctuation, and these are selected on the basis of the type of sentence. It has, therefore, been traditional to stress a classification of sentences which will correlate with these marks. In the fuller form, this recognizes four kinds: declarative, interrogative, imperative, and exclamatory. Declarative and imperative share the period; some grammarians, consequently, do not distinguish the two. Interrogative sentences are defined in such a way as to coincide with those usually punctuated with the question mark.

The practical utility of such a classification is obvious, but there are major difficulties. No straightforward definition of the exclamatory sentence is possible. Authors vary widely in their use of exclamation points, and it is hard to frame any sort of description, even of one writer's usage. Perhaps it would be better to treat it simply as an optional substitute for the period, to be used when it is desired to give special prominence for any reason. Its use or nonuse would, then, be a matter of personal choice or style, and not, therefore, a direct concern for grammar. The exclamatory sentence as the schools have known it would disappear.[3]

Interrogative and imperative sentences can be defined structurally, but not always simply. The school definitions are more often completely nonstructural: "An interrogative sentence asks for information."[4] There are exceptions to this from both sides. Rhetorical questions do not ask for information, and certain imperative sentences do: *Tell me where you have been.*

---

[1] C. C. Fries, *The Structure of English*, 1952, gives a critique of a number of these attempts in Chapter 2.

[2] Leonard Bloomfield, *Language*, 1933, p. 170. Note that Bloomfield goes on: "In most, or possibly in all languages, however, various taxemes [i.e. structural signals] mark off the sentence . . ." This can be construed as an important supplement to the definition, but is not always quoted with it, for example, not by Fries.

[3] This step is taken in R. W. Pence, *A Grammar of Present-Day English*, 1947, p. 17.

[4] Homer C. House and Susan E. Harman, *Descriptive English Grammar*, Second ed., 1950, p. 13.

Declarative sentences can be defined, either structurally or semantically, only by a negative statement: they are any sentences not falling into one of the other classes.

Certainly there must be rules for the use of the question mark. However, it seems unnecessary to make those rules into a fundamental classification of sentences.

The second classification of sentences is based on the number and kind of clauses that they contain. Three types are generally recognized, and a fourth is commonly added. Simple sentences consist of a single clause. Complex sentences "contain one principal clause and one or more subordinate clauses."[5] Compound sentences consist of two or more independent clauses, either or both of which may contain subordinate clauses. These are the most widely used definitions; another somewhat different set is the following: "Simple sentences consist of a single clause." "A compound sentence consists of two or more main clauses." "A complex sentence is a sentence containing at least one subordinate clause." "A sentence containing two or more main clauses and at least one subordinate clause is called a compound-complex sentence."[6] The differences between these two sets of definitions are appreciable, but seldom recognized.

At first sight such a classification is simple and definitive. This very simplicity, however, is its major weakness. Too great diversity of pattern is comprehended in these few categories. The lines are not as sharp as they seem to be. The distinctions are not always entirely relevant. A more detailed description of interclause relationship is required than any that can profitably be based on this simple scheme.

One of the complications can be seen by examining some of the ways in which three or more clauses can relate in a single sentence. The clauses are marked by X, Y, and Z under the first word other than a connector. The connectors are marked by c if they coordinate and s if they subordinate. In these examples the connectors are to be construed with the clause that follows:

While the teacher was out, the girls whispered and the boys talked. (1)
    s   X   Y   c   Z

Y and Z are coordinated and X is subordinated to the two jointly: $X \rightarrow (Y + Z)$.

While the teacher was out the girls whispered, but she heard them. (2)
    s   X   Y   c   Z

X is subordinated to Y, and this complex is coordinated with Z: $(X \rightarrow Y) + Z$.

The car skidded because he braked and the road was icy. (3)
    X   s   Y   c   Z

Y and Z are coordinated and then as a unit they are subordinated to X: $X \leftarrow (Y + Z)$.

---

[5] House and Harman, *Descriptive English Grammar*, Second ed., p. 202.
[6] Paul Roberts, *Understanding Grammar*, 1954, pp. 306, 307, 308.

The car skidded because he braked when the road was icy.   (4)
   X   s   Y   s   Z
Z is subordinated to Y and then the complex is subordinated to X: $X \leftarrow (Y \leftarrow Z)$.

The car skidded because when he braked the road was icy.   (5)
   X   s   s   Y   Z
Y is subordinated to Z and then the complex is subordinated to X: $X \leftarrow (Y \rightarrow Z)$.

The car skidded where the road was icy because he braked.   (6)
   X   s   Y   s   Z
Y is subordinated to X and then Z is subordinated to the complex: $(X \leftarrow Y) \leftarrow Z$.

He braked, and the car skidded because the road was icy.   (7)
   X   c   Y   s   Z
Z is subordinated to Y and the complex is coordinated with X: $X + (Y \leftarrow Z)$.

He braked and the car skidded, because the road was icy.   (8)
   X   c   Y   s   Z
X and Y are coordinated and Z is subordinated to the complex: $(X + Y) \leftarrow Z$.

Some of these sentences differ in only minor ways: (4) and (5) are alike in that both have a pair of clauses in a subordinate-head construction which in turn is subordinated to a third; they differ in the order of these elements. Others differ in more significant ways: (1) and (2) have the same order of elements in every respect: s X Y c Z, but the relations signaled by the connectors are quite different. (7) and (8) even have identical connectors joining identical clauses, but differ in structure. It is not adequate to subsume all these differences under a classification as compound, complex, or compound-complex.

Moreover, different grammars would classify these differently. The second set of definitions given above would label (4), (5), and (6) as complex; (1), (2), (3), (7), and (8) as compound-complex. The first set would assign (3), (4), (5), and (6) to complex; (2) and (7) as compound; but makes no provision for (1) and (8). The latter do not have one main clause, but two, and so cannot qualify as complex under the definition. Though the sentences each contain a subordinate clause, it is not contained in either of the main clauses, and so the sentences do not qualify as compound.

It would seem better to look at such sentences in terms of immediate constituents. On this basis, (1), (3), (4), (5), (6), and (8) are sentences formed by a subordinating construction, while (2) and (7) are formed by a coordinating construction. One of the partners in (2), (4), (5), (6), and (7) is built on a subordinating construction — the head in (6), the subordinate member in (4) and (5), and one coordinate member in (2) and (7). In (1), (3), and (8) the second level of sentence structure is coordinate. To look at sentences in this way, however, is to shift away from the traditional school classification — or from any classification of sentences for that matter — to a focus on successive levels of relationship within sentences. Such a shift is essential if the more complicated sentences are to be understood.

COORDINATION AND SUBORDINATION

A second difficulty in the familiar classification of sentences lies in the distinction between coordinate and subordinate clauses. A simple dichotomy is not adequate and plays down certain important distinctions. There are at least four different kinds of subordination, illustrated in the following:

If you feel that way, don't go.	(9)
I asked the man a question which he did not know.	(10)
I gave him what he wanted.	(11)
I asked the man the last question, which he did not know.	(12)

In (9) the subordinate clause, *if you feel that way,* is connected somewhat loosely to the main clause as a whole. In (10) the subordinate clause, *which he did not know,* connects specifically to one element in the main clause, the noun *question.* It can be removed from the sentence, making some change of meaning of course, but without making any change in the basic structure of what remains. This is not the case with sentence (11), where the subordinate clause, *what he wanted,* is itself a basic sentence element rather than a modifier of one. If this is removed both the structure and the meaning of the sentence are drastically changed, since such a sentence cannot have an indirect object in the absence of a direct object. Another element must be substituted if the structure is to be preserved: *I gave the man something.* These three patterns represent three degrees of integration into the structure of the main clause. Traditional grammarians have not been, of course, unaware of this difference. They generally have taken care of it by discriminating adverbial, as in (9); adjectival, as in (10); and nominal, as in (11), subordinate clauses. The question is whether it is really useful to gather these types together under one class in contrast with independent or coordinate clauses, and it is not at all clear that it is. The fourth pattern, as in sentence (12), is superficially similar to that in sentence (10), but it is much looser even than that in sentence (9). The subordinate clause, *which he did not know,* seems hardly a part of the sentence at all, though it is written within it. Any subordination that there may be is purely formal, and perhaps even a little artificial. This pattern, the nonrestrictive relative clause, is discussed further in a later section of this chapter.

Not only are the places of subordinate clauses in larger constructions various, the clauses themselves are of different structures. One type is marked as subordinate merely by adding a marker, *because, while, since, if,* and so on. The internal structure of the clauses is not altered in any way as a consequence of the subordination. In this regard such clauses differ in no important respect from some coordinated clauses. The latter have different markers, that is all. The second type has a special form, a relative, as one of its clause elements, and often the order is different from what would be normal in independent clauses. The marks of connection, then, are integral in the clause rather than added to it. These two types clearly demand separate descriptions.

Some subordinate clauses have the same structure as some coordinate clauses. Moreover, the distinction between the two is not always clear. Subordination is commonly defined in terms of the logical relationship between the concepts expressed in the clauses. This is inadequate. Consider the following sentence:

> *I have no doubt that life exists on Mars.* (13)

There is no way of telling out of a context which clause expresses the logically subordinate idea. If the author is writing primarily about Mars or about extraterrestrial life, then the first is. But if he is writing an intellectual autobiography, then the second is. In one case the sentence is essentially synonymous with:

> *Undoubtedly, life exists on Mars.* (14)

In (14), *undoubtedly* is clearly a subordinate element, and the equivalent, *I have no doubt*, must also be, if only logically. In the other case the approximately synonymous sentence would be:

> *I have no doubt about the existence of life on Mars.* (15)

Logical coordination and subordination have no necessary connection with grammatical coordination and subordination. As we shall see, this is an important fact about English and a basic consideration in understanding some aspects of literary style.

Few grammars really attempt any definition of subordination. When this is done on any basis other than logic, the usual criterion is the ability of the clause to stand alone as a sentence. Subordinate clauses are said not to be able to do so, whereas coordinate clauses can. There are difficulties from both sides.

> *When are you going to the store?*
> *When John gets home.* (16)

Such a definition requires an independent criterion for excluding the answer in such a dialog as a sentence. And, for the conservative who disallows *and* and *but* in sentence initial position, many clauses that he would like to call independent will be unable to stand alone as sentences.

Absolute coordination should imply complete interchangeability. If, then, two clauses in a sentence can be interchanged without altering meaning, they may be safely considered to be in coordination. This is the case in the following:

> *Birds sang and squirrels chattered.*
> *Squirrels chattered and birds sang.* (17)
> *Either John ate it or James took it to the picnic.*
> *Either James took it to the picnic or John ate it.* (18)

There is clearly some touch of subordination in the following, where reversal, if possible at all, alters the meaning more or less:

> *It rained and so I stayed home.*
> *I stayed home and so it rained.* (19)
> *You go or I will be mad.*
> *I will be mad or you go.* (20)
> *He came but he didn't stay long.*
> *He didn't stay long but he came.* (21)

With other connectors, the subordination (that is, the noninterchangeability) would be still stronger. We do not claim that there is no distinction between coordination and subordination, for the examples demonstrate that there is. But the two are not sharply separate; they intergrade imperceptibly.

In practice, grammarians have generally distinguished coordinate and subordinate clauses by the connectors. Even here they do not agree. *And, or, but, both...and, either...or* are generally agreed to be coordinating conjunctions. But *for, yet, so, still* are variously treated.[7] The reason for this disagreement is fundamentally that the line between coordination and subordination is not sharp.

Still another difficulty with the classification of sentences as simple, compound, and complex may be seen in a series such as the following:

> *I saw a horse which was running.* (22)
> *I saw a horse running.* (23)
> *I saw a running horse.* (24)

By the traditional definitions, (22) is clearly complex, and (24) is just as certainly simple. Yet the two do not seem as distinctly separated as the

---

[7] "Some grammarians insist that *for* is a subordinating conjunction, the argument being that *for* never joins anything but clauses. The principal reason for classing *for* as a coordinating conjunction is the fact that *for* may be used at the beginning of an independent statement or even of a paragraph. *Yet* is now generally regarded as a coordinating conjunction — at least as far as punctuation is concerned. And *so* seems well on the road to acceptance as such." Pence, *A Grammar of Present-Day English*, p. 106.

classification would suggest, and sentence (23) is in some ways intermediate. Students who understand the definitions have no difficulty with sentences like (22) and (24), but sometimes hesitate or make errors with ones like (23), particularly when the troublesome element is longer as in (25).

> *I saw a horse running rapidly around the track without a rider.*   (25)

In any case, there seems to be some very strong relationship between sentences such as (22), (23), and (24). This relationship is obscured or concealed by the school grammar treatment.

Transformational-generative grammar accounts for all three sentences in very similar ways, deriving them by sequences of transformations from strings that would underlie such sentences as *I saw a horse.* and *A horse was running.* (22) is then the simplest of these, (23) and (24) differ in the application of additional transformations that further remove or disguise the clause structure of the modifier. If such sentences are described in this way, the distinction between simple and complex sentences becomes otiose. Even if this form of description is not used, the relation between such sentences must receive some sort of recognition. The transformations linking the three must be described in a complete grammar. They deserve mention in an English class because they are useful in certain practical applications of grammar.

RELATIVE CONSTRUCTIONS

One of the most important types of clause connection is that involving a relative clause modifying a noun. It is one of the places where a modified transformational approach[8] can be most useful in teaching. It will be profitable to discuss it in some detail within the framework of such an approach.

Sentences such as (26) and (27) are to be derived from pairs of sentences such as (28):

> *I saw the man who went home.*   (26)
> *The man whom I saw went home.*   (27)
> *I saw the man.*
> *The man went home.*   (28)

---

[8] That is, the kind of approach used in Paul Roberts, *English Sentences,* 1962. Transformations are grafted onto a basic grammatical apparatus which is only minimally adjusted to them. The general treatment is certainly not generative and hardly transformational. This type of grammar, however, seems a particularly fortunate choice for high school textbooks at the present time. It is fairly compatible with other systems in classroom use. It has considerable merit in comparison with those which leave sentence relations unmentioned. It is more flexible than a more strictly generative model.

The rules can be stated as follows: 1) The two clauses to be connected must have some noun phrase in common. In this example it is *the man*. 2) In one of the two (the choice is grammatically free, though of course sometimes one choice produces an undesirable sentence), this common element is removed and replaced by the appropriate *wh*-word or *that*. Both possibilities are illustrated:

I saw the man	*The man went home*
I saw whom	*who went home*

3) The *wh*-word or *that* is moved to the initial position in its clause if it is not already there:

I saw whom	*who went home*
whom I saw	(no change required)

4) The relative clause is inserted into the other clause immediately after the remaining one of the original pair of common phrases:

The man⟍
     ⎩*whom I saw*   *went home.*

I saw the man⟍
     ⎩*who went home.*

This gives the desired sentences, (26) and (27).

For many students one of the common difficulties with complex sentences is the "misplaced modifier". The rules as stated above for the insertion of relative clauses into sentences can be helpful with this. Since they call for placing the relative clause immediately after the noun phrase which originally matched in the two clauses, they automatically lead to the correct construction. However, to obtain this result it is necessary to insist that the whole noun phrase, including any postnoun modifiers, be EXACTLY identical, and that the WHOLE noun phrase must be replaced. The only exception is in the case of pronouns where case may be disregarded, that is, *he* and *him* or *she* and *her* may be considered as identical. The following, for example, is not permitted. It will lead to a misplaced modifier:

> *The man in the sports car danced a jig.*
> *The man plays piano duets.* → *who plays piano duets*
> ×*The man who plays piano duets in the sports car danced a jig.*   (29)

If, however, the following two sentences, which do meet the requirements, were available to start from, a workable result would be obtained:

The man in the sports car danced a jig.

The man in the sports car plays piano duets. → *who plays piano duets*

The man in the sports car who plays piano duets danced a jig.   (30)

This technique is used by Paul Roberts in *English Sentences* to introduce relative clauses. However, he fails to insist that the two input sentences share phrases which are absolutely identical. The result has been confusion for some students. Moreover, the rules do not work out as effectively to prevent misplaced modifiers, or to help indicate the nature of the error. Roberts gives the following example on page 75:

It looked odd.

I bought a picture.

I bought a picture that looked odd.   (31)

It would be far better to build this complex sentence from the following pair:

A picture looked odd. → *that looked odd*

I bought a picture.   (32)

If the other sentence is altered, these could also lead to:

A picture which I bought looked odd.   (33)

It is possible, following the rules as given above, to start from the two sentences which Roberts gives, provided another step is taken. *It* is a pronoun, that is, a substitute for a noun phrase. If it can reasonably be assumed that *it* in this example can be a substitute for *a picture*, then the following steps are possible.

It	*looked odd.*
A picture	*looked odd.*
that	*looked odd*
I bought a picture that	*looked odd.* (31)

There is one very interesting variation in the rules for the relative transformation as given above. If the phrase used is the object of a preposition, then two alternative procedures are possible in the second step. Either the relative pronoun is moved to initial position, leaving the preposition where it was (often final in the clause!), or, the preposition is moved with the relative. The following example will show the difference:

The house is red.

I live in the house.

— *I live in which* —

in which I live   *which I live in*

The house in which I live is red.   *The house which I live in is red.*

(34)

The first pattern (*in which I live*) is used only in literary English; the second (*which I live in*) is used in both literary and colloquial English, but in literary use it is less formal than the first. Colloquial English would more often elect to use *that* than *which*. The preposition cannot accompany *that*. Moreover, *that* may be dropped. As a result, the following are also possible alternative outputs:

> *The house that I live in is red.*
> *The house I live in is red.* (34)

These represent still less formal usage. The description just given, then, accounts in a simple way for a very significant variation in English. This is one of its values.

PARENTHESES

A parenthesis is a statement that interrupts another with which it is only tenuously connected. This type of clause relationship is common in English, both written and spoken. But the devices by which it is signaled are quite different in the two. In speech the preceding portion of the matrix usually ends with a /↗/ juncture, a sign both of a fairly major break and of incompleteness. The parenthesis itself usually ends with a major juncture. When the parenthesis is short, a pair of /↗/ junctures around a short stretch is quite characteristic. There is often a change of the intonational key, and sometimes other modification of the pitch system extending over the whole. At the end of the inserted passage, normal intonation is resumed and the discourse is continued more or less as it was going originally. These pitch phenomena are reminiscent of the change to a smaller type face sometimes used in technical books to mark incidental material or minor notes. In written English the normal marking of parentheses is by parens[9] ( ), double dashes — —, or similar paired punctuation.

In either speech or writing, parentheses are commonly introduced by special markers: *incidentally, by the way, that is, i.e., for example, e.g.,* and so on. Sometimes connectors which are also used to coordinate or subordinate clauses in uninterrupted discourse are used to introduce parentheses, usually with some other mark. There are considerable differences between speech and writing in the selection of these introducers, but the details have never been worked out and stated formally.

---

[9] I have used the term "paren" for the mark rather than the more familiar "parenthesis", an abbreviation of "parenthesis mark". The desirability of this is apparent in this section, which otherwise would become completely unintelligible. The common use of "parenthesis" for this meaning has pretty well driven the word out of use in its meaning 'matter that is inserted'. This is unfortunate, since the latter phenomenon deserves thorough exposition in English classrooms.

Parentheses are more easily identified when they actually interrupt a clause. But not infrequently they can be clearly recognized when they come between closely connected clauses:

If it rains — and I don't think it will — we'll have the picnic indoors. (35)

When the connection is less close, parentheses become indistinct or completely indistinguishable. Strangely, punctuational marking of intruding material is most regular and most distinctive in precisely the cases that are most easily recognized with or without marking, as in sentence (35). Compare:

*My friend — he lives in New York — is a stamp collector. He has
a very fine set of British airmails.* (36)
*My friend is a stamp collector. He lives in New York. He has a
very fine set of British airmails.* (37)

In a sense, the clause that is a parenthesis in (36) is also in (37). It interrupts the transition between *My friend is a stamp collector.* and *He has a very fine set of British airmails.* But if we are to call it a parenthesis in (37), it is a very unobtrusive one, and it is not marked in normal written English by any punctuation, though parens ( ) would be possible. Simple but fluent English tends to place many of the parenthetical remarks in such places, where they are less obviously interruptions. A parenthesis of the type of (35) seems a little more elaborate, perhaps a little more literary.

This, however, is not the characteristically literary form for a parenthesis. That would be the nonrestrictive relative clause. It might come in the same place in the sequence of sentences as the parenthesis in (36), but it would take the form not of an independent clause, but of a relative clause with a *wh*-word. Its true relationship to its surroundings would be shown by punctuation appropriate to a parenthesis — a pair of marks, generally commas:

*My friend, who lives in New York, is a stamp collector. He has a
very fine set of British airmails.* (38)

A nonrestrictive relative clause is superficially similar to the normal "restrictive" relative clause. The latter, however, is by no means a parenthesis, since it has a function in the clause in which it is embedded, as the one in (38) does not. That function would be to identify the friend. Accordingly it does not ordinarily have surrounding paired punctuation:

*My friend who lives in New York is a stamp collector. He has a
very fine set of British airmails.* (39)

A restrictive relative clause cannot be moved away from the noun phrase within which it is a modifier. There must be an element within the sentence to which it clearly relates. The latter is not true of the nonrestrictive relative clause — "parenthetical relative clause" would be a better term. While attachment to a noun phrase is usual, vague reference is possible and fairly common:

> *Her husband washed all the dishes after her bridge party, which*
> *was a truly noble gesture.*   (40)

The nonrestrictive relative clause is peculiarly a literary construction. It is extremely rare in colloquial, even very formal styles. Some people seem never to use it in speech, though many of them write it fairly often. A native speaker, therefore, does not necessarily know it, unless he has learned it from written material.

English has a set of conventions by which everything written can be read, and parenthetical relative clauses are no exception. They are usually read with a pattern of intonation characteristic of parentheses. This includes rising terminals /↗/ both before and after, a vocal performance of the conventional surrounding punctuation. But this pronunciation is primarily a phenomenon of orally read English, not of spoken. The native speaker does not know and use or react to this intonation pattern, any more than he knows the construction, until he has learned it as a part of the standard reading conventions of literary English.

The nonrestrictive clause, then, is a pattern which is new and strange to most children in the schools. It must be taught as a new structure, in much the same way that an element of French syntax is presented. Preferably it should be related to the colloquial devices for parenthesis in much the same way that a French structure must be taught in relationship to the very different English constructions which perform similar functions. It will not do to teach it as a variety of the relative clause punctuated differently BECAUSE it is pronounced with a different intonation. The intonation is either unknown or not yet thoroughly natural to the child.

CONNECTORS

As we have already seen, there is intergradation between coordinating and subordinating conjunctions, and between these two and various types of sentence introducers. Taken all together, these elements constitute a very important set of devices to connect clauses or larger structures.

Each connector has a range of levels at which it is used. For example, *and, but, or* can be used to connect single words:

> *a bright and shiny dime*
> *any teen-aged boy or girl*
> *a tattered but beloved doll*

They are also frequently used to join phrases and clauses of various kinds:

> *He came in and went out again before I knew it.* (41)
> *He was in a hurry and I hardly had a chance to see him.* (42)
> *It was done brilliantly and with great imagination.* (43)
> *John will get his work done or I will know the reason why.* (44)
> *It was foolish but I did it anyway.* (45)

Conservatives generally disapprove of connecting sentences by *and, but, or.* But it is increasingly common practice to do so. However, the sentences so joined must always be fairly closely related. Since this is so, the change in practice may not be so much an extension of the use of these conjunctions as a change in punctuation. Sentences so joined are generally ones that might have been punctuated as a single sentence:

> *Conservatives generally disapprove of connecting sentences by* and,
> but, or, *but it is increasingly common practice to do so.* (46)

When much larger units (say paragraphs) are to be connected, *and, but, or* are not ordinarily used. Their range of levels extends only from words to clauses within sentences or closely connected sentences. In their place are used other elements, for example, *moreover, alternatively, however,* which indicate the same general types of connections, but are used specifically with larger units. The higher level ones do not join single words and seldom join phrases, but they extend upward to much larger constructions. The ranges of *and* and *moreover, or* and *alternatively, but* and *however* do overlap. There are constructions of intermediate grade in which the writer has an option.

The first classification of connectors, then, is on the basis of the units that they may connect. Not only does the closeness in structure determine what markers can be used; the markers signal something of the intended level of connection. Clauses can be pulled together slightly by using *and, but, or* or pushed apart a bit by using *moreover, alternatively, however.*

A second classification is on the basis of the kinds of connection they show. Among the latter, the following are important or frequently recognized. The list is not exhaustive by any means.

> Cumulative or Additive: *and, likewise, moreover, in addition, furthermore,* etc.
> Disjunctive: *or, nor, else, lest, otherwise, alternatively,* etc.
> Adversative: *but, however, nevertheless, on the contrary, on the other hand,* etc.
> Illative: *therefore, so, for this reason, then,* etc.

(The four types above are often defined as coordinating; those below as subordinating.)

Causal: *because, since, as, for, for the reason that,* etc.
Purposive: *that, in order that, so that, lest, for the purpose of,* etc.
Conditional: *if, unless, provided, provided that, whether,* etc.
Concessional: *though, although, in spite of the fact that, notwithstanding that,* etc.
Comparative: *as, than*
Temporal: *as, as soon as, while, before, until, since, when, ere,* etc.

This classification, while interesting, is vague at many points. Some of the categories overlap; some are heterogeneous. Nevertheless, it provides a framework to make an important observation: Some of these meaning-types form pairs of opposites. Two are worth illustration. Nearly synonymous but structurally contrasting constructions can be made with illative and causal connectors:

> *It is raining. Therefore I will stay home.* (Illative)
> *Because it is raining, I will stay home.* (Causal)   (47)
> *I don't speak French, so I need an interpreter.* (Illative)
> *Since I don't speak French, I need an interpreter.* (Causal)   (48)

Adversative and concessional form another pair:

> *I would rather stay home, but I must go.* (Adversative)
> *Though I would rather stay home, I must go.* (Concessional)   (49)

Such pairs have a special usefulness in that they allow the same clauses to be joined so as to give much the same semantic relationship, but with very different formal structure.

Another important difference among connectors is in the freedom of movement that they allow clauses. With certain of them, the clauses can be reversed with no change of meaning:

> *Although the roads were slippery, I had no trouble coming home.*
> *I had no trouble coming home, although the roads were slippery.*   (50)

But the nearly synonymous sentence with an adversative conjunction does not permit this inversion:

> *The roads were slippery, but I had no trouble coming home.*
> *ˣBut I had no trouble coming home, the roads were slippery.*   (51)

Those that show this reversability have an important stylistic flexibility that is often not shared by their mirror partners.

Compared with other languages, English has a remarkable variety of clause connectors, and these have widely varying patterns of use. This is one of the features of the language which give it great flexibility. It permits the signaling of complex interclause relationships with great precision when this is desired, or more loosely when that is preferred. Written English uses a much greater variety than does spoken. The connectors, therefore, constitute one of the important resources for writing to which students must be introduced carefully and thoroughly. They deserve a great deal of study against a structural framework.

ANAPHORA

We commonly connect clauses into sentences by *and* or other connectors. On this basis we might expect the following two clauses to combine to form (53):

> *John plays chess.*
> *James plays chess too.*   (52)
> *John plays chess and James plays chess too.*   (53)

That is perfectly possible, and similar sentences are actually used, but the following would seem much more natural:

> *John plays chess and James does too.*   (54)

Very much the same thing may occur in combining sentences into structures on a slightly higher level:

> *Don't touch the hot stove.*
> *If you touch the hot stove, you'll burn yourself.*   (55)
> *If you touch the hot stove, you'll burn yourself. Don't do it.*   (56)

In (56) *do it* is substituted for a predicate, *touch the hot stove*, just as in (54) *does* was substituted for a predicate, *plays chess*. Various forms of *do* or *do it* in these and similar examples are called anaphoric substitutes. This term identifies items that refer back to a previous occurrence of the elements for which they substitute. They are properly used only when the context shows unmistakeably what element they are replacing. The phenomenon itself is called anaphora.

Anaphora is an important structural device with interlocking functions. It serves to avoid repetition, though there are other devices available to do this. Much more important, it serves as a signal for connectedness between clauses or sentences. It has this latter function because each type of anaphora is restricted to elements occurring in some structural relationship.

The use of various forms of *do* and *do it* as anaphoric substitutes for predicates is restricted to instances when both occurrences (the one that is replaced and the one which remains unchanged) are in the same sentence as in (54) or in very closely connected sentences as in (56). Therefore, the presence in a clause of an anaphoric *do* or *do it* signals the close connection of its clause to some previous clause in which there is an appropriate predicate. If there are several patterns of anaphora running through a passage, as there commonly are, they can jointly indicate a number of intricately interwoven relations.

Other patterns of anaphora involve other classes of words or phrases. They vary widely in the scope over which they operate. One of the very narrowly restricted ones is that involving the reflexive pronouns. The latter are typically used when otherwise some noun phrase in the predicate would repeat the subject within the same clause:

> *John cut himself.*
> *Mary knows judo and can take care of herself.*   (57)

Reflexive pronouns cannot be used to refer back to a noun phrase in a previous sentence:

> *×I just saw my friend, Mary. Herself was in the supermarket.*   (58)

Instead we must use either the noun itself, or some other type of anaphora which is not restricted in this way. The second alternative is the most usual:

> *I just saw my friend, Mary. Mary was in the supermarket.*
>
> *I just saw my friend, Mary. She was in the supermarket.*   (59)

Occasionally a reflexive pronoun seems to refer back to a noun phrase in an earlier clause. In (60), *himself* seems to refer to *the man:*

> *This is the man who cut himself.*   (60)

This, however, is an illusion. This sentence might be formed by combining:

> *This is the man.*
> *The man cut himself.*   (61)

Himself does not refer to *the man* in the previous clause, but to *the man* within its own clause, though the latter has itself been replaced by *who*.

Because reflexive anaphora is restricted to single clauses, it does not serve as a signal of a clause connection in any direct way. It is of interest here merely because it represents one extreme. Every type of anaphora is restricted in some way, but most extend beyond single clauses, and operate within sentences or connected groups of sentences of various levels. Therefore, all other types have some function as signals of clause relationship.

The most important type of anaphora is that involving the so-called third person pronouns, *he, she, it,* and *they,* each of which comprises a set of inflectionally related forms, *he, him, his,* and so on. Conversely, anaphora is the most important function of these pronouns, though not the only one. Occasionally they serve merely as a reference point for a following relative clause:

> *He who hesitates is lost.* cf. *Whoever hesitates is lost.*   (62)
> *They have my undying gratitude who brought me here.*   (63)

Some pronouns are not substitutes for anything, but merely fillers of sentence positions. Most frequent in this use is *it:*

> *It is raining.* (64)
>
> *I 've always had to go it alone.* (65)

Sometimes pronouns are used in anaphora-like ways when the reference does not occur in the discourse, but is evident from the nonlinguistic context. For example, a mother goes to the crib and looks in and says: *She's asleep.* Someone points at something and says: *What is it?* But normally, and especially in written English where the situational context is less often obvious, the use of these pronouns is anaphoric.

When a discourse is initiated, noun phrases are used to introduce the *dramatis personae.* Thereafter, pronouns are substituted in the majority of possible occurrences. This means that pronouns are very much more frequent in noninitial clauses than in initial ones.

One way to describe the use of third-person pronouns is to consider the discourse as underlain by a sequence of clauses without pronouns. There are instead full noun phrases in every position calling for a nominal element. The actually used discourse is derived from this theoretical underlying sequence of clauses by substituting pronouns for noun phrases. So viewed, there are definite patterns of substitution, and these are characteristic of the language. (A translation into German, Greek, or Chinese, even if no other difficulties appeared, would probably result in different patterns of nouns and pronouns.)

The rules for pronoun substitution are not simple. A number of other factors may interact to obscure even their broad outlines. They represent, however, one of the important features of English discourse structure.

DETERMINERS

School grammar teaching has always given attention to the articles. It is a commonplace to contrast such pairs of sentences as:

> *I saw a book.*   *I saw the book.* (66)

The difference is generally formulated in terms of meaning: the first is said to be indefinite, to refer to some unidentified book; the second to be definite, to refer to a specific book. There are some situations where there is a contrast, but this is at best only a crude statement of the difference. Actually, the situations in which a speaker or writer is free to choose between such sentences are rather infrequent. In most positions only one of the two forms is appropriate to the context. The choice is determined by relationships within the sentence and, particularly, by the place of the sentence in the continuing discourse. Even when a choice is possible, it is often because at that point there are alternative ways to structure the sequence of clauses. The choice of a structure settles the determiner, and conversely.

The system is intricate, and to describe exactly how it works is difficult. A few generalizations have become more or less current among English teachers influenced by linguistics or the "new grammar". But these are reliable only if not carried too far. The factors are multiple and interact in complex ways.

The is most frequently used to indicate that the referent of the noun phrase may be identified with one already known, in most instances one already introduced into the discourse in some earlier clause or sentence. The absence of *the* and hence the presence of *a* or *an* in most cases signals that a new character or object is being introduced into the discussion. This is probably the normal or most characteristic use, but various other functions may override and obscure this simple pattern. Two of them will serve as a sample of many:

When nouns are modified by certain words, particularly superlatives and ordinals, *the* is used in many situations where it would not otherwise appear. Both the following sentences might naturally occur as the opening of a conversation.

> *I just saw the most wonderful bargain at Smith's.* (67)
> *I just saw a wonderful bargain at Smith's.* (68)

But the following sentence would occur in this position only under special conditions, for example, when the two people conversing have discussed the matter on a prior occasion:

> *I just saw the wonderful bargain at Smith's.* (69)

When nominal phrases are headed by adjectives, *the* is almost always used no matter where it comes in the discourse:

> *In that city the poor are everywhere.* (70)

If a noun is used, an initial sentence would most likely be different. The following are both possible. (72) is more probable. Neither pattern would be possible with *poor*, and only (70) is possible with *the poor*.

> *In that city beggars are everywhere.* (71)
> *In that city there are beggars everywhere.* (72)

Synonyms are commonly used to avoid repetition of noun phrases, particularly when anaphoric use of pronouns is not possible or convenient. In this connection there is a rather special use of *the* that is of great importance in signaling sequence. The noun may be completely new in the discourse, but the use of *the* suggests that it is not actually a new discourse element, but only a new label for an old one. That is, it marks the substitution and contributes to the reader's identification of the new noun as a member of a little system of alternative designations, which with the appropriate pronoun, carries one thread of the topic through the passage. For example:

> *Senator Phoghorne introduced a unique bill on the first day of the new session. It sets rigorous new state-wide standards for clam chowder...The proposal would require...Among its other provisions was...The measure would make it illegal to...*   (73)

It would have been possible to have used *it* throughout the excerpt except in the first sentence where the topic is introduced as *a bill*. However, this would be slightly infelicitous in the last sentence, which would then have two occurrences of *it* in two quite different functions: *It would make it illegal to...* This and the monotony of a long series of pronouns can be relieved by occasional use of noun phrases. *The proposal* and *the measure* are signaled as synonym alternates by the fact that they first appear with *the*. Avoidance of repetition in this way is highly developed in journalistic writing, and is carried to extremes on the sports pages.

The use of determiners is also controlled by various factors within the noun phrase itself. Mass nouns, proper nouns, and a few peculiar words like *intelligentsia* have characteristic rules for the use of determiners. The latter, therefore, have an additional function in contributing to the identification of noun subclasses. *The* (any single instance of the word) may thus operate simultaneously as a marker in two or more systems. For this reason, its use can seldom be decisive in any, but it can be important in all.

Other determiners have similar combinations of lexical meanings and grammatical functions. The latter are partly local, that is, determined within the phrase itself, and partly sequential, that is, determined by the place of the clause in discourse. Dual grammatical function is not restricted to determiners, but it is particularly well developed among them. This fact sets determiners and closely related words apart from other noun modifiers. Moreover, each determiner has its own set of patterns on both levels, so that the whole system is very complex.

There are, in addition, some important differences in practice between written and spoken English, and probably even between varieties of each. An interesting case is the growing use of *this* as a usual way of introducing a new person or object in speech. This is most consistently used in the least literary types, but is not restricted to them. It is most easily exemplified in a substandard narration:

> *I was just walking along down the street, and this guy comes up to me, and he says, "Where do you think you're going?" I don't say nothing, but then I see he has this big knife in his hand, so...* (74)

In this extreme type, *this* seems to be losing other uses that might be confused with its introductory function. Thus a simple and unambiguous device for introducing new discourse elements is being developed. *This* marks the element at the time of its introduction, whereas the standard pattern marks items recurrently as having been introduced earlier. As this new pattern becomes established, the function of determiners in all contrasting uses is inevitably altered, and the whole system is reorganized. For some kinds of substandard English, at least, the system of marking topics through a discourse is not simply the standard pattern badly used, but a separate, self-contained, and coherent system.

Students who bring such a pattern to school in their usual speech will have to learn the standard literary system as a whole new set of patterns. It cannot be taught simply as corrections of details. New patterns are best taught against an understanding of the old. Yet we know very little about patterns of sequence marking in standard English, and very nearly nothing about popular spoken usages.

"SEQUENCE OF TENSES"

In Chapter 13 it was pointed out that the predicate introducers of English fall into two major groups. We can conveniently refer to them as A (*can, shall, will, may, must, ought*), and B (*could, should, would, might, -ed*). The basis of this classification is their behavior in closely joined clauses. In general, in many kinds of sentences, all the clauses must have introducers of the same group:

If he can go, I will go too.	(A)	
If he could go, I would go too.	(B)	(75)
He says he will go.	(A)	
He said he would go.	(B)	(76)

This principle is commonly referred to as "sequence of tenses", and is thought of as a feature of conditional sentences especially and to a lesser extent of indirect discourse. Actually, there are other wider-ranging patterns of the same sort. Generally, whole discourses maintain one or the other type of predicate introducers for long stretches. A change of group — not simply a change of introducer within the group — usually signals a major disjunction within the discourse.

These restrictions are another place where literary and colloquial language differ. In common speech, -*s/-0*, the so-called "simple present" is neutral; it may occur either in a discourse otherwise using only A-group introducers, or in one using B. A very common pattern is to use -*ed* or some other B-group marker in the first clause, and thereafter to use mostly -*s/-0*. *Could, should,* and *would* are used when called for, but after the first sentence -*ed* is used only rarely, if at all, and seldom in two successive clauses. -*s/-0* is used in place of -*ed*. (74) is an example. The contrasting pattern would be to use A-group introducers together with -*s/-0*. In literary

English -*s*/-*0* is not neutral, but a member of the A-group. It is not, therefore, used in discourses employing the B pattern. When colloquial English would use it, literary English generally uses -*ed*.

> *I was merely walking down the street when a man came up to me*
> *and said, "Where do you think you're going?" I said nothing.*
> *Then I noticed that he had a large knife in his hand. So...*   (77)

The substandard colloquial passage in (74) is no less precisely structured than its literary translation in (77). The structures are merely different. In fact those of most colloquial speech are more rigid.

Since -*s*/-*0* is neutral in colloquial English, it is commonly used in narrating past events, where B-group markers are usual. The more rigid sequencing of literary English excludes it from many of these past uses. But -*s*/-*0* is not thereby excluded from all past contexts in literary language. It is simply much less frequent. That it does occur is shown by the existence of a special label, "historical present".

There is another interesting function of this kind of sequencing. It may serve to mark quotations off from the narrative in which they are embedded. Direct quotations operate independently of the matrix. They may be either A or B, when the surrounding material is either A or B. Often the quotations are A, while the narrative is B. In such a case the differentiation is unmistakable in literary English, though somewhat less clear in some colloquial patterns. Indirect quotations differ from direct among other ways in that they most often conform to the sequence of predicate introducers of the passage as a whole. Indirect discourse also shifts pronouns from first to third person, and makes various other changes, all of which merely integrate it into over-all sequences.

This chapter might have been labeled "The Sentence", but that would have been misleading. It has discussed a small selection of the devices by which clauses are joined into sentences but it has also shown that every one of them reaches out beyond the sentence to connect larger structures. The sentence is a somewhat arbitrary point on a ladder leading upward from clauses to total discourse. It is important as a basis for conventions of punctuation, but otherwise it does not stand out prominently as different from other structures just above it or just below it.

Part Three

POINTS OF CONTACT AND
IMPLICATIONS

Chapter 15

Language Variation

The description of a language may seem to isolate the grammar from all other questions. But, if it does so, it is only in the statement. In the study and research out of which the grammar comes, other problems have to be faced. Perhaps the most insistent of these is language variation. The grammarian may wish to describe just one kind of language, but to gather his materials he must sift through numerous, closely related but divergent, forms. He may push this variety aside as irrelevant to his present task, and leave its description for some other occasion or for some other linguist. Still, he must understand it well enough to separate correctly what he wants to study from the remainder.

In the classroom this separation is even more difficult. Any discussion of grammar that does not simultaneously face language variation is unrealistic, and students will recognize it as such. If the data is carefully chosen, variation can be eliminated, but to do so will detach grammar from the world of experience. If the data is assembled from the students' own usage, from their observation of the speech of others, or from their reading, it will inevitably embody more or less of language variation. It will not, therefore, suffice merely to introduce somewhere into the curriculum a unit on dialect. The problem must be faced at the very beginning of formal study of the grammatical system and at every point throughout its duration.

VARIETY IN SPEECH PATTERNS

It is a truism that no two people speak exactly alike. Speech is as distinctive as fingerprints.[1] Very few people can disguise their voice for more than a moment. But, though certain personal characteristics are always there, nobody speaks exactly the same at all times. Speech differs with a person's health, his mood, and, especially, with the social situation in which he finds himself.

Underlying this variation from individual to individual and from time to time, however, is a fundamental unity. There are profound and pervading similarities in the patterns of all speakers of any one language. These are the things described in a grammar. They are more extensive and intricate than any speaker himself recognizes. Their full complexity is not seen until the attempt is made to formulate them.

Against the background of a grammatical system, the diversities within a language seem mostly to be matters of detail. In an apparatus as complex as this, however, there is room for tremendous variety without destroying the essential similarity.

Not all the differences within language are of interest to a linguist or to an English teacher. For example, there are variations in speech which reflect mere physical environment. A voice sounds different in a small room than in a large, indoors than outdoors. Even weather conditions affect it in small but detectable ways. For the most part, we take no notice of these differences. Our ears adjust to such conditions and automatically make allowances, except when distortions are extreme. The mechanism by which this is done falls in the domain of the psychologist; the linguist need not give it any attention beyond noting its existence and pointing out the provisions — largely redundancy — that are built into language to make this adjustment possible. For example, of the thousands of possible speech sounds that the ear can distinguish under good hearing conditions, few languages use more than fifty to distinguish utterances. Most pairs of phonemes, therefore, are amply distinct, separated by a number of unused intermediate sounds. Each can suffer a great deal of distortion before it becomes indistinguishable from another.[2] Even if an occasional one is misidentified or missed completely, another kind of redundancy (see p.

---

[1] There has recently been developed a machine which produces a "voiceprint", a visible record of the characteristic features of a person's speech. It does so by discarding most of the information by which words or sentences can be distinguished, leaving largely that which is individually distinctive. Its counterpart is the vocoder, a machine that separates out of speech the features of language significance and feeds these into a second machine which produces a completely impersonal speech signal.

[2] The experience of a partially deaf person might seem to contradict this statement. But such a person has to cope with all the usual distortion plus a very ample amount arising from his deafness. Without this high redundancy, only the imaginary person with perfect hearing would be able to understand speech, and then only under perfect conditions.

457) generally prevents confusion. Utterances differing only in single phonemes — hence vulnerable to this sort of misunderstanding — are relatively infrequent.

The variation that is of interest to the linguist affects every aspect of language with which he deals. Differences in pronunciation come immediately to mind. These may be purely phonetic: Scots dialects typically use a rolled *r*, while Americans generally do not. For the most part, one pronunciation of this phoneme merely replaces another; the function in the language is unchanged. Or differences may lie in the phonemic system. One person may have a phoneme another lacks. Not all Americans, for example, have the same repertoire of vowels, though most use exactly the same list of consonants. One person may use some phoneme in a place another does not. For example, some Americans use the same consonant in the middle of *vision* and at the end of *garage;* others do not. Many of the latter never use the sound of *vision* at the end of any word. In this case, it is more than a difference in pronunciation of the single word *garage;* there is a basic divergence in patterns in use of at least one phoneme. The systems are, therefore, different.

Less fundamental disagreements are frequent. The same word may be realized by a slightly different set of phonemes in one person's speech than in another's. *Route* may rime with *boot* or with *bout; roofs* may contain the same consonant as *if* or as *of.* Every American is aware of many such examples. These intergrade into differences of vocabulary. A *roller coaster* in one area is a *leapty dip* in another. Some words, familiar in one part of the English-speaking world have no equivalent at all in another.

No two people ever wholly share the same vocabulary. Nor do they understand precisely the same thing by all the words they do have in common. *Evening* starts at midday in some areas, nearer sundown in others. Women may call some things *pink* that to men are *red* or *purple.* All such matters the grammarian can overlook or bypass, though the English teacher cannot: they inevitably intrude into the literature class, the composition class, or any discussion of language.

But differences are also found in the grammatical system. Morphology may differ: *dug* or *digged, shone* or *shined, woke* or *waked, cacti* or *cactuses.* One person may use a syntactic construction that another avoids: *You need not come.* or *You needn't come.* or *You don't need to come. Have you a ticket?* or *Have you got a ticket?* or *Do you have a ticket? If it be possible,* ... or *If it is possible,* ... Some of these may affect the formulation of the grammar at fundamental points, others only in details.

Most of the speech variation of linguistic interest can be conveniently classed into three somewhat overlapping sets. The first includes characteristics of a person's speech which are more or less fixed and are determined by his background and his group affiliations. These change only very slowly as his membership changes, if they change at all. They may indicate the speaker's regional provenience, social class, educational status, profession, age, sex, even politics or religion. The second set includes characteristics of a person's speech which are adjusted to the known or supposed position of the person spoken to. These involve the hearer's status, sex, age, education, and so on. The third set includes characteristics that are determined by the social situation, particularly in terms of the immediate interpersonal relationship between the speakers as understood by them at the moment. All of these variations have important social implications, and all speakers therefore give them close, if informal, attention.

We feel uncomfortable in the presence of strangers. We always want a certain minimum amount of information about them. We study their appearance carefully, if unobtrusively, to find any clue. Dress usually reveals something, sometimes a great deal. Mannerisms are probably much more informative, though harder to describe precisely. Often speech is the chief source of information. We desperately want, even need, to hear the language of people with whom we come in contact. We listen in on conversations, or we make conversation ourselves just to hear others speak.

Language, we like to think, is a means of conveying information. Yet if conversation is examined, it will be found that much of it is about topics of no significance to the people conversing. Another large part concerns items that are already common knowledge. In these cases, clearly, the communication is not in what is said, but in the way it is said. Each participant is interested in what speech reveals about the other: his background, his affiliations, his current mood, and particularly his appraisal of the situation and the role he is ready to assume in it.

This process functions at several levels. At one extreme are the small ephemeral groupings based on chance meetings or temporary association. Even here we feel a compulsion to converse. If there is a topic of known mutual interest we may get immediately into a serious discussion. More often we keep to certain conventional subjects, preferably ones which are general knowledge (and hence unlikely to embarrass by revealing unexpected ignorance) and noncontroversial. The safest, most convenient, and most conventional is the the weather. Most of our talk about it is done precisely when we are least interested in it.[3] Indeed, our attention may be so far from the actual meteorological facts that we may say obviously ludicrous things, though most of what we say about the weather is merely vacuous. The conversation is, nevertheless, serious and purposeful. Its function is to provide a medium for transmission of information that in other circumstances might be accessory to the "message". Here the subject matter is accessory, or even irrelevant.

---

[3] Mark Twain is said to have complained that everybody talks about the weather but nobody does anything about it. This misses the point completely: We talk about the weather precisely because nobody can do anything about it, and it is, therefore, a safe topic.

The difference between *Nice day* and *It is a nice day* is far more interesting than that between *Nice day* and *Rotten weather*. The sentence fragment signals one set of facts about the speaker and his view of the situation; the full sentence signals another. The way in which he pronounces *nice* tells a bit more. Indeed the signaling possibilities, even in a very short utterance, are numerous. The hearer picks up a number of clues.

His response tells whether he is willing to accept the first speaker's appraisal of the relationship. In the course of a short interchange, the two reach an understanding of a sort, a rough social adjustment. They know more or less where they stand in relation to each other. In a chance and temporary association this need not be very precise. The interchange may, therefore, be minimal. But both people are uneasy until some relationship is defined.

When the interaction between two people is of more importance, the whole operation takes on a very elaborate structure. Conversation is more extended, perhaps passing from the weather to other more-or-less safe topics — baseball, nonpolitical current events — and finally to less safe areas of mutual interest. Each feels out the other by subtle adjustments and observes the responses carefully. The two converge on a mutual definition of the relationship satisfactory for their purpose.

Of course, speech is not the only clue. Gestures are also of great importance. This is one reason some people carefully avoid the telephone for their more delicate contacts. Popular magazines like to speculate about the wondrous future when we will have "phonevision", that is, when all the signals will be available in all our interactions. We have learned for many purposes, however, to dispense with gesture and to rely on speech.

The basic language apparatus for this purpose is a system of speech types — keys,[4] each of which functions in a specifiable set of social situations. Five may be recognized:[5] Consultative is the central one. Deliberative and oratorical lie on one side, and casual and intimate on the other. Each of these has its own peculiarities, both social and linguistic. Each has its own set of minor variations within the major type. The three central ones, consultative, deliberative, and casual, are of primary concern in any American language curriculum.

---

[4] In the treatment of keys, I follow very closely Martin Joos, *The Five Clocks*, 1962. I have, however, made three terminological changes, two with Joos' concurrence: I have substituted *keys* for Joos' *styles;* the latter term I prefer to retain for a more general use. I have substituted *oratorical* for *frozen;* Joos included much written language in this, but I have kept speech and writing separate. I have substituted *deliberative* for *formal;* I have wished to retain the latter for written language. My indebtedness to Joos is heavy throughout this chapter.

[5] In the last decade or so, it has become usual in schools to distinguish two or three levels of speaking. The treatment here is quite different. Language variation is conceived of as having several dimensions, each with a range of types. It will not, therefore, be possible to equate the usual levels with keys.

THE FIVE KEYS

CONSULTATIVE key is the central point in the system. It is the one type of language which is required of every speaker. It is used in most orally conducted everyday business, particularly between chance acquaintances. It is the usual form of speech in small groups except among close friends.

The typical occurrence of consultative speech is between two persons. Most often they talk alternately, though one may hold the floor for a very long period. Neither, however, is inactive. While one is speaking, at intervals the other gives short responses, mostly drawn from a small inventory of standard signals. These are a basic part of the system, essential to its operation. Among them are: *Yes. No. Uhhuh. N'n. Mmm. That's right. I think so.* A number of them are aberrant enough in phonology that they cannot be represented well in spelling. They are so seldom written that they do not all have standard spellings. Intonational contrasts separate several of those listed into two or more with quite different functions.

The speaker listens for these FEEDBACK SIGNALS as indications of how much is getting across and what the hearer's reactions are. He adjusts his rate and manner of delivery on the basis of this information. He slows down — not in rate of words per minute, so much as ideas per minute — when he senses that the hearer is having difficulty, and he speeds up when the hearer signals impatience.

If the hearer wishes to change roles, he may break in by saying: *Well.* This is another of the conventional signals of the system, largely restricted in this use to consultative key. The speaker may invite the change of roles by using the same word with a different intonation, perhaps best shown in writing as: *Well?*

There is usually a great deal of background information fed into the conversation. This is one way to dilute the flow of new ideas and lighten the load on the hearer. It is also a way of insuring that the two share the same presuppositions — or perhaps, of insuring that they realize that they do.

A consultative conversation is not planned more than a few words in advance. Nor is much thought given to clear connection of what is being said with what has preceded. The continual monitoring of the hearer's reaction makes elaborate planning unnecessary, and generally warns immediately if the message is not correctly received. Because of this looseness, it is common to change constructions almost imperceptibly in the middle of sentences in ways that suggest, on careful examination, that the speaker has lost track of what he started to say. Usually, however, any stretch of six or seven words is consistent within itself structurally. The difficulty appears only when longer sequences are considered — sequences beyond the span of structural attention of either the speaker or the hearer. Occasionally, however, the shift is abrupt enough to be quite noticeable. I recently heard the following in a conversation: *It takes so much time consuming to do that.* Apparently the speaker started to say: *It takes so much time to do that.* Then before completing it he shifted to: *It is so time consuming to do that.* Sometimes successive sentences are telescoped, the end of one also serving as the beginning of the next. *I think what we need for the dance is a good orchestra will be a lot better than records.*

Patterns of clause connection are generally simple. From the viewpoint of literary standards they are usually monotonous. *And* is used very heavily. Connectors of greater range, like *nevertheless, moreover, alternatively*, are very rare; they are practically unused by many, including some who would write these frequently and who would employ them regularly in more formal speech. This fact is probably associated with the lack of long-span integration in structure. Consultative speech is simply not organized at a level where these would be useful. The so-called "run-on sentence" of school compositions is modeled on the use of *and* in consultative key, where it is unobtrusive or even quite normal for most speakers.

The consultative key makes use of certain characteristic items of vocabulary. *On* as a general duty preposition is one: *I have to see him on a matter. He cut himself on a knife.* Other words are just as conspicuously missing: *may* expressing permission, for example; *can* is the invariable consultative equivalent.

When people have well-established relationships with each other and the situation is informal, they are likely to shift to CASUAL key. This differs from consultative in certain important respects.

Casual key implies a complete rapport and mutual interest. The background information so freely inserted into consultative conversation is not needed — indeed, it is carefully avoided, since to give it would imply a lack of confidence that the hearer shares all pertinent assumptions.

Positively, casual key is characterized by the use of slang. This is a prime indication of in-group relationship. True slang is a sort of semi-private language. It is used only with insiders, and it is assumed to be known only by members of the group. When it becomes inescapably evident that this fiction is no longer tenable, slang no longer has any function. It must be replaced. Most of it is simply dropped and soon completely forgotten. The process of invention goes on steadily, so that a supply of fresh new words and usages is always at hand.

Instead of being dropped, a few words simply change their function. With no further implications of privacy, they begin to be used in the less formal varieties of consultative conversation. A small number become firmly established and slowly work their way upward into more and more formal speech. Words of this sort are listed in dictionaries with the label "slang", but they no longer have true slang characteristics. They are now merely ex-slang, informal words in the public domain. True slang is always restricted to specific groups, for example, to teenagers or to som. clique among adolescents.

Another characteristic feature of casual speech is the omission of unstressed words, particularly at the beginning of sentences. Those most often involved are articles, pronouns, auxiliaries, and *be*. *Car broke down. Got a match? Need help? Anybody home?* Such expressions are a highly diagnostic feature of the casual key; they will generally be interpreted as signaling informality. However, most speakers are not aware either of the phenomenon or of its significance. That is, they do not know what it is about an utterance that gives them the impression of informality. They simply sense it somehow.

An example is in order. I once visited a junior high school class which had been asked to bring in some sentences that they had heard but which they thought would not be written. One boy read his list to the class. In it appeared: *Won't say a word about it.* In the course of the discussion, the source was identified as a girl present in the class. The teacher asked her to say it. She said: *I won't say a word about it.* She seemed not to have noticed the difference. The teacher asked her again for confirmation, and she gave it again with *I*. I guessed the circumstances under which the sentence had been recorded. After class I checked with the teacher and she confirmed my guess. The speaker was the reporter's girl friend. She had spoken to him, as one would expect, in casual key. In class she automatically, and probably unconsciously, shifted to consultative. She was adjusting her speech to the situation as would any normal American. She not only was unaware of the difference, but seemed unable to hear it when it was pointed out.

The DELIBERATIVE key-is typically used in speaking to medium or large groups. The feedback of response and encouragement characteristic of consultative key is not possible. The speaker is, therefore, left on his own to maintain the proper pace of delivery. He can no longer proceed freely, adjusting momentarily to the observed response. Instead, he must plan ahead, framing whole sentences before they are delivered. It is this advanced planning which gives the key its name.

Deliberative key may also be used in speaking to a single hearer. To do so, however, indicates that the speaker feels little mutuality with the hearer. It is used, therefore, sometimes to show deference and sometimes to show contempt or impatience, but always distance. When used in a situation where casual is expected, it indicates strained relationships. Thus when a mother calls *Johnny* (casual), *John* (consultative), and *John David Smith* (deliberative), a child rightly expects quite different treatment, and responds accordingly.

Deliberative key is characterized by sentence structures more complex and varied than in consultative. The sentence is a more sharply defined unit. Run-on constructions are less frequent, and with more adept speakers, practically nonexistent. There is a much greater variety of sentence transitions. Overlapping constructions are avoided.

The vocabulary is more extensive and includes a number of words that are avoided as "too fancy" for consultative speech. There is some effort to avoid repetition of the major words, and this necessitates a stock of synonyms or near-synonyms.

Anacoluthon, the abrupt starting on a new construction without finishing the first, is common with some speakers. I have heard as many as five starts before a sentence was finished in a public address by a well-known professor, a leader in his field. This differs sharply from the gradual shift of construction characteristic of consultative key. There is usually a sharp break clearly marked in the intonation. This is usually reinforced by special hesitation signals, most commonly what is sometimes spelled *er*. Excessive anacoluthon is often an indication that the speaker is not really at home in deliberative key or that, because of the complexity of the subject matter, he is having difficulty organizing his sentence structure far enough in advance. To speak in deliberative key is a difficult art to learn.

Few children have any command of deliberative speech when they enter school, and few have any opportunity to acquire it out of school. Their first attempts to speak before the class are often obviously difficult for them. This is not necessarily because they lack any fluency in English, nor because they are frightened. Rather they have always depended, when they speak, on feedback from the hearer, and in the formal speaking situation they are deprived of this. Their problem is to learn to speak as an individual rather than to participate in the group activity of conversation.

ORATORICAL speech is still more elaborate. Structure is planned over still longer spans, often whole declamations. Not only are sentences carefully constructed individually, but sequences of sentences are intricately related. There are elaborate rhetorical devices of various kinds. Obviously it must be very carefully planned, and to be well done requires high skill. The oratorical key is used almost exclusively by specialists — professional orators, lawyers, preachers.

At the other extreme, the INTIMATE key is a completely private language developed within families or between very close friends. Since it is not used in public, it is of little concern to the schools.

ADJUSTMENTS TO THE HEARER

Four dimensions of speech adjustment to the hearer can be mentioned. Each of these is independent of key. That is to say, each of them can operate in more than one key. They must be thought of as a set of added variations superimposed on those just discussed.

The first of these relates to status. There are a few situations where the operation is fairly simple and obvious. For example, in some schools the boys address the masters with *Sir*. Failure to do so is a punishable infraction. On the other hand, for a master to address a boy with *Sir*, except in the most obviously sarcastic context, would be an even more serious breach. Boys and masters can speak to each other in either consultative or casual key when they meet individually. In class they generally use deliberative English. Within each of these keys, however, the status differences are maintained.

In most organizations there is a line of protocol that finds expression in speech. People far apart in the hierarchy generally avoid casual speech entirely, varying between consultative and deliberative. It is not that casual key is prohibited, but that the kind of relationship that would call for casual speech is impossible. People nearer together usually avoid deliberative English, varying between consultative and casual. In addition, there are always differences in the way the higher addresses the lower and the lower the higher. Very often the marks of status difference are harder to isolate than the simple *Sir* of the school, but they are nonetheless real for their subtlety.

In some languages, the status system is very much more obvious. Bengali, for example, has three different sets of pronouns, one for near equals, one for inferiors, and one for superiors. The same distinction shows up in the inflection of the verb for person. That is to say, status is built into the basic grammar of the language. That status differences are much less obvious in English has led some to overlook them and to assume, mistakenly, that English differs sweepingly from languages like Bengali. This is certainly an exaggeration.

A second adjustment is made to the knowledge or assumed knowledge of the hearer. We speak in one way to those in our profession or to those who seem to have an understanding of our field. We speak in another way to outsiders. This is partly a matter of technical vocabulary. We reserve this for those who we think will understand. We use a less technical — and often less precise — vocabulary with others. However, the difference goes far beyond vocabulary. There are characteristic styles of speaking. A physicist talks like a physicist — if he is talking to a physicist — almost regardless of the subject of the conversation.

There is not the same compulsion to make the adjustment in technicality as there is to make that to status. The man who does not "respect his superiors" is considered dangerous; the man who "talks professional gobbledegook" is simply incomprehensible, perhaps a bore. Some specialists are unable to make the adjustment of technicality easily; among them are the "ivory-tower professors". Others are very adept; among them are the "excellent popularizers".

Technicality is independent of key. I occasionally speak technically and in deliberative key giving a paper before an audience of linguists, but technically and in consultative key in small groups after the meeting. In a very informal situation, I might use professional slang or near-slang, thus marking my speech as casual or a very informal variety of consultative. Most professions have both a formal technical vocabulary and at least a little professional slang. The latter, of course, is used largely in casual key. On the other hand, I must occasionally speak about linguistics to a non-linguist audience. In this case, I make an effort to speak nontechnically, and in whatever key the situation seems to demand.

The third adjustment is in the matter of dignity or polish of language. At one extreme, speech may contain a great deal of profanity and obscenity. At the other, there may be an extreme use of euphemism. Very few speakers range over the whole length of this scale. But almost everyone shows some variation, and this depends largely on the speaker's assessment of his hearers. Men think of certain speech features as appropriate when ladies are present, and others as suitable for an all-male group. Differences of this sort occur in all three of the central keys, but are probably more pronounced in casual than in deliberative. The variation on this dimension is largely a matter of vocabulary (and nonlinguistically, of subject matter), but not entirely so. *Damn* as an all-purpose modifier occurs in some grammatical patterns which are unusual in more polished speech: *You damn well better go!*

A fourth adjustment is in conformity to socially approved grammatical norms. This is conditioned in part by the known or supposed attitudes of the hearer toward language, and in part by the impression we wish to make. In speaking to some people we are either a little less careful than with others, or even deliberately choose solecisms. Even the most fastidious use slightly different grades of English with different hearers, though the range may be wholly within what is generally considered as correct and proper. Other speakers vary widely. Still others merely cut down slightly on usages known or thought to be wrong when in the presence of, for example, school teachers. This dimension, too, works within each of the keys, but is probably more pronounced in consultative than in any other. In casual speech we tend to be more relaxed, and hence to be less concerned about "grammatical propriety". In deliberative key we tend to favor more socially accepted uses.

SEMI-PERMANENT SPEECH TYPES

Of the variations in speech which are not subject to the immediate control of situation or hearer, the most familiar is geographic dialect. Americans are conscious of certain widespread regional types, for example, the "Southern accent", and of certain very local ones, for example, the speech of Boston and that of "Brooklyn". These popular stereotypes, however, are not always accurate. In every instance much of the interesting and important detail goes unnoticed. Part, at least, of what is commonly believed about these dialects is wrong or misinterpreted. The assumed geographical spread is generally incorrect. For example, though there is a kind of speech that can conveniently be labeled "Southern", it does not by any means cover the whole South.

Geographic dialects are, in fact, usually difficult to delimit exactly. The boundaries are seldom sharp. Instead they are separated by broad zones of intergradation. This does not alter the reality of geographic dialects, but does make their classification difficult and subject to differences in interpretation.

Moreover, dialects are subject to change. Population mobility has brought many people into communities where they are surrounded by speakers of other forms of English. Radio and television have greatly increased the hearing range. The increasing contact between speakers of different dialects inevitably affects the speech of all, and diminishes differences. Many people, particularly those farthest displaced by migration, slowly lose the characteristics which mark their origins. A dialectologist, however, usually has no trouble in recognizing their provenience. Their conformity to their neighbors' pattern is usually only partial, most conspicuous in some of those features that are popularly identified as dialect earmarks. A much larger number of old habits are retained unchanged or only slightly modified. Many of these are in phonologic features, which are found to be particularly resistant to change in adults.

That is to say, within whole populations and over the dimensions of generations or centuries, dialect change is fairly rapid. Within the speech of single individuals and over the dimensions of months and years, change is very limited. Certainly change from moment to moment is of no consequence in most Americans, though there are a few unusual individuals who are able to switch back and forth between two regional dialects.

The social dimension of language variation is almost as familiar as geographic dialect, but even more likely to be misunderstood. We are generally aware that people from different social classes speak differently. We do not expect the same kind of English in a slum area and in the "best" residential neighborhood. There are, however, certain things that make it difficult to get any clear understanding of these differences. The first is that the class structure of American society itself is not understood. In many parts of the country it is extremely difficult to delimit the significant groups in any meaningful way. There is no denying that class differences exist, but if they cannot be categorized it is impossible to define their correlation with language.

Moreover, it has long been customary to look at these language diversities in an entirely different way. This seriously obscures their significance. All speech differences except geographic dialect (and sometimes that!) are fitted into a simple two-valued categorization in terms of "good" and "bad" English. "Good" has often been defined to coincide, more or less, with upper-class deliberative key.[6] It is taken as an important status symbol, particularly among the upward-mobile groups.

That "good" English has become so important a status symbol is the result of many factors. The schools' contribution to this development is probably minor. The schools are, however, directly responsible for much of the oversimplified scheme of evaluation as simply "good" or "bad". The schools should, therefore, accept the responsibility for replacing this by a more realistic, and necessarily more complex, set of scales. There are numerous reasons why it is essential that it be changed.

For one thing, it makes the task of the school very much more difficult in those instances where some change of language habits seems called for. If the objectives are thoroughly misunderstood by children, parents, and teachers alike, no very effective program is likely. Efforts are misdirected. Expectations may be unrealistic. A common result is an obviously affected, ineffectual imitation of alleged "good" English that is less useful to the speaker than his more natural "bad" English might be.

Social and regional dialects are never single speech forms. They are rather whole systems of keys. Even the most "substandard" type of speech differs from situation to situation. It is absolutely essential that it should, of course. In every segment of American society, speech cues are used to identify and define social situations. Every regional and social dialect must provide the mechanism by which this can be done by its speakers. The cues which mark the keys may differ from dialect to dialect. An outsider is never quite as sensitive to them as he is to those in his own dialect. This is an even more serious source of misunderstanding than an occasional vocabulary difference.

Much more striking than most dialect differences are those that are correlated with age — a perpetual source of concern to everyone dealing with young people. Actually, there are two very different factors at work here and they need to be clearly distinguished. One of these is a difference in generation. The second is a difference in age-grade. We can never observe these directly except in combination, but they cannot be understood until they are separated.

Each stage in the life history of an individual has a set of characteristic behavior patterns. As a person passes from one to another, he gives up one

---

[6] In recent years there has been a very profound shift in attitude toward "correctness" on the part of many teachers and most of the leadership in the English profession. At the same time, there has been a similar change in usage, both oral and literary, even by the most conservative speakers and authors. As a result, there is less and less dogmatism as to what "good" English is, but old formulations die slowly and the attitudes held by the most straight-laced English teachers of the last generation persist very widely in the general public.

set of patterns and assumes a new one. Probably the most striking of all these are the patterns of adolescence. These are passed down from one teenage group to the next. They will not normally persist, but will in due course be replaced by those appropriate to the next stage of life.

Among these patterns are many features of speech. Everyone seems to be aware of this, but many tend to think of the matter in terms of the deterioration of the language in the hands of THIS generation of teenagers. They are alarmed because these young people will be the next generation of adults.

It is, of course, true that the speech of this year's adolescents is different from that of all former groups, but these differences need to be seen in perspective. Every group of teenagers has been different from all that preceded. So likewise has every group of octogenarians differed from every preceding group. Indeed, they have differed in exactly the same ways. From late childhood onward, one's speech becomes quite resistant to change in some features (for example, phonemic patterns), while remaining very open to change in others (for example, vocabulary). Each generation preserves with very small change some language patterns as they were learned in childhood. A group born in the 1940's will, therefore, be different at every age from a group born in the 1920's, even if they are compared at the same age. This persistent difference between generations, of course, becomes more pronounced the farther apart the two are. It is but a small sample of the long-term historical development of the language. The differences from generation to generation summed over four centuries can be seen in the differences between Elizabethan English and that current today. We are not privileged to hear this difference directly, but we can see reflections of it in literature. We can easily hear speech differences spanning three-quarters of a century, though these will always be compounded with a similar difference of age.

The generation differences are usually in basic matters of pronunciation and in grammatical habits of the most basic sort. The age-grade differences are more likely to be superficial — embellishments on the fundamental structure. They most often affect vocabulary and style, the most changeable elements in language. For example, teenagers use more slang (or slanglike consultative vocabulary) than the groups either ahead of them or behind them. The slang vocabulary changes from generation to generation, indeed from week to week. (It is only the transience that makes it slang!) The patterns of use are more or less permanent characteristics of a stage in life history, going on as one group after another passes through.

Teachers and parents are traditionally distressed over teenage language. They have forgotten about their own adolescent speech. They can only see the current patterns as permanent, destined to be carried into adult life, unless the schools somehow apply firm corrective measures. Actually, the schools can probably do nothing, and in any case nothing is needed. The age-grade component of the teenagers' language is transient. What is permanent was probably fairly well fixed before adolescence. Moreover, there are aspects of language behavior, other than those which cause this concern, which deserve more attention and which can more profitably be treated.

WRITTEN AND SPOKEN ENGLISH

In addition to the complex system of spoken language types, there is another at least partially independent set of patterns: written English. A literate American must control a very considerable number of forms of language, both spoken and written, and must understand and react to the functional significances of each. Literacy is no small attainment, and it should not be surprising that it requires years to get a full working command.

Most Americans are unaware of the depth and extent of the contrasts between written and spoken English. If an extempore but formal speech is taped and transcribed without editing, the problem becomes immediately evident. Competent appraisal of the speech when heard from the tape and when seen on paper will be dramatically different. Generally the reaction to the transcription will be strong rejection or total disbelief. We are not accustomed to seeing spoken deliberative English in unedited written form, and it is so strange when we do see it that we are unable to judge it on its own terms. Certainly it does not measure up to minimum standards if judged by the norms we expect of written composition.

The opposite experiment is much less impressive. A good written passage, when read aloud more or less verbatim, is generally accepted and almost no notice is taken of any of the peculiarities in it. Yet it is as different from normal speech as is the transcribed address from normal written language. We have become accustomed to hearing literary English read aloud. Every fully literate person learns a set of special conventions that apply. That is to say, orally executed literary English is a conventionally established form of the language, to be distinguished from speech, and in many ways also from written literary English.

A few people learn to compose orally a close approximation to literary English, so that their addresses require minimum alteration when printed. When delivered, however, such speeches are not necessarily more effective for this literary quality. But, of course, many people speak "for the record", that is, with more thought to the effectiveness of the transcription than of the delivery. This is an interesting evidence of the place of writing in our culture, though this is changing. It has been only recently that a speech by a public figure could be heard by as many people as would read it.

A similar phenomenon is the ability to dictate letters, especially to a machine. Many people have great difficulty. This is variously ascribed, but part of it is the inability to compose writable English orally.

Even in special cases, when spoken material is carefully conformed to literary usage, transcription always involves editing to some extent. That is to say, it is not merely written down, but translated from one language form to another. Unnecessary signals are deleted, others are added, many are changed in form. The minimum level of editing is unobtrusive — perhaps nothing more than substitution of punctuation for intonation — and even the transcriber is unaware that he is doing it. For most speakers, however, this unconscious editing does not suffice, and the material must be restructured more extensively to become acceptable in print.

To an extent few of us realize, an opposite translation operation is applied in reading aloud. It is instructive to make a tape of a good oral rendition of a highly literary passage and then carefully collate it with the text. For many readers — including many outstandingly good ones — there are differences. Words are added or changed, but very seldom omitted; word order is inverted. Often these minor adjustments result in fairly major restructuring of sentence patterns. The changes are overwhelmingly in the same direction — from more literary toward more colloquial.

Like many others, I find reading absolutely verbatim a difficult task and one requiring a conscious effort. I must keep my attention strictly off the content of the passage and focused completely on the clause or phrase being read at the moment. If the passage is in a language I know only poorly, this is easy enough, but in English it is difficult. I make entirely different sorts of errors, depending on the familiarity of the language and the subject matter. In English, on topics I understand, most deviations from the precise text are the substitution of a synonymous word or construction. That is, they are freer translations. They seldom alter the meaning in any material way. In German or Latin, say, I may mispronounce a word, sometimes rendering the sentence gibberish, but relatively seldom do I read a synonym.

One of the most urgent tasks in English language research is to examine a large body of oral readings to determine exactly how this translation process is done. It would be very revealing of fundamental structural relationships and of psycholinguistic processes. Ultimate applications in the teaching of reading, literature, and composition would be numerous and significant.

In the meantime, we know that written and spoken structures differ to some extent, and that there are differences in the underlying grammatical structure, but we have no accurate idea of their magnitude. At some points they are probably overestimated, at others equally certainly underestimated. Perhaps some have hardly even been noticed.

The characteristics of written English are best seen in edited writing — writing that has been done with care and then revised in accordance with established conventions of form and style, either by the author or by another person. Such editing removes many features that might be carried over from speech and many individual peculiarities. The resulting language, nevertheless, is not uniform, but varies in a number of dimensions. Many of these are parallel, though not identical, to those found in speech. The variation in written language must be studied on its own terms, and cannot be treated merely as a projection of speech variation into a new medium.

Historical differences may be great. Most educated Americans have read not only twentieth-century English but also Elizabethan literature, and works from all periods between. This is a span of nearly four hundred years — at least five times the span of speech differences we can hear at any one time. The permanence of written records makes this possible. This dimension of variation poses crucial problems in the teaching of English literature.

Regional differences are slight: *colour* and *gaol* against *color* and *jail*, *the committee are* against *the committee is*. Within either American or British English, regional variations are almost nonexistent, though occasionally some very minor regionalisms may be seen. It is one of the very significant features of all written languages that they tend to be relatively uniform over areas within which speech varies appreciably, but to change abruptly at national boundaries, though the speech may not.[7]

Professional differences are conspicuous. For example, anyone can sense the contrast in professional writing between linguistics and literary criticism. This is not restricted to the technical terminology, but extends to many other features of the language. There are a few instances of differences in grammar, mechanics, or usage in certain disciplines. For example, in some subjects *data* is regularly used as a mass noun, in others as a plural. In many sciences the exclam! is used where others would write *sic*. Most of the differences are in stylistic preferences, and hence in the frequency of use of various constructions.

These differences are the source of one minor irritation that some professors feel toward English departments. Freshman composition courses have long taught various matters of style and conventions that are unacceptable in certain other disciplines. Scientific papers should no more be written in a belletristic style than literary essays should imitate chemical reports. It may, indeed, be the function of English courses to teach a non-

---

[7] For example, most of southwestern Europe speaks some Romance dialect. These tend to merge into each other, and thus the folk speech shifts gradually from place to place. There is little difference of speech on either side of, say, the Portugal-Spain boundary, while there are great cumulative differences across the width of Spain. At the boundary, the written language changes abruptly, the people in one village writing standard Spanish and in the next standard Portuguese. There is little difference in the Spanish written and taught in schools from one end of Spain to the other. The same thing can be found at many other places in Europe and elsewhere.

scientific kind of prose, but this should be done without deprecating other genres, equally effective for their special purposes.[8]

Edited English shows variation parallel in general effect to the keys of speech, and we can conveniently describe it in terms of literary keys. The three central ones can be labeled formal, semiformal, and informal. These are less sharply delimited from each other than are the speech keys, but any thoroughly literate person is quite sensitive to their differences. The features by which they are distinguished have not all been identified, but a few can be mentioned: Contractions such as *don't, it's, I'll* are common at the informal end of the scale, but avoided in the more formal keys. "Sentence fragments" occur, though generally with restraint, in informal writing, but only exceptionally in formal. Certain highly elaborate syntactic patterns are characteristic of formal keys. There are many vocabulary differences.

As with the spoken keys, some features are very characteristic of one and are felt to be out of place if they are used in another. Others are used more commonly at one end of the scale than the other, grading in frequency in the intermediate keys. Probably more of the differences between written keys are of the latter type than of those between spoken keys.

These written keys define the purpose of a piece of writing and indicate the relationship that the author considers as existing with his intended readers. Their function is, in broad lines, similar to that of spoken keys. However, since there is never the immediate interaction which is basic to casual and consultative keys, this function is never as definitive in writing as in speech. Nevertheless, we can say that formal writing has much the same function as deliberative speech, semiformal as consultative, and informal as casual. Hyperformal, belletristic writing can be compared to oratorical. These equations are only approximate, but indicative.

Not only are the differences between literary keys less sharp than with speech keys, but they are less in magnitude as well. That is to say, there is less difference between a passage in informal and one in formal edited English than would be observed between two discourses, one in casual speech and one in deliberative. There are certain features of written language in which a high degree of uniformity is demanded, for example, spelling and punctuation. Whereas casual speech may differ from deliberative in having sentence boundaries very ill-defined, this is not possible in most informal writing. Sentences have to be marked with periods, and all edited

---

[8] Composition teachers should become acquainted with some of the style books published to guide scientific writing. A good example is Conference of Biological Editors, Committee on Form and Style, *Style Manual for Biological Journals*, rev. ed., 1964. One warning, however, is in order. All style books are more conservative than actual practice. None can be believed as a straight description of how writing is actually done, or even of what editors demand, but only as a statement of what editors think they are demanding.

English must be organized into sentences. There are internal differences in sentence structure, for example, the semicolon is infrequent in informal, but a minor mark of highly formal writing.

It is difficult to match written and spoken keys in terms of form. A rough idea can be had by rendering passages from writing into speech and then comparing them with spoken keys, or vice versa. The renditions must be, of course, as nearly verbatim as possible. For example, if informal literary English is read orally, it sounds more like deliberative speech than like either consultative or casual, though, of course, it does not match exactly. Conversely, a transcription of deliberative speech seems to fall most naturally into the informal portion of the literary scale. Formal literary English (not hyperformal!) carefully read often sounds more like oratorical than deliberative.

On the diagram which follows we have attempted to indicate these relationships by lining up the two spectra opposite each other, the literary somewhat higher on the page. Dotted lines join points that are functionally equivalent, that is, that indicate much the same appraisal of the situation or definition of relationship between transmitter and receiver. The diagram suggests that if something is to be written so as to convey the same impression as would deliberative speech, it must have a somewhat more elaborate or formal structure. If a match for casual conversation is to be written, the difference in structure will be extreme.

Literary Keys   Spoken Keys

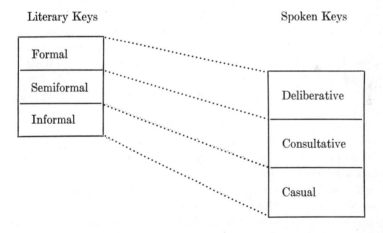

If one listens, unobserved, to a conversation, the language used will convey a great deal of information about the participants and the situation as they see it. Dialect, polish, technicality, key — all these dimensions will be picked up and interpreted by any competent observer. He may sift out of this mass of information whatever is relevant and interesting. The reader of a novel is in many ways comparable to such an unobserved listener. The novelist writes dialog, as it were, designed to be overheard. Nothing ostensibly directed to the reader can be said in the dialog, though the novelist has the option of interposing, whenever he chooses, narrative passages that are written for the reader.

Art involves presenting just those details that the artist considers relevant for whatever purpose he may be pursuing. The art of the dialog writer lies in giving, in his representation of speech, suggestions of just those features of the situation and of the background that he judges his reader should have at that point. He does this by varying the kind of language that appears in his dialog. Literary keys may be used to suggest spoken keys. The occurrence of a colloquial word or two may reinforce this. Social or regional dialects may be suggested by what are conventionally established as literary earmarks of these, or occasionally by an innovating introduction of some representation of a cue from speech. And so with every other dimension of speech variation.

All of this is done by use of forms of literary English as they arrange themselves along the multiple dimensions of language variation within the literary tradition and by occasional borrowings from speech. Dialog almost never records precisely what might actually be said. In general, to do so would give entirely the wrong impression. A precise transcription of speech will almost always be interpreted in a way quite different from the speech itself. That is, in part, the import of the diagram of keys above.

As we have noted, written dialog may borrow elements from spoken language, just as literary English may occasionally borrow from French or Latin. The use of really colloquial elements in writing is an important technique, but it will not ordinarily suffice to produce a colloquial effect. These borrowed elements must be embedded in the proper form of literary English. The greater part of the task of suggesting the social situation must be carried by this matrix. It must accordingly be a form of literary English that is the functional equivalent, rather than any sort of a direct portrayal, of the spoken form which it is intended to suggest.

Actually, many of the earmarks of varieties of written English are conventionally established, and sometimes bear little, if any resemblance to any feature of spoken English. A clear, if somewhat special, case is the spelling *wuz* occasionally used to indicate "substandard" speech. This can represent nothing directly other than a perfectly standard pronunciation of *was*. But the function of *wuz* is not to say anything about the pronunciation of an individual word, but to identify a whole utterance as departing, in unspecified places, from standard in a certain socially significant direction. Other cues, though less obtrusive, generally work in much the same way.

These things are, of course, controlled by established literary convention, gradually built up through the history of English writing. Any author may innovate, but sparingly. Some of his innovations may find their way into the changing conventions of the art. At no time are the conventions identical with those of speech. There are forces pulling functionally equivalent keys of speech and writing together and forces keeping them apart.

Dialog is not a transcription of speech. If it were, anyone with an accurate ear and a little phonemic training could write dialog. But not everyone can. Accurate dialog is not normally convincing. Convincing dialog is not — in a phonographic sense — accurate. The novelist is an artist, not a recorder. He operates within, or just outside, the established conventions of his art. Those conventions both control him and allow him freedom for artistic creation.

BILINGUALISM

The coexistence of two language systems — either spoken and written or two spoken dialects — naturally suggests comparison with bilingualism. A true bilingual seems to shift easily and cleanly from one language to another as occasion demands, using either with equal facility. On closer inspection, however, there are some special complexities which are of great significance.

The first of these is functional specialization. Every speaker has certain limitations on his language competence. It would be most remarkable if the bilingual's range of abilities exactly coincided in the two languages. In most cases, the difference is considerable. Only one language is available for certain uses, or one comes more easily than the other for certain purposes. Usually each language has some area in which it is preferred.

When a whole community is bilingual, this division of labor becomes conventional, and sometimes rigid. There are several communities in South India who speak only Telugu within the group, and only Tamil to outsiders. This arrangement has persisted in one group for seven hundred years.

Such an arrangement is reminiscent of the functional specialization within a single language, each situation calling forth some slightly different variety. Speakers of two dialects come to use the dialectal differences as an additional means of signaling the relationship which exists between themselves and their hearers. In many situations a regional dialect becomes an important means of establishing a community of interest.

A second characteristic of bilingualism is interference. A "foreign accent" is the most familiar example. In a few cases, the phonology of the mother tongue, only slightly altered, is used for both. More often, the bilingual uses two different phonologic patterns, but each is conformed somewhat to the other. This modification of one system on the model of another is interference. The amount may be great or so slight as to escape casual notice, but it is always present. Grammatical interference is just as universal — syntactic patterns of one language intrude into the other. Or the meaning of a word in one is conformed more or less to that of an assumed equivalent in the other. The shift of speech form, though definite, is never as complete as it sometimes seems.

Interference between spoken dialects is particularly strong. Indeed, many people cannot keep two spoken dialects apart, but speak a mixture, at best shifting a little toward one set of patterns on one occasion, and more toward the second on another. A command of two dialects is most often the ability to shift across a continuum of speech types, rather than to jump from one to another. For example, I normally use a largely Northern dialect with a sprinkling of usages from Midland and Southern speech. But when I talk with people from the Southern mountains, my speech shifts, becoming very much more Midland. The change is gradual, the effect becoming more obvious the longer I talk. There is a kind of functional specialization involved also; the shift is more rapid and more complete when certain subjects are discussed. Indeed, an increase in Midland characteristics is noticeable when I talk about the mountains for a period of time, even if no Midland speakers are present.

Interference between spoken and written English is equally important. Every literate person tends to bring literary expressions into his speech, particularly into deliberative key, and he tends to bring colloquialisms into his writing, particularly into the more informal. Since the American population is dominantly literate, this is not an individual matter, but is strongly reinforced by similar interference in other people. This is an important factor which keeps spoken and written language reasonably close together. It is counterbalanced, of course, by the fact that the demands of spoken and written communication are so different that each is subject to strong pressures not experienced by the other. Interference of spoken English in written is one of the major problems in composition teaching.

Very rarely will you hear two people conversing in two languages. One speaks, say, German, and the other answers in English. With most pairs of languages, this makes both speakers uncomfortable. Each will try, if at all possible, to shift to answering in the same language as he is addressed in, or, if he is unable to do so, he will hope the other will.

With two regional dialects of the same language, however, there may be little embarrassment. Most Northerners will make no effort whatever to shift their dialect when talking to a Southerner and will not expect the latter to attempt to accommodate either. Indeed, most Americans feel a little strange about changing dialect, and even interpret an effort to do so as mocking (which it sometimes is!). As a matter of fact, speakers of two dialects conversing for very long will each shift slightly toward the other's patterns. But this accommodation is almost never deliberate and often the speakers are not conscious of it.

A person with other than the most narrow contacts needs to understand a much wider range of dialects than he himself speaks. For most reasonably cosmopolitan Americans, no form of American English nor any reasonably standard variety of British is unintelligible. They very seldom hear English which gives them any trouble. They forget that this receptive flexibility must be learned.

I have known children who have had very little contact with anybody from outside their own community. I have seen them having great difficulty understanding the speech of a person from another dialect area. In fact, on a few occasions I have had to translate into their local dialect for them. Older people in the same community had much less trouble. They had had wider contacts and had learned to understand additional dialects. As the children have similar outside contacts and hear a variety of types of English, they will rapidly approach the normal American ability to speak one dialect, but understand a very large number.

Greater receptive control than productive is just as important in writing as in speech. An educated American should be able to read many varieties of literary English, but he need not learn to compose in all of them. Perhaps the clearest case of this kind is with certain historical types. He probably will never need to write in Elizabethan English, but he must be able to read the language of Shakespeare. This is different enough from any modern form that he will have to learn it, and this task will not be an easy one.

Chapter 16

Changing Syntactic Patterns

The speech of one generation differs slightly from that of the preceding. A speaker of English pays little attention to such differences, though he is often aware of them. They are, after all, not great compared to the range of other speech variation he hears every day. But this is only because his sample is small: seldom do more than four or five generations coexist at any one time. The differences are cumulative, however. If a modern American could hear the speech of the Mayflower immigrants, he would immediately be struck by its strangeness, though he might quickly learn to understand it.

A millennium of language change is quite a different matter. Few present-day Americans would recognize Old English as in any way their language. It would be just as unfamiliar as any foreign tongue. Fortunately, written documents do record English of a thousand years ago and the spoken language can be reconstructed with fair detail from them. It not only sounds unintelligibly foreign when read aloud but a description of its grammar seems very queer and un-English. Yet this strange language is quite appropriately labeled "Old English". We can trace an almost continuous history of small changes which have transformed it into the language we now speak and read.

Conventionally, we consider English as a separate language to have started in the fifth century A.D. when Germanic-speaking tribes from the continent of Europe began to establish themselves in Britain. Its millennium-and-a-half history is conveniently broken into three major divisions: Old English down to the Norman Conquest beginning in 1066, Middle English down through the fifteenth century, and Modern English to the present. These are roughly thirds of the total span. They are traditionally designated by abbreviations: OE, ME, and MnE. Within MnE it is useful to distinguish the first two centuries as early Modern English and the last two as late Modern English. The language of the late sixteenth and early seventeenth centuries is also sometimes referred to, very loosely, as "Elizabethan English"

EARLY MODERN LITERATURE AND LANGUAGE

Early Modern English is most commonly seen in the schools in two sources — the plays of Shakespeare and the King James Version of the Bible. Though roughly contemporary, they differ in very important and interesting respects. These need to be taken into account in teaching either the language or the literature.

The King James Version was the work of a committee of scholars. It was done with meticulous care and it was reviewed and edited in detail. The committee had been charged with preserving as much as possible of earlier versions, hence the inscription on the title page "with former translations diligently compared and revised". Every circumstance of its production would work for conservative language, consistent and precise.

Shakespeare wrote much more freely and for the stage. His works come much closer to representing the colloquial usages of the time. The language varies in formality. He made much use of dialect, drawing his material from many parts of Britain. There is none of the conservatism of the King James, and much less of consistency in his grammar or his diction.

While not meticulously edited before publication, Shakespeare's works have been extensively edited since. Much of his original language has been emended, particularly in school editions. Occasionally rime inhibits editors:

> *Unless you would devise some virtuous lie,*
> *To do more for me than mine own desert,*
> *And hang more praise upon deceasèd I*
> *Than niggard truth would willingly impart:*
> Sonnet 72

In other circumstances most of his grammatical "errors" are seldom seen — school editors have "corrected" them. Something can be said for such emendation, of course, but the result is, if anything, linguistically less consistent than unedited printings.

The King James Version, on the other hand, stands very much as it was originally published. The spelling is almost invariably modernized — somewhat differently in British and American printings, of course. A few verbal changes have become established, most of them soon after 1611. On the whole, however, it stands as a faithful record of very conservative "Elizabethan" syntax, at places archaic.

Taken together, the King James Version and the plays of Shakespeare give a binocular view of the language of the early modern period. As such, each illuminates the language and style of the other, provided, of course, that both can be taught against a perspective of the historical development of English.

The chief reason for recognizing three major periods in the history of the English language is that there have been two eras of sweeping linguistic change. OE and ME are traditionally separated by the year 1066 and the Battle of Hastings. Linguistically, of course, no transition was that sudden. The Norman Conquest, however, did break established patterns of language behavior and language status. It thus led to a realignment that took place slowly but effectively in a few generations.

The Renaissance was the new force that seems to have accelerated change at the end of the ME period. Power shifted again in Britain, not to an invading people but to a new mercantile class arising in growing urban centers. A new standard language gradually arose. The introduction of printing into England stimulated the development of spelling conventions. Changed attitudes toward language led to the establishment of conventions of usage and style. The ultimate outcome was the remarkably consistent patterns of present-day edited literary English.

No similar rigidity appeared in speech. Colloquial English went its way. Modern local dialects arose out of the regional varieties of ME. In time, however, all of these came under the influence of standard English in one or another of its forms. The interaction has increased with the appearance of effective mass literacy.[1] Standard words, standard forms, and standard syntax have made their way into the dialects, but the latter show remarkable resiliency, both in Britain and America. Dialectal features have made themselves felt in the standard. Literary English is not immutable; it does change, but comparatively slowly, held back by an elaborate system of conventions.

Early Modern English differs most conspicuously from present-day language in that the literary conventions were not yet fully established. There was much greater variety in every dimension of language in early Modern literature than in that of any later period. Some dying ME forms lingered on, occasionally supported by deliberate archaism. There was competition among regional variants of many forms.[2] There was experimentation of many kinds. The great variability of Shakespeare was not, therefore, abnormal for his period. It was the extreme consistency and conservatism of the King James Version that was unusual. In many ways this was only an anticipation of later, present-day rigidity. Today's edited writing achieves its great uniformity by being highly conservative.

[1] In very recent times this has been reinforced by radio and television, but the process was already well started before these were invented. It remains to be seen whether radio and television will accelerate the process a great deal. It is conceivable that they may have more effect in conforming literary uses to colloquial than the converse.

[2] This is most often noticed in the third person singular ending: -s, a northern form, competed with -th, a southern form. Both are familiar in Elizabethan classics.

CASE

The syntactic differences between early and late Modern English are the primary interest in this chapter. They constitute the essential grammatical equipment for careful study of Shakespeare, the King James Version, or any other Elizabethan literature. However, some of the syntactic features rest on morphologic forms, so that we must start by looking at the inflection of nouns and pronouns.

Certain syntactic relationships were signaled in OE by the selection of the proper form of the noun or pronoun. Thus, 'man' when subject was *guma*, but when object, *guman;* 'son' when direct object was *sunu*, when indirect object *suna;* 'stone' when modifying another noun was *stānes*, when subject *stān*. No single noun made all three of these distinctions, but to account economically for all the facts it is convenient to recognize four cases in all nouns. Each case was characteristically used in a set of syntactic positions. The four OE cases are traditionally labeled nominative, genitive, dative, and accusative. The personal pronouns also showed these same cases. The paradigms (overlooking some variations) for the three nouns cited and the first person pronoun were as follows:

Singular	Nom.	*guma*	*sunu*	*stān*	*ic*
	Gen.	*guman*	*suna*	*stānes*	*mīn*
	Dat.	*guman*	*suna*	*stāne*	*mē*
	Acc.	*guman*	*sunu*	*stān*	*mec*
Plural	Nom.	*guman*	*suna*	*stānas*	*wē*
	Gen.	*gumena*	*suna*	*stāna*	*ūre*
	Dat.	*gumum*	*sunum*	*stānum*	*ūs*
	Acc.	*guman*	*suna*	*stānas*	*ūsic*

By the end of the ME period, the case system had largely disappeared from the noun. Nominative, dative, and accusative had become alike and needed no longer to be distinguished at all. Only the old genitive remained in any way distinct. Four cases had been reduced to two. Moreover, much of the variety in inflection had been lost. Instead of -*an*, -*a*, -*es*, and other endings for the genitive singular as in OE, one ending was used for all nouns. This was one which traced back to -*es*. It and what had become the commonest plural ending had come to be alike. Most nouns, therefore, had only two audibly distinct forms, one serving for the genitive singular and all cases of the plural, the other for the non-genitive singular. These are continued in present-day English by nouns like /pet pets/. The s-genitive, originally used only in the singular had also spread to the genitive plural of words like *man* and *child*, and these had four forms, retained today as /mæn mænz men menz/.

Some early modern writers interpreted what has become /mænz sən/ as a contraction and spelled it as three words: *man his son*, or the like. Others indicated the assumed contraction by an apostrophe. In due course the spelling was standardized as -'s, and by analogy the spelling -' became established for the common form of the genitive plural. The result was, in most cases, the orthographic distinction of four forms: *pet pet's pets pets'* parallel to *man man's men men's.*

However, even that does not reflect the true state of affairs in modern English. As was shown in the section beginning on p. 164, the function of -'s has also changed. Today it is no longer a case ending, but an element behaving more nearly like a preposition. That is, it is appended to whole noun phrases. This was already true in Elizabethan English:

> *My wife and children's ghosts will haunt me still.*[3]
> Macbeth v:7:16

> *By Suffolk and the Cardinal Beaufort's means*
> II Henry VI iii:2:124

> *The Duke of Norfolk's signories*
> II Henry IV iv:1:111

The case system remained in the personal pronouns. Dative and accusative had ceased to be distinguished, old dative forms taking over the function of both cases. Early MnE, therefore, had only three of the four cases of OE. The following can be given as a conservative MnE paradigm. The spelling is somewhat modernized. (In Shakespeare's time it was not yet as highly standardized as it is today.)

				Singular	Plural
First:	Nominative			*I*	*we*
	Genitive			*mine, my*	*our*
	Objective			*me*	*us*
Second:	Nominative			*thou*	*ye*
	Genitive			*thine, thy*	*your*
	Objective			*thee*	*you*
Third:		Masc.	Fem.	Neut.	
	Nominative	*he*	*she*	*hit*	*they*
	Genitive	*his*	*her*	*his*	*their*
	Objective	*him*	*her*	*hit*	*them, hem*[4]

In the early Modern period, the case system in pronouns, already changed from that of OE, seemed to be tending toward further reorganization, particularly in the second person. The first step was the confusion of

---

[3] Shakespeare quotations are conformed in both text and reference to John Bartlett, *A New and Complete Concordance . . . [to the] Dramatic Works of Shakespeare*, 1894.

[4] In most modern speech the *h* in *he, him, his, her* is unpronounced in many positions, being retained for the most part only when the word is stressed or after a terminal. The dropping of *h* from *hit*, went further in most dialects, disappearing entirely in many, but there are some dialects in which the *h* is still pronounced in /hit/ in the same places in which it would be pronounced in /hiy/ or /him/. *Hit* is occasionally seen in some early printings of Shakespeare. *Hem* remains as modern *'em*, now used only in unstressed positions.

nominative and objective forms, each being used occasionally where the other would be proper by a continuation of OE rules. This can be observed in most Elizabethan literature.

The King James Version is a conspicuous exception. It very carefully preserves the distinction between the nominative and the objective, using *thou* and *ye* for subjects and predicate nominatives, and *thee* and *you* for direct and indirect objects and after prepositions. Modern readers seldom understand the distinction, thinking of *ye* as merely a strange spelling for *you*.

The consistency of the King James Version, however, is nothing more than archaism or pedantry. Shakespeare, like most of his contemporaries, used the two almost interchangeably. For example, in the following quotations, each form is used where the other would be "correct":

> *Stand, sirs, and throw us that you have about ye.*
> Two Gentlemen of Verona iv:1:3

> *I do beseech ye, if you bear me hard.*
> Julius Caesar iii:1:157

Similar confusion can be found between the second person singular pronouns, *thou* and *thee*. It has been suggested that the similarity of the nominative *ye* to the objective *thee* contributed to the loss of distinction.

In the first and third persons there are many instances of objective forms where we might expect nominative, and vice versa, though by no means the complete confusion seen in the second person. Many of these are of a pattern still familiar in current colloquial:

> *All debts are cleared between you and I.*
> Merchant of Venice iii:2:321

> *Yes, you have seen Cassio and she together.*
> Othello iv:2:3

All this is evidence that the old case system was disintegrating in the pronouns, as it already had in nouns. The process had merely gone farther toward completion in the second person than elsewhere, but it was starting in the first and third also.

Subsequently, however, this trend was arrested in the standard language, but only after *ye* had been lost completely. *You* came now to stand in two places in the paradigm, as *her* and *hit* (*it*) already did. The literary language came to be, in theory at least, quite rigid in the use of pronoun cases.

In colloquials the outcome has been quite various, but seldom conforms to the standard in all details. In some dialects the old nominatives are used for single pronoun subjects: *I went*... Whenever two pronouns are joined by a conjunction, both are in the old objective form: *Me and him went*... In other dialects, the objective form is used after any verb, preposition, or conjunction: *I and him went*... There are many other patterns, some of them not so simply stated.[5]

The schools have struggled valiantly to make the standard pattern universal, but with various degrees of success. Most American speakers follow the school prescriptions in at least some situations, but few conform in every instance. *It's me* is, perhaps, the most widespread of the departures from the proclaimed norms, so widespread that *It's I* impresses many as prim or pedantic. However, there are differences from one person to another and from one situation to another in the actual compromises that are followed.

In addition, there is a great deal of overcorrection. Constructions like *between you and I* are formed on the pattern of *you and I went*, often in an effort to be correct. They indicate that, whatever attitudes may be, understanding of the normative pattern is not always complete. All these confusions in the use of pronoun cases have been present throughout the MnE period and show very little promise of reaching a stable solution.

The use of pronouns is one place where "correct" and "incorrect" forms occur together in the speech of a very large part of the American population, and where most speakers are aware that there are differences in "correctness" among the forms that they use or hear. The variation can easily be given a secondary signaling function. As a result, speakers tend to shift their use with the circumstances, adjusting to their hearer and to their own moods and needs. Unwillingness to conform or detachment from the conventions can be signaled by a judicious use of "incorrect" forms. One hoping to make a contrary impression can do so by speaking with meticulous "correctness" — if he knows how. The use of pronoun cases has become an important element in one type of language variation (see p. 363).

Strangely, at the same time that the case system was moving toward further simplification, it was also elaborating by the split of the old genitive. The change seems to have originated in the first and second persons singular.

OE *mīn* and *þīn* became MnE *mine* and *thine*. These forms tended to drop the final consonants, much as did *an* to form its alternant *a*. Thus *my* and *thy* came to exist beside them. In the paradigm above, both variants have been given. They were, at first, merely alternant forms. In part they followed the rule that later became regularized for *an/a*: the *n* was dropped before a consonant in an immediately following word.

It is hard to determine Shakespeare's usage in this matter. Lacking

---

[5] The word order in these constructions also presents an interesting problem. Colloquial dialects almost universally place the first person first. The contrary order has long been insisted on by purists. Unlike most such prescriptions, this one does not have a Latin origin. Both Greek and Latin placed the first person first — indeed, that was the origin of the designation. The present prescriptive rule apparently traces back to medieval customs. It has become, however, a pan-European feature, see p. 405 ff.

his original manuscripts, we must rely on editions which passed through the hands of many others: stenographers, editors, compositors, and proof-readers. They do not agree. For example, the first three folios agree in having *mine* in the following:

> *I'll prove mine honour and mine honesty.*
> A Comedy of Errors v:1:30

But the fourth folio reads *my honesty.* In the following only the first folio has *mine:*

> *He that commends me to mine own content.*
> A Comedy of Errors i:2:32

As usual, the King James Version is very much more consistent. *Mine* and *thine* are regularly used before vowels, but in Eph. 6:21 we find *my affairs,* and there are a few instances of *thine* before consonantal *h: thine head,* Mt. 6:17; *thine house* Mt. 9:6; *thine hand* Mt. 12:13. Surely, this can be nothing but a deliberate effort at regularization based on what was believed to be the conservative (that is, archaic) pattern.

This use of *mine* as a deliberate archaism has continued into modern times:

> *Mine eyes have seen the glory of the coming of the Lord.*
> Julia Ward Howe.

Except for a few such instances, *my* has completely replaced *mine* when a modifier in a noun phrase. *Thy* and *thine* have both disappeared.

In early MnE, *mine* and *thine* were also used when final in a sentence or a phrase, that is, presumably, when immediately preceding a terminal, or where the stress pattern might be assumed to have been different. There were several possibilities:

> *You, brother mine, that entertain'd ambition,*
> Tempest v:1:75
> *Mine and my father's death come not upon thee.*
> Hamlet v:2:341
> *I will chain these legs and arms of thine,*
> I Henry VI ii:3:39
> *She was mine, and not mine, twice or thrice in that last article.*
> Two Gentlemen of Verona iii:1:365

The first two of these patterns have now disappeared, and *mine* has now been regularized to all occurrences where the pronoun is not a modifier in a noun phrase. Whether the form is *my* or *mine* does not, therefore, depend in any way on the phonology (stress, terminal, following vowel), but simply on the syntactic position. That means that the two, today, represent two different cases. The personal pronouns now have four cases: *I, me, my, mine,* each with a characteristic set of syntactic positions it can occupy.

ITS *AND GENDER*

The genitive form of the neuter pronoun was *his* in OE, and this form was preserved in early MnE as *his*. This is quite usual, for example, in the King James Version:

> *If the salt have lost his savor, wherewith shall it be salted?*
> Mt. 5:23

Apparently, English speakers were already uncomfortable with this form, and as a result many alternatives were experimented with in the sixteenth and seventeenth centuries. The King James, conservative as it is, seems deliberately to avoid *his* in some passages by several devices. This is seen clearly in the following quite parallel verses:

> *And they shall make an ark of shittim wood: two cubits and a half shall be the length thereof, and a cubit and a half the breadth thereof, and a cubit and a half the height thereof.*
> Ex. 25:10

> *And Bazaleel made the ark of shittim wood: two cubits and a half was the length of it, and a cubit and a half the breadth of it, and a cubit and a half the height of it:*
> Ex. 37:1

Shakespeare, as usual, shows much greater variety, verging on confusion. *His*, the conservative form, occurs very frequently:

> *How far that little candle throws his beam!*
> Merchant of Venice v:1:90

> *Dark night, that from the eye his function takes.*
> Midsummer Night's Dream iii:2:177

Of it, a device used in the King James, also occurs:

> *And the tears of it are wet.*
> Anthony and Cleopatra ii:7:55

It, identical with the nominative, is also used:

> *The hedge-sparrow fed the cuckoo so long,*
> *that it's had it head bit off by it young.*
> King Lear i:4:235
> *It lifted up it head.*
> Hamlet i:2:216

This last usage occurred once in the original form of the King James:

> *That which groweth of it own accord of thy harvest thou shalt not reap.*
> Lev. 25:5

However, in 1662 this verse was emended to read *its*. This is now the only occurrence of *its* in the Version. Most of the places commonly quoted with *its* actually read *his*.

Its was, in fact, a very late entry in the contest — too much of a neologism to be acceptable to the King James committee. The earliest attestation in the Oxford English Dictionary is from 1598, though it has since been found from at least a year earlier. Bartlett lists only ten occurrences in Shakespeare.[6] (Many places have been emended to read *its* in some school editions, of course!) By the end of the seventeenth century, however, *its* was firmly established and all other forms were either disused or looked upon as deliberately archaic. (Note that Lev. 25:5 was not changed to *his.*) The rapidity with which the new form was accepted is remarkable.

The disuse of *his* in the neuter seems to have been associated in some way with a drastic change in the gender system. In OE gender was an arbitrary assignment of nouns to classes. Only to a limited extent could any semantic basis be discerned. Male beings were often, but not invariably, named by masculine nouns, and female beings were more often than not designated by feminine nouns. But sexless things might be in any gender: *stān* 'stone' was masculine, *bōk* 'book' was feminine, and *scip* 'ship' was neuter. Some assignments were quite contrary to our expectations: *wīfmann* 'woman' was masculine, and *mægden* 'girl' was neuter. Sex, clearly, was not the major basis for the system.

Gender, moreover, had considerable significance in the syntax. Determiners and adjectives had to agree in gender, number, and case with the nouns they modified. This agreement had some importance in signaling structure within sentences.

In Modern English syntax gender has become less important (for example, agreement has disappeared) and has greatly changed in nature. It is perhaps best to say that we now have only two genders, each of limited use. Masculine includes almost exclusively nouns referring to male beings. Feminine includes nouns referring to female beings, and to some inanimate objects when given personal affection. (A well-liked old jalopy is *she* to its owner; any other car is *it.*) All the remaining nouns (most of the singulars and all plurals) are genderless — in the singular commonly called "neuter". Even nouns referring to people can be neuter: *child* is genderless, unless we wish to make a point of sex, in which case either *he* or *she* can be used. In any case, arbitrary assignments are no longer a feature of English.

This change was well along in the early Modern Period. *He, his, him* and *she, her, her* were coming to be thought of as indicating sex-gender. *It* was increasingly used where sex was absent, unknown, or irrelevant. The use of *his* for genderless referents was in conflict with this emerging pattern. This seems to have stimulated experimentation to find a substitute. *It, of it, thereof* were all efforts in this direction. None was entirely satisfactory.

---

[6] By comparison, his concordance lists twelve occurrences of *it* as a possessive. The listings are not complete for such words, so that there is no guarantee that there may not be more instances of either *its* or *it*. However, *his* is certainly much commoner. Bartlett, *A New and Complete Concordance.*

Meanwhile, the element -'s, a remnant of the old genitive ending, had become available. It was found that it could be added to *it* as well as to other types of nominal constructions. When *its* was tried, late in the sixteenth century, it was very quickly accepted. It not only supplied the needed form, but did so in a way that fit neatly into the patterns of the language, and so brought a kind of regularity into the paradigm. The formation of *ours, yours, hers,* and *theirs* are further examples of the extension of this morpheme into new uses.

AUXILIARIES

The verbal system has remained the same in certain broad outlines throughout the history of the language, but there have been extensive changes in details. Only two tenses are marked by inflection, a "present" and a "past".[7] In OE both were further inflected to show person and number. In MnE this has disappeared in the past and been reduced to a vestige in the present (except for *be* which retains a slightly fuller set of forms). Other tenselike distinctions are made in all stages of the language by means of auxiliaries. There are, however, a number of differences between the auxiliaries of OE and of MnE.

The OE perfect was formed, as it still is, by an auxiliary and the participle. OE had two such auxiliaries, *habban* (modern *have*), generally used with transitive verbs, and *beon* (modern *be*), generally used with intransitive verbs. The contrast in structure can be seen in *he hafað onfunden* 'he has found' and *hit is geworden* 'it has happened', more literally 'it is become'.

The passive also made use of the participle and either of two auxiliaries, *beon* or *weorðan* 'become'. There was a slight difference in meaning between the two in some cases, but many writers seemed to use the two more or less interchangeably with some verbs. The perfect with *beon* and the passive with *beon* could not ordinarily be confused, since the first occurred only with intransitive and the second only with transitive verbs.

There was no regular OE construction parallel to the modern use of *be* + *-ing*, nor was there an auxiliary *do* comparable to the present one.

Between OE and the present time, the whole system of verbal auxiliaries has been reconstructed and reinterpreted. The process was a long one; the first steps were already visible in OE in embryo, and it was by no means complete in the Elizabethan period. As a result we find many verbal constructions in Shakespeare that are strange to us. There are others which look familiar, but function differently from the superficially similar modern forms.

---

[7] The "present" is so marked only if a zero-suffix is recognized. The labels "present" and "past" are not fully satisfactory; see p. 323 ff.

Perhaps the first change to be completed was the loss of the old passive with *weorðan*. This left the passive construction much as it is in MnE, briefly describable as marked with *be* + *-en*. There is, therefore, no particular difficulty with the passive in Elizabethan literature. That, however, is not the end of the story, since MnE has reestablished the old distinction in a new form. A second passive with *get* has gradually been developed (colloquially one might say "gotten started"): *He got hit by a car. Podunk is going to get beat for sure with Jones out of the game.* For the most part, this new passive has not yet been fully accepted into standard written use. It is, therefore, difficult to document its history. A few instances have been found before 1700, and it has become steadily more frequent, though only in informal passages. Whenever the two passives show any differences, the *get* passive has much the same meaning as the older *weorðan* passive.

ME still made, in general, the distinction between perfects with *be* for intransitive verbs and perfects with *have* for transitives. But departures from the strict pattern increased through the period. By the beginning of MnE, the trend toward one uniform perfect formation with *have* + *-en* was already unmistakable. Perfects with *be* linger on, however, particularly with verbs expressing motion. Thus we find:

> *My life is run his compass.*
> Julius Caesar v:3:25
> *His lordship is walk'd forth into the orchard.*
> II Henry IV i:4:1
> *When they were come to Bethlehem . . .*
> Ruth 1:19

It is only the fact that *be* + *-en* for the perfect is restricted to intransitive — and, indeed, largely to verbs of motion — that prevents these being mistaken for passives.[8] There was from late ME onward a trend toward easy transitivizing of intransitive verbs. This meant that the safeguard just mentioned became less and less adequate. The difficulty can be seen by comparing *His lordship is walked...* with a more modern *The dog is walked...* The perfect with *be* has practically disappeared from late MnE. The few that remain current are more or less stereotyped and are no longer felt as perfects. The commonest, perhaps, are *I am done* 'I have finished' and *He is gone* 'He has left'.[9]

The present-day formation with *be* + *-ing* was a later development. It is very seldom found in Shakespeare and is completely absent from some other Elizabethan writers. OE and ME have, rarely, structures that look a little like it. These are probably always to be interpreted in some other

---

[8] These have been discussed as "passives of intransitives". See, for example, E. A. Abbott, *A Shakespearean Grammar*, 1870, p. 206.

[9] This is commonly contracted: *He's gone.* In this case it is not evident whether the auxiliary is *is* or *has*, but the question is usually: *Is he gone?* Somewhat less frequent, but by no means rare is: *Has he gone?*

way. The construction with *be* + *-ing* expressing limited duration is a late development within MnE.

Shakespeare uses simple verb forms in most of the places where a modern author would use phrases containing *be* + *-ing*. This can lead to minor misunderstandings. Serious difficulties are rare because of the very nature of the contrast in late MnE. *Be* + *-ing* signals a very complex set of factors depending on the verb with which it is used (see p. 326). Its absence, however, does not signal any opposite set of factors, in most cases, nor even the necessary absence of these. Rather, if *be* + *-ing* is not used, these matters are simply left unspecified. Thus the present-day reader is not likely to read into Shakespeare anything that is not there. But not infrequently he may misjudge Shakespeare's style rather badly. One possibility open to the twentieth-century author was simply unavailable three centuries earlier.

The present-day English verb phrase can be described by some such formula as the following:

$$\begin{Bmatrix} \text{-}s \\ \text{-}ed \\ \text{Modal} \end{Bmatrix} + (have + \text{-}en) + (be + \text{-}ing) + (be + \text{-}en) + \text{Verb}$$

This is intended to suggest that all possible combinations occur, and apparently for some speakers they all do. That is, using *can* as representative of all the modals, the following third person singular forms would seem possible:

eats	*ate*	*can eat*
has eaten	*had eaten*	*can have eaten*
is eating	*was eating*	*can be eating*
is eaten	*was eaten*	*can be eaten*
has been eating	*had been eating*	*can have been eating*
has been eaten	*had been eaten*	*can have been eaten*
is being eaten	*was being eaten*	**can be being eaten*
*has been being eaten	**had been being eaten*	**can have been being eaten*

Quite understandably, these are not all equally frequent or familiar. In general, the ones toward the top of the list (with fewer elements) and the ones in the first two columns (with *-s* and *-ed*, the latter combining with *eat* to form *ate*) are commoner than those at the bottom of the list or in the last column. All of them have been found in speech or writing composed without conscious attention to verb forms.

Some native speakers of English, however, will not readily accept the phrases marked with asterisks. The four have one feature in common: they contain two *be* auxiliaries and these are assonant. Notice that there is no objection to the presence of two forms of *be* if they are quite different; *is being eaten* and *was being eaten* are not only wholly acceptable, but actually fairly frequently used — so far as we can see, by all fluent speakers of standard English.

This peculiarity can be explained by euphony, but some other facts raise doubts. No similar rejection applies to *had had: He had had it ten years before it began giving him trouble.* A second, historical, explanation also seems possible.

Each of the elements in the formula given above has its history. Some are very ancient, as the *-ed;* others quite recent, as *be + -ing.* If each were traced in detail, this would not constitute a full history of the English verb phrase. Equally important and interesting are the patterns of combination of these elements. Actually, the free combining which the formula indicates seems to be a new phenomenon.

In older forms of the language, the auxiliaries were much less freely combined. Perfect passives do not occur in the older period when both perfect and passive were already well established. The combination of *have + -en* with *be + -ing* seems to be appreciably later than the use of *be + -ing* alone. Perhaps, the rejection of constructions of the type of *has been being eaten* by some speakers and their acceptance by others represent just the last stages of generalization of the pattern. Free combining of all the elements in the verb phrase has been being attained gradually over the last few centuries. With it has undoubtedly gone a restructuring of the function and meaning of the various elements in the system. The differences between Elizabethan and present-day verbal constructions are often more extensive than they seem at first sight.

QUESTIONS AND DO

For a modern American reading Shakespeare for the first time, the most strikingly strange feature of the syntax is usually the construction of interrogative and negative sentences. Some are so nearly identical with modern patterns that they attract no attention:

> *Is that true?*
> > Othello iv:2:227
> *Do you know me?*
> > Measure for Measure v:1:329
> *Where is your master?*
> > Merchant of Venice ii:2:183
> *Who should I swear by?*
> > Titus Andronicus v:1:71

But one question in three is of a form now practically impossible, difficult to understand, or even misunderstood:

> *What means this shouting?*
> > Julius Caesar i:2:79
> *Know I these men that come along with you?*
> > Julius Caesar ii:1:89
> *Who comes here?*

Many of the differences are the result of changes already discussed in this chapter. Thus the last example would today be understood to ask who habitually comes whereas it meant the same as the modern question *Who is coming here?*[10] There would be an exactly comparable change in the form of the equivalent statement: *Someone comes here* to *Someone is coming here.* The unfamiliarity is not, therefore, a matter of the form of the question, but of another change in the verbal system. Some questions give trouble only because they use second person singular pronouns, now largely obsolete.

Many of the questions, however, differ from what we would use today primarily in the absence of some form of *do.* Thus we would expect:

What does this shouting mean?
Do I know these men that are coming along with you?

The equivalent statement forms have not changed, at least in the part we are concerned with:

This shouting means...
I know these men that...

In Modern English, questions can be described as formed from statements by transposition of the first auxiliary. Whenever there is an auxiliary in an Elizabethan declarative sentence, the same rule holds. The strange constructions are usually those without auxiliaries. In these the first word of the verb phrase — the main verb — is moved. In present-day English, a *do* is supplied. The rules are essentially identical for positive sentences except at one point: Both move the first word of the verb phrase, but contemporary English adds a restriction that this cannot be the main verb unless it is *be* or *have* (with dialectal differences in the case of *have*). The following examples make the difference clear:

Statement	Shakespearean Question	Current Question
He will go.	*Will he go?*	*Will he go?*
He went.	*Went he?*	*Did he go?*

In Modern English, *do* has two major sets of uses: as a main verb, and as an auxiliary. In the latter it is used exclusively in sentences where the grammar requires an auxiliary, and as such it is effectively meaningless. There has obviously been some change in the use of *do,* and an understanding of this might be important.

The main verb uses of *do* largely continue ones known in OE, though there have been changes in frequency. Three can be distinguished: 1) It is a pro-verb, replacing some other verb and functioning anaphorically: *Christ weox swa swa oþre cild doþ.* 'Christ grew just like another child does.'

[10] In certain fixed or semi-fixed expressions, the old form is preserved, for example, in the sentry's challenge: *Who goes there?*

2) It is used with *what* in questions: *Hwæt sculon we do?* 'What must we do?'
3) It is used with certain nouns expressing action in idiomatic phrases: *Eall hiera weorc hie doþ þæt mann hie geseon.* 'All their works they do that men might see them.'

Do is occasionally used in a concatenation of verbs in OE, but never as a true auxiliary. The latter usage is a late ME and MnE development. A common ME construction was to use *do* with another verb to form causatives: ...*to do me live or deye*... 'to cause me to live or die' (Chaucer). This pattern continues into early MnE, but becomes less and less frequent. It does not occur in Shakespeare, and is now extinct.

Apparently, it was from such uses that *do* developed into an auxiliary. In late ME and early MnE, the distinction between simple and causative constructions weakened. (Today we say both: *The dog walked.* and *The man walked the dog.*) Do continued to be used with certain verbs, but the combination lost its causative meaning, becoming at first merely intensive, and finally nearly meaningless. In due course, it became completely dissociated from its original function. By the fifteenth century it was used very freely and contributed little if anything to the meaning of the sentences in which it occurred. Do had become largely an optional auxiliary, having more stylistic than semantic or grammatical significance. Often there seems to be no other motivation than to supply a syllable to fill out the meter.

In early MnE, *do* was frequently used as an unstressed auxiliary in positive declarative sentences, a position no longer possible. Evidence for this can be seen very readily in metrically scanable poetry:

> *Beasts did leap, and birds did sing,*
> *Trees did grow, and plants did spring.*
> Passionate Pilgrim 377

The natural inclination of a modern speaker of English is to stress *do* when not in a question or a negative sentence. In a passage such as that just cited, this is almost impossible, but in others one can easily miss the scansion and misread. With Elizabethan literature, particularly with poetry, one must always be on his guard against automatically stressing all occurrences of *do*.

Of course, *do* was frequently involved in negative constructions and in question inversions, but in Elizabethan English this was incidental — any auxiliary might be. In these cases, *do* is present for some other reason, often metrical or stylistic. As a result, sentences can be deceptively modern in appearance:

> *Do you understand me?*
> Tempest ii:1:268
> *Do you know Ford, sir?*
> Merry Wives ii:2:280
> *We do not know what's brought to pass under the profession of fortune-telling.*
> Merry Wives iv:2:183

Subsequently, however, the use of the auxiliary *do* was regularized. It became compulsory in certain situations and impermissible in others. In the process, it necessarily lost any remaining semantic significance and all stylistic implications. It is, in present-day English, simply a meaningless bit of grammatical machinery.

There are three important uses for the auxiliary *do* in current spoken English: 1) To provide an auxiliary for the question inversion, 2) To allow attachment of the negative suffix, *-n't*, and 3) To receive one kind of emphatic sentence stress. In written English, the stress is almost never written. (Occasionally, italics or some similar device may be used.) Since *do* without a negative is not used outside questions unless it has emphatic stress, a written *do* is usually taken as emphatic. Indeed, *do* is frequently thought of as being, itself, a mark of emphasis. A case can be made for this in current written forms, but not in speech.

NEGATIVES

Negative sentences have been subject to the same change as interrogatives. In most instances, the negative follows the first auxiliary. In speech it is usually an affix, sometimes spelled *-n't*, but in writing it is usually a separate word *not*, regardless of the pronunciation. Thus, Elizabethan *I know not* has been replaced by *I do not know* or *I don't know*.

However, other constructions suggest that there has been more of a restructuring than appears in these simple examples. In the following, *not* clearly precedes the verb that is negated:

> *He is the only man I know who can dive but not swim.*
> *I said if you want to go you will have to wear a coat and tie. If you don't, you can just not go.*
> *Try not to make a fool of yourself for a change.*
> *If you would rather have it as it is, I can not paint it.*

In the last example, the speaker is not asserting 'it is not possible for me to paint it', but 'it is possible for me to not paint it'. It therefore contrasts in structure with the following:

> *The wood is so dirty, I cannot paint it.*

That there is a structural contrast is clearly demonstrable in at least two ways: The second would most often be pronounced contracted, *I can't paint it;* this is not possible with the first. The word *just* can be inserted into either, but only in different places:

> *If you would rather have it as it is, I can just not paint it.*
> *The wood is so dirty, I just can't paint it.*   OR
> *The wood is so dirty, I can't just paint it.*

In fact both kinds of negative seem quite possible in the same sentence:

> *I couldn't just not paint it; I'll have to put some clear varnish on it, or something.*

This is certainly not a double negative of the familiar type of *We ain't got no bananas*. Still, we have become so terrified of double negatives (some of us, at least), that on our best behavior we would be more likely to say:

 I couldn't just leave it unpainted; . . .

But this may be a touch of hyperpurism!

All of this suggests that, contrary to the Elizabethan practice, we now place *not* immediately before whatever we desire to make negative except with auxiliaries and modals. The latter are never preceded by *not*, but can be followed by *not* (usually as a suffix *-n't*). There is, thus, a case of complementary distribution. That is, there is no contrast between the two positions, following auxiliaries and modals, and preceding everything else. This is justification for some transformational-generative grammars introducing *not* before the verb phrase, then inverting by a rule such as: *not + could ⇒ couldn't*.

Actually, it is rather difficult to get clear examples of a contrast such as *can (not paint)* vs. *(can not) paint*. In most instances, negating either part of the construction has about the same effect. There is however one modal construction that has two quite different negatives, that with *must*. One would mean 'it is not necessary that...', the other 'it is necessary that...not...'. Just as the comparable difference with *can* may be made by careful use of stress and juncture, something similar might be possible with *must*. Instead we have a synonymous modal, *need*, with the arbitrary convention that each is used in only one of the two negative meanings. The modal *need* is, therefore, not needed in the positive and does not occur. Thus, *you must go* has two negative equivalents, *you mustn't go* and *you needn't go*.[11]

So far as we can see,[12] Elizabethan use of negatives is different from modern patterns in small but significant ways. With nouns, adjectives, or infinitives marked with *to* the pattern seems the same: *not* precedes that which it makes negative. In uninverted verb phrases it almost always follows immediately after the first word, whether this is the main verb or an auxiliary. In this position it seems to make the whole verb phrase negative.

---

[11] Constructions with *have to* are generally synonymous with those with *must*. The two negatives would be amply distinct: *you don't have to go* and *you have to not go*. Actually, the second form is very rare, usually replaced by *you mustn't go*. or *you can't go*. The first is common, and generally replaces *you needn't go*, which is often felt to be bookish. But, however complex the facts may be, the basic principle is clear: possible contrasts on the basis of the place or relationship of the negative tend to be avoided, totally different constructions being used instead.

[12] Work on the grammar of an older form of a language always presents special problems. With a living dialect, the normal recourse is to elicitation from native speakers. It is possible in this way to obtain examples of constructions that might require months of searching through texts to find. In the absence of informants, we have to rely on the textual evidence, always partial and generally difficult to interpret. Yet, in spite of these difficulties, we certainly have accomplished only a very small part of what we can do with Elizabethan English. Here is one of the least occupied frontiers of English research.

If a construction in which a part of the phrase was negative were possible in Elizabethan English — say, one comparable to *can (not paint)* — I have not found an example. They would, of course, be rare. Shakespeare has a handful of examples which seem to have *not* preceding the verb:

> *I not doubt He came alive to land.*
> Tempest ii:1:121
> *Whereof the ewe not bites.*
> Tempest v:1:38

These, however, are considered parallel to constructions such as *I nothing doubt*, also found in Shakespeare. It is assumed that the pronunciation of *not* here was different from that of the usual simple negative,[13] and that the modern equivalent would be *naught*.

In older English, *not* was most often after the verb phrase, occasionally at some distance, and this construction is still occasionally found in Shakespeare:

> *Give me not the boots — No, I will not for it boots thee not.*
> Two Gentlemen of Verona i:1:27

The long-term trend has been for the negative to move forward in the predicate. The modern result is close association with the predicate introducer. The common Elizabethan placement after the first word of the verb phrase is a step in that development.

Questions give us a test of the attachment of the negative to the auxiliary. Two patterns are found, both in the King James Version and in Shakespeare. In the more conservative, the first element of the verb phrase is moved without the negative:

> *Will't not be?*
> King John iii:1:298
> *Hast thou not signed a decree?*
> Daniel 6:12

In the other, the negative is moved with the auxiliary:

> *Were not you here?*
> Love's Labors Lost v:2:433
> *Is not this great Babylon?*
> Daniel 4:30

In modern colloquial, of course, unemphatic *not* is always moved. In literary English, *not* may or may not be shifted, but when left in place, there is often an archaic flavor.

In Elizabethan times, *not* had not yet become a suffix to the auxiliary. Kökeritz[14] found only eight places in the entire Shakespeare corpus where it seemed to be elided. Not only does the scansion demand that *not* be

[13] See W. Franz, *Shakespeare-Grammatik, zweite Auflage*, 1909.
[14] Helge Kökeritz, *Shakespeare's Pronunciation*, 1953, p. 280.

given full syllabic value, but in nearly half the cases, *not* must be treated as accented. The grammatical attachment of *not* to auxiliaries was well on the way to establishment in Elizabethan English, the phonologic attachment came later.

Somehow related to this shift in the position of the negative is a change, apparently now in process, in the use of the limiters, *just, only, hardly,* and so on. One basic and old use of these is to modify phrases. This often gives rise, in literary English, to structural ambiguities of a peculiar sort. For example in *only twenty-five boys, only* is followed by a numeral phrase, *twenty-five,* and by a noun phrase, *twenty-five boys.* It could modify either. Occasionally context will distinguish:

> *He sent me only twenty-five boys; I asked for thirty.*
> *He sent me only twenty-five boys; I asked for men.*

As a matter of fact, it is not often that such a structural ambiguity would affect the meaning of the sentence in any way. The problem is, therefore, usually only academic.

In colloquial English, limiters are tending to move forward from complements into the verb phrase. Here they tend to precede the one word verb phrase or to follow the first auxiliary. In this position they would, in literary English, modify the verb phrase or some part of it. Teachers object to

> *He only sent me twenty-five boys.*

when, as is often quite evident, the intended meaning is what in conservative literary usage would be written

> *He sent me only twenty-five boys.*

As a matter of fact, as a spelling representation of colloquial, the sentence is triply ambiguous. The three can be easily distinguished by context in favorable instances:

> *He only sent me twenty-five boys; I asked for thirty.*
> *He only sent me twenty-five boys; I asked for men.*
> *He only sent me twenty-five boys; I asked him to bring them.*

If these are read aloud, it will be seen that there is another difference clearly correlated with the contextual difference. In the three, the primary stress in the first clause is on *twenty-five, boys,* or *sent* respectively. *Only* in a colloquial predicate signals only that some phrase is limited; stress tells which one. This device is unavailable in writing, and literary English must continue to distinguish as best it can by the position of *only* alone.

This pattern is paralleled by distinctions made by stress in colloquial negative sentences:

> *He didn't send me thirty boys; he only sent twenty-five.*
> *He didn't send me twenty-five men; he only sent me boys.*
> *He didn't bring me twenty-five boys; he only sent them.*

In literary English, if the context does not make the intention clear, a sentence such as *He didn't send me twenty-five boys* would probably be restructured to avoid ambiguity.

The syntax of negative sentences has been undergoing change for several centuries and has not yet reached an equilibrium. Several stages of this long development coexist in present-day colloquial and literary usage. In Shakespeare's language we also find several stages coexisting. The assortments are, however, different. Some have finally disappeared in the interim. Some new ones have appeared. We cannot speak either of THE Elizabethan pattern or of THE twentieth-century pattern — only of different mixtures of patterns.

So it is also with other syntactic matters. Old and declining patterns linger on alongside young and advancing usages. In some areas, Elizabethan practice is sharply different from modern; in others there are puzzling mixtures of similarities and differences. To understand earlier literature, a reader must often be aware of changes. Otherwise he may be trapped in misinterpretations. Literature and speech, however innovating they may be, retain within themselves much evidence of their history. To understand deeply the language of even this single year, a knowledge of historical processes is needed. Today's language cannot be fully appreciated without attention to its early modern roots, nor can today's literature if such antecedents as Shakespeare and the King James Bible are neglected.

Chapter 17

Language Comparison

The grammar of English, like that of any other language, may be looked at from three quite different points of view. A hasty or incautious statement of any one of them might seem to rule out either or both of the other two, yet all three are supplementary and, therefore, necessary to a full understanding.

In the first, the grammar of English is autonomous, concerned only with the facts of the English language itself. Nothing that we know about any other language is relevant. Swahili, for example, has agreement of adjectives with nouns, but that is no reason to expect that English would have the same thing or anything like it. Swahili nouns are inflected to show singular and plural; so are English, but we must not expect any similarity of detail. The rules of English grammar are proper to the English language. They are to be found only by investigating suitable samples of English. They can be tested only by applying them to additional samples of English. If they look outlandish from a Swahili point of view — and in many places they do — that is of no significance.

From a second point of view, English is not so completely isolated. It has a long history of development, partly known and partly hidden in the inaccessible past. It shares antecedents with certain other languages. It has been molded by forces both within and outside itself, and some of these have been shared with neighboring tongues. English does, therefore, have significant resemblances to other languages. These are revealing of the history of English. They help, moreover, in elucidating certain features of English grammar itself, some of them otherwise obscure. The carefully directed comparison of English with properly selected other languages is, therefore, important to the grammarian, often suggesting interpretations that are unlikely to be found from looking at English alone, but which do prove useful even in a strictly English context. Yet nothing suggested by a comparison can be accepted as a fact of English grammar until it has been confirmed as fitting the behavior of the language itself.

From a third point of view, English is a language among languages, a special case of a phenomenon much wider than English itself. Its study can be illumined by comparison with any language, however remote geographically or culturally. Yet we do not here get clues as to specific facts of English grammar so much as insights into the fundamental framework of language and human communication. Moreover, it is from such comparative work that we develop and test our methods. The techniques of investigation and description that stand behind our English grammars are crucial, and the grammar is never any better than the theory on which it is based. The methods learned in the study of one language may be applied in another, but only to guide the examination of the language itself, never as a substitute for data.

In the past chapters, the focus of attention has been on the facts of English. General principles of linguistics have, however, frequently entered the discussion in one way or another. It could not have been otherwise. Very little was said about the comparison of English with other languages, though there were many places where the results presented were suggested to scholars in the first instance by such comparison. It will now be worthwhile to examine a few places where English can profitably be compared — largely with German — and see, thus, some of the ways that English grammar can be clarified by such a procedure.

ENGLISH AND GERMAN VERBS

The verb inflection of English is not extensive. *Be* has eight forms in regular use[1] (*be, am, is, are, was, were, been, being*). Other verbs have three, four, or five. For convenience in description, *be* is usually laid aside for special treatment and the remaining verbs are all treated as having exactly five forms[2] two or three of them being alike in some instances:

Infinitive	Past	Past participle	3d sing. present	Present participle[3]	
drink	*drank*	*drunk*	*drinks*	*drinking*	(five forms)
break	*broke*	*broken*	*breaks*	*breaking*	
come	*came*	*come*	*comes*	*coming*	(four forms)
sting	*stung*	*stung*	*stings*	*stinging*	
cut	*cut*	*cut*	*cuts*	*cutting*	(three forms)

[1] *Art* may be considered as a ninth form, but is hardly in regular use. *Wert* is even less used, but is seen occasionally in older texts.

[2] Most of these verbs also had second person singular forms in the older language, and many of these are still in sporadic archaistic use, but are here overlooked.

[3] We will use the traditional labels throughout this chapter, though certain of them are quite unsatisfactory if taken as anything more than simply labels.

Of these, the present participle can always[4] be formed from the infinitive by simple rules. Likewise the third person singular present can be so formed, except in three verbs:

have	/hǽv/	*has*	/hǽz/	not	/×hǽvz/
do	/dúw/	*does*	/dɔ́z/		/×dúwz/
say	/séy/	*says*	/séz/		/×séyz/[5]

The vast majority of verbs form both their past and their past participle by adding *-ed* (/-d ∼ -t ∼ -id/). However, a considerable number, including many of the commonest, follow other patterns. For these there are no simple rules, and the three forms, infinitive, past, and past participle, are traditionally listed in grammars and dictionaries. Such a list is known as the "principal parts" of the verb.

In many other languages similar principal parts are listed in the dictionaries or presented for memorization in vocabularies. In Latin, for example, four forms are traditionally given: present, infinitive, perfect, and perfect participle. These exhibit all the basic forms of the stem and show which set of endings is to be used. There are many more verb forms than in English (nearly 150), but with a few minor exceptions (comparable to *has, does,* and *says*) all of them can be formed by rules if the principal parts are known:

pōtō	*pōtāre*	*pōtāvī*	*pōtātus*	'drink'
frangō	*frangere*	*frēgī*	*fractus*	'break'

In German also it is customary to list principal parts. These are sometimes given as follows, the forms being the same three used in English:

trinken	*trank*	*getrunken*	'drink'
brechen	*brach*	*gebrochen*	'break'

There are interesting similarities. In part, this is a matter of technique of description. Very much the same conventions are used in the traditional grammars of all three languages: Latin, German, and English. But underlying this, there are also certain basic similarities in the grammatical systems.

German and English are more similar to each other than either is to Latin. In some instances, *drink* and *trinken*, for example, the internal changes in spelling from one verb form to another are exactly the same. (Of course, the pronunciation of these vowels is not the same in the two languages, but the parallelism remains striking.) It would be difficult to

---

[4] There are some irregularities in a few dialects, but the formation is entirely regular in all regional standards and most local dialects. The rules, however, are not the same in all dialects.

[5] In some dialects some of these forms are regular, for example, in certain areas of the United States /séyz/ is frequent.

find any Latin verb which shows this same similarity in detail to an equivalent English verb, though several such pairs can be found between English and German. Here, then, is a specific similarity which must be explained and which may reveal something significant.

Striking as some of the similarities between English and German verbs may be, they become even more so if Old English is used in place of Modern English. OE verbs also are usually described on the basis of principal parts, though for complete information it seems necessary to list five forms:

Infinitive	3rd sing. present	Past		Participle	
		3d sing.	3d plur.		
drincan	*drincð*	*dranc*	*druncon*	*gedruncen*	'drink'
brecan	*bricð*	*bræc*	*bræcon*	*gebrocen*	'break'

The additional principal parts are required because OE has a more complex inflection than MnE. The full paradigm of the present and the past may be compared with German and MnE. All forms that are different in any verb are shown. The forms within each box are based on the same principal part.

Present	German		Old English		Modern English	
sing. 3	*trinkt*	*bricht*	*drincð*	*bricð*	*drinks*	*breaks*
2	*trinkst*	*brichst*	*drincst*	*bricst*	*drink*	*break*
1	*trinke*	*breche*	*drince*	*brece*	"	"
plur. 3, 1	*trinken*	*brechen*	*drincað*	*brecað*	"	"
2	*trinkt*	*brecht*	"	"	"	"
past						
sing. 3, 1	*trank*	*brach*	*dranc*	*bræc*	*drank*	*broke*
2	*trankst*	*brachst*	*drunce*	*bræce*	"	"
plur. 3, 1	*tranken*	*brachen*	*druncon*	*bræcon*	"	"
2	*trankt*	*bracht*	"	"	"	"

There are many evident similarities in these paradigms, especially between German and OE. Some of the endings look much alike. Both form the second and third persons singular present in certain verbs from a stem with a different vowel from the infinitive and the rest of the present. (As a result, a fourth principal part is often listed in German: *brechen, bricht, brach, gebrochen*.)

All German past forms have the same stem; many OE verbs, including the two examples, do not. Old High German may conveniently be taken as an older form of German roughly contemporaneous with OE.[6] In OHG

---

[6] If the direct line of descent for present-day standard German is traced back, it will not pass through Old High German. But the latter is very closely related on a collateral line, and represents fairly well the condition of a direct ancestor. The same thing is true of OE, most familiar in its Wessex form, which is not the direct ancestor of modern standard English.

there are two stems in the past: *trank, trunken* parallel to OE *dranc, druncon.* That is, the verbal system of OHG is still more closely similar to that of OE than is that of Modern German.

In their modern forms, English and German show interesting grammatical similarities in many details. Millennium-old forms of the two languages are more similar. If we might go back another millennium, we would expect to find still more convergence. Unfortunately, we cannot do this in the same way, since we do not have the necessary documentary evidence for this period for either language. However, it would seem reasonable to extrapolate from what we do know. The most reasonable guess would be that two millennia ago the two languages were very much alike indeed. This should be no surprise: OE arose from the speech patterns carried to Britain by invaders from northern continental Europe. They were closely related to other tribes who stayed behind and whose speech gradually developed into the various historical stages and dialects of German.

That is to say, many of the similarities of German and English must be explained by their common origin out of a complex of very similar dialects spoken by a group of closely related peoples in prehistoric northern Europe. We recognize this fact by saying that English and German are genetically related, or by classifying them together in a group usually labeled "Germanic". Dutch, Danish, Swedish, Norwegian, and Icelandic are other languages of the same group. In many parts of their grammars all of them show similarities of the kind just examined, and they all seem still more alike whenever we are able to compare older forms rather than the modern languages. This last fact is a test of genetic relatedness. In addition, the Germanic languages all show many similar vocabulary items — words that seem to trace back to a period when they were only slightly divergent dialects of one language.

GRAMMATICAL DIVERGENCE

While the grammatical similarities between the Germanic languages are interesting and significant, the differences also demand attention. They must be accounted for, and they, too, may shed some light on language history and interlanguage relationships.

The basic phenomenon, of course, is linguistic change, the subject of Chapter 16. The attention there was more on the fact and form of change than on the mechanism. Properly, linguistic change is not one process but an assortment operating in various ways and affecting all parts of a language. For the present, it will suffice to distinguish three general types of change, though a more detailed classification is possible and necessary for certain purposes.

Part of the change in English verb inflection originated outside of language in a change in social habits involving language use. The disuse of *thou* was the result of such a series of social changes. It led to linguistic consequences, since the verbal ending *-est* was used only with *thou*. The verbal inflection was already greatly simplified from other changes, hence the disappearance of this one ending had a profound effect on the system.

Such a change is likely to come to completion very slowly. That is true in this case. *Thou* and *-est* persist in two kinds of specialized uses in present-day English. They are very rarely used to impart an archaic effect, and rather more commonly in certain religious contexts.

A second kind of change also originates outside the language in changes in habits of pronunciation. For the most part, these build up gradually over long periods of time, so that the phonetics of one generation is only slightly different from that of the preceding. The course of change is often different in different dialects. Thus such gradual change has resulted in the rolled /r/ of Scots and the familiar American /r/, technically a fricative. This change has not affected the phonemic system: both dialects retain a phoneme /r/ with much the same patterns of use.

Sometimes, however, such phonetic changes obliterate the distinctions by which phoneme contrasts are marked, thus forcing changes in the phonemic system of the language. There have been many such cases in the history of both English and German. For example, at one stage in the history of English there were a number of different vowel phonemes which could occur in unstressed syllables. Gradually the distinctions between these were lost — but only in weakly stressed syllables — and the vowels involved became indistinguishable one from the other. At this point all these formerly distinct vowels became the same phoneme, /ə/, and numerous changes were forced in the system, among them that the distribution of /e/ was changed: it no longer occurred with weak stress.

As a separate process of change, what had been final short vowel in OE became less and less distinguishable from the absence of any vowel. Thus what had been OE *drince* became indistinguishable from what had been OE *drinc*. A brief way of stating the facts is to say that final short vowels disappeared. But this *-e* was an inflectional suffix. The phonetic change had phonemic consequences and these led to morphemic consequences also. In general in the history of Germanic languages, many inflectional endings simply disappeared. Others became indistinguishable. Much of the change in inflection has followed from phonetic change.

Other changes center in the grammatical system itself. Less than 150 verbs form their past in Modern English in any other way than by simply adding *-ed* (/-d ∼ -t ∼ -id/) to the infinitive form. When new verbs come into the language they usually automatically go into the larger group taking *-ed*. From time to time, old verbs are given new past forms, usually following this dominant pattern. The result has been a continuing decrease in the number of verbs following other patterns. Moreover, some features of these patterns have been lost completely or very strictly limited. The details may be complex, but some examples will suggest something of the process.

OE verbs fall, on the basis of their past tense forms, into two major classes, each of which can be further divided. Weak verbs form their past tense by adding a suffix. This takes the forms -d-, -t-, or -od-. There may be various other changes, but these need not concern us here. Weak verbs use the ending -e in the first and third persons singular. Strong verbs do not form their past by the use of a suffix, but generally by various other changes. Many of them have two stems, usually with different vowels, but sometimes also with different consonants. They have no ending in the first and third person singular. The following list gives a sample of past forms of one pattern from each major class. They are followed by the MnE past forms of the same verb.

	OE past		MnE past		
weak	*fylde*	*fyldon*			*filled*
	lifde	*lifdon*			*lived*
	dēmde	*dēmdon*			*deemed*
	hringde	*hringdon*	*rang*		
strong	*dranc*	*druncon*	*drank*		
	sang	*sungon*	*sang*		
	begann	*begunnon*	*began*		
	stang	*stungon*		*stung*	
	sprang	*sprungon*	*sprang* ~ *sprung*		
	sanc	*suncon*	*sank* ~ *sunk*		
	swamm	*swummon*	*swam* ~ *swum*		
	clamb	*clumbon*		*clumb* ~ *climbed*	

Most OE weak verbs that persist (some of course have totally disappeared) now form their past with -ed, the direct descendant of the old suffix and have principal parts comparable to *fill, filled, filled*.

The pattern of having two different stems in the past has now almost completely disappeared. *Was, were* is the only remaining example, the past tense of a verb that is unusual in many other respects as well. Modern strong verbs have had to settle, in any given form of the language, on one past stem. In the first three strong verbs in this list, the form with *a* (which has changed somewhat in pronunciation, of course) has become dominant. It has displaced the form with *u*, and is now used with both singular and plural subjects. Part of the stimulus of this was undoubtedly the weak verbs which in OE had only one stem in the past. The result is a set of principal parts of the type *drink, drank, drunk*.

In some others of this OE pattern, the form with *u* (again with a change of pronunciation and with loss of ending) has come to be used in the singular as well as in the plural. The result is a set of principal parts like *sting, stung, stung*.

English dialects do not agree in their choice of past tense forms for some of these verbs. Some use *sprang*, others *sprung;* some use *swam*, others *swum*. The alignment of dialects is different for each verb. Moreover, in a few dialects both forms occur, sometimes associated with different keys, sometimes carrying different meanings. I would say: *The boat sank. He sunk the boat.* Some others would distinguish: *The bucket sprung a leak. He sprang to the rescue.*

In OE *climb* was just like the others in the list. In MnE it has been transferred to the much larger class taking -*ed*, and both original forms have disappeared — or nearly so: *clumb* remains in some dialects, though now looked on as substandard.[7] The opposite change has affected *ring*. In OE this was a weak verb. Its principal parts were *hringen, hringe, hringde, hringdon, gehringed*. In Modern English we would expect *ring, ringed, ringed*, but because of the shift to another class we have *ring, rang, rung*.

The effect of this type of change, of course, is to gradually obliterate the evidence in any language for its past history. Since much the same process was occurring in German, though often different in details, the further effect is to obscure the relationship between the two languages. Comparing OE with OHG and then looking at MnE and German shows roughly how much two languages can drift apart in about a millennium of this sort of change. A few more thousands of years and the relation might be visible only to a specialist. Still more time for change and even he might be unable to detect what little evidence still remained.

Latin verbal inflection does not show the same obvious similarities to English that German does. But there are significant resemblances and they can be found by careful examination. Naturally it is easier if Latin is compared with an older Germanic language rather than a modern one. For example, the following are the endings of the present tense:[8]

		Latin	OHG			Latin	OHG
Sing.	1	-ō	-u	Plur.	1	-āmus	-amēs
	2	-ās	-is		2	-ātis	-et
	3	-at	-it		3	-ant	-ant

Similarities are evident. If, however, Spanish were compared with modern German, much less would be visible.

There are frequently vowel changes involved in the formation of the principal parts in Latin — compare *frango, frēgi*.[9] It is difficult to match these in detail with those of Germanic languages, but they can be traced

---

[7] The table does not list all the variants. *Clumb* is the only one given which is definitely substandard, but there are such forms for several other verbs. Some of these are also direct descendants of older forms.

[8] In the case of both languages, the endings given are those appropriate to a single class of verbs. Other classes would show similar resemblances.

[9] In addition to the vowel change, there is the insertion of /n/ into the present stem. This is a characteristic IE feature, traces of which remain in English *bring, brought* and *think, thought*.

back to a common origin in a much older ancestral language. Similar vowel changes are found in Greek, Sanskrit, and various other languages.

These facts, and many other similarities in grammatical details, indicate that we can group Germanic with these other languages into a comprehending family, Indo-European. Germanic is, then, one of several branches. Some of the more familiar branches and languages are the following:[10]

Germanic: Icelandic, Norwegian, Swedish, Danish, German, Yiddish, Dutch, Frisian, English.
Celtic: Welsh, Breton, Gaelic.
Italic-Romance: Latin, Portuguese, Spanish, Catalan, French, Italian, Romanian.
Greek: Greek.
Baltic: Lithuanian, Latvian.
Slavic: Serbo-Croatian, Bulgarian, Czech, Polish, Russian, Ukranian.
Armenian: Armenian.
Iranian: Persian.
Indic: Sanskrit, Hindi, Urdu, Bengali.

All of the languages of Europe are Indo-European, with only the following important exceptions: Basque (in Spain and France), Finnish, Estonian, Hungarian, Turkish, and a number of languages in Eastern Russia and the Caucasus.

WESTERN EUROPEAN UNITY

For two millennia the Latin language has had a series of unique and significant roles in Western Europe. Whatever have been the integrating institutions — and they have shifted from time to time — Latin has always been associated with them in some way as the unifying linguistic base.

For much of the area, the dawn of history came with incorporation into the growing political unity of the Roman Empire. Starting as a very minor contender among the warring city states of the Italian peninsula, Rome grew to become the first region-wide political unit in the Western Mediterranean. Roman hegemony was extended northward into Central Europe. This large area was maintained under one integrated governmental system for several centuries — long enough to establish one unified set of political traditions. Latin was the language of this growing military and political unit until Greece was conquered, after which Latin was gradually restricted to the West and Greek became the language of Rome in the East.

[10] For a more complete and detailed tabulation, the most convenient source is the entry at Indo-European in *Webster's Third New International Dictionary*.

The traditions of the two were much the same, but just different enough to have eventuated in two partially dissimilar culture spheres which persist today.

The political structure of the Empire was destroyed by Germanic-speaking invaders from the north. They replaced it with a series of contending units of various sizes and constantly shifting status. Even so, many of the political traditions were maintained — witness the constant struggle among the new dynasties to establish themselves as the legitimate successors of the emperors and their dominions as the continuing Roman Empire. These traditions were only a small part of a solidly established common culture that held Western Europe together. Prominent in this were the Christian religion, the ecclesiastical institutions which embodied it, and a common heritage of learning. For all of this, the medium was almost invariably Latin.

Even during this period of political fragmentation, the common Latin-based culture of Western Europe extended itself northward beyond the limits that the Romans had reached, all the way to the Arctic Ocean. For this to have happened, Europe could not have been so disorganized as is implied by the common label "the Dark Ages".

From about the twelfth century, there was a new birth of learning as scholars rediscovered older Latin literature, some of it neglected and forgotten for centuries. The Greek classics became better known. A new scholastic Latin was developed to meet the new needs, and it was through this medium that the new learning was disseminated. As the pace of these movements quickened, Scholasticism was transformed into the Renaissance. Printing came to Europe, and with it further increase in scholarly work. The major vehicle remained Latin.

As a result of the new forces released by the Renaissance, the vernacular languages of Europe began to achieve a new dignity. Only a few (for example, Old English and Icelandic) had had any flourishing literature in the medieval period. Now, one after another, they were given standard written forms and literary conventions were established. Invariably this work was done by men steeped in classical learning who looked to classical literature — mostly known to them in Latin — for a model. Every literary language of Western Europe received a strong Latin stamp from its formation.

For many years Latin and the vernacular languages coexisted symbiotically. All educated men were bilingual, at least, and interference was heavy. Latin had a profound and continuing influence. The standards of oratory, for example, were Cicero and Quintillian. Students learned rhetoric in their own language from manuals based on those of classical times. Virgil, Horace, Ovid, and Juvenal set the styles for much of European poetry.

To this was soon added interaction between the various modern literatures. Dante, for example, has been widely influential in every Western

European language. This meant, in part, that though the ties with classical models and with the Latin language became increasingly indirect, they were never cut off. The old Latin unity broadened into a pan-West European tradition with many new sources added. It might be less obviously Latin, but fundamentally it was the old extended.

Long after belles lettres had come to be written largely in modern languages, serious philosophical and scientific writing continued in Latin. Today science has become the conspicuous new force for unity in Western Europe and far beyond. Science is international, and so is its language. Most of the terminology is Latin or latinized Greek in origin, but it is a new kind of Latin — neither classical nor medieval, but the culmination of the long development of which these were stages.

Only a few scientists today write obvious Latin;[11] superficially they seem to be using English, French, German, Russian. Still their language remains international. The same words appear in the same meanings, but with slightly different spelling conventions: *phoneme, phonème, fonema, Phonem*. Even when the word elements are vernacular, the pattern of formation is usually international. *Medklanker* is the Dutch form of the international *consonant, consonante. Med-* is the regular Dutch substitute for *con-, klank-* for *son-* and *-er* for *-ant/-ent*. Ultimately, Latin provided the model for Dutch *medklanker* as surely as it did for English *consonant*.

This "International Scientific Vocabulary" is not restricted to the university and the research laboratory. *Thermometer, radiator, photograph, stenographer, telephone, accelerator* are common everyday words from this source. Every European uses hundreds of them regularly.

There is much more to this international scientific language than terminology. Style, conventions, and even many points of syntax are common. Scientific English, French, and German are more nearly alike than are belletristic English, French, and German, and the latter are, in turn, more alike than rustic colloquial forms of the three languages.

It is hard to assess this latinization of European languages when they are looked at from a purely European point of view. The modern languages of India provide a very closely parallel case which an American can appraise from the outside. Sanskrit has had much the same roles in India as has Latin in Europe. Each of the modern vernaculars has grown up in a Sanskrit-dominated milieu and each has been profoundly influenced by it. Literary style, syntax, idioms, and vocabulary have all received the impress of classical patterns.

I once heard a student reciting poems he had written in his native Telugu to an audience from all over the country. The applause was obviously more than simply polite. I questioned one of my friends who

---

[11] The custom lingers on in plant taxonomy, where the international rules require that a new species be described in Latin.

knew no Telugu. He explained that of course he did not get everything, but in the highly classicized language of such poetry so much of the vocabulary, metaphor, and theme was Sanskrit that he had little difficulty in filling out what he did not understand. One might compare the poems to a Sanskrit mosaic only held together in Telugu mortar.

On another occasion, I taught linguistic field methods to a class of north Indian students, all speakers of Indo-European languages. We used as an informant a speaker of a Dravidian language from the south. Repeatedly I found myself having difficulty with syntactic points that seemed completely obvious to the students. So much of a pan-Indian syntax has seeped into every language of the country (including even this unwritten language of a minor hill people) that there is little strange to one Indian in another's speech.

Pan-West-European patterns are hard to identify because they have become so thoroughly naturalized in literary English. It is, however, fair to say that almost every construction that is more common in literary than in colloquial English is in some way or another pan-European. Most of the patterns found in late MnE but not in earlier forms of the language can also be ascribed to the common interlanguage of Europe.

But the reverse is not necessarily true. Latin influence is not a new feature in English, but can be detected in standard OE. One example is the development of a passive infinitive consisting of the infinitive *beon* 'be' with a participle: *we magon beon getrymede mid Iohannes cuide* 'We can be strengthened by John's voice'. This construction, of which there are something over 600 examples in the extant literature, is very much more frequent in translations or in works obviously influenced by Latin than in the more strictly native writing.[12]

One of the clearest cases, though not of ultimate Latin origin, is the pattern: *King of Kings, Lord of Lords, Holy of Holies*. These appear in the King James (and other versions of the Bible) as renderings of the overliterate translations into Latin of Hebrew superlative constructions. The last, for example, might better be translated as 'most holy place'. This is an odd construction in Latin, and it has had a rather restricted use both there and in English. But even so, it has spread outside Biblical and theological contexts in a limited way. An actor is sometimes spoken of as a *star of stars*, quite a shift from the original use!

The core of this set of pan-West-European patterns is found in most of the languages of the area, producing a similarity in grammar that is striking when examined from a broader base. It extends beyond the Indo-European languages. Hungarian, Finnish, and Basque show many similarities to their neighbors that can only be explained as the result of the pervasive influence of these regional patterns. Conversely, the Indo-

---

[12] Morgan Callaway, Jr., *The Infinitive in Anglo-Saxon*, 1913.

European languages of Asia, being in a different regional system, seem to us much more different from English than is, say, French or Czech, even though they are only a little less closely related genetically.

ENGLISH AND GERMAN NOUN PHRASES

The English noun phrase has a complicated structure involving at least six distinguishable positions before the head, each fillable by a class or a set of classes of words or phrases. Much of this can be duplicated in German:

N − 6	N − 5	N − 4	N − 3	N − 2	N − 1	N
all		*three*		*new*		*houses*
alle		*drei*		*neuen*		*Häuser*
	the	*three*	*other*	*new*		*houses*
	die	*drei*	*anderen*	*neuen*		*Häuser*
all	*the*		*other*	*new*		*houses*
alle	*die*		*anderen*	*neuen*		*Häuser*
all	*the*	*three*	*other*	*new*	*school*	*houses*

Five of the six positions are duplicated in German and these five are fillable by classes quite comparable to those used in the same slots in English. The full phrase with all six positions filled is possible, but most unusual in English. I could not find a phrase with all five positions filled that was acceptable to the German informant. This suggests that there are some differences, perhaps only minor, in the rules for combinations of modifiers.

This extensive, though not perfect, parallelism suggests that the structural patterns are inherited. This can be confirmed by comparing Old English:[13]

	N − 6	N − 5	N − 4	N − 3	N − 2	N − 1	N
OE	*ealle*	*his*			*leofan*		*halgan*
Eng.	*all*	*his*			*beloved*		*saints*
Ger.	*alle*	*seine*			*geliebten*		*Heiligen*
		þa		*oþoro*			*lond*
		the		*other*			*land*
		das		*andere*			*Land*
			ænne		*blacne*		*stedan*
			one		*black*		*stallion*
			ein		*schwarzer*		*Hengst*
		min	*twa*				*wergeld*
		my	*two*				*wergelds*
		meine	*zwei*				*Strafzahlungen*
		þære			*gesættredan*	*deofles*	*lare*
		the			*poisoned*	*devil's*	*teaching*

[13] OE examples are from Charles Carlton, *Word Order of Noun Modifiers in Old English Prose*, 1963, Journal of English and Germanic Philology, 62:778–783. Carlton's analysis of OE, independent of mine for MnE in Chapter 7, is followed.

Each of the examples, except the last, can be paralleled word for word in either English or German. The last example is parallel if the genitive *deofles* is properly translated as a descriptive rather than a possessive.[14] In MnE, the latter would go in N − 5.

There are some interesting differences between the three systems, some of which deserve comment here:

At first sight there is nothing in German syntax which corresponds with N − 1 position in MnE. This is occupied most commonly by nouns, but occasionally by other forms in attribution to the head noun. However, many of the sequences of noun-adjunct and noun can be translated into German by compound nouns: *school house, Schulhaus; fish market, Fischmarkt; university city, Universitätsstadt.* That is to say, the German equivalent of the N − 1 position is WITHIN the noun, rather than before it. On this basis, the last example can be translated into a parallel construction: *die vergiftete Teufelslehre* — parallel morpheme for morpheme but not word for word.

The German parallel here reinforces the feeling that the N − 1 position in English is different in some basic way from the others. There are frequently several elements which seem to be in this position, for example, *Miami ball park ticket collector, toll gate supervisor examination application fee,* but close examination shows that these must be described in terms of two-part constructions nested within each other, and there may be contrasts in the IC structures of rather similar appearing constructions. If there are two or more adjectives in the N − 2 position, no such contrast seems to occur. Indeed a full description of the MnE noun phrase is probably considerably simplified by recognizing the noun head and the N − 1 position modifiers as forming an inner unit within the larger phrase. On this basis, the difference between the German and MnE structures is little more than one of spelling.

Another interesting difference is in the treatment of *both* and its German equivalent *beide.* The differences are shown in the following phrases:

N − 6	N − 5	N − 4	N	
all	*the*		*houses*	
alle	*die*		*Häuser*	
both	*the*		*houses*	
	die	*beiden*	*Häuser*	'both the houses'
alle		*beiden*	*Häuser*	'both the houses'
alle		*zwei*	*Häuser*	'both the houses'

---

[14] I do not know whether any such contrast occurred in OE. It is, of course, very clear in MnE. Compare: *He sells the best men's hats.* (descriptive) and *The men's best hats were hanging in the coatroom.* (possessive).

alle		*drei*	*Häuser*	
all		three	houses	'alle drei Häuser'
all	*the*	*three*	*houses*	'alle drei Häuser'

Although usually translatable by 'both', *beide* goes into position N − 4, the usual place for numerals. The result is that there are at least three German phrases for which the nearest English translation is 'both the houses'. The differences are, from an English point of view, subtle, and not expressable in brief form. On the other hand, German does not as easily as English allow a determiner between *all* and a numeral. The result is two translations for *alle drei Häuser*. An English speaker feels a subtle difference here, but it cannot readily be carried over into German.

The basic pattern is the same in the two languages; the differences are only in detail. They indicate a change in one or both languages. Only an examination of the use of 'both' in OE and Old High German, or in other Germanic languages, would permit a decision as to which pattern is original and which has changed.

The recognition of two slots before the numeral is partly arbitrary. *All, both,* and *half* can precede *the, this, that,* and *his.* Constructions such as *all the men, both these books, half that quantity* are common. They can be adequately described only if two positions, N − 5 and N − 6, are set up. However, there are a number of other words that also precede numerals but which do not clearly fall into either of these slots. Among them are *some, any, every, each.* If constructions such as ×*all some men*, or ×*some the men* occurred, there would be no problem. But *some* neither precedes any of the words known to go in N − 5 nor follows any of those going into N − 6. We may arbitrarily assign it to either, noting that the other must remain vacant with *some*, or we may simply state that its position is indeterminate, N − 5/6. The situation is similar with many other words.

Moreover, while it is convenient to class *all, both,* and *half* together since they are the three most common words falling into N − 6, there is really little justification for doing so. Each one has many uses not open to either of the others: *all three houses*, but not ×*both three houses*. A full treatment would have to mention a great deal of detail which the brief description here has overlooked. In particular, it would have to recognize a very large number of very small classes, many of them with only a single member.[15]

---

[15] One might object that the difficulty with ×*both three houses* is semantic rather than grammatical. But this can be argued both ways, and no conclusive answer is possible. When grammatical classes are small — and *both* must fall into a very distinct single-membered subclass — it is difficult or even impossible to draw the line between grammatical and semantic features. This is an important source of the difficulty in attaining a satisfactory description of the N − 5 and N − 6 positions in the noun phrase. Most of the words occurring in these positions are members of very small subclasses.

It is not surprising, therefore, that there are many differences in detail in $N - 5$ and $N - 6$ between the three systems we have compared. One example is worth noting: OE *sum þæt lond* shows *sum* 'some' before a determiner and hence in $N - 6$ position. NE *some* cannot occur in this place. The phrase must, therefore, be translated in some nonparallel way: 'some land' or 'some of that land'. A German translation must be even less closely parallel, perhaps 'ein Teil jenes Landes' ('a part of that land') or 'ein Teil diese Landes' ('a part of this land').

These minor shiftings within the general framework of the system are entirely comparable to those we saw in the verb inflection. Individual verbs have shifted from one class to another, but the over-all system has changed much less. So likewise in noun phrases, there have been greater changes in the use of individual items than in the patterns as a whole.

There are occasional departures from the basic order we have discussed. One of these is worth mention here: the placing of a single adjective after the noun. This is commonest today in relatively fixed phrases, for example *notary public, heir apparent, body politic*. The pattern was fairly common in Shakespeare:

> *Speak from thy lungs military.*
> Merry Wives iv:5:18
> *Sport royal, I warrant you.*
> Twelfth Night ii:3:187
> *My presence, like a robe pontifical,*
> I Henry IV iii:2:56

It is striking that the instances of this sort in Shakespeare all involve adjectives derived from Latin or French. While a similar order occurs in German (for example, *Röslein rot* 'little red rose'), there are differences which make one hesitant to match them directly. All the facts suggest that this construction is borrowed. It can be taken as an instance of the West European Latinate influence.

It is not simply Modern English that shows this. Old English has one very common example: *God ælmihtig* 'God Almighty', certainly a literal translation from *Deus omnipotens*. The identical phrase occurs in German, here also clearly a translation: *Gott almächtig*.

In MnE the use has spread somewhat, taking on a poetic flavor in some cases, for example, *rubies red*. At the same time, some of the fixed phrases have become reinterpreted. *Attorney general*, as long as it is of this pattern, would have a plural *attorneys general*. For some it has become a compound noun; for others, *general* is interpreted as the head with *attorney* as a modifier. In either case the plural becomes *attorney generals*. In both developments, the origin of the pattern becomes less clear. Nevertheless, it is quite certain that both inheritance and pan-West European influence have affected, in different measures, the syntax of the noun phrase in English.

SUPERLATIVES

The superlative form of the adjective presents many puzzling problems in English grammar. In the scheme for the noun phrase we have used on page 140 and in the last section, it occurs most typically in the N − 3 position, that is, before other adjectives:

N — 5	N — 4	N — 3	N — 2	N
the	three	best	new	houses
die	drei	besten	neuen	Häuser

There is a simple objection to this analysis, and it has been raised several times: There are many examples of nouns preceded by two or more adjectives, for example, *the three good new houses*. If both *good* and *new* are to be put into the same group,[16] why should not *best* also be in N − 2? There are several reasons for treating *best* and *good* differently.

First consider the sentences agnate to the phrases:

the new houses	⇔ *The houses are new.*
the good new houses	⇔ *The good houses are new.*
	⇔ *The new houses are good.*
	⇔ *The houses are good and new.*

The second group suggests that *good* and *new* are coordinate. Either can be moved to the predicate separately, but if both are they must be joined by *and*. But:

the best new houses	⇔ *The best houses are new.*
	⇔ *The new houses are the best.*
	×*The houses are best and new.*

Only under the most unusual circumstances can a superlative be coordinated with any other type of adjective.[17] It is, however, quite possible to coordinate an absolute and a comparative: *a new and better way.*

---

[16] Westbrooke Barrett's analysis, followed in A. A. Hill, *Introduction to Linguistic Structures*, 1958, distinguishes three positions and three classes of adjectives where I have recognized only one. I would claim that the differences in use between *good* and *new*, for example, are stylistic. That is, *the three new good houses* is grammatically acceptable but seldom used because of a strong PREFERENCE for the other order, but ×*the three new best houses* is either rejected outright or interpreted as parallel to the phrase in: *When John got sick, they had to find a new best man for the wedding.* Here *best* is in N − 1. Almost any class of elements can be used in the N − 1 position, including superlatives. But the latter cannot be used in N − 2.

[17] The King James Version has *This is the first and great commandment.* Mt 22:38. This seems to be an overliteral translation of the Greek, in which language the contrast between superlative and absolute is apparently different. As such, it is a rather subtle grammatical error, and probably was in 1611 as much as today. There is a tendency for

There is similar resistance from native speakers to coordination of adjective and noun modifiers: *Wood and plastic furniture* is generally preferred to *wooden and plastic furniture*. *Californian and Nevadan customs*, or *California and Nevada cars*, are acceptable but not [×]*Californian and Nevada...* nor [×]*California and Nevadan...*; *ocean and river water*, but not [×]*salty and river water*. There is some reason to believe, however, that resistance to mixed coordination of this sort is relaxing at the present time. If this is the case, it probably portends a significant restructuring of patterns of modification.

There are many restrictions on combinations of determiners and superlatives, but much greater freedom with other adjectives:

the good house	*the better house*	*the best house*
a good house	*a better house*	[×]*a best house*
any good house	*any better house*	[×]*any best house*

The excluded constructions may occur in certain special contexts:

In any town there is always a best house.

All the others, however, are quite general.

In the predicate, superlatives usually require special constructions. This is even clearer and more regular in German than in English:

the best house	⇔ *The house is the best.*
das beste Haus	⇔ *Das Haus ist das beste.*
	⇔ *Das Haus ist am besten.*

Either *am* or an article (*das* with a neuter singular subject) is required with the superlative. The two constructions have slightly different meanings. The English parallel usually has *the;* absolute and comparative adjectives seldom behave like this.

Finally, superlatives, but not other adjectives, can be used as modifiers of numerals. In this way they are like the specifiers, *other, same, different,*

Americans in quoting this passage to correct it unconsciously to *the first and greatest*, thus indicating a deep-seated feeling for the grammatical pattern formulated here. To test this, verses 37 to 40 were duplicated, with 38 reading: *This is the . . . and . . . commandment.* A sample of students, staff, and faculty at the Hartford Seminary Foundation filled out the blanks from memory with the following results:

the first and great	15
the first and greatest	46
the first and the greatest	1
totally deviant answers	4

Since some would be expected to know this passage so thoroughly that they would be able to quote it verbatim, the results show a nearly universal tendency to make *great* a superlative, if the passage is not remembered in full detail.

. . ., and the ordinal numbers, *first, second, third,* . . ., all of which can occur in the N − 3 position.[18]

the two best houses	*the best two houses*
the two same houses	*the same two houses*
the two other houses	*the other two houses*
the two new houses	×*the new two houses*

The use of the superlative has been one of the neglected aspects of English grammar, and one of the most puzzling. Perhaps this has been because of a predisposition to think of it in the same terms as other adjective forms. Most traditional grammars have made very little of the differences in syntax which have just been pointed out. At the same time, it is easy to make too much of them. If the formulation just given is accepted, there remain many exceptional instances. The puzzles are reduced but by no means cleared up. Probably the confusion is the result of some process of language change currently in progress; new patterns are being superimposed on old; both coexist though partly contradictory to one another.

In such a situation, direct analysis of current usage will not easily disentangle the two or reveal the facts of either pattern. The comparison with German is instructive, since it shows, much more clearly and decisively than does English, a pattern which is possibly one component. This checks out to be consonant with the facts of English usage to a very considerable extent. In this, the significant difference between superlatives and comparatives is that they are used in two different sets of positions for two different grammatical functions.

The second component pattern centers in a distinction in number of objects compared. Comparative is used when two are involved, superlative for three or more. Quite probably this familiar distinction is basic in Latin — without having reexamined the question carefully, I know no evidence to the contrary. Probably, then, this component of the usage of the superlative and comparative in present-day English is an example of pan-West European syntax, superimposed on the Germanic pattern without as yet obliterating it.

Certainly the patterns of use of superlative and comparative are changing today, though it is a little difficult to see clearly what may be the direction of movement. It is probably safe to suggest that whatever may be the outcome, it will resolve some of the conflicts in current patterns and work toward a new and more consistent distinction or toward the disappearance of one of the two forms.

[18] Many of these words can also be used in N − 2 position, but always with a difference of meaning. For example, *different* in N − 3 means 'not identical with the one mentioned', but in N − 2 'unique' or 'unusual'. In general, words in N − 3 most often answer the question *which?*, those in N − 2, *what kind of?*.

Incidentally, the mere presence of comparative and superlative forms of the adjective is evidence of a fundamental unity. These forms are very infrequent outside the Indo-European languages, and the inflectional affixes in Germanic and Latin can be, in part, shown to be cognate.

LANGUAGE UNIVERSALS

As long as experience was largely restricted to the languages of Western Europe, many details (such as the inflection of adjectives to form comparative and superlative) seemed to be universal or nearly so. It was thought that languages might differ in how such categories were expressed, but if any were missing, it could only be regarded as a regrettable deficiency. A common core of features abstracted from the grammars of the familiar languages could be taken as a standard from which languages might depart only in primitive societies.

As experience widened, however, a different conclusion became inescapable. More and more instances were found of languages lacking some of these "fundamental" patterns, yet without evident ill effects. For example, inflection of nouns for singular and plural is far from universal — some languages mark other but similar contrasts, and many have nothing of the kind. Extensive practical acquaintance with such a language soon demonstrates that the singular-plural dichotomy is not in any way essential to effective communication. At the same time, almost every language which has been examined thoroughly has shown features not previously known, and many of these have evident usefulness within the systems where they occur. As linguists became acquainted with an ever-widening roster of possibilities, they were led to re-examine the familiar languages of Western Europe. Often they found that many interesting and significant details had been overlooked. English is not as much like French as had been supposed, nor German like Spanish. Some of the old "universals" evaporated when the basis on which they had been established became more thoroughly understood.

We have had to reconcile ourselves to much greater diversity in detail than we formerly assumed. For example, neither noun nor adjective, nor, indeed, any other part of speech is subject to the same patterns of inflection or use in all languages. This has been a difficult notion for many people, but it is only the beginning. The parts of speech themselves are by no means universal. Many languages lack adjectives as a distinct group, for example. What we would expect to be adjectives and nouns are not separable, or the equivalents of our adjectives and verbs show identical patterns. Indeed, the only parts of speech that approach universality among the languages of the world are nouns and verbs, and then only if some looseness of definition is allowed. Languages have been reported where even this distinction is either absent or of only minor significance. Not only most of the details, but also the general outline of the grammar has had to be stricken from the list of universals.

If, in this way, the familiar points of grammar have been disqualified, are there any universal features? We cannot expect to find them lurking in our traditional grammatical descriptions. Instead, there are two other approaches open to us, both important.

One is to compare human language with some similar nonhuman system to see what, if anything, sets them apart in basic structure. Perhaps the most familiar languagelike system, at least to rural Americans, is that of crows. This includes a number of recognizably different signals, each with a distinct meaning. It serves among crows at least some of the functions served by language among humans. It is a more limited system in that the signals are far fewer in number. More significant, they seem to be fixed. The crow does not have any method for inventing and establishing new signals. In contrast, men create new words constantly. Here is at least a symptom of a basic difference.

Human speech is extensible because there are in its basic plan two or more separate but interacting systems. Crows lack, so far as we can tell, anything comparable to the distinction between phonology and grammar. Because of this, they do not have a stock of unused but possible words from which they can draw for new needs. Nor do they have the complex syntax which enables human speech to define a place in the system for the newly selected words.

True language universals are to be found, then, not in the generalization of the features usually discussed in grammars, but in something more fundamental, in the underlying architecture of language, in the principles of organization that make possible the familiar kinds of grammatical facts. These characterize human language and set it off from communication systems of other animals.

A second approach to the discovery of language universals is through the examination of an increasing number of speech forms. The tremendous diversity in superficial detail from language to language is actually very helpful here. To some extent, the superstructure always hides the foundation. As a result only part is discernable even to the most careful investigator of any one language. Fortunately, it is not always the same parts that are hidden. If, then, what seems to be a fundamental feature appears in an Amazonian language, is also found in one from New Guinea, and is further suggested by a tongue from Central Asia, this may be a facet of the basic architecture of language. If it is, it will lie, more effectively hidden perhaps, behind the grammar of every language. Given a hint from field workers on these obscure and remote tongues, linguists can test the suggestion on other languages, including English.

Linguistic theory advances largely through the stimulation of new observations flowing in from the most unlikely sources. Today, when data is accumulating at a quickening pace, our understanding of language is deepening at an encouraging rate.

The study of English stands to gain more from linguistics in the future than it has in the past simply because linguists will have more to offer. It will have gained this both from intensive study of individual languages and from the careful comparison of one language with another. Much of the contribution will stem ultimately from remote tongues, often themselves of minor social or political importance or even on the verge of extinction.

Linguistics will serve not only to sharpen our analytic tools and so enable us to write better grammars, but also to put English into perspective as having certain features inherited from its past and shared by its relatives, as influenced from many directions, but primarily from the pervading Western European tradition, and as a language among languages sharing the common features of human speech.

Chapter 18

Literary Form and Style

In many ways the grammarian and the literary scholar seem remote from one another, and, indeed, the relationships between the two have not always been either cordial or understanding. If it can be said that the warfare of the "two cultures" exists within a single discipline, the most likely instance is between these two wings of the English profession.

Yet there is a great deal of similarity in methods and convergence in aims, once some superficial matters of terminology and technique can be laid aside. Both work with texts — actual samples of language use — and for both it is not the text itself that is central so much as something that lies concealed within the text. Both are interested in finding patterns — interrelations of various kinds between parts. Literary and linguistic patterns coexist, but not in such a way that either the literary scholar or the linguist can simply seek the one and neglect the other. Rather, they interact in various ways, so that neither can be fully understood without attention to both. Neither kind of scholar is interested solely in specific texts, but both seek principles that underlie the features of individual samples and that, therefore, characterize language or the literary use of language as effective systems of communication.

Linguists and literary scholars may operate with exactly the same material. Both, for example, might examine Spenser's *Faerie Queene*.[1] Such use of the same data is more likely with older materials than with contemporary. It is also perhaps more common with other literatures and languages than with English. The *Iliad* and the *Odyssey*, for example, have had a great deal of intensive work from both sides, and will continue to have.

---

[1] There is, in fact, a grammatical monograph on this text, Herbert W. Sugden, *The Grammar of Spenser's Faerie Queene*, 1936.

Working on the same materials, each might be expected to turn up results of interest and value to the other. That is, grammatical and literary scholarship should be complementary and mutually assisting. Indeed, this seems to be the case, for example, with the study of Homer. But there is little evidence in work on Modern English that either party recognizes any significant contribution from the other. Grammar and literary studies generally go their separate ways, most probably to the detriment of both.

There are, however, several problems which fall clearly into the purview of both approaches. In this chapter mention will be made of a sampling of such problems centering around literary form — particularly poetic — and style. Nothing more can be attempted than some broad principles, just enough to suggest how grammatical and literary scholarship come together in these areas.

POETIC FORM

In its broadest sense, poetry certainly transcends the boundaries of individual languages. But one specific poem cannot; it must first be English, French, Zulu, or some other speech form. Only after it has qualified as a sample of some specific language can the question be raised as to whether it is poetry or not, for a poem is always a text that uses the resources of its language in a characteristically poetic way. To give a general definition of poetry requires that this fact be taken account of. We shall say little about imagery, allusion, or any other characteristic of the content of the poem. Although these are important, it is on the poetic use of language that we must focus here.

We have said that a poem must first of all be in a language. By this we mean, of course, that it must follow the normal phonologic[2] and grammatical patterns of some language in one of its many variants. Perhaps a little license is occasionally permitted, but never much. That is, an English poem must first of all be English, just as a Japanese poem must first of all be Japanese.

The formal patterns which define a language are conventional. It is the grammarian's task to describe these, separately for each language, since they differ from language to language. A literary genre typically has a formal component which is also conventional, imposing further constraints beyond those of the phonology (or graphemics) and grammar of the language. These do not nullify or replace any of the patternings of the language — except occasionally in quite minor ways — but are superimposed and operate within the freedom that the language system allows.

[2] Poetry is with rare and insignificant exceptions basically an oral form. It may be composed in a very literary variety of the language, but if so, it is a spoken literary — comparable to the oral language used in reading aloud rather than that used in speaking. This is not necessarily the case in nonpoetic genres, many of which are clearly written for the eye. Poetry is for the ear, and the phonology is controlling.

In the case of poetry, some of these additional constraints are phonologic, that is, they can be stated in terms of phonemes. Rime is a familiar example; it can be precisely defined only in terms of a specifiable degree of similarity[3] of a specifiable sequence of phonemes. Meter is another; in English it can only be defined in terms of a certain patterning of stresses, elements in the English phonologic system. But poetic form may involve other phonologic features in other languages, and indeed has not always involved rime and the familiar types of meter even in English. In Old English each line had four stressed syllables, but no fixed number or arrangement of unstressed syllables, and the first three stressed syllables were alliterated,[4] that is, began with similar[5] consonants or with no consonant:

Fore	fytum	þu,	freond min Beowulf	
F	F		F	—
and for	ar-strafum,		usic	sohtest.
0	0		0	—

'You have sought us, friend Beowulf, for battles and for honor.'
(Beowulf 920, 921)

To obtain a definition that will transcend English, and indeed to obtain one that will cover all types of English poetry, it will not be possible to specify any kind or kinds of patterning as specific as rime or meter, but to provide for any sort of PHONOLOGICAL pattern whatever. We will accordingly define poetic form, or versification, as any conventional patterning superimposed on the normal (or near normal) phonologic structure required by the language in which the poem is composed. The three important components of this definition are (1) conventional, (2) superimposed, and (3) phonologic. Certain literary texts may show very significant patternings that do not meet all three conditions, but it will only confuse the issue if these are not treated under some other rubric.[6]

[3] The usual definition in terms of identity of pronunciation is inadequate. English-speaking poets quite happily use rimes that are not absolutely identical. The allowable departure from identity is set by convention — in exactly the same way that convention requires a certain rime scheme. These conventions are such that they make certain rimes acceptable to readers even when their phonology is different from that of the poet. That is, rime is largely neutral as between dialects.

[4] Or either the first or the second alone alliterated with the third. The fourth usually did not alliterate. The alliteration is indicated below the example, 0 indicating an alliteration of consonantless syllables. The nonalliterating stressed syllable is marked with a dash.

[5] OE alliteration is, like MnE rime, not a matter of identity but of definable similarity. It can best be described in terms derived from a linguistic description of OE phonology, but that alone is not enough. A full statement must indicate the required degree of similarity along each of the phonetic dimensions proper to the language.

[6] For example, if a modern English poem uses alliteration, this is not covered by the definition, since alliteration is not regulated by the basic conventions of MnE poetry. Instead, it would be a matter of style.

While a great deal of diversity in poetic forms can be demonstrated within English, even within MnE, it will be worthwhile to see an even greater range by examining versification in two other languages.

For our first example we will take classical dactylic hexameter. This was developed by the Greeks and is used in the Homeric literature. Latin phonology is similar to Greek in most of the respects significant for meter. As a result dactylic hexameter could be adapted to Latin with only minor modification. It is typographically easier to use a Latin example, the first seven lines of Virgil's *Aeneid:*

> *Arma virumque cano, Troiae qui primus ab oris,*
> *Italiam fato profugus, Lavinaque venit*
> *Litora multum ille et teris jactatus et alto,*
> *Vi superum saevae memorem Junonis ob iram,*
> *Multa quoque et bello passus dum conderet urbem,*
> *Inferetque deos Latio, genus unde Latinam,*
> *Albanique patres atque altae moenia Romae.*

Certain facts about Latin (or Greek) phonology must be kept in mind in order to understand the nature of classical hexameter. Latin vowels are either short or long. The orthography did not mark this contrast, but it is sometimes indicated in modern editions by a macron ⁻, and will be so marked below. Each vowel or diphthong is the nucleus of a syllable. Before it may be one or two consonants or none, and after it may be one or two consonants or none. Clusters within syllables are infrequent, initially mostly a stop plus /r/ or /l/, for example, /pr/, /tr/, /pl/. One consonant between two vowels normally belongs with the following syllable. Word division is of no significance in syllable structure, and hence not in meter.

The first unit in meter is the syllable. Syllables are, for metrical purposes, of two kinds. A light syllable ends in a short vowel. A heavy syllable ends in a long vowel, a diphthong, or a consonant. Syllable-initial consonants have no metrical significance. In metrical recitation, at least, a heavy syllable was pronounced twice as long as a light syllable.

A line of hexameter cannot be described directly in terms of syllables, but the latter are organized into another unit, the foot. In a hexameter there are only three types of foot: a spondee consists of two heavy syllables; a dactyl of one heavy and two light; a trochee of one heavy and one light. A line of hexameter consists of six feet. The last is either a spondee or a trochee. The other five may be either spondees or dactyls, though the fifth foot is almost always a dactyl. A trochee is always followed by a pause; considering this as equivalent in timing to a light syllable, every foot has a total length equal to four light syllables.[7]

The following transcription gives the same example with the syllables

---

[7] There are some additional constraints on classical hexameter, but these are not pertinent to the present discussion. One is mentioned on page 434.

separated and vowel lengths indicated. /q^u/ is a single phoneme, traditionally written with two letters, just as x is a single symbol for two phonemes /cs/. Elided vowels have been indicated by an apostrophe. Below each line the scansion is indicated. Heavy syllables are marked — and light ∪.

```
ar  ma vi |rum  qᵘe ca |nō  troi  |ae   qᵘī  |prī mu sa |bō ris

ī   ta li |am   fā     |tō  pro fu |gus  lā   |vī  na qᵘe |vē nit

lī  to ra |mult' mil   |le't tē    |rīs  jac  |tā  tu se  |tal tō

vī  su pe |rum  sae    |vae me mo  |rēm  jū   |nō  ni so  |bī ram

mul ta qᵘo|qᵘe't bel   |lō  pas    |sus  dum  |con de re  |tur bēm

in  fē    |ret  qᵘe de |ōs  la ti  |ō   ge nu |sun de la  |tī nām

al  bā    |nī   qᵘe pa |trē sat    |qᵘ'al tae |moe ni a   |rō mae
```

Classical Chinese poetry is in almost every respect different from that of Latin or Greek, but there is one fundamental similarity in that both are subject to phonologic constraints over and above the basic sound patterns of the languages. Poetic forms are necessarily different, of course, because the languages are different; hexameter would be impossible in Chinese, just as Chinese versification rules would not make any sense in Latin. But the two poetries differ more than their languages would force them to. Poetic forms are conventional, and radically different types of conventions have become established in the two traditions. Nevertheless, in both cases the conventions rest on the phonology of the language.

There are many details of classical Chinese phonology which are inaccessible to us. But while we have little precise information about phonetic details, we do know a good deal about phonemic patterning. For example, we can only guess at the pronunciation represented by such symbols as /i/, but we can be quite sure that the various syllables transcribed with /i/ all share some feature of pronunciation not found in syllables transcribed without /i/. This phonemic, rather than phonetic, information is, however, precisely what is needed to understand the versification of classical Chinese poetry. Indeed, it is largely because this information is what is needed to understand poetic form that we can be as sure of it as we are. The Chinese produced a number of very comprehensive riming dictionaries, that is, listings of phonemically similar syllables. These, with the evidence of modern Chinese pronunciations, enable us to reconstruct the ancient phonemic system.

Syllables not ending in /p/, /t/, or /k/ could be pronounced in several contrasting pitch patterns. That is to say, Chinese of the classical period had phonemic tone, as modern Chinese still does. In the transcription tones are written as diacritics above the syllables. Tones were — and are — basic constituents of the syllables, and indeed from the point of view of metrics the most important element, as classical Chinese poetry is based largely on tonal patterns. For metrical purposes, syllables fall into two types: *ping*, with the tone indicated — (perhaps indicating a level pitch) and non*ping*, having any other tone or ending in /p/, /t/, or /k/. For scansion non*ping* tones can be indicated by a slash /.

The example selected is of one of the shortest and most rigid forms of what may be called regulated poetry.[8] It consists of four lines, each of five syllables, and each having a caesura after the second syllable. Typically all lines must have different tone patterns, and in the example they do. In addition, there is a special relation between the patterns in lines one and two and in three and four. The first couplet shows this perfectly: Wherever line 1 has *ping*, line 2 has non*ping* and vice versa. Lines 3 and 4 show the maximum departure from this pattern that is allowable. They are to be considered as implying:

$$/ \ /, \ — \ — \ /$$
$$— \ —, \ / \ / \ —$$

Under certain circumstances breaks in the pattern are allowed in the first or the third syllable in the line, never in the other three. Finally, lines 2 and 4 rime — syllables rime if the tones are alike and if the vowel over which the tone is written and everything thereafter are alike. The example is as follows:

山	中	相	送	罷	— —, — / /
sɛ̇n	ţiɛ̆ŋ,	siɑ̄ŋ	suɨŋ	pħɛ̆i	
日	暮	掩	柴	扉	/ /, / — —
ņiɨ̇t	muɨ,	qiɛ̆m	tsħɛ̄i	pɨ̄ai	
春	草	明	年	綠	— /, — — /
ţşhiuɨ̄n	tsħɑ̆u,	miǣŋ	nɛ̄n	liɨk	
王	孫	歸	不	歸	— —, — / —
ħiuɑ̄ŋ	suɛ̄n,	kiŭɛ̄i	puət	kiŭɛ̄i.	

RIME

---

[8] Regulated poetry, of which there were several varieties, developed during the T'ang period. Other types of poetry, some of them much older, were also in use at the same time. What is described here, therefore, is only one of many Chinese poetic genres.

'Amid the hills we have taken leave of each other
And at evening I have shut the brushwood door.
When the spring grass is green next year
Will you, Sir, return or not?'
                    Parting by Wang Wei

If other poetries were examined, we would find other kinds of patterning. They may require definable similarity at certain points — rime, alliteration, assonance, or other patterns — or they may demand differences — as the tone balance in regulated Chinese poems. They may involve consonants, vowels, tones, stress, length, or any other phonologic feature. But the requirement of phonologic patterning is widespread and profitably studied as a basic feature of poetries.

CHOICE AND POETIC FORM

Certain requirements in the writing of classical hexameter are very rigid: Every line must have exactly six feet, and each foot must be equivalent in duration to four light syllables. However, there is also much freedom of choice within these strict prescriptions: The last foot may be either spondee or trochee, the others spondee or dactyl. The choice is not equally free at every place: there is a strong preference for a dactyl in the fifth foot, though a spondee may occasionally be used.

Six choices, each between two alternatives, permit a total of sixty-four different hexameter scansions. These range from

$$— — \;/\; — — \;/\; — — \;/\; — — \;/\; — — \;/\; — —$$

with no short syllables at all to

$$— \smile \smile \;/\; — \smile \smile \;/\; — \smile \smile \;/\; — \smile \smile \;/\; — \smile \smile \;/\; — \smile$$

with eleven. Five of the possibilities occur in the seven lines of the *Aeneid* quoted; more would, of course, be found in a longer passage. Different types of hexameters have different effects, most marked in the case of the more extreme. A skillful poet uses these differences to assist in conveying, or in highlighting, the impression he desires. That is to say, the choices may have a stylistic implication.

Not only so, but since there are different types of heavy syllables, there are further differences possible, and these too figure in the total impression made by any small part of the poem. For example, the sequence of consonants in the second foot of the third line (*mult' mil*) stands out prominently, giving a very different effect than, say, the last foot in the seventh line (*rōmae*). Both, however, are spondees. Not all feet of the same metrical type are stylistically equivalent.

There is, thus, a kind of style that operates within the poetic form.

It consists of a patterning of the options elected within the freedom of choice allowed by the versification. To meet the conventional requirements of the poetic form may require nothing more than cleverness — though when the rules are very strict it may require a very high order of cleverness. To meet them in a pleasing way, however — that is, to make an effective use of the choices — is a very different matter. It is here that a significant part of the poet's creative ability can be seen. The writing of good poetry is, then, both a craft and an art. Craftsmanship is conventionalized; art, that is style, is free. Both, however, have a component which is grounded in the phonology of the language and can be studied in detail and in depth only against the phonologic system of the language.

English poetry is of various kinds. Each kind has its own conventions of versification, and each leaves room for choice and hence for style. Each can be examined in terms of the way it uses the resources of English phonology. However, the principles that apply to all English poetry are very general, and their detailed working out can be seen only as they are applied to one type or one tightly knit group of types.

The commonest meter in English is iambic.[9] That is, a line is organized into feet — five is a common number — most of them iambs. Each iamb consists of two syllables with an accent on the second.

The iambic metric pattern must be rooted in English phonology in some way, as was hexameter in Latin or regulated poetry in Chinese. In the latter cases, this can be understood only by dividing the several types of syllables, as the phonology would describe them, into two types for metrical purposes. The distinction between heavy and light syllables is not a fact of Latin phonology, but a schematization of the phonology for a particular purpose. So likewise the distinction between *ping* and non*ping* is presumably not a basic distinction within Classical Chinese phonology, but a classification imposed for defining poetic form. There must be some similar schematization for English metrics.

English scansion is defined in terms of a two-way contrast between accented and unaccented. English phonology may be described as involving four stresses — in order: primary/ˊ/, secondary /ˆ/, tertiary /ˋ/, and weak /ˇ/. Basic to English poetics is a schematization that relates the two units of one system to the four of the other. This is more complex than its equivalents in either Latin or Chinese. Whereas a Latin syllable is, by itself, either light or heavy, and a Chinese syllable either *ping* or not, an

---

[9] The term "iamb" is of classical origin. In Latin or Greek it labeled a foot consisting of one light and one heavy syllable. Many of the classical types of feet have English namesakes, but their definition can be only superficially the same. To make the transfer, English accent is taken as equivalent to classical heaviness.

Modern English phonology is not hospitable, as was Latin, to the importation of Greek metrical patterns without drastic alteration. However, so important in our culture are the pan-Western literary patterns that classical scansion has been fundamentally reinterpreted to allow at least terminologic continuity.

English syllable can be identified as accented or unaccented only in a context. The rules are as follows:

1. A higher stress surrounded by lesser stresses is accented. /´/, the highest stress, is therefore usually accented, as in the following environments: /˘´˘/, /^´^/, /`´`/, and so on. But /`/, tertiary stress, can also be accented when flanked by /˘/.

2. A lower stress surrounded by heavier is unaccented. /˘/, the lowest stress, is usually unaccented, as in the following environments: /^˘´/, /`˘`/, /^˘`/, and so on. But /^/, secondary stress, can also be unaccented when flanked by /´/, a rather unusual occurrence.

3. The second of two identical stresses is accented, the first unaccented.

As a result of these rules, any one of the four stresses may count as accented, even weak stress when in a sequence of weak stresses. Conversely, any one of the stresses may count as unaccented, even primary when in the sequence /´ ´/. Without going into any further details,[10] there are, then, the following types of iambs:

```
 ´ ´
 ^ ´      ^ ^
 ` ´      ` ^      ` `
 ˘ ´      ˘ ^      ˘ `      ˘ ˘
```

With at least ten kinds of iambs to choose from in each foot, there would be some 100,000 differently scanning pentameter lines. No wonder there can be such a difference from one poem to another, even though both follow the same conventions!

Epstein and Hawkes make a detailed examination of twenty-one lines of *Samson Agonistes*. In this passage every one of the ten types of iambs is used at least twice. The commonest one, /˘´/, averages only once per line. This diversity of feet is one of the features of the poem which can be said to characterize its style.

For comparison, *Trees*, an iambic tetrameter of very different quality, contains nineteen feet of the form /˘^/ out of forty-eight and uses in all only seven of the total possible types of iambs. Part of the difference in style which anyone will sense between these two poems is reflected in this very different patterning: One tends to concentrate very heavily on a few kinds of iambs — generally those with sharp difference between the stresses. The other tends toward full exploitation of the resources of the iambic meter.

In both there are places where different interpretations are possible,

---

[10] See Edmund A. Epstein and Terence Hawkes, *Linguistics and English Prosody*, 1959. These authors further consider the junctures, thus giving more than the ten types of iambs listed here.

and another reading might give slightly different results. But no feasible reading could obscure the difference. Indeed, it is easy enough to exaggerate it. *Trees* seems to present a constant temptation to recital in a style that approaches / ˘ ˄ ˘ ˄ ˘ ˄ ˘ ´ ↘ /, that is, to simple singsong or doggerel. Such manner of recitation is perhaps possible with *Samson Agonistes* also, but rather than slipping into it, a reader must make a conscious effort to do so. Every verse is open to a doggerel rendition, some only with great difficulty, some easily, and some permit no other. This is associated with a range of style.

The preceding discussion may be very misleading. To make the point it was necessary to select examples for comparison that were grossly different. Another pair of poems, even with very obvious differences, might not show a significant contrast if nothing more were done than simply to count types of iambs. This is because counting neglects the most important feature of style, the patterning of the choices. Statistical studies always discard part of the data in order to concentrate attention on some selected bit. In the treatment of style, the simple statistical methods so far used discard the most significant part, and, therefore, are usually extremely crude and often totally unrevealing.

The patterns that exist within a poem are frequently subtle and very difficult to define, but good style is never simply random. It is one task of literary scholarship to delineate the stylistic patterns and to investigate how they contribute to the effect of a poem. To do so, of course, it is necessary not simply to be able to identify accented and unaccented syllables but also to distinguish the different kinds of iambs. For a yet more thorough study this must involve also an examination of junctures and various other features. That is to say, deep searching into poetic style requires a thorough understanding of English phonology.

STYLE AS CHOICE

Our discussion has concerned itself with one particular level of style, and indeed with only one aspect of that. A much broader definition along the same lines can profitably be made: Style is the patterning of choices made within the options presented by the conventions of the language and of the literary form. The key phrases here are 1) patterning of choices and 2) presented by the conventions. We have looked only at the phonologic options presented by the conventions of English and of iambic verse. Wider aspects of style can be seen in poetry as well as in other genres.

Perhaps the familiar kind of style that fits most obviously into this definition is that sometimes called "diction", the choice among synonyms or near synonyms. It is characteristic of languages that they have effectively equivalent expressions in their vocabularies. Some carry this to an extreme, seemingly having numerous words at hand to express any given idea.

English is certainly well supplied, but cannot match Arabic or Sanskrit in this regard.

Of course, no two words are precisely equivalent in all regards. If they were, the choice between them would be of little consequence.[11] For the most part, synonyms carry different associations or connotations and this makes their choice significant. Moreover, they fit into vaguely defined systems, so that it is meaningful to compare the choice made at one place with that made at another. Without this, it would be impossible to see patterning in the choices, and vocabulary would have little stylistic importance.

Among the information that we would like to get from a dictionary entry are the stylistic implications of a word. They are, however, very difficult to define precisely, and a lexicographer would have an impossible task if he were to undertake to do so for every item. A more feasible procedure is to give illustrative citations. If he is skilled, he picks sentences which indicate — largely by the other words in them — something of the stylistic values of the entry. To do this in all fullness is impossible, but then, a dictionary is not intended to be self-sufficient. A person acquires a basic feel for diction from wide reading. A lexicon cannot replace this, but it can and should supplement it at various points.

Less widely understood than diction, but in many ways more interesting, are the stylistic implications of grammatical constructions. Almost any sentence in the language has at least one synonymous agnate sentence. Many have a considerable number. The choice between these is not always entirely free. Sometimes the context will require one of the set rather than another. More often the context will weight the choice heavily in one direction or another. We have seen an analogue in poetic style: The fifth foot of a hexameter is almost always a dactyl; the poet's choice here is less free than at any other place in the line. So it is with sentence forms. In some positions the choice is quite free, in others it is more or less restricted, occasionally severely. Seldom is it completely closed. Moreover, the choice made at one point may alter the freedom of choice at another.

A convenient source of examples to show how grammatically equivalent structures can affect style is to be found in the many translations of the Bible. Many of these make a very strenuous effort to remain close to the meaning of the original and yet produce good, idiomatic English. Some pairs of versions are quite obviously different in style. Since they are saying

---

[11] In addition to the differences in connotation and stylistic affiliations, synonyms may differ significantly in phonology. One may have more syllables than another, a different pattern of stresses, or a different rime. They may then present a choice directly relevant to poetic form.

Phonologic differences between near-synonyms may be of value in prose also. For example, in one version of Chapter 15, I had written *casual is usual*. This was changed to *casual is expected* for purely phonologic reasons, here a matter of style since there is no phonologic constraint proper to the genre.

the same thing,[12] a point-by-point comparison is possible. This will reveal many places where the difference in effect is traceable to different choices between agnate constructions. An excellent pair of translations for this purpose is the Revised Standard Version and the New English Bible. Both are recent and both intend to use contemporary language. For example, Mark 1:19 reads as follows:

> RSV   *And*   *going on a little further, he saw James the*
> NEB   *When he had gone*   *a little further   he saw James the*
> *son of Zebedee and*   *John his brother, who were in their boat*
> *son of Zebedee and his brother John*   *, who were in the   boat*
> *mending   the   nets.*
> *overhauling their nets.*

There are two examples of lexical differences: RSV uses *go on* and *mend*, whereas NEB uses *go* and *overhaul*. These pattern with RSV's *preach* and NEB's *proclaim* in verse 14 and many other comparable instances. Such vocabulary choices contribute a great deal to the obvious stylistic contrast between the two translations.

The example also shows three differences of construction: RSV uses a sentence introducer, *and*, whereas NEB omits this. The use of *and* in this way reflects Greek patterns. It might be considered simply as a case of overliteral translation. However, it is so frequent in older translations that it has come to be a mark of Biblical style. The other two are *going* vs. *when he had gone* and *his brother John* vs. *John his brother*. Both these contribute significantly to the stylistic contrast. Both fit into patterns; compare in verse 16:

> RSV   *And*   *passing along by*   *the sea of Galilee,*
> NEB   *Jesus was walking*   *by the shore of the sea of Galilee*
> *he saw Simon and*   *Andrew the brother of Simon*
> *when he saw Simon and his brother Andrew*
> *casting a net into the sea;*
> *at work on the lake with a casting   net   ;*

This verse shows an even more far-reaching restructuring of sentences, involving several transformations and the addition or deletion of some material of little semantic significance. There are two excellent illustrations of stylistic use of anaphora. The NEB might have read *He was walking...* This would be perfectly clear, since *Jesus* appears in verse 14, and there is nothing else to which *he* might conceivably refer. Indeed the RSV has no difficulty using *he* as the subject in this verse. There is a genuine option here,

---

[12] Some may reject the notion that two sentences can mean the same thing and differ in style, on the grounds that style itself carries meaning. This is perhaps only a terminologic matter. I am using "meaning" of that which remains invariant through certain changes of sentence form. Stylistic effect may be meaningful, but it is not meaning in this sense. This distinction, whether using this label or not, is essential if style is to be identified and understood.

either the noun or the pronoun is quite acceptable. The choice made by the NEB has the effect of giving a little less close connection between verse 16 and what precedes. The second example is in *the brother of Simon* and *his brother*. The use of the proper name in the RSV gives a slightly archaic flavor, lacking in the NEB at this point.

Further comparison of the same sort will show that a very large part of the difference in style that is so evident between the Revised Standard Version and the New English Bible can be accounted for in terms of choices between synonymous words, between agnate constructions, and between patterns of anaphora.

Every sentence might present an author with innumerable choices. Probably he remains unaware of most of the options. At some points the selection is real but quite unconscious, at others he simply follows his own personal habits. Careful authors do choose deliberately at certain places, weighing the alternatives carefully, perhaps trying several before a final choice is made. Here is the witness of one to his own writing processes taken from a discussion of a point in Chinese poetics:

> Chinese, especially as written, is abundantly rhythmic, and often gives the impression of being artificially so cast. But real rhythm is a rhythm of real words, and it is difficult to imagine any people taking enjoyment in an imperfect melody patched up with noises. In writing the last sentence, which the author modestly considers euphonious, he hesitated between *actual* and *real* for the eighth word, weighed *hard* against *difficult*, and tried *enjoying* instead of *taking enjoyment in*. In each case the choice was made according to his personal conception of rhythm and style, but the alternatives were always living. We have no stock of thumps in English whereby a sentence can be pounded into rhythmic form, and unless there are strong reasons to the contrary, we should not assume such accessories in Chinese.[13]

Certainly the sentence under discussion presents many more choices than the three listed. Perhaps Kennedy chose to mention only these, though he had actually weighed a number of others. But he could not have considered every possibility with the same care. Some selections were probably simply random. Others were chosen in accordance with his established personal writing habits. Most of these went by unnoticed.

The advent of computer processing has reawakened interest in stylistic determination of authorship. The machine can count and tabulate vast multitudes of little features with inhuman accuracy. And this is precisely what is required. The notion is that each writer does favor certain choices in these unnoticed details. If enough of these are examined each writer will be seen to have an established profile of peculiarities that appear in any document he composes. If, then, we inspect two documents minutely, we may find either that the same combinations of features appear, suggesting identity of authorship, or that they are so disparate as to effectively rule

[13] George A. Kennedy, *A Study of the Particle* yen, 1940, JOAS 60:1–22.

out the possibility of the same writer. For the evidence to be meaningful, numerous patterns must be compared.[14] No handful can be sufficient to distinguish adequately between many thousands of possible authors. Moreover, the constant personal features must be distinguished from those which are deliberately controlled and varied for effect and from those which are merely random. This can be done effectively only if all aspects of style are thoroughly studied.

Perhaps underneath those variables which we manipulate for our literary purposes there are patterns as individual as fingerprints. If so, they are still personal choices — however habitual — within the over-all patterns of the language as it prevails in the community. Style is choice, whether it be made consciously or unconsciously, anew each time or semi-permanently. But not all choices are of the same significance.

PATTERNINGS OF STYLE

As we have digressed into distinguishing an author's persistent personal style from the style artfully used at a given place, we have tended to focus on individual choices. Choices are inevitable when we speak or write. But if all choices are either random or predetermined, style can be only haphazard or ineffective. It is the patterning of choices that makes style interesting. And the patternings may be fairly complex.

Perhaps an oversimple but familiar example will make the point as well as a more elaborate one. One variety of the run-on-sentence disease shows in compositions consisting of long sequences of quite unvaried clauses, all joined into one long chain by *and*. Its polar opposite seems to be "short choppy sentences", where a similar sequence of clauses is made into an equal number of sentences, all of the same pattern. Actually, the two are but different symptoms of the same fundamental difficulty. Each is the invariant use of a single technique of joining clauses. The stylistic failing is monotony.

In either case some improvement can often be made by a very simple expedient: merely mix the two kinds of transitions randomly. Variety, even when purposeless, seems better than a deadening uniformity. But the gain is usually small. Much more can be had by carefully selecting which transitions are to be marked with *and* and which by sentence separation. To make maximum use of the resources, the choices must be patterned in two regards. First, we must avoid, say, a simple alternation, but find a pattern

---

[14] Most of the efforts at establishing authorship by computer have been unconvincing. Too often they have examined only rather superficial features, frequently ones that may well be under conscious control, such as sentence length, or affected by the subject matter, such as vocabulary choice. The possibility of using computers for this purpose cannot be ruled out, but much more sophisticated programs will be required. Moreover, these must be based on a much more penetrating understanding of style and a large body of empiric data on styles.

which shows a proper balance of continuity and change within itself. Second, the patterning of clause transitions must be made to fit appropriately with other patternings in the passage, for example, the connection of sense from clause to clause. It is this twofold patterning that makes the style.

The example just discussed is much too restricted to be realistic, but it will take on significance as it is broadened to cover more of the possibilities for clause transition. Not only are connectives numerous in English, but they can be classified in at least three ways: by keys (deliberative English may use *thereupon*, consultative, *so then*), ranks (*but* joins smaller structures than does *however*), and types (coordinating as *and*, subordinating as *if*, with further subclassification, see p. 342). Selection of connectives from different ranks and types and their arrangement into patterns gives opportunity for interesting stylistic differences, even within one key.

Again, this can be looked at in two ways. First, there may be patterning internal to the system of clause transitions, a movement from one type to another and from one rank to another. Second, and often more significant, there may be external patterning, the interplay between this system and one or more others.

For example, a narrative has a structure in the form of a sequence of events and circumstances. These relate to one another in an internal pattern: One occurrence is a consequence of another and at the same time the background for a third. One feature relates to a whole complex of happenings, while another relates specifically to one detail only. As a whole, the pattern may be simple or very intricate. If we take this structure for the present as given — though, of course, it is also the work of the storyteller — we may ask how the patterning of clause connections matches.

In the simplest and most straightforward kind of narrative prose, the relationship is quite direct. Subordinate events are stated in subordinate clauses. Tightly connected facts are recounted in a single sentence, but more loosely associated ones are separated. That is to say, the structure of narrative and the structure of clause sequencing run as nearly parallel as the resources of the language permit. But in another kind of narrative prose, the parallelism is only partial. Occasionally a subordinate idea is made grammatically superordinate. At one place a series of events is stated in one long sentence, whereas another series just as closely connected is expressed by a number of short separate sentences. It is the patterning of one structure against another that is stylistically most significant.[15]

---

[15] Many passages in Rudyard Kipling's *The Jungle Books* show this technique carried to an extreme. Part of the quaintness of the style is ascribable to frequent coordination of clauses that are not logically closely connected, and subordination of a clause to another to which it is not logically subordinate. That this is so may be demonstrated by rewriting a passage, replacing transitions by ones more nearly in accord with normal usage, but making no other changes. The flavor is completely altered.

Another simple example of this interplay of two structures can be seen in poetry. Meter imposes a structure of units within units — perhaps of feet within verses, verses within couplets, and couplets within stanzas. (Different poetic conventions, of course, impose different patterns, and some make the structure much more rigid or more obvious than others.) The syntax of the passage involves another structure of units within units, words, phrases, clauses, sentences, and so on. Here, then, are two structures of the same general hierarchical type coexisting in the same text. They are seldom absolutely parallel, and they are probably never completely divergent. They may run closely together for a while and then separate, or they may continue throughout approximately parallel. Most often cuts coincide, but differ in rank in the two.

For example, in *Trees*, every clause end coincides with a line end. Four line ends are not clause ends, but all four are within couplets. That is to say, in this poem major grammatical boundaries coincide throughout with major metrical boundaries. In *Samson Agonistes* the situation is quite different. Clause ends come about as often within lines as at line ends. However, in the passage examined every line ends with a phrase boundary of some kind. There is thus much more than a simply random relationship between the two, but it is far from mere parallelism. Much of the effect of the poem is achieved by this subtle patterning.

Before the influx of Greek metrics, Latin poetry was based on stress. After the hexameter was introduced, the Romans retained something of their previous feeling for patternings of accent in their verse. This led to a compromise — the basis of the most evident differences between Latin and Greek hexameters — in which both stress and syllable length were taken account of. It was generally demanded that the two patterns run together at the ends of lines, but they were allowed — or better, preferred — to show more independence in the first part of the line. One consequence was a strong preference for disyllabic words at the ends of hexameters (six of the seven in the example), since this was the easiest way to obtain the necessary coincidence. Another was an additional dimension of poetic style, as the interrelation of the two was varied in the first part of the lines.

Taking a poem as a whole, the interweaving of the various patterns may be much more complex than any of the examples mentioned. There are, of course, a number of independently variable systems, all of which may contribute in some measure to the style of a text. Seldom does any one carry more than a small share of the whole stylistic burden.

Quite typically, through the greater part of a text these strands are woven together in such a way as to give no particular prominence to any one feature, but to give an interesting background texture to the whole. It is much like the slight irregularities in the thread, and perhaps also in the dyeing, which give an interesting texture to handspun cloth. A sort of pattern is there, but it is seen as a whole rather than as a collection of parts.

The whole of a text may be of this sort, but equally often this unobtrusive variation is only the background against which a few selected features are made to stand out.

This sort of prominence is often given by the simultaneous occurrence of a number of features in various strands of the structure. A striking word, an unusual phonologic pattern, an emphatic word order, an unusual figure — any of these may give a small measure of prominence within the structure to which it belongs. But in most instances, this minor prominence sinks into the general texture because it is not reinforced by other features. But let these coincide — say, an unusual word is placed in the riming position in its verse and further strengthened by alliteration, or by primary stress — and this point stands out from the background. Unless prominence is desired, the writer must carefully keep the various patterns out of step one with another, maintaining in each the amount of variation needed to produce the proper texture. However, where prominence is needed, the patterns must be made to converge, each reinforcing the other.

An interesting extension of this principle has recently come to attention in connection with Bible translation. The most widely used Spanish version is the Reina Valera. This uses very elegant and somewhat archaic language. It is therefore quite difficult for many people, particularly those for whom Spanish is a second language. To meet their needs, a translation in a much simpler kind of language is being produced. It has been found, as might have been expected, that it is indeed possible to attain very much the same level of fidelity to the original in a very different style from that of the Reina Valera. That is to say, the same message can be put into Spanish in a variety of ways, ranging from extremely simple to very elaborate. Comparable simple versions are now being prepared in a number of other languages including English.

It might seem that a translator for such a rendition should settle on a level of difficulty and stick with it throughout. Experience shows that this invariably produces an unsatisfactory result. The chief complaint of the reader is LACK of uniformity. To make it appear uniform, it must in fact be made nonuniform. The message varies widely in its own complexity. At one place there is straightforward narrative, at another, involved and very condensed theological reasoning. The language must vary inversely, becoming simpler when the argument becomes difficult, and more elaborate when the argument is simpler. This condensation pushes the variation in the message into the background, where for easy reading it must be.

FOREGROUNDING

One general type of style is characterized by a fairly uniform background. Selected features are pulled into the foreground and given greater or lesser prominence as suits the author's purposes. This can be done in a number of ways. One has been mentioned — the coincidence of several small features, which if used out of concert form the background texture. This is a delicate device, and its effective use requires skill and foresight. It is perhaps more characteristic of enduring literature than of the more ephemeral language of every day.

Less subtle devices are more commonly heard in oral English. One of these is a sudden, often drastic shift in the variety of language. The very unexpectedness of such a change produces a sharp discontinuity which almost inevitably brings prominence of some sort to the point at which it occurs. For example, occasionally a speaker will outline an elaborate argument using deliberative English, perhaps in a fairly formal and polished style. Then suddenly the effect is shattered by *But it just ain't so!*, a locution which not only contrasts strongly in key with the language that has preceded but also has in itself a certain shock value. All this may be reinforced by its phonologic treatment — perhaps a slower, more measured delivery and often short pauses on both sides. This stylistically intrusive sentence marks a change in direction of the whole presentation. In most cases, the speaker returns immediately to deliberative English and then endeavors to demolish the previous argument, point by point.

Less strong, but still quite dramatic, can be the use of a "slangy" expression. (That is, one using words of the sort labeled in dictionaries as "slang", usually recent promotions into consultative use, but still remembered by the conservative as less than fully respectable. Real and current slang is usually too little known to be generally understood.) The same effect can be had by an opposite shift. The sudden intrusion of a decidedly deliberative English pattern into a consultative matrix will do much the same, particularly if reinforced by the delivery. It is the mismatch, the sudden change, that produces the effect.

Indeed, this can be heightened by making the intrusion not only a break with the general context but even incongruous in itself. I once heard a college admissions officer speaking to a group of high school students in a somewhat relaxed but still formal way. Into this came the sentence *I kid thee not!*, a shift simultaneously to consultative vocabulary and to archaic (and therefore effectively very formal) structure. In no sense was this artistic, but it certainly did give prominence.

In a discussion of literary style, such examples seem almost out of place. But the same technique can be used with much more finesse, and hence a quite different effect. Of the well-respected poets, probably the one who most often uses a shift in language is Robert Burns. In a poem in Scots, a point may be foregrounded by use of standard English. More rarely, he uses the opposite device in an English poem.

In most cases, this technique can be thought of as merely shifting from one variety of the language to another, much as one might shift if he were to include a Latin quotation. But it can be viewed in another way. Each type of English has its own proper set of conventions, not of course wholly different from those of other types, yet certainly distinctive. A shift of key, for example, is evident only when the intrusive bit exhibits one or more features in which the conventions of the two keys differ — that is to say, only if in some respects there is what amounts to a deliberate breach of conventions.

Discussions of style from a linguistic background have tended to fall into two approaches. One emphasizes style as choice within the patterns of the language. The other stresses the stylistic significance of breaches of the patterns.[16] Some of the difference between these points of view rests in one's view of the language system. A broader and more flexible kind of grammar allows for more choice within, and a more rigid makes more to be infractions. But beyond this, both have something to contribute to a total understanding of style. Each approach handles certain aspects of style better than the other.

We are most familiar with departures from normal language structures in poetry, where they are often referred to collectively as "poetic license". Words may be shortened or lengthened to fit the meter or unnaturally stressed. Word orders not used in prose are fairly common. An interesting and rather simple example can be seen in the following metrical psalm:

> The King of Love my shepherd is,
> Whose goodness faileth never.
> I nothing lack, if I am His,
> And He is mine forever.

The first line must be considered as a subject and a predicate nominative both preceding the verb. A more normal order would be either *The King of Love is my shepherd* or *My shepherd is the King of Love*. It is not at first sight clear which of these two to consider as behind the inversion in the verse.[17] (Actually there would be little difference in meaning in any case!) One reason for this uncertainty is that an inversion of order in a copulative sentence is so unusual that there is no established pattern, that is to say, the phenomenon can be considered as lying outside the regular conventions of English.

The inversion of other types of complements is not unusual. The third line includes an instance, *I nothing lack*, and many can be found even in everyday speech, though today more common in fixed expressions like

---

[16] This view has been most thoroughly developed in eastern Europe. Much of the most important work is in Czech and deals with Czech literature. A suggestive sampling has been made available in English in Paul L. Garvin (ed.), *A Prague School Reader on Esthetics, Literary Structure, and Style*, 1964.

[17] There is a basis for choice, but it would not be immediately apparent to most people. Proper nouns are more often subjects than predicate nominatives. *The King of Love* can be construed as a proper noun; the capitalization indicates this, for one thing. On this basis the underlying sentence must be: *The King of Love is my shepherd*.

This I must see. There are various motivations for sentence inversions in prose, a few of which will be mentioned below. None of them, however, is likely to produce the inversion of a predicate nominative such as we have just seen. Rime or scansion, on the other hand, might provide a motivation.[18] It would, therefore, be possible to say that the difference between prose and poetry is not in what is allowed, but what is motivated. Much of "poetic license", then, consists only in the slightly more common use of constructions that are permissible but extremely rare in nonpoetic discourse.

In this manner we might shift the emphasis toward viewing style as choice among permitted alternatives and away from seeing it as controlled infraction of conventions. In any case, there are some limits on the possibilities. If the rules are breached they can be breached only in some small degree, and not too frequently within any one text. In a sense it is a little like the folklore about highway laws: It is permissible to exceed the speed limits, but ordinarily only by about five miles per hour. If this were so, it would perhaps be better to consider that the effective legal limit is five miles above that which is posted. Moreover, of course, as most drivers know, if the limit be exceeded it is even more important that every other aspect of one's driving be unexceptionable. If you must go forty in a thirty-five mile zone, stay in your lane!

The last part of the analogy is as good as the first. Infractions of language patterns — or exceptional constructions — must be used singly in other than the most exceptional circumstances.

In Elizabethan times a great deal of attention was given to figures and schemes of rhetoric. This was basically a heritage from the classical rhetoricians, particularly Cicero and Quintilian. An extremely elaborate terminology and classification was worked out.[19] Peacham in 1577 listed as many as 184 named types. Among them were "schemes of words", such as prosthesis, the addition of an initial syllable; epenthesis, the addition of a medial syllable; diastole, stressing an unstressed syllable; antisthecon, change of a vowel to provide a rime; and so on. Then there was a group called "schemes of construction", including tmesis, the interrupting of a compound; eclipsis, the omission of certain words; polysyndeton, the use of excess conjunctions, and so on. Many, but not all, of these are easily

---

[18] In the verse cited above, the motivation is clearly rime. In Longfellow's *The Builders* it is just as clearly scansion:

> *Nothing useless is, or low;*
> *Each thing in its place is best;*
> *And what seems but idle show*
> *Strengthens and supports the rest.*

[19] A thorough discussion of Elizabethan rhetoric can be found in Sister Miriam Joseph, *Shakespeare's Use of the Arts of Language*, 1947, or in the paperback abridgment, *Rhetoric in Shakespeare's Time*. Specific facts in this section are from this source.

considered as infractions of conventions. Interestingly, some of them are now very rarely used in most prose, but perhaps more common in advertising copy than anywhere else.

The most frequently used and most important of the figures that involve clear breach of established patterns are those that work at the semological stratum. The metaphor, for example, when fresh and not yet reduced to a cliché, is simply one pattern for using a word in a meaning not hitherto associated with it. Our attitude toward semological innovations is in sharp contrast to that toward grammatical, phonologic, or orthographic inventions. Metaphor is prized, and is almost a necessity in certain kinds of writing. Other deviations are, at best, tolerated. In principle, there is little basic difference. Nonconformity, one might protest, is always nonconformity. However, in English literature, the limits writers have learned they must respect are quite different — wide in semology, narrow in grammar.

These limits cannot be codified. Nor, when the choices can be specified, can the basis of choice be reduced to rule. What is required of a writer is that he know the resources of his language, that he have a flair for creation, and that he be judicious.

Chapter 19

Clarity, Redundancy, and Ambiguity

Style, as we have defined it, has many facets. The writer's choices must meet a number of demands, often at variance and sometimes sharply opposed. Writing, then, becomes a series of compromises between competing requirements and the bypassing, or even skillful exploitation, of unresolvable conflicts. It is never sufficient to ask what, in any given place, is the most artistic use of language. Rather, what must be sought is that use which most successfully meets all the desiderata while maintaining some over-all unity of treatment.

In the last chapter, grammar, literary form, and style were set one against the other. It was suggested that these three show a kind of precedence in the order listed. Only quite exceptionally may the demands of style override those of grammatical structure or the conventions of the genre. For this reason, we started from a definition of style that subordinates it to the grammatical system of the language and secondarily to the literary conventions.

Style, itself, is no simple entity. Within it are at least four general qualities of a text that must be balanced one against another. These, however, do not fall into any fixed order of precedence. A writer is free to stress any one more heavily than the others, though only in very special situations dare he totally neglect any. In most writing, the four must be kept in balance.

The first of these four qualities of a text, artistry, is certainly the most difficult to define. Probably no part of it is open to full specification in terms derived from grammar, though of course, like every other aspect of style, it is based on the language resources, grammatical and other. Much of what was said about style in Chapter 18 applies to its artistic component — and to other aspects of style as well — and little more will be added here.

The remaining three qualities of a text we will present under the rubrics of clarity, redundancy, and ambiguity. Each of these falls in large part under our general definition of style. Each is of considerable interest as a point of contact between English grammar and the study of literature or the teaching of composition.

CLARITY

It is possible, as every composition teacher is painfully aware, for a passage to be grammatically correct under the strictest application of the rules, yet fail in some other quality, seemingly rather closely akin to grammar. The exact nature of the difficulty is often hard to specify. In grading papers, "awkward" is commonly written against the focus of the trouble. While this does locate the problem, it does not identify it. The notation gives the student no aid in correcting it. He knows nothing else to do but to try again, more or less at random. The teacher is frequently unable to give any specific help, not even to indicate in the most general way what is awkward about the passage. A more precise diagnosis might be more effective in suggesting a cure, both for the individual case and for recurring types of awkwardness.

Much of what is labeled "awkwardness" is simply the antithesis of a stylistic quality which we will designate as clarity. Neither will be precisely defined, but, in general, clarity is a quality of a text — apart from any character of the content — which makes it possible to read it easily and smoothly. There are a variety of difficulties that interfere with clarity, and therefore commonly receive the comment "awkward". Some of these, at least, can be fairly easily specified in ways that suggest precise techniques for treatment. Such awkwardness is the result of undesirable choices within the grammatical options. The opposite choices, therefore, may remedy the difficulty. Many grammatical alternatives in English seem to have as their chief function the avoidance of awkwardness or the improvement of clarity. Others make contributions to several aspects of style, clarity among them.

Of the many kinds of awkwardness, we shall examine and exemplify only three: front-heaviness, excessive embedding, and poor transitions. Probably several others can also be defined, diagnosed, and treated, as these can be, in grammatical terms.

FRONT-HEAVINESS

The following is an almost classic example of one kind of "awkwardness".[1] It is grammatically correct in every detail, as may be seen by

---

[1] This example is from Victor H. Yngve, *A Model and an Hypothesis for Language Structure*, 1960, Proc. Amer. Philosophical Soc. 104:444–466. The notion of front-heaviness is largely a restatement of Yngve's depth hypothesis in a form that is easier to apply, though not, perhaps, so elegant. Similarly, in the following section, the use of example (27) derives from the same source.

thorough parsing, but it is quite difficult to read — one tends to lose track somehow in the process.

> *If what going to a clearly not very adequately staffed school really means is little appreciated, we should be concerned.*　　　　(1)

There is a fairly simple and straightforward technique by which the chief difficulty in a sentence such as this can be precisely identified and then corrected. The next several pages will be devoted to showing this step by step. In the course of the demonstration, some other problems — in part side effects of the treatment — will come to light, but their discussion will be postponed to the last. We will agree that the sentence will be maintained intact — though further improvement might well be made by dividing it — and we will make only such changes as can be made by specifiable grammatical rules. A writer or composition teacher might want to make other changes for other reasons, but the purpose of this presentation is to point out some of the ways in which the sentence can be improved by the application of statable rules based on grammatical principles.

Sentence (1) is complex, falling clearly into two subsentences,[2] as is recognized in the punctuation:

> *if what going to a clearly not very adequately staffed school really means is little appreciated*　　　　(2a)

and

> *we should be concerned*　　　　(2b)

These two are quite disparate in length.

There is a principle of English style that can be stated somewhat as follows: If, in any two-part construction, there is an appreciable difference in length between the two, then it is usually preferable for the shorter one to precede. Note that this is expressed in terms of a preference. It is this feature that makes the rule one of style rather than of grammar. A convenient designation for a construction which runs counter to this preference is "front-heavy". The sentence under discussion clearly presents a case of front-heaviness. It should be stylistically improved (perhaps only in small measure, of course), if the subsentences are reversed. Whether such reversal is possible and how it is to be done is a matter to be determined by the grammar of the language.

Any native speaker of English will see immediately that the inversion of the two subsentences (2a) and (2b) is easily possible. This is not a feature

---

[2] That one of these can be further divided need be of no concern at this stage. The term "subsentence" rather than "clause" is used to emphasize the fact that the internal structure of the unit is not relevant at this point.

specifically of this sentence, but rather of any sentence of the same type. That is, a general grammatical rule can be stated:

$$\text{if } X, \text{ (then) } Y \Leftrightarrow Y, \text{ if } X \tag{3}$$

This rule is of the type that most often has stylistic significance; it relates pairs of synonymous agnate constructions.

The application of the inversion rule (3) to sentence (1) produces the following:

> *We should be concerned, if what going to a clearly not very adequately staffed school really means is little appreciated.* (4)

This version impresses some people as slightly better, but others see no improvement. The reason is clear: we have removed only one instance of front-heaviness, and perhaps not the most serious one. What was originally the first part, and is now the second, divides obviously into *if* and all the rest. Certainly there is no trouble here. But this remainder divides into:

> *what going to a clearly not very adequately staffed school really means* (5a)

and

> *is little appreciated* (5b)

Another reversal of order is called for, and this is most easily done on the basis of a general grammatical rule:

$$\text{Clause is } X \Leftrightarrow \text{it is } X \text{ Clause} \tag{6}$$

This is sometimes called the "*it*-inversion". Taking (5a) as *Clause*, and *little appreciated* as X, this rule may be applied to sentence (4), giving:

> *We should be concerned, if it is little appreciated what going to a clearly not very adequately staffed school really means.* (7)

This is better, perhaps, but still awkward.

Again, close examination points to front-heaviness, this time within the fragment (5a), which seems to break down into three parts:

> *what* (8a)
> *going to a clearly not very adequately staffed school* (8b)
> *really means*[3] (8c)

The trouble seems to arise from the long element (8b) preceding the

---

[3] *What* is part of the predicate here, shifted forward in forming a relative clause. A good case might be made for considering this construction to have only two constituents, the second being *really means what*. The structure is front-heavy in any case.

markedly shorter (8c). These can be reversed by application of another slightly different form of the *it*-inversion.

> *We should be concerned, if it is little appreciated what it really means going to a clearly not very adequately staffed school.*   (9)

This does not seem to be an improvement. Two things can be picked out as sources of the new infelicity in (9). Both are side effects of the changes made so far to remove front-heaviness. Each of these might be corrected at this stage, but we will hold them in abeyance and examine version (9) for any further instance of front-heaviness.

There is clearly one more occurrence of the trouble we are focusing on:

> *clearly not very adequately staffed | school*   (10)

The preferred position for any such complex modifier is after the head. This preference is a special case of the dislike for front-heaviness. If it is shifted, the result is:

> *a school, clearly not very adequately staffed*   (11)

However, simply to shift the participial phrase makes little improvement, though it does provide a base for further changes that will produce a better sentence. The first of these is to make the long modifier into a relative clause, using another very general grammatical relationship:

$$N \ X \Leftrightarrow N \begin{Bmatrix} which \\ that \end{Bmatrix} is \ X$$

where X is either an adjective phrase or a participle with or without modifiers. This gives:

> *a school that is clearly not very adequately staffed*   (13)

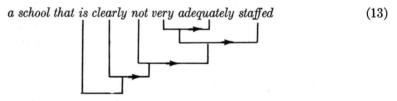

A dislike for piled up modifiers can be placated by shifting *clearly* to modify the whole predicate. If this is done, *not* will almost automatically shift its relationship, becoming attached to *is*. The grammatical principles involved were suggested on page 395.

> *a school that clearly is not very adequately staffed*   (14)

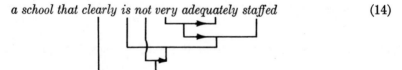

The result of all these changes is as follows:

We should be concerned, if it is little appreciated what it really
means going to a school that clearly is not very adequately staffed. (15)

This is not yet a good sentence, but we would claim that it is better than the original version (1), and in particular that it is greatly improved in one respect, clarity. The reader no longer loses track, but is able to keep the development clearly in mind from beginning to end. The difficulties have been found and eliminated by the use of techniques based directly on grammatical principles: first, patterns that enabled us to segment each construction into ICs and so pinpoint the problems, and second, rules that guided us in inverting. Grammar, therefore, has been shown to be relevant to more than mere correctness, having an essential part to play in achieving clarity as well.

However, in the process of correcting front-heaviness, we have introduced two new difficulties. To fully substantiate the claim of grammar's relevance to style, it will be necessary to pick these up again and show that they too can be diagnosed and treated in a similar way, that is, by techniques based on, but not subsumed by, grammar.

One difficulty is the occurrence of two *it*-inversions. The familiar school rule against the repeated use of the same word — when properly qualified, as we will see below — applies to constructions as well. We would, therefore, like to eliminate one of the two *it*-inversions. One way to do so in some cases is by a rule that can be roughly stated as follows:

$$\textit{it is V-en X} \Leftrightarrow \textit{there is V-nom of X} \tag{16}$$

In this formula, *V-en* stands for a participle and *V-nom* for a noun formed from the same stem by a nominalizing suffix. There are a variety of such suffixes, but such a noun is not formed from every verb. For *appreciate*, however, the required noun is in common use, and hence readily available. We may, therefore, make the change:

$$\textit{it is little appreciated what} \Leftrightarrow$$
$$\textit{there is little appreciation of what} \tag{17}$$

The second difficulty that we noticed but left for later attention was with the use of *going*. Verbs with their complements can be used in non-predicate positions if marked with either *to* or *-ing* (see p. 323). In most places these are interchangeable, though in a few contexts there is a subtle difference of meaning. Much more often the only contrast is stylistic. In this sentence, *to go* seems preferable to me. Making both changes we finally bring sentence (1) to the following form:

We should be concerned, if there is little appreciation of what it
really means to go to a school that clearly is not very adequately
staffed. (18)

There are several other options by which the infelicities of sentence (15) might have been removed. We will not state the grammatical rules on which they are based, but simply show two additional alternatives:

> *We should be concerned, if it is little appreciated what is the real meaning of going to a school that clearly is not very adequately staffed.* (19)

> *We should be concerned, if there is little appreciation of the real meaning of going to a school, that clearly is not very adequately staffed.* (20)

These are not all equally good,[4] but the choice among them must be made on some basis other than clarity — artistic effect, perhaps. Indeed, the difficulties with sentence (15), which stimulated us to try some further alterations, were very rudimentary matters of artistry. The requirements of clarity may exclude, or weight the choices heavily against, some versions of a sentence, but they seldom leave the writer without some effective choice by which he can seek to meet the demands of other aspects of style.

As we have seen in earlier chapters, a sentence can be analyzed on the basis of repeated divisions into immediate constituents.[5] That fact has been the basis of the discussion in this section. If we underline all but the last constituent in each construction — in most instances, the first of two — we can see something of what we have done and why it affects clarity. There will ordinarily be one line terminating with each word in the sentence except the last. The length of the lines will vary from a single word to many. This is shown below for both the initial and final versions of our example.

If what going to a clearly not very adequately staffed school

really means is little appreciated, we should be concerned. (1)

We should be concerned, if there is little appreciation of

what it really means to go to a school that clearly is not

very adequately staffed. (18)

---

[4] For example, two occurrences of *-ing* close together is not good. The most likely way to resolve this would be by substituting a synonym, giving perhaps: *what is the real significance of going* in (19). However, in this section we are restricting discussion to grammatical changes. Many would also want to eliminate one or all of *really, clearly,*

The difference between the two versions is striking. In sentence (1), one word, *very*, is marked six times as being included in a first constituent, and three other words are underlined five times. In the second, only one word reaches three. An underline represents unfinished business that the hearer or reader must keep in mind if he is to follow the sentence as it is presented to him. The average load in version (1) is almost as great as the maximum in version (18).

Careful reading of good expository writing will reveal many instances where sentence inversions seem to be motivated by a desire to avoid front-heaviness. The easiest way to see this is often to reconstruct an equivalent sentence which has a more basic order and compare the two. Sentences (21), (23), and (25) are as found,[6] (22), (24), and (26) are in uninverted order.

Thus there arose an important new type, the upside-down spider which hangs from the filaments with toothed tarsal claws. (21)

×An important new type, the upside-down spider which hangs from the filaments with toothed tarsal claws, arose thus. (22)

It appears highly improbable that chemical action is the cause of more than a slight dulling of the sharpest angularity of quartz grains. (23)

×That chemical action is the cause of more than a slight dulling of the sharpest angularity of quartz grains appears highly improbable. (24)

To the electrical engineer this large current density suggests several lines of application: miniaturization of components, very high power levels or — perhaps most interesting — a means of attaining the high "information rates" required in electronic devices ranging from fast oscilloscopes to compact X-ray machines for studying high speed phenomena. (25)

×This large current density suggests several lines of application, miniaturization of components, very high power levels or — perhaps most interesting — a means of attaining the high "information rates" required in electronic devices ranging from fast oscilloscopes to compact X-ray machines for studying high speed phenomena, to the electrical engineer. (26)

---

very. This raises, however, another kind of question, also outside the limits set at the beginning of the discussion. See page 460 for this.

[5] There is, of course, no agreement either on the use of ICs or the details of division. This, however, affects the argument in only minor ways. The formulation "all but the last constituent" is designed to make it applicable to a slot-and-filler analysis as well. The resulting underlining will be very little different from that obtained by a strictly binary IC analysis.

[6] Sentences (21), (23), (25), (36–39–40), (43–44), (46) are taken from various issues of the *Scientific American*. This journal has a justifiable reputation for good semitechnical scientific writing.

EMBEDDING

A second example will show a somewhat different variety of awkwardness. For this we may start from a passage from a familiar bit of folklore:

> *This is the dog that worried the cat that killed the rat that ate the malt...*   (27)

It is easy enough to describe the formation of a sentence such as this in terms of a number of short clauses and a transformation discussed on page 338. Stated as simple sentences, these clauses would be:

> *This is the dog.*
> *The dog worried the cat.*
> *The cat killed the rat.*
> *The rat ate the malt.*   (28)

Now suppose our interest shifted so that we wanted to start from

> *This is the malt.*   (29)

The first step would be to change *The rat ate the malt* to *that the rat ate*, and insert this relative clause immediately after *the malt*. The result is a quite satisfactory sentence:

> *This is the malt that the rat ate.*   (30)

The next step would be to form the relative clause, *that the cat killed* and insert this immediately after *the rat:*

> *This is the malt that the rat that the cat killed ate.*   (31)

Something is definitely wrong, and it gets worse at the next step:

> *This is the malt that the rat that the cat that the dog worried killed ate.*   (32)

Though formed by the rules, and hence strictly grammatical, this is now totally unintelligible except by a process of meticulous dissection. Here is sentence awkwardness carried to the extreme. Yet the original sentence continued on without trouble: *...that lay in the house that Jack built.* Why is it that sentence (27) can continue seemingly without limit, whereas (31) is very awkward and (32) hopeless?

The test for front-heaviness will immediately show where the trouble is: *that the rat that the cat that the dog worried killed | ate.* Yet it seems so much worse here than in sentence (1) that we must conclude that, if this is the same disease, it represents a particularly virulent strain. It certainly deserves some special treatment.

When one clause is inserted in this way into another, interrupting it, we may say that it is embedded. We have in (32) an example of embedding within embedding within embedding. From the point of view of English grammar, this can go on forever — the rules merely specify that a noun phrase be identical in any two sentences to permit one to be inserted as a relative clause into the other. From the point of view of English style the limit is very quickly reached. The option to embed cannot always be elected without dramatic consequences. Excessive embedding is a serious fault in writing—and rather common, even if extreme instances like (32) are infrequent.

Suppose, however, that we did in fact want to start with *this is the malt* and pack all the rest into the same sentence. There is a way we can do this. As a first step, the simple sentences can all be inverted to passive:

> *This is the malt.*
> *The malt was eaten by the rat.*
> *The rat was killed by the cat.*
> *The cat was worried by the dog.* (33)

Now, using the same procedure as before, we get:

> *This is the malt that was eaten by the rat that was killed by the cat*
> *that was worried by the dog.* (34)

And such a sentence can be continued indefinitely: . . . *that was owned by the man that*. . . If we use passive forms starting from *this is the dog*, we again get into a totally impossible muddle.

One important function of such sentence inversions as the passive is to assist, in certain sentences, in avoiding front-heaviness or excessive embedding. It does this by virtue of the fact that it reverses the order of major sentence elements, bringing either actor or undergoer to the end position where modifiers can be attached without embedding.[7]

POOR TRANSITION

The two types of awkwardness discussed above are features of a single sentence — kinds of structure that make it difficult to see the relationships within the sentence. There are similar phenomena which affect larger constructions. They obscure the relationships between sentences. In correcting compositions, these are sometimes labeled "awkward transition" or "unclear reference", or something of the kind. These rubrics, like the

---

[7] Only two functions of the passive are commonly mentioned: to avoid mention of the actor, and to emphasize the undergoer. "Emphasis" is a very indefinite concept, so that the second of these is very imprecise. Actually, many of the instances which are usually considered as emphasizing might better be treated as efforts to meet the demands of clarity. In scientific exposition, of the type represented in *Scientific American*, avoidance of front-heaviness seems to be the commonest use, followed by inversion for smooth transition. Writers of this kind of prose seem to show no particular reluctance to state the actor — *we* and *I* are both rather common.

comment "awkward", cover a variety of pathologies which deserve to be distinguished and more precisely diagnosed.

A smooth transition is often obtainable by selecting the proper form of a sentence. The following example will indicate how this works. One sentence is given in three versions, (37), (38), and (39). Each of these should be read in context, that is, between (36) and (40), as a continuous sequence of four sentences.

> *One person in five shows no alpha rhythm at all — only small, complex, irregular pulsations from all parts of the brain, with no fixed frequency. In one in five also the alpha rhythms go on even when the eyes are open.* (36)

We have established a tentative classification of brain types in human beings on the basis of such personal differences.	*A tentative classification of brain types in human beings has been established on the basis of such personal differences.*	*On the basis of such personal differences we have established a tentative classification of brain types in human beings.*
(37)	(38)	(39)

> *This system indicates differences in ways of thinking, rather than the relative success of people's thinking, as "intelligence tests" do.* (40)

Sentence (37) is the uninverted form. Sentence (38) is the passive (with *by us* from *we* dropped out as it almost certainly would be in this context). Sentence (39) has the adverbial phrase moved up to presubject position. In isolation all three are quite acceptable and very nearly equally good; at least there is no problem of front-heaviness or embedding in any of them.

However, as soon as the preceding and following context is read with them, sentence (39) becomes evidently superior to the other two. This can be only because it makes a better transition from the sentence before, to the sentence after, or at both places. To see how this obtains, it is convenient to consider the sentence as having three major components: a) *we have established* or *has been established*, b) *a tentative classification of brain types in human beings,* and c) *on the basis of such personal differences.* These are indicated in the diagrams below by the words *established, classification,* and *differences* — the key words in each fragment. The previous context, though it does not contain the word, is talking about differences. The following context is concerned with classification, indicating this by the use of a synonym *system.* We may, then, show the structure in which we are interested by the following diagrams:[8]

---

[8] I find useful an analogy with dominoes, where plays are made so that the end of one matches the abutting end of another. Unfortunately, the game is not popular today, and the comparison loses some of its punch.

differences (36)	established (37)	classification	differences	system (40)

differences (36)	classification (38)	established	differences	system (40)

differences (36)	differences (39)	established	classification	system (40)

Version (39) has the effect of bringing the sentence element concerned with differences next to the context dealing with the same topic, and the sentence element dealing with classification next to the context for which *system* is the keynote. Other things being equal, putting likes together in this way smooths the transition from one sentence to another. Sentence inversions of all kinds, therefore, find an important function in English prose in easing transitions from sentence to sentence. The more complex the writing, the greater is their importance. But even in fairly straightforward prose, order within sentences is a major device alongside of specific connecting elements (such as *therefore, on the other hand*) and pronoun anaphora.

CONFLICTS AND THEIR RESOLUTION

If the choice between agnate sentence forms can be used both to avoid front-heaviness and to ease transitions, we might expect occasional conflicts between the two. We do find them. Consider the following:

> *No sharp distinction between a temporary halt and the final goal can be made, however.*   (41)

This is front-heavy. The following, related by a series of changes, is agnate and avoids this difficulty:

> *It is not possible, however, to make a sharp distinction between a temporary halt and the final goal.*   (42)

The previous context is as follows:

> *...Its* [a grain of sand's] *movement is intermittent, and the periods of stagnation vary from a few minutes in a river bed to eons on a flood plain or beach ridge. But ultimately it finds a final resting place where the sand is covered by younger deposits and is no longer disturbed.*   (43)

Sentence (41) affords a smoother transition from (43) than does (42). The demands of clarity within the sentence are in conflict with those between sentences. The author resolved this by the following:

> *No sharp distinction can be made, however, between a temporary halt and the final goal.* (44)

Splitting a constituent in this way is a device available at various places in the syntax of English to reconcile conflicting demands. Two simple cases are the constructions: *a better product than any now on the market,* the constituents of which are *a | better than any now on the market | product,* and *three score years and ten,* analyzed as *three score and ten | years.*

Another device can be seen in the following. The basic form of the sentence would be:

> *The helicopter that had started tracking the cloud had been forced to return to the base when...* (45)

This sentence presents no internal difficulty. The transition from the previous context, however, involves *cloud.* It would be smoother if this word could be moved to the beginning of the sentence. Unfortunately, this is almost impossible by any simple inversion. Instead, an independent mention is placed in front of the sentence which remains uninverted, and *cloud* is changed to *it.* The following is the way the author wrote it:

> *As for the cloud, the helicopter that had started tracking it had been forced to return to the base when...* (45a)

This construction with *as for the* seems to be a special device for resolving problems such as the one presented by this sentence.

Front-heaviness, excessive embedding, and rough transitions are only some of the problems that must be met in order to write in good style. There are other ways in which a passage can fall short of a satisfactory level of clarity. All of these must be avoided or minimized. Clarity, in turn, is only one of several dimensions of style. Taking all of them together, the requirements that must be met are both numerous and diverse. There are many opportunities for conflict among them.

The resolution of these conflicts makes one of the major demands on the technical skill of an author. Good writing is difficult enough, but superior writing requires extraordinary competence in the handling of the language, as well as the development and organization of content. It is no disparagement of writers, however, to suggest that we frequently overlook a complementary point: the extreme flexibility and resourcefulness which is demanded of language. We too easily take the medium for granted. Yet it is only the intricacy of grammatical patterns that allows anyone, however skillful, to meet the conflicting demands of style.

This complexity of language is brought home if, when writing and revising, we ponder what is involved in the choices we make. It is not simply that at every point there are numerous alternatives before us, but rather that these differ in so many ways besides grammatical structure. Careful reading of the work of a skillful writer will almost always show us additional grammatical resources which we might not ourselves think of using. The good writer usually is one who has a command of a wider spectrum of patterns as well as a finer feel for their stylistic effects.

Our natural tendency is to lose patience with language complexity, particularly in someone else's language. Certainly it is a nuisance to the learner, or to the half-fluent reader. We might ask why this heavy burden of apparatus is maintained. In some measure, of course, it is merely inertia, since language — especially literary language — is conservative and changes only slowly. But for the most part, it is because the complexity is functional. That is, language is as it is because no simpler mechanism would enable it to do as well what its users expect of it. Those demands are so complex that a language must approach in complexity to the limit of the users' capacity. Under these circumstances, totally useless features will either soon be abandoned or given new functions.

The demands of day-to-day oral communication and belletristic literature are quite different. Yet spoken and written language are both under this same pressure. Both must somehow maintain a level of complexity just within the limits of workability, so that each may optimally perform its functions. The two may be expected to differ most pronouncedly at what might be called the outer limits — the less central features useful in meeting the more specialized demands.

Actually, the individual demands are not so extreme in either speech or writing. It is rather that a number must be met in the same material. A passage must simultaneously be artistic and clear, and the requirements are not always compatible. As we shall see, the writer must at the same time meet the claims of redundancy and ambiguity, running so often counter to one another. Grammatical complexities exist, primarily, because they allow us the luxury of meeting these demands concurrently — that is, because they allow good writing or effective speech.

The grammatical basis of style, then, is not in the simpler patterns, but primarily in the most elaborate. Grammar can illuminate stylistic problems, but only if it can be carried beyond the fundamentals. To look at the problem superficially is only to trivialize it.

WEIGHTING OF CHOICES

Stylistic choices cannot be made independently. Each influences many others, and a web of interdependencies extends throughout a text. This can be demonstrated in proper literary passages by examining not single options but combinations of alternatives at two or more places near each other. It will usually be found that a different choice at one point puts the choosing at several others on a different basis. However, when the options are themselves complex, the careful evaluation of very many sets of alternatives is laborious. The principle is far better illustrated in a situation where the choices presented are of the simplest possible kinds. Even then it is tedious to discuss all the possibilities explicitly. Anyone, however, who will take a few minutes to work through a passage for himself will find it revealing.

Below we give a possible sample for this purpose.[9] As it stands it is hardly a connected discourse of any kind, appearing rather as a list of separate sentences. Excepting the third and seventh sentences, each is quite correct as it stands if examined in isolation. Most are not satisfactory in context, but the difficulties are restricted to two features: no pronouns have been used, and there are no clause connectors.

> [1]*Joe reached the barn.* [2]*Nellie stood patiently.* [3]*Nellie was waiting for Nellie's oats.* [4]*Joe went to the feed bin.* [5]*Joe took down the scoop.* [6]*Joe was about to measure out the oats.* [7]*Joe heard someone behind Joe.* [8]*Joe spun around.* [9]*Joe saw Tim.* [10]*Tim was slipping furtively out of the box-stall.* [11]*Tim had a bridle in one hand.* [12]*Tim had a strange instrument in the other hand.* [13]*Joe called to Tim.* [14]*Tim ran.* [15]*Tim disappeared in the woods.* (46)

The problem is to transform this list of sentences into a narrative paragraph by altering just the two features mentioned. Pronouns can be substituted for nouns, or under certain circumstances the noun may simply be dropped. Clauses can be connected into compound or complex sentences, or into "simple" sentences with compound elements. There are several possible solutions — each a paragraph using only the material given and using it all except for certain redundancies. That is to say, the resulting narrative can be in any of several styles.

In the text above the word *Joe* occurs nine times. Some of these can be changed into *he* or *him;* some can be dropped entirely, but at least one must remain unchanged. This three-way choice must be made at each occurrence of *Joe* in (46). The decision at each of these places, however, affects the choice at the next. In addition, there are seven occurrences of *Tim,* and for each of these a similar choice must be made. These choices are also interrelated, not only among themselves but with the choices pre-

---

[9] The sample passage was written for this purpose, but in general it is better to prepare such exercises by reversing the operations illustrated. That is, a well-written passage is selected, and then nouns are substituted for pronouns, connectors are deleted, all sentences are made active, or whatever is desired. An exercise of this kind forces close attention on one or a few problems at a time. AFTER students have produced their versions, and stylistic differences among them have been discussed, the original can be compared. This will often bring out certain features of an author's style very sharply and revealingly.

sented by *Joe*. If the two sets of decisions are not made in relation to each other, there is a very serious probability that the pronoun references will be confused.

As you rewrite this passage, you will find that the choice is not equally free at every point. For example, it is very nearly required that *Joe* remain in the first sentence. In the third, *Nellie's* must be changed to *her*. At other places there are real options, but the attractiveness of the alternatives varies from place to place.

Another set of choices must be made in clause connections. It is hardly possible to leave the fifteen simple sentences as they now stand, even if most of the proper nouns are replaced by pronouns. For example, while not required, there is every inducement to combine the eleventh and twelfth sentences: *He had a bridle in one hand and a strange instrument in the other.* rather than: *He had a bridle in one hand. He had a strange instrument in the other.*[10] At other places the choice is much freer: *Joe went to the feed bin and took down the scoop.* or *Joe went to the feed bin. He took down the scoop.* or *Going to the feed bin, Joe took down the scoop.* These are the sort of choices of which style is composed.

Notice that these alternative transitions directly affect the choices between *Joe*, *he*, and nothing. We have advanced (46) as an example presenting two systems of choices. There are interdependencies not only within each but also between the two. No two systems of grammatical choices are ever completely separable. These two are, perhaps, more closely bound together than most: signaling of clause connections is one of the chief functions of pronoun anaphora (see p. 344 and following).

At each point where there is a choice, we can think of each alternative as having a certain probability. For example, we have observed that in the first sentence of (46), *Joe* has a high probability; *he* has a low one. In the third sentence, the probability of *her* is even higher,[11] approaching certainty, while that for *Nellie's* is negligible. In some other sentences, alternatives can be found with nearly equal probabilities. Thus probabilities for a given choice may range all the way from near certainty to near impossibility and through all intermediate values.

The probability for any one selection may be altered, either upward or downward, by previous choices. For example, if the first occurrence of *Nellie* is allowed to remain, the next has a very high probability of replacement by *she*. But if the first does not remain, the next has a very high probability of being retained. Usually, however, the change in probabilities

---

[10] The use of *the other* for *the other hand* is part of the system of substitution of pronouns for noun phrases.

[11] When no choice is available, no question of style arises. The substitution of *her* for *Nellie's* is a case in point, and most linguists would agree that it is grammatical rather than stylistic. However, it is best to include it in an exercise dealing with style so that the distinction between grammar and style can be made clear.

is less dramatic. If one occurrence of *Joe* is preserved, there is slightly less probability that the next one will be and conversely. Or, putting it another way, each choice that is made weights the probabilities at many subsequent points.

We mentioned above the familiar principle that a word or construction should not be repeated. Stated thus, it is hardly helpful; too many exceptions can be seen in good writing. Yet there is some validity in it — enough to warrant reformulation. In the first place, it obviously does not apply to the more frequent items. There can be no objection to repeating *the, of,* or a subject-verb-object clause pattern, even within a single sentence. It is with the less frequent words or patterns that the preference applies most strongly. In the second place, it is never absolute. There are circumstances where a repetition is quite acceptable, and some where it seems indisputably the best decision. We cannot state a stylistic preference in the absolute fashion in which we state grammatical rules. It must be formulated in terms of weighting of choices.

Whenever an item has been chosen, that fact weights the choices in immediately following places against that item. How far the effect continues and how strong it is depends, among other things, on the unusualness of the item. I sometimes find myself rejecting a word because I had used it a page or two earlier. With other words, after a sentence or two has intervened, a prior use seems to matter little. It also depends on the kind of writing. In a scientific paper, technical terms are very little affected, though not entirely immune.

This weighting of choices against an item does not mean that it cannot be selected, but only that it is less likely than under other circumstances. And it does mean that the choice of the item is stylistically more significant. An unexpected — that is, less probable — item is always more striking. Think for a moment of the impression made by a pair of sneakers with tuxedo and black tie, or of a hot dog at a formal banquet. The stylistic impact of any item is related to its probability[12] and this in turn is determined by other choices that have been made in its context.

This dislike of repetition is a canon of style in English, and in at least most other modern Western languages. It is not a universal. For example, in some Semitic languages the preference seems at certain points to be exactly opposite. Even reading the Old Testament in translation, one is often struck by repetitions which seem to an English reader inelegant. The original text has many more repetitions — they tend to be eliminated in translation. For example, the King James Version's *ye shall surely die* is more literally *dying you shall die*, with two verb forms from the same root.

---

[12] This suggests that certain insights from the mathematical methods of information theory may be helpful in the interpretation of style. It does not justify the reductionism that treats style as dominantly, or even wholly, amenable to statistical investigation.

Reading the Hebrew, one inevitably gets the feeling that repetition was an important and generally positive matter of style for the writers.

Stylistic preferences are one of the matters that have diffused through Europe from classical antecedents. While there is no uniformity, there is a high degree of similarity in the canons of style in modern European languages. This makes literary translation of works in French, German, or Italian relatively easy.[13] The resulting versions often show both high fidelity and excellent literary quality. Putting Oriental classics into English is a much more difficult operation for many reasons. One of these is the wide disparity in stylistic values. Even when a fairly literal translation is grammatically possible (and it often is not), the effect can be very different. A translator, then, must not only replace sentence with equivalent sentence but also stylistic feature with equivalent stylistic feature. A translated metaphor can be annotated,[14] but footnotes explaining implications of stylistic devices of other kinds are almost unthinkable.

REDUNDANCY

It is said that a composition teacher once commented that a paper was "redundant, tautologous, and pleonastic". Obviously, this was not intended as a compliment. Redundancy is commonly considered one of the great errors in writing. Yet all writing, and all speech, is redundant. This must not be considered a fault, but a very necessary quality of language if it is to be successful as an instrument of communication. What the composition teacher decries is not redundancy as such, but an excess, or a crude handling, of redundancy.

Redundancy is familiarly defined as saying something more than once. It is only the grosser instances that are noticed and condemned; the subtler types escape interdiction.

Consider a sentence such as the following:

The ducks quacked at the top of their voices.   (47)

Almost every bit of information conveyed by the verb stem *quack* is duplicated elsewhere in the sentence. This can be seen by deleting it, leaving:

The ducks____-ed at the top of their voices.   (48)

---

[13] Note that this statement reads "relatively easy". Translation is, even in the most favorable situations, a very involved process, requiring meticulous attention to many details.

[14] They may need to be. For example, in Sanskrit literature, a graceful woman may be said to walk like an elephant. More familiarity with elephants than we Americans generally possess would make this more apt than it at first appears. Some metaphors are purely conventional — as the owl for wisdom (in India the owl is the symbol of complete stupidity) — and some have a real basis. Since, however, people do not all observe in the same way, even the latter type often needs annotation.

Only *quack* can be inserted easily and naturally into the blank. There are a number of verbs that will fit well with *ducks* as their subject: *swim, sleep, waddle*, and so on. Likewise there are many that are compatible with *at the top of their voices: bark, howl, sing*, and so on. To fit in sentence (48) a word must belong to both these lists. *Quack* is alone or almost alone. It fits because it means something like 'make a vocal noise like a duck', that is, because its meaning includes information already given in the sentence by *voice* and by *duck. Quack* in (47) is nearly one hundred percent redundant.

We have just seen that redundancy in sentence (47) is associated with the fact that *ducks* as a subject imposes restrictions on the possible verbs, while *at the top of their voices* does likewise. Any sort of restriction on occurrences is equivalent to redundancy. Grammar consists of restrictions on possible structures. It must therefore produce redundancy. In a few instances it is easy to see that this is so since it produces actual duplication of a very evident sort. For example, a phrase like *these stones* is marked as plural twice, once by *-s* and once by *these* rather than *this*. If this phrase is the subject of a sentence, the number may be marked a third time by the verb form, perhaps *are* rather than *is*. In a sentence such as:

The wisdom of Solomon was unparalleled.   (49)

the word *wisdom* is known to be a noun from its form. In addition, we expect *the* to be followed by a noun; *of* is more often than not preceded by a noun; and *wisdom* is in the subject position, a place by no means restricted to nouns, but nevertheless most often filled by nouns. At least four indications point to the same fact; this constitutes high redundancy.

Throughout the remainder of this chapter, we will use "redundancy" in the technical sense suggested in the last two paragraphs. It is a measure of excess of linguistic signals above the minimum that could carry the message. Equivalently, it is a measure of the extent to which each element is predictable from the context.

One way to estimate redundancy is by the "cloze" technique. Words are systematically deleted from a text. Then it is determined how much damage this does to the intelligibility. The more redundant, the more words can be taken out without serious difficulty. In the following passage[15] decreasing portions — indicated by a fraction at the left — have been removed:

1/2   *In ...... second ...... of ...... Christian ......, the ...... of ......*
       comprehended ...... fairest ...... of ...... earth, ... the
       ...... civilized ...... of .... The ...... of ...... extensive ......

1/3   *were guarded ...... ancient renown ...... disciplined valour.*
       ...... gentle but ...... influence of ...... and manners ......
       gradually cemented ...... union of ...... provinces. Their

---

[15] The opening paragraph and part of the second from Edward Gibbon, *The Decline and Fall of the Roman Empire*, 1776.

1/4   *peaceful ...... enjoyed and abused ...... advantages of wealth*
      ...... luxury. The image ...... a free constitution ...... was
      preserved with ...... reverence: the Roman ...... appeared to

1/6   *possess the sovereign ......, and devolved on the emperors ......*
      the executive powers of government. ...... a happy period of
      more ...... fourscore years, the public administration ......

1/8   *conducted by the virtues and abilities of ......, Trajan,*
      Hadrian, and the two Antonines. It ...... the design of this,
      and of the two ...... chapters, to describe the prosperous

1/10 *condition of their empire; ...... afterwards, from the death*
      of Marcus Antoninus, to deduce ...... most important
      circumstances of its decline and fall; a ...... which will

1/12 *ever be remembered, and is still felt by the ...... of the*
      earth. The principal conquests of the Romans were
      achieved ...... the republic; and the emperors, for the most
      part, were satisfied ...... preserving those dominions
      which had been acquired by the policy of ...... senate,
      the active emulation of the consuls, and the martial
      enthusiasm ...... the people.   (50)

The intelligibility is very poor when one half of the words are omitted, but increases until in the last section, with only one word in twelve missing, there is little difficulty for a competent reader of English.

Actual reading is more like the cloze technique than it might at first appear. Almost every text contains some vocabulary items which will be unknown to some of the intended readers. A small number of unfamiliar words will cause a good reader no trouble; he will merely determine their meaning from the context and go on. That is, he will treat them more or less like blanks in the last section of passage (50).

Moreover, everyone has a much larger recognition vocabulary than his active vocabulary. This means, simply, that there are many words which he reads without difficulty but does not himself use in speaking or writing. Many of these he is unable to recall at will. Some of them he cannot recognize at all out of context. In a sense, he only partly knows these words. That they give him no trouble in reading is largely because this partial understanding is supplemented or confirmed by the context in which he finds them — that is, by redundancy. They might be compared to items that are partly removed in a cloze experiment.

Nor is this the end of the matter. Any dictionary will show that all common words, and even many of the rarer, have two or more meanings, often quite distinct. It is virtually impossible to understand language by merely knowing, however thoroughly or precisely, the meanings of words. We must have at our command the ability to select the correct meaning for the passage at hand. Thus, even with perfectly familiar items, it is imperative that we use contextual redundancy. The model, then, is not a cloze experiment with blanks, but something much the same with multiple choices.

Intelligible writing, therefore, must have enough of the right sort of redundancy to meet the needs of the intended readers — to enable them to guess meanings of words new to them, to assist their recall of words only partly known, and to help them select the right meaning for words with two or more. How much redundancy there will be depends on many factors, including the nature of the subject matter, the way in which it is to be read, the importance of correct understanding, and the ability of the readers.[16] On the other hand, excessive redundancy is not only wasteful of paper and of the reader's time and effort but also very annoying. The proper CONTROL of redundancy, then, is an important responsibility of the writer.

Various choices affect the redundancy of a passage, including many of those which figure in other aspects of style. For example, sentence (1) near the beginning of this chapter contained twenty words. It was altered by a series of operations which do not affect meaning. The result was sentence (18) with twenty-six, an increase of thirty percent.[17] An improvement in clarity was achieved at the cost of additional redundancy. We may judge that this was a reasonable price in this case. There are times, however, when clarity must be balanced against redundancy and where a compromise must be reached.

Choice among agnate constructions may affect redundancy more or less, but the use or nonuse of modifiers is usually more important. Many people would consider that both sentence (1) and sentence (18) would be improved by simply deleting *really*, *clearly*, and *very*. That such a change can even be considered is a consequence of the high redundancy in these words. That is to say, they contribute so little to the sentence that their removal hardly alters the meaning. Their function is largely stylistic, and most would judge their value to be negative.

Comparison of two closely parallel versions will often show places where one has material lacking in the other, but where the meaning is effectively the same. For example, the Revised Standard Version and the New English Bible differ in this way in Acts 27:13:

| RSV: | *they . . .* | *sailed along* | *Crete* | |
| NEB: | | *. . . they sailed along the coast of Crete* | | (51) |

If, as seems quite certain to me, these two mean very nearly the same, then *the coast of* is almost wholly redundant. Part of the meaning of these words is contained in that of *sailed along* and the remainder in *Crete*.

---

[16] The ability to make efficient use of redundancy is one of the characteristics of a good command of language. For this reason, the cloze technique is an excellent device to measure reading ability in either a first or a second language.

[17] We must not assume that thirty percent is a measure of the redundancy in sentence (18). Sentence (1) had appreciable redundancy to start with.

How highly redundant modifiers can be is easily seen by experimenting with a set of contrasting adjectives — the eleven basic color terms (*red, orange, yellow, green, blue, purple, brown, pink, black, gray, white*) are excellent. The possible combinations of these with a suitable set of nouns may be examined. It will be found that some combinations are very likely, others highly improbable. *Red rose* or *blue lupine* is much more likely than *blue rose* or *red lupine*.[18] This reflects redundancy. In a cloze experiment, *red* is an excellent guess for . . . . . . *rose*, whereas *blue* is a very poor one.

If, then, in a sentence about roses, the word *red* is added, there is an increase in redundancy. The same effect is obtained by adding to a sentence containing *red* the phrase *as a rose*. Many of these similes are quite standard — that is, highly redundant — and their usefulness is determined by that fact, for example, *black as coal, white as snow, green as grass, gray as ashes*. They must be avoided in texts where redundancy is not needed, but are useful in certain special situations where it is needed.

AMBIGUITY

It is a commonplace that everything we say or write is open, somehow, to misinterpretation. This cannot be charged simply to the carelessness of the reader; the greatest skill and care cannot always abstract from the text the meaning the writer intended. Nor is it wholly the shortcoming of the author; feasible techniques for forestalling misunderstanding are not always available to him. The problem lies, in part at least, within language itself. There is no way in which words can be selected or constructed into sentences that will automatically assure a single unambiguous meaning. The best that is ordinarily possible is to make one meaning so overwhelmingly more likely than any other that the lesser alternatives can be safely disregarded. Even this is not always easy, and may, indeed, entail a cost that the writer cannot assume.

Ambiguity, like redundancy, is a characteristic of language. It is less easy to show that it is a useful feature, but much easier to show that it is pervasive. While the popular view of redundancy is too narrow, that of ambiguity is too broad. A very disparate collection of phenomena is often gathered together under this heading. Any muddy thinking or any poor phrasing is sure to be called "ambiguity" by someone. The extremes aside, "ambiguity" is used of two quite different things.

---

[18] One might object that at this point I am talking about facts of nature rather than facts of language. We speak more often of red roses than of blue simply because the former are common and familiar, the latter rare, unknown, or freakish. Yet it is still redundancy. It has the linguistic function (a linguistic origin is not necessary) of helping a reader over rough spots in a text, or a hearer to fill in words that have been masked by noise. Moreover, some comparable combinations are not so easily laid at the door of nature: *blue Monday, purple prose*. These are also highly redundant.

One is a matter of what is NOT said. Consider a very prosaic sentence:

He looked at the table.   (52)

This might refer to a large dinner table or a small coffee table, to one with chrome legs and a plastic top or to one of hand-carved cherry wood. Many quite different things may be referred to, but this sentence applies equally well to all. If the writer had judged it to be worthwhile, he might have added any specification he desired. A good writer fills out no more of the details than suit his purpose.

There is a second kind of ambiguity which lies WITHIN what is actually said. Reading sentence (52), one person may visualize a piece of furniture. Another may imagine a page in a mathematics book. (Whether he thinks of logarithms, trigonometric functions, or multiplication facts is an instance of the first type of ambiguity.) In each case there are additional details that might have been given. But whether the sentence is interpreted as referring to a piece of furniture or an array of data is on a different level. *Table* has two (at least) basic meanings, not apparently connected in any way except that they are expressible by the same word. Only one of these can, ordinarily, apply in any one sentence. In (52) nothing tells the reader which the author had in mind.

We will restrict the term "ambiguity", for this discussion, to the second phenomenon. So limited, it can be given a reasonably precise meaning in terms of the lexical, grammatical, or other systems of the language. It is a basic feature that must be taken account of in the study of language, or of any single system within language. Moreover, it is a crucial matter in literature. Genres differ in the ways that they either exploit, tolerate, or seek to avoid ambiguity. Types of ambiguity differ in the values that are put on them in literature. These questions, however, are outside our scope here. Rather, we are concerned with the language basis for ambiguities, their resolution and control. Three types might be distinguished:

The first and most familiar is a matter of vocabulary, already illustrated in sentence (52). Many words, including almost all the common ones, have two or more distinct meanings. The combinations, taking any of the available meanings for each word in a sentence, may be extremely numerous. Actually most of these are ruled out, one way or another. A sentence is said to be ambiguous when there is nothing that will make one set of meanings for its components — hence one meaning for the sentence as a whole — definitely preferable to all others.

A second kind of ambiguity rests not in the vocabulary but in the grammar. A syntactic construction is more than a mere sequence of words or morphemes. There must be some identifiable relationship between the elements. It is possible, therefore, to have the same words in the same order but representing two quite different constructions. Any such sequence is ambiguous — each construction suggests a different meaning or list of meanings. Several classic examples have been mentioned in earlier chapters — *old men and women, flying planes, Virginia ham packer.*

A third kind of ambiguity is also grammatical, but rests not in the syntactic relations of elements, but in the identification of elements. Probably the most elaborate and familiar short example is the ambiguity in speech between: *The sons raise meat.* and *The sun's rays meet.* (See p. 168.)

RESOLUTION OF AMBIGUITY

The reader or hearer must have some mechanism by which to resolve ambiguities, that is, to select the most likely interpretation for a sentence or longer sample.

In the resolution of vocabulary ambiguities, one important factor is grammatical structure. It is easy to create sentences, as the examples above, which are unresolvably ambiguous on the basis of the two meanings of *table*, 'article of furniture' and 'array of information'. It is more difficult to find one where the ambiguity is between one of these and a third meaning 'to postpone discussion'. The reason is obvious: the first two are meanings of *table* as a noun, the third as a verb. Nouns and verbs usually occur in quite different places in the sentence. The grammatical context, therefore, prevents some pairs of meanings being confused except in very rare instances.

A second factor often resolving ambiguity is redundancy between words in the sentence. A set of examples will show something of how this operates. For simplicity, we will consider that each of the words which are our central concern has only two meanings:

> *table:* 'article of furniture',   'array of data'
> *chair:* 'article of furniture',   'endowment for a professorship'
> *scholarship:* 'endowment for student aid',   'academic performance'

Abbreviating still further, we will list these glosses under the words concerned:

> *He gave the university a table   and a chair.*   (53)
> 　　　　　　　　　　'furniture' ↔ 'furniture'
> 　　　　　　　　　　'data'   'endowment'
> *He gave the university a chair   and a scholarship.*   (54)
> 　　　　　　　　　　'furniture'   ⟶ 'endowment'
> 　　　　　　　　　　'endowment' ⟵ 'performance'

Table potentially brings both its meanings to sentence (53) as does *chair*. The similarity in meaning expressed by glossing each as 'article of furniture' strengthens the probability for that meaning in each case. An arrow has been added to point out the redundant relationship between the two words.

Similarly, in (54) the common meaning 'endowment' is strengthened in each word by the possibility of such a meaning in the other.

But this effect can be overridden if a conflicting pattern of redundancy is present:

> He gave the university a very valuable hand-carved antique table
> and a chair in the history of furniture design.   (55)

The way this works is best seen by considering the result if certain parts of the sentence are omitted or altered.

> He gave the university a very valuable hand-carved antique table
> and a chair.   (56)

Table is marked as meaning 'article of furniture' not only by the context *and a chair* as in (53) but also by the modifiers *antique* and *hand-carved*. In turn *table and* seems to determine the meaning of *chair* even more strongly than in (53). Conflict arises when *in the history of furniture design* is added. This points to the meaning 'endowment for a professorship' for *chair*. In turn, this is strengthened by *university*, as may be seen by substituting *his wife:*

> He gave his wife a very valuable hand-carved antique table and a
> chair in the history of furniture design.   (57)

The conflict remains, but it cannot now be so easily resolved and the sentence seems nonsensical — the kind where we automatically start searching for a typographical error. Moreover, in (55) the redundancy between *antique* and *history* strengthens the interpretation — try omitting all the modifiers of *table:*

> He gave the university a table and a chair in the history of furni-
> ture design.   (58)

Or again, try the following:

> He gave the university a table and a chair in history.   (59)

Such experiments — and many more could be performed with this same sentence as a starting point — demonstrate that very many of the words in the sentence figure in the context determining the correct meaning for *table* or for *chair*. When there are conflicts, one bit of context pulling in one direction and one in another, there seems to be something about their places in the structure of the sentence which determines which has the greater effect.[19]

---

[19] To state in detail how this operates would be to give a large part of a full theory of semantics, a thing which we cannot, at present, do. Perhaps the most important effort in this direction in recent times is Jerrold J. Katz and Jerry A. Fodor, *The Structure of a Semantic Theory*, 1963, Language 39:170–210. This is based on a transformational-generative view of grammar.

The reader's problem in working out the meaning of a passage seems much like that of the writer in attempting to achieve a balanced style. In the latter case, every choice of construction or vocabulary item weights the probabilities at the remaining points where a choice must be made. Conflicts arise and must be resolved, sometimes by seeking an additional more elaborate option which had not been considered before. In reading, the words are given but each presents a choice among its meanings. Each choice of a meaning affects all others nearby. Alternatives become weighted. Weightings cumulate in a favorable circumstance until one meaning for each word seems far more probable than any other. In this case, the sentence may be considered unambiguous.

A third factor involved in resolution of ambiguity may be called "unity of the discourse". The reader or listener must assume, unless there is clear evidence to the contrary, that any given word carries the same meaning throughout the passage. In good writing, it generally does. Thus we would avoid using a sentence like:

> *He got up from his chair and announced that he had given a chair*
> *to the university.* (60)

Instead:

> *He got up from his seat and announced that he had given a chair*
> *to the university.* (61)

Paronomasia must be clearly signaled.

The resolution of potential grammatical ambiguities is more complex. The same principles of vocabulary redundancy and unity of discourse operate, however, though in an opposite way. Consider *old men and women* and *old men and children*. The first is ambiguous, the second not. One reason is that there is a meaning for *old* which is compatible with both *men* and *women*, but none which is easily compatible with both *men* and *children*.

Or consider the following:

> *He is a Virginia ham packer from North Carolina.* (62)

The phrase *Virginia ham packer* is, by itself ambiguous. The most likely interpretation for the structure *Virginia (ham packer)* is 'ham packer from Virginia'. This is not compatible with *from North Carolina*, and so is ruled out. For the structure *(Virginia ham) packer*, the most probable interpretation is 'packer of a certain type of hams'. This is compatible with the rest of (62), and the hearer or reader will generally select this analysis. Much the opposite argument and conclusion apply in the following:

> *He is a Virginia ham packer specializing in sugar-cured meats.* (63)

Something much like vocabulary redundancy resolves the structural ambiguity.

Probably the most complex operation in reading is the resolution of potential ambiguities. It is the writer's responsibility to provide the necessary help and to control ambiguity. This does not necessarily mean simply to avoid it, or even to minimize it. Ambiguity may be deliberately used for some special purpose, as in much poetry, belletristic prose, advertising copy, or humor, but this must be done with care. If there is too much, if it is of an inappropriate kind, or if it is badly handled, the desired effect may be spoiled. In other kinds of writing, straightforward exposition for example, ambiguity should be minimized.

This can be done in several ways. One is the careful choice of vocabulary. A word with fewer meanings might be selected in preference to one with more. But there are limitations. Often the less ambiguous words are little known. It may be necessary to increase redundancy to insure that they will be understood. Too many such words will interfere with readability for many audiences. Often the most precise words are to be found in specialized terminologies, but if these are used they will give a highly technical cast to the whole, and this may be undesirable.

Often a more satisfactory strategy is to focus attention on the contexts rather than the words themselves. Even the most polysemous words may be unambiguous if they can be used in the right environments. The trick is to see that they are provided, at their first appearance, with sharply defining contexts. Often this is best done by careful selection of modifiers — words so closely related syntactically that they are clearly relevant context, and semantically compatible with only the desired meaning. *Hand-carved* in sentence (55) is an example; even if the writer had no interest in the details of the table, this might be added to assist in making the noun unambiguous.

Careful attention to grammatical constructions is as important as vocabulary selection. But the two are not independent. The sentence pattern determines how the context applies, and hence whether individual words are ambiguous or not. Similarly, the words inserted in a sentence pattern determine whether it is grammatically ambiguous or not.

We can illustrate this by considering the following sentence which has a grammatically ambiguous phrase for a subject:

> *The killing of the lion was a wanton act.* (64)

At least four ways are available to render this sentence unambiguous: First, we can replace the phrase by an agnate phrase which has only one meaning:

> *To kill the lion was a wanton act.* (65)

Second, we may replace a word in the phrase by a near synonym which will fit into only one of the two possible constructions:

The shooting of the lion was a wanton act. (66)

Third, we may replace a word remote from the point of ambiguity but significant as context:

The killing of the lion was an illegal act. (67)

Finally, we may add a largely redundant expression of some kind:

The killing of the lion was a wanton act and the hunter should not have done it. (68)

These and other techniques may reduce ambiguity very materially, but they never wholly eliminate it. Beyond a certain point, further reduction is only at a cost, most often in the form of excessive redundancy and diminished clarity. This mounts steeply, and may soon become prohibitive. How soon depends on the purposes behind the writing. Extreme examples can often be seen in legal documents. The following example shows this:

Ordered, that six months from the 2nd day of July, 1964, be and the same are limited and allowed for the presentation of all claims against the said estate to the executor thereof and said executor is directed to cite all creditors of said decedent to bring in their claims within said time allowed by publishing the same once in some newspaper having a circulation in said Probate District within thirty days from the date of this order.[20] (69)

From any point of view, this is highly redundant. It is by no means easy reading. Yet it cannot properly be considered bad writing. It does precisely what it is designed to do in the most effective way known to do it. Ambiguity is cut to a minimum; high redundancy and poor clarity are the price. For its purpose, however, such a cost is bearable. Legal proceedings can tolerate almost any feature of language more readily than ambiguity. In this context, we are willing to put up with great difficulty in reading, provided, once the meaning is made out, it will be certain and precise. To insure this, we leave both the writing and the reading of contracts to

[20] This formula is repeated day after day, with only a change of date, in every notice of this kind in the state of Connecticut. The specific example was found in the *Hartford Times*, July 7, 1964, where there were three such notices. The fact that these notices are so highly standardized means that from some broader point of view the whole formula is entirely redundant. A regular reader of probate notices (say, a lawyer) never bothers to read the formula at all; he already knows exactly what is in it. Moreover, he knows exactly what it means as it has been interpreted through years of judicial consideration and legal practice. The relevant context is not contained in the notice, but in many volumes of legal decisions. These make it ALMOST completely unambiguous.

specialists. A lawyer has more than one function, but not the least is simply to handle the special kind of language required to avoid costly misunderstandings.

For other purposes, such a price cannot be paid. The relative values of artistry, clarity, brevity, and unambiguousness may vary from one kind of writing to another. In each situation an appropriate compromise must be found between the several conflicting demands. To write well, one needs a feel for the proper balance, as well as an understanding of the devices available to effect the best possible resolution of the tensions.

Chapter 20

The Rehabilitation of Grammar

The 1950s saw a turning point in American education. Among the new developments, none seems more significant than the growing movement for curriculum reform. In many academic subjects there is now intense activity, and in all there is, at least, widespread discussion. There has been an unprecedented degree of public support. Significant new resources are becoming available, both in funds and in personnel. Some of the projects have now been in operation long enough that concrete results are to be seen. Their evident success is taken as confirmation of the basic premises of the movement, and the leaders are now emboldened to suggest even more far-reaching changes. It seems certain that within the next decade the school curriculum will have undergone the most extensive transformation in its history, both in content and in method. The most profound change, however, will be one not immediately evident to the nonprofessional: a fundamentally new understanding of the educational process.[1] This underlies the whole and gives the movement unity and direction.

At present, the leadership in this movement rests largely with mathematics and the sciences. In these subjects, curriculum reform projects are proliferating. They range from cautious readjustments to profound restructurings. The first efforts were carried out within the traditional curricular framework of the schools. But as the work has gone on, the familiar organization of subject matter has increasingly been questioned. Already integrated curricula are being worked out for subjects long kept separate.

---

[1] Probably the most accessible formulation of this understanding is to be found in Jerome S. Bruner, *The Process of Education*, 1961. This is a report of a conference of leaders in curriculum reform held in 1959. It therefore represents only the thinking of the earliest years of the movement.

Within individual sciences there has been a trend toward greater freedom in selecting and organizing material. Topics hitherto considered far too complex or advanced for the schools have been successfully taught, often by rigorous pruning off of nonessentials and simplification of terminology or notation. In many projects fewer topics are covered than in the older curricula, but each is carried to much greater depth. Much more attention is being given to the more basic questions of theory and scientific method, and less to the presentation of results. Interrelationships of fundamental concepts, in particular, are receiving greatly increased attention. Efforts are being made to reduce the hitherto very pronounced difference in attitude between the schoolroom and the research laboratory. The aim is to present science as it is, not as it was a generation ago.

While the more cautious projects are important as interim programs, often being the only feasible way for a school to start in curriculum modernization, it is increasingly clear that the future is with the more radical restructurings. Already some leaders are looking beyond the most daring reforms of the present wave. They foresee that in a decade or two the needs of the schools will have gone beyond the best current schemes, and new projects will be needed. They recognize the immenseness and complexity of fundamental curriculum rebuilding, and feel that it is not too early to start preliminary work now on the new curriculum for the late '70s and the '80s.[2]

In this movement for curriculum reform, English seems to be lagging far behind. There are many efforts directed to improvement in details, but few which look at the subject as a whole. An impartial appraisal can characterize these only as conservative or halting. In part this is because of the small resources available for curriculum work. In part it is because of the magnitude of the job. English is, after all, a far larger part of the total school curriculum than any of the subjects in which comprehensive projects are now underway. We must expect a major attack on the problem to be at least commensurately larger. This same fact, however, makes the neglect more tragic. It is not simply that English is large; the major share of the child's time in school which is assigned to English is certainly a reflection of its generally recognized central importance. For this to remain antiquated and inadequate will mean a serious deficiency in the quality of schooling as a whole — one not easily compensated for by high quality elsewhere.

Yet the situation is not without its encouraging side. While there has not yet been any major project in English, there has already been accomplished much which prepares for it. Curriculum reform has deep and

---

[2] Probably the most important statement of this position can be found in Cambridge Conference on School Mathematics, *Goals for School Mathematics*, 1963. The introductory portion of this report (to p. 30) has a significance that extends far beyond mathematics. Work on a curriculum along the lines suggested was started in the summer of 1964.

significant roots in English, perhaps more so than in most subjects. There has been a long-term development pointing toward fundamental changes. This would have led sooner or later to a major attack on the problems of curriculum modernization, even if the reform movement in other disciplines had not provided an outside stimulus. The next task of the profession is to carry forward these internal developments, to learn what it can from the successes and failures of ventures in other subjects, and on this dual basis to get underway a major reformation of the English curriculum.

In Chapter 1, three recent steps in this progression were traced. First the "survey of errors" movement called into question some of the details of the grammar teaching in the schools. As this went on, it led inevitably to the "usage movement". This raised the related but much broader question of the criteria for correctness. In its turn this made possible the first stirrings of a movement for a "new grammar", that is, for a still broader and deeper reform. The trend for some decades has been toward the raising of progressively more fundamental questions.

This trend has continued. In the last few years the concern with grammar has broadened, so that this part of the curriculum is now more often referred to as "language". This is no mere change of label: efforts are being made to include some discussion of dialect, of the social implications of language, of linguistic history, and of various other topics. The desire is clearly for a comprehensive and integrated treatment of language in every aspect.

With this widening of scope, the relationship to literature and composition has come under scrutiny, and the tripartite division of English has been questioned. Inevitably, the possibility of a "language-centered curriculum" has been raised. With this proposal, the stream of development in one sector of English has come in contact with the ever-widening circles of discussion in other sectors. The groundwork is being laid for a concerted attack on the curriculum as a whole and for a radical rethinking.

None of these movements has ever become firmly consolidated. Before each has attained the support of a majority of the English teachers, the concern of its leadership has moved beyond it. This is the origin of part of the chaos which seems so to beset the profession. It is the confusion of accelerating development. Through it runs a trend toward increasingly fundamental concern. English is, on the basis of its own internal development, coming rapidly to a position where a broadly based, thorough, and imaginative reconsideration of its total curricular structure is both possible and imperative. Curriculum reform projects of major dimensions must certainly lie just ahead. Though unaware of the direction it has been traveling, the English teaching profession has, for two generations, been preparing for revolutionary changes.

It is still too early to discern the shape of that new curriculum, but a few characteristics can be predicted. One feature must be the pulling together of the various strands now loosely federated under the catch-all rubric "English". Recent discussion of the "language-centered curriculum" is one set of probings in this direction, and probably the most promising. It has, of course, not really delineated a new curriculum, only vaguely adumbrated certain possible lines of development. Many fundamental problems are still to be worked out, and in many cases even to be raised. The questions to be faced are not all matters of selection, organization, and presentation — that is, properly curricular questions — but there are questions of content as well. Even our best scholars do not at present understand some of the matters that we should be teaching. Prominent here are certain features of English grammar, and even more of the grammatical bases of style. English must face a revolution, not only in its representation in the school curriculum, but equally in its organization for research.

The "language-centered curriculum" easily arouses misapprehensions, many of them arising from the use of "language" as a label for one segment of the present structure. It cannot be a matter of one component swallowing up the others. There must be as profound a reorganization within "language" as in composition or literature. In all three there must be increased recognition of the unity of the study of the English language and its use.

In such a new curriculum, grammar must certainly have a central place as one of a small number of basic subdisciplines. That language has structure and system is fundamental, not only to the study of language in the abstract, but equally to the scholarly consideration of the use of language — that is, to major dimensions of the work in composition and literature. Grammar is the study of structure and system in one of its most significant aspects. An integrated English curriculum must make grammar an important element if it is to deal adequately with many of its proper concerns.

Grammar as it has been known in the American schools, however, cannot bear such a responsibility. It is too narrow in scope, too shallow, too isolated from other disciplines, and too intellectually sterile. It is, in fact, only a caricature of what it ought to be. To serve in a new curriculum, grammar must be rehabilitated, given a new content and a new image.

STANDARDS

As the first and most essential step in this rehabilitation, grammar must be relieved of police duty as the sole arbiter of "correctness". The instrument is not fitted to the task. Both grammar and standards have suffered severely from the unnatural assignment. Trivialization and sterility in the grammar section have been the immediate penalties, and others have flowed from these to contaminate every branch of English studies with at least a taint of anti-intellectualism and superficiality.

The American public, taking up a notion that was long popular in the schools, has closed-mindedly assumed that grammatical rules constitute the only possible standard for correctness. It has, therefore, received every suggestion that the two should be divorced as a threat to any standards at all. If grammar is not to rule, the only alternative is believed to be first "permissiveness" and then complete collapse.

Yet it is precisely the need for effective standards of good writing that most powerfully demands a change. The employment of grammar for this purpose has failed demonstrably and miserably. To be sure, the rules might be made a little more realistic, or a little more effective. But the improvement needed is of an entirely different order of magnitude than the best we might hope for from any such emendation. The problems of good writing are simply too large and too complex to yield to any such weak instrument as a handful of prescriptive rules.

Much bad writing conforms explicitly to the rules, and most good writing is actually somewhat free in its conformity. This is evidence, if evidence were needed, first, that mechanically precise application of rules is not what is demanded, and second, that there is much more to good writing than what the present type of rules is able to specify. Mechanical correctness is not enough — even for what is condescendingly called "simple expository writing". Some, at least, of the features of style must be considered in even a minimum program. They are not amenable to formulation as prescriptive rules.

Since standards, in their completeness, cannot feasibly be formulated in a set of rules of the traditional kind, they must be set forth in some other form. The standard of good writing can be based only on the practice of good writers, and this must be seen in their works. Standards must be rooted, somehow, in the body of English literature.

One possibility that immediately suggests itself is an agreed upon corpus of writings. Indeed, English teachers have often acted as if they believed such a corpus existed, at least as a standard of literary excellence. Actually, there would probably be insurmountable difficulties in finding any general consensus.[3]

It is, nevertheless, worthwhile to consider how such a corpus would operate as a standard. If such were available, a grammatical statement might be drawn up, reflecting in any desired degree of detail the patterns that actually occurred. This would be useful in teaching writing, but would

---

[3] The difficulties in setting up a corpus of writings as a standard are not only practical. To set forth any official list of either approved or disapproved works verges closely on literary censorship. It is doubtful that the English-teaching profession has any greater moral justification in doing so than governmental bodies or self-appointed guardians of public purity. It is also doubtful that censorship based on the quality of language is fundamentally different from that based — or alleged to be based — on artistic quality, propriety, or political conformity.

be a description of the standard, rather than the standard itself. The function of such a statement would be primarily to organize observation and to provide an instrument for the comparison of any piece of writing against the standard.

In such an arrangement, a variety of grammatical techniques would be advantageous, since each might point out certain characteristics of the standard corpus more effectively than the others. New and better grammatical techniques would be welcome. There would no longer be any reason to hold grammar sacrosanct, as it now seems to be, even in the face of known deficiencies. There would be freedom to experiment, to speculate, and to evaluate. Such freedom is absolutely necessary if grammar is to become an intellectually respectable subject.

The shift from prescriptive rule to standard corpus would, therefore, remedy one of the two great difficulties that are rooted in the use of grammatical rules as the standard. Grammar would no longer be sterilized and would cease to be a focal point for anti-intellectualism within the English curriculum. But it would do very little to meet the other need. Standards cannot be very much more effective if a legislatively selected corpus is substituted for a set of prescriptive rules.

Writing must vary with the situation, the purpose, and the audience. There is no one single form of English that has general usefulness. Nor would it be possible to agree on a set of standards for any reasonable number of specific varieties. Good written English does not fall into any finite number of definable types. Instead, there is multidimensional variation, producing an infinity of kinds, each with characteristics which may be useful in some situation.

Moreover, there is a continual but gradual drift in literary taste, just as there is in fashions of other kinds.[4] The conservative may wish for immutability, but this hope is vain and totally antithetic to central values in literature. Great writers are always innovators, and innovation is essential to their art, yet at the same time they are always traditionalists. The problem of standards is to maintain a balance between continuity and development. Neither rules nor a corpus, if either is set forth once for all, can give proper recognition to these two. Only the on-going practice within the language community can serve as an acceptable base for standards.

But simply to say that the usage of others is a standard is to excuse the writer from his personal responsibility in the matter. Standards of

---

[4] The wild and erratic shifts in fashions of dress and coiffure are a special phenomenon. Here the balance between innovation and tradition has been destroyed or seriously distorted, presumably as the result of a peculiar commercial premium on innovation. It is one task of literature teaching to keep a sufficient spread of literary types and periods before the public that no similar distortion is likely. Fortunately, there is a large homeostatic element in the balance, so that it tends naturally to correct SMALL departures.

language must be partly discovered and partly created by their user. They are an abstraction, a summarization, of his past experience with language. The more perceptive his observation has been, the more adequate and useful they are. The "teaching" of standards is not the presentation of a ready-made body of rules or exemplars, but help and guidance in building something that is at once personal and within a tradition.

A native speaker of a language has a most remarkable ability to subject his speech, as it is spoken, to continuous comparison with a standard. This is of his own compilation, based on his observation of the speech of all those with whom he comes into contact. It is continually modified as his experience increases and as the speech around him changes. Moreover, this standard is not monolithic. Both his speech and the model against which he assesses it vary with his mood and intention, the situation, and the audience. In effect he is always trying to speak in the way that his observations have led him to feel is appropriate and effective for the particular conditions of the moment in the light of his continuing responsibilities. There is a personal element in this, but it is always checked by a responsiveness to observable consensus in the community.

A good writer does much the same thing in much the same way. His language, committed to paper rather than to the air, is his best effort to match the language he has observed to be effective in similar situations. He has an internalized grammar[5] of literary English to guide him as he writes. He has also a sensitivity to situation and an ability to appraise language effectiveness. These are combined with a feel for balance between the various stylistic demands. The poor writer, for the most part, simply lacks an adequate image of prevailing practice, is insufficiently sensitive to appropriateness, or is less competent in manipulating the resources of the language.

There are, however, significant differences between the processes of speaking and writing. One of these is that written material can be, and usually is, edited. An author goes back over his manuscript, changing a word here and a construction there. Or, in his writing he halts, sometimes for protracted periods, while he weighs alternatives, actually composing mentally several structures from which he can choose. Often he seeks — or has imposed — the advice and help of another. This editing process means that written English is a very much more precise production than spoken. We expect both more complex structures and more exact conformity to the conventions. Good writing demands a greater competence with the patterns of the language and a greater sensitivity to certain aspects of style than does ordinary speech.

---

[5] That is, a set of patterns which have become habitual, so that they are followed without conscious effort. A person is often totally unaware of the nature of these patterns, or even of their existence.

GRAMMAR AND THE TEACHING OF COMPOSITION

One learns literary English much as one learns spoken,[6] that is, by copious observation of the language of others and by a great deal of personal experimentation. These two activities are essential for everyone, but sufficient for only a few. That is, an occasional person has become a good writer simply by extensive reading and by practicing with pen or typewriter until he can produce material of quality. While we must admit this possibility, English teachers have shown no great faith in it. Instead, we have always assumed that, for most people, some direct help is necessary, and we have sought to provide it. That is to say, we have acted on the conviction that the composing process must be taught.

If this last assumption is accepted, the question remains: What form should we give this intervention in the "natural" learning process? Since there are three basic components in the skill[7] that is sought, there are three general approaches, each supplementary to the others.

First, the teacher should aim at increasing sensitivity to structure and to alternatives in structure, that is, to the subject matter of grammar. For free and fluent writing, this means strengthened competence in the student's internalized grammar of literary English, and the assimilation of additional structural patterns. For editing, it means sharpened ability to deal explicitly with grammatical questions of the sorts that arise in seeking a rephrasing to replace a construction judged unsatisfactory.

Second, the teacher should aim at increased appreciation for differences of situation, intention, and audience, and the correlation with these of variations in language. Again, this has an informal component for free writing, and a more formal one for the editing process.

Third, the teacher should aim at a deeper understanding of the dimensions of style (artistry, clarity, redundancy, ambiguity), a sensitivity to the balance between them, and the ability to see and resolve conflicts. A good writer manipulates these outside awareness, but must be able to bring recalcitrant problems into focus for editorial attention when needed. Stylistics, then, like the others, has both an informal and a formal aspect.

---

[6] There are, however, significant differences: (1) Literary English is ordinarily learned at a more mature age. We have every reason to believe not merely that language learning ability changes with age, but specifically that there is a shift in the kind of approach that is more effective. (2) Interaction between producer and receiver is less immediate in written than spoken. This means that practice is not as automatically helpful. (3) Few devote nearly full-time to literary language learning, whereas spoken language learning verges on a full-time activity for most children over a period of years. All three of these differences suggest that the learning of literary language is less efficient and that active intervention in the process is usually needed.

[7] We are here concerned with the learning of the use of language. Quite parallel things might be said about other aspects of the composition process. For example, there must be the acquisition of a feel for the structure of discourse, or for the use of rhetorical schemes and figures.

As has been pointed out in Chapters 15, 18, and 19, these three areas of writing skill are intimately interrelated. It is only in their systematic discussion that they can be separated. In practice, they always appear together, each interacting with the others. They have much in common: the first is grammatical, and the other two have strong grammatical foundations and implications. It is here that the rehabilitation of grammar will make its impact on the teaching of composition.

There is a danger in a grammar-based approach to composition teaching. There are two halves of the writing process: free writing and editing. It is the latter that is the direct point of attack for any teaching. It is easy to concentrate so heavily on the conscious analysis of writing problems as to seem to give editing a real priority over the more basic writing process. The more wooden and prescriptive the teaching of grammar, the more likely this is to occur. In particular, it is essential that the attention always center on the phenomena of language and their functions, rather than on terminology and rules. It is here that composition teaching makes its demands for rehabilitation of grammar.

GRAMMAR AND THE READING OF LITERATURE

The reading of literature makes demands on the reader that are seldom fully appreciated. Finding the meaning in a passage is a complex operation at best, requiring a good command of the grammar and vocabulary of the language, and resting heavily on the redundancy within and between these. Literary writing differs in important respects from most forms of language with which a person comes in daily contact. It is often grammatically more complex and almost certainly more precise, its vocabulary is commonly more extensive or at least somewhat special, and there tends to be a great deal less redundancy. This combination of factors produces special difficulty for many readers — certainly for most student readers.

The schools have long been aware of one side of the problem and have given it concerted attention. "Vocabulary building" is heavily weighted (as it probably should be[8]) toward literary words. Instruction in the use of dictionaries is standard, and students are expected to use them regularly in their reading. A sizable part of the discussion in literature classes deals with the author's choice of words, and consequently with details of their meanings. When classics are annotated, vocabulary receives the lion's share of attention.

Grammar, by comparison, is neglected. Seldom a topic of discussion in literature classes, it is equally seldom the subject of annotations. The concentration on prescriptive rules has made the application of grammar to

---

[8] But it is probably much less effective than it should be, in part because words are too often taught in isolation. The trend is apparently toward more and better contextualization. This should improve performance appreciably.

accepted literary pieces both embarrassing and presumptuous and has hidden any possible relevance of grammar instruction to reading. Reference grammars having a role comparable to that of dictionaries are unheard of.

Yet grammatical problems are present in all the literary pieces commonly read in the schools, and acute in some. Writers are no less likely to use a construction unfamiliar to a high school student than they are to use a word he will not know. Other things being equal, the strange construction is more of a problem, since we do not have the same flexibility in grammar as in vocabulary.

It is hard to estimate how the responsibility for reading difficulties should be apportioned between these two factors. Indeed, an exact figure would probably be meaningless, for structural and vocabulary problems are not sharply separated. As we have seen, vocabulary contributes to the resolution of potential grammatical ambiguities and vice versa. Redundancy in one helps elucidate problems in the other. As a result, many points of difficulty that come up in reading can be interpreted as examples either of trouble with a word or with a structure. Were the construction understood, the meaning of the word would become clearer, and, conversely, identification of the word meaning would render the construction less obscure.

It is probably inefficient, however, to place so much of the burden on either one factor or the other. Reading would become easier and more natural if attention were given to both vocabulary and structure. Certain misconceptions about literary language would also be dispelled.[9]

It is with the reading of older authors that the problem is most generally acute. The majority of high school students have great difficulty with Shakespeare, and as a consequence they tend to be repelled. Some of the trouble is certainly lexical, but a large part is grammatical. A more balanced set of annotations would help in a small way, but only in a small way, since disjointed notes are not an efficient device for handling anything as systematic as fundamental grammatical patterns.

A more comprehensive strategy to promote acquisition of receptive control of Elizabethan English is to increase the redundancy in the students' early contacts with Shakespeare. New patterns are understood when the

---

[9] Many people recognize a kind of "fancy" literary language characterized primarily by big and difficult words. The notion apparently arises from seeing such words in passages where the reader is unable to sense the care with which they have been selected or their contextual appropriateness. Word choice can only appear erratic if the structures in which the words are embedded are not understood. Certainly, any niceties of style are lost, and the one thing remaining that can make a definite impression is sesquipedalianism. So viewed, literary language is often ridiculed by deliberate parody: *Gyrating petraceous aggregates accumulate no bryophytes.* Just as often it is subject to unconscious parody when efforts are made to "fancify" a piece by meaningless and erratic use of literary vocabulary. Basically, the problem is a particularly acute form of conceiving language solely in terms of words, and less virulent forms of the disease are widespread. In whatever form it occurs, the tendency to think of language in terms of words is a serious problem for every aspect of English (and foreign-language) study. Its eradication must stand high on the list of objectives in any language-centered curriculum.

context makes clear their meaning, and they are learned when repeatedly heard and understood. One way to assure this is to present Shakespeare first in oral form. If read aloud with proper intonation,[10] there is always more redundancy than on the printed page. A still better way is to introduce the plays through stage performances. Thus, visual redundancy is added, and most students are able to understand in spite of language difficulties.

It is striking to see a group of boys return enthusiastic from a Shakespeare theater when those same boys, a few weeks earlier, were in open rebellion against *Julius Caesar*. The change of attitude is the result of a marked difference in level of understanding. The additional redundancy of the stage performance brings them across a threshold between dislike and enjoyment and in so doing drastically alters the learning conditions.

The shortcoming of any approach that rests solely on exposure — whether it is simply to the printed text or to dramatic renditions — is that more may be required than it is feasible to provide. The interests of efficiency demand other supplemental approaches. As in the teaching of composition, some deliberate intervention in the process is called for.

The standard technique has always been the close reading of the text with discussion of interesting or difficult points as they arise. This will be better, of course, if the play has already been seen, so that it is understood as a whole. Even so, there are difficulties, and it is easy for such a reading to wander off into unprofitable sidetracks. The method itself may become either pedantic wrestling with minutiae or vacuous generality. There are, in any passage of Shakespeare, innumerable topics deserving attention, and these must be kept in balance. It is too easy to neglect all but the teacher's special interest. Language, in particular, often drops out of sight, since only a minority of teachers are specially challenged by it. Yet language is basic to any detailed reading, and must have its due share of attention or the whole effort may become unproductive.

Clearly, close reading of text is successful only if certain conditions are met, and of these one of the most important is the proper preparation of the students.[11] We cannot expect them automatically to be qualified to

[10] By "proper intonation" is meant one which will carry a suitable meaning to a modern hearer. This may or may not bear any close relationship to the original Elizabethan patterns, which, in any case, we know only very poorly. This modernization — and the parallel use of current pronunciation — is probably harmless enough, but should be recognized for what it is.

[11] We assume, of course, that the teachers must have a much deeper and more comprehensive preparation than the students. That is, they should not only be perfectly at home in Elizabethan English but they should also be well acquainted in a formal way with all the essential elements of early MnE grammar, with the general processes of language change, and with techniques of analysis. Indeed, one of the causes of the current sad state of grammar is that teachers have been content to know very little more than that which they are to teach. Moreover, to guide students into an understanding of the language of Shakespeare, it is essential to have at least a general knowledge of the problems of the text and its transmission, a subject which I would not consider particularly worthy of systematic presentation in a high school classroom.

discuss language problems intelligently and revealingly. They must have both a technical vocabulary adequate to the task[12] and some skill in approaching language analytically. That is to say, they must have some prior training in grammar that is more than just memorization of definitions and rules. They must have been taught to compare and contrast constructions, to observe regularities, and to generalize. Faced with an Elizabethan sentence that is obscure to them, they must know how to dissect it into its component constructions, to seek parallels, and to formulate hypotheses for testing.

The first demand that the literature segment must make on rehabilitated grammar is, then, that it be reoriented toward analysis, the observation of data, and the framing of descriptions.

In the case of Shakespeare, this is not enough. Differences between Shakespearean English and ours are so profound — and to the uninitiated so strange — that they demand some explanation. The only possible one, of course, is historical. Before a student does very much with Elizabethan literature, he should have been introduced to the basic operations of language change.

Much of this can be done by systematic examination of certain features of Elizabethan English and their comparison with later structures. This has the further virtue of preparing the student specifically for commonly recurrent patterns in the plays. Chapter 16 suggests some of the kinds of problems that might profitably be discussed.

Many progressive English teachers have introduced material on the history of the language into their classrooms. When well done, this has had excellent response from the students. Much of it has dealt with word histories — the material for this is at hand in any good dictionary, and there are good treatments of a more discursive nature readily available. There has been some work on phonologic history, or on the development of English morphology. Again, sufficient details are available in handbooks. There has been, however, relatively little instruction in historical syntax. The reason is obvious enough — the required information is generally not available. But this would be at least as interesting and probably more meaningful than many other aspects of language history. The most significant principles of the grammar of current English are syntactic, and they would profit from a historical undergirding. And, of course, it is syntactic problems that loom largest in Shakespeare.

The teaching of English literature thus makes a second demand that must be met in the rehabilitation of grammar: its broadening to include the historical dimension, particularly in syntax.

---

[12] The common assumption of school grammar seems to be that everything needs a label, and every label a definition. The proper principle is rather that we must provide just as many terms as contribute to clear and decisive discussion, and no more. Moreover, no term is to be admitted until AFTER its referent is understood.

It is not only archaic language that causes difficulty. The more elaborate forms of late Modern English raise nearly as many problems. Indeed, almost every literary work gives continual trouble to some students, and occasional to many more. We have come to expect a certain part of the high school population to be poor readers, and have established remedial programs for them. Here much of the effort is concentrated on "word-attack skills", and for some this is certainly needed. We have, however, very largely failed to cope adequately with the reading difficulties of the group not poor enough to warrant remedial work, or with some of the less immediate problems of the poor readers.

The students' difficulties with the more formal kinds of literary English can be looked at from two points of view. Their language abilities are rooted in colloquial speech where patterns are comparatively simple, language redundancy is high and generally supplemented by situational redundancy. A rather crude order of skill is sufficient to find meanings with adequate accuracy. There is far less redundancy in literary English, and, therefore, a more efficient use is demanded of what there is. Practice, preferably carefully graded, can gradually raise the level of performance, and in any case is probably essential. It is not likely, however, that it can fill the need alone, even in the most favorable cases.

If we consider the variety and intricacy of patterns rather than the level of redundancy, another approach is suggested. Specific attention to constructions not commonly used in colloquial is indicated. This is much the same as what was found to be required in the case of Elizabethan English, but there is a notable difference. The obvious problems with Shakespeare are in divergences at central points in the system — for example, a quite different set of verb-phrase patterns, different negative structures. These require a contrastive, historical treatment. With modern belles lettres, the problems are more peripheral. The central parts of the grammatical system are much the same as those the student already knows well. Trouble stems from structural intricacies involving more elaborate combinations of familiar patterns, from more frequent use of patterns rare in speech, and from additional patterns which are probably totally unfamiliar.

The grammar taught in school has been of very little help in these problems. It deals almost exclusively with patterns with which the student will have little trouble.[13] To be useful, it must be extended outward from the central features of the system to the constructions over which the student has inadequate receptive control. What is needed, then, is a grammar that penetrates more deeply into its traditional subject matter, the

---

[13] There are, of course, some students who do have trouble with some of the central patterns normally included in the grammar syllabus. The majority do not have any RECEPTIVE difficulty, though they may not use these patterns actively.

structure of sentences, so that it can be helpful with the more unusual patterns.

But that is not all. The tight structure of high quality prose is not found only within sentences, but just as much in the sequencing of sentences within the passage. Indeed, there is probably more difference between good literary English and good colloquial in the matter of transitions than in any features of the sentences separately. Readers not thoroughly accustomed to this kind of language have real and troublesome problems here, and this is a place where they need help. The scope of grammar must be extended to include the grammatical features of sentence connection, and this brings in a number of topics hardly touched on in existing textbooks. Most of them are inadequately handled in the reference grammars as well.

If we were to think of grammar as relevant only to the finding of meanings in a passage that might be all. But literary study must also concern itself with style, that is, with the patterning of the choices made within the options presented by the language. If it is to do this, there must be available reasonably precise information about the alternative grammatical structures that are available. That is, it must be based on a grammar that treats of the relationships between agnate sentences. This is a matter that has been touched only lightly and unsystematically in school grammar and is not even mentioned in some competing systems.

The rehabilitated grammar needed for the effective study of literature in a language-based curriculum must, then, be expanded in at least four directions: more deeply into its own traditional subject matter, back into history, upward into larger structures and into the sequences of sentences, and outward into the relations between stylistic alternants.

ENGLISH, MODERN LANGUAGES, AND LINGUISTICS

Some of the most dramatic changes in American education in the last two decades have been in foreign-language teaching. At one time considered a luxury for the academically talented, second language instruction is coming to be accepted as essential for everyone. Languages are started earlier in the school career and continue longer. Methods of teaching are being modernized, and a better balance is being sought between spoken and literary language. More high school graduates are able to use two or three languages, and this ability is more highly valued.

But, while this movement is going forward, language needs are changing even more rapidly. It is becoming ever more obvious that an educated American will have greater need for foreign languages in the near future, but it is becoming more and more difficult to see which ones will be required. A few years ago the problem was very much simpler. Latin, French, German, and Spanish were taught in the best high schools, and only two or three more in most colleges and universities. It was assumed that these languages would fill the needs. And indeed it was often possible to make a reasonable choice among them.

For example, a prospective scientist should take French and German — these would be the languages he would need in his future work, and this fact was recognized in the prescribed examinations for graduate study. This is no longer true; scientific papers are now written in a far greater variety of languages than they were a generation ago. Russian has become more important than French and German in some fields and is a strong competitor in most. Japanese, Chinese, Hindi, and several others are of increasing importance. Few scientists today can effectively cover the literature of their field through as few as half a dozen languages, and the situation seems to be becoming steadily more complex.

Spanish or French always used to be the choice for commercial students. But today international business — and an increasing part of business is international — may find Arabic, Urdu, or Indonesian indispensible.

One response to this situation has been the marked increase in the number of languages taught. Universities which once were quite satisfied with a half dozen may now be teaching thirty or more. The list differs from institution to institution. Considerably over a hundred languages are regularly available somewhere in the United States and the number increases every year. High schools are experimenting with Chinese, Swahili, and Arabic.

This increase in variety cannot, alone, offer any solution. While we are convinced that languages should be taught earlier, we also know that the selection of a language must come later than it did a few years ago. Even if a child of six did know that he was going into international trade, he might not know until he got his first overseas assignment whether he would need Turkish, Thai, or Tagalog.

Faced with this problem, we must have a thoroughgoing reassessment of our language programs. The whole question must be faced on a broader basis than it has been hitherto. Three major things must be done, it would seem to me:

First, the trend toward more, earlier, and better learning of some specific language must be continued. Ultimately, every elementary school child should have a second language, and in most cases a third should be added in high school. But the justification for this will have to be shifted to give less prominence to the values of the specific language and more to the general values of any second language.

Second, both the language instruction itself and other related parts of the total curriculum must be biased more toward preparation for language learning. Perhaps, after all, the best argument for foreign languages in the the elementary school is not that the child learns a language so much as that he learns how to learn a language. But having said that, we must recognize that this is not necessarily true of second-language teaching as it is now done.[14]

Third, students must be prepared to understand and live with "the language problem". They will be influenced for the remainder of their lives by things said and written in languages they do not speak. Much of the world's most significant communication is across language boundaries and is accordingly subject to special, often serious, stresses. It is crucial that educated adults understand the implications of these facts and be able to deal critically with them. For this they must know something of the nature and function of language, of the differences between languages, and of the process of translation.[15] This demands that we build into their education — in whatever niche may be appropriate — a great deal of the subject matter of general linguistics.[16]

The first and second of these are largely the obligation of the modern-language teachers. Yet the program as a whole, and especially the third requirement, poses both an opportunity and a responsibility for a language-centered English curriculum. No such curriculum can be planned without full and detailed consideration of what it may contribute to this larger problem. Nor should it fail to recognize what it stands to gain from any such broadening of the neighboring curriculum. It will not be enough merely to keep informed of developments in modern languages; parts of both curricula will have to be planned, tested, and probably even taught, jointly.

English teachers too often have had their attention centered on English and its literature and their vision limited to its parochial confines. They

---

[14] This is not the place to make any specific recommendations for changes in modern-language instruction. It would seem to me, however, that the field is due for an over-hauling as fundamental as that needed in English — in spite of the fact that there have been basic reforms in the last two decades.

[15] I know of very few efforts to give students any systematic treatment of translation problems. We have, therefore, very little basis for planning a program. Old-fashioned translation exercises, when well done, do give some unsystematized experience, and are valuable. I feel that some formal translation — preferably both ways — should be included in ADVANCED language classes. (Beginners have too much difficulty with the language to get full value from the experience.) But beyond that, something more systematic needs to be done. One thing, also possible in advanced language classes, is the reading of a text and a parallel translation with detailed comparison. Another thing is systematic examination of differences of semantic structure, such as that shown in an elementary way in problems 1.A., 1.B., and 1.C. in H. A. Gleason, Jr., *Workbook in Descriptive Linguistics*, 1955. A third technique is the detailed comparison of two or more translations of the same passage. This was suggested on pages 430 and 460 as a technique for studying style. The same exercises can be used to make some important points about translations.

[16] Certainly linguistics should not be added to the school curriculum as an additional subject at any level. But certain basic notions must be worked into the curriculum of existing subjects. English and modern languages will be most affected, but all social sciences certainly, and mathematics possibly, will also be involved. This must reach down into the lower elementary grades in language arts and second-language instruction.

have felt no need to broaden their students' view, or, if they have been interested in world literature, have done nothing comparable in language. Yet it is impossible to achieve any deep understanding of English from such a narrow base. The language has its roots in its Germanic ancestry and in the Western European unity. It has both its own individuality and its own expression of the language universals. All these are put into a new and revealing light by comparison. These wider aspects are no extraneous additions to English studies, but integral to a full understanding of the language and its use.

Not only so, but some important facts about English are hidden from sight if they can be viewed only from within. Native speakers of English are so accustomed to certain basic patterns of their own language that they are effectively unable to examine them critically. Yet the language is a system, and its coherence is not readily visible if certain central features are forever taken for granted.

The most basic problem in the creative teaching of English grammar is certainly this very fundamental one: Students must be led to think objectively about their language, to raise questions, and to seek answers. They must be able to do these things, above all, with the points that are most familiar and most easily overlooked. These are the features most often basic to the functioning of the whole. Unless they are understood, the system falls apart and the interrelations are not seen. Only some vantage point outside English can serve as a base for some of the crucial investigations.

That this is true of research in English grammar is amply demonstrated by examining the list of important contributors to recent progress in this subject. Some have been continental Europeans: Jespersen, Poutsma, Kruisinga. Some have been linguists prepared through field work on other languages: Trager, Smith, Nida. All have had this extra-English viewpoint from some source or other. It is also true in the classroom study of English grammar. Whatever second language a student knows is important background for his work. In addition, it will often be desirable to give him some passing acquaintance with other language structures simply as background for the presentation of significant concepts of English grammar or linguistics.[17]

---

[17] I have used Swahili noun-phrase patterns to introduce elementary, junior high, and high school students to an examination of English noun phrases, and Hindi questions to introduce problems in English question structure. The experiences, though limited in number, have been very successful. Regular teachers who have tried either the same materials or others of their own devising have been equally enthusiastic. Quite usually, the small amount of time necessary to introduce and work through the non-English problems is more than made up by the much more rapid progress made in the English material. This technique should, of course, be used sparingly. Its function is primarily to introduce a method of attack. Once this has been established, only a very occasional incidental comparison is called for.

Students need to see that more than one way of conveying a message is possible; that the familiar pattern is only one method, neither inherently better nor worse than any other; and that the structure used in any one language can be judged only in the light of its place within that coherent language system. The only feasible way to get such ideas across is by comparison. This must be carefully and systematically done, with thoughtful consideration of the materials used. And to be effective, it must be undergirded with a comprehensive and defensible general view of language.[18]

The rehabilitated grammar which will be needed for the new English curriculum must be firmly anchored in general linguistics. The horizons, both in research and teaching, must extend far beyond the single language of chief concern. It must give a central place to principles which can be understood only in a broad context of interlanguage comparison. It must therefore use such comparison as one of its basic teaching tools.

At the same time, the English curriculum will make use of every opportunity to develop general linguistic principles of the widest possible significance. In part, this is simply accepting its responsibilities within the total process of education. The building of a comprehensive, reasonable, and realistic view of language should be a major obligation in a liberally conceived educational system.[19]

English has a crucial place in this. It is the language best known to most American students. It is the one in which the deepest probings are possible. Some of the more subtle aspects of the nature and functions of language can be adequately presented only in a context such as this. No general teaching about language will be meaningful or successful unless it can be tied in with English, and particularly with the grammar of English.

COHERENCE

A new English curriculum, however it is organized, will differ from the present in making much less of the boundaries between areas within it. There will be much more use of the results of one in the study of another, and there will be more attention to common problems which can be attacked within different frameworks and from different directions. Style is just such a common problem, a meeting ground for language, composition, and literature.[20]

Grammatical ideas and techniques will be employed more extensively

[18] It is not enough that the curriculum planners and lesson writers know a good deal of linguistics. To teach this comparative approach well, classroom teachers must have a good grounding also. They do not, however, need to be acquainted with all the languages used, beyond what is feasibly provided in a teacher's guide to a single lesson.

[19] H. A. Gleason, Jr., *What Grammar?*, 1964, Harvard Educational Review 34:267–281.

[20] H. A. Gleason, Jr., *What Is English?*, 1962, College Composition and Communication 13:1–10.

and effectively in composition and literature.[21] In turn, more of grammar teaching will make use of the data and discoveries in these areas.

For this to be effective, each section of the curriculum must be planned to make the maximum contribution to the others. Yet no part of the whole can be left simply to determination by such external needs. Each must be, within itself, a coherent, intellectually respectable, and teachable system.

In the last three sections of this chapter, there were pointed out some of the requirements which other related areas of study will make of grammar. If these are merely listed, they might seem to be pulling grammar in a number of different, perhaps even contrary, directions. In the past, grammar has suffered terribly from disconnectedness and diffuseness. Any further scattering of effort must be resolutely avoided. The demands must be met within a consistent over-all structure for grammar, or they must be rejected as impossible.

Fortunately, if the demands are brought together and compared, it will be seen that they can be made to fit into a fabric with intellectual dignity. But this can be done only if less basic demands are interpreted in the light of the more basic. That is to say, the organization must be dictated by the needs of grammar, but if it is, the demands of other areas can still very largely be met.

One of the key requirements was developed in a discussion of common problems between English and modern languages: that grammar should be solidly based in general linguistics, on a perspective wider than that of the English language alone. This does not mean, of course, that grammar should be replaced in the curriculum by linguistics. The chief focus of specific attention must unquestionably remain English. It does mean that English is to be looked at in the light of the broadest and most basic generalizations about language as a fundamental human characteristic. It is to be seen as one special case of the much broader phenomenon, language. Accordingly, there need be no apology if data or conclusions from some other speech form are occasionally brought in to illuminate some question in English.

Closely related to this is the second key demand: that "attention center on the phenomena of language and their functions, rather than on terminology and rules" (p. 477). This can be read in two ways, both of them important. First, understanding must be made more central than the apparatus. Second, language must be looked at in a broad context. It must not be simply formal grammar, a neat — and to those who like that sort of thing, satisfying — statement of pure relationships within the structures of English sentences and the systems that underlie them. Rather, it must place all these things within a broad system of communication and show

[21] It may well be that composition and literature do not remain as distinct segments in the curriculum, but just how they may be realigned is not at present visible. Certainly their functions must be discharged somewhere in the new structure. What is said here will apply either to them or to their successors.

how the grammatical features are adapted to the meeting of a complex set of human requirements. Grammar must be functional,[22] not in the simplistic sense of selecting only those points that are directly useful, but in the sense of emphasizing the function along with the internal architecture of language.

Several of the other demands are really nothing more than corollaries of these two. This fact not only permits their inclusion in a rehabilitated grammar, but actually necessitates it. A linguistically and functionally oriented grammar must be broadened in several specific ways.

The functions of language can be seen fully only in the use of whole discourses. A functional view of language cannot recognize anything short of this as an arbitrary endpoint of its concern. It can no more be a grammar of sentences than it can of phrases or of words. Much of what connects sentences in a passage is not grammatical, even nonlinguistic. The structure of longer passages, therefore, transcends grammar. Yet the grammatical features are crucial. A broadly conceived functional linguistic base demands, just as insistently as do other areas of English study, that grammar be extended to larger structures and to features of sentence connections. And it gives this extension a natural place within the whole, so that it need not seem an addendum, but is in fact an integral part of grammar.

Similarly, as has been pointed out (p. 453), much of the grammatical apparatus of a language such as English seems mere needless complexity until its function in resolving stylistic conflicts is recognized. Here the notion of structural alternatives grammatically formulatable — that is, agnate relationships — becomes essential. Grammar has two kinds of statements to make about sentences, for example: one relates to their structure, the other to their relationships. A grammar that does not undertake both tasks is, particularly in a functional context, inadequate of itself.

For exactly the same reason, the significant functional questions about language are missed entirely as long as one takes a superficial and simplistic view. Much of school grammar in restricting attention to the minimum of detail forces such a view. It is not possible within the confines of a school curriculum, of course, to lay out and examine minutely all the details of a language like English. Yet it is essential that the examination move outward from the central basic patterns to a sampling of the peripheral. Only so can some of the most significant functional adaptations of language be made plain. To meet its own objectives, grammar must plunge more deeply into its subject matter.

Clearly, grammar must be related to social context. The ways in which

---

[22] Jespersen uses this term to indicate an emphasis on the function of structure within the language. I am using it to indicate a yet broader emphasis on the function in human communication. It is unfortunate to introduce "functional grammar" in a third meaning, yet no other phrase seems to describe what is intended. I hope that it will not become a label for another entry in the contest between approaches to grammar.

language patterns vary from speaker to speaker, from audience to audience, and from situation to situation are just as crucial to a basic understanding of language and its function as they are to the practical use of language skills. How this variation makes use of grammatical resources and how it affects grammatical patterns give significant insights into the functions of grammatical variety.

Just as certainly, the historical dimension must be examined. Languages change, and in intricate ways, yet through it all they maintain a close adjustment to their functions — which of course may also be changing. Moreover, grammatical patterns preserve in themselves relics of their past history, sometimes with reduced function (and hence perhaps on the road to extinction), sometimes with changed function. A static view of language or of grammar can never serve as a base for deep understanding of either the nature or the function of language.

The emerging patterns of a rehabilitated grammar, then, run closely parallel to the demands laid upon grammar by composition and literary study. We need not fear the further fragmentation that would certainly be disastrous.

TEACHABILITY

All this reinforces an uneasy feeling that will have come over many readers through the first part of this chapter. Both the demands of other areas and the needs of a coherent, intellectually respectable grammar point to a very sizable increase in total content. Will this also be teachable?

Indeed, part of the problem may have been sidestepped by glossing over a difference in the requirements of grammar and of other areas. For example, on page 481 it was suggested that past grammar teaching had failed literature because it had not extended far enough into some of the more minor patterns, that students would be helped with their reading to the extent that these might be included in the syllabus. Then in the last section, we asserted that for a coherent grammar curriculum it would be necessary to treat a "sample" of these minor constructions. Will this "sample" include the construction soon to be encountered in a literature assignment? If it does not, will the needs of literature be served?

We seem to be caught in a dilemma of coverage. A sample may serve to establish the functional significance of language intricacy, but not necessarily to give help whenever the need arises. More complete coverage looks dangerously like the reinstatement of an old enemy. If anything, the traditional grammar syllabus has had an oversupply[23] of "facts", isolable statements about constructions. We certainly cannot go on forever cramming more of these into our program.

---

[23] The "oversupply" is really a matter of bad balance, more facts than can be supported by the weak framework. As more content is put into the syllabus, the theoretical foundations must be strengthened commensurately.

The issue, of course, is a familiar one these days. The basis of inclusion in the curriculum can never again be simply usefulness. The body of useful information is many times larger than what can go into the fullest syllabus. The responsibility to provide a student with what he will need must be met in some other way than by simply giving it to him.

We cannot inform a student in advance of every detail of English grammar that may some day be required. Nor can we fall back on showing him where to look it up — certainly not until good reference grammars become available and in general use.[24] Instead, we must teach him to extrapolate from the known to the needed, to work out the problem for himself when he meets it. A key notion in the grammar curriculum must be extrapolation. This can justify the teaching of a sample, and it must determine something of the sample we will choose to teach.

This brings us back to one of the demands that was raised above: that grammar be "reoriented toward analysis, the observation of data, and the framing of descriptions" (p. 480). That is, we must teach not only a body of facts and theories but also a technique — a technique by which the body of facts and theories can be augmented as needed. This is often referred to today as the "inductive method" of teaching.[25]

We are in a fortunate situation here. A native speaker of English carries around with him a vast store of language habits and of observations of the language of others. He need never lack for an adequate base for extrapolation, provided he knows techniques to make effective use of all this data. Good language work is extrapolation from sound principles and verifiable data, never simply creation *ex nihilo*.

The "inductive method", then, can help us in limiting the total amount of content in the grammar syllabus. Instead of attempting to teach everything which might prove useful — the ponderous scholarly grammars should warn us of the magnitude of such an undertaking — we can be satisfied with a much smaller body of content. It is required only that it exhibit the coherence of the whole and that it provide a suitable base for extrapolation.

Nevertheless, the teaching of grammar must remain a large undertak-

---

[24] Perhaps there is a silver lining here. We are spared the excessive dependence on grammars that has developed with regard to dictionaries. Let us hope that when reference grammars do become available, we will have prepared for their intelligent use by building an attitude of critical respect for their scholarship.

[25] "Inductive teaching" has been applied in various ways ranging from the use of small problems, so set up that the student is practically forced to arrive at precisely the desired formulation, to free-wheeling investigation of language, following whatever leads arise. The most highly programmed versions are easiest and probably least productive. The freer type yields most insight when it can be moderated by a teacher thoroughly acquainted with the technique, the basic facts of language, and the possibilities and limitations of the students. In any case, however, I am concerned here only with those types which do actually provide practice in genuine analytic processes and so train students to observe language and give them the tools to do so effectively. Not all "inductive teaching" necessarily does this.

ing. The content of the new grammar syllabus must certainly be larger than that of the old, and by no small margin. A substantial increase in content raises the question of teachability in a different form. We can certainly expect no increase in the time allotted. Can the new content be handled within the practical dimensions of any reasonable curriculum?

The question can be looked at in terms of teaching efficiency. In the past this has been very low. Grammar has seemed a particularly refractory part of the curriculum. More sheer time and effort seem to be required to obtain even the temporary retention demanded by examinations than is the case in most other subjects. Annual repetition does not lead to mastery. Either grammar is intrinsically unteachable, or the teaching is open to dramatic improvement. Nothing leads me to accept the first alternative, which indeed runs counter to every conviction I have about either grammar or the learning process. Curriculum reform must assume the second and seek ways to make the teaching of grammar distinctly more efficient.

In a book about grammar rather than about method, only the most general principles, particularly those rooted in the nature of the subject itself, can be mentioned. It would seem that at least four features of a rehabilitated grammar curriculum can be expected to contribute significantly to improvement in teachability.

The first of these will be the "inductive method". This has been successful in parallel tasks in other disciplines, notably in modern mathematics. There is every reason to believe that grammar is particularly suited to this approach. No special equipment is needed. The data is plentiful and easily available. Young children have a deep interest in language. Sometimes this curiosity has been suppressed before adolescence, but it is easily re-established in high school if language can be presented as something to explore without prescriptive injunctions casting their shadows. Grammar presents many interesting and instructive problems, of every degree of difficulty. A skillful teacher can guide a class, of whatever ability, into areas where they will find the right balance of success and challenge. There is ample opportunity for a change of pace as needed. Many of the problems can arise naturally out of other work — for example, composition and literature — and others will come to the students' attention as they observe language use among their fellows. Relevance is, therefore, evident.

No one can responsibly suggest that ALL grammar instruction should be inductive, but it is possible for inductive teaching to set the tone for the whole. Grammar then becomes a subject where authority need never be accepted blindly, where a textbook statement is open to verification if desired, and where as yet unanswered questions can be accepted as a part of the normal condition of human knowledge.

The second feature contributing to a new teachability will be closer attention to the most basic central principles. Again modern mathematics can provide a model. Instead of beginning with addition as a manipulation of numbers and a set of "arithmetic facts" to be memorized, more and more curricula are starting with the patient development of the basic concept of number. The result is slower progress at first, but much more solid and rapid progress later. Addition now has real meaning. Much the same is needed in grammar teaching. Formal instruction must start with principles antecedent to the definitions of parts of speech. As we have mentioned, it is particularly difficult to give the required attention to these as long as the sole focus is English. It is too easy to take familiar things for granted. Here is one place where the judicious use of cross-language comparison is demonstrably fruitful.

The third feature is perhaps only a variation of the last. This is increased attention to "pregrammar" instruction, that is, to the development of basic linguistic notions and attitudes long before any separate segment of the curriculum can be labeled "grammar". A very large part of primary education deals directly with language. In addition to the skills of reading, writing, spelling, and new forms of speech, a child inevitably picks up unformulated but powerful ideas and feelings about language. Some of these rise up to plague English teachers in later years. Instead, there might be planted seeds of sound insights and constructive attitudes. For example, the improvement of phonics instruction, so that it will exploit our best phonetic and phonemic understandings,[26] will start one stream of development. Increased attention to sentence structure in beginning reading[27] will give another. The extension of foreign-language instruction through the early elementary grades will provide a third. These — and others — can bring students to the upper elementary grades with important foundations well laid. In the long view, every element in the language arts curriculum must be re-examined and probably redesigned to contribute toward ultimate linguistic understanding of a basic sort.

Fourth, we must assume that the increased over-all coherence of the new grammar curriculum will contribute in a marked way to its teachability. There is a growing conviction among learning theorists that integration is one of the most significant factors. Meaningful, interrelated material is not only more easily learned but far better retained. The emphasis in grammar teaching must be shifted to the more general and more widely relevant principles. Details — and many must be treated in a grammar class, of course — must always be clearly related to these fundamentals.

We must not, however, place too high hopes on any one of these changes alone. It is the combination of all four — together with other reforms of the same general nature — that must be counted on. These four do fit together as mutually supporting. With the changes suggested in content, they should go far toward making the rehabilitated English grammar coherent, intellectually respectable, and effectively teachable.

[26] See Charles C. Fries, *Linguistics and Reading*, 1963.
[27] See Carl A. Lefevre, *Linguistics and the Teaching of Reading*, 1964.

CRITICAL THINKING

The suggested recommendations for the rehabilitation of grammar make it more useful to other areas of study and at the same time render it a more viable unity. In addition, they converge on a major objective of curriculum reform in any field: the development of the ability to think critically, in this case about language. There is no need to document past failure in this regard beyond what was done in Chapter 1. The sources of the difficulty rest largely with prescriptivism, a static and simplistic notion of language, and the confusion of arbitrary English patterns with universal logic. These three sets of errors are intimately related, each reinforcing the others. Any thoroughgoing reform must attack all three as decisively as possible and work for their complete and permanent banishment from the classroom.

To effect the needed rehabilitation, it is not simply the content or the methods of teaching that must be changed, but just as much the attitudes toward grammar. Traditionally, it has been looked on largely as a tool useful in the teaching of correct speech and writing, but of no independent intellectual value. It has been a Cinderella consigned to scouring the grimiest pots in the composition classroom.

The reforms which have been discussed in the last sections will go a long way toward changing this. If prescriptive notions of correctness are abandoned and if language is approached inductively against the background of a broad set of fundamental principles, attitudes toward language will inevitably improve. There is one essential additional step: We must also develop a critical attitude toward the tools with which language is investigated and the framework within which it is discussed. We must not simply replace naïveté about English with dogmatism about linguistics. A critical approach to language must turn back on itself and examine its own instruments. An educated person needs to understand not only the nature and function of language but equally the nature and function of grammars, for these also have their strengths and limitations, and our understanding of language is inevitably colored in various ways by them.

Fortunately, we have a great deal of direct evidence which we can marshal to this question. English grammar has been approached from many different directions, some of them with quite disparate philosophical foundations and conflicting basic assumptions. The contrast of one grammar with another can give us much insight into the nature and functioning of grammars. Beyond this direct comparison, we have a priceless resource in the continuing debate among linguists. These range from mere bickerings to very fundamental discussions of the basis and validity of our knowledge of language.

Much of this should be known to every teacher of English. Indeed, it has been one of the major objectives of this book to show some of it. A smaller part should be shown to students in the schools. That is, we should give them more than one system of grammar, and help them come to grips with the basic differences between them. They must learn to approach grammars as thoughtfully as we hope they will language.

The commonly asked question, "Which grammar should we teach?" is, therefore, a false one. We must teach two or more — not from indecision, but from deliberate choice. This is the only way there is to exhibit to the students the basic strengths and weaknesses of any one system and the fundamental questions that cluster around every theory.

In grammar, as in everything else, students must learn something of the limits and validity of their knowledge. This is the essence of a liberal education.

Bibliography

Bibliography

ABBOTT, EDWIN ABBOTT. *A Shakespearean Grammar.* London: Macmillan, 1888.

ALLEN, HAROLD BYRON (ed.). *Readings in Applied English Linguistics,* second ed. New York: Appleton-Century-Crofts, 1964.

ALLEN, ROBERT LIVINGSTON. *A Modern Grammar of Written English.* New York: Macmillan, 1965.

ATWOOD, ELMER BAGBY. *A Survey of Verb Forms in the Eastern United States.* Ann Arbor, Mich.: University of Michigan Press, 1953.

BACH, EMMON WERNER. *An Introduction to Transformational Grammars.* New York: Holt, Rinehart and Winston, 1964.

BARTLETT, JOHN. *A New and Complete Concordance . . . to the Dramatic Works of Shakespeare.* London: Macmillan, 1894.

BAUGH, ALBERT CROLL. *A History of the English Language,* second ed. New York: Appleton-Century-Crofts, 1957.

BLOOMFIELD, LEONARD. *Language.* New York: Holt, Rinehart and Winston, 1933.

BORGH, ENOLA M. *Grammatical Patterns and Composition.* Oshkosh, Wisc.: Wisconsin Council of Teachers of English, 1963.

BRONSTEIN, ARTHUR J. *The Pronunciation of American English, An Introduction to Phonetics.* New York: Appleton-Century-Crofts, 1960.

BROOKS, GEORGE LESLIE. *English Dialects.* New York: Oxford, 1963.

BRUNER, JEROME SEYMOUR. *The Process of Education.* Cambridge, Mass.: Harvard University Press, 1961.

BRYANT, MARGARET M. *A Functional English Grammar.* Boston: Heath, 1959.

———. *Current American Usage.* New York: Funk & Wagnalls, 1962.

CAMBRIDGE CONFERENCE ON SCHOOL MATHEMATICS. *Goals for School Mathematics.* Boston: Houghton Mifflin, 1963.

CARROLL, JOHN BISSELL (ed.). *Language, Thought, and Reality: Selected Writings of Benjamin Lee Whorf.* Cambridge, Mass.: Technology Press, 1956.

CHATMAN, SEYMOUR. *A Theory of Meter.* 's-Gravenhage: Mouton & Company, 1965.

CHOMSKY, NOAM AVRAM. *Syntactic Structures.* 's-Gravenhage: Mouton & Company, 1957. (Janua Linguarum, Series Minor, no. 4)

CURME, GEORGE OLIVER. *Syntax. (A Grammar of the English Language,* Vol. 3). Boston: Heath, 1931.

———. *Parts of Speech and Accidence. (A Grammar of the English Language,* Vol. 2). Boston: Heath, 1935.

EPSTEIN, EDMUND A., and TERENCE HAWKES. *Linguistics and English Prosody.* Buffalo, N. Y.: Studies in Linguistics, 1959. (Occasional Papers, 7)

FODOR, JERRY A., and JERROLD J. KATZ (eds.). *The Structure of Language: Readings in the Philosophy of Language.* Englewood Cliffs, N. J.: Prentice-Hall, 1964.

FRANCIS, WINTHROP NELSON. *The Structure of American English.* New York: Ronald, 1958.

———. *The English Language: An Introduction.* New York: Norton, 1965.

FRIES, CHARLES CARPENTER. *American English Grammar.* New York: Appleton-Century-Crofts, 1940.

———. *The Structure of English: An Introduction to the Construction of English Sentences.* New York: Harcourt, Brace & World, 1952.

GARVIN, PAUL L. (ed. and trans.). *A Prague School Reader on Esthetics, Literary Structure, and Style.* Washington, D. C.: Georgetown University Press, 1964.

GIMSON, A. C. *An Introduction to the Pronunciation of English.* London: Edward Arnold, 1962.

GLEASON, HENRY ALLAN, JR. *Workbook in Descriptive Linguistics.* New York: Holt, Rinehart and Winston, 1955.

———. *An Introduction to Descriptive Linguistics*, rev. ed. New York: Holt, Rinehart and Winston, 1961.

HALL, ROBERT ANDERSON, JR. *Linguistics and Your Language.* New York: Doubleday, 1960.

———. *Introductory Linguistics.* Philadelphia: Chilton Books, 1964.

HALLIDAY, M. A. K., ANGUS McINTOSH, and PETER STREVENS. *The Linguistic Sciences and Language Teaching.* London: Longmans, 1964.

HILL, ARCHIBALD ANDERSON. *Introduction to Linguistic Structures: From Sound to Sentence in English.* New York: Harcourt, Brace & World, 1958.

HOCKETT, CHARLES FRANCIS. *A Course in Modern Linguistics.* New York: Macmillan, 1958.

HORNBY, ALBERT S. *A Guide to Patterns and Usage in English.* London: Oxford, 1954.

———, E. V. GATENBY, and E. WAKEFIELD. *The Advanced Learner's Dictionary of Current English*, second ed. London: Oxford, 1963.

HOUSE, HOMER C., and SUSAN EMOLYN HARMAN. *Descriptive English Grammar*, second ed. Englewood Cliffs, N. J.: Prentice-Hall, 1950.

IVES, SUMNER. *A New Handbook for Writers.* New York: Knopf, 1960.

JAKOBSON, ROMAN, and MORRIS HALLE. *Fundamentals of Language.* 's-Gravenhage: Mouton & Company, 1956.

JESPERSEN, JENS OTTO HARRY. *Language, Its Nature, Development, and Origin.* London: G. Allen, 1922.

———. *A Modern English Grammar on Historical Principles.* København: Ejnar Munksgaard, 1909–1949.

———. *Growth and Structure of the English Language*, ninth ed. Oxford: Basil Blackwell, 1960.

———. *Essentials of English Grammar.* New York: Henry Holt, 1933. Reprinted, University of Alabama Press, 1964.

JOOS, MARTIN. *The Five Clocks.* Bloomington, Ind.: Indiana University Press, 1962. (Indiana University Research Center in Anthropology, Folklore, and Linguistics, Publication 22)

———. *The English Verb, Form and Meanings.* Madison, Wisc.: University of Wisconsin Press, 1964.

KATZ, JERROLD J., and PAUL M. POSTAL. *An Integrated Theory of Linguistic Descriptions*. Cambridge, Mass.: M. I. T. Press, 1964. (Research Monograph, no. 26)

KÖKERITZ, HELGE. *Shakespeare's Pronunciation*. New Haven, Conn.: Yale University Press, 1953.

KURATH, HANS. *A Word Geography of the Eastern United States*. Ann Arbor, Mich.: University of Michigan Press, 1949.

——. *A Phonology and Prosody of Modern English*. Ann Arbor, Mich.: University of Michigan Press, 1964.

——, and RAVEN I. McDAVID, JR. *The Pronunciation of English in the Atlantic States*. Ann Arbor, Mich.: University of Michigan Press, 1961.

KRUISINGA, ETSKO. *A Handbook of Present-Day English*, fourth ed. Utrecht: Kemink en Zoon, 1925.

LEES, ROBERT B. *The Grammar of English Nominalizations*. Bloomington, Ind.: Research Center in Anthropology, Folklore, and Linguistics, 1960.

LEHMANN, WINFRED PHILIPP. *Historical Linguistics: An Introduction*. New York: Holt, Rinehart and Winston, 1962.

LEONARD, STERLING ANDRUS. *The Doctrine of Correctness in English Usage, 1700–1800*. New York: Russell and Russell, 1929.

——. *Current English Usage*. Chicago: Inland Press, 1932.

LEVIN, SAMUEL R. *Linguistic Structures in Poetry*. 's-Gravenhage: Mouton & Company, 1962. (Janua Linguarum, Series Minor, no. 23)

LLOYD, DONALD J., and HARRY R. WARFEL. *American English in its Cultural Setting*. New York: Knopf, 1957.

LONG, RALPH B. *The Sentence and Its Parts: A Grammar of Contemporary English*. Chicago: University of Chicago Press, 1961.

McINTOSH, ANGUS. *An Introduction to a Survey of Scottish Dialects*. Edinburgh: Thomas Nelson & Sons, 1952.

MARCKWARDT, ALBERT HENRY. *American English*. New York: Oxford, 1958.

——, and FRED WALCOTT. *Facts about Current American Usage*. New York: Appleton-Century-Crofts, 1938.

MARTINET, ANDRÉ. *A Functional View of Language*. Oxford: Clarendon Press, 1962.

——. *Elements of General Linguistics*. London: Faber, 1964.

MENCKEN, HENRY LOUIS. *The American Language: An Inquiry into the Development of English in the United States*, abridged ed. New York: Knopf, 1963.

MIRIAM JOSEPH, SISTER. *Shakespeare's Use of the Arts of Language*. New York: Columbia University Press, 1947. abridged as *Rhetoric in Shakespeare's Time*. New York: Harcourt, Brace & World, 1962.

NESFIELD, J. C. *English Grammar, Past and Present*. London: Macmillan, 1898.

NEWSOME, VERNA L. *Structural Grammar in the Classroom*. Milwaukee: Wisconsin Council of Teachers of English, 1961.

NIDA, EUGENE ALBERT. *A Synopsis of English Syntax*. Norman, Okla.: Summer Institute of Linguistics, 1960.

ORNSTEIN, JACOB, and WILLIAM W. GAGE. *The ABC's of Languages and Linguistics*. Philadelphia: Chilton Books, 1964.

The Oxford English Dictionary. Oxford: Oxford University Press, 1933.

PALMER, HAROLD E., and F. G. BLANDFORD. *A Grammar of Spoken English on a Strictly Phonetic Basis*, rev. ed. Cambridge: W. Heffer & Sons, 1939.

PEDERSEN, HOLGER. *Linguistic Science in the 19th Century*. John Webster Spargo, trans. Cambridge, Mass.: Harvard University Press, 1931. Reprinted as *The Discovery of Language*. Bloomington, Ind.: Indiana University Press, 1962.

PENCE, R. W., and D. W. EMERY. *A Grammar of Present-Day English*, second ed. New York: Macmillan, 1963.

POSTMAN, NEIL, HAROLD MORINE, and GRETA MORINE. *Discovering Your Language*. New York: Holt, Rinehart and Winston, 1963. [The teacher's edition contains additional pages.]

POTTER, SIMEON. *Modern Linguistics*. London: André Deutsch, 1957.

POUTSMA, HENDRIK. *A Grammar of Late Modern English*, second ed. Groningen: P. Noordhoff, 1914–1929.

PYLES, THOMAS. *The Origins and Development of the English Language*. New York: Harcourt, Brace & World, 1964.

QUIRK, RANDOLPH. *The Use of English*. London: Longmans, 1962.

ROBERTS, PAUL. *Patterns of English*. New York: Harcourt, Brace & World, 1956. [The teacher's edition contains a *Teacher's Guide*.]

——. *English Sentences*. New York: Harcourt, Brace & World, 1962.

——. *Teacher's Manual, English Sentences*. New York: Harcourt, Brace & World, 1962.

——. *English Syntax: A Book of Programmed Lessons*. New York: Harcourt, Brace & World, 1964. [There are several editions for different markets.]

ROBERTSON, STUART. *The Development of Modern English*, second ed. Englewood Cliffs, N. J.: Prentice-Hall, 1954.

ROBINS, R. H. *General Linguistics: An Introductory Survey*. London: Longmans, 1964.

ROGOVIN, SYRELL. *Modern English Sentence Structure*. New York: Random House, 1964.

SAPIR, EDWARD. *Language: An Introduction to the Study of Speech*. New York: Harcourt, Brace & World, 1921.

SCHEURWEGHS, G. *Analytical Bibliography of Writings on Modern English Morphology and Syntax 1877–1960*. Louvain, Belgium: Nauwelaerts, 1963–

SCHLAUCH, MARGARET. *The Gift of Tongues*. Reprinted as *The Gift of Language*. New York: Dover Publications, 1955.

SEBEOK, THOMAS A. (ed.). *Style in Language*. Cambridge, Mass.: The Technology Press, 1960.

SLEDD, JAMES. *A Short Introduction to English Grammar*. Chicago: Scott, Foresman, 1959.

——, and WILMA R. EBBITT. *Dictionaries and That Dictionary*. Chicago: Scott, Foresman, 1962.

STAGEBERG, NORMAN C. *An Introductory English Grammar*. New York: Holt, Rinehart and Winston, 1965.

STEWART, WILLIAM A. (ed.). *Non-Standard Speech and the Teaching of English*. Washington, D. C.: Center for Applied Linguistics, 1964.

STOKOE, WILLIAM C., JR. *The Calculus of Structure, A Manual for College Students*. Washington, D. C.: Gallaudet College, 1960.

STRANG, BARBARA M. H. *Modern English Structure.* New York: St. Martins Press, 1962.

TRAGER, GEORGE LEONARD, and HENRY LEE SMITH, JR. *An Outline of English Structure.* (Studies in Linguistics, Occasional Papers, no. 3). Reprinted, Washington, D. C.: American Council of Learned Societies, 1957.

TUCKER, SUSIE I. (ed.). *English Examined: Two Centuries of Comment on the Mother-Tongue.* Cambridge: Cambridge University Press, 1961.

TWADDELL, WILLIAM FREEMAN. *The English Verb Auxiliaries,* second ed. Providence: Brown University Press, 1963.

WATERMAN, JOHN THOMAS.   *Perspectives in Linguistics.* Chicago: University of Chicago Press, 1963.

Webster's Third New International Dictionary of the English Language, Unabridged. Springfield, Mass.: G. & C. Merriam, 1961.

WHITEHALL, HAROLD. *Structural Essentials of English.* New York: Harcourt, Brace & World, 1956.

ZANDVOORT, REINARD WILLEM. *A Handbook of English Grammar.* London: Longmans, 1957.

Linguistics

DESCRIPTIVE There are four acceptable textbooks. Each has its own characteristic emphasis, so that they are complementary in many respects, and it would be worthwhile to read two or more of them. Robins' *General Linguistics* is the shortest, easiest, and most literate, and is the best place to start for a person whose background is in English studies. It is British, and so presents a neo-Firthian point of view, but it does not neglect other approaches. The other three are American and all generally Bloomfieldian, though none is strictly orthodox. Taken together they indicate rather well the range of variation in position within the mainstream of American linguistics. Hockett's *A Course in Modern Linguistics* is probably the most difficult and also the most strongly oriented toward linguistic theory. Hall's *Introductory Linguistics* tends to emphasize systematic presentation of results rather than either theory or method. Examples are largely drawn from modern European languages. Gleason's *An Introduction to Descriptive Linguistics* has the heaviest emphasis on the analysis of language, and tends to prefer less well-known languages for examples. It is best studied in connection with his *Workbook in Descriptive Linguistics*, which gives graded problems from a wide range of languages.

Two books by Martinet, *Elements of General Linguistics* and *A Functional View of Language*, give a significant European view useful as a counterbalance to American prejudices. The first is a rather easy textbook, almost a popularization. The second is a series of lectures dealing with rather fundamental issues and giving minimum attention to details. Sapir's *Language* is a classic—well written, insightful, and remarkably undimmed by age. It provides a perspective that many of the newer books fail to give, and should be considered essential reading for everyone seriously interested in language.

TRANSFORMATIONAL-GENERATIVE To go beyond the treatment of transformational-generative grammar in this book, the next step should be Bach's

An Introduction to Transformational Grammars. This gives a good treatment of every aspect of the theory in textbook form. It is written for persons who already have some fundamental orientation in linguistics. After that, turn to the article by Edward S. Klima, *Negation in English*, in Fodor and Katz' *The Structure of Language*. This discusses a set of structures in a semi-inductive way that gives insight into the rationale of the theory as its adherents see it. Chomsky's *Syntactic Structures* is now the classic formulation of the position, and as such must be read carefully by anyone deeply interested in English grammar or in linguistics. It has a reputation, not wholly deserved, of being difficult, and partly for this reason should be studied after Bach's book and Klima's article. Transformational-generative theory is in a state of rapid evolution, and Chomsky's *Syntactic Structures* has now been superseded at many points, though it is still frequently referred to. A much more recent stage in the development is recorded in Katz and Postal's *An Integrated Theory of Linguistic Descriptions*. This will be difficult reading, but it is essential if current work is to be understood. It attempts to bring together the theory of syntax stemming from *Syntactic Structures* with the theory of semantics developed in Katz and Fodor's *The Structure of a Semantic Theory*, which is now reprinted in Fodor and Katz' *The Structure of Language*. This collection includes several other papers of importance, among them two by Morris Halle which present the approach to phonology usual among transformational-generative linguists. Lees' *The Grammar of English Nominalizations* should be studied as an exemplification of the theory in application to a specific problem.

HISTORICAL   Hockett's *A Course in Modern Linguistics*, Hall's *Introductory Linguistics*, and Robins' *General Linguistics* all include treatments of historical and comparative approaches to language, and any one of them will serve as a good introduction. Another useful recent treatment is Lehmann's *Historical Linguistics*. Bloomfield's *Language* is now quite obsolete in some parts, but the treatment of historical material is still excellent, and in some places superior to any later statement. It would be well to work through two or more of these sources.

English Grammar

SCHOOL GRAMMAR   Most high school textbooks are based on school grammar, but generally with so much abridgment that the system cannot be seen clearly. For reference purposes or for systematic study, two books can be recommended: House and Harman's *Descriptive English Grammar* and Pence and Emery's *A Grammar of Present-Day English*. There are small differences (for example, House and Harman follows Reed and Kellogg very closely, whereas Pence and Emery introduces some minor modifications), but they are too much alike to supplement each other effectively. For a contrasting treatment within the same general frame of reference, it is useful to go outside the American tradition. Nesfield's *English Grammar, Past and Present* presents a full and conservative statement of British school grammar.

SCHOLARLY TRADITIONAL GRAMMARS   The major works are discussed on pages 77 and 78. For any serious research all of these should be consulted, not only for their analysis but primarily for their excellent and copious examples. For ready reference there are three useful one-volume works: Jespersen's *Essentials of English Grammar* is the smallest of these, giving a convenient summary of the approach used in his seven-volume grammar. Zandvoort's *A Handbook of English Grammar* represents the conservative central position in traditional grammar and is probably the most convenient for quick reference. Long's *The Sentence and Its Parts* gives a wealth of details and many original suggestions. It is more influenced by recent linguistic work than the others. Nevertheless, it has a very weak theoretical framework and a sometimes idiosyncratic terminology. These features make it essential that it be used in conjunction with some other book, but when so used it is very useful. Bryant's *A Functional English Grammar* is an American textbook heavily influenced by scholarly traditional grammar, primarily by Jespersen. It would be a desirable subsidiary textbook in many English grammar classes.

RECENT INNOVATIONS   Structural grammar stems largely from Fries' *American English Grammar*, and more especially from Fries' *The Structure of English* (see pp. 19–20 and 79–81). The influence of these books can be discerned in almost all of the many "linguistically oriented" grammar textbooks, perhaps most strongly in Roberts' *Patterns of English.*

A second major line of development was first comprehensively formulated in Trager and Smith's *An Outline of English Structure* (see pp. 82–84). This is essential background for any serious work in the teaching of English grammar. Most of the "linguistically oriented" textbooks have depended heavily on Trager and Smith for their phonology, and indeed even the amount of attention devoted to phonology is a reflection of the influence from this source. Some have modified the analysis more or less—most drastically in Sledd's *A Short Introduction to English Grammar.* Influence in grammar proper has been much less. It is, however, strong in Stokoe's *The Calculus of Structure.* Much the same approach as in Trager and Smith is further elaborated, with some modifications, in Hill's *Introduction to Linguistic Structures.*

A pure IC approach is seen in Nida's *A Synopsis of English Syntax.* (see p. 85). This book is a useful source of information, but unfortunately not organized for easy reference.

Allen's *A Modern Grammar of Written English* uses a slot-and-filler approach. It is written as a reference grammar primarily for the use of teachers.

British teachers of English as a second language were experimenting with new grammatical frameworks before there was much thought of such a possibility in America. Two of these are very suggestive and deserve to be much more widely known in this country. Palmer and Blandford's *A Grammar of Spoken English* attempted to build a new approach to the structure of the language based largely on phonetics. Its handling of syntax is sketchy but there are a few grammatical points which it treats well. Hornby's *A Guide to Patterns and Usage in English* gives a very full treatment of sentence patterns with copious examples, and for that reason is an indispensible reference work for anyone concerned with English grammar.

TRANSFORMATIONAL-GENERATIVE GRAMMAR   Most treatments of transformational-generative theory use English examples, often giving a restricted grammar, but there is no comprehensive grammar on this model yet available. The most complete treatment of English to date is to be found in Lees' *The Grammar of English Nominalizations*. We now have two textbooks based squarely on this approach: Roberts' *English Syntax*, a few points of which are discussed in Chapter 12, and Rogovin's *Modern English Sentence Structure*. Both are programmed. Rogovin's book penetrates less deeply and uses quite traditional terminology throughout. It would probably be suitable at a lower grade level than Roberts'.

SPECIAL TOPICS There have been many special studies of English syntax published as monographs or in periodicals. A convenient listing of some of the more significant of these can be found in Scheurwegh's *Analytical Bibliography*. For work more recent than 1960, some of the journals must be examined. Among the most important are *American Speech, English Studies, Language,* and *Word*. In the last few years a great deal of attention has been focused on the verbal system. Several monographs have appeared reflecting a variety of approaches. Twaddell's *The English Verb Auxiliaries* is the basis for the treatment in this book, particularly in Chapter 13. Joos' *The English Verb* is a later and fuller work following in general the same approach. Others can be found through the current periodicals.

LINGUISTICALLY ORIENTED TEXTBOOKS The following textbooks for high school or junior high school have appeared: Roberts' *Patterns of English* will serve as a reference point. Postman, Morine, and Morine's *Discovering Your Language* can be used at a level a grade or two below this. Rogovin's *Modern English Sentence Structure* would seem useful at about the same level. Roberts' *English Sentences* has been used successfully in the next year after *Patterns of English*. Roberts' *English Syntax* would seem to be best suited for the same level as *English Sentences*. A series including Postman, Morine, and Morine's *Discovering Your Language* as the first volume has recently been announced, and three others should be available by the time this is in print.

College textbooks are more numerous and, if anything, more diverse: Francis' *The Structure of American English*, Ives' *A New Handbook for Writers*, Lloyd and Warfel's *American English in its Cultural Setting*, Sledd's *A Short Introduction to English Grammar*, Stokoe's *The Calculus of Structure*, and Whitehall's *Structural Essentials of English*. In addition, at least Roberts' *English Syntax* is being marketed for both high school and college use—the latter labeled "Alternative Edition". Strang's *Modern English Structure* is a British textbook on a level somewhat above the typical American freshman English course. After a short lull, there seems to be renewed activity in the publication of linguistically oriented college textbooks. Francis' *The English Language* and Stageberg's *An Introductory English Grammar* represent two such published this year, and there are others in preparation.

Related Topics

ENGLISH PHONOLOGY In addition to treatments in all introductory linguistics textbooks, there are a number of good books on English phonetics. We list only two recent works, one American and one British. These reflect not only differences in pronunciation but also lesser differences in phonetic theory: Bronstein's *The Pronunciation of American English* and Gimson's *An Introduction to the Pronunciation of English.*

In America the most widely used analysis of the English phonemic system is that first stated in full in Trager and Smith's *An Outline of English Structure.* A quite different approach is presented rather fully in Kurath's *A Phonology and Prosody of Modern English.* The transformational-generative linguists have been sharply critical of the whole phonemic theory as developed by Sapir, Bloomfield, and their followers. The phonetic theory on which their work is based can be found in Jakobson and Halle's *Fundamentals of Language.*

LANGUAGE VARIATION   A survey of American dialects has been underway for over three decades, and we will soon have coverage of the whole country. However, it takes a long time after completion of field work before the data can be organized into useful general statements. The three summary statements that have appeared are, therefore, limited to the East: Kurath's *A Word Geography of the United States,* Atwood's *A Survey of Verb Forms in the Eastern United States,* and Kurath and McDavid's *The Pronunciation of English in the Atlantic States.* The best brief summary of this work is that by McDavid included as Chapter 9 in Francis' *The Structure of American English.*

The initial publication of data for a comparable survey of England is just getting started, and summary studies based on it have not yet appeared. What is known of British dialects is most conveniently seen in Brook's *English Dialects,* and this will lead to some of the important monographs. The best introduction to the objectives and methods of such investigations can be found in McIntosh's *An Introduction to a Survey of Scottish Dialects.*

Material on social dialect is both scant and scattered. There is no single work that can be recommended as giving an overview of the problems. Some suggestions of the implications for the schools can be found in Stewart's *Non-Standard Speech and the Teaching of English.*

The fundamental work on situational variation is Joos' *The Five Clocks,* a most unusually provocative book. It should be considered essential reading for all English teachers.

HISTORY OF ENGLISH   There are a number of textbooks. Baugh's *A History of the English Language* has long been the standard, but concentrates very heavily on the external history, and hence skimps on the history of the language system. Robertson's *Development of Modern English* is much the same kind of book, but some consider it better balanced and less shallow. Pyles' *The Origins and Development of the English Language* is the most recent, and perhaps the most satisfactory for an introductory course. There is a great need for a book at a somewhat higher level that makes full use of recent research. Jespersen's *Growth and Structure* is an excellent older work.

For American English specifically, Marckwardt's *American English* is a useful introductory treatment. For a vast store of details, Mencken's *The American Language* has a pre-eminent place. It has recently been abridged and annotated by Raven McDavid.

It is easier to find good sources on OE and ME than on early MnE. Abbott's *A Shakespearean Grammar,* though not easily obtained and often very wrong in detail, remains the best we have in English. If used with Bartlett's *A New and Complete Concordance*, it can lead to many important examples. Early MnE phonology is somewhat better covered in Kökeritz' *Shakespeare's Pronunciation*. Sister Miriam Joseph's *Shakespeare's Use of the Arts of Language* is indispensible for an understanding of the rhetorical aspects of early MnE literature.

LEXICOGRAPHY Two dictionaries should be considered essential primary sources: For any work on the history of English, either lexical or grammatical, *The Oxford English Dictionary* is always the basic tool. Only a few high school libraries own it, but any one which intends to give strong support to the English program should. Students should be made acquainted with it and given experience in using it. For the modern vocabulary, *Webster's Third New International Dictionary* is essential. Every English teacher should make a careful study of the front matter, where, for example, is given an excellent and thorough treatment of English spelling and pronunciation.

Every classroom in which grammar is taught should have Hornby, Gatenby, and Wakefield's *The Advanced Learner's Dictionary*. This gives more detailed information on grammatical points than any other dictionary. It is, moreover, in effect an index to Hornby's *A Guide to Patterns and Usage*, where copious parallel examples can always be found.

Sledd and Ebbitt's *Dictionaries and That Dictionary* gives full documentation of the attitudes of the public toward dictionaries.

HISTORY OF LINGUISTICS AND OF GRAMMAR We are badly in need of a moderate-length treatment of the history of linguistics based on a thorough restudy of the sources. The best recent work is Waterman's *Perspectives in Linguistics*, a small book and necessarily very limited in coverage. With this should be read Pedersen's *The Discovery of Language* and the relevant parts of Jespersen's *Language*.

A history of English grammar is even more badly needed. There are casual remarks or even short chapters in many books on English, but these all tend to be colored unduly by present-day polemic, and in particular seldom come to grips with the development of basic points of view. Leonard's *The Doctrine of Correctness* treats one aspect over a century. Tucker's *English Examined* gives an assortment of passages from a number of authors of the formative period; in those where I am familiar with the original works, the selection seems to be good. For a more recent period, a few of the landmark books should be read: Leonard's *Current English Usage*, Marckwardt and Walcott's *Facts about Current American Usage*, and Fries' *American English Grammar* among them.

USAGE Apart from the numerous handbooks, which exhibit various degrees of conservatism, the most useful source is Bryant's *Current American Usage*. This summarizes a large number of empiric studies on specific points.

LINGUISTICS AND LITERATURE There is a rising interest in the applications of linguistics to the study of literature. This has focused, for evident reasons, most heavily on poetry. Two books treat English metrics from a linguistic point of view. Epstein and Hawkes' *Linguistics and English Prosody* is based on Trager and Smith's analysis of stress and intonation; Chatman's *A Theory of Meter* is based on that of Dwight Bolinger. Though approaching the problems in quite different ways, both demonstrate the necessity of a foundation in phonology for any further advance in the study of poetic form. Levin's *Linguistic Structures in Poetry* deals primarily with the grammatical dimension. Sebeok's *Style in Language* is the report of a conference of linguists, literary scholars, and others. The papers are notably uneven in value, but some are of considerable interest. The whole symposium demonstrates something of the difficulty of bringing together in a fruitful way all of the competences which must be applied in a comprehensive approach to literature. The papers gathered by Garvin in *A Prague School Reader* represent an earlier and very significant effort to bring together the study of language and literature. Joos' *The Five Clocks* and certain of Whorf's papers in Carroll's edition of *Language, Thought, and Reality*, though addressed primarily to other questions, are very suggestive.

TEACHING Books on the teaching of English generally give little attention to grammar and particularly to the implications of linguistics in the teaching of grammar. They are often completely silent on any possible applications of either grammar or linguistics to basic problems of literature or composition. This deficiency has been partially made up by a number of pamphlets, two of which are listed: Newsome's *Structural Grammar in the Classroom* and Borgh's *Grammatical Patterns and Composition*. Other suggestions can be found in the professional journals or in the publication lists circulated periodically from the National Council of Teachers of English.

Less directly concerned with classroom procedures is a recent book by three British linguists. Halliday, McIntosh, and Strevens' *The Linguistic Sciences and Language Teaching* covers both second language teaching and the teaching of English as the mother tongue

The basic understandings behind current efforts at curriculum reform are best seen in Bruner's *The Process of Education* and in the first thirty pages of the Cambridge Conference's *Goals for School Mathematics*. (Beyond p. 31 only a mathematician can read with profit, but the first part setting forth general principles is both readable by the nonmathematician and general in its relevance.) English teachers would do well to read both of these works and to discuss recent developments in their fields with colleagues in mathematics and science.

INTRODUCTORY BOOKS Anyone who has worked through this book should be ready for solid textbooks in linguistics. But you may be asked to recommend suitable popularizations for friends or colleagues. This is a difficult matter. There are many, but most, including some of the most widely circulated, are poor or even pernicious. The following four are acceptable: Hall's *Linguistics and Your Language*, Ornstein and Gage's *The ABC's of Languages and Linguistics*, Potter's *Modern Linguistics*, and Schlauch's *The Gift of Tongues*. Sapir's *Language* is in a class by itself, a classic that every advanced student should know, and a book that a beginner can read. For a general introduction to the applications of linguistics to the teaching of English (and a number of related topics) the best is certainly Quirk's *The Use of English*, a series of popular talks given over BBC. Allen's *Readings in Applied English Linguistics* is a collection of reprints useful as general orientation to linguistic viewpoints in English.

Index

Index

Index to Symbol Definitions